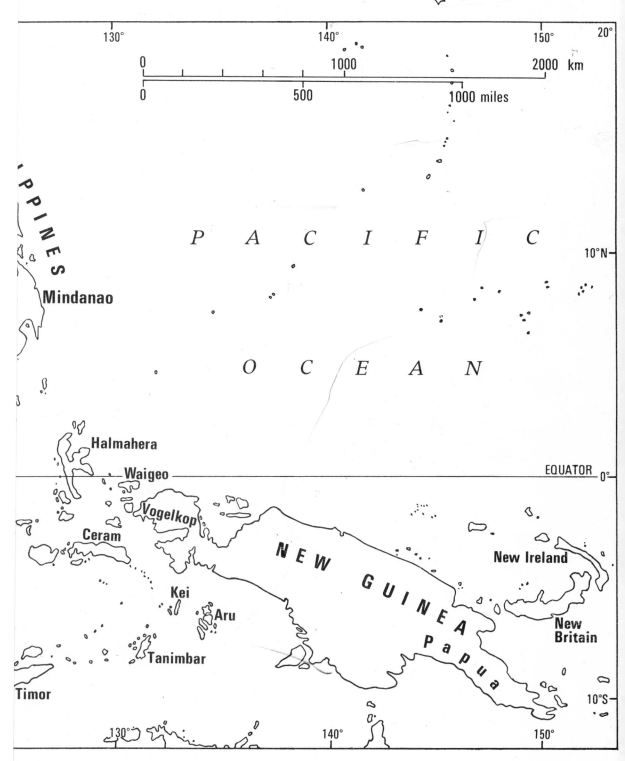

Tropical rain forests
of the Far East

Tropical rain forests of the Far East

T. C. WHITMORE

WITH A CHAPTER ON SOILS BY
C. P. BURNHAM

CLARENDON PRESS · OXFORD

1975

Oxford University Press, Ely House, London W.1

GLASGOW   NEW YORK   TORONTO   MELBOURNE   WELLINGTON
CAPE TOWN   IBADAN   NAIROBI   DAR ES SALAAM   LUSAKA   ADDIS ABABA
DELHI   BOMBAY   CALCUTTA   MADRAS   KARACHI   LAHORE
DACCA   KUALA LUMPUR   SINGAPORE   HONG KONG   TOKYO

ISBN 0 19 854127 9

SET IN MONOPHOTO EHRHARDT 10/11 pt
PRINTED IN GREAT BRITAIN BY THOMSON LITHO LTD, EAST KILBRIDE, SCOTLAND

Foreword

It was with the greatest pleasure that I accepted Dr. T. C. Whitmore's invitation to write a Foreword to *Tropical rain forests of the Far East*. Tim Whitmore, whom I first met in Malaya shortly after his arrival in the region, has spent 17 years working intensively on the forest botany of south-east Asia and the Pacific islands, including over 10 years in the field. He is therefore eminently qualified to have undertaken this mammoth task and will have readers in no doubt concerning both his excellent field knowledge and wide and yet deep appreciation of the subject and of the problems that beset these forests in this modern age. The result is an authoritative and comprehensive work which will fill a long-standing need.

The book has been written, according to the author, for all those who have some concern with the tropical forests of the Far East, probably the richest and oldest forests of the world, and principally for the large and increasing numbers of students and their teachers at universities and colleges throughout the region. This is, however, no ordinary textbook in the presentation of the scientific content and in the moral issues raised. I have been fascinated, as I am sure others will be, by the broadly based and dynamic ecological approach to the subject and intrigued with the contents of the three concluding chapters 'Man and the tropical rain forest', 'Secondary forest and shifting cultivation', and 'Looking ahead'.

The appearance of this book is particularly timely.

The increased and almost explosive rate of exploitation of the dipterocarp forests of the Far East during the last two or three decades, both for the valuable resource they possess and for the agricultural development of the land on which they grow, is posing a very serious threat to their survival and viability in their natural form beyond the next few decades. In consequence, the survival of many of the animals, both large and small, living therein is threatened. It is hoped, therefore, that this work will go a long way in assisting the people of these countries to understand, appreciate, and conserve viable samples of their forests, forests which have given me personally such pleasure for nearly a quarter of a century. The tropical rain forests of the Far East are such a priceless global heritage that these ecosystems must surely not be completely lost in the face of necessary world development. World development in the generally accepted modern sense will not in fact have taken place if *viable* samples of the tropical rain forests of the Far East are not conserved for posterity. In Dr. Whitmore I believe these forests have found a champion and I would not be surprised if the publication of this masterly work will not be found in the future to have contributed substantially to the turning of the tide.

Shillingford,   J. Wyatt-Smith
Oxfordshire,
May 1975

Preface

IN 1898 A. F. W. Schimper published his monumental *Plant geography upon an ecological basis* (English edition 1903), which included a general account of the tropical rain forest, and indeed introduced this term for the evergreen forests of the humid tropics. No further general treatise appeared until 1952 when the first edition was published of *The tropical rain forest—an ecological study* by P. W. Richards. This immediately became, and has remained, the standard work, an important source and reference for all subsequent investigations.

Tropical rain forest occurs in South America, Africa, and the Far East. In the present book the field of study is narrowed still further and only the tropical rain forests of the Far East are included. The emphasis is also slightly different and can be simply stated.

Richards has described the structure and physiognomy, the environment and the floristic composition of tropical rain forest, its main variants, its occurrence under limiting latitudinal and altitudinal conditions, and the influence of man. For a general outline on a world basis his book remains the essential synthesis. The time now appears ripe for a new account, emphasizing particularly the three main subjects in which there have been substantial progress during the last two decades, and written in such a way as to be accessible to everyone who is interested in or needs to know something of the Far East rain forests.

The three main fields of advance are, first, knowledge of the seasonality of climate, especially rainfall, even within the wettest parts of the region, and its consequences for plant and animal life. Secondly, much has now been discovered about the growth rates and the ecological requirements of individual tree species, notably their response as seedlings to brightly illuminated gaps in the high forest canopy. The consideration of the autecology of individual tree species leads into an analysis of the forest as a dynamic, continually rejuvenating community, necessitates a reinterpretation of the much-discussed concept of stratification in the canopy, and makes possible a discussion of the ecological basis of rain forest silviculture. In fact, it is largely due to foresters that we now know so much about the behaviour of individual tree species, and their knowledge, which

has accumulated over many years, was not fully covered by Richards. The third important field of advance over the last two decades has been in our understanding of the nature of variation within rain-forest communities. Richards' book aroused a lively controversy on this topic and was the spur to the considerable volume of work subsequently undertaken. Much of the new work has been carried out in the Far East, and recently modern numerical techniques of community analysis have been utilized. In addition, our knowledge of the ecological requirements of individual tree species now throws considerable light on the nature of variation within rain forest.

There have been substantial advances in tropical soil science in recent years. Chapter 9 (by C. P. Burnham) is devoted to an up-to-date account of tropical soils and their occurrence in the region. It is perhaps the first such account written especially for an audience of biologists.

Other themes which are appraised or reappraised in the present book are the ecology of animals in the rain forest (in which virtually all the work is recent); the interactions of animals and plants (which is subject of recently renewed interest); quantitative measures of plant growth and studies on the productivity of rain forest; the nature and position of the change in forests north of Malaya in the Kra isthmus; conifers in the forest, especially the three genera of high commercial interest; and secondary forest together with shifting cultivation.

Different forest Formations are treated in varying degrees of detail. A very full account is given of the peat swamp forests, both because of their intrinsic ecological interest and also because they are, and are likely to remain, an important part of the permanent forest estate. Considerable advances in our understanding of plant–environment interaction allows a new appraisal to be made of mountain forests and their change with increasing elevation. Similarities are demonstrated between certain mountain forests, heath forests (on which important eco-physiological work is described), peat swamp forests, and certain forests over limestone. The directions future investigations on these related forest Formations should take can now be clearly indicated.

The book concludes with an appraisal of the

alarming rate at which tropical rain forests are being cut down and a reasoned argument as to why man, purely out of self-interest if for no higher motive, needs to take steps now to conserve adequate samples. By the mid-1980s it will surely be too late.

The published results of research into the Far East rain forests are very scattered in a large number of periodicals, books, and government reports. An attempt is made to give access to this literature by copious references to original and secondary sources, which at first sight might appear excessive in a book of this kind. It has been impossible to include in the book a detailed account of all the work which has been done or to which reference is made. It has not been felt necessary to repeat much of the description of the rain forest, its environment, and its variation under different conditions which is so elegantly and adequately covered by Richards; *The tropical rain forest* remains an essential source for this information. Nor has a detailed account been given of all the forest types of the region, on which a volume of *Flora Malesiana* (series I, vol. 2) is in preparation. In particular, vegetation of monsoon climates — monsoon forest and savanna woodland of Schimper — which lies adjacent to the rain forest, receives only brief attention. In this direction it has proved difficult to strike a balance as some account is necessary to complete the framework of the book.

The book is written for all those who have some concern with the tropical rain forests of the Far East. This means principally the large and increasing numbers of students at Universities and Colleges throughout the region and their teachers, who as agriculturists, biologists, foresters, or administrators have need to know the state of our knowledge of what is still the principal vegetation of the region, if this is to be wisely conserved and utilized for continuing national and international benefit. The development of rain-forest ecology in the Far East has been so rapid over the last twenty years, and now in most directions so far leads the field, that the book should also be useful outside the region.

My justification for venturing to write this book is seventeen years' work on forest botany of the tropical Far East including ten years' first-hand experience. It is hoped that, despite the inevitable imperfections and bias, the new synthesis which the book provides might be useful in indicating topics now needing further study. And the best indication of success will be that it is rendered rapidly out of date.

T.C.W.

Saffron Walden, Essex
September 1974

Acknowledgements

THANKS ARE due to the numerous foresters and biologists who, on many a steamy day in the rain forest, have answered questions and discussed ideas during the years through which I have been gathering the information for this book, and to the many others who have helped by correspondence while I have been writing it. Special mention must be made of the men of Kwara'ae who were my constant companions in the Solomons and the orang asli, friends and relations of Soh bin Tandang, who formed our team of tree climbers in West Malaysia; at least a little of their inherited lore was transmitted and has been, of course, of immense value.

The book could not have been written without a grant from St. John's College, Cambridge, for which I express the deepest thanks, and these must be shared by my wife for her help with typing and indexes, at a time when I had no other assistance.

Mr. C. P. Burnham nobly agreed, during a period when he was exceptionally busy, to contribute the chapter on soils and to review the other mentions of soil. Professor P. W. Richards, whose own book was one of my main original stimulants, has read a draft and made a number of helpful comments. My daughter Katy must be especially thanked for sterling assistance with checking the references and compiling the species index.

The late Mr. L. F. H. Merton read critically the entire manuscript, made many detailed and lengthy comments, which have nearly all been incorporated, and gave me great encouragement at times when it was very much needed. To him I owe an enormous debt. Mr. J. Wyatt-Smith, Principle Forestry Adviser to the Ministry of Overseas Development, has similarly contributed criticism, comment, and encouragement, from his deep understanding of dipterocarp forest ecology and silviculture, and has contributed the Foreword.

Other individuals who must be singled out for special mention from amongst the numerous persons who have assisted in various ways are Dr. J. A. R. Anderson, Dr. P. S. Ashton, Dr. E. F. Brunig, Mr. P. F. Burgess, Dr. D. J. Chivers, Dr. H. C. Dawkins, Dr. G. C. Evans, Sir Frank Engledow, F.R.S., Mr. C. J. Folland, Mr. B. Gray, Dr. P. J. Grubb, Mr. J. R. F. Hansell, Mr. J. J. Havel, Mr. Loh Hoy Shing (flowering and fruiting statistics in Chapter 4), Dr. J. A. MacKinnon, Mr. K. D. Marten, Lord Medway, Mr. J. R. Palmer, Dr. M. E. D. Poore, Professor C. G. G. J. van Steenis, Mr. F. White, Mr. J. S. Womersley, and the librarians of the Cambridge University Botany School and the Commonwealth Forestry Institute at Oxford. In places where I have made use of unpublished information from these persons and others the name of my informant has been appended in brackets.

The following acknowledgements are made for the figures:

Dr. J. A. R. Anderson (10.15, 10.16, 11.2–11.5, 11.7–11.13, 14.3, 16.6, 16.7);
Dr. P. S. Ashton (2.2, 2.6, 6.5, 7.3, 10.1, 10.10, 10.13, 11.6, 11.14, 11.15, 14.5);
Dr. E. F. Brunig (2.32, 10.5–10.9, 10.12, 12.1, 12.2, 14.2, 15.3, 18.2);
Mr. P. F. Burgess (4.3);
Dr. D. J. Chivers (2.27, 4.1);
Mr. P. F. Cockburn (7.2);
Dr. Ding Hou (17.9);
Dr. J. Dransfield (2.5);
Dr. G. W. Gillett (7.4);
Dr. D. J. Gobbett (17.1);
Mr. B. Gray (14.7);
Dr. D. J. Hill (2.7, 2.9, 2.19);
Dr. J. A. MacKinnon (2.26);
Lord Medway (2.11);
Mr. J. S. Womersley (7.5);
Mr. J. F. U. Zieck (14.6);
Australian Journal of Forestry (15.2);
Biological Journal of the Linnean Society (2.31, 6.2);
British Museum (Natural History) (4.2, 16.3, 16.4, 16.9);
Clarendon Press (1.6, 2.1, 10.4, 10.11, 15.4, 15.16);
Commonwealth Forestry Institute (14.1);
Ecological Monographs (3.2, 3.3, 14.1);
Flora Malesiana (1.2);
Forest Research Institute, Kepong (2.15, 2.17, 2.21, 6.3, 15.5, 17.2, 17.4);
Journal of Ecology (6.7, 14.8, 15.7, 15.15);
Journal of Tropical Geography (3.4);
Macmillan (15.8);
Malayan Nature Journal (9.15, 16.5, 17.6);
Malayan Forest Records (15.6);
Malayan Forester (7.1, 15.14, 16.2);
New South Wales Forestry Commission (1.7);

Acknowledgements

Overseas Development Ministry and Dr. J. E. D. Fox
(6.8, 15.4);
Oxford University Forest Society (8.1);
Oxford University Press (1.8, 2.22, 10.3, 11.1, 15.12);
Quarterly Review of Biology (1.9);
Reinwardtia (12.3);
Rimba Indonesia (8.2);
Singapore Government Printer (2.24);
University of California (18.2);
University of Hull, Geography Department (10.14,
14.1);
Witherby (4.4, 12.5).

Contents

NOTE ON UNITS AND NOTE ON PLACE NAMES   xiii

Part I: Introduction
1. TROPICAL RAIN FORESTS OF THE
FAR EAST   3
   1.1. Flora   5
   1.2. Fauna   10

2. FOREST STRUCTURE   12
   2.1. The rain-forest ecosystem   12
   2.2. The synusiae   12
   2.3. The forest growth cycle   13
   2.4. Stratification   16
   2.5. Tree form   18
   2.6. Epiphytes, climbers, and stranglers   26
   2.7. Animals in the forest   32
   2.8. Plant and animal interactions   34

Part II: Seasonality
3. THE FOREST ENVIRONMENT: CLIMATE   43
   3.1. Systems to characterize climates   43
   3.2. Climates within the tropical Far East   44
   3.3. The water balance   46
   3.4. Water balance within the wettest climates   47
   3.5. Rare climatic events   49
   3.6. Microclimates   49

4. SEASONAL CYCLES IN PLANTS
AND ANIMALS   52
   4.1. Seasonal cycles in plants   52
   4.2. Seasonal cycles in animals   58

Part III: Growth of the forest
5. SEED DISPERSAL TO SEEDLING
ESTABLISHMENT   63
   5.1. Dispersal   63
   5.2. Seed dormancy and germination   64
   5.3. Seedling establishment   65

6. GROWTH OF SEEDLINGS INTO TREES   67
   6.1. The gap phase of the forest growth cycle   67
   6.2. Light-demanding and shade-bearing
tree species   69
   6.3. Forest dynamics: Solomon Islands   73
   6.4. Forest dynamics: Malaya   74
   6.5. Seedling survival   77

7. THE ECOLOGICAL BASIS OF
RAIN-FOREST SILVICULTURE   81
   7.1. Silviculture in lowland dipterocarp
rain forest   82
   7.2. Commercially important pioneer species   84

8. GROWTH RATES AND FOREST YIELDS   89
   8.1. The foresters' measures   89
   8.2. Tree age   93
   8.3. Productivity studies   94
   8.4. The quantitative analysis of plant growth   98

Part IV: Kinds of forest
9. THE FOREST ENVIRONMENT: SOILS
by C. P. BURNHAM   103
   9.1. General features of zonal soils   105
   9.2. Ultisols (red–yellow podzolic soils)   108
   9.3. Oxisols (latosols)   109
   9.4. Laterite   110
   9.5. Soils on volcanic ash   110
   9.6. Soils on coarse, siliccous deposits (podzols)   112
   9.7. Soils on limestone   113
   9.8. Soils on ultrabasic rocks   114
   9.9. Soils on finer marine alluvium   115
   9.10. Fresh-water alluvial soils   116
   9.11. Soils of seasonally dry climates   117
   9.12. Mountain soils   118

10. FOREST FORMATIONS:
(1) THE DRY-LAND RAIN FORESTS   121
   10.1. Tropical lowland evergreen rain forest   122
   10.2. Tropical semi-evergreen rain forest   126
   10.3. Heath forest   129
   10.4. Forest over limestone   138
   10.5. Forest over ultrabasic rocks   140
   10.6. Beach vegetation   141

11. FOREST FORMATIONS:
(2) THE WET-LAND RAIN FORESTS   143
   11.1. Mangrove forest   143
   11.2. Brackish-water forest   143
   11.3. Peat swamp forest   144
   11.4. Fresh-water swamp forest   156

12. MONSOON FOREST FORMATIONS   158
   12.1. Monsoon forests and savanna   158
   12.2. Tropical moist deciduous forest   162
   12.3. Transition from rain to monsoon forest
north of Malaya: the Kra ecotone   163

13. ANIMAL LIFE AND
FOREST FORMATIONS   166

14. CONIFERS IN THE FORESTS   169
   14.1. *Agathis*   172
   14.2. *Araucaria*   174
   14.3. *Pinus*   176

Contents

15. VARIATION WITHIN THE TROPICAL
    LOWLAND EVERGREEN RAIN FOREST   179
    15.1. Variation through the region   180
    15.2. Regional variation within dipterocarp forest   181
    15.3. Local variation within dipterocarp forest   186
    15.4. Variation within a rain forest in the
          Solomon Islands   193
    15.5. On the nature of variation within
          lowland rain forest   196

16. MOUNTAIN RAIN FORESTS   199
    16.1. Montane forest Formations   199
    16.2. The tree line and beyond   206
    16.3. The mountain floras   206
    16.4. The upper montane and heath-forest
          Formations compared   207
    16.5. The montane environment   208
    16.6. Correlations between elevational changes
          in forest and environment   210
    16.7. Zonation of animals on tropical mountains   212

Part V: Man and the tropical rain forest

17. MAN AND THE TROPICAL
    RAIN FOREST   217
    17.1. The three ages of man   217
    17.2. Man's current impact on the forest   220
    17.3. Effect of intensive logging on the
          rain forest   224
    17.4. The effects of logging on the rain-forest
          animals   225

18. SECONDARY FOREST AND
    SHIFTING CULTIVATION   228
    18.1. Shifting cultivation   229
    18.2. General course of secondary successions   232

19. LOOKING AHEAD   234
    19.1. Trends in forestry and forest industry   234
    19.2. Importance of the rain forest   235
    19.3. A plan for the future   236

APPENDIX   239
Select list of publications containing descriptions of tropical
rain forest in the countries of the Far East

BIBLIOGRAPHY   241

INDEX OF PLANT NAMES   259

GENERAL INDEX   270

*The front end-paper shows a map of the tropical Far East,
and the back end-paper a map of Malesia, Australia,
Melanesia, and Micronesia.*

Note on units

THROUGHOUT this book S.I. units are used. Many of the original measurements were made in Imperial measure. These have been converted to an appropriate number of significant figures. The conversion results in many plot areas and girth limits which are on first sight curious.

Note on place names

ON OCCASIONS in this book parts of the region are referred to by their older name. The following is a list of the place names used here accompanied by the names now in common use.

Billiton	Belitung
Ceram	Seram
Celebes	Sulawesi
Ceylon	Sri Lanka
Indochina	Vietnam, North and South; Cambodia (Khmer Republic); Laos
Indonesian Borneo	Kalimantan
Java	Djawa
Lesser Sunda Islands	Nusa Tenggara
Natuna Islands	Kepulauun Bunguran
North Borneo	Sabah
Siam	Thailand
Sumatra	Sumatera
West New Guinea	Irian Jaya

Part I: Introduction

1 Tropical rain forests of the Far East

TROPICAL RAIN FOREST (*tropische Regenwald*) is a term coined by A. F. W. Schimper in his great classic work *Plant geography* (1898, 1903), and has been generally used ever since. It describes the forests of the ever-wet tropics where there is no, or only minimal, seasonal water shortage, and as a general term will be used in this sense in this book. Schimper (1903, p. 260) gave, as a brief diagnosis of dry-land tropical rain forest, that it 'is evergreen, hygrophilous in character, at least thirty metres high, rich in thick-stemmed lianes, and in woody as well as herbaceous epiphytes'. Schimper contrasted this with monsoon forest with which the rain forest merges at its latitudinal and climatic limits. Dry-land monsoon forest he defined as 'more or less leafless during the dry season, especially towards its termination, tropophilous in character, usually less lofty than the rain forest, rich in woody lianes, rich in herbaceous but poor in woody epiphytes'.

Rain forest also occurs outside the tropics, for instance, in the Far East, southwards, in eastern Australia, and northwards to 28° in southernmost China (Taiwan, Fukien, Kwangtung, and parts of Yunnan and Kwangsi) (Wang 1961) where, however,

it has been largely cleared except from the slopes of wet valleys. Towards the latitudinal limits it differs somewhat in structure and physiognomy (Baur 1964*a*) and is now usually called subtropical rain forest. Further away from the equator temperate rain forest is found, for example, in south Japan, along the wall of the Himalaya (Stainton 1972), and in New Zealand. Within the tropics there are changes associated with increasing elevation and various montane types of rain forest are now recognized.

There are three great blocks of tropical rain forest in the world (Fig. 1.1). The most extensive is the American rain forest, centred on the Amazon basin, extending to parts of the shores and islands of the Caribbean in the north and down the eastern Andean foothills in the south, and with outliers on the western slopes of the Andes and the Atlantic coast mountains. The extent of this forest is about 400×10^6 ha; it comprises about one-sixth of the total broad-leaf forest of the world (Pringle 1969).

The Indo-Malayan rain forest, the subject of this book, is the second most extensive block and is estimated to cover about 250×10^6 ha (Pringle 1969). This extent is less than that of the American block,

FIG. 1.1. Distribution of tropical rain forest: South America after Richards (1952); Africa and Madagascar after Keay (1959, his 'moist forest at low and medium altitudes'); Far East after Richards (1952 updated).

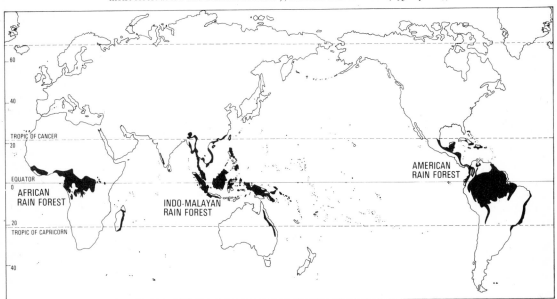

and the Indo-Malayan rain forest has been more extensively disturbed or destroyed by timber extraction.

The third block, the African rain forest, centred in the Congo basin and extending along the north coasts of the Gulf of Guinea and with outliers in Uganda, is the least extensive and the poorest in species. Pringle (1969) estimated that the evergreen and semi-deciduous forests of Africa cover 180×10^6 ha.

In addition there are a few relicts of rain forest remaining on the east coast of Madagascar and on the islands of Mauritius, Reunion, Rodriguez, and the Seychelles. These rain forests of the south Indian Ocean islands were never very extensive.

The structure of the various kinds of rain forest and the physiognomy of the species are similar throughout the world, in all three blocks. Despite this the species are entirely different and there are few genera in common. At the family level there is more in common. Similarity of life-form between totally different floras in different continents is not, of course, restricted to rain forest, but is generally the case. It is beyond the scope of this book to make detailed comparisons between the rain forests of the Far East and elsewhere. It will be shown that, despite over-all similarity, there are important differences and that in the tropical Far East occur the world's rain forests of grandest structure and of probably greatest richness in both plant and animal life.

The Far Eastern tropical rain forest lies as a belt of evergreen vegetation extending through the Malay archipelago from Sumatra in the west to New Guinea in the east (front end-paper map). It extends from the shoreline to the tops of all except the few very highest mountains. This rain-forest belt is broken into western and eastern blocks by monsoon forests in the seasonally dry central part of the archipelago. To the north-west, on the Asian continent, rain forest persists only in the wettest sites north of about the isthmus of Kra at latitude $10\frac{1}{2}°$N in southern Thailand, and is found in the Andaman Islands and on restricted areas in parts of Burma and Assam. There is a small outlier in south-east Thailand, which extends across the border into Cambodia, and on to the islands off-shore. There are further outliers on the western Ghats of India and in south-west Ceylon.

Tropical rain forest penetrates Queensland (back end-paper map), and subtropical rain forest reaches as far down the eastern seaboard of Australia as New South Wales. As at its north-west limit in Asia, here also it occupies only the wettest sites or most fertile soils; details have been worked out by Webb (1959, 1968).

Tropical rain forest extends eastwards and southwards from New Guinea into the Melanesian archipelagos—the Solomons, New Hebrides, Fiji, Samoa, and Tonga—and into Micronesia and Polynesia (back end-paper map). Here it becomes progressively attenuated with the increasing floristic poverty eastwards into the Pacific, and it is confined to islands or parts of islands with ever-wet climate.

Within the lowland humid tropics it is now known that there is very considerable variation from place to place in the rain forest, and a number of types with different structure and physiognomy can be recognized. The most luxuriant type, which is also the most species-rich, grandest in stature, and most complex in structure, is here called tropical lowland evergreen rain forest.† It occupies the best sites, on well but not excessively drained soils which are not excessively poor in mineral nutrients, and tends to be replaced by less luxuriant, simpler, species-poorer types of forest where environmental conditions are less favourable.

Man has profoundly affected tropical forest, especially those parts in a slightly seasonal climate which are easily burned in the drier months. The traditional cultures of the Far East thus have extensively degraded these drier primary forests to open savanna woodland or treeless grasslands, or, in the wettest places, replaced the tall virgin forest of complex structure mainly with a lower, simpler secondary forest, and only patchily with open woodland or grassland.

Modern man over the last century or so has made an even greater impact, clearing extensive areas for plantation agriculture and removing timber from tracts which are so huge that well before the end of this century primitive untouched tropical rain forest will be restricted to a few inaccessible pockets and such National Parks and other special reserves as survive increasing economic pressures. Fast-rising populations, following the more or less effective control of malaria and other endemic diseases about the middle of this century, plus rising human expectations in an age of speedy world-wide communication, have increased the demand for the products of the rain forest and for the money to be derived from the sale of those products. In addition there has been an increasing demand to use land occupied by forest to produce greater annual wealth from agricultural crops.

† Nomenclature after Burtt Davy (1938), see Chapter 10.

4

1.1. Flora

The wet tropics of the Far East have a distinctive flora which does not merge gradually with those of adjacent drier regions. This has been dramatically shown by van Steenis (1950*a*) (see Fig. 1.2). The

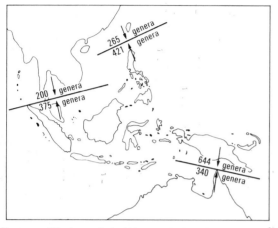

FIG. 1.2. The three principal 'demarcation knots' of the Malesian flora. (From van Steenis 1950.)

number of genera which reach the southern end of their range at the isthmus of Kra is about 200, and another 375 reach their northern limit there. The sum of these genera (575) may conveniently be termed a 'demarcation knot'. The boundary between New Guinea and north Australia is even more strongly defined with a demarcation knot of 984, and the boundary north of the Philippines with one of 686. By contrast, there is no sharp boundary eastwards; the demarcation knot between the Bismarcks and Solomons, for example, is only 282 (van Balgooy 1971). It is no coincidence that the strong knots coincide with the major forest-type boundaries already described, and that eastwards into the Pacific where there is no such change in forest type the knot is weakest. A coherent floristic region can be defined, therefore, and this area is called Malesia,† which is naturally bounded to north-west, north, and south, and arbitrarily bounded east of the Bismarck archipelago.

The flora of Malesia is exceedingly rich, and is conservatively estimated to comprise 25 000 species of flowering plants (van Steenis 1971) which is about 10 per cent of the world's flora. Malaya (Peninsular Malaysia + Singapore, 132 100 km²) has, according to the most recent estimate, about 7900 species and 1500 genera of seed plants (Whitmore 1973*k*). The

† To avoid confusion with the State of Malaysia. Note also that zoologists formerly used Malaysia as a general term for the islands on the Sunda shelf (see later) together with the Malay peninsula.

British Isles (311 000 km²) in the north temperate zone have by contrast 1430 species (18 per cent) and 628 genera (42 per cent) native, with an area about 2·3 times greater.

Some 40 per cent of the genera in Malesia are endemic and so are still more of the species. The biggest family is the Orchidaceae with 3000–4000 species. Amongst the woody plants the Dipterocarpaceae have some 500 species, mainly in the west, *Eugenia* (Myrtaceae) and *Ficus* (Moraceae) some 500 species each, and the Ericaceae 737 species (including 287 *Rhododendron*, 239 *Vaccinium*). Long series of species of largely overlapping geographical range and apparently identical, or at least very similar, ecological range are characteristic of these and other genera. For example, Malaya is known to have 102 species of *Ficus*, 59 of *Shorea*, 49 of *Garcinia*, 45 of *Calophyllum*, and 38 of *Lithocarpus*, to cite only a few tree genera (Whitmore 1972*b*, 1973*c*).

The great richness of flora is to some extent a consequence of the very complex structure of the vegetation, lofty trees providing a framework and an environment within which smaller trees and plants of a wide range of life-form grow. These features are discussed in Chapter 2.

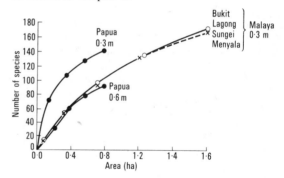

FIG. 1.3. Species–area curves for small plots in tropical lowland evergreen rain forest Malaya and Papua (minimum girth shown). Malayan curves: Wyatt-Smith (1966, Fig. 4), 541 and 3 m elevation; Papuan curves: Paijmans (1970, Fig. 11), plot 4 at 825 m.

Considering solely the trees, there is commonly a great number of species growing together, and the number increases with increasing size of the sample area. This is clearly shown on Fig. 1.3 for small plots in Malaya and Papua. These curves are mostly based on samples down to a minimum girth limit of 0·3 m, which is common in rain-forest ecological studies.† The number of tree species encountered per

† The data on Fig. 1.3 are plotted from contiguous sample areas. Many published species–area curves are from non-contiguous plots (for example, those in Ashton (1964)) these are not strictly comparable and can be expected to rise more steeply.

5

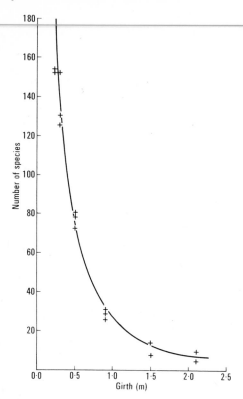

FIG. 1.4. Relationship between species number per 0·4 ha and different minimum sample girths. (From Wong 1967, Fig. 1; based on 3 plots of 0·4 ha at Kemasul forest, Malaya.)

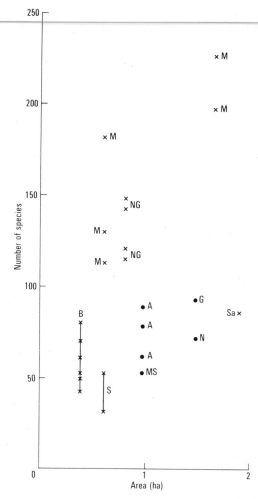

FIG. 1.5. Species richness (trees ⩾ 0·3 m girth) on small plots in mixed species tropical lowland evergreen rain forests. × Malesia (B: Brunei; M: Malaya; NG: New Guinea; Sa: Sabah; S: Solomons). (After Ashton 1964; Wyatt-Smith 1966; Cousens 1951; Paijmans 1970; Austin and Greig-Smith 1968; Whitmore 1974, respectively.) ● Elsewhere (A: Amazon; G: Guyana; M: Mauritius; N: Nigeria). (After Ashton 1964; Richards 1952, respectively.) Lines connect sample plots which lie near together.

unit area decreases rapidly as the girth limit is raised as is shown in Fig. 1.4 (see also the Papuan forest on Fig. 1.3). For forest-survey purposes a minimum girth limit of 1·2 m or 1·8 m is commonly used; it can be seen that this greatly reduces the number of species encountered and hence reduces the practical problem of species identification.

Figure 1.5 shows that small areas of the Malesian rain forest are richer in tree species than similar areas in Africa and South America; and there is no reason not to expect similar relationships if climbers, epiphytes, etc., were added in. They are in fact the most species-rich communities known from anywhere in the world. Samples of Fynbosch of the Cape region of South Africa, which is the most nearly comparable vegetation in terms of richness, have been estimated to have a total vascular species complement of between 61 and 119 per hectare (Werger 1972), which is comparable to the numbers of trees greater than 0·3 m in girth in some of the poorer tropical rain forest samples (see Fig. 1.5). It can also be seen in Fig. 1.5 that the Solomon Island sample is less species-rich than the other

tropical forests. This exemplifies the fact, mentioned already, that the Malesian flora becomes attenuated eastwards into Melanesia, where there are fewer families, genera, and species of all groups of vascular plants, only partly compensated by a very small Melanesian element. In the Solomons an important floristic difference from New Guinea is the absence of many of the groups characteristic of mid-mountain forest, for example, Fagaceae, *Engelhardtia*, and *Araucaria*. Concomitant with the relative floristic poverty of the Solomons some species have wider ecological ranges than they have further west, for

Fig. 1.6. Tropical lowland evergreen mixed dipterocarp rain forest on a ridge at Andulau, Brunei. Plot area 60 m × 7·5 m, all trees over 4·5 m tall shown; mature phase forest except extreme right-hand end. (From Ashton 1964, Fig. 25.) Species and stem numbers: Anacardiaceae: A.1, *Mangifera havilandii* (11); A.2, *Mangifera* sp. (1); A.3, *Melanorrhoea torquata* (1); A.4, *Parishia* (?) *insignis* (8); A.5, *Semecarpus rufovelutinus* (1); A.6, *Swintonia schwenckii* (1). Annonaceae: An, *Polyalthia sumatrana* (1). Burseraceae: B, *Dacryodes expansa* (6). Celastraceae: C, *Lophopetalum subovatum* (1). Dipterocarpaceae: D.1, *Cotylelobium melanoxylum* (3); D.2, *Dipterocarpus globosus* (3); D.3, *Dryobalanops aromatica* (2); D.4, *Shorea acuta* (1); D.5, *S. dolichocarpa* (5); D.6, *S. geniculata* (1); D.7, *S. multiflora* (5); D.8, *S. ovata* (1); D.9, *Vatica micrantha* (1). Ebenaceae: Eb.1, *Diospyros buxifolia* (1); Eb.2, *D. ferruginea* (1); Eb.3, *D. hermaphroditica* (1); Eb.4, *D. bantamensis* (1); Eb.5, *D. toposoides* (1); Eb.6, *D.* sp. (1). Linaceae: Er, *Ixonanthes reticulata* (1). Euphorbiaceae: E.1, *Agrostistachys longifolia* var. *leptostachya* (1); E.2, *Aporusa elmeri* (1); E.3, *Cleistanthus winkleri* (4); E.4, *Coelodepas* sp. (8); E.5, *Mallotus griffithianus* (2); E.6, *Pimelodendron griffithianum* (2). Guttiferae: G, *Garcinia parvifolia* (1). Icacinaceae: I, *Platea fuliginea* (1). Lecythidaceae: L, *Barringtonia* sp. (2). Melastomataceae: Me, *Memecylon* sp. (1). Moraceae: Mo.1, *Artocarpus odoratissimus* (1); Mo.2, *Prainea frutescens* (1). Myristicaceae: Mi.1, *Knema cinerea* v. *patentinervia* (1); Mi.2, *Knema kunstleri* (1); Mi.3, *Myristica lowiana* (1). Myrtaceae: M.1, *Eugenia* sp. (2); M.2, *Whiteodendron moultonianum* (1). Olacaceae: O, *Gonocaryum* sp. (1). Rosaceae: Ro, *Parastemon urophyllus* (4). Rubiaceae: R.1, *Canthium* sp. (1); R.2, *Gardenia tubifera* (1); R.3, *Randia jambosoides* (1). Sapotaceae: S.1, *Madhuca crassipes* (1); S.2, *Payena* sp. (1); S.3, *Payena lucida* (3). Simaroubaceae: Si, *Eurycoma longifolia* (1). Theaceae: Te, *Adinandra cordiifolia* (1). Thymelaeaceae: Th, *Gonystylus velutinus* (1).

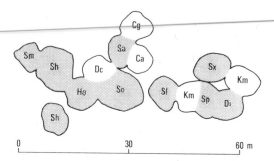

0   30   60 m

FIG. 1.7. Canopy-top trees, tropical lowland evergreen mixed dipterocarp rain forest at Kemasul, Malaya (Baur 1964*a*, Fig. 6). Ca, *Canarium* sp.; Cg, *Sarcotheca griffithii*; Dc, *Dyera costulata*; Km, *Koompassia malaccensis*. Dipterocarpaceae hatched: Di, *Dipterocarpus costulatus*; Ho, *Hopea* sp.; Sa, *Shorea acuminata*; Sh, *S. lepidota*; Sl, *S. leprosula*; Sm, *S. macroptera*; So, *S. ovalis*; Sx, *S. maxwelliana*.

example, *Pometia pinnata* is common in a range of habitats, whereas in Malaya it is restricted to riverine forest. *Campnosperma brevipetiolatum* is wide-ranging, whereas in New Guinea and the Bismarcks it only inhabits seasonally flooded sites (Whitmore 1966*a*, 1969*a*).

There is considerable variation in flora within the vast Malesian region. Ecologically, as well as commercially, the most important feature is undoubtedly the occurrence of extensive dipterocarp forests only in the western half of the archipelago, that is, in the western block of tropical lowland evergreen rain forest. Dipterocarpaceae here grow as very lofty trees, and the top of the canopy is commonly at 45 m, sometimes 60 m, not consisting of isolated emergents but of extensive groups of giant trees. Figures 1.6 and 2.1 (see p. 14), using data from Brunei, show typical mature Bornean dipterocarp forest, and Fig. 1.7 shows in plan view the contiguous crowns of the emergents in a Malayan dipterocarp forest. Tropical rain forest of this stature and with this density of top-of-canopy trees is unique in the world (see by contrast the profile diagrams of New Guinea and Solomons forests in Figs 15.3, 15.18, and 15.19, pp. 182 and 194–5), and the region is justly famous because of it. Typically, in any one place several species of several dipterocarp genera grow together, although their timber can be considered commercially as one or a few grades. The combination of a relatively few timber groups, a very high stocking of trees of huge stature with clear bole lengths commonly attaining 20 m or more, and timbers of relatively light weight has contributed to the explosive increase in the exploitation of these forests since the end of the Second World War which threatens to eliminate all extensive virgin tracts well before the end of this century (and from Malaya before 1980), as will be shown later in Part V. In Chapter 15 we give a detailed discussion of the ecology of dipterocarp low-land rain forest.

Table 1.1 shows the range of volume and mass of wood and bark per hectare from three 0·4 ha plots in

TABLE 1.1

Volume and mass per hectare of above-ground wood and bark on small plots in Malaya and the Solomons

	Malaya†	Solomons‡
(a) Volume over bark of all stems and branches 0·3 m or greater in girth (m³).	575 –731	236–492
(b) Commercial timber as percentage of (a).	44 – 59	22– 41
(c) Volume of same parts but over 225 mm girth (m³).	580 –735	—
(d) Excess of (c) over (a) percentage.	0·9– 0·5	—
(e) Approximate mass in tonne of parts over 0·25 m girth.§	230 –290	95–195

† Kemasul forest from Wong (1967).

‡ Kolombangara and Viru-Kalena forests. (From Self and Trenaman 1972.)

§ Using the formula of Ogawa *et al.* (1965*b*).

highly stocked dipterocarp forest at Kemasul in central Malaya and four average or poor plots in the New Georgia Islands of the Solomons group, and dramatically illustrates the difference. No comparable figures from New Guinea are available; they would come somewhere between those shown here, and nearer the figures for the Solomons.

The western rain-forest block is characterized not only by the important role the dipterocarps play. Numerous other genera and species are restricted entirely or nearly so to the Sunda-shelf countries and thus to this forest block. Two examples are given in Fig. 1.8. The nine genera of climbing palms, the rattans or Lawyer Vines (Palmae, subfamily Lepido-caryoideae), are strongly centred on this region (Fig. 1.8(a)). In fact, of the eight subfamilies of the Palmae in the tropical Far East, only the evolutionarily advanced Arecoideae are more strongly developed in the eastern rain-forest block. Figure 1.8(b) shows the Sundaic distribution of one section of *Artocarpus*, the genus of the Jack and Bread Fruits.

Sumatra, Malaya, and Borneo, which all lie on the Sunda shelf and at the heart of the western rain-

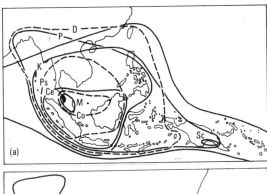

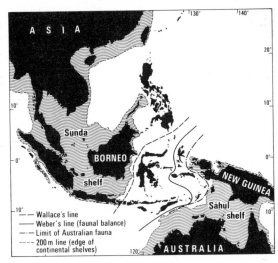

FIG. 1.9. The Sunda and Sahul shelves with Wallace's and Weber's zoogeographic border lines. (From Mayr 1944, Fig. 1.)

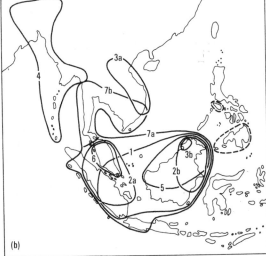

FIG. 1.8. Plants centred on the Sunda shelf. (a) The Asian rattans. D, *Daemonorops*; P, *Plectocomia*; C, *Calamus*; K, *Korthalsia*; Ps, *Plectocomiopsis*; Ce, *Ceratolobus*; M, *Myrialepis*; Co, *Cornera*; Sc, *Schizospatha*; *Calospatha* in solid black. (Whitmore 1973b, Fig. 93.) (b) *Artocarpus* section *Duricarpus*. L, *A. anisophyllus* (? also in the Philippines); 2, *A. lanceifolius*, a, ssp. *lanceifolius*, b, ssp. *clementis*; 3, *A. melinoxylus*, a, ssp. *melinoxylus*, b, ssp. *brevipedunculatus*; 4, *A. chaplasha*; 5, *A. odoratissimus* (probably introduced in the areas enclosed by broken lines); 6, *A. hispidus*; 7, *A. rigidus*, a, ssp. *rigidus*, b, ssp. *asperulus*. (After Jarrett 1959, Fig. 11.)

forest block, have close floristic similarities. An analysis based on the results of recent work in Malaya shows them to be even more similar than was formerly thought. Thus, of 395 genera and 1759 species in 43 tree families, only 3 per cent and 5·5 per cent are restricted to Sumatra/Malaya and Malaya/Borneo respectively, and these are not more common in the adjacent part of Malaya than elsewhere in the peninsula (Whitmore 1973k). Over 90 per cent of the species investigated occur throughout the three countries. There are, despite this, some very marked differences. Thus, *Crudia*, a genus of mostly small or medium trees, is extremely rare in Malaya and common in Borneo and *Iguanura*, an under-

growth palm, vice versa. The palm *Johannesteijsmannia* occurs in east Sumatra (1 species), throughout Malaya (4 species), and just reaches west Sarawak (1 species). The palm *Eugeissona* has 3 species in Borneo, 2 species in Malaya, and is absent from Sumatra (Whitmore 1973b).

Much less is known in detail about the phytogeography of the eastern block which mainly comprises the single vast island of New Guinea.

The plant geography of the tropical Far East is to be interpreted against the geology. The Malay archipelago spans two continental shelves: the Sunda shelf in the west and the Sahul shelf in the east (Fig. 1.9). The Sunda shelf is the largest continental shelf in the world; on it lie Sumatra, Malaya, Java, Borneo, and Palawan. The Sahul shelf runs north from Australia around New Guinea and offshore islands. Between these two shelves lies a region of deep seas in which lie most of the Philippines (except Palawan), Celebes, and the Lesser Sunda Islands.

There is now clear evidence from the existence of thick deposits of fluviatile alluvium below sea-level on land and by erosion features on the adjacent seabed that, at times in the Pleistocene period, sea-levels around the Malay peninsula have been lower than they are now by amounts of up to 100 m (Haile 1971).† Therefore much of the area of both the

† By contrast Haile shows that there is no evidence that sea-levels, round Malaya at least, have been more than 3 m higher than at present at any time during the Pleistocene or Holocene periods; earlier reports were all due to misinterpretation. Yancey (1973) presents convincing evidence that sea-level was about 3 m higher than now over much of Sundaland about 5000–6000 years ago.

Sunda and Sahul continental shelves has, in all probability, been dry land. Indeed the deeply penetrating estuaries of the coasts of Malaya and Sumatra facing the Malacca straits, for example, are signs of a rise in sea-level. Sea-level lowering was probably due to the extension of the polar ice caps during glacial epochs. The close floristic similarities now known to exist between the countries of the Sunda shelf are certainly the result of evolution, migration, competition, and possibly extinction, against a background of rising and falling sea-levels during the Pleistocene period. And there is also the possibility that some places have at times had a more seasonally dry climate (Chapter 12). Animal distributions, described in the next section, show a similar picture.

1.2. Fauna

Animals are even more sharply divided into two groups, corresponding to the Sunda and Sahul shelf areas, than are plants. To consider the mammals (excluding bats), the Sunda group is exclusively placental and of clearly continental Asian ancestry; it includes apes, tiger, elephant, monkeys, and ungulates. The endemic New Guinea mammals, by contrast, consist of monotremes and marsupials of Australian affinity, with the addition of murine and hydromyine rodents most of which are endemic. Full lists are given by Medway (1972b). The only mammals found throughout the whole region are bats (several genera but few species), the genus of true rats (*Rattus*) and other commensals with man, and introduced species (for example, the feral pig, *Sus scrofa*). The pattern of variation of other groups of vertebrates varies in detail. The strictly freshwater fishes of the Orient and Australia do not meet at all. Amongst amphibians there is a considerable overlapping of Oriental and Australian groups, mostly different families, at least from Bali and Celebes eastwards. Of reptiles and birds there is overlapping of some families, and also of many genera and species, in a still wider area from within the Sunda-shelf region to northern and eastern Australia. Some of the charges in avifauna are conspicuous: barbets reach east to Bali; cockatoos reach west to Lombok and south-east Borneo. The complexity, level, and width of the transition from an Oriental to an Australian vertebrate fauna varies with the probable ability of the different groups to cross saltwater barriers. More or less the entire Oriental fauna reaches the edge of the Sunda shelf, the area dry during the eras of low sea-level during the Pleistocene; east of this is an area of subtraction and transition

to the predominantly Australian fauna, which is reached at the line of the Sahul shelf west of New Guinea and including the Aru Islands and Salawati, Batanta, and Waigeo off the coast of the Vogelkop peninsula, but not the Kei Islands (Fig. 1.9).

The boundary of the rich Oriental fauna coincides with Wallace's line (Fig. 1.9), a faunistic limit first detected over a century ago (Wallace 1860). The line where the Oriental and Australian faunas are more or less equally represented is known as Weber's 'line of faunistic balance'. The whole intermediate region of transition and subtraction between the Oriental fauna of the Sunda shelf and the Australian fauna of the Sahul shelf has been named 'Wallacea' (Dickerson, Merrill, McGregor, Schultze, Taylor, and Herre 1928). (Fuller discussion of fauna and its variation will be found in Mayr (1944) and Darlington (1965).)

Within Sundaland extinction on some islands has occurred, as in plants, and this has been a Late Pleistocene phenomenon. Thus, for example, the tapir (*Tapirus indicus*), now restricted to Malaya and Sumatra, survived in Sarawak till at least 9000 years ago (Medway 1960), and fossils of the orang utan (*Pongo pygmaeus*), a species now restricted to Sumatra and Borneo, have been found in Java.

Amongst the amphibians there is a distinctly Sundaic fauna with many endemic genera and species. In the Kra peninsula the number of species of this group drops sharply between 10° and 14° N coincident with the occurrence of an extended dry season (Chapter 3), and more continental species extend southwards towards Malaya than Sundaic species extend north. This is because the southwards barrier for the former group, which are all of necessity adapted for seasonal drought, is less than the northwards barrier for the Sundaic species of ever-wet climates (Inger 1966). North of the Philippines the limit of the Sundaic amphibian fauna is less sharp than its eastern boundary, probably because there have been isthmian connections with the continent at epochs of low sea-level.

Within Sundaland some mammals are strictly arboreal, adapted to the closed forest as habitat and food source; examples are apes, monkeys, and squirrels. Other mammals, for example, elephant, deer, and cattle, are grazers or browsers, essentially adapted to grassland or savanna and feeding in primary rain-forest country largely on the lush herbs of swamps and valley bottoms, bamboo thickets, and landslip regrowth. The grazing and browsing mammals are well adapted to take advantage of man's destruction of the forest; indeed the gaur or seladang

(*Bos gaurus*) is believed to be a recent invader of Malaya following Neolithic man, and dependent on his forest clearings (Medway 1972*b*).

Amongst both birds and mammals the montane fauna has closer affinities with continental Asia, especially with the Himalaya, than does the more distinctively Sundaic lowland fauna. A similar pattern in flora is discussed in §16.3.

The mammal fauna is a very rich one despite extinctions which have occurred during the Pleistocene period. Malaya, for example, has 199 known species of mammals (11 orders, 32 families) including 81 species of bat (Medway 1969). The avifauna is also extremely rich. There are some 800 bird species known to occur on the lands of the Sunda shelf, 633 of them breeding there; some 70 per cent of the birds inhabit forest (excluding mangrove forest). The Sunda avifauna reaches about 10°N, with small outliers further north, paralleling the distribution of tropical lowland evergreen rain forest (Wells 1971; §12.3). Table 1.2 shows that small areas of lowland forest are richer in bird species in Malaya than is rain forest in Africa. They are comparable in richness to South and Central American samples. Concerning reptiles and amphibia, Lloyd, Inger, and King (1968) have demonstrated the very rich fauna of a lowland forest in Sarawak. In an area of 52 km^2, and during 1 year, 135 species were seen (72 of them regularly), comprising 48 species of amphibians, 40 of lizards, and 47 of snakes. This may be contrasted with 41 species in Fukkien and 43 in a small forest area in Mississippi.

TABLE 1.2

Several tropical forest avifaunas compared †

Place	Area (km^2)	Breeding species	Period
Africa			
Congo	52	128	
Nigeria: (i)	210	100	long
(ii)	65	117	
South America			
Panama: Barro Colorado	15	175‡	?
Costa Rica	2·6	269‡	?
East Peru, Balta	80	>300	long
Southeast Asia			
Malaya: Pasoh	10	175	4 days
Kuala Lompat	0·2	141	3 days
Ulu Sat	2·6	127	1 week

† After Wells (1971) except East Peru after Amadon (1973).
‡ May include migrants and birds of open places.

2 Forest structure

THIS CHAPTER is concerned with the structure of the rain-forest ecosystem, an introduction to its dynamic nature (which will be developed further in Part III), and a discussion of the interrelationships of plants and animals.

2.1. The rain-forest ecosystem

Rain forest is a complex community whose framework is provided by trees of many sizes. In this book the term *forest canopy* is used as a general one to describe the total plant community above the ground. Within the canopy the microclimate differs from that outside; there is less light, humidity is higher, and temperature is lower. Many of the smaller trees grow in the shade of the larger ones in the microclimate that these produce. Upon the framework of the trees and within the microclimate of the canopy grow a range of other kinds of plants: climbers, epiphytes, strangling plants, parasites, and saprophytes.

The trees and most of the other plants are rooted in the soil and draw nutrients and water from it. Their fallen leaves, twigs, branches, and other parts provide food for a host of invertebrate animals, amongst which termites are often important, and for fungi and bacteria. Nutrients are returned to the soil via decay of fallen parts and by leaching from the leaves by rain-water. It is a feature of tropical rain forest that most of the total nutrient store is in the vegetation; relatively little is held in the soil.

Within the forest canopy, especially in lowland forest, there live a large range of animals, vertebrates and invertebrates, some eating plant parts, some eating other animals. Complex interrelationships exist between plants and animals, for example, in relation to pollination of flowers and dispersal of fruits. Some plants, so-called myrmecophytes, provide shelter for ants in modified organs. Many plants, it is now believed, produce chemicals noxious to many insects and in this way attempt to protect themselves from being eaten.

The whole organic community and its immediate physical and chemical environment together make up the ecosystem (Tansley 1935) of the rain forest. If part of the forest is destroyed plants (and attendant animals) recolonize the gap, others invade in competition with them; there is a secondary succession of seral plant communities, until eventually a community similar to the original is restored. This is called the climax. On bare land surfaces, for example, that created in 1963 by the eruption of Gunung Agong in Bali, a primary succession, or prisere, occurs leading also to the climax.

Over a sufficiently large area the climax itself is in a state of dynamic equilibrium. There is no net increase in the biomass of living plants and animals; deaths are more or less balanced by replacements. This is true on time-scales comparable to a man's life-span, and may be so too over a few centuries. But on a long, secular scale there may be change in the geographical range of species following alterations in climate such as have occurred during the Pleistocene period, and there are hints of this having happened, as will be shown later in Part IV, Chapters 12 and 15. On a still longer time-scale new plants and animals have evolved and come to influence the ecosystem.

2.2. The synusiae

A synusia is a group of plants of similar life-form which fill the same niche and play a similar role in the community of which it forms a part (Richards 1952); that is, it is a partial life-form community.

Synusiae provide a good means for analyzing complex plant communities. Richards (1952) has introduced a convenient practical classification for the synusiae of tropical rain forest:

A. Autotrophic plants (with chlorophyll)
 1. Mechanically independent plants.
    (a) trees and treelets;
    (b) herbs.
 2. Mechanically dependent plants.
    (a) climbers;
    (b) stranglers;
    (c) epiphytes (including semi-parasitic epiphytes).
B. Heterotrophic plants (without chlorophyll).
 1. Saprophytes.
 2. Parasites.

These synusiae are elaborated at length in Richards' book. They will be mentioned only briefly in this chapter to provide a basis for later chapters, or where there is new information from the Far East, or to draw attention to topics ripe for fuller investigation.

Species of very diverse taxonomic affinity make up

12

the synusiae. As well as having a common life-form, many also have very similar physiognomy. The relative representation of these ecological groups differs in the various Formations of the tropical rain forest and is important in their definition. They are all represented in tropical lowland evergreen rain forest. The synusiae occur throughout the tropics wherever the Formations are found.

2.3. The forest growth cycle

Trees are mortal and eventually die of old age, commonly from the branch tips backwards to the centre of the crown, so that old moribund specimens ('overmature' in foresters' parlance) are 'stag-headed', with heavy limbs exposed by the loss of the more slender members; boles are commonly hollow at this stage. The crown falls to the ground in parts, and eventually the trunk and remaining limb stubs fall, often blown over by a high gust of wind preceding a storm. Alternatively the trunk disintegrates as a standing column. Many trees never reach such an advanced stage but are struck dead by lightning or are blown over singly or in groups at their prime maturity or earlier. Foresters attempt to harvest a tree well before its moribund old age.

The death of an individual tree or of a group produces a gap in the forest canopy into which other trees grow. These in turn reach maturity and perhaps senescence, then die. The forest canopy, therefore, is continually changing as trees grow up and die. It is a living entity in a state of dynamic equilibrium. It is convenient to analyze this growth cycle of the canopy into three phases: the gap phase, the building phase, and the mature phase (cf. Watt 1947).

The extent and arrangement of these phases differs from forest to forest, mainly because of different causative factors of death. This aspect is discussed further in Chapter 6. In a lowland evergreen dipterocarp rain forest in central Malaya, a region where small gaps are the usual kind, Poore (1968) measured their extent as 9·9 per cent of his survey area of 23·04 ha.

The amount of new plant matter produced per unit area per unit time, which can be called the net primary productivity of the forest, differs between the phases. It is low in the gap phase, increases to a maximum in the building phase, and declines during the mature phase (cf. Watt 1947). This aspect will be discussed further in Chapter 8.

The phases cannot be regarded as separate entities because the gap phase passes by growth into the building phase, which itself becomes mature by continuing growth; rather, they are convenient abstractions and they can be readily recognized in the forest. To use the terms of forestry, the gap phase contains juvenile, seedling and sapling, trees (conventionally plants to 2·7 m tall and to 0·3 m girth respectively); the building phase is a forest of still-juvenile trees of pole size (conventionally stems 0·3–0·9 m girth); and the mature phase contains trees in the foresters' strict sense, as well as smaller stems.

Forest structure is conventionally depicted by the *profile diagram*. This is a side-on sketch of all the trees on a narrow strip which is conventionally 7·5 m wide and usually about 60 m long; also by convention, trees shorter than either 4·5 m or 6 m tall are omitted. The profile diagram has been very widely used as an aid to the description of tropical rain forest since its introduction by Davis and Richards (1933–4) for a study in British Guiana; it had been earlier used for temperate forests, for instance by Watt (1924) in his study of English beechwoods. Profile diagrams are nearly always restricted to the mature phase of the forest growth cycle, though sometimes the building phase is included. They are also invariably chosen to include one or more emergent trees.

Figure 2.1 shows a profile along a ridge in tropical lowland evergreen dipterocarp rain forest at Belalong in Brunei. The mature phase is represented to left and right, the canopy top being formed of three giant mature dipterocarps, *Shorea laevis*, *S. parvifolia*, and *Hopea bracteata* (45 m, 40 m, and 40 m tall respectively). In the centre is a patch of building phase containing two dipterocarp poles, *Shorea glaucescens* (16·3 m) and *S. laevis* (23·7 m), still with deep monopodial crowns and which are both still growing in height (see below). Figure 2.2 is another Brunei forest seen in profile.

Figure 2.3 shows in plan view the mosaic of the three phases of the growth cycle in another small area of tropical lowland evergreen dipterocarp rain forest, this one 2·02 ha at Sungei Menyala in Malaya. Long narrow gaps due to the windfall of single dead trunks can be clearly seen. The larger gaps are due to the multiple windfall of trees on the edge of smaller original gaps. The biggest gap of all is centred on an area where all the trees have died, possibly from fungal attack of the roots (see §6.1). Regrowth of gaps, currently at the building phase, is visible. The plan was drawn in 1971. The extensive area of building phase at the north end of the plot is a reflection of the fact that the forest there had been cleared (but then abandoned 54 years previously, in 1917) for a rubber plantation (Wyatt-Smith 1966).

13

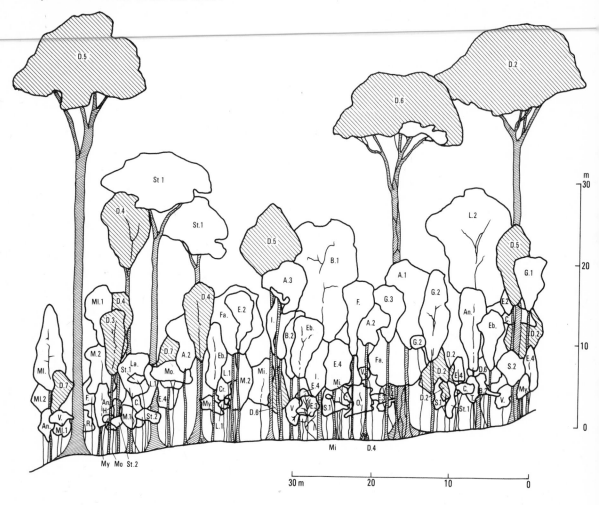

Fig. 2.1. Mature and building phases on a ridge at Belalong, Brunei, in tropical lowland evergreen mixed dipterocarp rain forest; plot area 60 m × 7.5 m, all trees over 4.5 m tall shown. Dipterocarps hatched, note that in the building phase these retain the tall narrow (monopodial) crowns of youth (see text). (Ashton 1964, Fig. 27.) Species and stem numbers. Anacardiaceae: A.1, *Buchanania insignis* (1); A.2, *Gluta laxiflora* (2); A.3, *Swintonia glauca* (2). Annonaceae: An, *Popowia pisocarpa* (3). Burseraceae: B.1, *Dacryodes rostrata* (2); B.2, *Dacryodes laxa* (2). Celastraceae: C, *Lophopetalum javanicum* (3). Crypteroniaceae: Cr, *Crypteronia griffithii* (1). Dipterocarpaceae: D.1, *Dipterocarpus caudatus* (1); D.2, *Hopea bracteata* (4); D.4, *Shorea dolichocarpa* (1); D.4, *S. glaucescens* (4); D.5, *S. laevis* (3); D.6, *S. parvifolia* (3); D.7, *Vatica odorata* (2). Ebenaceae: Eb, *Diospyros sumatrana* v. *decipiens* (3). Fagaceae: Fa, *Quercus argentata* (2). Flacourtiaceae: F, *Hydnocarpus pentagyna* (2). Euphorbiaceae: E.1, *Aporusa nitida* (1); E.2, *A. prainiana* (1); E.3, *Mallotus* sp. (2); E.4, *Pimelodendron griffithianum* (4). Guttiferae: G.1, *Calophyllum depressinervosum* (1); G.2, *C. rubiginosum* (2); G.3, *C.* sp. (1). Hypericaceae: H, *Cratoxylum sumatranum* (1). Icacinaceae: I, *Stemonurus umbellatus* (2). Lauraceae: La, *Litsea* sp. (2). Leguminosae: L.1, *Fordia filipes* (3); L.2, *Koompassia malaccensis* (1). Meliaceae: Ml.1, *Dysoxylum motleyanum* (1); Ml.2, *Sandoricum maingayi* (1). Moraceae: Mor, *Prainea frutescens* (2). Myrsinaceae: My, *Ardisia* sp. (3). Myristicaceae: Mi, *Knema latericia* (3). Myrtaceae: M.1, *Eugenia cuneiforme* (3); M.2, *E. rosulenta* (2). Olacaceae: O, *Ochanostachys amentacea* (1). Sapotaceae: S.1, *Ganua palembanica* (2); S.2, *Palaquium rostratum* (1). Sterculiaceae: St.1, *Scaphium macropodum* (4); St.2, *Heritiera sumatrana* (2). Tiliaceae: T, *Pentace macrophylla* (1). Verbenaceae: V, *Teijsmanniodendron coriaceum* (3). Rubiaceae: R, *Timonius borneensis* (1).

FIG. 2.2.   Tropical lowland evergreen mixed dipterocarp rain forest in profile with *Dipterocarpus crinitus* (right centre) and *Shorea curtisii* to its left; Brunei.

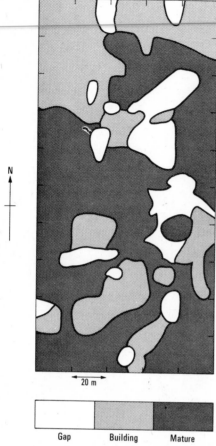

Gap · Building · Mature

FIG. 2.3. Canopy phases on 2 ha of tropical lowland evergreen mixed dipterocarp rain forest at Sungei Menyala, Malaya, 1971. Long narrow gaps result from windfall of single moribund giant trees. Big gaps result from multiple windfall increasing an originally small gap. The extensive area at the north end of building phase forest results from regrowth after partial clearance in 1917.

2.4. Stratification

The canopy of tropical rain forest is often considered to be layered or stratified and different forest Formations to have different numbers of strata. Strata (layers or storeys) are sometimes easy to see in the forest or on a profile diagram, and sometimes not. Few concepts are likely so quickly to divide a room-full of ecologists into two vociferously opposed groups as this one, and it is necessary to make a close examination of the features involved.

Different authors have referred to different aspects of layering, which they have not always clearly distinguished. Nor has it always been made clear whether a particular area is claimed to be stratified (for instance, the 60 m × 7.5 m plot on the profile

Fig. 2.1 or the area seen in Fig. 2.4) or whether the author is dealing in abstract terms with an extensive tract.

Probably the most common usage of the term stratification is to refer to layering of total tree height, which is sometimes refined as layering of tree crowns. The classic view of layering in tropical lowland evergreen rain forest is that there are five strata, A–E. The A stratum comprises the top layer of the biggest trees which commonly stand as isolated or grouped emergents 'head and shoulders' above a continuous B layer, the main canopy. Figure 2.1 clearly shows A and B layers. Under B is a lower storey of trees, the C layer, which in Fig. 2.1 merges into B except at two points near the left end. The D layer is woody treelets and the E layer forest-floor herbs and small seedlings. Together these five layers comprise the synusiae of mechanically independent autotrophic plants (see above). Correlated with this structural layering, it is frequently the case that in the lower strata the tree crowns are mostly taller than broad, and vice versa in the upper ones; this can be seen in Fig. 2.1.

The concept of structural layering loses sight of the dynamic nature of the rain-forest canopy, which is in fact growing up in patches all the time. Patches of various sizes are at the various phases of the forest growth cycle. In Fig. 2.1 the emergents represent two patches, to left and right, of the mature phase. The main or B stratum comprises the area of the building phase in the centre plus also some of the trees in the mature patches, and merges in with the lower or C stratum, which is only clear as a separate entity in part of the left patch of mature phase forest.

The layering of crown shape is correlated with tree growth (see §2.5). Young trees still growing in height are nearly always monopodial, with a single stem (there are a few exceptions, for example *Alstonia*), and the crown is usually tall and narrow. Mature trees of most species are sympodial, without a single central trunk, and the several limbs continue to grow adding to crown width after the mature height has been attained; most usually, sympodial crowns are broader than they are deep, increasingly so with increasing tree-age. More short trees are immature than tall ones. Layering of crown shape is thus to be expected.

Height growth of most tree species is completed when only between one-third and one-half of the final bole diameter has been reached. It follows that foliage will tend to be concentrated in layers wherever a species or a group of species of similar

FIG. 2.4. Tropical lowland evergreen rain forest, Bukit Bauk, Malaya, with emergent *Shorea* and *Canarium* but no other clearly distinct stratification. Note man.

mature height predominates in a stand, as, for instance, in the dipterocarp forest shown in Fig. 2.1. Layering will be most marked in stands containing a few species or only one, and is least likely in a forest of numerous dissimilar species where individuals of a given species are scattered. Species which are light-demanders (Chapter 6) usually grow up in pure stands. Commonly, slower growing individuals of such species die, as they are over-topped and become shaded, thus accentuating stratification. By contrast, slow-growing individuals of shade-tolerant species persist, and marked layering in stands of such species is less likely (Dawkins 1966).

Structural layering is sometimes visible on profile diagrams or in the forest and the number and height of the layers will depend on the phase or phases of the growth cycle represented. Three tree layers in tropical lowland evergreen rain forest is a convenient abstraction which represents the usual state of the building and mature phases considered together. But the

pooling of data from an area without regard to the phasic stages will usually obscure the existence of layering, except in forests with a few species or groups maturing at different heights.

Another use of the concept of stratification is of the height at which certain tree genera or even families commonly mature. For example, in Malaya the topmost or emergent layer is composed mostly of groups of Dipterocarpaceae and Leguminosae. Of the Dipterocarpaceae, *Dipterocarpus, Dryobalanops,* and *Shorea* provide most of the emergents and by contrast *Hopea* and *Vatica* are mostly small trees of the B and C layers. Only a few of the 53 species of Leguminosae trees in Malaya are common as emergents, principally species of *Dialium, Koompassia,* and *Sindora* (Whitmore 1972d). Dipterocarp lowland evergreen rain forests usually have the top of the canopy at 45 m, and individual trees reaching 60 m tall are common. The tallest trees recorded are *Koompassia excelsa* (80·72 m Malaya, 83·82 m

Sarawak;† Fig. 4.2, p. 54) and *Dryobalanops aromatica* 67·1 m (Foxworthy 1926). East of the Philippines dipterocarps are only locally important and the canopy is lower, for example, *Vitex cofassus–Pometia pinnata* forest in lowland Bougainville is usually 30–35 m tall with scattered emergents to 39 m (Heyligers 1967).

Burseraceae and Sapotaceae are abundant in the main canopy layer in west Malesia and the top canopy layer in east Malesia. At this region-wide level of generalization one can say that the C or bottom tree layer contains most species of the two biggest tree families, Euphorbiaceae and Rubiaceae, and many Annonaceae, Lauraceae, and Myristicaceae, amongst others.

Trees which attain the canopy top are exposed to the external atmosphere, intense insolation, high temperature, and considerable wind movement, and have to be suitably adapted physiologically. Within the canopy the microclimate is quite different, as was outlined in the introduction to this chapter and is elaborated in the next. It follows that one might expect to recognize certainly two distinct groups of species, adapted to these two sets of conditions; and it is interesting that whole genera, or even whole families, do exploit one situation or the other. Species which grow up in shade but reach the top of the canopy at maturity thereby live in two very different environments at different stages of life, and probably change physiologically, though experimental data are still largely lacking (see §8.4).

The lower part of the canopy contains young individuals of growing trees which will become taller as well as mature short trees. The rapid increase in the number of species enumerated at increasingly small girths on plots of 0·4 ha is dramatically depicted in Fig. 1.4 (p. 6). More species are adapted to live within the canopy than to reach the top, or emergent, stratum of the biggest girth trees.

2.5. Tree form

Trees are the predominant life-form of the rain forest. Even the undergrowth is composed mainly of woody plants of tree-form; true shrubs are rare, though the D stratum is sometimes loosely called the 'shrub layer'.

Crown

The most important aspect of tree-form for a forester has already been mentioned in the previous

† This is the tallest rain forest broad-leaf tree in the world and is only exceeded by the conifer *Araucaria hunsteinii*, of which an individual 88·9 m tall was measured in 1941 (Gray).

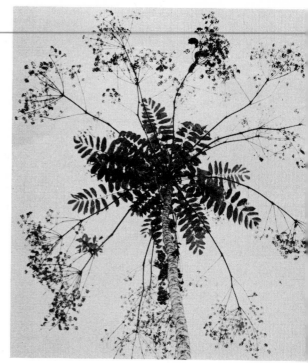

FIG. 2.5. Monopodial crown of the small secondary forest tree *Arthrophyllum diversifolium*, Araliaceae, in Malaya.

section: the distinction between monopodial and sympodial crown construction (Figs 2.5 and 2.6). The change to the latter is to some extent genetically determined, but trees grown in the open often lose their single leading shoot at a much shorter height than in the forest. This is well shown by trees planted isolated as specimens, for example, the arboretum of Dipterocarpaceae at Kepong, Malaya. Some species retain monopodial crowns throughout life, for example, all Annonaceae and Myristicaceae in the tropical Far East; this is especially common amongst small tree species which mature within the canopy (Fig. 2.7). A forester is interested in wood volume increment per area, and monopodial trees with their characteristic narrow crowns are better subjects for growing in plantations than most sympodial species. This is one reason why those conifers which will grow in the humid tropics have attracted so much attention, especially the tropical *Pinus* spp. and *Araucaria* (Chapter 14) and why *Shorea* spp. of the Light Red Meranti timber group of the Dipterocarpaceae and other fast-growing, light-demanding hardwood species indigenous to the region, such as *Albizia falcata*, *Campnosperma*, *Endospermum*, and *Octomeles*, have only limited attraction. Calculations of the bole-diameter/crown-

FIG. 2.6. A mature tree of *Shorea curtisii*, a giant dipterocarp, showing sympodial crown structure with discrete subcrowns. A strangling fig (note its descending roots) has commenced growth in the crown base. Brunei.

FIG. 2.7. Monopodial crown of *Chisocheton princeps*, a treelet of lowland rain forest, Malaya; note man.

diameter ratio have shown that a bole area of 19–23 m²/ha is the maximum possible in most even-aged tropical tree plantation crops without crown overlap (Dawkins 1963*b*).

There is a very wide range of types of crown construction amongst trees of the tropical rain forest (Figs 2.6–2.8), which comes as a surprise to a person brought up in a temperate country with its very limited tree flora. The result is a great diversity of tree-form, which is of considerable importance for species identification in the forest.

Hallé and Oldeman (1970*a*, 1975) have recently attempted an analysis of tropical tree-form, building on the earlier work mainly of Corner (1940), Holttum (1955, for Monocotyledons), and Koriba (1958), and have brought the subject to the point where experi-

ments might now usefully be devised. However, they had to restrict themselves to understorey species and the young stages of big trees growing within the canopy, because forest giants were found to vary too much with environment. The main factors which influence crown-form are apical versus lateral growth; radially symmetrical versus bilaterally symmetrical meristems; and intermittent and rhythmic versus continuous growth of leaves or flowers. Tree architecture does not correlate well with taxonomy, some families are rich in forms, for example, Euphorbiaceae (Hallé 1971), and others poor, for example, Myristicaceae. The number of orders of branching varies from nil, in nearly all palms and all tree ferns, to one or two, in *Pandanus* and *Sararanga*, most *Dracaena*, most Sterculiaceae and Araliaceae (Fig.

FIG. 2.8. The pagoda-like crown of *Alstonia scholaris* (Honiara, Solomon Islands).

2.5), many Annonaceae and Myristicaceae, to numerous, as in many Dipterocarpaceae and Leguminosae, to cite only a few examples. The sparsely branched species commonly have stout twigs, whereas copiously branched species tend to have slender twigs; these forms have been called pachycaul and leptocaul respectively (Corner 1949). There is a small group of unbranched treelets with palm-like construction, commonly with a head of big leaves, and some with stout stems, which are conspicuous by their curious construction; the latter have been called *schopfbäumchen* (Drude 1890, in Hallé and Oldemann 1970) or, in Corner's terminology, pachycaul treelets. These are noticeably more frequent in the Solomon Islands' forests than in Malaya and Borneo (Whitmore 1969b); examples are species of *Tapeinosperma* (Stone and Whitmore 1970), *Barringtonia*, and *Schefflera*. This group comes at one end of Hallé and Oldeman's scheme, as monocaul trees, which they divide into the *modèles Holttum* (inflorescence terminal) and *modèles Corner* (inflorescences lateral).

Horn (1971), using a theoretical model of the photosynthetic efficiency of different shapes of crown, has attempted to forecast which will be most successful in different situations. He predicted that crowns with a single layer of leaves (monolayer) should dominate in the shady forest understorey and multilayered crowns in the well-illuminated upper parts of the canopy. The change from monopodial to sympodial crown as tree height increases in tropical rain forest appears to counter this prediction, but Horn's approach illustrates a recent advance in the attempt to correlate form with function which will no doubt be developed in the future.

Bole

To the observer on the forest-floor bole-form is usually more or less columnar, at least up to the lowest limbs, and he feels as though in a lofty green-roofed cathedral. In fact there is usually some degree of taper, as can readily be seen on felled trees and for which allowance must be made when constructing volume tables for forestry purposes.

Buttresses

Buttress-height, spread, thickness, and surface-form are generally fairly constant within a species and therefore, like crown-form, buttresses are a valuable guide to forest identification (Figs 2.9 and 2.10). A simple practical classification was introduced by Wyatt-Smith (1954b; see also Whitmore 1966a). Within dipterocarp lowland evergreen rain forest in Malaya 40·7 per cent of 18 067 'timber-size' trees measured had buttresses reaching higher than 1·35 m; the range was from 87·8 per cent of *Intsia palembanica* stems down to only 0·8 per cent of *Calophyllum* (Setten 1953). For *Koompassia malaccensis* incidence of buttresses varied from 35 per cent (Kemahang) to 93 per cent (Bukit Mambai), and buttress-height increased with girth in this species, also in *Dryobalanops aromatica*, *Shorea leprosula*, and *S. parvifolia* but not in *S. curtisii* (Setten 1954a,b).

There is singularly little evidence from which to judge the truth or otherwise of the common generalization (for example, of Corner 1940, Richards 1952) that trees with deep tap roots do not form buttresses, and vice versa. Henwood (1973) has recently demonstrated by the analysis of the stresses to which a tree is subject, using a simple model and a formulation borrowed from engineering, that buttresses are indeed structural members which help to support trees on substrates that offer poor anchorage, as has long been suspected (see the review in Richards (1952)). They act as tension members which reduce the strain on the roots on which they occur (and indeed they resonate when hit with a bush knife). They thus make these roots less susceptible to withdrawal or breakage under strain. Flowering plants are known to form tension wood rather than compression wood. Buttresses

21

FIG. 2.9. The highly distinctive buttresses of *Kostermansia malayana*, a monotypic genus endemic to Malaya where it is confined to lowland rain forest.

develop on the windward side, where there is a prevalent wind direction, on the uphill side on slopes (for
example, on all trees in an extensive stand of *Shorea
curtisii* at Semangko forest, Malaya (Burgess)). In
trees with asymmetric crown or a heavy asymmetric
climber load, buttresses can be expected to form on
the side opposite to the bulk of the crown or
climbers. The different incidence of buttresses in
different species can be ascribed to intrinsic differences in construction of the root system and in the
tensile strength of the root wood. Differences
between sites and individuals reflect substrate and
loading differences. The incidence and size of
buttresses diminishes with altitude (Table 16.1, p.
199), part of the explanation must be that smaller
trees have a lesser need for support.

Bark

It is still a common fallacy that all or most rain
forest trees have pale, thin, and smooth bark (see
Walter (1973) for the latest statement). This is far
from the case. In fact, within rain forest there is a
rich range of colours and shades from black
(*Diospyros*) to white (*Tristania*), through fawn and
bright rufous brown (*Eugenia*). It is only trunks
exposed outside the forest microclimate, such as are
possessed by isolated trees and at forest fringes,
which are bleached to a uniform pale grey. Saplings
and small poles do have thin, smooth bark. Trunks
over about 0·9 m girth exhibit a great diversity of
surface sculpturings, crudely summarized as fissured
(Fig. 2.11), scaly (Fig. 2.10), or dippled (Fig. 14.4, p.
173), and some smooth (Fig. 2.12). After leaf, bark
surface characteristics and the appearance in section
('slash' or 'blaze') are the most important aids to
forest recognition of species (Whitmore 1962*d*,
1972*c*) and may have significance for taxonomy
(Whitmore 1963). Some families are fairly homogeneous in bark (for instance, most Lauraceae are
smooth) and others show the whole gamut of
patterns (for example, Dipterocarpaceae (Whitmore
1963)). It is now known that smooth barks are
slowly growing (Whitmore 1962*a,b,c*, 1972*c*) with the
surface long-persistent, and these are the barks on
which lichens grow, often as conspicuous splashes
of colour (Figs 2.12 and 2.13).

Went ((1940) reviewed by Richards (1952) and van
Steenis (1972)) demonstrated that in the mountain
forest at Cibodas in west Java, different tree species
have different epiphytes and that this is most
likely due to water-soluble chemicals in the bark. By
contrast, epiphytes growing on humus were far less
specific in their hosts. This interesting work has still

FIG. 2.10. Flying buttresses of a *Eugenia* in Brunei.

not been followed up or extended; some bark microlichens appear to be specific and aid, by their colour,
the forest recognition of particular species, for
example, the dark-green lichen on *Diospyros*.

Flowers

The frequency with which flowers are borne on
the trunk (cauliflory) (Figs 2.14 and 2.15) or
branches (ramiflory) varies between the different
tropical rain forest Formations. Cauliflory is

23

FIG. 2.11. The coarsely fissured bark of *Shorea curtisii* (Gunung Benom, Malaya). [above]

FIG. 2.12. The columner bole and pale, smooth bark, flecked with microlichen patches of a *Vatica* (Brunei). [top right]

FIG. 2.13. Microlichens on the old culms of a bamboo (Ulu Perak, Malaya). [bottom right]

commonest in lowland evergreen rain forest and diminishes rapidly with elevation (Table 16.1, p. 199). Merrill (1945) tells how Osbeck (on a voyage from Sweden to China), during a short stop in Java on 20 January 1752, was so deceived by this feature, unknown in northern Europe, that he described the cauliflorous inflorescence of the cultivated fruit tree *Lansium domesticum* (duku, langsat) as a leafless parasite *Melia parasitica*, 'a small rare herb growing on tree trunks'. Trunk-borne flowers may even be at ground level, as in some *Durio* spp. and *Baccaurea parviflora* (Figs 2.16 and 2.17), or below ground, as in several gingers and the so-called geocarpic figs where they occur on the end of whip-like strands reaching 6 m long (Corner 1940; 17 species). Richards (1952) gives a full account of cauliflory.

Roots

There is a growing, renewed interest in the root systems of tropical rain forest trees with the recent development of studies in productivity and mineral cycling. As is generally the case, most roots in the rain forest are to be found in the top 0·3 m or so of the soil. Many trees have entirely superficial root systems with no deeply penetrating roots at all. Some, probably a minority, have deep tap roots; but owing to the practical difficulties root systems have been very little studied. Nye and Greenland (1960) have drawn attention to the important role of the relatively few roots which do penetrate to depth in bringing up mineral nutrients from weathering rock particles or illuvial horizons, besides their role as stabilizers and anchors. It is believed that one important reason why most roots are concentrated near the surface is because most mineral nutrients are found there, resulting from the decomposition of fallen plant and animal remains. Mycorrhizas are known to be associated with many species in this superficial zone of the soil, but this subject is still mainly unexplored (Singh 1966; Went and Stark 1968). Some species have root nodules, containing nitrogen-fixing bacteria (for example, Casuarinaceae and Leguminosae except Caesalpinoideae); the importance of their role also remains uninvestigated. Kerfoot (1963) has drawn attention to the anaerobosis likely to develop at depth, especially in wet or compact soils and at the high respiration rates

FIG. 2.15. Cauliflorous *Baccaurea griffithii* (North Malaya).

FIG. 2.14. Cauliflorous *Dysoxylum caulostachyum* (Guadalcanal, Solomon Islands).

FIG. 2.16. *Baccaurea parviflora*, flowering at ground level (Malaya).

FIG. 2.17. *Baccaurea parviflora*, fruiting at ground level (Malaya).

at the prevailing high temperatures; he suggested this is likely to contribute to the occurrence of mainly superficial root systems. Odum (1970) suggested that in mountains or elsewhere where transpiration is low, trees will extract insufficient water from the soil to prevent waterlogging and hence anaerobic conditions.

The weight of the root system was calculated, in a tropical semi-evergreen rain forest in south Thailand (Ogawa, Yoda, Ogino, and Kira 1965b; §8.3), from excavation of samples, to vary from $\frac{1}{10}$ to $\frac{1}{3}$ of the weight of the above ground parts which is from 0·5–1·7 tonne per 100 m². This is $\frac{1}{2}$ to $1\frac{1}{2}$ times the weight of the tree crowns. The root system was about 80 per cent of the crown-weight for a forest of the same Formation in the Ivory Coast (and see Evans 1972, p. 525).

2.6. Epiphytes, climbers and stranglers

Richards (1952, Chapter 5) gives a full review of the available information on these dependent synusiae, and there is a review of terminology in

Grubb, Lloyd, Pennington, and Whitmore (1963). They are discussed here in so far as they bear on later chapters, for example, there are differences between different rain-forest Formations, and to draw attention to topics ripe for further investigation.

Epiphytes and climbers are stratified. Within each synusia two main groups can be recognized: a photo-phytic or sun-loving group, adapted morphologically and physiologically to the microclimate of the canopy top, and a skiophytic or shade-loving group, adapted to the cooler, darker, moister microclimates within the forest canopy; though the distinction is never absolute.

Epiphytes

Tree-crown epiphytes (Figs 2.18 and 2.19) include many orchids and Ericaceae (especially *Vaccinium* species). A special group of this synusia is the hemi-parasitic epiphytes which are attached to the host tree by haustoria through which mainly water and mineral nutrients, and in addition some photosynthate, are taken up. All Loranthaceae are in

FIG. 2.18. Epiphytic *Asplenium nidus* in light shade. Lower montane rain forest (Cibodas, Java).

FIG. 2.19. *Pandanus epiphyticus*, an epiphyte of the lower crowns of big trees in lowland rain forest (Johore, Malaya).

this class, the mistletoe of Europe being the most familiar example. Far Eastern Loranthaceae have long, conspicuous, vivid red and yellow flowers and are believed to be bird-pollinated (see §2.8). There are also several Santalaceous hemi-parasites, *Dendrotrophe*, *Dendromyza*, and their allies and including one genus, *Phacellaria*, which is hemi-parasitic on other Santalaceous or Loranthaceous hemi-parasites (Danser 1939; Whitmore 1973*h*). A few Loranthaceae are hemi-parasitic on other hemi-parasites, for example, *Viscum articulatum*.

Bole epiphytes range in their degree of adaptation to cool and dark conditions. It is sometimes useful to distinguish the vascular epiphytes (flowering plants and pteridophytes) from the non-vascular ones, that is, Bryophyta, Algae (including the orange-red coloured Green Alga *Trentepohlia*) and lichens.

Ability to resist or endure periodic drought is important for epiphytes. Walter (1964, 1973) has drawn attention to the two major strategies in his two classes: homoiohydres, plants which avoid desiccation, and poikilohydres, plants whose protoplasm resists drying out, and which revive on rewetting; in this latter class are most non-vascular plants, filmy ferns (*Hymenophyllum* and *Trichomanes*), and some dicotyledonous herbs, especially members of the

Fig. 2.20. Leaves with abundant epiphyllae and pronounced drip tips. Lower montane rain forest (Ecuador).

Gesneriaceae. Went's work at Cibodas, demonstrating that at least some epiphytes are host-specific, has been briefly reviewed above. Went mentioned in passing that the epiphytic fern *Pyrrosia nummulariifolia*, which frequently webs coffee twigs with its long, thin rhizomes, was believed by planters to contribute to the decay of the twigs. Ruinen (1953) was able to confirm this, and show that certain small orchids produce a similar effect. She coined the term 'epiphytosis' for what appears to be a form of mild parasitism. She also showed a similar influence for the tiny epiphytes·growing on leaves, the so-called epiphylls (Fig. 2.20), which are a characteristic feature of the more humid rain forests.

In a recent massive study of the effects of high levels of radioactivity on lower montane rain forest on Puerto Rico in the Caribbean, Odum and his collaborators discovered that there is a very high retention of radioactive fallout by the epiphyll flora, which was also shown to fix atmospheric nitrogen (Odum 1970). It is now well established that considerable quantities of minerals are leached from the canopy, mainly from the leaves (for example, Kenworthy 1971). Odum suggested that his findings indicate an important role of the so-called 'phyllosphere' in trapping minerals cycling in the forest ecosystem. The function of drip tips (the long drawn-out apices sometimes possessed by all or some of the leaves of many rain-forest species—Fig. 2.20) is ripe for review, in correlation with studies on the establishment and role of an epiphyll flora. There has long been a controversy (amply reviewed by Richards (1952)) as to whether drip tips increase the rate of run-off from the leaf lamina or not.

In the lowland rain forest of Kolombangara, an island in the Solomon archipelago, epiphytes were found to be consistently less luxuriant in an area believed to be first-generation regrowth from extensive clearings than in older forest (Whitmore (1974) and §15.4). On a regional scale, shade epiphytes are commoner in the lowland forest of the Solomons and Santa Cruz archipelagos than in the Malayan and Bornean forest, reflecting the extremely moist, tropical oceanic climate of these islands (Fig. 17.5, p. 223). In the dry-land lowland rain forests of Malaya, and probably of most other countries of the tropical Far East, epiphytes are inconspicuous. They are in general commoner in swamp forests and in particularly humid situations such as enclosed valleys. They are also in general commoner at high elevations rather than low, being characteristically abundant on mountain peaks subject to frequent fog (Chapter 16).

Climbers

Many climbers which reach the canopy top have crowns of the form, and often the size, of a tree crown. These climbers commonly have a freely hanging woody stem, and can be conveniently referred to as big woody climbers (see Figs 2.11 and 10.2, p. 124). They are represented in very many families of plants. All except two species of the curious gymnosperm *Gnetum* are big woody climbers (and are very readily identified from the raised hoops at nodes on the stems (see Fig. 2.21) (Whitmore 1972*e*)). Amongst the commonest big woody climbers are Annonaceae (for example, in Malaya 14 out of 38 genera and 67 out of 198 described species (Kochummen 1972)), *Bauhinia*,

Mezoneuron, Strychnos, and *Uncaria*. The climbing palms, the rattans (Fig. 2.22), are another important class of big woody climbers which are a particularly pungent feature of the rain forests of our region, especially the western part (Fig. 1.8b, p. 9). Most big woody climbers are photophytes and grow prolifically in clearings and on forest fringes, giving rise to the popular myth of the impenetrable dense jungle. They spring up in gaps and grow with the crowns of young trees, so are carried up with the growing height of the replacement canopy. They also spring up after logging operations and may prove a serious hindrance to the growth of a new forest; for example, *Mezoneuron sumatranum* is especially bad in Sabah and species of *Merremia* there and in the Solomons and *Uncaria* species are common in the whole region. In the survey on Kolombangara just mentioned it was found that there were more species (50 versus 38 per hectare) and individuals (470 versus 194) of big woody climber, and they were of smaller average girth (107 mm versus 143 mm) in

FIG. 2.21.   A climbing *Gnetum* showing the conspicuously hooped stem (Kemahang forest, Malaya).

FIG. 2.22.   The fiercely spiny stem of the climbing palm, rotan kertong (Gunung Stong, Malaya).

FIG. 2.23. Mixed Araceae climbers, some closely adherent to the bole, some with pendent roots, draping the trees along a small river (Roviana lagoon, Solomon Islands). A few fronds of the fern *Stenochlaena* are visible in the centre.

FIG. 2.24. The development of a strangling fig. (From Corner 1940, Fig. 250.)

FIG. 2.25. The strangling fig *Ficus glandulifera*. Lowland rain forest (Solomon Islands).

places believed on other grounds to be first regeneration regrowth forest (Whitmore 1974).

The other group of climbers are the bole climbers (Fig. 2.23), which grow close to a tree adhering by one of various means (Richards 1952). In the same survey in the Solomons there was found to be marked stratification within this synusia. Topmost, and distinctly photophytic, was the climbing pandan *Freycinetia solomonensis*, found on upper boles and in the lower parts of crowns and occasionally also seen in gaps in the canopy at or near ground level. Below this occurred a mixed group of Araceae, themselves stratified. Lowest was a belt of the fern *Stenochlaena*, most markedly skiophytic. Comparing forests in the Solomons of known approximate age, including areas near Munda which had regrown since felling by the Japanese in the Pacific War, the abundance and number of species of bole climbers and epiphytes was seen to increase markedly with age. It is a truism that these synusiae are sparse in secondary forest.

Stranglers

Stranglers are plants which start life as epiphytes and send down roots to the ground which increase in number and girth and self-graft on contact under pressure, ultimately encasing the host tree which often then dies. Figs are the most familiar example (Figs 2.6, 2.24, and 2.25), and true stranglers developing a dense, tight, stem-like structure of often-anastomosing roots must be distinguished from the banyan type which starts life similarly but forms a much more open structure of roots, descending

C

from the limbs and commonly covering an area up to 20 m across. Where banyans are common, as in the Solomons, they are a considerable hindrance to silviculture. Several species of *Schefflera* and *Fagraea* are stranglers, at least facultatively, and strangling species of *Timonius* (New Guinea and Solomons), *Spondias* (Philippines), and even a member of the Scrophulariaceae *Wightia* (see van Steenis 1972) are now known.

2.7. Animals in the forest†

The forest provides the dwelling place for the animals which live within it and also the food source, directly for herbivores and indirectly for carnivores. Producers and consumers can be recognized, the main producers being the autotrophic plants on which the whole ecosystem depends. The consumers comprise all the heterotrophic plants as well as the animals. The ecology of the rain-forest animals is more difficult to study than is that of the plants, not least because it is virtually impossible for the kind of short-term expedition on which so much of the earlier research depended. Resident zoologists have begun to redress the balance, and the complex interactions of animals with each other and with plants now begins to be understood.

Different animals occupy different niches in the rain-forest ecosystem, separated from others in space, in time of activity, or in the plants or other animals utilized for food. Harrison (1962) defined six communities of birds and mammals in tropical lowland evergreen rain forest based on the level of the canopy occupied and by the range of foodstuffs. These are as follows:

1. Above the canopy: insectivorous and carnivorous birds and bats.
2. Top of canopy: birds and mammals feeding largely on leaves and fruits and to a minor extent on nectar and insects also.
3. Middle-of-canopy flying animals: mainly insectivorous birds and bats.
4. Middle-of-canopy scansorial animals: mixed feeding mammals which range up and down tree trunks from crown to ground; also a few carnivores.
5. Large ground animals: herbivores and attendant carnivores.
6. Small ground or undergrowth animals: mammals and birds of varied diets taken from the forest floor, predominantly insectivorous or mixed feeders; plus some herbivores and carnivores.

It can be seen that the main group of phytophagous birds and mammals lives in the top of the canopy (Fig. 4.1, p. 53), the other zones contain fewer primary consumers and far more secondary consumers, animals which prey on other animals.

Within each layer community there is also a distinction between members active by day and those active by night, with, on, the ground, several which are active by both day and night. Figure 2.26 depicts this vertical and diurnal stratification for the non-flying mammals in tropical lowland evergreen rain forest in Sabah.

Wells (1971) pointed out the clear vertical stratification of birds which exists within the canopy of lowland dipterocarp rain forest in Malaya. The top-of-canopy group includes hornbills, barbets, and pigeons, feeding on fruits and insects. The undergrowth birds include pittas, thrushes, babblers, and pheasants. The group inhabiting the middle of the canopy is less clearly defined and in mountain forests becomes difficult to separate; it includes trogons, woodpeckers, and bulbuls.

Horizontal spatial separation of birds between grossly different adjacent habitats has been recorded at Kuala Lompat, Malaya, in an area of lowland rain forest bounded by two large rivers and with a few big clearings; and separation is also reported between mangrove forest and adjacent evergreen rain forest. Details will be given in Chapter 13.

Recent work on monkeys and apes in Sumatra, Malaya, and Borneo has clearly shown the different niches primates utilize within the forest itself. For example, in Sumatra (Wilson and Wilson 1973) the two widespread macaque monkeys have similar geographical distribution, but different habitat preferences. *Macaca fascicularis* (the long-tailed macaque or kera), probably the most abundant primate in the region, is very wide-ranging in disturbed secondary and primary forests, right down to the mangrove forest and seashore. *M. nemestrina* (the pig-tailed macaque or berok) occupies secondary and primary lowland forest, and ranges further from rivers in

† The extremely important account of invertebrate animals in the lowland rain forest at Bukit Timah, Singapore, by Murphy (1973) arrived too late for inclusion. This is by far the fullest work yet published on the ecology of these animals in rain forest. It includes observations on the fauna of different spatial niches, both vertical and horizontal and both continuous and discontinuous, and also major differences between day and night. The extreme richness of the fauna is vividly described, with numerous species and genera and a few higher ranks new to science. It is quite clear that very much can be discovered by continuing observation with a minimum of equipment in even small relict patches of near-virgin rain forest.

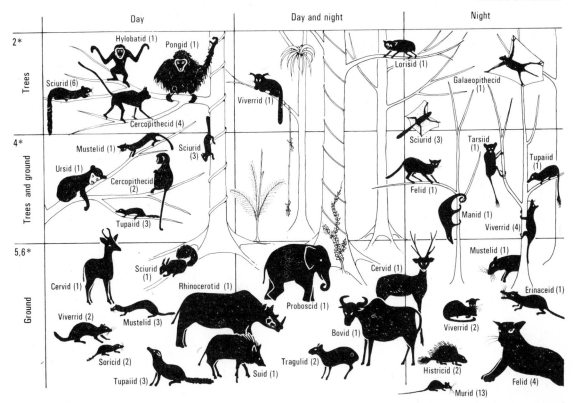

FIG. 2.26. Stratification of the non-flying mammals in the lowland rain forest of Sabah (MacKinnon 1972, Fig. 6). *Communities of Harrison (1962), see text.

primary forest. Where troops occupy the same forest *M. fascicularis* feeds mainly in the trees and *M. nemestrina* on the ground. These findings are confined by observations elsewhere. Of the gibbons, Wilson and Wilson (1973) found the siamang (*Hylobates syndactylus*) (Fig. 2.27) sympatric with the other two species *H. agilis* and *H. lar* in Sumatra but distinctly commoner in lower montane forest. By contrast, Chivers (1972) did not find any difference in elevational preference between *H. syndactylus* and *H. lar* where their ranges overlap in Malaya. Intensive studies of two sites in lowland forest in Malaya inhabited by both these species revealed that on average a troop consists of about four animals. A siamang troop occupies 23 ha, of which not all is utilized, whereas a troop of *H. lar* occupies on average 40 ha. There can be a complete overlap between the two species. Recent unpublished observations by MacKinnon suggest that the remarkable difference in niche-utilization (namely that a siamang troop of twice the biomass of a troop of *H. lar* occupies only half the area) can be attributed to differences in feeding behaviour. At Kuala Lompat he observed that siamang systematically strip trees of

much of their fruit; but *H. lar* is a much more selective feeder, choosing only the ripest fruit, and individuals travel about three times as far in a day as do siamang. MacKinnon believes that this difference in behaviour can be correlated with the energy the animals obtain from their food and that the smaller *H. lar* are able on energy grounds to travel further each day than the bigger and heavier siamang. The orang utan, *Pongo pygmaeus*, travels even less a day than the siamang where all three species co-exist in north Sumatra.

The full details of niche-specialization amongst primates are still being worked out. Wilson and Wilson (1973) estimated that in Sumatra there are on average 6·5 groups comprising more than 27 animals per square kilometre of forest. This island has four distinct races of leaf monkey besides those already mentioned.

The orang utan, the largest arboreal ape in the world (males reach 130 kg weight), has been intensively studied in the Ulu Segama forest of Sabah by MacKinnon (1971, 1972, 1974). The territorial range is large. Animals live solitary lives, with little social interaction except between mother and offspring, and

33

FIG. 2.27. A siamang gibbon, *Hylobates syndactylus* feeding on fruits of *Aglaia* (Kuala Lompat, Malaya).

keep in touch with each other by calling; they travel only a short distance each day through the lower canopy and on the forest floor, foraging primarily for fruits, which they are extremely good at discovering. MacKinnon found that *Pongo* eats a much larger proportion of the fruit crop of a tree than any other arboreal animal, systematically stripping the crown, over several days if necessary. He considered their success in competition with other frugivorous animals lies in greater tolerance of sour and bitter fruits, which they are able to consume before they become ripe enough for other apes, monkeys, and birds. He notes that the fruits taken are mainly the wild ancestors of the cultivated fruit trees of the region (cf. Chapter 17).

We shall consider the extent to which different kinds of forest are inhabited by different animals in Chapter 13 and §16.7.

2.8. Plant and animal interactions

We shall return to other aspects of these primate studies in Part V. To conclude this chapter some

of the specialized interactions between plants and animals now known to exist are considered. This is a field where, as van Steenis (1972) so rightly says, length of discussion is often inversely proportional to the precise information available. It is an important (though very difficult) field in which there is indeed a wealth of speculation, and this is because of the far-reaching implications for evolution within the rain-forest ecosystem. Simple, careful observations are urgently needed.

The forest provides more than a habitat for the animals which live within it. Many of them feed on parts of the plants, and this is believed to have led to co-evolution of plants and animals in several different ways.

Pollination

Flowers have a particular construction, shape, size, colour, and odour, and certain repeatedly occurring combinations exist which may be called 'syndromes' and which are associated with visits by particular classes of animals. For example, 'bird

Fɪɢ. 2.28. Bird-pollinated flowers of *Firmiana malayana*, harsh orange in colour and borne on the bare crown (Ulu Gombak, Malaya, February 1970).

flowers' are scentless, with contrasting harsh colours, often reds, oranges, yellows, and greens and of strong construction with abundant watery nectar (Fig. 2.28). Such are possessed, for example, by most Loranthaceae and the climbing gesneriad *Aeschynanthus*; these are visited by members of the sunbird family Nectariniidae, and are thought to be pollinated by them (McClure 1966; Doctors van Leeuwen 1954; Proctor and Yeo 1973). However, an observed visit does not actually indicate more than the menu of the visitor (van Steenis 1972); self-pollination may actually be the rule as in some Leguminosae and Orchidaceae with apparently highly adapted flowers. The fact that birds have been observed to visit some such flowers in some parts of the world does not necessarily mean that all flowers with this syndrome are visited by birds. It is, however, significant that species with bird flowers brought into cultivation in a different continent are nevertheless recognized and visited by the birds of their new home, for example, *Hibiscus rosa-sinensis* and *Spathodea campanulata* from tropical Africa grown in the Far East. Other flower-visiting birds in the tropical Far East are the White-eyes (Zosteropidae), the Flower-peckers (Dicaeidae), and (in New Guinea) the Honeyeaters (Meliphigidae). A good account of the details of the bird–flower syndrome is presented by Proctor and Yeo (1973).

Pollination ecology is thoroughly reviewed in recent books by Faegri and van der Pijl (1966, 1971) and Proctor and Yeo (1973), from which the following additional notes on the main flower syndromes in the tropical Far East are taken. The succinct and

critical account by van Steenis (1972) should also be consulted.

Beetle flowers 'are as characteristic of the tropics as bee flowers are of semi-arid and temperate lands', and 'the fragrance of tropical nights is almost beyond belief with the fragrance of beetle-pollinated blossoms'. Beetles eat pollen, the flowers are commonly simple, open dishes or bowls, and pollination is by clumsy scrambling. Annonaceae, Magnoliaceae, and Myristicaceae exhibit many examples. Beetles had already evolved greatly by the Jurassic and Cretaceous periods, before the higher Hymenoptera and Lepidoptera, which are important for pollination today, had developed.

Faegri and van der Pijl consider bees to prefer zygomorphic flowers, usually with dissected petals and of lively colour, often yellow, blue-green, or blue, weakly scented, and provided with footholds. Labiatae, Orchidaceae, Leguminosae subfamily Papilionatae, and Scrophulariaceae have many examples. Bees are strong and intelligent and can utilize the most complicated flowers.

Moths (mostly Sphingidae) with long tongues are bound to whitish or greenish, long-tubed, sweetly scented, nocturnal flowers. *Lonicera* and *Ipomoea alba* are good examples.

Butterfly flowers are erect, vividly coloured and trumpet-shaped, with nectar in a narrow tube or spur, and therefore inaccessible to bees unless they bite through the corolla. *Mussaenda* is in this group.

Flowers smelling of carrion or dung, such as *Amorphophallus* and *Rafflesia*, attract beetles and flies by deception, and are usually traps. They are usually

FIG. 2.29.   Bat-pollinated flowers of *Duabanga grandiflora*, borne pendulous at the ends of the twigs and nocturnal (Ulu Gombak, Malaya).

dark reddish or purplish in colour. *Tacca* is even more deceptive; it has the colour but not the odour.

Evolution has proceeded to produce pollination mechanisms of greater precision, concealment of pollen and nectar, and, concomitantly, availability to fewer visitors.

Pollination by vertebrates is well manifest in the tropics. Bats, besides birds, act as pollinators (van der Pijl 1956). These two syndromes are considered to have evolved recently, for they occur as isolated cases in numerous different families in the Old and New World tropics. The typical bat-flower syndrome is nocturnal opening, sour scent (curiously reminiscent of the smell of the bats), mucilaginous nectar, and pale colour. Bat flowers are either of the 'shaving-brush' type, exposing the stamens to the bat's breast (for example, *Parkia*), or are deeply campanulate so that the inserted head and foreparts get covered with pollen (Baker 1973). Bat flowers are held away from the main foliage of the crown, on long processes (as in *Parkia* and *Oroxylum*), at the tips of pendulous branches (as in *Duabanga*—Fig. 2.29), or at the stem apex (as in *Musa* and *Ensete*, the bananas), and this is termed penduliflory. Alternatively they may be borne on the main limbs (as in *Bombax valetonii*, some *Durio*, and many

Sapotaceae) which is termed ramiflory. Perhaps cauliflory is also an adaptation to bat-pollination, though lizards may also be involved (Medway); observations are lacking. There is some overlap between bat and bird flowers as in *Mucuna*, *Spathodea*, and perhaps *Erythrina*. Baker and Harris (1957) have some fine photographs of bats visiting *Parkia*, and give a review of studies on bat-pollination.

Flowers are believed to have evolved these 'syndromes' as an aid to pollination by particular animals, in a few extreme cases (such as some Orchidaceae) by a single species, but most flower-visiting animals cannot depend on a single plant species as a food source, because most species do not flower all the time. A selective advantage for related plant species to flower at different times from congenerics, and thus to avoid hybridization, can therefore be envisaged. *Shorea* species in Malaya and Borneo (Wood 1956; Ashton 1969; Fox 1972; Burgess) are well known to flower at slightly different times.

One of the most specialized of all pollination mechanisms is that of the big genus *Ficus*. In fig trees the numerous, tiny, unisexual flowers are arranged on fleshy receptacles which are hollow and bear the flowers on the inner surface. There are three kinds: male flowers, gall flowers, and female flowers. The latter are pollinated by specialized wasps of (in south-east Asia) family Agaonidae. The eggs are laid by the female wasp within the ovary of the gall flower, by placing her ovipositor down the style. The larva feeds on the ovary wall. Male and female wasps develop, which bite their way out and copulate; the male then dies and the female crawls out of the fig, getting pollen on her body from male flowers as she goes, and emerges from the orifice. She then searches, probably by scent, for another fig and either pollinates the flowers if it contains females or deposits her eggs if it contains gall flowers. There has been very precise evolution of one species of wasp for each species of fig or for a small group of closely related figs and also in the timing of maturity of male flowers and the receptive gall and female flowers. The full intricacies of this marvellous specialization are reported by Corner (1940) and Proctor and Yeo (1973).

Dispersal

Animals play a major role in the dispersal of the seeds of tropical trees. One syndrome of characters is an adaptation to dispersal by bats. Bat fruits contrast with bird fruits in their duller colours,

FIG. 2.30. *Dysoxylum angustifolium*, brownish-cream coloured pericarp and hanging scarlet seeds. In this species the seeds are eaten by fish whose flesh they taint and render poisonous. This species is a typical rheophyte with narrow, willow-like leaflets.

predominantly brownish or yellowish, and strong, musty odours. They ripen on the tree, and, as with bat flowers, are held away from the foliage to facilitate visits. (See van der Pijl (1957) for fuller details.) The larger fruits, which characteristically contain a single large seed, are carried by the bats to habitual roosting spots where the flesh is torn from the seed. The principal bats are *Pteropus*, the flying foxes, and these huge animals (wing span to 1·5 m in *Pteropus vampyrus*) can carry fruits weighing as much as 200 g. Fruits with small seeds are pressed against the palate to extract the juice. The remaining dry mass is ultimately ejected from the mouth and falls in heaps below feeding roots (Medway). Common examples are *Muntingia calabura*, *Melastoma malabathricum*, and *Ficus* spp. The spread of the South American treelet *Piper aduncum* round Kuala Lumpur (Whitmore 1967*b*) and Lae is due at least in part to bats. Van der Pijl contrasts a tropical fruit stall with the brightly coloured temperate one, based

on bird-dispersed plums, cherries, etc., and regards as bat-adapted fruits *Achras*, *Aegle*, *Annona*, *Artocarpus*, *Averrhoa*, *Baccaurea*, *Bouea*, *Cynometra*, *Detarium*, *Diospyros*, *Dracontomelum*, *Feronia*, *Lansium*, *Mammea*, *Mangifera*, *Manilkara*, *Musa*, *Persea*, *Psidium*, and *Spondias*.

Another syndrome is the brilliantly and contrastingly coloured capsule or follicle, most typically red, black, and yellow, with the seeds sometimes dangling (Fig. 2.30). Ridley (1930) argued that such fruits are adaptive to be conspicuous from a distance amongst the sombre greens and browns of the forest, and hence for dispersal by birds. Perhaps primates too are attracted. *Sterculia* species have a vermilion epicarp and dangling shiny black seeds. Connaraceae and *Durio griffithii* are similar, the seed being partly enveloped in a yellow aril. A similar effect is sometimes achieved by the colouration of other tissues. In *Talauma* the carpels split irregularly to expose black seeds set in red mesocarp. The syncarp of *Rejouia aurantiaca* splits to expose similar colours. Many undergrowth palms, *Licuala* and *Pinanga*, for example, have showy infructescences of bright, contrasting colours (Whitmore 1973*b*). In *Adenanthera bicolor* the seed is half black and half red and the aril function may be considered to have been 'transferred' to part of the testa. A particularly long series of transfers is shown by species of *Artocarpus* and *Parartocarpus* as described by Corner (1962). Spines are argued by Corner to be primitive, protecting the unripe fruit; and the bright, contrasting colours and edible, fleshy, sometimes highly smelling aril are regarded as acting as attractants to animal dispersers. This is the nub of the 'durian theory', named from the most famous Far Eastern fruit (Corner 1949; and see also van der Pijl 1969).

Fruit-eating carnivores, especially civets and mongooses (family Viverridae), and also bears are important fruit-dispersers in the rain forest; fruits form an important part of their diet. The syndrome which attracts these animals is not well established; it seems likely they are guided by smell rather than colour (indeed many are nocturnal), though they frequently consume brightly coloured fruits when they chance to come across them (Ridley 1930; Medway 1969). It is notorious that tigers have a passion for durians.

Primates and rodents feed partly on fruits and seeds and doubtless play a role in dispersal. The syndromes particularly attractive to animals of these orders have not been elucidated.

Some riverine species are known to be dispersed by fish, and the fruits of some of these provide bait for fishermen. Examples from Malaya are *Aglaia salicifolia, Dysoxylum angustifolium* (Fig. 2.30), and *Ficus pyriformis*. In Sarawak the small catfish *Clarias batrachus* (ikan kli) which inhabits the streams draining mixed-species peat swamp forest (§11.3) develops a peculiar flavour during the fruiting season of the codominant tree *Gonystylus bancanus* which is attributed to it having eaten the aril of its seed (Anderson 1961*b*) (see also Fig. 2.30).

Phytophagy

A characteristic of most kinds of tropical rain forest, which has attracted much speculation and a little investigation, is that trees of many species are scattered as single individuals. It has been argued that such a distribution pattern enables a species to escape predation of its leaves by insects and may result from predation of dense seedling populations (see, for example, Janzen 1971*a*).† Colour is lent to these suggestions by several reports. Anderson (1961*a*) has reported areas of several to many hectares of *Shorea albida*, which grows in huge pure stands in the peat swamps of Sarawak (§11.3), defoliated and killed by the caterpillar (*ulat beludu*) of an un-identified tussock moth (*Hymantridae*) (for details see §6.1) and also the almost complete defoliation of Sapotaceae (especially *Palaquium walsurifolium*) and of *Dactylocladus stenostachys*, though not killing the trees. Browne (1937) recorded repeated defolia-tion of a dense stand of *Endospermum malaccense* in Malaya by the caterpillar of the moth *Urapteroides astheniata*, which reduced girth increment by 20 per cent in its first year and by over 50 per cent after 6 years. Morel (1967) reported that young plantations of *Araucaria cunninghamii* in the Bulolo–Watut valleys of New Guinea had recently begun to be attacked by the Scolytid leaf miner *Hylur-drectonus araucariae*. Planting began in the late 1940s, and this trouble, which does not affect *A. hunsteinii*, did not arise for the first 20 years or so. To avoid it foresters are turning their attention to recreating semi-natural mixed conifer–broad-leaf rain forest instead of plantations (Havel 1972). Examples of similar problems with stands of teak and *Altingia excelsa* in Java, sal (*Shorea robusta*) in India, and *Pinus merkusii* in Sumatra are discussed by Atkinson (1953) and Kalshoven (1953). Gray (1972) gives a general review of the economically important insect pests of tropical trees.

However, many other tree species do exist pre-dominantly as clusters, for instance, in those which

† It is interesting to record that amongst arboreal vertebrates only a few mammals (primates mostly) are leaf-eaters (Medway).

have inefficient dispersal, family groups occur of big and small trees together, as in many Dipterocarpaceae (see Chapter 15). In cases like this it has been argued that the so-called 'secondary metabolites', for example, gums, resins, and latexes have the function of making a plant unpalatable, and that an insect which overcomes such a palatability barrier is at an advantage because it has an exclusive food source; the plant then evolves a further barrier which the insect in turn overcomes. Continuing step-wise co-evolution of plant and animal can be envisaged. 'Pest pressure' acting in this way was first argued by Gillett (1962) to have been a cogent driving force behind the prolific species formation which has taken place in many genera in tropical rain forest. It has been suggested that leaf-eating insects are far more restricted in the number of species utilized than are pollinating insects.

'The kind of substance a plant contains depends on the kind of plant that it is' (Bate-Smith 1971). Tannins, which have an astringent flavour because they precipitate proteins, are universally present in woody plants in the form of leucoanthocyanins, which are also the precursor of lignin. A useful review of the ecological role of these and other phenolic compounds in plants is given by Levin (1971). Anthocyanin pigments have been studied as an aid to the taxonomy of critical species of Diptero-carpaceae (Bate-Smith and Whitmore 1959); but, in general, chemotaxonomy of tropical species remains little developed. In herbs they are replaced as repellent compounds by painfully pungent sub-stances, often of disgusting taste or smell, as in Zingiberaceae and Compositae (for example, *Eupa-torium odoratum*); bitter-tasting alkaloids are also common, as in *Aristolochia* (Bate-Smith 1971). Some plants have physical repellents, thorns, leathery leaves, siliceous hairs (bamboos), or internal spicules (Araceae).

The relationship between plant and insect can go even further (Rothschild 1971). An insect which has overcome a chemical repellent itself repels, either while the food is inside it or even by accumulating the chemical so that it comes to taste and even smell of its host. Predators will avoid such insects, which often have warning coloration, and therefore the insects can afford to remain near to the host plant. This serves to attract other insects and in-creases the chance of pollination; in addition, the host plant has its distasteful odour reinforced. The well-known association of many butterflies with *Aristo-lochia* is of this nature, for example, the famous birdwings and some other Papilionidae in the tropical

Far East, which in Malaya are also mimicked by other papilionids and certain day-flying moths (Corbet and Pendlebury 1934).

Three general strategies can be recognized which minimize animal predation of seeds. Seeds may be so tiny there is no internal space and little food for would-be internal predators. Or they may be so numerous that some are likely to escape predation. Alternatively, they may be chemically protected, and this is generally the case with big seeds.

Damage to seed or seedling may conceivably some-times be important in determining the distribution of trees in the forest. In hill forests in Malaya ants destroyed germinating seeds of the dipterocarp *Shorea curtisii*; the survivors were a few of those which came up in dense patches, not isolated individuals (Burgess 1969a). This dipterocarp, like many others, has very poor powers of dispersal (Chapter 5), and ant damage reinforces the already

FIG. 2.31. The hollow twigs with punctured internodes and recurved stipules of *Macaranga triloba* are inhabited by ants.

strongly clumped pattern of its seedling populations. The extreme dangers of generalization are illustrated by the fact that Janzen (1971a) found for the Central American palm *Scheelea rostrata*, preyed on by a Brucid beetle, exactly the converse effect to Burgess: isolated seedlings stood a better chance of survival. Janzen (1971b) has written a comprehensive review of our scant present knowledge of this subject.

Termites play an extremely important role in many rain forest ecosystems, being, with Lyctid and Scolytid beetles, the principal wood-eating animals. It is remarkable that no other group of animals apart from the termites has developed the ability to break down and utilize lignin.

Myrmecophily

Association of ants with certain rain-forest plants is well known, and there are more diverse examples in the tropical Far East than anywhere else. In most cases careful observation is still needed to clarify benefits which either partner may be thought to receive.

Many species of *Macaranga* have hollow twig tips and recurved stipules bearing small starch-containing cells on the abaxial surface (Fig. 2.31). Ants (in Malaya, *Crematogaster borneensis* var. *macarangae*) inhabit the hollows where they cultivate sap-sucking scale insects (*Coccus* spp., Khoo 1974) and are presumed to eat the starch grains. Some species are only sometimes ant-inhabited (see Whitmore (1967a, 1973f) for further details). *Endospermum*, which is closely related to *Macaranga*, has a few species with hollow, ant-inhabited twigs. One of these, *E. formicarum*, is known as the Chief Tree in the Solomons because the crown of none other touches it (Whitmore 1966a). No one has investigated whether in either *Endospermum* or *Macaranga* ants play a role in warding off neighbouring plants or attacking animals. The ants which inhabit the enlarged swollen ocreae of the stem base of the climbing palm *Korthalsia* are claimed to have such a role (Corner 1966; Whitmore 1973b).

Several epiphytic ferns (for example, *Lecanopteris carnosa*, *L. sinuosa*) have hollow rhizomes; *Clerodendron fistulosum* and the rubiaceous genera *Hydophytum* and *Myrmecodia* have variously swollen hollow stems (Fig. 10.8, p. 130). The epiphytic genus *Dischidia* and some *Hoya* species have convex leaves adpressed to the host stem with hollows beneath. All these species are associated with ants which bring humic material into the hollows.

Merrill (1945) has a useful illustrated account of myrmecophytic plants.

FIG. 2.32. *Nepenthes ampullaria* on the floor of a Sarawak heath forest. Notice the fallen needle twigs of *Dacrydium beccarii* var. *subelatum*.

Plants as predators

The insectivorous pitcher plants *Nepenthes* (Fig. 2.32) trap, drown, and digest insects; the sundews *Drosera*, uncommon in our region, trap and digest insects. It is noteworthy that these and many myrmecophytes are especially abundant in habitats markedly poor in nutrients, for example, heath forest and the centre of some peat swamps (see §§10.3, 11.3) or ridge-crest forest in the mountains. The suggested nutritional benefits to the plant remain to be proved.

Conclusions

In conclusion, plant and animal interactions give a clue to some of the mechanisms which might have stimulated species formation in the tropical rain forest and to mechanisms which might be important in controlling species density. In both respects they are worthy of much closer study than hitherto, for

the light they may shed on two of the greatest enigmas of these great forests: their extreme richness in species, with many genera having long series of morphologically similar sympatric species, which yet occur at amazingly low density. Federov (1966) and later Ashton (1969) in a symposium on the topic (Lowe–McConnell 1969) advanced stimulating speculations on this highly controversial subject, from which it will be realized that what we now require are more observations, which in this field are technically extremely difficult to make.

Despite the substantial part Dipterocarpaceae play in the rain-forest ecosystems of the tropical Far East (discussed in detail in §15.1) there is little evidence that this family forms an important food source for the rain-forest vertebrate animals. This is remarkable. Mass migrations of pigs in search of illipe nuts occur in Borneo (§5.1), and fruit-eating bats and parakeets have been known to eat the whole fruit crop of *Dryobalanops aromatica* in Malaya (Wyatt-Smith 1963). But during a decade of observation in the Ulu Gombak forest, Malaya (Medway 1972a), it was conspicuous that dipterocarps were not fed on by either birds or mammals, and the general observation of forest botanists supports this finding. By contrast, fig trees, which are far less common than dipterocarps, play an extremely important role as food sources for numerous species of mammals and birds. Many species of *Ficus* fruit copiously several times a year. Congregations of animals can be observed in their crowns at these times. Chivers (1971) found that during a period of 12 months' observations a troop of siamang at Kuala Lompat, Malaya, spend a quarter of their total feeding time in fig trees.

Part II: Seasonality

3 The forest environment: climate

THE MOST important feature of tropical climates is the continuous warmth. Temperature is high, and typically the diurnal range is greater than any variation from one time of year to another. Frost is virtually unknown, except on the highest mountains.

There is a great variety of climates within the tropics from perhumid or ever-wet types through those which are dry for part of the year to a few which are permanently arid or almost so. The most important variable affecting the range of vegetation types is the availability of moisture, and this depends in a large degree upon the seasonal distribution of rainfall, rather than its total amount.

Tropical vegetation is limited away from the equator by temperature, though by what aspect of temperature is not clear; whether, for example, it is length of growing season, which is minimum above a certain level, or absolute minimum. The boundary of tropical climates has often been taken by climatologists to coincide with a mean temperature of 18 °C for the coldest month. Climates of the tropical Far East are ably summarized by Ho (1962) and Richards (1952, Chapters 7 and 8) gives a full and excellent account of rain-forest climate. It suffices here to discuss in detail only certain salient features, principally rainfall and its seasonality.

The most arid climates in the tropical Far East are confined to part of central Burma and to a large part of Australia. Away from these foci lie regions of increasing wetness of climate, culminating in the perhumid rain-forest climates lying along the equator. Taken as a whole the Malay archipelago has a tropical maritime climate, strongly influenced by the surrounding seas, by the Indian Ocean to the west and south, and by the Pacific Ocean to the north-east. Rainfall is more equably distributed, and indeed higher, than in large parts of the other two major rain-forest blocks of western Africa and South America, which are less influenced by surrounding sea. Nevertheless, there is a seasonal variation in the distribution of rainfall, even in the most equable parts of the region. This results from the two major wind systems which influence the area: the northern monsoon of about October to March and the southern monsoon of the middle months of the year. In many parts of the region one of the monsoons brings more rain than the other, and the climates which are seasonally dry are commonly referred to as 'monsoon climates'. Full details of the wind systems, and hence the origins of the monsoons, cannot be given in this book and can be found elsewhere (see, for example, Ho 1962).

3.1. Systems to characterize climates

Various attempts have been made to characterize climates and to map them. The most widely known and used of world climatological classifications is that of Köppen (1918, 1936). Köppen distinguished five world climate types—four on thermal grounds. Within them distinctions were made on seasonal incidence and amount of rain. The boundaries of the classes were arbitrarily chosen and are not based on consistent criteria (Carter and Mather 1966). For example, Köppen's tropical rainy climates (class A) have mean temperature t of the coldest month above 18 °C and annual total precipitation over $20t$ mm for winter rains or $20(t+14)$ mm for summer rains. This large group of climates is subdivided into Af (hot damp forest climates) with mean rainfall of the driest month not less than 60 mm, Am (monsoon type forest climates), and Aw (periodically dry savanna climates). Both Am and Aw regimes have less than 60 mm rainfall in the driest month. The Am climates are intermediate between the Af and Aw, and in them the total annual rainfall is sufficient to 'compensate' for the seasonal drought. Despite this subdivision Köppen's system only discriminates large regions of strongly contrasted rainfall which Ho (1962) has plotted for the region from India to Australia. The system is not sufficiently sensitive to discriminate types of climate coincident with the different kinds of forest of the tropical Far East. Agriculturists in what is now Indonesia found that it was not sufficiently sensitive to enable them to predict the limits within which particular agricultural crops could be successfully grown, and soil scientists needed a more precise measure of the availability of water for the study of pedogenesis. A serious limitation of Köppen's approach is, in fact, that the moisture regime cannot be characterized solely by water added by precipitation, because the amount lost by evaporation and by the transpiration of plants is also very important. Mohr (1933) attempted to allow for this in a scheme developed for Indonesia in which any month with over 100 mm of rain is regarded as wet (precipitation

43

exceeding evaporation), any month with less than 60 mm as dry (evaporation exceeding precipitation), and months with 60 mm to 100 mm as moist (precipitation and evaporation more or less in balance). Mohr distinguished climates by the number of wet and dry months. His climatic chart for Java produced from this basis had considerable practical application in agriculture. Schmidt and Ferguson (1951) pointed out that Mohr's system suffers from an identical weakness to Köppen's, namely, that average monthly rainfall from several years' figures are taken and that, because the rain-bearing monsoon may be early or late by several weeks, this obscures the intensity of the beginning and end of the monsoon and also obscures very dry months. They got over this difficulty by computing dry and wet months for each year, using Mohr's index, and then averaging the resulting figures. The result is expressed as a ratio

$$Q = \left(\frac{\text{dry months}}{\text{wet months}}\right) \times 100.$$

Records from all stations in Indonesia with at least 10 years' records between 1921 and 1940 were analyzed and a map produced showing seven successively drier climatic regimes, A–G. These are discussed further in the next section.

Two systems which have been widely and successfully used in studies in temperate climates must first be briefly mentioned (Penman 1963). One, due to Thornthwaite (1948, 1954), uses an empirical formula, developed from data from the north temperate zone, to calculate potential evapotranspiration (PE) from precipitation and temperature measurements. PE is then used to define a moisture index and a thermal scale, and fifteen climates are defined by a combination of an index and a scale value. This system has the virtue that it can be widely applied because precipitation and temperature are measured at most meteorological stations. It is the logical successor to Köppen's system and uses consistent criteria (Carter and Mather 1966). The system has been applied to parts of the tropical Far East and shown to produce rather coarse provinces which do not closely reflect details in vegetation distribution (see Ho (1962) and plate II in Carter and Mather (1966)); this would seem to be at least partly because the empirical formula on which the index is based is derived from temperate data (Schmidt and Ferguson 1951; Carter and Mather 1966); indeed Thornthwaite (1954) made this limitation clear. The other very well-known formula is due to Penman (1949, 1956, 1963). It has been greatly used in agricultural research but is difficult to apply to mapping climates

without a close network of sophisticated meteorological stations because its evapotranspiration estimate requires measurements of the duration of bright sunshine, mean air temperature, mean vapour pressure, and mean wind speed, and these, in practice, are seldom made.

Although temperature and available moisture are two important factors in determining plant growth and in delimiting vegetation types they are not the only ones; soil and the influence of man are also important. The boundary of forest types, even where it is sharp, thus usually represents a complex interaction of several different factors, and sometimes, as in the rain-forest–monsoon-forest boundary, a mosaic of types occurs (see Chapter 12).

Further information on climatological formulae and reviews of the different approaches which have been tried in the tropical Far East can be found in Schmidt and Ferguson (1951), Richards (1952), Mohr and van Baren (1954), Blumenstock (1958), Ho (1962), and Carter and Mather (1966). These sources also give full reference to the original literature.

3.2. Climates within the tropical Far East

The rainfall types of the tropical Far East are shown on the map in Fig. 3.1, using the scheme of Schmidt and Ferguson which has been simplified by uniting the four drier types into two and which therefore gives greatest definition for the wetter regions with which this book is concerned. On the scale of this map only the main pattern of climates is depicted, and inaccuracy in detail is likely also because of the small number of meteorological stations away from the coasts of most of the islands in Indonesia; nevertheless, there is a good correspondence between this map and vegetation types—very much better in fact than for any other climatic scheme yet developed.

The map clearly shows that the wettest climates (type A) occur in two great blocks lying about the equator and that, by coincidence, these roughly coincide with the Sunda and Sahul continental shelves; in the centre of the archipelago lies a north–south zone of seasonally dry climates, mainly types B and C/D, from the western side of the Philippines, through Celebes and the Moluccas and running into the even drier Lesser Sunda Islands, whose dry climate extends into east Java. Malaya, Borneo, and Sumatra are the heartland of the western wet block. Drier climates of type B occur in Malaya from about Alor Star (6°N) northwards, and north from about the isthmus of Kra type C/D

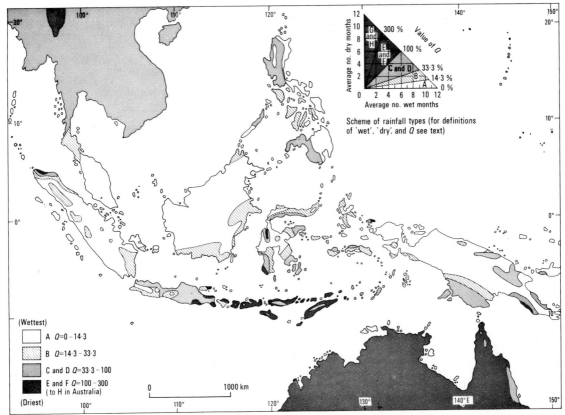

FIG. 3.1. Rainfall types of the tropical Far East based on wet/dry period ratios. Data of Schmidt and Ferguson (1951) for Indonesia, extrapolated using mean monthly figures in Walter and Leith (1960), and, for New Guinea, data by Fitzpatrick, Hart, and Brookfield (1966).

occurs.† This drier region just touches the north tip of Sumatra (Banda Aceh) and includes the Langkawi islands off the west coast of the peninsula. Type B climates extend in pockets southwards in the inter-montane valleys of northern Sumatra and recur in the lowlands of south-east Sumatra, north to Palembang, and in south and east Borneo.

New Guinea is the heartland of the eastern wet block, but has a broad, interrupted band of dry B and C/D type climates on the south coast, with a small area of E/F type around Port Moresby. There are also areas of fairly dry climate on the north coast, and Waigeo island off the north-west tip is very dry (E/F). The climates of the central cordillera of New Guinea change rapidly over small distances, and are

† Gaussen, Legris, and Blasco (1967) have published an excellent climatic map for Indo-China, Thailand, and the Malay peninsula which shows these features in greater detail. Consideration of their map together with the notes on the distribution of forest types in Chapters 10 and 12 reveals just how intricately rainfall, tempera-ture, and length of dry season together influence vegetation.

incompletely known. Certainly, the intermontane basins of the New Guinea highlands are fairly dry. Off the map, perhumid A climates extend into the Solomons, northern New Hebrides, parts of Fiji, and out to some of the islands of Micronesia. There are two tiny pockets of perhumid climate on the Queensland coast and the outlying fringes of tropical rain forest in south-west Ceylon and along the western Ghats of India coincide with pockets of A and B climates.

The influences of the monsoons can clearly be seen even on this small-scale map. The Lesser Sunda Islands are seasonally very dry, owing to the dry southern monsoon which blows off Australia during the middle months of the year. The west side of the Philippines is in the rain shadow of mountains down the east coast which receive most of the rain of the north-east monsoon. The south Papuan coast is dry because here the southern monsoon blows parallel to the coast. The west coast of the Malay peninsula north of Kra is wetter than the east, owing to on-

45

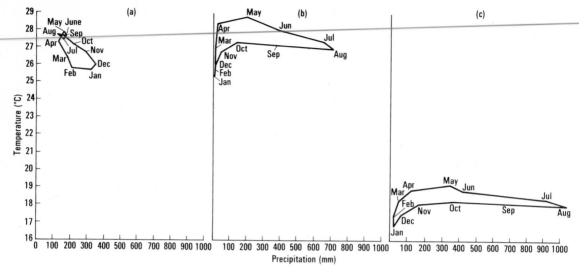

Fig. 3.2. Hythergraphs for three climate types in the Philippines (Kowal 1966, Fig. 2).
(a) Type A climate. Tropical lowland evergreen rain forest (Tacloban City, Leyte 11° N, 125° E).
(b) Type C/D climate. Monsoon forest (Vigan, west Luzon 17° N, 120° E).
(c) Type C/D climate (montane). Tropical lower montane rain forest (Baguio City, Luzon 16½° N, 120½° E).

shore monsoon winds; this is reflected in the vegetation but does not show in the map.†

The very equable nature of type A climates is shown in the hythergraph (Fig. 3.2(a)) for Tacloban City in the southern Philippines; there is little variation through the year in either rainfall or mean temperature. This is to be contrasted with the monsoon C/D climate of Vigan on the west coast of Luzon (Fig. 3.2(b)), in the north of the Philippines, which has a similar small annual range of temperature but a big range in rainfall. In the mountains at Baguio City (1480 m), south-east of Vigan (Fig. 3.2(c)), there is a similar rainfall range and an equable but much lower temperature. The precipitation and evapotranspiration curves for these three stations are shown in Fig. 3.3 and emphasize that in the monsoon climate evapotranspiration seasonally exceeds precipitation so that plants may be living in drought conditions.

Besides the orographic rain which they bear, the monsoons also cause boundary rain where airstreams converge, for example, along the north coast of Borneo at the onset of the north-east monsoon (Wycherley 1967). In addition, and not directly influenced by the monsoon winds, convectional rain is very important, usually in the afternoon and characteristically as heavy thunderstorms affecting only a small area and preceded by a build-up of cumulo nimbus clouds.

An important feature of wet tropical climates which contrasts them with more arid ones is the high degree of cloudiness and the concomitant small range of temperatures experienced at the ground. In the perhumid climates, and in the seasonally dry ones during the rainy season, diurnal temperature range rarely exceeds 11 °C and very high temperatures in excess of 37 °C occur rarely if at all. The average cloudiness is 5·2 (tenths) in the zone 0–10° N and 5·6 in the zone 0–10° S (Richards 1952).

3.3. The water balance

Rainfall P and evapotranspiration E have already been discussed briefly. The soil also plays an important role in the water balance; some rain runs off the surface or at depth (R = run-off) and some may be stored in the soil (and the change in storage expressed as ΔS). The whole water balance, therefore, may be expressed as the equation

$$P = E + R + \Delta S.$$

Evaporation is from the soil surface as well as of rain from leaves and limbs which never reaches the soil. Transpiration is mainly from leaves. The amount of water intercepted by the canopy varies with the intensity of the rain storm. Kenworthy (1971) found for a small part of the Ulu Gombak catchment in Malaya that it averaged 10 per cent and that more than 4·5 mm of precipitation were needed to increase the run-off. The actual evapotranspiration may be less than the potential because of water shortage. When soil water is limiting most plants reduce or eliminate transpiration by closing

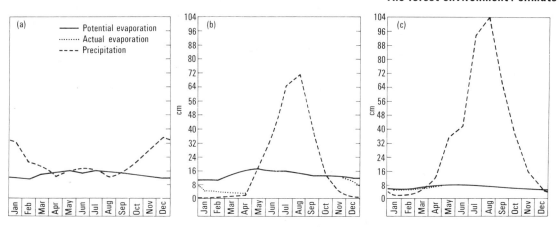

FIG. 3.3. Precipitation and evapotranspiration for three climate types in the Philippines (Kowal 1966, Fig. 3) (see Fig. 3.2 also).

their stomata. This is illustrated by studies of the catchment of the Pattani River in south-peninsula Thailand, where in years with different rainfall totals run-off and measured evaporation from pans remained the same because in the drier years actual evapotranspiration of water by the forest was reduced (Douglas 1971).

Run-off and soil storage depend on the physical characteristics of the soil. Water is held within the soil until the pores between the particles are filled; the soil is then said to be at field capacity and excess runs away in subsurface channels, which may be root channels or the tunnels made by termites and other subterranean animals. The greatest storage capacity is in soils with a loam texture. Finer soils have less available water at field capacity partly because plants can extract less. Coarsely textured soils can store less than finer ones, but may retain water as they dry out because capillary channels are broken. In heavy storms rainfall rate may exceed penetration rate (Guha 1969); the excess runs off the surface, often causing erosion. Run-off rate depends not only on the physical nature of the soil but also on gradient, the intensity of the rainfall, and on the presence of superficial materials, such as leaf litter, which impede flow. The nature of the vegetation cover also affects run-off. In one Malayan study, the run-off rate was greatest in the only one of five catchments under observation which had lost part of its virgin rain-forest cover (Low and Goh 1972). Different rocks weather to different depths, and age and topography also influence soil depth. Different trees have roots which penetrate to different depths, though most roots in tropical rain forest are within the top 0·3 m (Chapter 2). It follows that the volume of soil which can store water available to the forest is

variable and difficult to measure. The weathered soil mantle below a forest is a major reservoir for that forest, but the water is not always accessible to trees during dry periods.

The study of the water balance is thus seen to be an intricate subject. Recent investigations have indicated, despite the difficulties and the limitations of available data, that water relations play an important role in the lives of plants and animals and in the distribution of forest types, even within the equatorial climatic zone where it has been traditionally believed water is always freely available.

3.4. Water balance within the wettest climate

In Chapter 12 it will be shown that the distribution of climatic types as defined by Schmidt and Ferguson's 'Q ratio' of dry to wet months approximates closely to the distribution of forest Formations in the tropical Far East. It has become increasingly clear over the last few years that water balance is important even within the perhumid A type climate, which is the climate of tropical lowland evergreen rain forest, and that even here at certain times or in certain places evapotranspiration exceeds precipitation so that drought conditions can prevail. The work to be discussed has all been done in Malaya and Sarawak in the western Sundaland perhumid climatic block.

From long-term mean monthly precipitation figures and estimates of mean evaporation, based on measurement or regressions on sunshine records, Nieuwolt (1965) concluded that negative water balances occur annually in most parts of the Malay peninsula except for the southern tip and Singapore. But by tracing the water balance from monthly measurements over a continuous 3-year period

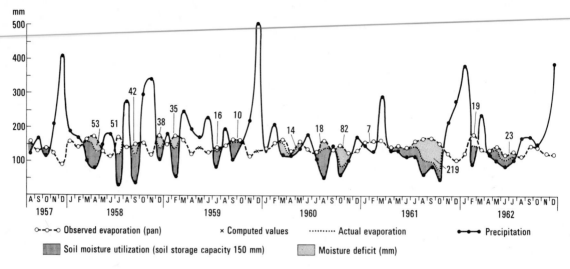

FIG. 3.4. Moisture balances for individual months 1957–62, Singapore (Nieuwolt 1965, Fig. 10).

(rather than from long-term means) he found that even in Singapore short periods of deficit occurred every year, which were obscured when averages are taken (Fig. 3.4). Such drought periods are, of course, one reason for the continual water-shortage crises and consequent water-conservation campaigns which have become a feature of contemporary Singapore.

Douglas (1971), from a 1-year study on the water balance of the Gombak catchment in the mountains near Kuala Lumpur, concluded that the cumulative evaporation from pans was greater than cumulative water loss from the catchment, indicating that the forest, although losing a lot, was in fact losing less water than that evaporated from an open water surface.

Rainfall in Sarawak is generally heavier than in most of Malaya (Wycherley 1967), and on a mean monthly basis precipitation exceeds evaporation throughout the year at all stations with evaporation pans. A more precise analysis was made by Brunig (1969b) who traced the running 30-day rainfall totals for five stations over 2 years. He found that there were spells during which the total of the preceding 30 days was less than 100 mm for several days on end, and that such periods increased in frequency from about once a year in the interior to 3–4 per year at the coast. At Miri, a station on the north-east coast, there are even days when the running 30-day rainfall total falls to 60 mm. Nieuwolt (1965) also found that in all months there is a general and rapid decrease of evaporation with increased distance from the coasts of Malaya. He believed this was due to greater cloudiness inland consequent on the con-

vectional rise of heated air; higher wind speeds near the coast due to sea breezes and lower friction near the earth's surface; and reduction of evaporation with increasing elevation.

The water-storage capacity of the soil determines when, in a period of greater evaporation than rainfall, water shortage affects plants. For instance Nieuwolt (1965) demonstrated a prolonged period from July to October 1961 in Singapore when, as a result of 7 consecutive months of water losses, the deficit reached 190 mm, 249 mm, or 316 mm for soil storage capacities of 254 mm, 152 mm, and 76 mm of water respectively (Fig. 3.4).

Baillie (1972b) refined Brunig's work by investigating for four Sarawak stations whether moisture-stress periods developed for soils of different water-storage capacity. He also utilized running 30-day rainfall figures and concluded that vegetation on deeper soils (that is, with greater storage capacity) is rarely subject to moisture-stress, even at the coast. On the shallower soils moisture-stress is much more frequent, severe drought being almost an annual event at the coast, whereas at Kapit, 200 km inland, mild moisture-stress was experienced in only 3 years of the 6 years investigated, and true drought was rare. Kapit has a lower but more evenly distributed rainfall than the coast with a higher frequency of convectional rain.

Prediction of soil moisture conditions from meteorological data is, as Lockwood (1971) and Baillie (1972b) discuss, a poor substitute for actual measurements, as severely simplifying assumptions have to be made. In practice, for example, evapotranspiration is unlikely abruptly to decrease at an arbitrary soil moisture content.

Guha (1969) made measurements of soil moisture near Kuala Lumpur and showed that, during 1 year, sandy soils were below 75 per cent field capacity for 9 months (with 100 days at only 0–25 per cent) and clay soils for 7 months (and never very low). He concluded that during this period lack of moisture limited the growth of rubber, but this could be compensated for by the use of fertilizers.

In conclusion, analysis of data for actual periods in Malaya and Sarawak, rather than long-period average values, has recently demonstrated periods of water deficit, whose frequency, duration, and severity varies from year to year, with situation and with soil. Correlation of water deficit with seasonal cycles in plants and animals is considered in Chapter 4 and with the distribution of forest types in Part IV.

3.5. Rare climatic events

Extreme climatic events of rare occurrence can be more important and critical to plant life than averages.

Rainfall and temperature

In Singapore and Malaya, within the perhumid A type climatic block of the Sunda shelf, there are sometimes spells of up to about 7 days' duration, and occasionally much more, when clear, cloudless skies result in unusually hot days and unusually cool nights (for example, the temperature at Kuala Lumpur may range from 34 °C to 20 °C). Such weather occurs especially at the end of the northeast monsoon in late January and in February. Afternoon convectional rainstorms frequently fail to develop at this time, so the spell is also one of lower humidities than usual and possibly of drought.

Mean rainfall data are particularly misleading in the humid tropics where the range of variability is far greater than anywhere else. It will be shown in Chapter 4 that exceptionally heavy flowering occurred in Malaya in 1963 and 1968 after particularly marked dry periods, and in the next section that in two places forest undergrowth plants were seen to be seriously affected in 1968. Concerning the 1963 drought Nieuwolt (1966) noted that much of south and east Malaya received only 40–80 per cent of the mean rainfall. He demonstrated striking deficits between precipitation and actual evapotranspiration from forests and soils; water rationing was introduced in Singapore and Malacca and there was severe loss to the rice crop of the north-west states

owing to the drought. Quite exceptionally strong droughts may occur at much longer intervals. For example, in 1902 Pekan on the east coast of Malaya received only 954 mm of rain, against an annual average of 3230 mm (Dale 1959). The disjunct distribution in Malaya of, for example, the palms *Johannesteijsmannia altifrons*, *Eugeissona tristis*, and some *Parinari* spp. can be most simply explained by patchy extinction breaking up formerly continuous ranges, and possibly dependent on some such rare exceptional drought period, most likely superimposed on a slow, secular climatic change (cf. Whitmore 1973b; Prance and Whitmore 1973).

Wind

In Chapter 5 the important role played by gaps in the forest growth cycle will be discussed. Gaps often form because trees are blown over. Freak high winds can cause freak gaps. Many big-tree species live to reach several centuries age, and a freak wind may therefore leave its mark on forest structure and floristics for several centuries. The 'storm forest' of Kelantan in Malaya which originated in November 1880 was still clearly recognizable in the late 1960s.

3.6. Microclimates

The general climate described in the earlier part of this chapter is the one measured by meteorologists in arbitrary but standard conditions, in a shaded screen in the open at about 1 m above the ground. It is only one of a whole family of climates which could be measured, and is chosen because it is approximately what is experienced by a human being in the open. The standard climate is the one prevailing in a large clearing in the rain forest, and also at a distance above the forest canopy.

There is a whole series of climates within the rain forest each with a whole series of aspects. Richards (1952, Chapter 7) gives a full and excellent account of rain-forest microclimates which should be consulted. He considers them under the aspects of air movements, precipitation, temperature, relative humidity, saturation deficit, and evaporation, light, and carbon dioxide; he also gives some consideration to the influence of forest type on microclimate and its importance to the physiology of the forest flora.

Three aspects of variation in microclimate will be discussed here to supplement Richards' account, and which have special relevance to the topics of later chapters of this book. These aspects are variation vertically in the forest canopy, variation through the year, and variation horizontally between phases of the forest growth cycle.

Vertical variation in microclimate in the forest canopy

The microclimate of the canopy top approximates to that on the ground in an extensive clearing and there is a progressive change downwards within the canopy. This is well documented by Richards (1952) and is also shown for temperature in Fig. 3.5, which includes mean air temperature at 24 m and 0·6 m above ground level and at 1·2 m below ground level in Semengo arboretum near Kuching, Sarawak. Probably the most comprehensive study of vertical variation and its annual march is that by Cachan (1963) and Cachan and Duval (1963) for the semi-evergreen rain forest of the lower Ivory Coast. Such vertical variation in microclimate is reflected by several aspects of forest floristics described in Chapter 2. Different families and species of trees, climbers, and epiphytes reach to different levels in the canopy. The microclimate experienced by the crown of a tree is likely to differ as it grows taller, and the change from monopodial to sympodial construction (Chapter 2) may coincide with a major change in microclimate experienced. During the day the air in the lower levels of high forest is cooler than that above. A temperature inversion exists. At night then the air above the canopy has cooled to below that inside convective mixing of the air masses occurs (Evans 1966). But dew does not form inside the forest, and this may be significant for the life of undergrowth plants, especially young tree seedlings.

Seasonal variation in microclimate

Richards (1952, 1962) graphically described the gloom, high humidity, and continuous high tempera-ture of the rain-forest floor and its great constancy and quoted Allee (1926) that 'the animals of the lower forest . . . would need only to avoid sunflecks in order to keep under environmental conditions that must excite the envy of every experimental ecologist with experience in trying to control environmental factors for land animals in the laboratory'. That there are small changes during a 24-hour period in temperature, relative humidity, and saturation deficit is made clear, and the daily march in light conditions he described was later amplified for a Singapore rain forest by Whitmore and Wong (1959).

There is also seasonal change. Figure 3.5 shows that at Semengo air temperature at all three levels measured is higher in the middle of the year, which is the drier season, and also that the maximum soil temperatures are reached in June, about 2–4 weeks after the peak air temperatures.

It will be shown in Chapter 4 that much flowering in rain forest follows a spell of water-stress. Such flowering is not restricted to trees of the canopy top but extends down to the undergrowth. The fact that all layers are affected by the stress indicates that a shortage of available water in the soil is more important than the concomitant lower relative humidity and higher day temperatures of dry weather (§3.5), which affects the canopy top more than the undergrowth. The author has seen in Malaya in February 1968 tracts of lowland forest in the Pahang valley on alluvium and near a scarp edge on sandstone in which the entire undergrowth was wilting, both herbs (for example, Acanthaceae and Scitamineae) and small trees to about 6 m tall. Later in

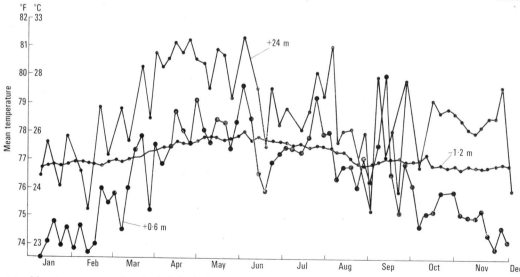

Fig. 3.5. Mean temperature at three levels in lowland rain forest at Semengo arboretum, Kuching, Sarawak, in 1969. (After Baillie.)

May of the same year on Gunung Belumut filmy ferns and Gesneriaceous herbs along mountain water courses were seen to be dead, and a 6 m stretch on a narrow ridge crest was also dead as a result of the same drought. The importance of extreme climatic events such as this widescale drought has already been stressed.

Horizontal variation in microclimate

Microclimates within the rain forest differ markedly horizontally at ground level between the gap and forested phases of the growth cycle and are discussed here as a setting for the description of forest regeneration in Part III. There are few precise measurements, and the differences, therefore, have largely to be described in general terms.

A gap is open to the sky, and direct light from the sun strikes the floor or ground vegetation at some time of day while it is shining and while it is over the horizon of the gap edge. The light reaching the ground under a forest canopy in sunny weather conditions comprises three distinct elements of different spectral composition (Evans 1956; Evans, Whitmore, and Wong 1959; Whitmore 1966*b*; Grubb and Whitmore 1967): direct sunflecks which move in a pattern across the floor, direct sky light coming through holes in the canopy, and the light which has been transmitted through one or more leaves and reflected from leaf and bark surfaces. The first two components are much more effective for photosynthesis than the third, from which the most useful wavelengths for photosynthesis have largely been filtered. But some sunflecks are probably so intense that they contain more energy of useable wavelengths than can be absorbed by a leaf (Björkman, Ludlow, and Morrow 1972). Whitmore and Wong (1959) calculated for a lowland tropical rain forest in Singapore that the total light energy on the forest floor was about 2 per cent of that outside. In sunny conditions 50 per cent of the total annual energy came from sunflecks (which occurred from 2 hours after sunrise to 2 hours before sunset), 6 per cent came through canopy holes, and 44 per cent was reflected or transmitted. In cloudy weather, which in Singapore occupied 47 per cent of the time, there are only the latter two components.

In a more recent study in a subtropical rain forest in southern Queensland (Björkman and Ludlow 1972) the energy transmitted was a similar fraction (2·5 per cent), but only 12 per cent of this came from sunflecks. In fact at this site the values of photosynthetically active radiation were believed to be very near the lower limit of light at which higher plants occur. Björkman and Ludlow go on to give the fullest analysis yet made of the energy flux in different weather conditions of the visible light (300–2400 nm) and of the quantum flux of the wavelengths utilized in photosynthesis (400–700 nm), as part of an investigation of the photosynthetic performance of deep-shade plants. Further details may be found in their paper.

In a gap, small moving sunflecks are replaced by big patches of sunlight, so that any one leaf lies in sunlight for a longer period. Also, the direct sky light component is bigger and the transmitted–reflected component is much smaller than in high forest. Thus, the two most photosynthetically useful elements of the light climate are increased, and the least useful one diminished. However, direct sunlight also has a series of other effects. It raises the air temperature, and so lowers the relative humidity and raises the saturation deficit (that is, drying power) of the air. It also raises the temperature of surfaces upon which it impinges, for instance, leaves in its path. Leaves keep cool by transpiration, by reflecting some of the incident energy, and by convection. Insofar as their temperature rises, despite these devices, so probably will their respiration (section 10.3). Presumably, as air temperature in a gap increases so convection is set up; the air rises and is replaced by cooler, moister air from the adjacent forest.

The smaller a gap, the shorter the period when the sun will be high enough in the sky to shine in and the shorter the period of the changes in microclimate which sunlight entails. A series of conditions progressively more different from those inside the forest canopy exists with increasing size of gap. It will be shown in Part III that there are important differences in the ecological strategies of species which succeed in gaps of different size; these different species succeed in the different microclimatic regimes which exist. Quantitative measurements on microclimate in a graded series of gaps, and of the response thereto of selected species, are badly needed. Some pioneering work on these lines has been undertaken by Schulz (1960) in Surinam.

4 Seasonal cycles in plants and animals

IT WAS shown in Chapter 3 that there are seasonal variations, even in perhumid tropical climates. Of these, variations in the availability of water to plants are probably ecologically the most important. In this chapter we shall describe seasonal cycles in plants, and show that there is now considerable evidence that they can be correlated with changes in the water supply. Some animals show distinct seasonality in behaviour, which it is believed results from changes in their food supply, that is to say, either directly or indirectly to seasonality in leaf, flower, or fruit production and hence also to seasonal weather. Most of the work to be described has been done in Malaya and Singapore.

4.1. Seasonal cycles in plants

Observations on leaf change can for convenience be discussed separately from those on flowering and fruiting.

Leaf change

Monthly observations (Medway 1972a) of top-of-canopy trees in tropical lowland evergreen rain forest in the Ulu Gombak valley in Malaya for 6 years between 1963 and 1969 showed an average annual pattern in leaf growth, with a distinct maximum of new leaf production and shoot extension in the period between February/March and May/June, as is shown in Table 4.1. In most years a second period of slightly heightened activity occurred during September/October to December. Rainfall observa-tions at and near the station and for west coastal central Malaya, where it lies, show that, although there is considerable variation in total rainfall and its seasonal distribution, a distinct pattern can be discerned of more or less regular fluctuation; the wettest months are October to December/January; February is dry and there is a second less-pronounced rainy season beginning about April followed by a longish period of diminished rainfall from about June to August (Dale 1959, 1960; Medway 1972a). The main peak of leaf growth comes just after the driest time of year; the second lesser peak begins before but extends into the wettest time of year.

Rubber (*Hevea brasiliensis*) in Malaya is briefly deciduous ('wintering') at the beginning of the year, following the onset of the early-year dry period, and early or late depending on the date the dry weather commences; the same clones winter at different times in different parts of the country. Wintering is followed by refoliation, shoot growth, and flowering. There is sometimes a second, but gradual, leaf change 5 or 6 months later and new shoot formation, branch by branch, but the whole tree does not become bare at once (Wycherley 1963). The pattern shows some similarity with that of the jungle trees at Ulu Gombak. There is a slight difference in onset and duration of wintering with age. Juveniles do not show marked seasonal foliage production, a feature which has also been found to be the case in mangoes (Alvim 1964), and this property is utilized in propagation by cuttings. Chua (1970a,b) discovered that

TABLE 4.1

Leaf flush expressed as the percentage of 58 observed trees undergoing leaf renewal or vigorous growth of new shoots and/or new leaves during any part of the month indicated (Malaya, Ulu Gombak forest)

Year	Jan.	Feb.	Mar.	Apr.	May	June	July	Aug.	Sep.	Oct.	Nov.	Dec.
1963	—	—	—	—	—	—	7	2	12	24	12	12
1964	7	3	24	3	12	17	5	7	5	16	2	12
1965	12	16	38	20	17	14	10	10	5	10	12	14
1966	5	10	28	26	16	12	12	7	10	10	11	21
1967	5	4	11	29	21	18	14	11	5	7	17	11
1968	15	17	33	17	13	6	6	4	9	6	13	13
1969	8	6	23	17	29	10	12	—	—	—	—	—
Monthly average	9	9	26	19	18	13	9	7	8	12	11	14

From Medway (1971a, Table 6).

the mechanism of leaf fall in rubber lies in the balance of concentration of abscissic acid and auxin; in the excess of either the leaf senesces and an abscission layer forms, but it is not known what triggers the regular annual change. Wintering is accompanied by the formation of a faint growth ring in the wood (Wycherley 1963) which Rao (1973) has shown results, in rubber and eight other species examined, from cell division in the cambium when water tension is high in dry weather.

The over-all pattern discerned in the Ulu Gombak forest (Table 4.1) obscures marked diversity between the 45 species (58 trees, 17 families) under observation. In only three trees (*Shorea laevis*, *S. platyclados*, *Artocarpus lowii*) were new leaves produced more or less continuously during the whole 6 years. Twenty-one species had annual, recurrent leaf growth, and several species had two seasons of leaf growth a year (Medway 1972a). The importance of Medway's observations is that most previous studies of leaf production have been on either relict or planted specimen trees not growing in virgin forest, and the rhythm of the forest as a whole had not previously been detected. One such survey is that by Holttum (1940), of trees in Singapore. He discovered regular, periodic behaviour in leaf production with only a small standard deviation, ranging from 6·1 months (coefficient of variation 10·1 per cent) in *Ficus variegata* to 32·0 months (c.v. 4·1 per cent) in *Heritiera macrophylla*. Singapore has a less marked annual rainfall seasonality than west central Malaya, but frequent water-stress has recently been shown to occur (Chapter 3).

Koriba (1958), also reporting on planted and relict trees, found that for several species leaf fall occurred during the dry season in both east Java and Ceylon, although it was at a quite different time of year. Further, the same species changed leaf in Singapore (where the dry season is much less marked) regularly at an interval ranging from 7·25 months (*Adenanthera pavonina*) to 12·9 months (*Tamarindus indica*). In addition, Koriba recorded several species which are evergreen in Singapore and deciduous in seasonally drier climates, for example, *Trema orientalis* and *Duabanga grandiflora*.

Fox (1972) noted that in north-east Sabah many species produce a flush of new leaves between October and December, often coinciding with the start of very wet weather; by contrast, leaf fall is more or less continuous, and is especially heavy in drought periods: many species around Sandakan were observed to have rather few leaves during a prolonged dry spell in early 1969. Nicholson (1958)

FIG. 4.1. The bare crown of *Intsia palembanica*, which in Malaya loses its leaves annually around February. The gibbons are *Presbytis obscura*.

noted that a tree of *Shorea smithiana* in Sabah changed leaf regularly in February during dry weather, and showed low girth growth at this time. Fogden (1972) found maximum new leaf production at Semengo forest Sarawak at the wettest time of year (about January), which there follows the driest time.

In seasonally dry forests of Ceylon maximum leaf fall was recorded at the time of year when evaporation exceeded precipitation and trees were utilizing the soil water store (Koelmeyer 1960).

By contrast to the whole of this body of data, in the western part of the Solomon archipelago, where there is no regular drier season (Brookfield 1969), no regular periodicity in leaf flushing or leaf fall has been observed amongst rain-forest species.

In conclusion, these studies clearly show that leaf

production and fall is commonly associated with water-stress, but the relation is not simple and there often appears to be some degree of endogenous control, a 'biological clock', despite the confident assertion of Coster (1923) to the contrary. Much remains to be learned on the mechanisms of control.

Koriba (1958) distinguished four kinds of periodicity in leaf growth: evergrowing (cf. Ulu Gombak, above), manifold, intermittent, and deciduous. The manifold habit, with different limbs behaving differently, is exemplified by rubber at its second leaf change of the year (above), sometimes by mango (*Mangifera*), and sometimes by *Peltophorum pterocarpum* in Malaya. Intermittent leaf growth is probably the commonest mode; Holttum (1940) and

Medway (1972*a*) give many examples. Intermittent growth is associated in some species with protection of the young leaves at the apex, between adpressed petiole bases (as in *Garcinia*), or stipules (*Magnolia*) or scale leaves (*Altingia*), but in many rain-forest species the apex is naked. The deciduous habit (Figs 4.1 and 4.2) is an extreme modification of the intermittent, in which the old leaves are shed before the new ones open. In essentially non-seasonal climates deciduous trees are often only bare for a day or two, as in, for example, *Terminalia catappa*, though the period may be prolonged, especially when flowering and fruiting occur on the bare shoots, as in *Firmiana* (Fig. 2.28, p. 35). Holttum (1953) noted that *Dyera costulata* is briefly bare in Singapore in dry weather, but in wet weather the new leaves expand a few days before the old ones are shed, so the

Fig. 4.2. The bare crown of the giant emergent tree *Koompassia excelsa* which changes its leaves early every year (Gunung Benom, Malaya, March 1968).

Fig. 4.3. *Pentaspadon velutinum*, with a flush of new pale-coloured leaves (Gambang, Malaya, April 1968).

transition to the deciduous habit is seen to be gradual. The principal ecological significance of deciduousness is that it strongly reduces water loss. Deciduous trees in rain forest are almost entirely confined to the top of the canopy, which is the part of the ecosystem where atmospheric water-stress is most marked; their saplings are not deciduous (for example, *Bombax valetonii* in Malaya). The abundance of deciduous trees and species increases in rain forests of progressively drier climates, and is used as a character to define the different Formations along this gradient (Chapter 10). Some species which are evergreen in perhumid climates are deciduous in seasonal ones (Ng).

At certain times of the year the rain-forest canopy is suffused red or pink. This is due to the colour of newly produced leafy shoots which sometimes hang down in limp tassels as, for example, in *Cynometra* and *Saraca*. At this time of year the unsuspected abundance of certain species is dramatically revealed, for example, of the wild nut tree perah, *Elateriospermum tapos*, over much of Malaya (Burgess 1969*c*;

Whitmore 1973*f*). Other species have pale green, sometimes almost white, young leaves (Fig. 4.3) and a few species (especially of Rubiaceae) even have them vivid blue. The significance of the high anthocyanin concentrations responsible for the striking pink and red coloration remains to be explored. The temperature of young leaves may be either higher or lower than of mature ones (Smith 1909); and such coloration is not confined to tropical plants. Bright coloration of old leaves is less common, and is of diagnostic value for tree identification (Corner 1940; Whitmore 1966*a*, 1972*c*); for example, most *Elaeocarpus* species have leaves senescing clear red.

Flowering and fruiting

It is commonplace to jungle dwellers in much of the tropical Far East that, although there are some trees in flower and fruit all the time, most species bear flower and fruit only periodically, many of them annually, and that some years are better than others. Wild fruit trees are productive at the same time as their descendants in orchards, and every year there

TABLE 4.2

Flowering expressed as the percentage of 55 observed trees blooming during any part of the month indicated (Malaya, Ulu Gombak forest)

Year	Jan.	Feb.	Mar.	Apr.	May	June	July	Aug.	Sep.	Oct.	Nov.	Dec.
1963	—	—	—	—	—	—	24	12	7	0	0	0
1964	2	9	12	3	9	7	7	2	3	3	2	2
1965	2	14	16	12	2	3	7	0	2	0	3	0
1966	0	7	10	12	16	17	12	2	7	7	2	2
1967	0	4	7	11	9	10	16	7	0	0	2	0
1968	0	11	11	22	30	35	24	2	2	4	6	0
1969	0	4	15	4	4	6	4	—	—	—	—	—
Monthly average	1	8	12	11	12	13	13	4	4	2	3	1

From Medway (1971*a*, Table 4).

TABLE 4.3

Fruiting expressed as the percentage of 58 observed trees in fruit (and in parentheses, the percentage bearing ripe fruit) during any part of the month indicated (Malaya, Ulu Gombak forest)

Year	Jan.	Feb.	March	April	May	June	July	Aug.	Sep.	Oct.	Nov.	Dec.
1963	—	—	—	—	—	—	43(3)	50(3)	57(24)	55(26)	34(28)	19(17)
1964	5(0)	3(0)	7(3)	7(0)	12(2)	14(3)	14(2)	21(3)	19(7)	16(5)	10(2)	12(3)
1965	12(3)	9(3)	9(3)	14(3)	21(2)	24(3)	19(3)	24(7)	21(10)	16(9)	16(9)	7(2)
1966	7(3)	5(2)	3(0)	10(2)	14(3)	12(2)	17(3)	16(2)	12(9)	3(2)	7(0)	9(2)
1967	5(2)	4(2)	4(0)	7(0)	14(0)	14(4)	14(2)	23(2)	27(4)	23(14)	9(7)	2(0)
1968	2(0)	4(0)	7(2)	13(0)	19(0)	39(2)	58(11)	55(9)	47(21)	41(34)	13(9)	8(4)
1969	2(2)	2(0)	6(2)	15(0)	17(2)	15(2)	13(2)	—	—	—	—	—
Monthly average	6(2)	5(1)	6(2)	11(1)	16(2)	20(3)	25(4)	32(4)	31(13)	26(15)	15(9)	10(5)

From Medway (1971*a*, Table 5).

D

is a major and a minor season of durian, rambutan, mangosteen, rambai, and langsat (*Durio, Nephelium, Garcina, Baccaurea, Lansium*), amongst others, in the lands of the Sunda shelf. The illipe nuts of Borneo, gathered from wild and planted trees of *Shorea macrophylla* and its allies, produce a crop only once every few years. By contrast, bananas and the introduced papaya and pineapple fruit continuously.

The study at Ulu Gombak, Malaya, already mentioned, monitored flowering and fruiting for the decade 1960–9 (McClure 1966; Medway 1972*a*). The sample as a whole showed a single distinct and marked annual peak of flowering between March and July then fruiting from about July to October, as can be seen in Tables 4.2 and 4.3. A minimum of 44 per cent of the 45 species flowered each year, and a minimum of 27 per cent fruited. Flowering followed the early-year dry season; the highest incidence of flowering was in 1963 and 1968, when that was most pronounced, and included gregarious flowering of the Dipterocarpaceae.

The species which flowered varied from year to year, the aggregate never falling below 20.

This pattern of a peak of flowering followed by a fruiting peak was found to be generally true of Malaya as a whole from analysis of nearly 4000 herbarium collections made from lowland and lower montane rain forest throughout the country during 1966–70 by the Forest Research Institute, Kepong. There was a distinct indication of a second peak at the end of each year, not shown in the Ulu Gombak study but reflected in the availability then of durians and other fruits in the towns and villages from itinerant merchants. A similar analysis of 1366 collections made in lowland rain forest in the Solomons during 1962–4 showed no trace at all of different seasonal abundance of flowering and fruiting. As already noted above, much of the Solomon archipelago has no marked seasonal variation in rainfall and no regular seasonality in leaf fall or production is detectable in Solomons' rain forest either.

Flowering of Dipterocarpaceae is notorious for its infrequency and gregariousness. 1963 and 1968, in which the early-year drought was unusually severe (§3.6), saw general flowering of the family throughout Malaya including Ulu Gombak. Poore (1968) has published figures for Temerloh in central Malaya showing that in 1963 evaporation exceeded rainfall in every month except October and November. Burgess (1972) has recently analysed all available data for Malaya in Forest Department files, covering the period 1925–70. He has been able to demonstrate that dipterocarps in general fruit heavily every 2–3

years with occasional intervals of up to 5 years and with some difference between species. Even in the best years only 40–50 per cent of mature trees in a given area are fertile, and in some cases groups of trees flowered together. Careful observations on a number of trees of both *Shorea curtisii* and *S. platyclados* revealed that with one exception none of the trees which flowered in 1968 did so again in 1970. This suggests that a given tree may need a prolonged period of physiological preparation before it is ready to respond to an external stimulus to flower (cf. Wood 1956; Fox 1972). Burgess also found that many dipterocarp species flower sporadically during any month of the year, and this has tended to obscure the existence of a single regular maximum of flowering in May. *Dryobalanops aromatica* is unusual; it has a first peak in April and a second one in October; it also tends to flower more often than other species. From examination of the rainfall figures Burgess concluded that there is considerable circumstantial evidence that gregarious flowering is in some way connected with drought periods occurring 3–5 months before flowering. He suggested that such a drought acts on the axillary buds which are at that time developing on newly flushed leafy shoots, and turns them into flower buds. Similarly Whitehead (1959) found that for the rambutan (*Nephelium lappaceum*) in Malaya heavy rainfall prior to flower-bud differentiation promoted subsequent vegetative growth instead of flowering. The nutritional status of the tree was also important. Burgess' final conclusion was that further progress will only come from study of individual trees and monitoring the weather they experience.

Not all droughts are followed by heavy flowering. Medway noted at Ulu Gombak that flowering was more copious in 1968, when a short dry season was followed by wetter weather, than in 1963 when the drought was prolonged. Baillie (1972*b*) found a good correlation between drought in 1968 at Kuching in Sarawak and a subsequent heavy crop of illipe nuts from an experimental plantation. No such correlation was found for 1970, when there was a good crop but no drought. Flowering of the illipe nut trees, as indeed of other dipterocarps, may not be followed by fruiting; heavy rain or high winds may destroy the crop. (In Sabah in 1951 high winds and rain damaged flowers over a wide area and little fruit was set (Fox 1972).) The size of the illipe crop harvested, which for most areas is the only measure available, further depends on what other source of income is available to the Iban gatherers at the time the fruits ripen. Fox (1972) noted that in high forest emergent dipterocarps seldom flower until they have grown to full height, whereas non-emergent species flower at small size. Ng (1966) recorded flowering at young age and low height of planted dipterocarps. Anderson (1961*b*) made the very interesting discovery that the dipterocarps in the peat swamp forest of Sarawak flower out of phase with those of dry land, that is, not during the dry season. In Ceylon in both the per-humid and seasonally dry forests flowering of forest trees has been shown to follow a period of low rainfall or humidity or both (Koelmeyer 1959, 1960).

In conclusion, there is now a substantial body of circumstantial evidence which indicates that flowering of many lowland rain-forest tree species is promoted by water-stress, but the relationship is not simple. Schulz (1960) has found a similar relationship for *Tabebuia serratifolia* in Surinam, and Webb (1958) reported that it is popularly believed that relatively dry years favour flowering in the Queensland rain forest. The part played by endogenous controls is not clear; that such controls exist is definitely shown where single limbs are out of phase, as in the tree of *Gluta renghas* observed at Ulu Gombak (Medway 1972*a*) and in species such as some figs which flower at regular intervals during the year.

There are also several external stimuli other than water-stress which are known to trigger blossoming. Several species are now known which blossom if the bud initial is chilled during its formation, usually by a sudden rainstorm. The pigeon orchid *Dendrobium crumenatum* is the most famous example (Coster 1925, 1926); it flowers 9 days after chilling. *Thrixspermum arachnites* (Coster 1925, 1926), *Bromheadia finlaysoniana* (Holttum 1949), and *Epiphyllum oxypetalum* (Holttum 1954*a*) are other orchids. *Murraya paniculata* and *Pterocarpus indicus* are trees of this group (Corner 1940; Holttum 1954*a*). *Zephyranthes rosea* requires chilling plus moisture (Kerling 1941). And in both *Zephyranthes* and *Dendrobium crumenatum* prolonged gradual cooling, such as provided by a succession of cool nights, functions as effectively as a single sudden chilling. Coffee (*Coffea*) has a complex of responses involving chilling and moisture (Alvim 1964).

Short days are necessary to promote flowering in Poinsettia (*Euphorbia pulcherrima* (Garner and Allard 1923)), and they shorten the period from sowing to emergence of ears in rice (Dore 1959).

It now appears likely that more-or-less regular periodic flowering is probably the rule for most tree species of primary lowland forest. But, on the other hand, some tree species flower continuously. This second group includes many species of secondary forest or forest fringe habitats, for example, *Adinandra dumosa*, *Commersonia bartramia*, *Dillenia suffruticosa*, *Glochidion* spp., *Melastoma malabathricum*, *Piper aduncum*, and *Ploiarium alternifolium*; and also of the seashore, for example, *Hibiscus tiliaceus*, *Scaevola taccada*, and *Thespesia populnea* (Koriba 1958). Regular seasonal flowering is also less marked in high mountain forest. For instance, on Mt. Pangrango, in west Java, at a height of between 2700 m and 3025 m there were species flowering at all times, some mainly in the drier or wetter seasons and some continuously (Doctors van Leeuwen, in van Steenis 1972).

Gregarious flowering at much longer intervals than of Dipterocarpaceae is the rule of almost all species of the forest-floor herb genus *Strobilanthes* which occur in India, Ceylon, and Malesia (Robinson 1934; van Steenis 1942; Santapau 1962; Mathew 1971). The period varies from 5 years to 6, 8, 9, or 12 years. For example, *S. cernua* on Mt. Gede in west Java has been seen to flower gregariously every 9 years between 1902 and 1956 (van Steenis 1972). The plants are monocarpic and die after fruiting. Some bamboos behave similarly, for example, the common Malayan hill-forest bamboos *Dendrocalamus pendulus* and *Gigantochloa scortechinii* (Burgess), also a species of *Schizostachyum* in entire river systems in Malaya. There are other examples amongst the palms, for example, in the tropical Far East, *Plectocomia griffithii* in Malaya (Whitmore 1973*b*), though in both bamboos and palms the phenomenon is commonest in markedly seasonal climates (Blatter 1929, 1930*a,b*), for example, the complete avenue of Talipot palm (*Corypha umbraculifera*) at Peradeniya, Ceylon, has flowered simultaneously then died.

It can be argued that it is advantageous for a species that individuals blossom together. The evolutionary strategy of long-lived trees is to maintain high variability (Stebbins 1950), and one means to this end is by outbreeding, by cross-pollination between individuals. Many species commence flowering in response to the external stimulus of water-stress, which is why they come in to flower more or less simultaneously, though it was noted in Chapter 2 that related species often blossom a few days apart. Simultaneous flowering will tend to lead to simultaneous fruiting and simultaneous germination; this might be advantageous in some cases in ensuring that at least some seeds and seedings avoid being eaten. Wood (1956) noted that in Sabah the fruit of late-flowering dipterocarp species matured faster.

The simultaneous, periodic flowering and fruiting of forest trees at long intervals can have important practical implications for forestry, as will be discussed in Chapter 5. As dormancy is short or nil, seed supply is sporadic. This is the main reason why promising dipterocarp timber species, such as the Light Red Meranti group of *Shorea*, have never been planted, even experimentally, outside the region. Secondly, seedlings will appear on the forest floor in occasional immense populations.

Contemporaneous flowering and fruiting of many canopy trees results in seasonal peaks in food for herbivorous animals. This has interesting consequences, to which we can now turn our attention.

4.2. Seasonal cycles in animals

When the dipterocarps are in flower the forest is pervaded by their scent and loud with the hum of their pollinating insects (mainly Diptera (Murphy)). Later the corollas carpet the ground like fallen, tinted confetti.

Most birds in Malaya have a distinct annual breeding season. Wells (1974) discusses all groups. Most interesting from our present viewpoint is the seasonal behaviour of the rain-forest inhabiting insectivores and partial insectivores (which are also

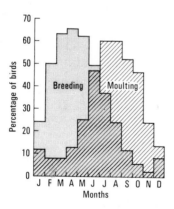

FIG. 4.4. Monthly incidence of breeding and moulting amongst insectivorous and partly insectivorous birds in Malaya (based on 245 and 146 species respectively) (from Wells 1974, Fig. 2).

the biggest group and that about which most is known). These birds show a marked peak of nesting in March/April and a low minimum in November (Fig. 4.4). Moulting follows nesting and is at a maximum in July/August, reaching a minimum in February/March. It is now believed that these two peaks depend, as in most seasonal situations, on the availability of food. Although to the casual observer insects and other small invertebrates are obvious at all times of year, marked seasonal fluctuations have now been recorded. For example, in the Ulu Gombak

valley a build-up in insects occurs associated with the seasonal peak in leaf and flower production. And it is well known in Malaya that butterflies are most abundant between April and September (Corbet and Pendlebury 1934), which implies an annual peak in caterpillar abundance a little earlier than this. October to January is a 'lean period'. Rainfall is heavy, flowering and fruiting sparse, and insects probably few. Breeding amongst birds is at a minimum, and moult declines sharply after about mid-October. Bird bodies have least fat.

Although seasonality is marked, the fluctuations are less than in the strongly seasonal tropics and the temperate zones. The fact that they occur at all is thought to be because many rain-forest insectivorous birds live closer to the food limit than species of more seasonal climates, and so are especially sensitive to relatively slight seasonal fluctuations in food supply. It is believed that in the case of birds which also eat fruit, seeds, or nectar the insect part of the diet is an essential high-protein component for feeding young nestlings and for moult, and that this is why partial insectivores show the same seasonality as obligatory ones.

A similar annual cycle of behaviour to that in the Malayan rain forest was found on Singapore Island for the Yellow-vented Bulbul (*Pycnonotus goiavier*), a small passerine bird of open places (Ward 1969), and for the Tree Sparrow (*Passer montanus*), an introduced species with the same urban and suburban niche as the House Sparrow in temperate regions (Ward and Goh 1968). Fogden (1972) found a similar pattern amongst rain-forest insectivores in Sarawak; most breeding occurs there between about January and June. Ward and Fogden both obtained evidence which suggests that a bird will come into a breeding condition whenever its protein level is sufficiently high, so there is a main annual peak at the principal time of insect abundance plus some breeding all the year round. In this connection it is interesting that the Barn Owl in Malaya is probably a year-round breeder. It lives around rural settlements, feeding principally on rats which are commensal with man and which themselves lack a breeding periodicity (Wells 1974). Breeding behaviour of insect-feeding Microchiropteran bats shows a similar seasonality to that of the forest-inhabiting insectivorous birds (Berry, Wells, and Wycherley, in press).

Davis (1945) found that, in strongly seasonal forest in Brazil, the reproductive and energy demands of birds and mammals changed according to food supply.

The exceptionally heavy fruiting of 1968 in the

Malayan rain forest, which has been mentioned above, coincided with heightened reproductive activity amongst groups of siamang studied at Ulu Sempan and Kuala Lompat. These primates also showed differences in behaviour at different times of year, correlated with the main wet and dry periods and hence with food availability and distribution (Chivers 1971). Forest rats in Malaya, for which fallen fruits are probably an important food, show maximum breeding activity more-or-less coincident with the annual peak in fruiting (Medway 1972*a*).

Twice-yearly seasonal production of fruit bodies by the higher fungi in south Johore and Singapore was attributed by Corner (1935) to revival of mycelial growth by rain following a dry spell. Murphy (1973) believes that there are peaks in the activity of the whole soil microflora at these times and, at Bukit Timah, Singapore, has traced peaks in numbers of soil invertebrates, which feed on this microflora as well as on the fungal fruit bodies.

In all these cases the most important single cause of periodically enhanced breeding behaviour is an increase in the food supply which in many cases follows from response of plants to seasonality in the climate.

It is noteworthy that, at Ulu Gombak, Medway found that in young shoot formation, in flowering and in fruiting there were consistent annual peaks, despite marked variations from year to year as to which particular individuals and species of plant became fertile.

Not all tropical rain forest animals show seasonal peaks in breeding. Besides the owl already mentioned, Inger and Bacon (1968) found no evidence of seasonal trends in various reproductive features of six species of frog in lowland rain forest in Sarawak or of another one associated with man in Kuching (Inger and Greenberg 1963) or of ten species of lizards (Inger and Greenberg 1967).

Periodicity or its absence in fruit production has implications for growth of the rain forest to which we now turn our attention in Part III.

Part III: Growth of the forest

It is important to concentrate attention on the dynamic aspects of the forest rather than on the futile pursuit of vegetation nomenclature which has so occupied the attention of tropical ecologists during the last half century. The crying need is for studies on the development of stands and the seral status of the desirable species.... (DAWKINS 1958)

5 Seed dispersal to seedling establishment

By GENERALIZATION one loses sight of important differences between species and in Part III particular studies will be described, dealing with individual species or small groups of species, mainly of timber trees, to illustrate first the kinds of problems a tree species has to overcome to maintain itself in the rain forest, and secondly the broadly different ecological strategies which have evolved as alternative solutions to the problems.

5.1. Dispersal

Of the fruit set by a tree much is eaten unripe by birds and other animals (Chapter 2), and even more when it is ripe. Frugivorous animals can be a serious pest in forest seedling nurseries, for example, squirrels at Lungmanis, Sabah, in 1971 (Fox 1972). Mass migrations of pigs (*Sus barbatus*) in search of fallen ripe illipe nuts (*Shorea* spp.) are famous in Borneo and formerly occurred in south Malaya (Medway 1969). The seed is the effective unit of dispersal, not the whole fruit, and syndromes of characters which are believed to attract different groups of animals to the fruit, so that they might disperse the seed or seeds, were described in Chapter 2.

Within the tropical rain forest dispersal by wind and by animal are the two principal modes. Dispersal by animals is presumably the answer to the old conundrum, 'how do big, heavy-seeded trees ever come to grow on ridge crests?' In addition some seashore and riverine species are dispersed by water. The definitive review of dispersal is Ridley (1930).

There is evidence that, amongst rain-forest trees, animal dispersal is more effective than dispersal by wind. *Terminalia calamansanai*, the only one of twelve species studied on Kolombangara Island in the Solomons which had seeds adapted to wind not animal dispersal, was also the least effectively dispersed; all seedlings were found immediately around parent trees (Whitmore 1974). Jones (1956) found wind dispersal less effective than animal dispersal in a Nigerian rain forest.

On a larger scale of time and distance is Wyatt-Smith's (1953a) study of Jarak, which is a small island of about 40 ha lying almost centrally in the northern approaches to the Malacca Straits, 64 km off the coast of Malaya. Jarak is believed to have been deeply blanketed by volcanic ash after the cataclysmic eruption of the volcano Toba in Sumatra, 224 km away. This occurred 34 000 years ago (Stauffer 1973). In the course of a survey Wyatt-Smith found only 93 species of flowering plants (76 genera, 44 families), far fewer than for a comparable area on the mainland (cf. Figs 1.3 and 1.5, pp. 5 and 6). All except 13 species were animal-dispersed, the exceptions being 8 seaborne species, 2 introduced by man, and 3 windborne ones (2 orchids, and *Hoya parasitica* with plumed seeds). In addition there were 16 fern species. There were no Dipterocarpaceae.† Wyatt-Smith commented on the clumping of many species, and suggested this might be because they were brought in by birds or fruit-eating bats.

The findings on Jarak contrast with those on Krakatau Island only 40 km off the coasts of Java and Sumatra, which had been recolonized in 1934, 48 years after its cataclysmic eruption, by 41 per cent windborne and 28 animal-borne species (Doctors van Leeuwen 1936, in Richards 1952).

The inefficient dispersal of fruits apparently adapted for wind-dispersal is vividly shown by several studies which have now been made on Dipterocarpaceae, most of which have 2–5 long wings developed from the sepals. Burgess (1970) found that a solitary tree of *Shorea curtisii* of bole girth 3·6 m and crown diameter 18 m, which was growing in forest on an exposed ridge, dispersed no fruits more than 80 m; 54 per cent, 83 per cent, and 97 per cent of the crop, estimated at 180 000 fruits, fell within 20 m, 40 m, and 60 m respectively, in an ellipse-shaped area with its long axis parallel to the prevailing wind. The fruits of *S. curtisii* are amongst the smallest of all species of the Red Meranti group of *Shorea*. Only 8 per cent of the fruits were viable, and these all fell within 25 m of the tree; the rest were attacked by a weevil, and were presumably therefore lighter. The first viable fruit fell in early October, the duration of fruit fall being from August to November. Another nearby tree fruited 2 weeks later and had a much higher percentage of viable seed. Fox (1972, Table 24) gives similar data for dipterocarps in Sabah, showing for two species of

† Rumbia Island, 22 km off the Malayan coast, did have a few dipterocarps.

Dryobalanops, three of *Parashorea*, six of *Shorea*, and a *Dipterocarpus* that there is a rapid decrease in amount of fruit fall to 40 m from the tree; 98 per cent of *Shorea fallax* fruits, a wingless species, fell within 10 m.

Occurrence in several dipterocarp species of a wide range of girths in discrete small patches of trees ('family groups') has been reported for Sabah (Fox 1972), and for the Jengka forest in Malaya (Poore 1968)—see Chapter 15 and Fig. 15.15 (p. 193). It clearly arises from inefficient dispersal, though interacting with gap formation (§6.4).†

The importance to dipterocarps of wings on the fruit is presumably that they slow down the rate the fruit falls. They also cause it to spin. Rarely, dipterocarp fruits are dispersed over distances of up to about 1 km by the high wind which precedes a convectional rainstorm. *Parashorea* fruit in Sabah has been seen carried 0.4 km (Burgess). Webber (1934) saw an ascending cloud of winged fruits in the Bubu forest, Malaya, which comprised six different dipterocarps as well as *Koompassia malaccensis* and an unidentified Anacardiaceae (rengas). After the storm which carried these fruits up from the crowns had passed, they fell like snow at a density of 3–4 per square metre up to 0.8 km away. A similar phenomenon with *Dryobalanops aromatica* has been reported from the former Lesong forest (Anon. 1972b), the rising fruit cloud in this case was compared to a swarm of white ants. By contrast Kochummen (1966) found a decrease in dipterocarp seedling numbers in an isolated block of old secondary forest at Sungei Kroh, Malaya, 5 km from a seed source, after old relict seed-bearing trees had died.

Havel (1971) found that the winged seeds of the conifer *Araucaria hunsteinii* were dispersed 60 m into a clearing north-westwards along the line of the monsoon winds, but only 20 m normal to them.

5.2. Seed dormancy and germination

Many rain-forest tree species have no dormant period or only a short one, and commence to germinate at once or within a few days. The large seeds of *Dipterocarpus* and *Durio*, which germinate at once, lack endosperm and cannot resist drying (Holttum 1953). Jensen (1971) investigated germination of the seeds of another dipterocarp, *Dryobalanops aromatica*. They were found to contain 44 per cent water on falling and soon began to germinate. Light did not limit either germination or storage. A tem-

perature of 5 °C killed the seed and storage was better at 12 °C than 20 °C or 30 °C; infection by micro-organisms increased with rise in temperature and was the major factor limiting storage. Tang (1971) was able to extend the viability of the seeds of *Shorea curtisii* and *S. platyclados* from 1 week to 3–4 weeks by reducing their moisture content from 40 per cent to 20–5 per cent at 34 °C and then storing them in charcoal, vermiculite, or sawdust. In further trials Tang and Tamari (1973) found that by markedly reducing seed moisture content and storing at 15 °C or even lower the viability period of several Malayan dipterocarp species could be considerably prolonged. Burgess (unpublished) found *S. curtisii* will normally germinate within 6 days of soaking by rain (10 days if only touched by damp litter) and loses viability in 6–7 days if not wetted. An atmosphere of 100 per cent relative humidity is no substitute for wetting by rain to produce the water content found in germinating seeds (which ranges from 90 per cent to 160 per cent of that of a freshly fallen seed). It is of interest that, in Malaya and Sabah, fruits of this and other dipterocarps are known to ripen and fall at about the time of onset of the wettest weather of the year. Cockburn and Wong (1969) found the starch and fat reserves in germinating seeds of *S. curtisii* had gone by 20 days.

Different species of *Shorea* have been found to have different viability in Malaya: *S. leprosula*, *S. macroptera*, and *S. ovalis* averaged 80 per cent, whereas *S. acuminata* had 100 per cent viability, possibly because of its small seed size relative to the larva of a common predatory weevil tentatively identified as *Alcidodes* (Burgess). *Dipterocarpus* species, which have bigger seeds than *Shorea*, are notorious for their high percentage of insect attack. Species of the seasonally dry far north-west part of Malaya have slightly longer viability than those from the ever-wet part (Wyatt-Smith 1963).

The lack of dormancy of the seeds of many rain-forest trees has serious implications for silviculture, especially of species which fruit infrequently. Flushes of seedlings will intermittently carpet the forest floor, and natural regeneration of the forest will depend to a great extent on whether enough survive until the time the forester wants to operate. The problem is nowhere more acute than in Dipterocarpaceae whose seedling survival is discussed in §6.4. Nor can the forester store seed in order to raise seedlings for planting at will, or to transport them for trial at a distance. Dipterocarpaceae have scarcely been tried outside their native region. Only recently has it been discovered that the viability of *Araucaria* seeds can be

---

† The occurrence of 'family groups' is not to be confused with same-age, more nearly same-size groups of trees which all grew up together in a gap (cf. §6.2).

prolonged, and plantations of the New Guinea species of this important conifer genus are now being established, from seed sent by air, in various parts of the tropics. *A. cunninghamii* is preferred to *A. hunsteinii* because of its smaller seeds of longer viability (Ntima 1968). The loss of viability after liberation from the cone is rapid. In *A. hunsteinii* it is about 10 per cent a week for 6 weeks, down to zero at 8 weeks (Havel 1971). Death can be delayed for a year by airtight, cold storage at 3 °C for *A. hunsteinii* and storage in jute sacks at −12 °C for *A. cunninghamii*. Seeds must be sown within 24 hours of removal from storage (Morel 1967). Seed fall is annual and is completed by the start of the wet season in November (Havel 1971), a synchronization comparable to that mentioned above for Dipterocarpaceae.

Seeds of the tropical *Pinus* species lose their viability less rapidly (though not from provenances of *P. merkusii* from continental south-east Asia) and can be dried for storage (Cooling 1968). They are extremely tiny (1000 *P. merkusii* seed weigh 16·7–37·0 g depending on provenance). These pines have been planted much more extensively than species of *Araucaria*.

Absence of dormancy complicates breeding for improved tree quality, which is becoming of considerable importance in developing plantation forestry. It also makes more difficult the breeding of improved strains of the many fruit tree species of the region whose ancestors are denizens of the rain forest. In conclusion, it is no exaggeration to state that the development of methods of inducing dormancy in the seeds of tropical rain forest trees still remains a virtually unexplored field of research on whose success awaits the opening of new vistas in silviculture and horticulture.

Some species show staggered germination over a period of several months; this device, which has obvious survival value in natural conditions, plays havoc with nursery schedules. Examples are *Dyera costulata* and *Koompassia malaccensis,* which in trials in Malaya germinated 24–130 days and 13–56 days after sowing, respectively (Wyatt-Smith 1963).

Some tropical tree seeds do have a dormant period before they germinate. Many Leguminosae are in this class, notably *Intsia palembanica*, though not all: *Koompassia malaccensis*, for example, germinates without prolonged dormancy (Fox 1972), a feature probably resultant from its having a soft testa, unusual in Leguminosae (Ng). *Albizia lophantha* may be cited as a legume which does exhibit seed dormancy. It is a small tree of upper montane forests from Sumatra, Java, Bali, Lombok, and Flores and is also found in south-west Australia. It is distinctly shade-intolerant and prefers open, stoney sites. Its seed has a thin, but hard and waterproof, coat and remains dormant for several years. Once the coat has become cracked, through the heat of ground fire or impregnation by acid from a solfatara, germination follows, hence even-aged, single-species groves result. Fruit is set abundantly at 5–6 years of age and the trees decline. The Javanese collect and eat the pods as a petai (*Parkia*) substitute and fire the forest to ensure a new crop (van Steenis 1972).

Anthocephalus chinensis seed have several years' dormancy (Fox 1972), and there are persistent reports that the whole class of species to which it belongs, namely, those which regenerate in open conditions, have seeds which can remain dormant. The evidence is not convincing and discussion is deferred until §6.2.

5.3. Seedling establishment

The seed must germinate in a suitable place for the seedling to become established and there is much wastage. For a few species we now have observations on reasons for failure to establish.

Terminalia brassii is a species of fresh-water swamps and moist, valley-floor alluvial soils, in the Bismarck and Solomon archipelagos (Coode 1973). It germinates freely in cleared forest on these sites and also on dry land, and seedling height growth is at first rapid; on dry-land sites the species succumbs to competition from others, initiated in dry spells of weather during which it shows signs of water-stress (Marten). The restriction of *T. brassii* to moist habitats probably results from these limitations in seedling establishment.

Species which establish in dense shade must be physiologically adapted to very low light. Experiments are awaited to demonstrate whether they have low respiration rates or unusually high carbon dioxide fixation rates at low light intensities compared to other species. Species of this group characteristically have substantial food reserves in the seed, which are an initial aid to establishment. For example, both *Calophyllum kajewskii* and *C. vitiense* of the Solomons have a massive endosperm and rapidly grow a hypocotyl 0·3 m long (Whitmore 1974); thereafter growth is much slower.

Our other examples on seedling establishment concern observations on Dipterocarpaceae in Sabah and Malaya.

Nicholson (1960), investigating five dipterocarp

species (*Dryobalanops lanceolata, Shorea leprosula, S. johorensis, Parashorea tomentella, Dipterocarpus stellatus*), found they all required some shade for seedling establishment, but showed decreasing tolerance in that order and then responded to full light after about 18 months by more rapid growth. Burgess (unpublished) found seedlings of *Shorea curtisii, S. laevis, S. leprosula,* and *S. platyclados* grew better in up to 50 per cent shade for establishment. Nicholson believed cool soil was an important component of the shade climate. By further experiments (Nicholson 1964, in Fox 1972) he was able to show that high soil temperature and low soil moisture become limiting for growth, so that in such conditions full exposure may not give an increased response. Another experiment showed that *Parashorea tomentella* seedlings failed to develop in non-forest soil (at 8 months only 32 per cent had leaves, and the rest were existing on their cotyledons); this may have been due to the absence of a necessary mycorrhizal fungus (Nicholson 1961, in Fox 1972). In all these experiments root competition was reduced or eliminated, although it is probably always important in the forest.

The most detailed study has been by Burgess (unpublished) on the establishment of Dipterocarpaceae seedlings in lowland evergreen rain forest in the hills in Malaya. Within the areas sampled and within dispersal range of fruiting mother trees observations after the 1968 year of heavy fruiting showed:

(1) recruitment was markedly better on granite-derived soils than on those derived from shale, but
(2) there was little difference with topography; valleys and lower hillsides received as much as ridges.

During the first year mortality was about the same on both sorts of soil, and 55 per cent of seedlings survived the first early-year drought after establishment; at 10 months, survival was 33 per cent (equivalent to 2 per cent of seedfall); much death was due to falling twigs. Mortality in valleys was much higher than on ridges. After some years both granite and shale carry about the same stocking of seedlings, which indicates that mortality must be much higher on granite-derived soils, and this could be because of their coarser structure and consequent greater proneness to drought. Heavier recruitment over granite could be because more trees there suffer water-stress and hence flower (Chapter 4), but observations suggest that at least part of the explanation lies in better establishment conditions on these sandier soils; the shale soils tend to form a hard surface skin where the clay almost puddles.

Burgess found much less recruitment (9600 seedlings per hectare) on all sites at higher elevations in the upper dipterocarp forest type (§15.2) than in steep lowland and hill dipterocarp forest ($2 \cdot 4 \times 10^4$ per hectare), and this was mainly because there is only one common species, *Shorea platyclados*, as high as this, contrasting with the many species at lower elevations. Litter depth proved no bar to recruitment, *S. platyclados* being able to survive for long periods just on water, and having notably long intercalary growth. Peat, found on the Malayan main range 1050 m upwards (Whitmore and Burnham 1969), seemed to be an absolute bar to dipterocarp establishment, and is probably the principal factor which limits the family upwards. It was discovered that an important reason for progressive reduction in dipterocarp seedling stocking with increasing elevation was that stocking falls with the micro-slope at the site of the seedling, rapidly so at slopes over 45° and reaching nil at 65°. At elevations of 150–450 m, 15 per cent of micro-slopes were over 45°; over 600 m this increased to 20 per cent.

Burgess' studies indicate the intricate relationships which exist in seedling establishment of Dipterocarpaceae in the hills of Malaya, involving both site (altitude, and the complex intertwined factors of topography, rock, soil, and micro-slope) and rainfall fluctuations (hence flowering and fruiting periodicity and seedling death by drought). His work throws some light on some of the mechanisms which might be important in determining the ecological range of different species, and on that long-standing foresters' enigma: why is it that timber-size trees are commonest on ridge crests? His findings will be considered further where variation within lowland dipterocarp rain forest is discussed in §15.3.

6 Growth of seedlings into trees

AT THE end of Chapter 5, the important roles which site and climatic fluctuations can play in seedling establishment were demonstrated. We must now turn our attention to another aspect of forest regeneration, namely, to consider in which phase of the forest growth cycle the tree seedling establishes itself. We shall then go on to investigate the conditions under which continued growth into sapling, pole, and mature tree can occur.

6.1. The gap phase of the forest growth cycle

It will be recalled (Chapter 2) that virgin rain forest consists of a mosaic of patches at different stages of maturity; from gaps, through stands of small saplings or poles, to mature high forest, often topped by giant emergent trees. For convenience, gap, building, and mature phases of the growth cycle are distinguished.

The cycle starts with the gap phase, and the size of the gaps formed in any given forest determines the size of the patches of regrowing forest, that is to say, the coarseness of the mosaic of structural phases. The microclimate within a gap becomes less like that of the closed forest canopy the larger the gap (§3.6). In this chapter it will be shown that different species are successful in growing up in gaps of different size. From this it follows that the size of gap has an important influence on species' composition and species' spatial arrangement in the forest.

Gap size

The tiniest gaps are formed by the slow death of a big tree, described in §2.3; the crown and then the bole falling to the ground, often in pieces. The crowns of big emergent trees are mostly about 15–18 m diameter. Many trees succumb to wind before they die of old age. The bole of a single falling tree cuts a narrow swathe through the forest, and its crown creates a gap of up to about 0·04 ha. Such gaps can be seen in Fig. 2.3 (p. 16), a plan of the structural mosaic on 2·02 ha of tropical lowland evergreen rain forest at Sungei Menyala, Malaya. Trees felled by wind usually have their roots torn from the ground, and forced in to a mound reaching 1–2 m high (sometimes called a root-plate), with a corresponding depression; eventually the wood rots away. Forest-floor micro-relief of hummocks and hollows is found in places where such tree fall is

common. The very strong local squalls which precede convectional rainstorms are a frequent source of tree fall. Such winds sometimes act on the edge of existing gaps and increase their size by felling or smashing the crowns of one tree or several, often in the same direction. Trees are especially susceptible to wind when the soil is very wet and has lost part of its cohesion, and especially where there are impediments to drainage either due to structural horizons, as in the B horizon of ultisols (Chapter 9), or where shallow bands of shale lie interbedded in coarser sedimentary rocks, as in the Belait formation of northern Borneo (Baillie). Sometimes a single falling tree will tear down others with it if their crowns are tied together with big woody climbers (this is especially frequent in Sabah).

Convectional storms are believed to be commoner in some places than others, for example, inland in Sarawak they are commoner than at the coast (Baillie), and in Malaya they are commonest in the foothills of the main east and west coast mountain ranges (Dale 1959). It follows that some forests are more prone to wind damage than others. Line squalls, associated with the movement of airstream boundaries, bring a short-lived belt of high winds across an extensive tract of land, for example, they sweep right down Malaya (Watts 1954) where they are probably the main cause of the gaps of up to 0·5–1 ha extent occasionally found in the lowland forest (especially swamp forest) in that country. Anderson (1964b) reported areas of over 80 ha thrown by single localized squalls in *Shorea albida* peat swamp forest in Sarawak, and Brunig reported a 77 ha fan-shaped extension to a felling area caused by a single storm.

Lightning, which is also associated with convectional rain storms, may kill forest trees. The pattern in the Solomons, where such damage is common, is of one or a few large trees completely killed, together with the small trees close by, and the surrounding forest scorched on the side facing the place of strike. The whole crown top of a 36 m tree of *Anisoptera megistocarpa* in the Singapore Garden's Jungle was blown off from 24 m up by a single stroke of lightning in 1964 (Anon. 1965a). Fire started by lightning has been recorded in Sarawak (Anderson 1966) and the Solomons, in trees where there was an accumulation of dry epiphyte detritus and despite rain. Brunig (1964) found that different communities in the *Shorea albida* peat swamp forests in Sarawak had different susceptibility to lightning strike, as reckoned from gaps in the canopy seen on aerial photographs, and the damage is sufficiently extensive in some types to influence forest management. Gaps of up to 0·6 ha affecting at least 70 trees are known (Anderson 1964*b*) in these rather flat-topped forests. The damage decreases outwards from a central point at which small trees are killed too. Occasional, exceptionally violent thunderstorms are believed to be responsible rather than normal afternoon ones (cf. §3.5). Mean gap size and number had increased between 1947 and 1961 in two areas studied in detail (Brunig 1964). Wind acts on lightning gaps in *Shorea albida* forest and fells trees in long narrow corridors (the longest over 8 km (Palmer)). Lightning damage is common in peat swamp and mangrove forest in Malaya (Wyatt-Smith 1963).

Gaps may be created by landslips in hilly country, especially when the soil is sodden after heavy rain. Size, position on slope, and frequency of slip varies from one rock type to another. In Malaya, granite, which weathers deeply and irregularly to leave huge boulders through the soil, is the rock by far the most susceptible to slip (Burgess). There is evidence from the United States that a forest cover may sometimes increase proneness to landslips (Oryness 1967), due to the localized heavy loading on the ground of big trees. Landslips expose subsoil at the surface, just as do trees overthrown by wind.

Gaps may be created because trees are killed by fungal attack, which may spread through the soil and increase the gap size. Bare patches in lowland forest in Malaya, in which all plants are dead including seedlings and saplings, may be due to this cause, but there has been no detailed examination. An example is the biggest gap in the Sungei Menyala forest (Fig. 2.3, p. 16), first noted in 1947 and still present in 1971, covering about 0·1 ha. These gaps are well known to foresters in Malaya as 'tempat kongkang beranak' (birth place of the slow loris).

The only reported example of gaps created by insects killing trees is in the *Shorea albida* peat swamp forest of Sarawak where the caterpillar of an unidentified tussock moth (Hymantridae) defoliates the crowns and the trees subsequently die. The scale may be spectacular, the largest area, killed over a 6-month period of 1948, was 31 km long; more commonly smaller patches are killed, to 60 ha extent, and about 12 000 ha of dead forest can be identified on aerial photographs. Successive aerial photographs show that there was a very rapid increase in the rate of damage between 1950 and 1960. Damage radiates from a centre and ceases suddenly (Anderson 1961*a*).

We have no measure of the importance of higher animals in creating gaps and maintaining them, but the larger herbivorous animals of the Sunda-shelf forests undoubtedly have a substantial effect. A mature elephant eats about 250 kg of plant material a day (Medway 1969) and tramples on much more. Elephant-damage in Sabah forests is thought possibly to be followed by an increase in the climbing bamboo *Dinochloa*, mainly *D. scandens* (Fox 1972). In Malaya the forest floor surrounding salt licks is trampled and the undergrowth plants destroyed, sometimes for up to a kilometre. West of Wallace's line, where there are numerous, large, ground-living mammals, game trails run through the forests and are especially prominent near salt licks and along ridges in mountainous country, making the exploring scientist's progress easy and rapid. In these ways the impact of animals is clearly visible, but how the forest growth cycle and composition are affected is not yet known.

Between 10° and 20° north and south of the equator lie zones where cyclones (typhoons, hurricanes, tornadoes) regularly form. These are storms of enormous violence which devastate all in their path. Damage to the forest consists of blowing trees over in the worst-affected zone, and over a wider belt causing crown-damage or defoliation, thus temporarily increasing the amount of light which penetrates to the forest undergrowth. The islands of the Philippines (except Mindanao), north Queensland (Webb 1958), the Solomons (Whitmore 1974), the New Hebrides, Fiji (Gane 1970), and Samoa (Wood 1970) are the parts of the tropical Far East lying in the two cyclone zones (Lamb 1972). Visher (1925) gives a very full review. In November 1880 a storm, the 'angin besar', probably an aberrant cyclone, devastated forests in Kelantan, north-east Malaya, over hundreds of square kilometres (Browne 1949; Wyatt-Smith 1954*a*). On Savai'i, one of the principal Samoan islands, over half the potentially exploitable forest was destroyed by cyclones in 1961, 1966, and 1968, the gaps became dense with the climbers *Merremia* spp. and *Mikania* '*cordata*', and tree stocking was reduced by as much as 90 per cent to 15 stems per hectare (Wood 1970). There is evidence that the zones have moved slightly closer to the equator since 1950; devastation is becoming more frequent in the Solomon archipelago between 7° and 11° S (Whitmore 1974).

The evidence just reviewed shows that size and

frequency of gap formation varies from place to place for a number of reasons, and is not entirely at random. Effects of these differences, on both a regional and a local scale, on forest structure and composition will be described in Chapter 15.

Gap microclimate

The many alterations to the microclimate which occur when a gap forms are all interlinked and have been discussed in §3.6. In addition to the aerial increase in temperature plus a concomitant increase in light and saturation deficit, there is a release of nutrients as fallen plants decay and a temporary decrease in root competition (the more so the larger the gap). Sometimes there is also a marked local alteration in micro-relief and soil profile.

Plant response to gaps

Shorea albida crowns can recover from wind damage. Out of 1006 trees surveyed, 128 showed signs of damage, including 43·5 per cent of those over 1·8 m girth and 82·1 per cent of those over 2·7 m girth (Anderson 1961b). In *Shorea albida* forest single-tree wind and lightning gaps and the long, narrow wind gaps mentioned above become filled by the expansion of the crowns of adjacent canopy-top trees, and bigger gaps decrease in size from the same cause (Brunig 1964). This is likely to happen also in some other forests. Otherwise, there are two broad alternative starts to the building phase of the forest growth cycle, either existing seedlings and saplings commence upwards growth or seeds germinate in the gap and new trees establish this way. (The seeds may either be lying dormant in the soil and germinate in response to the microclimatic changes of gap creation, or they may be borne in to the gap.) We must now turn our attention to a consideration of the details of these two alternative strategies of establishment.

6.2. Light-demanding and shade-bearing tree species

As a first generalization, it is found that established seedlings and saplings most often grow up to maturity in small gaps. By contrast, the drastic change in microclimate which occurs after the formation of a big gap is commonly followed by severe damage to, or death of, all or many of the young plants which previously became established in the cool, shady, humid microclimate of the closed canopy (see §6.5 for examples). And big gaps are found to be colonized by a group of species, rare or absent in the under-growth of high forest, which are equipped success-fully to exploit the very different microclimate of open sites.

Rain-forest trees can be divided crudely into two groups: those which regenerate *in situ*, in the shade of the high forest, and those which regenerate in gaps. These groups are respectively 'shade-tolerant' and 'light-demanding' in their early life.

Species which require gaps for regeneration cannot grow up even under their own shade. An evocative term for such species, and one which has gained common currency, is *biological nomads* (van Steenis 1958b), because, viewing the forest over a long period, they are continually moving, growing as populations of one generation duration in the scattered gaps caused by tree fall or landslip and in which they manage to establish, despite competition from other nomad species and from established seedlings. By contrast, the species which can regenerate in shade, and thus are potentially able to remain permanently in high forest, van Steenis called *dryads* (dryad—a wood nymph). The term nomad, however, does imply continuous movement, and an even more appropriate term, and one which will be used in this book, is *pioneer species*. They have sometimes also been called seral species.

Foresters have long recognized that the degree to which species are shade-bearers or light-demanders is an important key to other aspects of their behaviour. It is found that pioneers (light-demanders), characteristically have very rapid height growth in youth, and rapid girth growth, at least at first. Rapid height growth clearly has high selective value, as a pioneer tree which can over-top others in the same gap will suppress them by shading and by physical occupation of a volume of space, and so pre-empt that gap for itself for its whole remaining life. Wood of low density is a feature correlated with rapid growth, and it is usually pale in colour. (Balsa, *Ochroma lagopus*, is a South American pioneer.) Pioneer species characteristically flower and fruit copiously and continuously, without regard to season (Chapter 4), which is unusual in the flora as a whole. Individuals become fertile at an early age. A further important feature of pioneers is that dispersal is efficient. For all these characters, also, there is strong selective pressure. Most pioneers have big leaves, megaphyll and macrophyll in the terminology of Raunkiaer (1934), rather than mesophyll and notophyll (Webb 1959), which predominate amongst shade-bearers.

Euphorbiaceae, Malvaceae, Moraceae, Sterculiaceae, Tiliaceae, Ulmaceae, and Urticaceae provide many pioneer tree species. Van Steenis (1950b,

FIG. 6.1. *Macaranga gigantea* about 5 m tall, colonizing a roadside. Pahang, Malaya.

FIG. 6.2. *Macaranga triloba*. Pahang, Malaya.

FIG. 6.3. Leaf of *Macaranga gigantifolia*; Telaga Mas, Kalimantan. Several Macarangas have leaves almost as huge as this.

1958*b*) estimated that 20 per cent of the Malesian flora exhibits pioneering qualities, including the herbs of early seral stages which are mainly Amaranthaceae, Compositae and Labiatae (all with many ephemeral species), Gramineae, and Verbenaceae. *Macaranga* (Figs 6.1, 6.2, and 6.3) is the genus *par excellence* of pioneer trees; it is found throughout the tropical Far East, where most of its 280 species occur. In Malaya, for example, there are 27 species, of which 20 can be found along roadsides, 18 of them gregariously (Whitmore 1967*a*, 1973*f*)†; like other pioneers *Macaranga* has been able enormously to expand its populations as man has provided an ever larger area of suitable habitats, especially over the last century or so. One Malayan species, *M. constricta*, which was first discovered in 1967 on the slopes of Gunung Benom, was at that place moving for the first time from natural landslips and forest gaps, on to the sides of newly built logging roads (Whitmore 1969*d*; Whitmore and Airy Shaw 1971). The enormous expansion in range of *Macaranga* species presented an interesting situation for biosystematic study. In fact in Malaya man's intervention appears to have had little effect on species evolution, and no signs of introgressive hybridization or polyploidy could be detected (Whitmore 1969*d*; Whitmore, Soh, and Jones 1970). *Trichospermum* with over 30 species (Kostermans 1972) is also a genus entirely of pioneers, common and important from New Guinea to the Solomons, and so is *Homalanthus* (20 species). It is more usually the case that only a few species of a big genus have pioneering properties, for example, in *Mallotus* (notably *M. paniculatus*), which is mainly a genus of C storey, small trees of high forest (Whitmore 1973*f*).

There are several reports that the seeds of pioneers have a long dormancy and germinate after a gap forms on the stimulation of either bright light or high temperatures or both (Symington 1933; van Steenis 1958*b*; Nicholson 1970; Kellman 1970; Webb, Tracey, and Williams 1972; Fox 1972; (for west Africa); Keay 1960)). Critical experiments have yet to be performed in the tropical Far East to distinguish between the germination of dormant seeds and the rapid seeding-in of species whose propagules are produced continuously and which are efficiently dispersed, and to establish whether pioneer species have seeds capable of dormancy. The observations that pioneers usually occur in pure stands and that adjacent gaps created at different times—as

† In Borneo there are over 50 species (Whitmore 1975).

in logging areas—commonly have different species are indicative that invasion on a 'first come, first served' basis after gap formation may, in fact, prevail.

By contrast with light-demanders, seeds of shade-bearing species are able to germinate and establish in the gloom of the high forest, and some have substantial food reserves which they utilize to become established (§5.3). Seedlings can commonly persist for several years, growing only very slowly. As a generalization, shade-bearers are commonly slow growing in girth and height and have dense, dark timber. Examples are the Balau group of *Shorea*, *Hopea*, *Vatica*, and *Balanocarpus heimii* amongst the Dipterocarpaceae and species of Group (a) in Table 6.1 (p. 74) in the Solomon Islands. These features all contrast with the properties of light-demanding species, though a few hardwooded light-demanders are known, for example, *Securinega flexuosa* the prime house-post providing species of the Solomons and the pioneer *Casuarina* spp. of New Guinea.

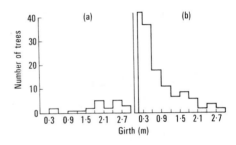

FIG. 6.4. Stand table for (a) a 'light-demanding'; (b) a 'shade-bearing' tree species (Kolombangara, Solomons). (a) *Endospermum medullosum*; (b) *Parinari salomonensis*. Populations on 13·35 ha in lowland rain forest. (From Whitmore 1974, Fig. 7.2.)

The population structure of light-demanding and shade-bearing species in a stand of high forest is markedly different. The former, illustrated in Fig. 6.4 by *Endospermum medullosum*, have a preponderance of big stems, simply because they cannot regenerate in shade. The latter have most stems in the smallest classes, as is shown by *Parinari salomenensis* in Fig. 6.4. Foresters often refer to these population structures as negative (that is, not reproducing, see also Fig. 15.20 (p. 196)) and positive stands, respectively.†

Extreme light-demanding and shade-bearing properties are two contrasting ecological strategies of

† There has been an unfortunate tendency amongst foresters to make predictions from stand tables alone about past and future performance of stands of a species without substantiating measurements made over a period of time. Such predictions are not justified.

forest trees with respect to perpetuation of the species. It must not be thought that all tree species fall neatly into one group or the other. Rather, there is a complete spectrum of responses to light, and these are the two extremes. The conditions which stimulate seedlings of shade-bearing species to commence and continue upwards growth are not well understood, and indeed are likely to vary from species to species. Some species probably need some increase in light, such as occurs in a small gap; this has now been shown for many dipterocarps (see below). Others may merely need a volume of space above ground, such as will develop after a small tree dies, and may be stimulated to grow by the reduced root competition which is concomitant with such a death.

Artificial small gaps of 0·1 ha area in primary forest on Gunung Gede in west Java were soon filled by surviving young individuals of primary forest tree species which made good growth in the gap. By contrast, in larger gaps of 0·2–0·3 ha, the primary forest trees were suppressed by a lush growth of secondary forest pioneers. This interesting early experiment has apparently never been repeated or extended (Kramer 1926, 1933).

The physiological basis of the difference between light-demanding and shade-bearing species remains largely uninvestigated (see §8.4).

Two groups of pioneers can be distinguished, those which are short-lived and long-lived respectively.

Fig. 6.5. *Trema cannabina*, a small short-lived light-demanding pioneer tree growing gregariously in heath forest after fire (Brunei).

Examples of short-lived pioneer trees which are common in the tropical Far East are *Commersonia bartramia*, all *Trema* (Fig. 6.5) and *Trichospermum*, some *Mallotus*, and most *Macaranga*. Kochummen (1966) found that a stand of *Macaranga gigantea* on an area farmed for one crop at Sungei Kroh, Malaya, had grown to 18–21 m tall and 1·2 m girth in 15 years and was beginning to die. Kellman (1970), working at 900–1200 m elevation in Mindanao, southern Philippines, distinguished *Homalanthus* spp. as very short-lived pioneers, which matured at 10 years and died after 15 years, from *Trema orientalis* and *Mallotus paniculatus* which lived to 30 years. Long-lived pioneers include the genera *Endospermum* and *Campnosperma* (Fig. 6.6), *Albizia falcata*, *A. minahassae*, *Anthocephalus chinensis* (Figs 7.2 and 7.3, p. 85), *Eucalyptus deglupta* (Fig. 7.4, p. 86), *Gmelina arborea*, *G. moluccana*, *Octomeles sumatrana* (Fig. 7.5, p. 87), and the two pines of our region,

Fig. 6.6. Sapling of *Campnosperma auriculatum* growing in a gap in logged lowland rain forest (Sungei Lallang forest, Malaya). The crown is still monopodial and the leaves are very much larger than on mature trees.

Pinus kesiya and *P. merkusii*. In Papua stands of the long-lived pioneers *Albizia falcata* and *Octomeles sumatrana* were dying at 84 years of age (§8.2). Long-lived pioneer species have very considerable economic importance, and will be discussed further in §7.2. Some of them have marked habitat preferences (for example, *Campnosperma coriaceum* for swamps—§11.4, Fig. 11.15, p. 156; *Pinus* for monsoon climates—§14.3). No sharp distinction exists against short-lived pioneers.

Light-demanding species which have been observed locally to colonize clearings, especially those made by man, but which are less widespread and common than those just considered, are *Symingtonia populnea* and *Weinmannia blumei* (for example, at Cameron Highlands and Fraser's Hill, Malaya); *Engelhardtia spicata* and *Harmsiopanax aculeatus* (east and central Java (van Steenis 1972)) all in lower montane forest; *Schima wallichii* locally in lowland and lower montane forest; and *Leptospermum flavescens* in upper montane forest. This group of species has some pioneer characters, but lacks the aggression of the true pioneers. In the Sarawak peat swamp forest (§11.3) *Cratoxylum arborescens*, *C. glaucum*, *Dactylocladus stenostachys*, *Lithocarpus sundaicus*, and *Macaranga caladiifolia* exhibit pioneer features. *Dyera costulata*, a giant emergent lowland tree in the Sundaland rain forests, is a very strong light-demander. It occurs scattered, never in stands, despite its frequently produced, windborne seeds. Its seeds take 24–130 days to germinate (Whitmore 1973*d*; Wyatt-Smith 1963). Why it exhibits only some pioneer characteristics remains to be ascertained.

Once a tree has grown to occupy a space in the forest it will remain there until its death, and that may be several centuries hence. It follows that an understanding of the conditions which lead to the establishment of one species rather than another are essential to an unravelling of the nature of plant communities in the rain forest. Foresters and botanists who work in the rain forest develop, from extensive observation and the results of experimental thinnings and planting trials, an acute idea of tree species' response to light, and are thus able from a quick inspection of a stand of trees to deduce from its composition, and to some extent too its structure, a good idea of the past history of the area. For example, a patch of small light-demanders indicates that there was a gap at some time recently in the past, and it will often be possible to date it roughly to within a few years. This kind of deduction is so much part of the stock-in-trade of rain-forest

scientists that it remains poorly documented by precise examples.† Despite this limitation instances can be given from two areas which illustrate the main features of species' ecological strategy so far described mainly in general terms only.

6.3. Forest dynamics: Solomon Islands

The whole populations—seedlings, saplings, poles, and trees—of the twelve main top-of-canopy tree species were kept under observation for 6·6 years on 22 sample plots (Fig. 15.7, p. 194), totalling 13·35 ha and distributed through the lowland evergreen rain forest which clothes the west and north parts of Kolombangara, one of the Solomon Islands (Whitmore 1974). Repeated counts were made of the small plants, and girth measurements made on the trees, and it was noted whether the individuals grew in gaps or within forest canopy. After 3·3 years the island was struck by a cyclone and 34·5 per cent of the canopy on the sample plots received serious visible damage tantamount to gap formation. This fortuitous event gave the chance to study the response of the twelve species to such major disturbance. Additionally, observations were made on the species' behaviour elsewhere in the Solomons, especially in areas regrowing after timber extraction, and in Forestry Department plantations and nurseries. The 13·35 ha of intense dynamic sampling were supplemented by an island-wide floristic survey (Greig-Smith, Austin, and Whitmore 1967; Whitmore 1974).

Table 6.1 summarizes the conclusions from this study (Whitmore 1974). The twelve species can be arranged in four groups on their response to gaps:

(a) those whose seedlings both establish and grow up under high forest;

(b) those which establish and grow up under high forest but show some signs of benefiting from gaps;

(c) those which establish mainly in high forest but definitely require gaps to grow up; and

(d) those, the pioneer species, which establish mainly or entirely in gaps, and only grow up in gaps.

These four groups show increasing dependence on canopy gaps and show clearly that 'shade-bearers' and 'light-demanders' are not two exclusive categories; even in the species-poor Solomons archi-

† This kind of qualitative observation is not, of course, a substitute for the measurements which must be made before any silvicultural treatment can be prescribed.

TABLE 6.1

Regeneration behaviour of the common big tree species, Kolombangara, Solomon Islands

Species	Seeds Dispersal†	Population size	Seedlings Conditions to establish	Conditions to grow up	Trees‡ Distribution
(a) *Dillenia salomonensis*	Poor	Medium	High forest	High forest	West only: common
Maranthes corymbosa	?	Small–medium	High forest	High forest	Uncommon
Parinari salomonensis	?	Medium	High forest	High forest	Common
Schizomeria serrata	Poor	Small	High forest	High forest	Mainly high elevation
(b) *Calophyllum kajewskii*	Poor	Big–huge	High forest or small gaps	High forest or gaps	Common
Calophyllum vitiense	Good	Small–medium	High forest	High forest or gaps	Mainly north
Pometia pinnata	Poor	Mostly small	High forest or disturbed	High forest and (?) small gaps	Mainly north
(c) *Elaeocarpus sphaericus*	Good	Medium	High forest	Gaps	More on north
Campnosperma brevipetiolatum	Poor	Mostly small	High forest/gaps	Gaps	Common
(d) *Terminalia calamansanai*	Very poor	Huge, ephemeral	High forest/gaps	Gaps	Mainly north
Endospermum medullosum	Poor	Medium	Mostly gaps	Gaps	Mainly north
Gmelina moluccana	Poor	Tiny	Mostly gaps	Gaps	Uncommon

† As judged from distribution pattern.   ‡ Taken to be stems $\geqslant$ 0·3 m girth.   Based on Whitmore (1974, Table 7.6).

pelago (Chapter 1) a gradation of response is found.

Table 6.1 also shows that the twelve species differ in other aspects of their behaviour: namely, effectiveness of dispersal, seedling population size, and distribution of trees. It is interesting to note that differences exist between the two species of *Calophyllum* which both have ubiquitous seedling populations (though larger in *C. kajewskii* than *C. vitiense*); only *C. kajewskii* is common as a tree in the northern forests. The two related species of Rosaceae subfamily Chrysobalanoideae, *Maranthes corymbosa* and *Parinari salomonensis*, also differ. Other more subtle differences between the twelve species for which there is no space here are described in Whitmore (1974). In detail every species was unique in its ecological strategy.

Height growth was measured of young trees of healthy appearance on a subplot of 0·28 ha in a small gap of about 0·04 ha in the Kolombangara forest, and found to be much slower than of the same species planted in open conditions, even for light-demanders capable of very rapid height growth of 2·1–2·7 m/year (see Table 6.2). Despite the different history of the samples being compared it is reasonable to deduce that root competition is an important cause of this slow growth, though the crowns of the

TABLE 6.2

Height growth in a small forest gap and in the open compared, Solomon Islands

	Gap (m/year)	Plantation (m/year)
Campnosperma brevipetiolatum	0·50 (6·6 years)	2·14 (6·5 years)
Elaeocarpus sphaericus	0·37 (6·6 years)	2·89 (10 years)

From Whitmore (1974, Tables 7.4, 7.5).

forest trees were not completely exposed to light either.

The twelve species studied on Kolombangara were differently represented in number and population structure in six forest types defined on floristic composition. Deductions made on the dynamic inter-relationships of these types are considered in §15.4.

6.4. Forest dynamics: Malaya

Two plots of 2·02 ha and two more of 0·40 ha each were established in lowland evergreen dipterocarp rain forest in Malaya in 1947 or 1949 and have been kept under continual observation ever since (most recently in 1971, 1972); a summary of findings

TABLE 6.3

Mortality at Sungei Menyala, Malaya, over 12 years, 1947–59, as percentages

Girth (m)	Mean	0·3–0·45	0·45–0·6	0·6–0·75	0·75–0·9	0·9–1·2	1·2–1·5	1·5
Primary forest (1·6 ha)	20·1	20·8	19·6	21·2	28·0	16·3	23·1	18·2
Secondary forest (0·4 ha)	25·0	22·2	23·2	40·0	34·6	11·1	20·0	23·1

From Wyatt-Smith (1966, Table 9); the whole 2 ha (primary and secondary forest) is included here.

TABLE 6.4

Deaths and recruitments at Sungei Menyala, Malaya

	Total number of stems	Number of ingrowth	Number of deaths	Years of death	Girths of deaths in sequence (inches)
(a) Pioneer and near-pioneer species					
Macaranga conifera	9	0	5	1957, '59 (4)	40, 29, 33, 34, 44
Macaranga gigantea	4	0	3	1951 (2), '53	33, 29, 41
Mallotus griffithianus	3	0	2	1959 (2)	13, 16
Pternandra capitellatas	9	2	4	1953 (2), '55, '57	21, 22, 20, 21
Sapium discolor	4	0	4	1948, '49 (2), '51	25, 30, 23, 30
(b) Shade-bearing species not reaching canopy top					
Alangium javanicum	16	3	4	1949, '51, '53 (2)	14, 13, 21, 15
Cyathocalyx pruniferus	7	2	3	1949 (2), '53	25, 38, 23
Horsfieldia fulva	7	0	2	1949, '57	13, 18
Horsfieldia superba	3	1	2	1949, '51	14, 21
Hydnocarpus woodii	11	2	3	1949, '59 (2)	13, 16, 18
Ochanostachys amentacea	22	0	3	1951, '59 (2)	41, 26, 42
Randia anisophylla	29	5	4	1953 (3), '57	16, 20, 21, 18
(c) Canopy-top species					
(i) without ingrowth 1947–59					
Canarium littorale	23	0	6	1949 (2), '51, '53, '55, '59	27, 13, 13, 16, 67, 30
Castonopsis wallichii	6	0	3	1949, '55, '59	35, 30, 26
Heritiera simplicifolia	8	0	2	1949 (2)	14, 20
Ixonanthes icosandra	36	0	8	1949, '51 (4), '55 (2), '57	27, 25, 32, 52, 57, 31, 47, 30
Koompassia malaccensis	15	0	3	1951, '53 (2)	24, 14, 86
Palaquium rostratum	5	0	2	1953, '57	23, 95
Shorea leprosula	16	0	4	1953, '55, '59 (2)	57, 18, 24, 62
Shorea parvifolia	26	0	7	1949 (2), '53, '55, '57 (2), '59	89, 93, 15, 17, 15, 58, 79
(ii) with ingrowth 1947–59					
Santiria laevigata	41	7	7	1951, '53 (2), '55 (2), '57, '59	63, 22, 54, 13, 13, 49, 14
Shorea macroptera	22	1	4	1953, '55, '57, '59	133, 18, 34, 14

Selection extracted from Wyatt-Smith (1966, Table 10), whole 2·0 ha (primary and secondary forest) is included here.

for the 12 years up to 1959 has been published by Wyatt-Smith (1966). These plots illustrate several aspects of the dynamic nature of tropical rain forest. Here we have only space to consider some of the findings from one of the main plots, that at Sungei Menyala, which has already been mentioned in connection with the spatial mosaic of structural phases (Fig. 2.3, p. 16), itself one expression of dynamics. The plot lies near sea-level in a small relict patch of forest rich in species of the Red Meranti group of *Shorea* and in *Dipterocarpus*, a forest type which was until recently very extensive in lowland Malaya but has now been largely cut down because of its high contents of valuable timber. One end of the plot,

0·4 ha, is old secondary forest, dating from clearance in 1917 (see Chapter 2) and presents interesting contrasts with the other 1·62 ha.

Table 6.3 shows that mortality occurred to trees of all girth classes, and that the mean mortalities over the 12 years of 20·1 per cent (primary) and 25·0 per cent (secondary) (1·7 per cent and 2·1 per cent per year respectively) conceal a much greater range in the secondary forest, with a maximum of 40·0 per cent mortality in the 0·6–0·75 m girth class.

Table 6.4 shows deaths and recruitments amongst trees exceeding 0·3 m girth for different species. Those species known to be pioneers or near-pioneers show death without recruitment, mostly within a short span of years and with similar girths, and this most probably represents mainly death by old age of trees which simultaneously colonized the area cleared in 1917. Six of the thirteen species Wyatt-Smith places in this category are Euphorbiaceae. The species which mature with crowns within the canopy showed most recruitment and death of a wider girth range and in several cases over more years. The species which reach the canopy top suffered mortality at a wide range of girths, over the whole 12 years in most cases, but only two showed recruitment.

There was a considerable change in species composition, equalling about 15 per cent (Table 6.5), involving the loss of eighteen species and (fortuitously) the gain of the same number, at the same time 233 trees died and 146 grew to reach 0·3 m girth. Only three of the eighteen species which disappeared had more than one stem on the plot (*Ptychopyxis costata* 3, *Sapium discolor* 4—both Euphorbiaceae; *Xylopia ferruginea* 3).

The total basal area per ha (in square metres) of all stems over 0·3 m girth on the 1·62 ha of primary forest was as follows:

1947	1949	1951	1953	1955	1957	1959
32·4	33·0	32·7	34·9	32·5	32·5	32·0

The fluctuation in basal area, as of stem and species number, reflects the incidence of tree death and in-growth on this small area between these chosen years (girths were measured to 2·5 mm and mensurational errors are very small). Over a large area of this climax forest type basal area, species number, and stem number will remain constant so long as do the gap-forming processes which initiate the forest growth cycle.

All saplings (defined as plants 1·5 m tall to 0·3 m girth) were counted on a subsample strip of 0·08 ha

TABLE 6.5

Change in numbers of trees and species ≥0·3 m girth over 12 years, 1947–59, at Sungei Menyala, Malaya

		a Individuals	*b* Species	Ratio *a/b*
In	1947	1075	237	4·5
Added by	1959	146	18	—
Lost since	1947	233	18	—
In	1959	988	237	4·2

From Wyatt-Smith (1966, Table 24). The whole 2·0 ha (primary and secondary forest) is included here.

running down the centre of the 1·62 ha of primary forest. There was distinct evidence of greater height growth in the period 1951–5, than in the period 1949–51, and which was correlated with the development of two small gaps. The most interesting finding was that 6 per cent of the saplings belonged to emergent species (that is, those which can grow to taller than 30 m), 22 per cent to main canopy (18–30 m), and 72 per cent to understorey (shorter than 18 m) species, despite the subjective nature of these classes and the rather arbitrary distinction between the latter two. 'Economic species' comprised 11 per cent (about 132 stems per hectare) of the saplings. Dipterocarpaceae were very sparsely represented; the two main commercial groups *Shorea* (Red Meranti) and *Dipterocarpus* comprised only 5 and 12 of the total 773 saplings in the 1955 enumeration. The conclusion is quite clearly that the emergents at Sungei Menyala (which include *Dipterocarpus* and *Shorea*) are very markedly light-demanding species, and the main canopy species strongly so. The principal shade-bearers in this forest are the species whose crowns never attain the canopy top. The plot was chosen to lie in high forest. The only gaps are small ones, and most of the 1·62 ha of primary forest are at the mature phase (Fig. 2.3, p. 16). On this very small area no big enough gaps have formed to enable the emergents to recruit sapling regeneration, and during the period of the observations shade-bearing species of ultimate smaller stature have been predominant amongst the saplings. It is clear from Chapter 5 that one wind-storm creating a big gap and coming at the right time after a dipterocarp fruiting year (Chapters 4 and 5) could change the whole status, structure, and composition of the forest on this sample plot.

The size-class distribution of most (that is, all the light-demanding) dipterocarps on the Sungei Menyala plot—namely, abundant seedlings, a dearth of saplings, and abundant poles and trees—is a feature of the mature phase of lowland dipterocarp rain forest on which Malayan foresters have frequently commented. The stand table for these species is somewhat like a reversed J (⌊). This population structure is a direct consequence of the fact that the seedlings of light-demanding dipterocarps require a patch of gap phase to continue growth to form saplings and that poles and trees can exist in mature phase forest.

6.5. Seedling survival

Consideration has now been given to dispersal (§5.1), dormancy (§5.2), seedling establishment (§5.3), and to the growth of seedlings into trees, showing how different species respond to gaps in markedly different ways (§§6.1, 6.2, and 6.3). The one remaining aspect of the growth of a tree, yet to be considered, is the period for which an established seedling can survive to await suitable conditions for continued upwards growth.

For a pioneer species, survival is a matter of success in the fierce competition for living space above and below ground in the gap in which it is growing. Seedlings of true pioneer species grow up without pause in gaps or succumb to death if shaded. Once over-topped in the upwards race in height growth, a pioneer seedling does not survive

for long (cf. §2.4 and Dawkins 1966); for example, *Terminalia calamansanai* in the Solomons produces dense carpets of seedlings to 20–30 m across which die within a few months if at all shaded.

The most shade-tolerant species, such as those which comprise the understorey at Sungei Menyala (§6.4), live in shade throughout their life. The observations on Kolombangara described above (§6.3) showed that there are also species of intermediate behaviour which can establish seedlings in high forest and which then need a gap for continued growth.

Agathis macrophylla, the Kauri Pine of the Santa Cruz Islands in the south-west Pacific (Fig. 14.4, p. 173), is a further example of a species with seedlings able to establish and apparently to survive for a long period under dense forest, growing to about 0·9 m tall. This Kauri requires a small gap to grow up; its seedlings are swamped by lush secondary growth in big gaps (Whitmore 1966c). It was found from a study on Vanikolo that seedlings are ubiquitous in lowland forest, and trees occur in mixed-sized stands, most commonly on ridges, probably because suitable conditions for the 'release' of seedlings are most common on such sites. The profile diagram (Fig. 6.7) shows a ridge-crest grove of *A. macrophylla* with, towards the right, a group of

FIG. 6.7. Ridge-top grove of *Agathis macrophylla* in lowland rain forest (Vanikolo, Santa Cruz Islands). Plot area 60 m × 7·5 m, all trees over 6 m tall shown. *Agathis* stippled. *Macaranga polyadenia* hatched horizontally, *Campnosperma brevipetiolatum* hatched vertically. (Whitmore 1966c, Fig. 1.)

TABLE 6.6

Recruitment and survival of dipterocarp seedlings in Sepilok forest, Sabah

Year of seed fall	?	1960	1961	1963	1967
Year of recruitment	1958	1961	1962	1964	1969
Total number recruited	405	89	31	892	63
Percentage survival after 1 year	88	79	77	63	90
2 years	68	62	48	47	
3 years	59	39	42	34	
4 years	51	30	32	25	
5 years	43	28	23	19	
6 years	37	22	19	16	
7 years	33	20	19		
8 years	30	17	19		
9 years	29	10			
10 years	26				
11 years	26				
12 years	26				

Computed to 1970; 0·0048 ha on research plot 51. (From Fox 1972, Table 28.)

small *Agathis* trees still with the deep monopodial crowns of immaturity, in a wind-fall gap, together with the two known light-demanding species *Campnosperma brevipetiolatum* (cf. Kolombangara, Table 6.1) and *Macaranga polyadenia* which also regenerate in gaps. It is noteworthy that *A. macrophylla* grown in the open branches at small size and produces a poorly formed, short tree.

Seedling survival has been most thoroughly investigated in the Dipterocarpaceae. Seedlings of dipterocarps require shade for establishment, as has been confirmed by experiments which were described in §5.3. They then more or less cease growing in height until 'released' when the canopy above them is opened, either by the development of a natural gap or by man.

Seedlings are recruited in huge populations after an occurrence of gregarious fruiting (Chapter 4), and there is very high mortality in the first few months, only a small fraction of the germinated seed growing into established seedlings. The established seedlings progressively die off, and the populations diminish until boosted by the next gregarious fruiting. Table 6.6 shows the recruitment and survival of established seedlings of all dipterocarps following five different seed falls on a small research plot (RP 51) at Sepilok forest, Sabah.† It is interesting to note that percentage survival of the later recruitments was lower than of the earlier. This is probably because seedlings arriving late succumbed in competition with earlier arrivals. On this plot total populations

varied in the range 57 000–230 000 seedlings per hectare between 1958 and 1970 (Fox 1972), but these figures conceal the marked patchiness of distribution which is a feature of dipterocarps. The fate of seedling populations from three seed falls is shown in Fig. 6.8 for the single species *Parashorea tomentella* on another small plot at Sepilok. It can be seen how seedling numbers increase after a gregarious fruiting and then fall away until the next one.

Dipterocarp species differ from each other in amount and frequency of recruitment and rate of seedling death. In Malaya it has been found that species such as *Shorea maxwelliana* and of *Hopea* which fruit infrequently tend to have longer-lived seedlings than species which fruit more frequently, such as the Red Meranti group of *Shorea* (Walton 1948). These former, and other species with dense, hard timber ('heavy hardwoods'), also have seedlings which can tolerate extreme suppression for several years and are even able to grow under moderate shade (Wyatt-Smith 1963).

Seedling population fluctuations of several species of the Red Meranti group of *Shorea* during the 12 years 1958–70 were reported by Fox (1972) for research plot 51 at Sepilok. Seed fall occurred in 1960, 1961, 1963, and 1968 (cf. Table 6.6). *Shorea parvifolia* had only two surviving seedlings of the period 1958–70, having had recruits in 1961 and 1964, and considerable fluctuations in population. *S. acuminatissima* had very large numbers of recruits in the seed-fall years, but most died at about 100 mm tall and only four survived over the 12 year period. *S. argentifolia* differed from the others in more rapid

† See also Liew and Wong (1973) and Fox (1973*b*) for further discussion of dipterocarp seedling population dynamics in Sabah, published too late for incorporation in this chapter.

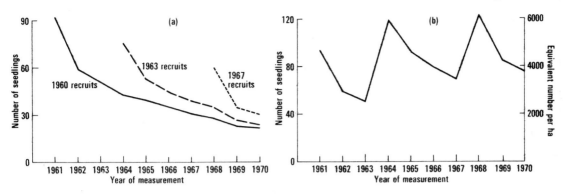

FIG. 6.8.   Fluctuation of *Parashorea tomentella* seedling populations (Sepilok, Sabah). (a) Fate of individual flushes; (b) total population. Numbers on 8 plots of 4×10^{-4} ha. (From Fox 1972, Fig. 46.)

early height growth, and although most seedlings died after each widescale recruitment a few are believed to have survived for a long time. Basically, all these species show the same pattern of a fast turnover in the seedling population—frequent recruitment followed by rapid death. By contrast, *S. johorensis* had recruits in 1964 only, and they persisted longer than seedlings of *S. parvifolia*. *S. macroptera* also only had recruits in 1964; they were very patchily distributed and showed greater longevity than any of the other Red Merantis in the area.

Following establishment, dipterocarp seedlings grow only very slowly in height in the closed forest. For example, twenty-one seedlings of *Parashorea tomentella* had an average height in 1961 of 230 mm after establishment, by 1965 the average height was 320 mm, and by 1970 it was 424 mm. These figures give some indication of what is believed to be the usual growth rate for Red Meranti species of *Shorea* as well as for *Parashorea* (Fox 1972). Height of a small group of seedlings on a plot from which other plants were removed increased by 56 mm over 8 months compared to only 20 mm in the control (Fox 1972), indicating the importance of root competition.

The dramatic increase in height once light is increased is shown in Table 6.7 comparing a seedling population in a Sabah forest before and 4 years after removal of most of the canopy.

The differences in response to light between dipterocarp species are of major silvicultural importance. In general, species with light timber ('light hardwoods'), mainly *Parashorea* and *Shorea* (especially the Red Meranti group), respond fastest to increased light and grow quickest, so also do *Dipterocarpus*. In fact they can compete with smothering climbers which rapidly invade large gaps. Most medium and heavy hardwood species, which include the Balau group of *Shorea*, *Hopea*, *Vatica*, and *Balanocarpus heimii*, are slower growing and respond less quickly to increased light; they are liable to be overtaken by faster-growing trees in clearings in less than 2 years (Barnard 1954, in Wyatt-Smith 1963). Moreover, in the extremely exposed conditions of big gaps, some (for example, Balau *Shorea* and *S. multiflora*) tend to die back at the tip and then to develop multiple leaders and hence to grow into poorly formed trees; *S. laevis* is killed by complete exposure; *Balanocarpus heimii* is very prone to attack by shoot-borers, as well as tending to branch if exposed to full light when small (Landon 1955); and *Dryobalanops aromatica* leaves may become heavily galled if seedlings are suddenly exposed to full light

TABLE 6.7

Growth of dipterocarp seedlings in Sabah following canopy opening, shown as percentage of whole population in different size classes

	Height			Girth			
Size of seedling	0–1·5 m	1·5–3 m	3 m–0·15 m	0·15–0·3 m	0·3–0·6 m	Total number
Year logged†	97·3	2·0	0·7			2250
4 years later	51·0	33·4	11·4	3·8	0·3	951

0·076 ha in 30 plots. (From Nicholson 1965*b*, Table 3.)
† Trees not logged were killed by poison-girdling.

79

E

(Wyatt-Smith 1963). In Sarawak, seedlings of *Agathis borneensis* benefit from increased light but are sensitive to sudden exposure, and other associated species usually grow faster (Brunig, in preparation).

The very high proportion of *Shorea parvifolia, S. leprosula,* and *S. pauciflora* (especially the first-mentioned) in the storm forest of Kelantan, Malaya (Browne 1949; Wyatt-Smith 1954*a*) shows that these Light Red Meranti species are well equipped to regenerate in certain circumstances even in very extensive gaps. They are almost pioneer species.

Nothing is yet known about the physiological basis of survival and growth of the seedlings and saplings of rain-forest trees. The relationships between respiration, photosynthesis, and temperature discussed briefly in §10.3 and summarized as Fig. 10.14 (p. 135) are obviously of fundamental importance. This is a field in which investigations on lines to be discussed in §8.4 are badly needed.

7 The ecological basis of rain-forest silviculture

Now THAT we have described the main alternative strategies available to tree species to ensure their perpetuation in the rain-forest ecosystem, it is appropriate to show how foresters have utilized these intrinsic properties to devise silvicultural systems to maintain or improve the rain forest as a source of commercially valuable timber.

The basic dicta are that liberation of a chosen tree is the most important phase of treatment and that maximum disturbance gives maximum response (Baur 1964b). *Liberation* implies freeing a desired tree from competition by increasing the light it receives; concomitant with this, root competition is usually reduced. In mixed species, rain-forest *refinement* is usually involved also, and this means assisting trees of the desired species by the removal of others ('weeds').

The silvicultural systems which have been applied to tropical rain forest belong to one of two kinds which are the polycyclic and the monocyclic systems respectively (Troup 1952; Dawkins 1958).

As the name implies, polycyclic systems are based on the repeated removal of selected trees in a continuing series of felling cycles, whose length is less than the rotation age of the trees. The aim is to remove trees before they begin to stagnate and deteriorate from old age, leaving all appreciating stems to swell the future yield. Because of the very species-rich nature of most tropical rain forest, and the relatively small number of species with timber which is commercial by current standards, extraction on a polycyclic system tends to result in the formation of scattered small gaps in the forest canopy.

By contrast, monocyclic systems remove all saleable trees at a single operation, and the length of the cycle more or less equals the rotation age of the trees. Except in those cases where there are few saleable trees, damage to the forest is much more drastic than under a polycyclic system, the canopy is much more extensively destroyed, and big gaps are formed. The monocyclic systems which have been used in the tropical rain forests of the Far East are those known as *shelterwood uniform systems* (uniform systems for short); the terminology implies a uniform (i.e. single) opening of the canopy in order to induce regeneration, plus also a uniform or even-aged condition of

the young crop produced thereby (Troup 1952). It can be seen at once that the two kinds of systems will tend to favour shade-bearing and light-demanding species respectively.

Silviculture came to the tropical Far East from Europe, where polycyclic systems have been practised for centuries. The introduction to Malaya in the early decades of this century was via India and Burma where silviculture had been practised since the mid-nineteenth century. In Malaya the early demand for timber from evergreen rain forest was for firewood, poles, and naturally durable constructional timber, the 'heavy hardwoods'. This favoured management on a polycyclic system, and the forests were manipulated to yield these products and at the same time to release from competition small specimens of the desired species. In some parts of Malaya far from any market, silvicultural operations were conducted towards these ends by the Forest Department, and were called regeneration improvement fellings (R.I.F.). (Wyatt-Smith (1963) gives an extended account of the history of silviculture in Malaya.)

The crucial matter in the operation of a polycyclic system is to control the damage done at each felling cycle, for, if damage rises beyond a small minimum, regeneration will be damaged and the yield will progressively fall off through a series of cycles. Several other factors make polycyclic systems difficult to operate. Dawkins (1958) has pointed out that girth increment in closed tropical rain forest, where basal area of the trees is usually about 31 m²/ha, is very slow, and suggests that a reduction to about 18–24 m²/ha basal area is needed to boost it appreciably. Moreover, many of the trees chosen for the crop in such a forest will not have full crown exposure or room to develop good crown-form. Measurements made in forest clearly show that poor crown exposure and form, especially the former, result in diminished growth rates; as is shown, for example, by the figures from Sepilok forest, Sabah (Nicholson 1965a). A vital further consideration is how quickly a poorly grown crown of a juvenile tree which has developed within the canopy can expand to full size, if at all. In addition, as Dawkins (1958) emphasizes, it is difficult to make an accurate visual assessment of any silvicultural treatment which might be desirable in a forest being managed selectively rather than uniformly, and an accurate system of growth measurements, which is very difficult to set up and maintain, is essential if such a forest is to be made to yield its maximum. Under modern conditions polycyclic systems are quite uneconomic (except possibly in the very special case of the Philippines dipterocarp forest described in §7.1 below); moreover they favour shade-bearing species whose timber is less in demand than that of light-demanders.

In Malaya all the more accessible forests were systematically worked for heavy hardwoods, especially *Balanocarpus heimii*, *Shorea laevis*, and *S. maxwelliana*, vast quantities of these being required for building construction and railway sleepers, before pressure impregnation made other species (particularly *Koompassia malaccensis* and *Dipterocarpus* spp.) durable in contact with the ground. These heavy hardwoods were felled by axe and converted by hand-sawing at stump into squares, baulks, and sleepers, which were then extracted by buffalo. For the supply of sawmills, soft-wooded *Shorea* (meranti), *Dipterocarpus*, and *Dryobalanops aromatica* logs were also felled by axe and either hand-sawn into halves and extracted by buffalo or extracted as whole logs by hand-hauling on wooden sledgeways (panglong). These methods were still practised until the late 1950s (Burgess). Nowadays the situation is completely different. Trees are felled by chain-saw and extracted by winch lorry or tractor. Hard, heavy, naturally durable timbers are less in demand than medium and light hardwoods, many of which can be impregnated with chemical preservatives if durability is required. An increasingly long list of species can be utilized as world-wide demand increases and prices rise. The necessity to get an adequate return on the substantial capital invested in vehicles, roads, sawmills, and plywood mills makes a uniform system in general the only commercially viable kind. Moreover, the extensive canopy damage which a uniform system causes favours regrowth of light-demanding species, whose rapid growth and pale, light timber makes them the desirable species to cultivate. Thus the *first managed rotation* under such a system will almost certainly contain a higher fraction of these economically desirable species than the original primary rain forest. Moreover, in a well-managed forest under a uniform system, the basal area per hectare will be lower than in only mildly disturbed virgin forest; crowns of the crop trees will have greater exposure to light and space to develop better form. All these three factors favour high growth rates.

Troup (1952) should be consulted as the definitive textbook on silvicultural systems and Dawkins (1958) more fully argues the case for and against the different systems which have been tried in tropical rain forest.

Areas in which natural regeneration of desired species after felling is inadequate or absent are sometimes planted up in patches or in lines with seedlings grown in nurseries or taken from the forest ('wildings'). Line planting has been extensive in Malaya, using especially *Anisoptera* spp., *Dryobalanops aromatica*, and *Shorea* spp. (Light Red Meranti), all fast-growing dipterocarps, but the rate of failure has been high. In the Solomons, the indigenous pioneers *Campnosperma brevipetiolatum* and *Terminalia calamansanai* have been most extensively used. Line planting into natural forest is a half-way step to plantation forestry, which is mainly based on pioneer species.

7.1. Silviculture in lowland d pterocarp rain forest†

The silviculturist working with lowland dipterocarp forest in its main zone from Sumatra to the Philippines is luckier than his counterpart anywhere else in the humid tropics. The most valuable timbers in today's markets are the light hardwoods, and so far as can be judged this will continue to be the case. With relative ease and at little cost he can manipulate the forest to produce a much higher stocking of these in the first managed rotation than existed in the virgin stand which preceded it, entirely because of the ecological behaviour of the light hardwood producing dipterocarps.

The Malayan Uniform silvicultural system is the best known. The system, which is a specialized kind of monocyclic shelterwood uniform system, is defined as 'the felling and removal in natural forest, in a short single operation, over an adequate number of selected natural seedlings determined by systematic linear sampling, of that part of the upper canopy which consists of the economic crop; to be followed immediately by the poison girdling of the uneconomic balance of the canopy of commercial-sized trees and of all the smaller trees and saplings down to a minimum girth over bark of 6–18 in (0·15–0·45 m) other than those of economic species of sound form' (Wyatt-Smith 1963). The key to the whole system is the presence in the forest at the time of felling of well-distributed seedlings of the

† The reader may find it convenient to consult, in conjunction with this section, §§15.2 and 15.3, where variation through the dipterocarp forest zone is described in some detail. This section should also be read with §8.1 in mind.

desired species. Advance growth is treated as bounty. The desired species are principally the fast-growing Shoreas of the Light Red Meranti group, amongst which *S. leprosula* and *S. parvifolia* are pre-eminent. They fruit gregariously, and seedling populations are replenished every 2 or 3 years (§4.1). Progressive mortality amongst the seedlings follows and just before a fruiting the seedling stock may be inadequate in amount and distribution to ensure a dense new crop (§6.5). The system also allows light-demanders other than dipterocarps to succeed, notably *Dyera costulata*, *Endospermum malaccense*, and *Pentaspadon officinalis* (Cousens 1958*b*). Felling kills many seedlings and saplings but releases the rest (§6.4). To establish the new forest, the system prescribed a poison-girdling of the relict stand immediately after felling to ensure good release and later, during the 10 years after felling, one or two diagnostic samplings, themselves followed, if necessary, by climber-cutting and canopy-opening. It is anticipated that a merchantable final crop of trees about 1·8 m girth will have grown by 70 years.

The Malayan Uniform system works well wherever there is an adequate seedling stand at the time of felling, and in fact, in many places, a satisfactory new forest will grow up even if the various post-felling silvicultural operations are omitted. Unfortunately, because of economic pressures, forest compartments are often felled at a time when the seedling stand is not adequate. Where this happens it is advisable not to poison-girdle and kill relict big dipterocarp trees, but to leave them as a seed source which will eventually provide a new dipterocarp forest. Indiscriminate poison-girdling in places where seedling stocking is poor or zero amounts to systematic elimination of Dipterocarpaceae from the rain forest.

In Sabah (Fig. 7.1), where dipterocarps form a larger proportion of the big trees, felling opens the forest more than in Malaya. *Parashorea* spp., also light-demanders, are very important as well as *Shorea* spp. There is evidence that there are nearly always adequate seedlings present on the forest floor (Nicholson 1965*b*). A system essentially the same as

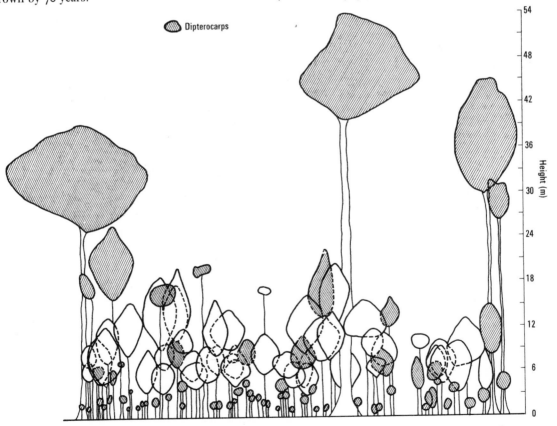

Dipterocarps

FIG. 7.1. Forest at Gum Gum, Sabah, showing how small dipterocarps were enabled to grow up by a light canopy opening 20 years prior to this profile being drawn. (Burgess 1961, Fig. 1.)

the Malayan one is advocated. Poles† ('advance growth') from the virgin stand supplement the first managed crop, but they are prone to attack by a Cerambycid borer, 'lobang pusing' *Cyriopalus wallacei* Pasc., which mainly attacks *Parashorea* spp. and *Shorea* spp. of the Yellow Meranti group, especially those 0·9–1·2 m girth (Anon. 1969). For this reason, and also because they are individually very much more susceptible to felling damage than seedlings, poles are not included in the estimation of the stocking of the new crop; they are regarded as bounty just as in Malaya. Big relict dipterocarps are not poisoned but left as potential mother trees (Liew 1971). *Merremia* spp. and *Mezoneuron suma-tranum* are climbers which become locally trouble-some.

In the Philippines, which have a preponderance of dipterocarps similar to that in Sabah, plus, in some places, a high stocking of poles (possibly due to temporary canopy-opening by cyclone damage, see §15.3) a selection system has recently been advocated (Anon. 1965*b*; Tagudar 1966; Nicholson 1970). By 1966, 70 000 ha on Mindanao had been treated this way (Brunig, in preparation). The system differs from the Uniform system practised in Malaya and Sabah in that the advance growth is counted in as part of the new crop. Success depends entirely on keeping felling damage down to an acceptable level (and one may doubt how practicable this is). The Cerambycid shoot-borer, so troublesome in Sabah, does not occur in the Philippines.

The only natural forest silviculture practised in New Guinea, on New Britain around Kerevat, uses a system similar to the Malayan Uniform, principally to regenerate *Dracontomelum puberulum* (*mangiferum*), *Pometia pinnata* (s.l.), *Pterocarpus indicus*, and *Terminalia* spp. (Morel 1967). A similar system is also used in the dipterocarp forests of the Andaman Islands (Dawkins 1958).

In the hill forests of Malaya, where the main timber stands are on ridges, the Malayan Uniform system has to be altered to allow for the less adequate numbers and distribution of seedlings, and problems which arise from exploitation in such country. One important modification is to omit the poison girdling of trees surviving felling (Burgess 1970).

It can be anticipated that in the future there will be a growing demand for wood to make pulp and particle board (see Part V). Nicholson (1970) has suggested that the whole gamut of small trees which

are not at present harvested could be removed before the main felling operation, leaving the young diptero-carps, whose growth would be stimulated by the operation (Chapter 8). There are grave biological objections to the drastic removal of a high percentage of the total biomass especially of the parts of small diameter; these will be discussed further in Part V.

7.2. Commercially important pioneer species

Modern economic considerations which will be briefly considered in Part V are increasingly leading forestry throughout the tropics into the cultivation of trees in plantations, rather than in semi-natural forest conditions. The demand is more and more for soft, pale timber, often as a source of cellulose or fibres and not for constructional timber. Pioneer species have the desired qualities and also grow fast. They occur naturally in pure stands and consequently can be grown in monoculture with less fear of decimation by fungal or insect attack (§2.8) which is an ever-present danger when species that occur naturally at low density in mixed rain forest are grown in plantations. Moreover, seed availability is good.

Several pioneer species of the tropical Far East are attaining importance.

Anthocephalus chinensis (*Figs* 7.2 *and* 7.3)

This species, widely known as kadam, kaatoan bangkal, kelempayan, or laran, occurs from Nepal and Assam eastwards to Indo-China and scattered through most of Malesia to New Guinea. Its optimum habitat is deep, moist, alluvial soils, and it is especially common along rivers. Extensive stands also occur on abandoned cultivations and old logging areas but only thrive on the deeper, moister, better-textured soils. The ecological amplitude is consider-able, from sea-level to 1000 m, rainfall 150–5000 mm, and mean annual temperature 3·3–37·7 °C. Kadam is frost-sensitive. Wild populations in Sabah have very low pest populations (Thapa 1969), but dense stands are prone to attack by caterpillars of the moth *Arthroschista hilaralis* (Pyralidae) (Mastan 1969).

Extensive planting began in the former Dutch East Indies in 1933 and by 1942 2640 ha had been established in Java and more in east Borneo, by the taungya system. The research results, published in Dutch, were summarized in English by Grijpma (1967); in addition Mastan (1969) and Fox (1971) have written reviews of experience in Sabah. Other work on the species is described by Sudarmo (1957), Anon. (1964), Monsalud and Lopez (1967), Soeharlan (1967), Zabala and Manarpaac (1968), Paa and Gerardo (1968), Fox (1968), and Chinte (1971).

† That is, stems 0·3–0·9 m girth, see §2.3.

• FIG. 7.2. *Anthocephalus chinensis*. Young trees by a logging track near Tawau, Sabah.

FIG. 7.3. Sapling *Anthocephalus chinensis* (Chomlong Kou, Cambodia).

The fleshy fruit contains numerous minute seeds ($(18–26) \times 10^6$ per kilogram dry weight) which are distributed by bats. They require a period of a few months after-ripening, one batch tested then gave 95–8 per cent germination. Old seed germinate best in full sun, and fresh ones in shade. Initial growth is very slow but then begins to accelerate. Mean height of 3 m can be expected 1 year after planting out and a mean increment of 2–3 m/year can be expected for 6–8 years with a diameter increment of 13–76 mm/year; after that growth slows down, and becomes particularly slow after 20 years. Trees 38 m tall and 0·65 m in diameter can be expected on a 30 year rotation, yielding 350 m³ timber gross per hectare; if thinnings are included the yield is about 23 m³/ha/year. Growth in plantations is nearly always very patchy; kadam is very sensitive to soil moisture and does not grow well in dry, heavy-textured or very poor soils. In Sabah growth has been very poor in unweeded grassy areas.

Kadam is under trial in Puerto Rico and Nigeria, as well as the Far East. Very little work has been done on the only other species of the genus *Anthocephalus macrophyllus*, native to the lowland monsoon forests of Celebes, Butung, Muna, Talaud, and the Moluccas. In two trials on Java it grew even faster than kadam and is clearly worth fuller study, especially as its range includes seasonally dry climates and possibly poorer, residual soils (Hellinga 1950).

Eucalyptus deglupta (*Fig.* 7.4)

This is a species of considerable interest as the only rain forest member of this huge genus (about

FIG. 7.4. A relict stand of *Eucalyptus deglupta* on riverine alluvium, at 300 m elevation near Bialla, New Britain. The tallest trees are about 60 m.

500 species) which is almost entirely confined to Australia. There are two or three species in the tropical Far East; except for *E. deglupta*, these are members of the monsoon forest and savanna woodland floras of the drier parts of east Malesia.

E. deglupta ranges from Mindanao (southern Philippines) through Celebes, the Moluccas, and New Guinea to New Britain (Merrill 1945) and New Ireland (Streets 1962). It has been widely planted as an ornamental and on an experimental scale throughout the lowland humid tropics where there is no dry season (Grijpma 1969; Lamb).

In New Guinea (Heather 1955) this species is known as kamerere. Its range is from sea-level to 1800 m (Chimbu valley) in places with at least 2000 mm rainfall per year. It can be seen colonizing newly deposited volcanic slopes, for example, to

1350 m on Mt. Ulawa; and growing through seral stands of *Macaranga*, *Mallotus*, etc., on abandoned cultivations. Kamerere cannot tolerate swampy conditions. It requires deep, moist, well-aerated soils of high fertility and grows best in pure stands on alluvial river banks and terraces in valleys flat enough to be subject to annual flooding at the height of the rainy season, and in such sites it may occur together with *Octomeles sumatrana* over a ground layer of grass. If such forests are burned the kamerere is killed out. Eventually these stands are invaded by *Dracontomelum*, *Pometia pinnata*, *Pterocarpus indicus*, and other 'dryad' species which grow up to form a continuous lower storey. Natural kamerere stands can contain 290 m³/ha of timber. The tree can reach the great height of 78 m and (in the Philippines) 7 m girth. The bole is sometimes strongly buttressed and fluted. Seeds are tiny, about 13.2×10^6 per kilogram. They can be stored under refrigeration for 4 years after fumigation (Lamb). In New Britain, near Keravat, kamerere is extensively planted on high forest sites after logging; average growth rate in well-maintained plantations gives trees of 45 m height (bole 31 m) and 6 m girth in 15 years at 100 stems per hectare (Lamb). In Malaya this species suffers from a stem-borer (Burgess).

Octomeles sumatrana (*Fig. 7.5*)

This pioneer is widespread through the tropical Far East from Sumatra to the Solomons but is absent from Malaya (van Steenis 1953). The trade name in New Guinea is 'erima'. Its range of habitats is similar to those of *Eucalyptus deglupta* and like that it is most characteristic of riverine alluvial soils, but it can resist waterlogging (Lamb) and is resistant to fire. Seeds soon lose their power to germinate. Trees can attain 48 m height and 1·05 m diameter in 60 years (Lamb). Bole-form is straight and cylindrical; buttresses go up to 2 m. A tree planted on the volcanic soils (andosols) at Bogor, Java, grew to 25 m tall and 0·47 m diameter in 4 years. Growth rates of young plantations at different spacings in Sabah are reviewed by Shim (1973). Ultimate size can be huge; in Borneo this species is, like *Koompassia excelsa*, a tree in whose crown wild bees nest. One old 3·2 ha stand comprised 62 trees of 10 species, of which 39 were *Octomeles* and contained 83 per cent of the timber volume; second was *Dracontomelum* with 12 trees and only 6 per cent of the volume (van Steenis 1953 and sources therein). The serious defect of *Octomeles* as a plantation tree is its huge crown.

Pinus kesiya and P. merkusii

The two pines of the tropical Far East are

FIG. 7.5. *Octomeles sumatrana* in New Guinea

restricted to seasonally dry climates. Both are true pioneers. They naturally inhabit landslips and lahars (volcanic mud flows), do not regenerate in their own shade, and persist as big old trees over a lower storey of mixed tropical rain-forest species. Both are fire-resistant, once established, and can colonize and persist in grassland which is fireswept every 5 years or less.

Nicholson (1970) has recommended that the pine forests of the Philippines should be managed by an extreme form of uniform silvicultural system known as the *seed-tree system*, in which a few mature trees are not felled but are left to provide seed after logging has taken place. The seed-tree system is clearly strongly weighted in favour of pioneer species, which produce copious seed frequently and can colonize open sites. Further consideration of pine forests will be given in §14.3.

8 Growth Rates and forest yields

8.1. The foresters' measures

THE FORESTER is interested in how much timber (of the desired quality) his forest will yield. The prime concern is with increment in volume or weight. It has been estimated that a mixed-species tropical rain forest, which is at low or medium altitudes under good silvicultural management and which has been manipulated to give the most productive species mix, will yield 3·6–12 tonne above-ground dry weight of bole timber per hectare per year, the highest yields being in places with high rainfall (Dawkins 1963a, 1964a). Plantations on medium to good sites of the best available local or exotic dicotyledons ('broad-leaf') species yield 6–17 tonne/ha/year (20–40 per cent more, that is, 10–20 tonne/ha/year, including branchwood), whereas plantations of conifers yield 12–25 tonne/ha/year (20–35 tonne/ha/year including branchwood). Certain *Eucalyptus* species (*E. grandis*, *E. saligna*, *E. tereticornis*) which thrive in sub-tropical or monsoon tropical climates are exceptional amongst dicotyledons and give yields similar to, or even exceeding, those of the conifers (Dawkins 1964b).

The ranges of annual yields for different species is shown in Fig. 8.1. Besides the substantial differences between the three groups, broad-leaf species, conifers, and eucalypts, there are also big differences in yield for each species, and these arise from three causes. First, species perform differently on different sites, and from place to place within a site, for example, *Anthocephalus chinensis* plantations are notorious for their patchy growth, differences in performance being in this case associated with variations in soil (see §7.2). The second reason for differences in growth lies in inherent genetic variability and, as a rough rule-of-thumb, the best-growing individuals can be taken to give some idea of what the species is capable of attaining (Dawkins 1964b). It is commonplace that an even-age stand of trees is never an even-size one (Fig. 8.2), and this is usually due to these two sources of variability.

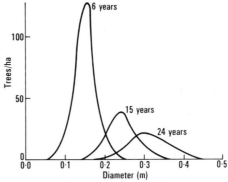

FIG. 8.2. The range of tree girths in 3 plantations of *Anthocephalus chinensis* at Bonita, Indonesia. (Soeharlan 1967.)

The third source of variability in the yield of a species arises from variation in crown size and exposure. There is now substantial evidence which clearly shows that for any given species a higher crown/diameter ratio at a stated girth indicates faster growth in diameter (and therefore in timber volume), that is to say, the trees with bigger crowns grow faster. This is not surprising, of course, as the leaves are the site of photosynthesis of the materials from which the tree is made. Table 8.1 summarizes increment of 150 stems of *Shorea macrophylla* of unknown age between 1·5–4·5 m girth which had been left behind after logging at Tenegang, Sabah; the trees with largest crowns are seen to have grown about twice as fast as those with the smallest crowns. At Sepilok, also in Sabah, Nicholson (1965a) found that, for 85 per cent of 1140 trees studied over 4 years, exceptionally fast or slow growth was correlated with crown-form. Only 17 trees were growing faster than 25 mm girth a year, and every one of these had a large crown receiving full light.

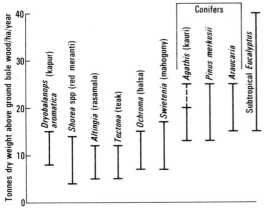

FIG. 8.1. Timber yields of various species grown in plantations. (Dawkins 1964a.)

TABLE 8.1
Correlation of girth growth (mm/year) with crown size in Shorea macrophylla

Period	Crown size			
	Large	Medium	Small	Mean
1962–3	35	27	20	30
1963–4	33	25	17	25
1964–5	27	23	13	25
Mean	32	25	17	

150 trees in all, 1·5–4·5 m girth. Logged forest in Tenegang forest, Sabah. (After Fox 1972, Table 2.1).

Silvicultural operations aim to give the crowns of the chosen trees room to develop and at the same time to increase their exposure to the sky. This is usually done by poisoning unwanted 'weed' trees and climbers; the death of which also very probably decreases competition underground between roots at least temporarily and releases mineral nutrients (though experimental evidence for this is so far lacking). The chosen trees are thus assisted in at least three ways, and it is not usually possible to distinguish between these. In practice it is found that crown growth must be encouraged in youth; big trees are unable to respond to silvicultural treatment much if at all. Table 8.2 shows how removal of competing weed trees and climbers increased girth increment mainly of the smaller stems in a plot at Madai, Sabah. It is the usual experience that girth increment is given a temporary boost and then slowly falls off; this can be seen for trees of all crown sizes in Table 8.1. This may be associated with depletion of the released mineral nutrients.

Different species respond differently to 'release' as it is termed. For example, it has been found in Malaya that heavy hardwood species respond more slowly and less in amount than do light hardwoods (Wyatt-Smith 1963). In virgin forest at Sepilok, Sabah, several species able to reach relatively large size, for example *Melanorrhoea wallichii*, showed no

difference in growth rate between different canopy conditions (Nicholson 1965a).

For most species there is found to exist a linear relationship between crown diameter and bole diameter (Dawkins 1963b). This is convenient because it means that the number of stems which can be accommodated per hectare and still have room for good crown growth can be readily calculated. In practice foresters commonly use basal area as a measure of the timber stand. Dawkins (1958, 1959) computed that the pantropical average basal area of most virgin lowland rain forests is about 36 m²/ha (140 ft²/acre) trees over 0·3 m girth, and estimated that this has to be reduced to 18–24 m²/ha to increase growth rate to an 'acceptable amount'. The pantropical mean figure is commonly exceeded in dipterocarp forests, and in the Queensland rain forest. For example, the 1·6 ha of primary forest at Sungei Menyala described in Chapter 6 has a basal area of 40 m²/ha (Wyatt-Smith 1966). Over small areas basal area may be even higher, for instance, 73·6 m²/ha on 0·048 ha at Gum Gum, Sabah (Burgess 1961). Basal area has also been used as the best measure available of the soil volume exploited (Dawkins 1963b).

It was noted above that in plantations conifers and, above all, subtropical and monsoon-tropical *Eucalyptus* have consistently higher timber yields per hectare per year than other broad-leaf species (Fig. 8.1). An important part of the explanation of this lies in their deep and narrow crown-form (they are characteristically monopodial, §2.5). Because they have a low crown-diameter/bole-diameter ratio (below 15, Dawkins (1964a)) they can grow well at close spacing and therefore more trees grown per unit area. Most broad-leaf species have crown-diameter/bole-diameter ratios of about 20 (Dawkins 1964a). Most pioneer tree species are notorious for their broad, spreading, shallow crowns at maturity with the ratio as high as 25 and do not grow fast at close spacing except in youth. No one has yet investigated

TABLE 8.2
Stimulation to girth growth (mm/year) by removing competition

Girth class (mm × 10⁻¹)	0–25	25–51	51–102	102–152	152–203	>203	Basal area m²
Current growth							
Control	9·6	18·0	18·2	33·7	32·2	30·0	28·7
Treatment	20·6	28·2	24·4	34·3	39·6	28·2	13·9
Difference	+11·0	+10·2	+6·2	+0·6	+7·4	−1·8	

Response of the best 100 dipterocarps on 1 ha at Madai forest, Sabah. (From Fox 1972, p. 193.)

timber yields for most of the multitude of indigenous tropical species with monopodial crown construction, for example, the whole Annonaceae and all Far Eastern representatives of the Myristicaceae.

Besides crown/bole ratio there are also likely to be important differences between species in the amount of light intercepted by the foliage and the efficiency of its utilization. An indication of the complexities of the kind of observations and analyses needed to unravel these effects can be seen in the recent study of tea in Assam (Hadfield 1974*a*,*b*, 1975). Such work has not yet been undertaken on tropical timber tree species.

Using a sensitive technique for measuring very small girth increments (developed by Dawkins (1956)) on five trees of *Shorea smithiana* in Sabah, Nicholson (1958) found a relationship (for trees of comparable size) between crown size and growth rate, and also found that there were two pauses in growth of which the first occurred in dry weather and was accompanied by the opening of a new flush of leaves. By the same method slight shrinkages in girth have been detected in Uganda, usually in dry weather (Dawkins 1956). There were substantial fluctuations in girth growth, between successive periods during 1964–7, of 854 measured trees over 150 mm girth and comprising 12 species on Kolombangara Island in the Solomons. The range in the mean was from 0·7 mm/year to 19·1 mm/year and could not be attributed to systematic errors in measurement. There was no correlation with the crude rainfall measurements available (Whitmore 1974).

Growth in height and girth of an individual tree, considered throughout its life from germination of the seed onwards, under very good conditions, follows a sigmoid curve (Fig. 8.3), with an initial slow phase as a seedling followed by a phase of accelerating growth which is approximately linear for some time and which eventually slows off and ultimately ceases.

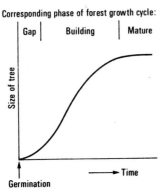

FIG. 8.3. Growth of a freely growing tree and its relation to the forest growth cycle.

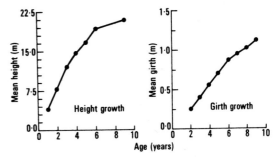

FIG. 8.4. Growth of young *Terminalia brassii* in plantations established 1964 in the Solomon Islands (Forest Department records).

Much of the growth of an established tree, solitary or well-spaced in plantations, is on the linear part of this curve, and girth growth is steady until large size is reached. The growth of *Terminalia brassii* in plantations, which is quite exceptionally fast, is shown in Fig. 8.4. Girth growth began to slow down at 7 years age at a mean girth 0·97 m.

By contrast, in closed forest it is common, at least at the smaller sizes, for girth increment to increase with size, as is shown for three species on Kolombangara and for all 1140 trees of 194 species at Sepilok, Sabah (Fig. 8.5). This relationship holds because those individuals with good genotype and on good micro-sites grow fastest, so that in the course of time the population of a species will tend to segregate into slow growers left behind in the small size classes, and fast growers which come to predominate in the larger size classes. Concerning indi-

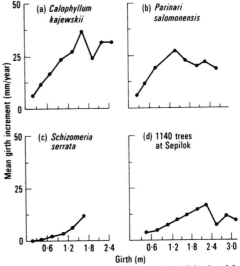

FIG. 8.5. Variation of girth growth rate with girth in closed forest. (a)–(c): Kolombangara Island, Solomons (Whitmore 1974); 6·6 year period. (d): Sabah (Nicholson 1965*a*); 4 year period.

vidual trees. Slow growers, for example, apparently start slow and continue slow; there is no evidence of change with age from being a slow grower to being a fast grower (Palmer).

Competition is an important cause for the slowing down or cessation of growth. The essence of the silviculturist's job is to reduce or eliminate competition, and in a plantation or a well-managed forest the stems he selects are kept growing at or near their maximum potential rate until ready to be harvested.

Height growth slows down and is nearly always completed before girth growth (as can be seen in Fig. 8.3). This is why basal area can be used as a simple, useful silvicultural measure of yield (that is, volume).

In virgin rain forest, the gap phase of the growth cycle (cf. §2.3) corresponds to the bottom part of the growth curve of an individual tree (Fig. 8.3), the building phase to the period of maximum growth rate, and the mature phase to the final slowing down of growth rate. A forest being managed for timber production will be harvested at about the time it would enter the mature phase, and it is the silviculturist's aim to convert his forest from a mosaic of gap, building, and mature phases to a complete building-phase forest (monocyclic systems) or a mixture of the gap and building phase (polycyclic systems).

Maximum girth growth rates of light-demanding tree species in well-maintained plantations may exceed 100 mm/year or even 125 mm/year for a few years; a sample series of figures is given in Table 8.3(a). Over longer periods, about 40 mm/year is more usual. In Table 8.3(b) are listed species which in natural or semi-natural forest in Malaya have been found capable of sustained fairly rapid growth.

At Sepilok, Sabah, Nicholson (1965a) found a large number of 'typical understorey species' including *Acronychia laurifolia*, *Alseodaphne bancana*, *Colubrina anomala*, *Ganua kingiana*, *Gluta* sp., *Mallotus glaberrimus*, *Pentace* sp., and *Teijsmanniodendron* sp. which did not attain a mean annual girth increment of as much as 13 mm, though individuals with big, well-exposed crowns grew somewhat faster than others. This contrasted with faster growth of species of the upper storeys. Nevertheless, a few understorey trees at Sepilok did respond strongly to good conditions, for example, several *Eugenia* spp., *Grewia*

TABLE 8.3
Some girth growth figures

(a) *Solomons, Guadalcanal, Mt. Austen: trial plantations†*

	Period (years)	Mean annual girth growth (mm)
Eucalyptus deglupta	12	140
Gmelina arborea	10·3	137
Elaeocarpus sphaericus	10	124
Terminalia calamansanai	4·6	114
Endospermum medullosum	6·6	104
Campnosperma brevipetiolatum	6·5	82
Pometia pinnata	10·1	89

(b) *Malaya: 'dominant' and 'codominant' trees in natural or semi-natural forest‡*

Artocarpus scortechinii *Bombax valetonii* *Campnosperma auriculatum* *Cyathocalyx* spp. *Dyera costulata* *Endospermum malaccense* *Macaranga* spp. *Randia scortechinii* *Sapium baccatum* Most *Shorea*, Light Red Meranti spp. All *Shorea*, White Meranti spp.	Capable of sustained growth of 38–51 mm/year; over short periods under optimum conditions capable of 76 mm/year or even more.

† Extracted from Marten (1972, Table 2).
‡ Cousens (1958b, Appendix V) and see also the extensive compilations by Edwards (1930) and Vincent (1961a,b, 1962).

cinnamomifolia, and *Symplocos* sp. It was also noticed in several dipterocarp species at Sepilok that those trees which retained monopodial crowns grew faster in girth than others of the same girth which had already developed the sympodial crowns which characterize maturity.

8.2. Tree age

The wood of most species does not have growth rings, and where such do occur they are not usually annual but are correlated with growth flushes (§4.1) and are quite frequently not annular, because if only one part of the crown flushes new wood may be laid down solely on the sector of the bole below it. Thus, ring counts, which are the principal means of determining the age of trees in temperate climates, are inapplicable or unreliable in the tropics. A few trees have been dated by radio-carbon (^{14}C) determinations. For the tropical Far East we have an age of (550 ± 85) years for a very

big tree of *Nothofagus pullei* (diameter 1·8 m) in lower montane rain forest in New Guinea (Walker 1966), and (800 ± 70) years for an overmature *Shorea curtisii* from hills in the Malayan lowland rain forest (Burgess). Both are younger than the age of (1000 ± 100) years for a 4·5 m diameter baobab (*Adansonia digitata*) in savanna woodland in central Africa (Swart 1963).

In other cases, the time a tree or forest began life is known, though the age of a planted specimen in, for example, a Presidential garden or on a golf course is little guide to performance of the species in closed forest. In Kelantan, north-east Malaya, there were, until recently, extensive tracts of forest which are known to have grown up after a freak storm in November 1880 followed by fire (Browne 1949; Wyatt-Smith 1954a). These are unusually poor in species for Malayan lowland dipterocarp forest, and probably give a good indication of the time taken for pure stands of the few species involved to reach

TABLE 8.4

Age of trees at Sepilok, Sabah, calculated from girth measurements

	No. of trees	Age at 1·2 m girth Mean (years)	Age at 1·2 m girth Min. (years)	Max. girth (m)	Age at maximum size Mean (years)	Age at maximum size Min. (years)	Range (years)
Emergent species							
Dipterocarpus acutangulus	62	260	120	4·8	570	400	⎫
D. grandiflorus	22	300	150	3	500	310	
Shorea mecistopteryx	16	300	170	2·1	400	230	130–570
S. smithiana	20	260	140	1·8	300	160	
S. argentifolia	10	140	90	2·4	190	130	⎭
Main canopy/emergent spp.							
Shorea beccariana	25	160	90	3	290	190	
Main canopy							
Shorea multiflora	58	200	100	1·8	260	120	⎫ 60–260
Hopea beccariana	42	110	60	1·2	110	60	⎭
Main/under canopy							
Lophopetalum beccarianum	40	450	180	1·8	720	350	
Eugenia sp.	20	310	160	1·2	310	160	
Under canopy							
Gluta sp.	27	720	270	1·2	720	270	⎫
Teysmanniodendron sp.	25	620	110	1·2	620	110	
Alseodaphne bancana	15	560	330	1·2	560	330	
Ganua kingiana	45	510	160	1·2	510	160	
Pentace sp.	26	—	—	0·9	490	250	110–720
Mallotus glaberrimus	32	—	—	0·9	360	130	
Moultonianthus leembrugianus	25	—	—	0·9	340	140	
Acronychia laurifolia	23	—	—	0·9	320	140	
Symplocos sp.	20	—	—	0·9	250	110	⎭

From Nicholson (1965a, Table 12). Mean age is calculated from all trees, and minimum age from the fastest grower in each 0·3 m girth class.

timber size. By 1953 most trees were 1·8–2·1 m girth and some concern was felt that most stems had brittle heart, a central zone of soft, useless timber, whose cause has not been discovered but which has possibly resulted from very fast early growth. In the Solomon Islands trees which grew up on land cleared of forest by the Japanese military forces in 1942–3 have been used to give an indication of potential performance in plantations and line planting schemes. Stands of the long-lived pioneers *Albizia falcata* and *Octomeles sumatrana* which colonized parts of the slopes of Mt. Victory in Papua after the eruption of 1870 were seen to be dying 84 years later, with shade-bearers coming up underneath (Taylor 1957, §6.2).

In all these direct methods extrapolation is risky, because of the very wide range of growth rates of which a given species—or even an individual tree—is capable at different stages of its life; these were described in §8.1. The same limitations apply to indirect methods of estimating age which are based on measuring girth growth rates and then using the measurements to estimate the age of a tree from its girth. A set of such computations for species in the Sepilok forest, Sabah, is given in Table 8.4, in which the markedly different mean and minimum ages are shown. Age at 1·2 m girth varies from 60 years to 720 years (*Gluta* sp. *Hopea beccariana*). The age of Santa Cruz Kauri, *Agathis macrophylla*, was determined by similar means to range from 270 years to 440 years at 2·4 m girth (Hadley 1959). The maximum age of trees in lower montane rain forest at Cibodas, Java, was estimated as 200–50 years and the mean average age of the measured trees as 130 years (Baas-Becking 1948, in Meijer 1959).

None of these methods of estimating age surmount the problem of how to allow for the period which elapsed between germination and the time when the established seedling began to grow and put on wood.

It can now be seen that there is no simple answer to the interesting question of how fast does the growth cycle of the forest turn; how old, on average will be a patch of the mature phase? This is due not only to the great variation between individuals and species in age to maturity, senescence, and death but also to the capricious operation of external gap-forming processes, which were discussed in §6.1.

8.3. Productivity studies

In §8.1 we considered productivity from the foresters' viewpoint (the annual production of wood per hectare expressed in tonnes), and showed that for management purposes basal area of the trees per hectare is also a useful measure. In some cases the forester is able to sell the boles of the trees, in others he can sell branchwood too, and in the case of plantations he can sometimes also sell thinnings. Thus, productivity has a different meaning and the economics are different in different circumstances and also depending on the species. In all cases, though, productivity (and hence annual financial yield) remains an important yardstick by which various timber crops can be compared with each other and with competing uses of the land.

Biologists have taken over the concept of productivity and applied it to whole ecosystems in different parts of the world and to comparisons of natural ecosystems with cultivated crops. As Evans (1972, Chapter 31, and see Chapter 13) has pointed out, once this is done new questions arise. He goes on to give a useful and critical discussion, which should be consulted in amplification of the rest of this section. In this section we shall consider productivity studies which have been made in tropical rain forest, and the term productivity will be used in the biologists' sense, which is defined in more detail below.

One basic biological interest behind the measurement of ecosystem productivity is that, if it is possible to estimate both the total dry weight of the community at any moment and also the rate of change, these can be converted into energy units to give a measure of the rate of energy flow through the system as well as the amount stored. Different natural ecosystems and crops can be compared with each other and their over-all efficiency in the utilization of incident solar radiation estimated (cf. Monteith 1972).[†]

The total dry weight of the plant community, including leaves, branches, trunks, and roots, but excluding fallen litter and decaying organic material, is termed the plant biomass. This dry weight is increased by the fixation of carbon from the atmosphere in photosynthesis, and the rate at which this occurs is the *gross primary productivity*. It depends not only upon the area of leaf exposed, the amount of light, and the temperature but also upon inherent characteristics of the plant which differ from species to species. A large part of this production is continuously and partly simultaneously lost in respiration. What is left after respiratory loss is the *net*

---

† Monteith also makes estimates for the production efficiency of a number of tropical crops by breaking down the over-all efficiency of utilization of solar energy into seven components. This has not yet been attempted for a natural ecosystem and would come up against many of the difficulties discussed in this section.

primary productivity and the accumulation over a period of time is the *net primary production*. Thus the concept of productivity in this sense is wider and differently defined from that of the forester.

Plants continuously lose a part of their biomass in the death and shedding of leaves, branches, and roots and of flowers and fruit, and by the attacks of animals and fungi. If these losses are high and the gains are low the biomass may remain more or less constant or even decline, as happens with overmature trees.

Climax tropical rain forest is, as we have seen (§2.3), a mosaic of the three phases of the forest growth cycle, gap, building, and mature. Over-all, building and degenerative processes are in balance, and net production is nil (except in those forests where peat is accumulated). The forest is in a steady state, and this is inherent to the idea of a stable climax community. The scale of the mosaic may be small or large (§6.1), and the rate of change determined in part by fortuitous external events (§6.1: gap formation). It will clearly be important therefore in any comparative study to relate findings to comparable phases of the forest growth cycle.

Annual net production (net productivity) is greatest during the building phase of the cycle when growth rates are fastest (Fig. 8.3). At the mature phase it slows down. The impressive stature and biomass of a mature rain forest are no guide to the productivity of the site, a common fallacy. Many of the giant trees may be growing little or not at all. Maximum productivity is found in stands of pole-size trees, of lesser height and lower biomass, and in areas of secondary forest regrowing in the larger clearings.

Let us now consider part of the growth cycle where upgrade processes predominate. In principle it is straightforward to estimate production by estimating the biomass at the start and end of a chosen period of time, and allowing for losses during that time resulting from litter fall and grazing by animals. To this figure for the net primary production an addition can be made for losses due to respiration to arrive at a figure for gross primary production. Animals form part of the rain-forest ecosystem, and if it is possible to estimate their biomass change we can arrive at a figure for *secondary production*.

Very few studies on rain-forest productivity have been published. We shall discuss two of these in more detail below, one at Khao Chong in Thailand, near the Malaysian border (Ogawa *et al.* 1965*a*,*b*; Yoda 1967; Kira and Shidei 1967; Kira 1969; Kira and Ogawa 1971), the other at Anguédédou in the

Ivory Coast, West Africa (Müller and Nielson 1965). First we must outline the methods which have been utilized to estimate the various components of productivity.

At Khao Chong biomass was estimated by allometry, that is to say, by weighing a small, representative sample of parts and determining the relationship between dry weight and an easily measured dimension, using a logarithmic scale. The Khao Chong study attempted to establish relationships between the logarithms of tree diameter and height and dry weight of (1) bole, (2) branches, (3) foliage, and (4) roots (Kira, Ogawa, Yoda, and Ogino 1967; Kira and Shidei 1967). Diameter and height of trees were then measured on a selected sample plot at the start and finish of a chosen period (just over 3 years) and an estimate calculated of biomass change. At Anguédédou biomass was estimated by felling and weighing trees outside the plot comparable to those inside it. Respiration was estimated from a small sample and multiplying up.

Litter fall was recorded at Khao Chong for a 42-day period on subsamples of the study plots, and the figure obtained extrapolated. At Anguédédou an estimate was made based on assumptions about the length of life of leaves. No attempt was made to estimate the amount of grazing. At Khao Chong 'field observation suggested that the consumption of leaves by herbivores was not so large in amount' (Kira *et al.* 1967, p. 156).

The reader will at once realize, from the discussions in this book so far, that every one of these estimates is liable to errors of several kinds. There are also difficulties not so far alluded to. Mixed-species lowland evergreen tropical rain forest is very rich in tree species (Chapter 1). The trees differ widely in architecture and in timber density (Chapter 2). A single allometric function for all tree species can only be considered a first approximation for dry-weight calculation, if that. Nevertheless, at Khao Chong more-or-less linear relationships were found for the fraction of the species sampled (Ogawa *et al.* 1965*b*; Kira *et al.* 1967; Kira and Shidei 1967), though Evans (1972) has shown that the leaf-weight estimate was exceedingly unreliable, and also that it is improbable that a simple relationship holds between root-weight and that of above ground parts, which is likely to vary through life as well as from species to species.

The dependent synusia of big woody climbers was estimated at Khao Chong, but bole climbers and epiphytes were neglected. At Anguédédou these synusiae were not measured. The biomass of these synusiae is only a very small fraction of the total, and this omission is probably not serious.

It is extremely important that girth increment is measured accurately, first, because where allometry is used the estimates of the various components of total biomass production all depend on it; and, secondly, because estimates of volume and mass depend on the square of the girth, so all errors are greatly magnified. We have shown (§8.1) that girth increment is often small in high forest and that the rate can fluctuate markedly; notably, growth may cease in dry weather. Thus it is singularly unfortunate that the first measurement at Khao Chong was at the height of the dry season of 1962 and the last measurement at the end of the 1965 dry season (Kira *et al.* 1967; Kira and Ogawa 1971).

We noted in Chapter 4 that even in the wettest climates, and more so in seasonally dry ones, there is marked seasonality in leaf fall and flushing and in flowering and fruiting. It follows that seasonal changes in litter fall are to be expected. Unfortunately, litter samples were only taken at Khao Chong for 42 days which occurred during the dry season when several of the biggest trees were bare for 1–2 weeks, and the extrapolated results are certainly a substantial overestimate of annual litter fall.

There are considerable difficulties in estimating respiration from measurements on samples. In the Ivory Coast study the rate of respiration of both small and large pieces of trunk varied considerably and systematically from species to species—the respiration of small branches was considerable, and the respiration of parts of large trees was consistently higher than that of parts of comparable diameter from small trees. At Khao Chong, where similarly complex relationships almost certainly hold, respiration was only measured on small members, and Evans (1972), after discussing the problems in considerable detail, concluded that total respiration was substantially overestimated.

Leaf-respiration measurements are subject to difficulties owing to differences between species, between sun and shade leaves on a single tree, and also owing to changes as the leaf ages. In making the estimation the danger of increasing respiration by wounding the leaves exists, and also the probably greater danger of underestimating it if they are poorly ventilated while respiration is being measured. Evans concluded that the estimate of leaf respiration at Khao Chong (Yoda 1967) was certainly much too high.

An adult Indian elephant eats about 250 kg of fresh vegetation a day, a tapir eats 4–5 kg (Medway 1969). Both animals roam widely and are indigenous to the Khao Chong region as are sambhur and smaller deer, two macaque monkeys, one ape, numerous squirrels, and other smaller mammals (Chapter 1). Aborigines extract rattans and poles and must be considered part of the natural ecosystem (Chapter 17). The magnitude of the effect of these consumers, and of birds, reptiles, and invertebrates, on a small sample stand of forest is imponderable, but might certainly be considerable.

In addition to all these sources of uncertainty Evans (1972) points out other minor ones in the course of his critical analysis of these studies.

The Khao Chong sample plot was 40 m × 40 m (0.16 ha), a small size relative to the mosaic of structural phases. It was selected in high forest near the confluence of two streams (Ogawa *et al.* 1965a). Khao Chong lies in tropical semi-evergreen rain forest (§12.3), which is a Formation of limited extent in the Far East (§12.2). No dipterocarps occurred on the plot; Kira and his coworkers note that they had been removed by logging. It can be deduced from this and from their description that the plot lies in a patch of old secondary forest not yet reverted to climax rain forest. A quarter of the top stratum of trees are light-demanding or seral species (*Alstonia spatulata, Anthocephalus chinensis, Carallia brachiata, Commersonia bartramia,* and *Pterospermum jackianum*); these also formed 20 per cent of the next layer and were present in the understorey too. It was noted that the closed stratum at 15–26 m was very heavily entangled with climbers, with only a few trees poking through. These climbers would have been carried up with the seral species as the forest regenerated after logging (§2.6). The canopy was probably completely removed by the logging operations because near streams at this latitude the shade-dwelling arecoid palms *Areca, Iguanura,* and *Pinanga,* which do not survive in openings, are common, yet the only palm present was *Wallichia* (Caryotoideae). For the purpose of production studies this sample of the Khao Chong forest can probably best be regarded as late building phase, though in species composition it differs markedly from climax rain forest of the area.

Mortality of trees was about 1 per cent each year (Kira 1969), reducing the mean estimated rate of biomass increase from 6.5 tonne/ha/year to 5.3 tonne/ha/year. In the Anguédédou forest the loss from death was greater, reducing the estimated rate of biomass increase from 9.0 tonne/ha/year to 4.2 tonne/ha/year.

This detailed analysis has served to show the

extreme practical difficulties which face any attempt to measure total production in tropical rain forest, the most complex of ecosystems. The measurements at Khao Chong are in a forest fairly far removed from climax lowland rain forest, and some of them are subject to severe criticism. In several respects the measurements at Anguédédou in the Ivory Coast can be accepted with less reservation although this is a place with a much more strongly seasonal climate, comparable to that at Chieng Mai in north Thailand (Kira and Ogawa 1971), and the vegetation is poorer in species and probably more markedly seasonal in behaviour.

We shall conclude this section by making a brief comparison of the main differences between these tropical forests and a 46-year-old planted Danish beech forest.

The mean rate of increase of dry weight of stems, branches, and roots was estimated to be 9·0 tonne/ha/year at Anguédédou, closely comparable to 9·6 tonne/ha/year in the Danish beech plantation and greater than 6·5 tonne/ha/year at Khao Chong. These figures are to be compared with the foresters' yield from managed rain forest of 3·6–12 tonne/ha/year of bole timber (§8.1).

To this must be added an estimate for the fall of branches and loss of roots of 2·3 tonne/ha/year and of leaves of 2·1 tonne/ha/year at Anguédédou and of 1·2 tonne/ha/year and 2·7 tonne/ha/year respectively in Denmark. The Khao Chong estimate of 23·2 tonne/ha/year (of which 51 per cent was leaves) is certainly very much too large (see above). The

measurement in two other Ivory Coast forests of a total fall of 8·3–13·4 tonne/ha/year (leaves 5·7–8·2 tonne/ha/year) (Bernhard 1970) suggest the Anguédédou estimate is almost certainly too low.

The net productivity of the Anguédédou and Danish forests are closely similar at 9·0 tonne/ha/year and 9·6 tonne/ha/year respectively (see Fig. 8.6).

Respiration at Anguédédou was estimated to be 22·2 tonne/ha/year and 16·9 tonne/ha/year of boles, branches, and roots and of leaves respectively. This is very much higher than the figure of 4·5 tonne/ha/year for each component in Denmark. The Khao Chong estimates which are probably much too high (see above) were 32·1 tonne/ha/year and 57 tonne/ha/year respectively.

It is thus extremely interesting to see that although the net production of the semi-evergreen rain forest at Anguédédou is similar over a year to the 46-year-old Danish beech forest, it has a gross production of 52·5 tonne/ha, over twice the Danish figure of 23·5 tonne/ha, and this is entirely because of its very much higher losses from respiration (respiration accounting for 75 per cent of gross production as opposed to 43 per cent in Denmark).

Respiration rate increases as temperature increases, and the Danish beech forest is leafless for about 7 months of the year when the leafless trees are subjected to much lower temperatures. These factors account for its much lower annual loss from respiration. It is of considerable interest to note that in the tropics tree plantations at some elevation are consistently more productive than plantations at sea-

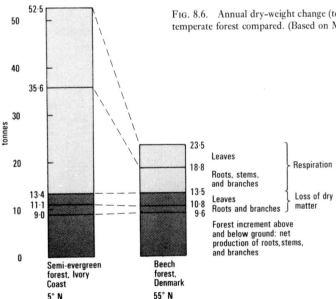

FIG. 8.6. Annual dry-weight change (tonne/ha): a tropical and a temperate forest compared. (Based on Müller and Nielsen 1965.)

level; low night temperatures which result in low respiration are probably the cause (Dawkins 1964b).[†] Löhr (1969) showed that, if reduced to the value at 20°C, there was very little difference in respiration rates between species in the Ivory Coast forest and beech in Denmark, for extreme sun and shade leaves the values were $0 \cdot 8 \, \text{mg} \, CO_2 / 50 \, \text{cm}^2$ leaf area/h and $0 \cdot 1$ mg $CO_2 / 50 \, \text{cm}^2$ leaf area/h; for trunks and branches the value varied greatly with diameter and nutritional condition and, reduced to 20 °C, was 700–150 mg CO_2/kg fresh weight/h for 5–20 mm diameter parts and 3–5 mg CO_2/kg fresh weight/h for trunk sections over $0 \cdot 2$ m diameter.

The gross annual production at Anguédédou of $52 \cdot 5$ tonne/ha is equivalent to about 100 tonne/ha of carbon dioxide, which is about twice the whole carbon dioxide content of the air over a hectare and which, as Evans (1972) points out, is sufficiently startling even on the weekly basis of $1 \cdot 8$ tonne/ha, or about a twenty-fifth.

Tropical lowland evergreen rain forest probably has a higher biomass per unit area on average than the tropical semi-evergreen rain forest at Anguédédou or Khao Chong, and we have seen in Chapter 1 that dipterocarp rain forests of Sundaland have greater stature than any other tropical rain forests in the world. It remains to be discovered whether net and gross productivity of the building phase of lowland dipterocarp rain forest also exceed the figures obtained in the Ivory Coast and south Thailand. It is doubly unfortunate that these figures have gained wide currency as measurements of the 'productivity of lowland tropical rain forest' (for example, in Duvigneaud 1971). First, because both sets of observations were made in forests where water is definitely seasonally limiting; and secondly, because, as the analysis by Evans and in this chapter have clearly shown, in both studies certain of the observations and calculations were not very accurate. It will be of the greatest interest to have critical and meaningful figures for the productivity of climax rain forest in which at least the major sources of uncertainty are controlled; for a start it will be essential to define the phase of the forest growth cycle to which the observations refer.

In connection with the growing concern of man at his interference with the 'regulatory systems of spaceship earth' it has been suggested that the destruction of the extensive tropical forests of the globe is removing an important carbon-dioxide absorbing and oxygen producing system. We may

[†] Soils also differ and experiments to elucidate the importance of pedological factors have not yet been devised or conducted.

note, as a final corollary to these productivity studies, that if net productivity is of the same order of magnitude in tropical as temperate forest the oxygen production will also be about the same (except in those exceptional forests in which peat is accumulating (§§10.4, 11.3, 16.1)). Moreover, a fast-growing crop, be it herbaceous or woody, may be a much more important oxygen source than natural forest; we noted in §8.1 that the best coniferous plantations in the humid tropics can yield 20–35 tonne/ha/year of stem and branchwood, $3 \cdot 5$ times the annual production of these components in natural rain forest. But, more important, climax rain forest is in a state of dynamic equilibrium, a mosaic of upgrade and downgrade phases, of which we have been considering the former. It follows that over-all it is in balance with the aerial environment. There do, however, remain ample reasons for alarm at the rapid current destruction of tropical rain forest, especially in the Far East, to which we shall return in Part V.

8.4. The quantitative analysis of plant growth

We have seen that an important part of the strategy of a species, enabling it to compete successfully with others for a niche in the rain-forest ecosystem, lies in its growth rate and response to light.

Two questions immediately arise. The many micro-environments within the forest differ in the quantity and quality of the light received (§3.6); not only is it darker on the forest floor of a mature phase part of the forest, but the incident light has also had much of the wavelengths useful for photosynthesis filtered out by successive layers of foliage. Do plants differ in their efficiency in utilizing light? Secondly, growth implies that photosynthesis exceeds respiration (cf. Fig. 10.14, p. 135), so that there is a net gain of fixed carbon to the plant; do plants differ in the ratio of photosynthesis to respiration?

Surprisingly, very few studies have yet been made on tropical rain-forest plants, and we remain in almost complete ignorance as to whether it is at this level that we have to seek for the basic difference between shade-bearing and light-demanding tropical rain forest species or whether there are important differences at this level between plantation performance of pines and eucalypys and other broad-leaved species (cf. Fig. 8.1). This remains largely an unexplored field of enquiry, ripe for investigation by methods which are now well established. There are a few clues.

Two fundamental measures of a plant's growth are the unit leaf rate (or net assimilation rate), which is the mean rate of increase of dry weight per unit leaf area, and the relative growth rate which is the mean rate of increase of dry weight per unit of total dry weight of the whole plant. It is beyond the bounds of our enquiry to consider these quantitative measures and their determination in full and the reader is referred to the recent monograph on the subject by Evans (1972).

Experiments on a number of species have shown that unit leaf rates and relative growth rates are lower in woody plants as a class than in herbaceous plants, and the few tropical trees investigated (*Camellia sinensis, Elaeis guineensis, Hevea brasiliensis, Musanga cecropioides, Theobroma cacao, Trema guineensis*) are similar to temperate species in this respect (Coombe 1960; Coombe and Hadfield 1962; Jarvis and Jarvis 1964). Maximum unit leaf rates of woody plants lie within the range 20–50 g dry weight/m²/week, and most are about 30 g/m²/week; these are low compared with unit leaf rates of herbaceous plants whose maxima lie in the range 70–150 g/m²/week (Jarvis and Jarvis 1964). In the few cases where woody plants and herbs have been grown together so that conditions are identical the same differences hold. For example, two tropical species, both common west African pioneer trees, were grown together with sunflowers (*Helianthus annuus*). Of these, *Trema guineensis* showed mean unit leaf rate of 14–15 g/m²/week against 33–4 g/m²/week for sunflowers (Coombe 1960) and *Musanga cecropioides* 6 or 10 g/m²/week (at leaf area index 1 and 4 respectively) against 43 g/m²/week for sunflowers (Coombe and Hadfield 1962).

Net photosynthetic rates of woody plants measured on single leaves or shoots are also low compared with those of herbaceous plants. The maximum uptake of most woody plants lie in the range 5–20 mg CO_2/dm²/h and mostly at about 15 mg CO_2/dm²/h; a few herbaceous plants may attain 50 mg/dm²/h, though the range is mainly 20–5 mg/dm²/h (Jarvis and Jarvis 1964). The only rain-forest tree species so far investigated, the pioneer *Anthocephalus chinensis*, had a maximum fixation rate of 9·5 mg/dm²/h (Stephens 1968). It is now known that there is a whole group of plants with a rate of net photosynthesis which may be two- to three-fold higher than others. These photosynthesize via the C_4-dicarboxylic acid pathway as well as via the earlier-discovered reductive pentose phosphate cycle. The groups also differ in leaf anatomy and several physiological respects. So far only herbs, many of them tropical and including maize, sugar-cane, and numerous other grasses and many Centrospermae

(but not sunflower) have been discovered to belong to this ecologically important class (Black 1971). Investigations have not yet proceeded far enough to elucidate why woody plants are inferior to even 'C_3' herbs in these fundamental respects. Jarvis and Jarvis (1964) reviewed the scanty evidence and speculated that woody plants as a class possibly had a greater resistance to carbon-dioxide diffusion in the mesophyll cells of the leaf.

Measurements in Puerto Rico by Odum, Lugo, Cintron, and Jordan (1970) of total net photosynthesis in the daytime of attached leaves contained in transparent plastic chambers, and of respiration at night, by analysing the carbon-dioxide content of air passed over them, showed the highest ratio in the two pioneer trees *Cecropia peltata* and *Anthocephalus chinensis* which were investigated and the lowest in shade leaves of climax-forest tree species. This was due to higher respiration in the latter. In some old shade leaves, night respiration actually exceeded net daytime photosynthesis. Sun leaves of climax species were similar to leaves of pioneer species. Odum and his coworkers inferred from these findings that pioneers maximize production at the expense of maintenance whereas climax species have low net production, grow slowly (cf. §8.1), and live to great age (§8.2), and speculated that part of their production goes into chemical defence mechanisms against animal predators (cf. §2.8).

Undergrowth herbs in an Ivory Coast forest were found to have lower respiration rates (compared at the same temperature) with the leaves of emergent trees and with temperate plants from similar situations, but at the prevailing high temperatures in the tropical forest respiratory losses are high, and net increase small (Löhr and Müller 1968; Evans 1972). Many pioneer species have large leaves (§6.1), and lobing is common; some are very shiny (that is, reflective) and many have a very pale undersurface with the lamina covered by a dense weft of hairs. The physiological significance of these features remains at present in the realm of speculation.

In a Queensland subtropical rain forest *Alocasia macrorhiza* and *Cordyline rubra*, plants of deeply shaded undergrowth, were shown to photosynthesize at remarkably low light intensities. They had an extremely low light compensation point for CO_2-exchange in natural shade light, about 50 times less than that of species grown in open sunny habitats. The diurnal course of CO_2 uptake closely followed that of light, with the peaks when the leaf under study was hit by relatively bright sunflecks, thus clearly demonstrating the important contribution of sunflecks to the total amount of daily photosynthesis (see §3.6). Further analysis showed that differences between photosynthetic capacities of sun and shade species result from several different factors, and these include the capacity of the photosynthetic electron transport chain as well as that of the carbon-fixation system (the shade plants were shown to invest more than the sun plants in the production of an effective light trapping system relative to the carbon fixation system). The sun species used in these studies was *Atriplex patula*. For full details the reader should consult Björkman, Ludlow, and Morrow (1972), Boardman, Anderson, Thorne, and Björkman (1972), and Goodchild, Björkman, and Pyliotis (1972).

To conclude this section we can note that the luxuriousness and appearance of unbridled growth given by the vegetation of the perhumid tropics does not therefore arise from an intrinsically higher growth rate than exists amongst temperate species.

The unfamiliar life-forms of palm, pandan, the giant monocotyledonous herbs of the Scitamineae (gingers (Fig. 8.7), bananas, and their allies), and the abundant climbers make a vivid impression of 'vegetative frenzy' on the botanist brought up in a temperate climate. The appearance of rapid growth of pioneer trees of forest fringes and clearings, which forms the other part of the impression, does not result, as far as we yet know, from a particularly efficient dry-weight production or energy conversion but arises from the architecture of the tree (§2.5), which results from the capacity for unrestricted elongation of internodes and production of leaves in the continually favourable climate. Temperate herbs, by contrast, die down annually, and although their annual production is impressive, growth is not cumulative and in many cases does not extend higher than eye-level to dwarf the observer.

Fig. 8.7. Giant gingers colonizing a roadside (Pahang, Malaya).

Part IV: Kinds of forest

9 The forest environment: soils: *by C. P. Burnham*

NEXT TO climate, soil conditions, taken in the broadest sense, constitute the most important controlling factor in the distribution of plants. Since the development of soils is itself guided by climate and affected by the plant communities present, and even the climate at the earth's surface is appreciably influenced by the vegetation, it follows that the distribution of plants, soil types, and climates must be considered as part of an integrated whole. It is not surprising therefore to find that the broad zone of the tropical rain forest lies within a corresponding climatic zone, the humid tropics, in which a dry season is short or altogether lacking (Chapter 3) and also that there is a corresponding soil zone in which particular soil types are characteristically widespread.

Soil zonality is not a fashionable concept outside the Soviet Union, but it is difficult to find an alternative philosophy for a coherent and useful, if inevitably greatly simplified, account of the soils of a large region such as the tropical Far East. Typical, well-developed soils formed from parent materials and in topographical situations which are in no way extreme were considered by the early Russian author Sibirtsev (1899) to be *zonal*. Later Russian pedologists (for example, Gerassimov and Ivanova 1959) have called the zonal soils of the humid tropics red earths (krasnozems) and yellow earths (zheltozems). Western authors have often grouped all or most of these as lateritic soils (for example, Mohr and van Baren 1954; Mohr, van Baren, and van

TABLE 9.1

Current United States Department of Agriculture Soil Classification
(7th Approximation): some categories important in the Far East

Order	Key concept	Selected suborders	Key concept
Entisol	Weakly developed	Aquent	Gleyed
		Psamment	Sandy
		Fluvent	Alluvial
Inceptisol	Distinct profile, moderate weathering	Tropept	Tropical
		Andept	Allophanic
		Aquept	Gleyed
Vertisol	Clay, with strong swelling and shrinking	Udert	Always moist
		Ustert	Seasonally dry
Alfisol	With clay enriched B horizon, relatively base rich	Udalf	Always moist
		Ustalf	Seasonally dry
Ultisol	With clay enriched B horizon, relatively base poor	Aquult	Gleyed or with plinthite
		Udult	Always moist
Spodosol	With 'podzol' B horizon	Aquod	With gleying
		Humod	Humus B only
		Orthod	Humus and iron in B
Oxisol	Highly weathered, low cation-exchange capacity	Aquox	Gleyed or with plinthite
		Orthox	Low in humus
		Humox	Humose A horizon
Histosol	Soil mainly organic	Saprist	Well decomposed

Notes. Of the two remaining Orders, mollisols are rare in the tropical Far East and aridisols are absent. Plinthite is unhardened laterite. This table is based on Soil Survey Staff (1967); definitive publication of a slightly modified scheme is imminent.

F

Schuylenborgh 1972) but as the term laterite is now generally restricted to features of iron and/or aluminium segregation which do not occur in all 'lateritic soils'; this name has been dropped. Since a predominance of kaolinitic minerals in the clay fraction is general in zonal soils of the humid tropics, Sys (1961) proposed the name kaolisol. A commoner approach of recent authors has been to subdivide the group, calling some red–yellow podzolic soils (for example, Dudal and Soepraptohardjo 1957) or ultisols (Soil Survey Staff 1960, 1967) and others latosols (Kellogg 1949), ferrallitic soils (Aubert and Duchaufour 1956), or oxisols (Soil Survey Staff 1960, 1967). From this discussion the reader will conclude rightly that international agreement about soil nomenclature is still remote. Useful recent general accounts of tropical soils have been given by Sys (1967), Buringh (1968), and Mohr, van Baren, and van Schuylenborgh (1972).

Dudal and Moormann (1964) produced a most useful review of the soils of south-east Asia, which has been brought up to date by Dudal, Moormann, and Riquier (1974). The latter is based on the new classification being used for the F.A.O./UNESCO *Soil map of the world* (1968). It is evident that there is a confusing multiplicity of names for similar soil categories. A summary of the more relevant orders and suborders of the new American classification

(Soil Survey Staff 1967) is therefore given in Table 9.1, and a correlation of nomenclature is attempted in Table 9.2.

Scientists studying soil formation and classification concern themselves with the whole soil profile, which consists of a sequence of layers, called horizons, from the surface to unaltered geological material. In a forest soil profile the layer of fallen leaves and other plant debris is called litter (L), and is sometimes underlain by partly humified plant remains (F) and well-decomposed humus (H). Where the H layer is sharply bounded and not mixed into the mineral soil below, the humus type is called mor. Mor develops in aerobic conditions. In anaerobic conditions peat may form instead (Fig. 9.1). A surface layer, composed mainly of mineral particles with some well-incorporated humus, is called an A horizon, and when it lies almost immediately under a thin litter may be referred to as mull. In some soil profiles the layers containing humus are underlain by a pale-coloured E horizon, sometimes called A_2, from which eluviation has removed some clay or iron and aluminium sesquioxides. Below the E horizon, or directly beneath the A if no E is present, there may be weathered layers and these are indexed as B. If enriched with clay a subscript t is introduced to distinguish a B_t horizon. If iron and aluminium sesquioxides have moved in from above it is a B_s

TABLE 9.2

Approximate equivalents of older terms, as used by Dudal and Moormann (1964), in the classification systems used for the World Soil Map (F.A.O./UNESCO 1968) and by the United States Department of Agriculture (Soil Survey Staff 1967)

Dudal and Moormann (1964)	F.A.O./UNESCO (1968)	U.S.D.A. (1967)
Alluvial soils	Fluvisols	Fluvents / Aquents†
Acid sulphate soils	Thionic fluvisols	Aquents†
Regosols	Regosols	Psamments / Orthents†
Grumusols	Vertisols	Vertisols
Andosols	Andosols	Andepts
Brown forest soils	Cambisols	Tropepts†
Podzols	Podzols	Spodosols
Non-calcic brown soils / Red–brown earths	Chromic luvisols	Ustalfs
Low humic gley soils	Gleysols	Aquepts†
Red–yellow podzolic soils / Grey podzolic soils	Acrisols	Ultisols
Dark red and reddish-brown latosols / Red–yellow latosols	Nitosols / Ferralsols	Oxisols
Organic soils	Histosols	Histosols

† Boundary criteria for the U.S.D.A. soil groupings normally differ from those in the other classifications. Dagger indicates that the correlation applies to some examples in south-east Asia but would be misleading as a generalization.

horizon; if finely divided humus it is a B_h horizon. The presence of diagnostic horizons is often a characteristic of a soil group, thus podzols have a B_h or B_s horizon, or both, as seen in Figs 9.11 and 9.12 (pp. 113, 114). In latosols the B horizon is very deep and highly weathered but has not usually received clay or sesquioxides by vertical translocation. However, iron and aluminium are concentrated by the removal of other constituents. In any soil the C horizon means its parent material. The new American classification (Soil Survey Staff 1960) dispenses with horizons designated by letters in favour of names, calling, for example, a more rigidly defined equivalent of the latosolic B an oxic horizon. The technical description of soil profiles has been described by Soil Survey Staff (1951), Leamy and Panton (1966), and Clarke and Beckett (1971).

The most active mineral component of soil is the clay fraction, that is, the fine particles less than 2 µm in mean dimension which are composed mainly of layer lattice silicates. When single layers of silicon and oxygen and of aluminium and hydroxyl ions alternate the mineral has a 1:1 layer lattice, as in the case of kaolinite and halloysite. Where two layers of silicon and oxygen alternate with one layer containing aluminium or magnesium and hydroxyl ions the mineral has a 2:1 layer lattice; examples are the micas, illite, and montmorillonite. To a soil, clay particles impart the property of swelling and shrinking with changing moisture content and also the power to retain and exchange cations, that is, the cation-exchange capacity. Both these properties are more strongly developed in 2:1 minerals, particularly montmorillonite, than in kaolinite. The low cation-exchange capacity of kaolinitic soils, which are extremely widespread in the tropics, means that these have poor retentivity of several important plant nutrients.

A considerable part of the tropical Far East is occupied by soils in which the overriding pedogenic factor is characteristic of the local rather than the regional environment. Some have a well-developed soil profile, but a factor such as location in a poorly drained part of the landscape or situation on an unusual parent material, for example, a pure limestone, has exerted a predominant effect. In the scheme proposed by Sibirtsev (1899) these were called *intrazonal soils*. Other profiles in which the effect of soil formation has been weak, usually owing to recent erosion or deposition, for example, of blown sand or alluvium, were termed *azonal*. While the terms intrazonal and azonal are no longer in general use, the categories they represent still need separate

FIG. 9.1.   Peat soil (saprist) under elfin woodland facies of upper montane rain forest dominated by *Dacrydium*. (Summit of Gunung Ulu Kali, Malaya, 1800 m elevation.)

description in a regional account such as this. So do those soils which by reason of high altitude really belong to cooler climatic zones. For the purposes of this book these terms are retained as usefully denoting general groups of soils.

9.1. General features of zonal soils

Weathering is strong in the humid tropics, being favoured by both warmth and moisture. The high rainfall frequently wets the soil throughout, with a surplus to penetrate to the ground water. Thus constituents which can be carried in solution are continually removed; this is the process of leaching. The temperature and water content of a well-drained tropical soil favour a high level of biological activity, including the continuous production of organic

FIG. 9.2. Quartz porphyry weathered to deeper than 10 m near Raub, Malaya. Soil surface is about 3 m above upper (vegetated) step. The lowest 2 m at the base is incompletely weathered with residual core stones. Man about 1·6 m tall.

FIG. 9.3. Weathering of granite at Tampin, Malaya. Lower right hard rock; upper left soft rock in which mineral grains are in place but felspar and biotite thoroughly decomposed. Photograph about 0·1 m across.

matter by the vegetation and its rapid degradation by macro- and micro-organisms in or on the soil. High levels of weathering, leaching, and biological activity control the properties of typical soils.

The strong weathering in the humid tropics leads generally to deep soils (2–15 m or more). The silicates of igneous and metamorphic rocks are usually decomposed to a much greater depth than soil mixing is effective, so that soils on crystalline rocks are underlain by considerable thicknesses of saprolite (rotten rock) in which each crystal apparently remains in place although most are completely altered to secondary products (Figs 9.2 and 9.3). For the same reason fresh rock fragments and grains of weatherable minerals are rarely found in soils of the humid tropics, thus excluding an important source of slowly available plant nutrients.

Complete weathering of all common minerals, except quartz, to kaolinitic clay and to iron and aluminium oxides and hydroxides leads to soils richer in clay than would be the case in an otherwise similar temperate environment. Another consequence of deep, complete weathering is that soil erosion rarely removes, or even exposes, any large amount of unweathered parent material relatively rich in plant nutrients. Thus, not only are the deep, sedentary soils of low fertility, but even soils on eroded slopes and on transported materials such as colluvium and alluvium are often poor also.

It is hard to separate weathering from leaching, for weathering is much assisted by the removal of soluble products. The most soluble products are base cations such as sodium, potassium, calcium, and magnesium, which are depleted to very low levels in the great majority of soils in the humid tropics. These are replaced by aluminium ions on the exchange complex, which in turn are active in sorbing soluble phosphate. Soil acidity is only moderate (for example, pH 4·5–5·5), even though by temperate standards the base content is extremely low.

Silica is very slightly soluble in water and is slowly leached, and even quartz suffers some attack. In time this has the effect of removing silt and fine sand particles from the soil, so that the mineral fractions of well-developed soils in the humid tropics have low silt/clay ratios and consist mostly of kaolinitic clay and coarse sand composed of quartz and iron-stone nodules. Silica dissolved in the soil solution can combine with gibbsite (aluminium hydroxide) initially formed from felspars and other silicates to produce kaolinite, a process known as resilication. This may be one reason why soils derived from basic igneous rocks low in silica and containing no quartz

are normally rich in gibbsite while soils derived from granite (with quartz) do not normally contain much gibbsite. Once formed, the kaolinite is very stable. The micaceous minerals common in shales may also weather to kaolinite, but the process may be relatively slow compared with the weathering of igneous rocks, partly because weathered shale subsoils tend to be impermeable.

The kaolinitic nature of the clay of most well-drained, well-developed soils of the humid tropics has several important consequences. Such clay does not swell and shrink much on wetting and drying, so that prominent cracking defining a well-developed blocky or prismatic structure is rare. On the other hand, kaolinite unmixed with humus or other clay minerals is hard to disperse in pure water; it flocculates to stable, fine aggregates so that subsoils are permeable and relatively resistant to erosion. Also, such subsoils retain much water available to plants and are easily penetrated by roots.

Kaolinite has low cation-exchange capacity, especially at a low pH. Therefore, in soils of the humid tropics, nutrient-holding capacity is mainly a function of humus content, and is very low where humus content is low, as is usual in subsoils; in fact in many cases more than half of the adsorbed bases in 1 m of soil are in the top 0·25 m (Nye and Greenland 1960; van Baren 1961). Humus both tends to reduce the phosphate-fixation capacity of associated mineral colloids and to release phosphate as it decomposes. It follows that the phosphate available to plants is also concentrated near the surface, falling to negligible values in the subsoil. These facts help to explain why roots are concentrated in the surface soil (§2.5) and are few in subsoils, even though many tropical subsoils are easily penetrated physically.

The high level of soil biological activity means that in well-drained situations litter is thin and the content of organic matter in the soil is not high. Mound-building termites seem to become prominent only where there is a dry season, but in lowland rain forest the activity of termites in destroying wood and in excavating galleries and chambers to considerable depths is great. Through the biological activity nutrients are rapidly released, and, through the efficient root system concentrated at the very point of release, they are quickly recycled into living tissue. As mentioned in §2.5, mycorrhizas, which are present on the roots of most trees in tropical rain forest, play a part in the uptake process, but the extent of their role has not yet been elucidated. In primary forest, this rapid recycling partly offsets the low level of chemical fertility. The annual return of vegetable matter to the soil is 3 or 4 times as great as in temperate forest (Bray and Gorham 1964) and, as the available evidence points to the likelihood of plant nutrients being in about the same concentration, the amounts returned each year are about 3 times as great.

A deep, strongly weathered soil mantle minimizes the effect of parent material on the nutrient content of surface soil and plants. Lemée (1961) observed that 'apart from soils whose oligotrophy is extreme it does not seem that the nutrient content of the soil plays an important part in the differentiation of forest communities'. There are now a number of detailed studies which throw light on this complex subject, and these will be discussed in Chapter 15. Soils on recent volcanic deposits, notably in Indonesia, constitute another exceptional group and are described in §9.5.

While differences in fertility are relatively slight the soils being described vary appreciably in colour, texture, and sesquioxide content and in the distinctness and nature of layering seen in the profile. As has been indicated they have usually been subdivided in soil classifications on these characteristics, but it should be noted that none of the schemes are easy to apply, since, wherever the limits are set, intergrade soils abound and the data required to apply any specified criterion are often lacking. Despite these difficulties recent authors have attempted to separate soils with a clay-enriched B horizon, which have been called podzolic soils (Dudal and Soepraptohardjo 1957; Dudal and Moormann 1964) or ultisols (Soil Survey Staff 1960, 1967) from deep, friable, generally sesquioxide-rich soils lacking marked subsoil horizons which were called 'latosols' by Dudal and oxisols by the U.S.D.A. Soil Survey Staff. The U.S.D.A. terminology will be used here as far as possible. These two groups will be considered in a little fuller detail in §9.2 and 9.3. Broadly, in typical areas such as lowland Malaya ultisols occur on younger surfaces and relatively quartzose materials and oxisols on old surfaces and basic parent materials. Inceptisols (resembling brown earths) occur occasionally on steep slopes (Fig. 9.4).

In the U.S.D.A. classification nomenclature is developed in a systematic manner. Each of the ten Orders (Table 9.1) has a name ending in -sol, for example, entisol and inceptisol. All subdivisions of an Order end in a characteristic syllable; for entisols this is -ent and for inceptisols it is -ept. Orders are first divided into Suborders, for example, entisols are divided into aquents, arents, fluvents, orthents, and psamments. Suborders are then divided into Great Groups by the addition of a further syllable or syllables. A quartzose psamment, for example, is a quartzipsamment. Subgroups can then be distinguished by the addition of an adjective, thus 'typic quartzipsamment'. In this way the position of a Subgroup at all levels in the heirarchy is evident from the name. The definitions of units at all levels are very specific, often quantitative, and during the development of the classification some have been changed. For this reason, and especially since analytical methods are specified which sometimes are not yet in general use, application of the classification to soils outside the United States can only be tentative at present, and in a few cases is still impossible.

9.2. Ultisols (red-yellow podzolic soils)

The distinguishing feature of ultisols is the so-called 'argillic' or 'textural B' (B_t) horizon in the subsoil. This has at least 1·2 times as much clay as the top-soil, and not infrequently has more than twice as much. The structure of the horizon is produced by fissures a few centimetres apart, giving a medium to coarse, blocky structure with clay coatings on the fissure surface, which appear in thin section to have uniformly fine particles with parallel orientation; features suggesting transport in suspension from higher horizons. Bright yellow–brown or reddish

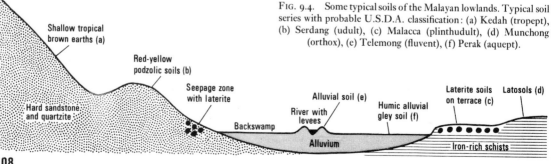

FIG. 9.4. Some typical soils of the Malayan lowlands. Typical soil series with probable U.S.D.A. classification: (a) Kedah (tropept), (b) Serdang (udult), (c) Malacca (plinthudult), (d) Munchong (orthox), (e) Telemong (fluvent), (f) Perak (aquept).

colours are usual in the argillic horizon, often becoming paler above, but the distinct, very pale E horizon, found between the humose A and the B_t in the classical red–yellow podzolic soils of the south-eastern United States, is usually absent. Ultisols with pale, often greyish, colours throughout the profiles are common in Burma, Thailand, and the countries bordering the lower Mekong river, but occur only occasionally (soil d in Fig. 9.7) in the wetter parts of south-east Asia (Dudal and Moormann 1964) where more brightly coloured ultisols are general, for example, throughout Malaysia (Leamy 1966; Sarawak Soil Survey Staff 1966; Folland and Acres 1972) and in the non-volcanic parts of Indonesia (Dudal and Soepraptohardjo 1957). In Africa, ultisols are found on Upper and Middle Pleistocene erosion surfaces within the humid tropical belt. They are replaced on the much more extensive older surfaces and peneplains by oxisols (Sys 1967). In the young landscape of south-east Asia, affected by extensive recent mountain building, old erosion surfaces and peneplains are rare, and ultisols are therefore much more extensive than oxisols—the reverse of the situation in Africa.

Ultisols have, by definition, a low base content (less than 35 per cent saturated in the subsoil). Despite their comparative youth, the high level of leaching ensures that the south-east Asian examples are infertile from the chemical point of view. As shown in Fig. 9.4, ultisols tend to occur on relatively siliceous materials whilst basic rocks, yielding more sesquioxides on weathering, give oxisols.

9.3. Oxisols (latosols)

Oxisols (Soil Survey Staff 1967) are characterized by the presence of an oxic horizon in the subsoil and usually by the absence of an argillic horizon. The oxic horizon has a low cation-exchange capacity (less than 13 milliequivalents per 100 g clay), and the clay has a low activity (that is, does not disperse appreciably when shaken in plain water). It lacks significant amounts of weatherable materials (2:1 lattice clays, feldspars, micas, glass, or ferromagnesian minerals). Very sandy soils are excluded from the oxisol Order.

Typical oxisols in south-east Asia are generally confined to intermediate to basic igneous rocks, for example, basalt (Fig. 9.5), although some are known on other parent materials, especially old alluvium, in stable landscapes. Oxisols on basic igneous rocks have high sesquioxide contents, often with gibbsite as well as ferric oxide minerals present, and they have a characteristic strong coloration, frequently dark

Fig. 9.5. Latosol (orthox) of Kuantan series, near Kuantan, Malaya. Road cutting with two steps. Note the accumulation of sand-size crumbs on the lower step from the friable, well-structured 5 m thick oxic horizon above (dark and somewhat reddish-brown in colour). Just above the step is a 'stone-line' and near the base the changkol is leaning on a residual corestone of partly weathered basalt.

red. The clay content is high (50–95 per cent) but stickiness low, so that the subsoil is friable and easily penetrated by roots. Examples may be drawn from the Kuantan area of Malaya (Leamy 1966), the Semporna peninsula in Sabah (Paton 1961), Indonesia (Mohr and van Baren 1954), the Philippines (Tamesis and Salita 1971), and the Solomon Islands (Lee 1969). Although these soils are strongly weathered and leached they may be marginally more fertile for agriculture than nearby ultisols on more siliceous materials. Conversely, oxisols on siliceous materials (for example, some older alluvial deposits) may have an appreciable content of quartz sand and are more infertile than adjacent ultisols, which implies a very high degree of infertility.

Intergrades between ultisols and oxisols are common. For example, they predominate over large areas of Malaya underlain by granite and shale. Since the distinction between the two groups is so difficult to make and has so little relationship to soil fertility, it seems hardly worth making. Intergrades to inceptisols are also common on steep slopes, for example, in Sarawak and Sabah (Folland and Acres 1972).

9.4. Laterite

'Laterite' formation implies the redistribution and concentration of sesquioxides within the profile. Features which may be broadly grouped under this heading are widely distributed in the zonal soils of south-east Asia, both ultisols and oxisols. They are rare in the wettest areas, become commoner in climates which are seasonally or absolutely drier and are most common in the regions of monsoon climate outside the rain-forest zone proper (§9.11).

The commonest and most widespread form of laterite is a subsoil layer of compact clay with bright reddish and pale yellow or grey mottling, lacking any hardening. An alternative name for unhardened laterite is plinthite. In seasonally dry areas similar material may be found near the surface as a con-

tinuous layer or as blocks with the reddish phase hardened (Fig. 9.6); unhardened mottled clay commonly occurs below. In Malaya such profiles are commonest in Malacca (hence their designation— for example, in Figs 9.4, 9.7—as the Malacca soil series) and in Kedah. It is notable that these are regions with a slightly more marked dry season than much of Malaya; this emphasizes the association between widespread laterite and seasonally dry climates. The mottled clay impedes rooting and hardened laterite prevents it, so such soils are considered relatively infertile although they are not more weathered than comparable 'non-lateritic' soils. Other 'lateritic' profiles are those with ironstone gravel (Fig. 9.7), either developed *in situ* or transported, and those with cementation due to the seep-

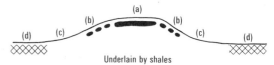

Underlain by shales

FIG. 9.7. The occurrence of laterite in relation to topography in central Malaya. (a) Relict ('fossil') laterite, *in situ*, partly hardened; (b) ironstone debris moved downslope from relict laterite; (c) yellowish-brown ultisol, with somewhat redder mottling in subsoil; (d) greyish-brown ultisol, with strongly contrasting red mottling in subsoil (unhardened, contemporary laterite); (a) and (b)—Malacca soil series, (c) Durian series, (d) Batu Anam series. (After Eyles 1967.)

age of iron-rich water at a spring line as in Fig. 9.4. General accounts of laterite have been given by Sivarajasingham, Alexander, Cady, and Cline (1962) and Prescott and Pendleton (1952). Occurrences in Indonesia have been described by Mohr and van Baren (1954) and in Malaya by Panton (1957) and by Eyles (1967: Fig. 9.7), who notes that in the area he describes there are annually three consecutive months with a mean soil moisture deficit.

It should be emphasized in conclusion that 'laterite' in these forms is not a dominant feature of the rain-forest zone of south-east Asia, and has not been shown to have any floristic effect.

9.5. Soils on volcanic ash

Volcanic activity has been very extensive on many of the islands of south-east Asia, and most particularly on the Sunda group (Sumatra, Java, Bali, Lombok, Sumbawa, and Flores). Java alone has 112 volcanoes, of which 34 have been active since 1600. Where volcanoes are formed by magma relatively low in silica, most of the discharge is lava with a subordinate quantity of volcanic ash, but where the magma is high in silica ash predominates. Volcanic

FIG. 9.6. Mottled clay from a laterite profile. Dark areas are reddish and hardening; pale areas are grey and remain soft. Scale in centimetres.

ash is principally composed of pumice debris, that is to say, shreds of silicate glass, although crystals of igneous minerals usually occur in it also.

The soils first formed on recent lavas are usually tropepts and resemble brown earths. With time these evolve in the lowlands to give oxisols (latosols), which are described in §9.3. Andosols (F.A.O. 1964; Mohr, van Baren, and van Schuylenborgh 1972) are the initial product of weathering of volcanic ash in most climatic zones, their distinctive properties depending on the presence of allophane. Allophane is an X-ray amorphous association of hydrous silica and alumina with a large active surface. This large, highly charged surface gives the soil a high porosity and a low bulk density, expressed in the field as a 'fluffy' consistence, a high capacity for water retention, for cation exchange, and for phosphate sorption, and an ability to form stable associations of mineral and finely divided organic matter which give top-soils a characteristic dark colour (Fig. 9.8). Andosols range from shallow soils with sandy, sometimes stony, textures where little weathered pumice still predominates to deep loamy or silty soils with a greasy feel, which are nevertheless not sticky and have a relatively low content of crystalline clay minerals. They are very difficult to disperse by standard procedures for particle-size analysis. A yellowish or reddish-brown subsoil may occur beneath the thick, dark top-soil in deeper profiles. Andosols are generally andepts in the U.S.D.A. soil classification.

Under well-drained conditions in humid climates allophane is changed in a few thousand years to halloysite and then to kaolinite. Dudal and Soeprap-tohardjo (1960) estimated that it takes 50 000 years to produce 1 m of kaolinitic soil from volcanic ash in Indonesia. It follows that andosols only occur in late Pleistocene and Holocene volcanic ash. Mohr and van Baren (1954) envisaged the evolution of andosols in time into kaolinitic red earths and eventually into lateritic soils, as shown in Fig. 9.9. Probably only the first stage is of universal occurrence because soil development in an ever-wet climate ends, in typical environments, with a deep, strongly weathered red earth (oxisol). Laterite formation occurs in the seasonal climate of Java which they had in mind. In practice rejuvenation by a fresh fall of ash usually intervenes.

In a world context the andosols are moderately fertile, with some favourable and some unfavourable properties for plant growth. Compared with other soils of the humid tropics, however, andosols are of distinctly superior fertility. They have a good natural supply of combined nitrogen and are moderately well provided with potassium, but phosphorus available to plants is often seriously deficient. Minor elements, notably manganese, are also sometimes deficient. Andosols formed in permanently humid climates may dehydrate irreversibly when thoroughly dried. A hard pan about 0·2 m thick often occurs at a depth of 0·4–1·0 m from the surface, owing to cementation by silica or by iron and manganese oxides, and is not easily penetrated by roots.

Fig. 9.8. Andosol (andept) of Olaa series, Hawaii. Thick crumbly A horizon of low bulk density over pumice debris. Scale is 0·3 m.

Tropical rain forests of the Far East

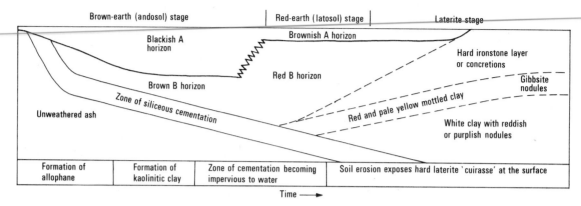

FIG. 9.9. Tropical soil profile development on volcanic ash in Java. (Partly based on Mohr and van Baren 1954.)

Soils on recent volcanic deposits, including ando-sols, are extensive in Java where the magma is mainly low in silica (andesitic or basaltic) and often occur at relatively high elevations giving soils with a very high cation-exchange capacity (Tan, in F.A.O. 1964). In north Sumatra the more siliceous magmas (andesitic or dacitic) have their greatest extent at lower elevations, and soils with a proportion of gibbsite and with a relatively moderate cation-exchange capacity have been reported. Young volcanic deposits are also common on some of the Lesser

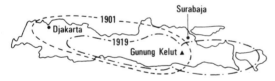

FIG. 9.10. Distribution of ash from the Kelut eruptions on Java in 1901 and 1919 showing the effect of wind. (After Kemmerling 1921.)

Sunda Islands and occur locally in Celebes and central Borneo. Several Indonesian volcanic eruptions have spread fine ash to considerable distances (Fig. 9.10) modifying and enriching soils which are not typical andosols. Mud flows of volcanic ash (lahars) have been important locally (Mohr and van Baren 1954). New Guinea, New Britain, the Solomon Islands, and the New Hebrides have active volcanoes, but these have ejected mainly basic, low-silica lava; volcanic ash, however, covers two-thirds of Bougain-ville, and most soils in the New Hebrides are affected by ash falls as are some in New Guinea. In the Philippines, andosols are confined to small areas in south Luzon and a rather larger part of Mindanao.

112

9.6. Soils on coarse, siliceous deposits (podzols)

Podzols (spodosols) occur in places where parent materials consist predominantly of quartz, for example, beach sand, sandstone, or quartzite, or much more locally on unusually siliceous volcanic rocks (a major example is the Usun Apau plateau in Sarawak). These parent materials are low in clay and in bases and also in minerals that might weather into these products. The soils are readily permeable and are well drained, except that the influence of ground water may sometimes cause subsoils to be waterlogged. In these circumstances podzolization is possible wherever rainfall substantially exceeds evapotranspiration. In the Far East podzols are rare unless the mean annual rainfall exceeds 2000 mm.

The podzols of the tropical Far East resemble those found in sands in southern England. Under a raw humus layer in undisturbed sites, or elsewhere under a dark grey sandy A horizon, lies a bleached E (formerly called A2) horizon, below which is a very dark or strongly coloured B horizon enriched in colloidal organic matter (humus podzol or humod) or in organic matter and sesquioxides (humus–iron podzol or orthod, as in Fig. 9.11). The constituents which have accumulated in the B horizon have been moved by percolating water from the upper part of the soil profile. Mobilized sesquioxides often originate from the chemical breakdown of clay which commonly occurs to some extent in the very acid conditions characteristic of podzols.

The most widespread environment where podzols are formed is on old beach deposits lying just inland in the form of low ridges or terraces. These sediments are in their second or third weathering cycle and are very deficient in bases.

Lowland podzols further inland on consolidated

A

E

B$_h$

B$_s$

C

FIG. 9.11. Podzol (orthod) of Rudua series, Kuantan, Malaya. Bleached E over very undulating B$_h$ and orange–brown B$_s$ horizons; on beach sand.

rocks, usually sandstone but also acidic volcanics, quartzite, and conglomerates, are restricted mainly to Borneo (see §10.3). Podzols are also frequent among mountain soils, as described in §9.12.

Much information about tropical podzols generally has been summarized by Klinge (1968), and a detailed study including podzols on both consolidated and unconsolidated materials has been made in Sarawak by Andriesse (1969).

The characteristic vegetation of lowland podzols is heath forest (§10.3). The intricate relationship

between this and some mountain forests is described in §16.4.

On stranded beach deposits, particularly where these consist of a series of low sand ridges becoming older in order inland (for instance, along the east coast of Malaya where they are known as tanah beris), a sequence of soil development can often be traced (Fig. 9.12) from regosols in which a weak A horizon is the only indication of soil formation, through podzols with shallow, weakly expressed horizons and humus–iron or humus podzols of moderate depth but with a bleached E and a strongly expressed B horizon, to 'giant' humus podzols in which the bleached E horizon is 1·5–2·0 m thick or even more and the blackish humus-enriched B horizon is near the water table (Burnham 1968). The natural vegetation of these beach deposits is heath forest, under which raw humus is found, often thin (for example, 50 mm) but passing to a thicker, more peaty accumulation on the sandy ground-water gley soils which occur in the elongated depressions (swales) separating ridges (Fig. 9.4, p. 108). The forest of the swales has some affinities with peat swamp forest (§11.3).

The soils on the beach ridges are developed in sand in which silt, clay, calcium, and potassium may be almost undetectable. A little exchangeable sodium and magnesium is present, derived no doubt from salt spray.

In Sarawak and Brunei there are extensive remnants of terraces at about 8–30 m above present sea-level which are partly of marine and partly of riverine origin (Wall 1964). They are often composed of loamy sand or sandy loam, but beds of clay also occur and sometimes support a perched water table. Well-developed humus podzols occur on the flat, undissected remnants of the marine terraces with a compact humus B horizon (pan) below 1 m, which may itself hold up water, and even be so cemented that blasting is needed to disintegrate it. Riverine terraces are less strongly podzolized.

Lowland podzols on sandstones, quartzites, and conglomerates occurring inland have shallower horizons than those in looser materials, and podzols seem here to be confined to sites where soils are not rapidly truncated by erosion (cf. §14.1).

All podzols and associated soils tend to have very poor natural fertility, coupled with a very low capacity to retain water and cations.

9.7. Soils on limestone

The areas occupied by relatively pure limestones cover in total only a small part of the tropical Far East, but are generally made evident by a distinctive

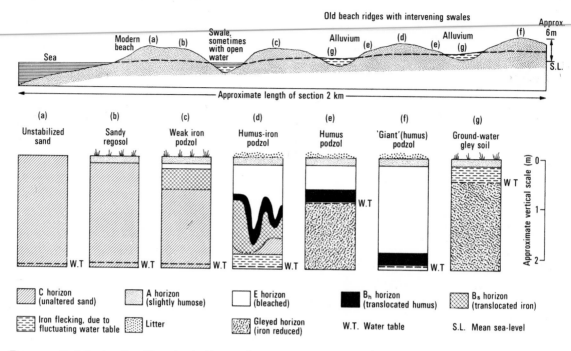

FIG. 9.12. Variation in soil profile on beach ridges on the east coast of Malaya. Probable U.S.D.A. names: (b) quartzipsamment, (c) spodic quartzipsamment, (d) haplorthod, (e) and (f) tropaquods, (g) includes aquic quartzipsamments.

karst landscape which occurs in south China, Indo-China, central Sumatra, Malaya, Sarawak, Java, the Lesser Sunda Islands, Celebes, the Moluccas, and New Guinea (Verstappen (1960) gives a useful review). Two forms of karst seem to be peculiar to the humid tropics and subtropics: cockpit (or labyrinth) karst and tower karst (*Karstkegel*). Cockpit karst has a regular series of conical or hemispherical hills and hollows with slopes ranging up to 30–40°. In tower karst (see, for example, Jennings 1972), isolated hills with precipitous sides (60–90°), 100–50 m high and often riddled with caves, are separated by flat depressions. Recent coral limestone exposed by falling sea-level or uplift forms a third kind of limestone landscape and is extensive, as a usually narrow coastal plain, especially in Celebes, New Guinea (notably the Vogelkop peninsula), the Bismarcks, and the Solomons.

The steeper parts of karst landscapes are mostly bare limestone with a little soil here and there in fissures. On crests and shelves in high-rainfall areas an acid, highly humose, peat-like surface layer may lie directly on pure, hard limestone as reported from central New Guinea (Reynders 1964a) and Sarawak (Wilford and Wall 1965). On gentler slopes and hollows brownish-red latosolic soils occur locally in Malaya, where tower karst is predominant, more

extensively in Java, associated with cockpit karst in Gunung Sewu (meaning thousand hills), and also on the coastal coral limestone terraces already mentioned. These soils are clay-rich and are leached, but slightly higher in base content and cation-exchange capacity than comparable soils on other parent materials. Montmorillonitic clay soils, often gleyed, have been reported from west New Guinea under a rainfall of nearly 4 m annually. Dark-grey montmorillonitic soils, deeply cracked in the dry season and with little sign of gleying (vertisols, generally usterts), are common where the rainfall is relatively low as in Java and the Lesser Sunda Islands. These are mostly on argillaceous limestones. Red, clayey, so-called 'terra rossa' soils are found on purer limestones and are probably ustalfs in the American classification.

9.8. Soils on ultrabasic rocks

Serpentinites and associated rocks such as peridotite have a high iron and magnesium and a low silica content. They are also characterized by high concentrations of phytotoxic elements, notably nickel, cobalt, and chromium. Morphologically the soils do not differ greatly from those on basic igneous rocks in the same area (oxisols, see above) and like them are characteristically high in clay and sesquioxides

(Mohr, van Baren, and van Schuylenborgh 1972). There have been few examinations of such soils in the tropical Far East. In the Solomons they were found to be excessively poor in all major plant nutrients (Lee 1969), and the distinctive vegetation on these rocks in the Solomons must be in part due to this; local dominance by *Casuarina papuana* may be due primarily to its ability to fix atmospheric nitrogen. The extent to which phytotoxic elements influence the vegetation has not been explored in the tropical Far East. In the north temperate zone the high ratio of magnesium to calcium has been shown to prevent some plants from obtaining their calcium requirements (Martin, Vlamice, and Stice 1953), and in Shetland serpentine, soil infertility was due to phosphorus deficiency associated with low nitrogen and potassium (Spence and Miller 1963).

The most extensive ultrabasic outcrops in our region are in New Caledonia (Tercinier 1962), where nickel and chromium toxicity were considered to be the major cause of the infertility of derived soils (Birrell and Wright 1945). Ultrabasic rocks on the flanks of Mt. Kinabalu in Sabah at about 2400 m, near Tanah Grogot in east Kalimantan, in the Solomons, and in northern New Guinea all bear vegetation of distinctive structure and physiognomy, whereas those in Malaya and at the foot of Mt. Kinabalu near Ranau do not. The soils on the Ranau outcrop are very porous (Fox and Tan 1971); those in Malaya are a very greasy clay, sometimes containing talc. The diversity exhibited by the forests over ultrabasic rocks, which are described more fully in §10.5, must reflect the still poorly investigated variation in the soils.

9.9. Soils on finer marine alluvium

Where coastal sedimentation is of medium or fine particles (mud rather than sand), mangroves are the usual initial colonizers. At first the mud flat is invaded by the tide twice daily, but the pneumatophore shoots of the pioneer species of *Avicennia*, followed at a later stage by the many-stemmed stools of *Rhizophora*, trap sediment with such efficiency that the coastline may advance seaward at a rate of several metres per year (cf. §11.3). The new alluvium is a more or less uniform bluish or greenish grey with rusty traces along roots, and sometimes contains shells. It is saline and neutral to alkaline in reaction, and there is a very significant sulphate content. Mounds made by mud lobsters (*Thalassina anomala*) may occur. Further from the sea, inundation is less frequent and brings less saline water. The soil is still permanently waterlogged, and the subsoil is unripened (that is, has low bearing capacity) but the content of partly decomposed organic matter builds up. Under these circumstances sulphate ions are microbiologically reduced and, reacting with the iron in the soil, produce pyrite (FeS_2) and ferrous sulphide (FeS). Still the soils are no more than slightly acid, but, with rain- and river-water replacing sea-water, the content of sodium ions is much reduced, and fresh-water swamp forest or peat swamp forest replaces mangroves. Sometimes such soils derived from marine or estuarine alluvium become extremely acid on drainage, when the sulphides oxidize to produce basic ferric sulphate and basic potassium ferric sulphate (jarosite), which are both bright yellow in colour, together with sulphuric acid which drastically lowers the pH (for example, to pH 2–3) and brings phytotoxic amounts of aluminium into the soil solution (van Beers 1962). It should be noted, however, that these acid sulphate soils (sulfaquents) are produced by attempted reclamation. The acidification does not normally occur under natural conditions; occasional exceptions are associated with levees or (in Sarawak) with old *Thalassina* mounds.

Apart from the 'acid sulphate' soils, most soils on marine alluvium are very fertile, for example, the alluvial gley soils on the west coast of Malaya (Fig. 9.13), where a natural shell content contributes calcium. The marine sediments are much richer in 2:1 lattice clay minerals (illite, montmorillonite) than nearby riverine sediments, and the soils therefore have a higher cation-exchange capacity as well as a higher base content. In Java and Malaya there is little forest left on these soils which are so attractive

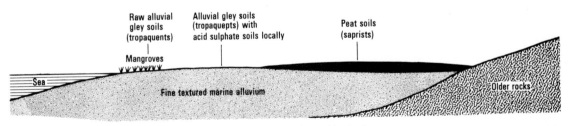

FIG. 9.13. Some soils of coastal lowlands.

for agriculture. Substantial areas of sub-recent marine alluvium are overlain by peat (§11.3; Fig. 9.13).

In the U.S.D.A. soil classification recent soils on fine marine alluvium are usually aquents, unripened ones being hydraquents. Older, somewhat better drained soils are aquepts.

9.10. Fresh-water alluvial soils

Soils formed from the recent alluvium of rivers and lakes are set apart from most others by the relatively short time which has been available for soil formation and by their special geomorphological position (usually low in the landscape and near a water table). They also have an intricate variability imposed by the inherently variable parent material and the special microtopography of flood plains. River alluvium varies very much in mineral constitution according to the lithology of the geological formations outcropping in the particular catchment and the surrounding topography. Relief largely governs how much material is offered to the river by erosion and how well weathered it is. In such new soils leaching *in situ* is not important, but in the humid tropics eroded soil generally will have been strongly leached already. On the other hand, soil waterlogging, leading to reduction of susceptible constituents, is almost ubiquitous. This may be present throughout the profile, reaching the surface, but sometimes has only occurred at considerable depth. Waterlogging results in the development of grey colours, usually with mottling, a process known as gleying.

Fresh-water alluvial soils are found in all climatic zones and occur throughout the tropical Far East. In Burma, Thailand, Cambodia, and Vietnam, where they are most extensive, the rivers (such as the Irrawaddy and the Mekong) drain extensive, geologically young mountain ranges, and this, together with the occurrence of a dry season, ensures that the alluvial soils are rich in bases and weatherable minerals. Elsewhere the river basins are smaller, and the alluvial deposits consequently vary much from one to another in their content of bases and weatherable minerals. For example, if the catchment is mainly occupied by calcareous sediments or basic igneous rocks and the rainfall is not too high the alluvial soils are usually dark-coloured heavy clays, which may contain montmorillonite, for example, in Java (Dames 1955). Siliceous parent materials and higher rainfall, associated with ultisols and oxisols in the catchment, give base-poor alluvial soils, often more loamy, dominated by 1:1 lattice clay minerals

such as kaolinite. Collectively, these smaller river basins have extensive alluvial plains, particularly in New Guinea. Even in mainland Malaya, a small country lacking large rivers, there are about 1 000 000 ha of fresh-water mineral alluvial soils. In Java and Sumatra lacustrine alluvium deposited in lakes formed by volcanic activity is of significant extent.

The two main alluvial soil environments are the levee and the backswamp (cf. Fig. 9.4). On the levee, a natural embankment adjacent to a present or former course of the river, the deposited materials are relatively coarse, and, since the water table can fall nearly to the level of the river, the soils are generally well-drained, at least near the surface. Beyond the levee the backswamp may extend a long distance from the river, with fine-textured, ill-drained soils. In the case of rivers which flood periodically, fan-shaped deposits of coarse-textured alluvium usually extend in places over the backswamp from points where the levee has been breached. Other coarser-textured 'fans' may occur where small tributary valleys join the main stream. Coarse and fine are relative terms. All the deposits of a briskly flowing mountain stream will often be sandy or gravelly. By contrast, a fairly large river, such as the lower Pahang in Malaya, has silt–loam or silty clay loam soils on its levees and clay soils in the backswamps.

The levee soils have a brown A horizon 0·2–0·5 m thick, weakly differentiated in colour, with a low organic content and a low C/N ratio. Where locally there has been recent deposition, no A horizon is evident. Below any A horizon, depositional bands can usually be detected, but mottling may not be encountered until a depth of several metres from the surface is reached. In the backswamp the A horizon may in some cases actually be thinner, but is much more evident, and has a relatively high organic content and C/N ratio. It may be peaty, and pass in some sites to thicker peat. Mottling may extend to the surface, but in some cases only appears a few centimetres beneath the A horizon (as in Fig. 9.14). Light grey, bluish, or greenish-grey colours dominate most subsoils, although yellowish-red staining follows root channels into layers which are apparently permanently waterlogged. This suggests that some plants can introduce a significant amount of oxygen into an otherwise anaerobic environment.

Recent fresh-water alluvial soils in the tropical Far East mostly support some kind of swamp forest, though there are extensive areas of herbaceous vegetation, especially in New Guinea. Fresh-water swamp forest is described in §11.4. Over great expanses the alluvium is overlain by peat. Peat swamp

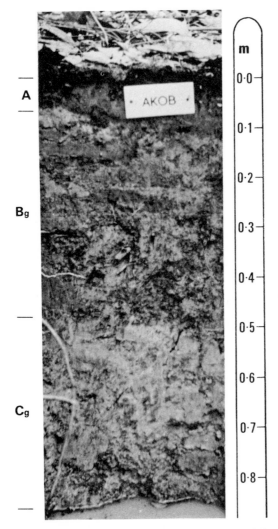

FIG. 9.14. Ground-water gley soil (aquept) of Akob series, Pekan, Malaya. The thin peaty A and brown, mottled B_g horizons are seasonally waterlogged and the alluvial, grey C_g horizon always so. Scale in feet.

forest and the circumstances which are believed to lead to the development of peat are described in §11.3. Mountain peat is described in §§9.12 and 16.5.

Chemically, recent alluvial soils are usually more fertile than the soils on the surrounding slopes, but not so fertile as some of the soils on recent marine alluvium or volcanic ash. In some cases areas may be enriched by bases contained in ground and seepage waters. This effect is noticeable even in Malaya within a few hundred metres of limestone outcrops, but is much more widespread in drier climates.

At a slightly higher level in the landscape, older alluvial deposits are often found, sometimes forming distinct river terraces. While the younger of these are not so different from recent alluvium, very well-developed profiles, sometimes with laterite, are often found on older alluvium. The soils derived from older alluvium, in Malaya at any rate, are commonly infertile (Gopinathan 1968; Arnott 1957). In Borneo the coarser, more siliceous deposits develop podzols, as was described in §9.6.

Such variation in the soils entails the use of many names. Fresh-water alluvial soils are often inceptisols in the U.S.D.A. soil classification. Where a fluctuating water table rises to within 0·5 m of the surface, these are aquepts. Some better drained soils on older loamy or clayey alluvium are tropepts, although some are oxisols and in areas with a dry season vertisols occur. Most other alluvial soils are entisols, because they are considered to show only relatively weak soil forming changes. Well-drained sandy ones are psamments; well-drained loamy and clayey soils on actively accreting alluvium are fluvents. Very poorly drained soils with a permanent water table within 0·25 m of the surface are generally aquents. Peat soils are placed in the histosol order, well decomposed ones are saprists.

9.11. Soils of seasonally dry climates

In Ceylon, Burma, Thailand, and Indo-China and in the drier parts of Indonesia where the mean annual rainfall is less than 1500 mm, brown and reddish-brown soils are widespread which differ from those of the ever-wet region in having a much higher base content and a more distinct subsoil horizon of clay accumulation. Following Californian precedents the brown soils were called non-calcic brown soils by Dudal and Moormann (1964), and are found on relatively acid or quartzose parent materials. The reddish soils were called red–brown earths (cf. east Australia), and are associated with limestone and basic igneous rocks. Both groups have affinities with the tropical ferruginous soils of Africa; they are ustalfs in the new American classification (Soil Survey Staff 1967). These soils have a pH of 5–7. The cation-exchange capacity is typically between 20 milliequivalents and 40 milliequivalents per 100 g of clay, much higher than in the ever-wet region, and even in the subsoil the content of exchangeable bases is more than 35 per cent of the capacity. Some 2:1 lattice clay minerals (for example, illite) are present, together with much kaolin. On flat, relatively low-lying sites, these soils tend to pass into dark-coloured montmorillonitic clay soils (vertisols). The assemblage of soils carries relatively little undisturbed forest and is occupied by poor secondary forest,

117

scrub, and grassland or by agriculture. Within the limits imposed by rainfall and relief these are moderately fertile soils, considerably better for non-tree crops than those of the ever-wet region. Teak forests occur, however, particularly on red–brown earths and vertisols in Burma, Thailand, and Java. Laterite, in the sense of sesquioxidic concretions or pans or thicker layers with a mottled or reticulate pattern which is either hard or hardenable on expo-sure, is extensive in the seasonally dry tropics. Soft or 'active' laterite is found where there is subsoil water-logging at the present time, notably on old river terraces and low peneplains. Hard or 'fossil' laterite tends to occur on plateaux, which are often being dissected, liberating laterite gravel to be incorporated in local colluvial and alluvial deposits (see Fig. 9.7). Laterite is only detrimental to plant growth where it seriously limits the rootable volume of the soil, and hence the water supply to plants. Soils containing laterite are sometimes highly weathered, but not invariably, indeed the feature has no necessary rela-tionships to chemical fertility. The nature and occur-rence of laterite in Thailand was extensively studied by Pendleton (for example, 1946).

9.12. Mountain soils

Large parts of south-east Asia are mountainous, giving great climatic variations in short distances. The resulting changes in the forest cover will be described in Chapter 16; concurrent changes in soils also occur, which are conveniently regarded as 'altitudinal zonation'. A neat pattern of soil changes occuring at predictable altitudes is often disturbed by the effect of parent material (as Reynders (1964*a*) found in New Guinea) and by the position of the examined site in relation to local topography. Ridge-top soils, for example, may differ from those deve-loped in valleys (for example, on Mt. Kinabalu (Askew 1964)). The incidence of landslides and soil erosion is another important factor on steep slopes. Regional changes in rainfall regime are of the greatest importance in that a dry season of significant length restricts leaching and prevents peat formation other than in depressions.

The soils of seasonally dry mountains

Despite the absence of peat, a progressive increase in the organic matter content of soils and in C/N ratio occurs with elevation, as has been described from Indonesia by Mohr and van Baren (1954) and Tan and van Schuylenborgh (1961) and from south Thailand by Kira and Shidei (1967). Soil descriptions from Ceylon and parts of the Philippines also show montane soils which are more humose than those of the lowlands, but which are not normally peaty. In the cooler, montane climate weathering is less severe, so that the soils are shallower. The cation-exchange capacity is high, indicating the presence of 2:1 clay minerals. Most of the montane soils of seasonally dry climates are only moderately acid (for example, pH 5–6), being less leached than those of the ever-wet climates.

Most profiles resemble brown earths (syn., brown forest soils) of oceanic temperate climates. In the new American classification (Soil Survey Staff 1967) they are tropepts. The whole depth is brown and friable, without strongly differentiated horizons. The humus form is mull, and over-all textures tend to be clayey. In volcanic areas, however, andosols (andepts) are often present (§9.5). The transition from the reddish well-weathered soils of the lowlands is either grada-tional or determined by local factors.

Some variations from this simple pattern have been reported. Van Schuylenborgh and his co-workers have studied soils on tuffs at high elevations (700–2000 m) in various parts of Indonesia, where the dry season is short. The soils formed depend on the base content of the parent material (van Schuylenborgh and van Rummelen 1955). Brown earths are found on basic basalto-andesitic tuffs, grey–brown podzolic soils (udalfs) on moderately basic andesitic tuffs, and humus–iron podzols (pre-sumably orthods) on acidic, rhyolitic, or dacitic tuffs (Tan and van Schuylenborgh 1961).

The soils of ever-wet mountains

Altitudinal changes in the soils of the ever-wet tropics are much sharper and are marked by a zone of peaty soils corresponding roughly with the 'cloud zone' and the mossy facies of upper montane rain forest (as shown in Fig. 9.1). These changes (Fig. 9.15) have been described in Malaya (Whitmore and Burnham 1969; Burnham 1974), Sabah (Askew 1964), and New Guinea (Reynders 1964*a,b*). Up to 1000 m elevation, or a little higher, the normal low-land soils occur, ranging from latosols (orthox) on basic parent materials in stable sites, through red–yellow podzolic soils (udults) to shallow soils re-sembling acid brown earths (tropepts) on steep slopes, as shown in Fig. 9.4.

On coastal mountains peaty soils are found as low as 1000 m elevation; indeed on Kolombangara in the Solomons (Lee 1969) they are found from 850 m. Inland the continuous blanket of peat associated with the cloud zone is found above about 1500 m on the main range of Malaya, 1700 m in the Star Mountains

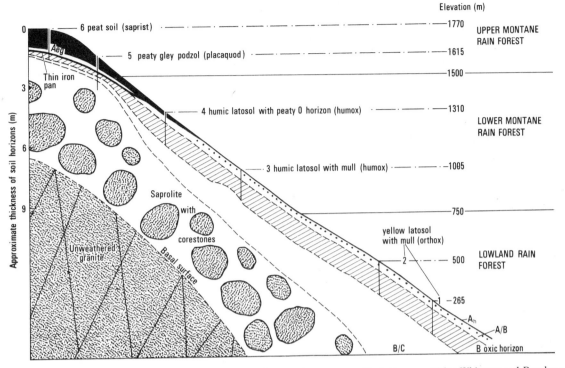

FIG. 9.15. Altitudinal sequence of soils on granite in the Malayan main range near Kuala Lumpur. (After Whitmore and Burnham 1969, Fig. 1.)

of New Guinea, and 1800 m on Mt. Kinabalu. Between about 1000 m and the cloud zone, within the lower montane forest Formation, rainfall is not necessarily higher than in the lowlands, but cloudiness and humidity are higher and evapotranspiration is sharply reduced. Soil formation is markedly affected by the greater amount of water available, which leads to increased leaching, podzolization, or soil waterlogging, depending on local circumstances. At the same time biological activity and chemical weathering are retarded by the lower temperatures. Brown earths, podzols, and peaty gley soils all occur in the lower montane zone, together with intergrades. The lower rate of weathering is reflected in soils which are shallower than those of the lowlands, with a higher cation-retention capacity. Commonly the soils are very acid. Some are extraordinarily low in calcium; Burnham noted an example in the Cameron Highlands in Malaya. It is noteworthy, therefore, that Grubb (1974) found that a sample of sun leaves from lower montane forest in the Cameron Highlands had only 39 per cent of the calcium content found in a sample from lowland forest. Reynders (1964a) quotes remarkable examples of soils developed over limestone which contain only traces of

exchangeable calcium. In Malaya unusually strong phosphate 'fixation' has been noted in a brown earth from the Cameron Highlands at 1430 m.

In the cloud zone, peat (Figs 9.1 and 9.16) is virtually continuous, even on steep slopes (for example, 25°). The thickness varies from about 0·3 m to considerably more than 1 m. In the field it is almost invariably wet, with a water content of 80–90 per cent. Except in its lowest part the mineral content of the dry matter is low, less than 10 per cent, and sometimes less than 1 per cent. pH values in the peat are extremely low, often between pH 3·0 and pH 3·5 in water and around pH 2·5 measured in potassium chloride solution. Hardly any data exists concerning the base content, but there can be little doubt that this is low. Very low fertility is suggested by the leaf analyses of Grubb (1974), who recorded that the content of nitrogen, phosphate, and calcium in leaves from three peaty montane sites in Malaya was much lower than that of lowland leaves. Potassium was slightly below the lowland level, but not magnesium. The subsoil sometimes has an appreciable base content, but this is not reached by roots. Thus extreme nutrient deficiency may have something to do with the low stature of upper montane rain forest. The

119

Fig. 9.16. Peat soil (saprist), Gunung Ulu Kali, Malaya, at 1670 m. Thick peat, thin A and E horizons underlain by multiple iron pans and granite saprolite with white pseudomorphs of kaolinite and gibbsite after felspar. Scale in feet.

interrelationships between soil, aerial environment, and mountain forest types, which are highly complex, are reviewed in Chapter 16.

Beneath the peat various mineral horizons occur. On granite a bleached layer underlain by a thin iron pan, often multiple, is frequently found, comparable with the peaty gleyed podzol (placaquod) of perhumid cool temperate regions (Fig. 9.16). On argillaceous sediments a gleyed horizon with mottling or iron concretions is usual. Weathered parent material occurs at no great depth, and, where permeable, is strongly leached. The removal of silica from granite saprolite, for example, leaves substantial amounts of gibbsite in material that would not on other criteria seem extremely weathered.

Above the cloud zone drier conditions prevail and the soils resemble those of a cool temperate oceanic area, such as Britain. Peaty soils are no longer dominant above about 2900 m on Mt. Kinabalu, above 3000 m on the Antares mountains, and above 3700 m on the Juliana mountains in west New Guinea. Mt. Kinabalu and the Antares mountains are of granodiorite. The deeper soils on both are generally acid brown earths (tropepts) with podzol intergrades (brown podzolic soils), and, locally, peaty gleyed podzols with a thin iron pan (placaquods). Shallow soils (rankers) and bare rock are also extensive. A remarkable feature of the soils in this zone on Mt. Kinabalu is the strong earthworm activity (Askew 1964), despite the isolation of the area by a broad band of peaty soils in which earthworms are not found. As might be expected from the presence of earthworms the soils are not extremely acid. On the Juliana mountains rendzinas are interspersed with the bare limestone rock. In general these small areas of very high mountains are not continuously forested, for reasons discussed in Chapter 16.

10 Forest Formations: (1) the dry-land rain forests

FROM A high-flying jet aeroplane or a manned satellite, the lands of the tropical Far East, glimpsed through breaks in the clouds, appear clothed in a dark blue–green carpet, a sombre girdle about the equator, increasingly patterned to the north-west and south-east with shades of brown, and mottled with brownish patches in some parts of the archipelago too.

There is considerable variation from place to place in this forest carpet, and it is possible to define very different kinds of forest which occur in distinct and different habitats. These kinds of forest are mainly sharply bounded because the habitats are bounded, but where habitats merge over an intermediate zone sharp boundaries do not occur in the forest and a blending region or ecotone occurs between two kinds.

The kinds of forest are often called *Formations* and differ from each other in structure, physiognomy, and floristic composition. The same Formation can be recognized from its structure and physiognomy in different parts of the Far East (and indeed in the tropics generally), although between distant areas there are substantial or complete differences in flora. Numerical analysis of data from eighteen sites in forests scattered through eastern Australia between 11° S and 19° S confirmed the importance of structural and physiognomic characters in defining forest types, irrespective of flora (Webb, Tracey, Williams, and Lance 1967*a*).

It is a convenient aid to understanding the distribution and interrelationships of the forest Formations to arrange them into groups according to the habitats they occupy, and the habitats can be arranged roughly into a hierarchy of decreasing wideness of occurrence, though it must be emphasized that habitat factors are not used in defining the Formations. The forests of the tropical Far East are arranged according to such a scheme in Table 10.1. It will be seen that availability of water plays the most important role in this hierarchy. The first division is between ever-wet (perhumid) and seasonally dry climates, and these two great groups more or less correspond with the greens and browns of our aeroplane or satellite view.

Within the Formations of ever-wet climates the second division is on a crude measure of the amount of water available to plants in the soil. The further, finer divisions of the dry land types of ever-wet climates are on other features of the soil, segregating forest Formations on limestone and ultrabasic-derived soils and those on quartz-rich, porous sands wherein podzols develop (5, 6, and 7 in Table 10.1).

TABLE 10.1

The main forest Formations of the tropical Far East

Climate	Soil water	Localities	Soils	Elevation	Forest Formation	
Ever-wet	Dry land	Inland	Zonal soils	Lowlands to 1200 m	1. Tropical lowland evergreen rain forest	
				Mountains (750) 1200–1500 m	2. Tropical lower montane rain forest	
				(600) 1500–3000 (3350) m	3. Tropical upper montane rain forest	
				3000 (3350) m to tree line	4. Tropical subalpine forest	
			Podzolized sands	Mostly lowlands	5. Heath forest	Tropical rain forests
			Limestone	Mostly lowlands	6. Forest over limestone	
			Ultrabasic rocks	Mostly lowlands	7. Forest over ultrabasic rocks	
		Coastal			8. Beach vegetation	
	Water table high (at least periodically)	Salt-water			9. Mangrove forest	
		Brackish water			10. Brackish-water forest	
		Fresh-water	Oligotrophic peats		11. Peat swamp forest	
			Eutrophic (muck and mineral) soils	Almost permanently wet	12a. Fresh-water swamp forest	
				Periodically wet	12b. Seasonal swamp forest	
					13. Tropical semi-evergreen rain forest	
Seasonally dry	Moderate annual shortage					Monsoon forests
	Marked annual shortage				14. Tropical moist deciduous forest	
					15. Other Formations of increasingly dry seasonal climates	

Based on van Steenis (1950*b*).

These are described later in the present chapter. On the remaining zonal or 'normal' soils (Chapter 9, p. 103) forest Formations can be recognized at different altitudes (2, 3, and 4 in Table 10.1); discussion of the intricate elevational changes in forest and in water relations, temperature, soil, and mineral availability is deferred until Chapter 16. Forest Formations of wet land (9–12 in Table 10.1) are described in Chapter 11.

Within the second major group in this hierarchical scheme there is a series of Formations found in increasingly dry habitats. The first Formation in this group, tropical semi-evergreen rain forest (Formation 13: §10.2) is of limited extent in the Far East, and occurs where water begins to be regularly and annually limiting, as an intermediate type between evergreen rain forest (Formation 1: §10.1) and the first of the monsoon-forest Formations, tropical moist deciduous forest (Formation 14). Fuller discussion of monsoon forests will be found in Chapter 12.

All Formations have in part been degraded by man by cultivation, grazing, and burning (as will be discussed more fully in Part V). Fire is the most potent agent. The drier types are more readily inflammable so have become more extensively degraded. Man has been the main source of fire ever since he learned its use (cf. Bartlett 1955*a,b*, 1957, 1961), before that lightning during dry periods probably started serious fires in the 'drier' Formations.

As mentioned above, the forest Formations themselves have each a distinctive structure and physiognomy throughout the region. There is as yet little understanding of this epharmony, as it is called, or convergent evolution of different floras in similar environments. Functional significance for certain physiognomic and structural features has now been claimed for heath forest (§10.3) and for some of the changes which take place with increasing elevation (Chapter 16). Further advances can be expected as rain-forest ecosystems are analysed by the newly developing techniques of model building and computer simulation of performance (see Parkhurst and Loucks (1972) for an attempt to apply this to leaf size). For the moment we are largely restricted in this and the next two chapters to description without being able to specify function.

It is not possible within the scope of this book to give full accounts of all Formations and emphasis is given to those in which there has been important recent ecological research which has advanced our understanding. *Malesian plant life* (Series I, vol. 2 of *Flora Malesiana*), which is currently in preparation, will give a fully referenced floristic description of the vegetation of Malesia region by region from the isthmus of Kra to the Torres Straits and the Bismarck archipelago, and will be an important compilation and reference work to fill out the accounts given here. A list of publications which include descriptions of vegetation of individual countries will be found in the Appendix (p. 239). The forest Formations described below have been widely recognized and described by numerous authors, and reference is given to the more important studies where additional details can be found.

The names used for the different Formations have varied greatly, and in some cases one feels there are almost as many names as authors. The nomenclature used here follows with only minor modification the scheme of Burtt Davy (1938) which is valuable in giving clear, concise descriptions of the Formations plus correlations, on a world-wide basis, with earlier schemes and especially with the important study of India and Burma by Champion (1936) (recently revised by Champion and Seth 1968). These correlations are followed in the present book. Burtt Davy's scheme has been widely used, for example, in the admirable analysis of the vegetation types of Malaya by Symington (1943). The recent UNESCO-sponsored scheme (Ellenberg and Mueller Dombois 1967; UNESCO 1973) is essentially the same as Burtt Davy's, but is fuller than is necessary for our present purpose and uses less familiar names, for instance, rain forests are called ombrophilous forests.

10.1. Tropical lowland evergreen rain forest
General description

For profile diagrams of tropical lowland evergreen rain forest see Figs 1.6, 2.1, 7.1, 15.3, 15.4, 15.18, and 15.19 and for photographs see Figs 10.1, 10.2, 10.3, 15.2, 15.10, 15.11, 15.12, and 15.13.

This is the most luxuriant of all plant communities and occurs under what are probably the finest dryland growing conditions found anywhere in the world. It is a lofty, dense, evergreen forest 45 m or more high, only occasionally less, characterized by the large number of trees which occur together. Gregarious dominants (consociations) are uncommon and usually two-thirds or more of the upper-canopy trees are of species individually, not contributing more than 1 per cent of the total number. This Formation is conventionally regarded as having three tree layers: the top layer of individual or grouped giant emergent trees, over a main stratum at about 24–36 m, and with smaller, shade-dwelling trees below that. Ground vegetation is often sparse, and mainly of small trees; herbs are uncommon.

FIG. 10.1. Looking into the crown of a giant emergent tree of *Shorea agami* in tropical lowland evergreen mixed dipterocarp rain forest (Kuala Belalong, Brunei).

Some of the biggest trees have clear boles of 30 m and reach 4·5 m girth, and may be deciduous or semi-deciduous without affecting the evergreen nature of the canopy as a whole. Boles are usually almost cylindrical. Buttresses are common. Cauliflory and ramiflory are common features. Pinnate leaves are frequent; laminae of mesophyll size predominate. Big woody climbers, mostly free-hanging, are frequent to abundant and sometimes also bole climbers. Shade and sun epiphytes are occasional to frequent. Bryophytes are rare.

All other rain-forest Formations differ from this in simpler structure, and in some cases in having fewer life-forms and fewer species.

Within the tropical lowland evergreen rain forest there is a great deal of variation from place to place, mostly gradual and not sharply bounded. The most gross variation is a major difference between the western and eastern blocks (cf. §1.1). The western block has family dominance of the Dipterocarpaceae in the emergent stratum, and these forests are of greater height than any other broad-leaf tropical rain forests in the world. Frequently, several genera of dipterocarps (especially *Anisoptera*, *Dipterocarpus*, *Dryobalanops*, *Parashorea*, and *Shorea*) and numerous species grow side by side. Malaya has 9 genera and about 160 species, and Borneo 10 genera and about 270 species, with probably more awaiting discovery in Kalimantan. No other tropical rain forests anywhere in the world show such abundance and diversity of a single family of big trees. And, out of a total 12 genera and about 470 species of Dipterocarpaceae in Asia, 10 genera and about 350 species are found on the Sunda shelf. A fuller discussion of variation within this Formation is reserved until Chapter 15.

123

FIG. 10.2. Inside tropical lowland evergreen rain forest on Kolombangara, Solomon Islands.

FIG. 10.3. A stand of the elegant undergrowth palm *Rhopaloblaste singaporensis* in tropical lowland evergreen rain forest: Johore, Malaya.

Habitat and Far East distribution

This is the predominant Formation of the tropical Far East and occurs throughout the two great perhumid blocks, that is, where water-stress is absent or only brief and intermittent (Fig. 3.1, p. 45), from sea-level to 1200 m elevation or less (see Chapter 16) and on dry-land sites where special soil conditions do not lead to its replacement by one of the Formations described below. In the north-west it reaches to about the latitude of the Malaysia–Thailand border (§12.3) but reappears as pockets in lower Burma, possibly on the Thailand–Cambodia border around Chantaburi, in south China, Hainan, and Taiwan, along the south wall of the Himalaya in upper Burma and Assam, in the Andamans, in a small area of south-west Ceylon, and in a narrow strip along the whole length of the western Ghats in peninsula India. In the east it reaches into Melanesia and possibly Micronesia, but not Australia.

World distribution

This Formation is found in parts of tropical America, especially in the region near the mouth of the Amazon River, on the foothills of the Andes and in the Guianas. It is probably absent from Africa.

General floristics

Tropical lowland evergreen rain forest has the greatest number of species of any rain-forest Formation. It is doubtful if any other vegetation type in the world exceeds it in this respect. This is partly due to the very large number of species of trees of all sizes, but also due to the extreme wealth of the other life-forms present. Besides the Dipterocarpaceae, the western block is characterized by a rich, ground-layer palm flora of shade- and moisture-loving genera, principally *Iguanura* and *Pinanga*, and to a lesser extent by *Areca*, *Nenga*, and *Rhopaloblaste* (Fig. 10.3).

It is estimated that in Sarawak and Brunei there are between 1800 and 2300 species of trees of diameter $\geqslant 0.1$ m in this Formation, compared with only 849 in heath forest and 234 in peat swamp forest (Anderson 1963; Brunig 1973).

Economics

The impact made by traditional cultures on this Formation varies through the region. In much of Malaya and Sumatra man has had little effect until recent times, the Malay peoples being essentially coastal and riverine and the aborigines sparsely distributed except in the malaria-free hills where, as in Borneo and New Guinea also, shifting cultivation has transformed huge tracts to secondary forest. Within the last century plantation agriculture has made extensive inroads notably in Sumatra and Malaya. The dipterocarp forests have become one of the world's major sources of hardwood timber, especially since the end of the Second World War, and exploitation is taking place at an ever-increasing pace. Exploitation has also begun in the less valuable forests of the eastern block. These aspects will be discussed in more detail in Part V.

Important references (tropical lowland evergreen rain forest)

Champion (1936, pp. 24–51), Champion and Seth (1968, pp. 57–81) as tropical wet evergreen forest; Burtt Davy (1938, pp. 28–33); Symington (1943, pp. xii–xvi) as lowland and hill dipterocarp forests; Beard (1944) as rain forest; Wang† (1961, pp. 155–64) as rain forest; Baur (1964a, pp. 76–7) as equatorial rain forest; Richardson (1966); and Hou, Chen, and Wang (1956) as tropical monsoon forest.†

† Referring to south China. This appears from Wang's account to be true evergreen rain forest; it is floristically rich with abundant epiphytes and climbers and is almost entirely evergreen. The total annual rainfall is 1300–3500 mm and the dry winters (rainfall < 100 mm) are presumably compensated by the low temperatures of those months.

10.2. Tropical semi-evergreen rain forest

General description

Semi-evergreen rain forest is a closed, high rain forest in which the biggest trees sometimes attain large size. It includes both evergreen and, in the top of the canopy, deciduous trees, in an intimate mixture but with a definite tendency to gregarious occurrence. Deciduous trees may comprise up to one-third of the taller trees, though not all are necessarily leafless at the same time. The number of species is high but less so than in evergreen rain forest. Buttresses continue to be frequent and occur in both evergreen and deciduous species. Bark tends to be thicker, and rougher and cauliflory and ramiflory rarer. The stature tends to be slightly less than evergreen rain forest and the emergents to occur as scattered individuals which are sometimes rare. Big woody climbers tend to be very abundant. Bamboos are present. Epiphytes are occasional to frequent and include many ferns and orchids.

Habitat and Far East distribution

Tropical semi-evergreen rain forest forms a belt between evergreen rain forest and moist deciduous forest. It occurs in places where there is regular annual water-stress of at least a few weeks' duration. This can be due to particular soil conditions as well as to the rainfall regime (Chapter 3), and a mosaic of the three Formations may occur at their mutual boundaries. It follows that no precise delimitation of the extent of this Formation from climatic data is possible. Tropical semi-evergreen rain forest is of very limited extent in the Far East compared to evergreen rain forest. Observations on its occurrence north of Malaya in the Kra isthmus are described in §12.3 (see also Fig. 12.2, p. 159). It forms the extension of rain forest into eastern Australia where detailed work has been done on its interdigitation with other Formations of suboptimal sites (Webb 1959). It also occurs marginally to evergreen rain forest in Indo-China, Thailand, Burma, the Andamans, Ceylon, and the Indian subcontinent. We have little detail on its extent within the Malay archipelago, though presumably it bounds the zone of monsoon climates which runs south from the Philippines to the Lesser Sunda Islands (Fig. 3.1, p. 45), and it occurs, possibly extensively, in New Guinea in rain-shadow areas.

World distribution

Semi-evergreen rain forest is probably the most extensive of all the tropical rain-forest Formations. It occupies much of the central part of the Amazon basin, occurs widely through the Caribbean area, and makes up some of the moister African rain forests. The dry season may extend for up to 4 months, and in some sites, for example, in parts of Amazonia (where edaphic water supply compensates for the seasonal lack of moisture), for even longer.

General floristics

In the Kra isthmus (§12.3) there is a slight decrease in total number of species of Dipterocarpaceae in the semi-evergreen rain forest compared to the evergreen rain forest to its south; some are characteristic of one Formation or the other. Characteristic species of semi-evergreen rain forest also occur in suitable sites within the evergreen rain forest. For example, a small island of semi-evergreen forest occurs surrounded by evergreen forest in central Malaya in Taman Negara in the intermontane valley of the upper Tembeling river, in the rain shadow of both monsoons and on riverine, alluvial soils. This forest is markedly deciduous in the regular early-year drought and contains much *Tetrameles nudiflora*, a species mainly of monsoon climates (van Steenis 1953; Whitmore 1973e). *Anisoptera oblonga*, a dipterocarp of the semi-evergreen and deciduous dipterocarp forests of continental Asia, also occurs in the upper Tembeling basin (Symington 1943; Wyatt-Smith 1963).

Economics

The forests of this Formation have been logged in the Kra isthmus and in eastern Australia, so that only small virgin fragments now remain. The most valuable commercial semi-evergreen rain forest stand is of a colline variant, namely, the broad-leaf—*Araucaria* forest of the Bulolo–Watut valleys in New Guinea, which will be described more fully in Chapter 14.

Because of the dry season, semi-evergreen rain forest and its secondary forest derivatives are more easily destroyed by fire than is evergreen rain forest, and therefore this Formation is more easily replaced by open grassland (principally of *Imperata cylindrica*, alang alang, cogon, kunai, or lalang), sometimes with scattered, fire-resistant trees. The extensive area around Bulolo in New Guinea is an example of such a replacement.

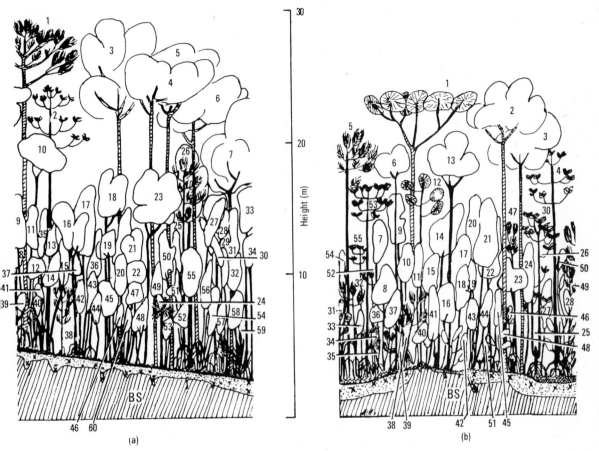

FIG. 10.4. Heath forest, Merurong plateau, Sarawak, overlying sandstones of the Belait formation (Brunig 1968, Fig. 4). (a) 750 m; (b) 735 m (see also Fig. 10.7). (a) 1, 25, 38, *Casuarina nobilis*; 2, *Ploiarium alternifolium*; 3, *Diospyros ferruginea*; 4, *Tristania obovata*; 5, *Parastemon urophyllus*; 6, 29, 33, 34, 40, 57, *Palaquium leiocarpum*; 7, *Castanopsis foxworthyi*; 8, 41, *Ardisia hosei*; 9, 16, *Ternstroemia magnifica*; 10, *Linociera evenia*; 11, 44, *Tetractomia montana*; 12, *Ixora havilandii*; 13, *Eugenia* cf. *myrtillus*; 14, 17, *E.* cf. *syzygioides*; 15, *Garcinia* sp.; 18, 35, 46, 47, 51, 60, *Palaquium rostratum*; 19, *Eugenia spicata*; 20, *Prunus arborea*; 21, *Ashtonia excelsa*; 22, *Eugenia corallina*; 23, *Elaeocarpus* sp.; 24, *Cyathea recommutata*; 26, *Shorea scabrida*; 27, *Tristania grandifolia*; 28, *Diospyros ferruginescens*; 30, *Garcinia bancana*; 31, *Litsea crassifolia*; 32, 37, 45, *Memecylon myrsinoides*; 36, 56, *Aromadendron nutans*; 39, *Campnosperma squamatum*; 42, *Eugenia oblata*; 43, *Gymnacranthera*

eugeniifolia var. *griffithii*; 48, *Santiria rubiginosa*; 49, *Elaeocarpus angustipes*; 50, *Eugenia myrtillus*; 52, *Vatica umbonata*; 53, *Ixonanthes beccarii*; 54, *Dialium laurinum*; 55, 58, Indet. (SAR 18780); 59, *Pandanus scandens*. (b) 1, 12, *Dacrydium elatum*; 2, 6, *Shorea coriacea*; 3, 10, 21, 51, *Parastemon urophyllus*; 4, 25, 26, 53, 55, *Ploiarium alternifolium*; 5, 32, 38, 39, 47, 49, *Casuarina nobilis*; 7, 11, 33, 50, *Garcinia rheedii*; 8, *Ctenolophon parvifolius*; 9, 36, *Ternstroemia* sp. nov.; 13, *Shorea scabrida*; 14, 15, *Eugenia subdecussata*; 16, *Canthium didymum*; 17, 37, *Palaquium rostratum*; 18, *Garcinia bancana*; 19, *Actinodaphne pruinosa* var.; 20, 23, *Tristania obovata*; 22, 45, *Palaquium leiocarpum*; 27, *Symplocos* sp. SAR 7327; 28, 30, 42, 48, *Rhodamnia cinerea*; 31, *Podocarpus neriifolius*; 34, 35, *Pinanga disticha*; 40, 43, *Ilex sclerophylloides*; 41, *Lithocarpus rassa*; 44, *Ternstroemia magnifica*; 46, *Sterculia rhoidifolia*; 54, *Eugenia* cf. *syzygioides*.

Fig. 10.5. Heath forest on a Quaternary terrace, Pueh, Sarawak. This forest is a relatively species-rich heath forest. The dark tree is *Palaquium leiocarpum*, to the left of it *Diospyros evena* and *Calophyllum* sp. The soil is a well-drained sandy-humus podzol over a clay subsoil.

Champion (1936, pp. 52–64), Champion and Seth (1968, pp. 81–103) as tropical semi-evergreen forest; Burtt Davy (1938, pp. 33–4); Beard (1944) as ever-green seasonal forest; Webb (1959) as mesophyll vine forest; Baur (1964a, pp. 78–81) as evergreen seasonal rain forest.

10.3. Heath forest

General description (Figs 10.4–10.13)

On soils derived from siliceous parent materials which are inherently poor in bases, and commonly coarsely textured and freely draining, evergreen rain forest is replaced by heath forest and this is strikingly different in flora, structure, and physiognomy.

> Even the botanically inexperienced casual wanderer will notice the change when he enters the kerangas forest from the lowland dipterocarp forest, not only because of the change in species (with which he may not be familiar) but also because of the striking difference in the structure, texture and whole colour of the forest. In the lowland dipterocarp forest the entire growing space is loosely and evenly filled with green foliage and the general impression is of a sombre but fresh green. In the kerangas forest the storey formed by large saplings and small poles predominates and forms a tidy and orderly but forbidding phalanx which is dense and often difficult to penetrate. The canopy is low, uniform, and usually densely closed with no trace of layering. Single emergents may occur and usually indicate extreme site conditions. Brown and reddish colours prevail in the foliage of the upper part of the canopy and the sun fills the forest with a rather bright light of reddish-brown hue which in spite of the dense canopy appears to be considerably brighter than the light in the lowland dipterocarp forest with its higher and more irregular vegetation. [Brunig, in Ashton (1971), writing on the heath forest at Bako National Park, Sarawak.]

To this description must be added that there are more trees with small leaves than in evergreen rain forest and many leaves are distinctly sclerophyllous (that is, thick and leathery), though precise statistics seem not to have been published; deciduous species are absent. The ground commonly has a bryophyte cover. Trees of large girth are rare; buttresses are smaller, but stilt roots commoner. Big woody climbers (including climbing palms) are rare, but slender, wiry, independent climbers frequent. Epiphytes are frequent and photophytes occur nearer the ground than in evergreen rain forest. Myrmecophytes are abundant, in the more open and stunted heath

FIG. 10.6.   Heath forest, Merurong plateau, Sarawak. Emergent *Shorea albida* over a dense pole forest.

FIG. 10.7. Heath forest with *Dacrydium* spp. Merurong plateau, Sarawak. This plot (no. 51.1) is depicted on the profile diagram, Fig. 10.4(b).

FIG. 10.8. *Hydnophytum* and *Myrmecodia*, epiphytic myrmeco-phytes with swollen stems, in the crown of *Dacrydium elatum* (needle leaves and behind it *Anisophyllea* sp. and *Cratoxylum glaucum* with shiny reflective leaves. Heath forest, Bako National Park, Sarawak.

forests, for example at Bako, and including there *Hydnophytum* and *Myrmecodia* (epiphytes with swollen stems—Fig. 10.8) and *Clerodendron fistulosum*. Amongst the herbs the insectivores *Drosera*, *Nepenthes*, and *Utricularia* may also be common in open places. On aerial photographs the flat canopy is highly distinctive due to its pale tone and its very fine texture which results from tree-crown structure and small leaf sizes (Fig. 10.9). Species with leaves held obliquely vertical may be common, for example, *Agrostistachys longifolia*, *Melanorrhoea beccarii*, *Ploiarium alternifolium* (Fig. 10.10), *Tristania* spp., and several Sapotaceae.

The streams draining areas of heath forest are tea-coloured by transmitted light, and opaque black by reflected light owing to the presence of colloidal humus. They are usually acid (pH < 5·5), and with a low oxygen content (Johnson 1967).

Variation in heath forest

In Bako National Park in west Sarawak, Brunig (1965) recognized a series of forest types (con-

FIG. 10.10. *Ploiarium alternifolium* in open degraded heath forest (Brunei).

FIG. 10.9. Interdigitation of heath forest (small crowns, even canopy) on waterlogged infertile soil and tropical lowland mixed dipterocarp rain forest (rough canopy) on deep clay–loam soil in the interior of Sarawak.

veniently summarized by Ashton (1971)) which he related to decreasing soil depth and increasing variability of water supply and which in turn can be correlated with variation in the degree of podzol development and in soil texture. Under the most favourable conditions there is considerable similarity with evergreen rain forest; dipterocarps are prominent among the larger trees, the canopy is 27–31 m high, and palms are common in the understorey. At the other extreme the canopy is only 4·5–9 m; *Cotylelobium burckii* is the only dipterocarp, patches of single tree species are frequent, palms are very rare, and there are abundant bryophytes on the ground and lower boles. The biomass of this extreme community is considerably less than of the others.

Similar variation occurs throughout Sarawak and elsewhere. For example, in Malaya the coastal heath forests are dominated by dipterocarps (*Shorea glauca* at Tanjong Hantu on the west and *S. materialis* on the east coast with subsidiary *Hopea semicuneata* throughout—Wyatt-Smith (1963); Robbins and Wyatt-Smith (1964)), and the small occurrences of the Formation inland on quartzite ridges are a low bushy scrub. And from Sarawak, forests have been described which are intermediate both floristically and structurally to evergreen dipterocarp rain forest (for example, Ashton 1971; Baillie 1972*a*).

Heath forest is easily degraded by felling and burning to an open savanna of shrubs and scattered trees over a sparse grass and sedge ground layer; this is often called *padang*, from the Malay word for an open space. The secondary succession is a slow-growing community of xeromorphic shrubs and trees, quite lacking those species of *Macaranga*,

Mallotus, etc., which are so characteristic of secondary evergreen rain forest (see Chapter 17). Trial planting on the east coast of Malaya showed that the possibility of re-establishing productive forest on such degraded sites is slight (Mitchell 1963).

Habitat and Far East distribution

Kerangas is an Iban term for land carrying forest which, when cleared, will not grow hill rice. The term *Heidewald* was used in the first major description of the Formation by Winkler (1914) for south Borneo and translated as heath forest by Richards (1936) in his important study of the Formation in north Sarawak. Heath forest develops mainly over coarse siliceous deposits which give rise to podzolized soils as has been described in the previous chapter (§9.6). The greatest extent of heath forest in the Far East is in Borneo where it occurs around much of the coastline on raised terraces of poorly consolidated coarse, sandy, marine, and riverine sediments left stranded by the fluctuating sea-level of the late Pleistocene. Similar but less extensive terraces which also bear or once bore heath forest occur along the south coasts of Thailand and Cambodia; in Malaya extensively down the east coast as parallel strips separated by swampy hollows (see §11.4) and on the west coast in north Perlis and near Satun (Setul) across the Thai border and also at Tanjong Hantu, Perak; on east-coast Sumatra; extensively on the islands of Bangka and Billiton; on the Karimatas, Anambas, and Natunas; and in south-west Ceylon.

Coastal heath forest has been extensively converted to secondary savanna (padang) maintained by grazing and burning; for example, on the whole of the east coast of Malaya only two small semi-natural stands of heath forest remain, at Jambu Bongkok and Menchali (Wyatt-Smith 1963).

In Borneo, lowland heath forest also occurs extensively inland, mainly on sandstone plateaux and cuesta formations. In Sarawak, Brunei, and Sabah it is usually on the dip slopes in hilly country, where sandstone beds lie close and parallel to the surface. The scarp slopes carry evergreen rain forest on less stable, continually rejuvenating soils. This catenary complex, frequently completed by the type of evergreen rain forest known as empran along rivers (§15.3), has been well described for Sarawak by Browne (1952), Brunig (1971), and Baillie (1970, 1972a), and by Fox (1973a) for the Kabili–Sepilok forest of east Sabah. It occurs on the Dulit range in north Sarawak, which was the site of the classic studies of Sarawak rain forest by Richards (1936, 1952). Fig. 10.11 shows an example from Brunei, where it can be seen that the most common species on each soil type are those found on the same soils elsewhere in the State. It is likely that the same catena will be shown to occur in Kalimantan. On flatter sites interdigitation also occurs, similarly correlated with differences in soil (see Figs 10.9 and 10.12).

In parts of Sarawak (and probably elsewhere in Borneo), mainly inland, podzolic soils become tem-

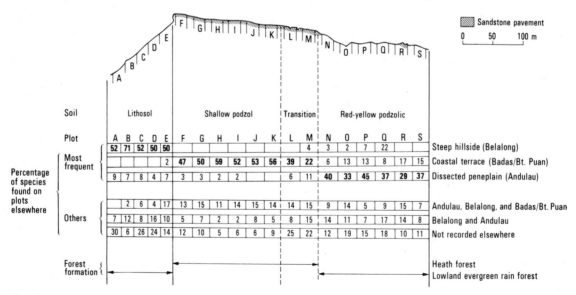

	Plot	A	B	C	D	E	F	G	H	I	J	K	L	M	N	O	P	Q	R	S	
Soil		Lithosol					Shallow podzol						Transition		Red-yellow podzolic						
Most frequent		52	71	52	50	50								4	3	2	7	22			Steep hillside (Belalong)
						2	47	50	59	52	53	56	39	22	6	13	13	8	17	15	Coastal terrace (Badas/Bt. Puan)
		9	7	8	4	7	3	3	2	2			6	11	40	33	45	37	29	37	Dissected peneplain (Andulau)
Others			2	6	4	17	13	15	11	14	15	14	14	15	9	14	5	9	15	7	Andulau, Belalong, and Badas/Bt. Puan
		7	12	8	16	10	5	7	2	2	8	5	8	15	14	11	7	17	14	8	Belalong and Andulau
		30	6	26	24	14	12	10	5	6	6	9	25	22	12	19	15	18	10	11	Not recorded elsewhere

Percentage of species found on plots elsewhere

Forest formation: Heath forest / Lowland evergreen rain forest

Sandstone pavement

0   50   100 m

FIG. 10.11. Forest Formation and soil type at Bukit Patoi, Brunei. Plots of 0·042 ha. All trees ≥ 50 mm girth enumerated. (Based on Ashton 1964, Fig. 59.)

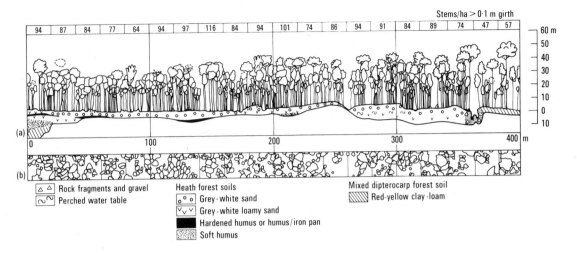

Stems/ha > 0·1 m girth

| 94 | 87 | 84 | 77 | 64 | 94 | 97 | 116 | 84 | 94 | 101 | 74 | 86 | 94 | 91 | 84 | 89 | 74 | 47 | 57 |

Rock fragments and gravel
Perched water table

Heath forest soils
Grey-white sand
Grey-white loamy sand
Hardened humus or humus/iron pan
Soft humus

Mixed dipterocarp forest soil
Red-yellow clay-loam

FIG. 10.12. Transect through the Sabal forest, Sarawak, developed over sandstone. (a) In profile; (b) in plan view from above. Heath forest (kerangas and kerapah) over sandy soil, dense and with small crowns. Evergreen mixed dipterocarp rain forest (extreme right) over clay–loam soil, less dense with big crowns. (After Brunig, in preparation.)

porarily, to more or less permanently, waterlogged because of imperfect subsoil drainage or because the hard pan in the soil forms an impermeable layer. The forest is here known as *kerapah*, an Iban term denoting swampy conditions. In structure and physiognomy this is heath forest, though some species are particularly common in these sites. The summit plateau of Gunung Panti in south Malaya carries heath forest over a waterlogged soil developed over sandstone, which is perhaps comparable to kerapah forest, otherwise there is no record of kerapah from outside Borneo. It is equally curious that extensive stands of inland heath forest have also not been recorded elsewhere. In Malaya, for example, the extensive outcrops of siliceous sedimentary rock in the lowlands east of the Main Range carry evergreen rain forest. Hills along the east coast from the Gunung Besar massif northwards to south Trengganu have dense stands of the fan palm *Livistona saribus* which Wyatt-Smith (1963) believed to be associated with the drying effect of strong winds plus poor, shallow soils. Some quartz dykes and quartzite ridges in Malaya carry a low stunted heath forest (Wyatt-Smith 1963); they only cover a tiny area; comparable sites and forests have been described in Brunei (Ashton 1964).

Lowland heath forest has many features in common with upper montane rain forest (partly on sandstone in Malaya as well as Borneo); description is deferred until the discussion of mountain rain forests in Chapter 16.

Small areas of inland heath forest are reported from Bangka, Billiton, central Celebes, and New Guinea (van Steenis 1957). In the area of the Star Mountains in central New Guinea they are all on river terraces, some of which have impeded drainage, and some of which carry *Agathis labillardierei* forest (Reynders 1964*b*). The apparent absence of extensive areas of inland heath forest from the huge land mass of New Guinea serves, if it is confirmed by more thorough studies, to emphasize even further the uniqueness of Borneo in this respect.

World distribution

Heath forests are widespread in the Amazon basin, as small pockets in the evergreen and semi-evergreen rain forest, developed on both quartzite and granite. They are known as carrascos or humirizal (where dominated by the family Humiriaceae) or as campinas where degraded by fire to open savanna (for a general account see Aubréville (1961)). The main tributary of the Amazon, the Rio Negro, is black because it drains an extensive area of heath forest. Heath forests also occur in the Guianas where the best-known example is a type dominated by wallaba (the legume *Eperua falcata*) (Richards 1952). The only heath forests known in Africa occupy a small area in Gabon, on coastal sands (Richards (1961).

General floristics

There are substantial differences in flora between the various primary and secondary heath forest types, which cannot be described fully here (see general

133

references below, especially for Borneo and Malaya).

Concerning heath forest in general, Brunig (1973) estimated that in total there are 849 species of tree (428 genera) in the heath forests of Sarawak and Brunei; of this total, 220 species also occur in lowland dipterocarp rain forest. For example, many of the Dipterocarpaceae of the Sarawak heath forest are found in evergreen rain forest, and these are found mainly in the most favourable heath-forest sites. Heavy-wooded species are prominent, especially of *Shorea* (notably *S. coriacea* and *S. havilandii*) and *Hopea. Cotylelobium* species (*C. burckii*, *C. melanoxylum*) extend through to less favourable sites than other dipterocarps. There are also 146 species common to both heath forest and peat swamp forest (Brunig 1973), including the big timber trees *Shorea albida*, *S. pachyphylla*, *S. scabrida*, *Dryobalanops rappa*, and *Cratoxylum arborescens*. There is no species known which occurs both in peat swamp forest and lowland dipterocarp rain forest but not also in heath forest. Heath forest also has some species in common with upper montane rain forest, details will be given in Chapter 16. *Casuarina* * *nobilis*† (Fig. 10.13), widespread in heath forest, is abundant in the Lawas peat swamp forest (Fig. 14.3, p. 171) and, together with other heath forest species, also on the summits of limestone hills.

Myrtaceae are a prominent family in heath forest, especially *Tristania* * but also *Eugenia* and *Whiteodendron moultonianum* (Borneo) and *Baeckia* * *frutescens*. The last is found in open shrub communities fairly well protected from fire, together with *Alstonia spatulata*, *Cratoxylum cochinchinense*, *Dacrydium* spp., *Dillenia suffruticosa*, *Ilex cymosa*, *Licania splendens*, *Myrica esculenta*, *Pittosporum* * *ferrugineum*, *Podocarpus polystachys*, *Rhodamnia cinerea*, *Styphelia* * *malayana*, *Vaccinium bracteatum*, and *Cycas rumphii* amongst others. In areas frequently burnt, *Anacardium occidentale* (east-coast Malaya, introduced), *Fagraea fragrans*, *Melaleuca* * *kajuputi* (*leucadendron*), *Melastoma malabathricum*, *Morinda citrifolia*, *Ploiarium alternifolium* (Fig. 10.10), *Rhodo-*

† This species name cannot validly be used without a short latin description and citation of a type collection as follows: Arbor. Ramuli dense fasciculati internodi circa 1 cm longis. Strobili feminei 2 cm diametri, bracteolis valde 2–3 mm exsertis. Holotypus (K) Cuadra A3292, Sepitang, Sabah.

FIG. 10.13. *Casuarina nobilis* regrowth on the margin of fire-induced grassland and heath forest (Brunei).

myrtus tomentosa, and *Vitex pubescens* are commonest (Wyatt-Smith 1963). *Ploiarium* favours periodically wet sites, and because it coppices vigorously has become gregarious in places, such as around Kuching, where the scrub is repeatedly cut for firewood and poles (Browne 1955; Brunig 1965, 1969a).

The striking difference in flora of heath forest from lowland evergreen rain forest was found to be as equally marked amongst the mosses as the trees on Mt. Dulit, Sarawak (Herzog 1950).

A much-commented-on feature of the heath-forest flora is the abundance of genera with an Australian centre of distribution. To the trees and shrubs of this affinity (marked * above) can be added the sedges *Cladium* and *Gahnia,* and also *Dianella* (Liliaceae).

Economics

Heath forest, if carefully managed, can provide a continuing source of timber. Selective felling has been practised at Menchali in Malaya since early this century and is recommended for the remaining small areas on the east coast of Malaya (Beveridge 1953; Wyatt-Smith 1963).

Re-establishment after clear-felling and burning might be possible if care is taken and has been suggested for Sarawak to produce crops for domestic timber, poles, and firewood. *Casuarina nobilis* (Fig. 10.13) is a good species for these purposes.

Agathis borneensis (Chapter 14, Fig. 14.5, p. 174) which grows in some Bornean forests (including 30 000 ha in south Kalimantan (Manaputty 1955)) is a valuable timber species. Little work has yet been done on re-establishment after felling the virgin stands but Brunei hopes to re-establish *Agathis* on 4000 ha by about 1980.

Heath-forest soils are too infertile and acidic for traditional agriculture and quickly become degraded. Areas which have been cultivated are seen today as open sandy savannas, as along the Malayan east coast. These savannas, and the patches of trees and forest with which they are interspersed, have a recreational value there, as also at the Bako National Park, which will be increasingly appreciated as man becomes ever more an urban animal in the decades ahead. The cultivation of pineapples is a successful venture on heath-forest soils around Kuching.

Important general references (heath forest)

Heath forest is not included in the Formation schemes of Champion and Burtt Davy. Symington (1943, pp. xix and xxii), as heath-forest and coastal padang Formation; Richards (1952, esp. pp. 244–7); Browne (1952), as kerangas lands (1955, esp. pp.

10–12); van Steenis (1957), as siliceous vegetation; Wyatt-Smith (1963, pp. 7/17–19 and Chapter 13) also including his 'vegetation of quartz dykes, quartzite ridges and other sterile habitats with severe drainage or lacking available moisture' (1963, pp. 7/36–7); Baur (1964a, pp. 85–6), as xeromorphic rain forest; Brunig (1965), a full account for Bako National Park; Brunig (in press), an exhaustive and definitive monograph for Sarawak and Brunei, in both as kerangas and kerapah; Ashton (1971), an excellent general description of structure and floristics of the various kinds of forest found at Bako; Fox (1973a), Sepilok–Kabili forest, Sabah.

Eco-physiological studies in heath forest

Botanists have for long taken an interest in attempting to elucidate the causes of the very curious structure and the xeromorphic physiognomy of heath forest. Because the Formation is restricted to soils developed on siliceous deposits which are podzolized to a varying degree, the question to be answered is whether periodic water deficiency or an unusually low supply of mineral nutrients is the cause. Brunig (1970, 1971) has made the most comprehensive study of this subject and concludes that several features of heath forest are all adaptations to survival of the community in conditions of periodic drought. This is contrary to the view of Richards (1952, p. 244) who, on the basis of much less evidence, thought mineral deficiency of the very acid soils the more likely cause.

Certain basic physiological properties of plants must be considered briefly before Brunig's findings can be discussed. In general, respiration and photosynthesis both increase with temperature up to about

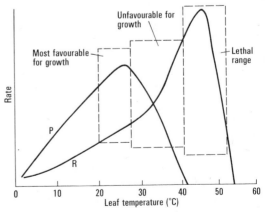

FIG. 10.14. Variation of photosynthesis (*P*) and respiration (*R*) rates with temperature. (After Grubb 1974.)

25 °C for many species (Fig. 10.14). At such temperatures conditions are favourable for growth, and net photosynthesis occurs. At higher temperatures photosynthesis declines while respiration rises sharply, conditions which are unfavourable for growth. Finally, temperatures of over about 40 °C are lethal for most species because the tissues are irreversibly damaged.†

Leaves are cooled by three processes: namely, by convection, by the latent heat absorbed by the evaporation of water transpired, and by re-radiation of incident energy. In many species these processes are of decreasing importance in this order.

Drought periods represent a serious danger to plants, in that the water supply for transpirational cooling is then cut off. We have shown in Chapter 3 that periodic droughts occur in even the perhumid parts of the Far East. In addition it was shown how the amount of water available to plants depends also on the storage capacity of the soil. Heath-forest soils are mostly porous, coarse, and freely drained. Roots do not penetrate the hard podzol pan. It follows that the total soil volume available to plants is less than in soils with no pan. Hence the available-water-storage capacity of heath-forest soils is less than in others, and water shortage is more likely to occur. It is noteworthy that the heath forest at Bako is coastal, and that it has now been clearly demonstrated that droughts are more frequent in Sarawak at the coast than inland (§3.4).

Brunig demonstrated that several of the striking structural and physiognomic features of heath forest are likely either to minimize water loss, thereby conserving the water available to the forest, or to reduce the heat load on the leaves, which could be vital to survival in drought periods.

1. Brunig pointed out that there is a decrease in roughness of the canopy surface from evergreen rain forest to heath forest, and the roughest canopy is in the riverine variant of rain forest known as empran (§15.3), which occurs on deep, permanently moist soils with moving ground water. These differences are conspicuous from the air (Fig. 10.9). Reduced canopy roughness has two effects. First, there is a reduction in the amount of incident radiation intercepted, greatest at low elevations of the sun and nil when the sun is overhead. Secondly, the aerodynamic roughness of the canopy decreases and consequently so does the turbulence from free and forced convection. The effects of this are manifold and complex, but important amongst them, at the wind speeds which prevail in Sarawak, is a tendency to decrease the rate at which water vapour is lost from the canopy.

2. Mean leaf size in heath forest is less than in evergreen rain forest, and it is noticeable that within heath forest some species show leaf-size reduction from relatively mesic and fertile sites to less favourable ones. It can be shown that air flow is greater round a small leaf, which therefore cools better by convection and, other things being equal, will therefore have a lower temperature excess above that of the surrounding air than a broader leaf. In the extreme case (needle-leaves) the temperature excess will be very small. The significance of this enhanced convectional cooling of small leaves is that they can limit their temperature excess with less transpirational cooling than broader ones, that is, in conditions when water is not freely available they use less water to keep cool.

3. Steeply inclined leaves and twigs are frequent in heath forest and most so on the driest sites. These features reduce the amount of incident radiation per unit leaf area, especially around noon when the sun is overhead, and hence the heat load on the leaves. The crown shape of *Casuarina* (Fig. 10.13) and *Dacrydium* (Fig. 10.8) is determined by the inclined twigs with, in the latter genus, inclined needle leaves too. Extending the argument to other crown shapes, Brunig concluded that, on the drier sites, types of crown geometry dominate whose effect on energy dissipation has advantages for cooling under conditions of water-stress and high incident radiation.†

4. Heath forest appears pale in tone on aerial photographs owing to its high reflectance of radiation (the so-called short-wave albedo). Gregarious species with particularly high albedo are *Shorea albida*, *Vatica brunigii*, and *Xylopia coriifolia*, which all appear grey. Other common species have glistening leaves and appear (dark) reddish-green to the eye (Fig. 10.8), most markedly *Melanorrhoea inappendiculata*, *Tristania stellata*, and *Whiteodendron moultonianum*. These reflective devices also serve to minimize the heat load on the foliage.

---

† These general relationships between respiration and photosynthesis are clearly also of critical importance in the survival and growth of seedlings and saplings in the forest (see §6.5).

† For a very detailed analysis on the interactions of tree-crown structure, light, temperature, and water relations see Hadfield (1974*a,b*, 1975), on tea in Assam.

FIG. 10.15. Bukit Krian, a limestone hill at Bau, Sarawak. The summit forest has been burned off at some time in the past and shows stunted regrowth. The vertical walls are the habitat of an endemic *Boea* sp.

There are then, in heath forest, a number of features of structure and physiognomy that can be considered to be adaptations to minimize the effect of periodic water-stress, which occurs at heath-forest sites more than at sites occupied by other lowland forest Formations.

The interrelationship between a forest and its environment is, however, exceedingly complex. For instance, for as long as there is ample water, bright conditions increase photosynthesis. It follows that dry spells of weather which are associated with clear skies and high incident radiation either increase or decrease primary production depending on water availability, that is, on site conditions. Brunig's conclusions are only tentative, and not all adaptations apply to all sites. They give a new insight into forest structure and physiognomy, and clearly it would be of the greatest interest to extend this kind of observation, especially by measuring the water and heat budgets of selected forests.

Despite Brunig's penetrating analyses certain features of heath forest do point to mineral deficiency, as he himself suggested:

1. The biomass of heath forest is lower than that of evergreen rain forest, and lowest on the most extreme sites. Three heath forests in Sarawak on progressively shallower humic podzols had standing biomass of 1000 tonne/ha, 750 tonne/ha, and less than 200 tonne/ha. This may be because of longer drought periods (see above) during which growth is suspended or it may be due to a smaller total amount of mineral(s).

2. As was mentioned above, heath forest is very easily degraded to a low scrub if burned or cultivated. By contrast, Browne (1952) described an area near Kuching that was simply clear-felled and then abandoned during the war to improve access to an airfield, which regrew as a fine pole forest, and the Menchali forest in Malaya has been selectively logged since early this century.

3. Plants with supplementary means of mineral nutrition are common, namely, myrmecophytes and insectivorous plants. *Casuarina nobilis*, an abundant species in the Sarawak heath forest, has (as do all Casuarinaceae) nodules containing nitrogen-fixing bacteria on its roots. It is not yet known, however, if mycorrhizas play a more important role in heath forest than elsewhere.

4. Sclerophylls have been shown to be related to shortage of nitrogen and phosphorus, especially from work in Australia (Beadle 1853, 1954, 1962, 1966). Sclerophylls in heath forest include several genera with an Australian centre of distribution.

It is tempting to suggest that the small-leaved aspect of heath forest might in part at least have a 'nutritional explanation'.

We have, as yet, no data on the rates of production or mineral-cycling in heath forest; indeed there is very little information for any forest Formation. The impression is that these rates are lower than in more mesic forests; this impression is enhanced by the virtual absence of deciduous species.

It will be quite clear to the reader of the preceding discussion that the importance of the various facets of water relations and mineral nutrition in heath forest will only be resolved by further study. It is probable that in different sites of this wide-ranging Formation a different balance of factors obtains. As in the case of mountain forests to be described in Chapter 16 and the forests of the centre of some Sarawak peat swamps (§11.3) both oligotrophy and drought appear to have similar effects on forest structure and physiognomy, and at present these effects can only be disentangled by a painstaking investigation of particular, well-chosen examples. In conclusion, it is pertinent to note that on the eastern seaboard of Australia, where rain forest and sclerophyllous (eucalypt) forests interdigitate, the former occupy the more fertile sites and those less liable to extreme water-stress (Webb 1965, 1968; Tracey 1969).

10.4. Forest over limestone

Craggy limestone hills (Fig. 10.15) form a striking part of the landscape in many parts of the tropical Far East, as was described in §9.7. They are apparently absent from the humid tropics of Africa and are rare in Latin America except the Caribbean region. The total extent of limestone is tiny and mainly at low elevations. This brief account is intended to draw attention to the literature and to make comparisons with other habitats.

Limestone landscapes (karst) whether of the tower (*Karstkegel*) or cockpit kind provide a diversity of habitats and soils which have been fully analysed by Anderson (1965).

1. The alluvial soils at the base of limestone hills, although derived from other rocks, are under the influence of run-off water and erosion from the limestone. In Sarawak the lowland evergreen rain forest of these sites has several characteristic species, notably *Eusideroxylon malagangai*, *Gonystylus nervosus*, and *Mammea calciphila*, and so does its nearby riparian variant. In Malaya vegetable cultivations often extend right up to the

foot of limestone cliffs on these more base-rich, fertile soils.

2. The base of cliffs and ravines in the hills, sometimes with small scree slopes of limestone boulders, have a number of distinctive species. *Cleidion spiciflorum* is abundant in Malaya, as are the palms *Arenga westerhoutii* and *Caryota mitis*. The nature of this habitat in Sarawak is complicated because ravines have formed along igneous intrusions. It is here and in deep soil pockets on ledges and in sink holes that most of the few Dipterocarpaceae associated with limestone occur; in Malaya mainly *Hopea helferi*, *H. latifolia*, *Shorea sericeiflora*, and *Vatica cinerea*, and in Sarawak mainly *Dipterocarpus caudiferus*, *Hopea andersonii* spp. *andersonii*, *H. argentea*, *H. dasyrrachis*, *Shorea guiso*, *S. isoptera*, and *S. pauciflora*.

3. The limestone slopes have a dense, irregular forest with trees clinging precariously, their roots penetrating to great depths in crevices. Sheer cliffs bear scattered shrubs and a characteristic herb flora, amongst which Gesneriaceae (*Boea*, *Chirita*, *Monophyllaea*, *Paraboea*) are prominent, many of which resist dry periods by reversible desiccation of the tissues (poikilohydry: see Chapter 3).

4. The summits of the limestone hills provide a peculiar habitat. There is a deep mat of peat-like humus, held together by tree roots and anchored by them to the limestone pinnacles underneath. This soil is acidic (pH ranges to 4·5), and in Sarawak the low forest it supports has affinities with lowland heath forest. *Casuarina nobilis* is the most prominent dominant, and other species also more typical of heath forest are *Agrostistachys longifolia*, *Cotylelobium malayanum*, *Palaquium leiocarpum*, *Shorea coriacea*, *S. havilandii*, *S. multiflora*, *Tristania obovata*, and *Vatica brunigii*. There are also several shrubby *Rhododendron* and *Vaccinium* species, both acidophilous genera, and in addition *Nepenthes albomarginata* is found. In Papua, *Casuarina papuana* clothes pinnacles of karst limestone (Paijmans 1969). *Agathis labillardierei* has been reported abundant, and in places dominant, in forest on the limestone hills of Waigeo Island off north-west New Guinea (van Royen 1963), and one may surmise that it is on deep, acid peat. This habitat resembles heath forest in both its deficiency in plant nutrients and also in its free draining status, which implies that periodic water-stress most probably occurs.

Limestone is known to occur at high elevations in New Guinea (Reynders 1964*b*), and also in the

FIG. 10.16. Limestone pinnacles at 1200 m (Gunung Api, Sarawak).

Gunung Mulu National Park in Sarawak on Gunung Api (Fig. 10.16) and Gunung Benarat, both of which rise to over 1200 m. In Sarawak the montane limestone habitats are similar to those of lower elevation. On the less precipitous pinnacles there is about 0·6 m of peat and a low forest which has distinct similarity to that on the adjacent sandstone mountain Gunung Mulu: the conifers *Dacrydium beccarii* and *Phyllocladus hypophyllus* are frequent, and in the more open areas *Myrica esculenta* is common. On exposed limestone calcicolous, plants such as *Boea*, *Impatiens*, and *Cyrtandra oblongifolia* occur. As on lowland limestone summits, the similarity with forest over sandstone suggests response to the same factors: oligotrophy and/or periodic water-stress.

The forest of recently emerged, pericoastal coral limestone platforms apparently differs little from adjacent lowland evergreen rain forest. For example, in the Solomons, *Celtis* spp. and *Pimelodendron amboinicum* are common in this habitat and also on soils derived from basic andesite, which suggests that they are basicolous rather than calcicolous species (Whitmore 1969*a*). *Pometia pinnata* is abundant here as well as in other habitats (Whitmore 1966*a*). In several localities pure stands of *Calophyllum kajewskii* have been reported, on platforms still submerged by the highest spring tides, yet the trees of this highly exacting environment show no morphological differ-

139

ences from others of the same species growing inland on ultisols.

In New Guinea lower montane beech (*Nothofagus*) forest, a community of ridges, extends below the lower montane zone on limestone karst pinnacles and doline rims (Robbins and Pullen 1965).

Most of the habitats of limestone hills are drier than those in surrounding country (though dolines and ravines may be highly humid) and also the mineral nutrient supply must often be extremely deficient. No investigations have yet been made on the relative importance of these habitat factors or into the details of mineral deficiency. We do not yet know, for example, if phosphorus is limiting or if calcicolous species are aluminium-sensitive as are some European calcicoles; the soils of limestone of the tropical Far East are exceptional amongst others in the region in not being rich in aluminium. Certainly, limestone has a large number of endemic species. The fullest investigation has been for Malaya where limestone, in the form of tower karst, occupies about 260 km²— about 0·2 per cent of the land area (Henderson 1939). Of 747 species recorded on limestone 195 (about 26 per cent) are in Malaya confined to it, and of these about 130 (67 per cent) are endemic to the country. Of those found on limestone but not confined to it 80–100 species are cremnophytes (crevice plants) rather than calcicoles; they always inhabit rocky sites but appear indifferent to the nature of the rock upon which they grow. Some 50 of the species confined to limestone in Malaya are species of monsoon Asia to the north, and most of these are restricted to the extensive limestone out-crops of the far north-west in Perlis, Kedah, and the Langkawi Islands. It would appear that they pene-trate south into the perhumid tropical zone only in the periodically dry limestone habitats where alone they can compete successfully (cf. Chapter 12). The limestone hills of Malaya also harbour two endemic monotypic genera, the palms *Liberbaileya gracilis* and *Maxburretia rupicola*, each of which is confined to a few adjacent outcrops. There is a third related monotypic palm genus, as yet undescribed, on lime-stone in south Thailand, west of Surat Thani. These three palms are closely related to each other and to *Rhapis* of continental east Asia, and are of consider-able interest to students of evolution in the family (Whitmore 1970, 1971a, 1973b).

Forest on limestone has no commercial value, though some very showy herbs (especially Balsa-minaceae, Begoniaceae, and Gesneriaceae) deserve greater attention from horticulturists; the forest is sometimes destroyed by deliberate burning by tin

and gold prospectors in Malaya and Sarawak. The forest on the high limestone mountains Api and Benarat in Sarawak is occasionally damaged by fire which according to local observations is started by lightning (*api* = fire). After fire the ground may remain bare for many years before a slow succession of bryophytes and ferns re-establishes, and then, in litter and soil pockets, a shrub flora (see Anderson (1965) for details). Earliest man probably made greater use of limestone areas, living in caves; both Java and Sarawak (Niah) have extensive fossil and subfossil remains.

Important references (forest over limestone)

Malaya: Henderson (1939); Symington (1943); Wyatt-Smith (1963, Chapter III/7). Sarawak: Anderson (1965).

10.5 Forest over ultrabasic rocks

Along the north coast of Waigeo Island and of New Guinea to its east (for example, along the northern foothills of the Cycloop mountains) is a belt of low shrubby vegetation, open in places and sharply bounded against tall lowland evergreen rain forest. This vegetation coincides exactly with red–purple soils derived from ultrabasic rocks. Common woody species are *Alphitonia* sp., *Dillenia alata*, *Myrtella beccarii*, and *Styphelia abnormis* (van Royen 1963).

In the Solomons the most distinctive lowland forest Formation is that found over ultrabasic rocks. It is sharply demarcated from adjoining forest and over large areas is dominated by *Casuarina papuana* or *Dillenia crenata*. Geologists have mapped the extent of the ultrabasics from aerial photographs, on which this forest Formation is easy to see. Only four species are known which are restricted to ultrabasics in the Solomons: *Gulubia hombronii* (a palm), *Myrtella beccarii*, *Pandanus lamprocephalus*, and a *Xanthostemon* sp. (Whitmore 1969a). In both New Guinea and the Solomons, *Gleichenia* (s.l.) and *Lyco-podium cernuum* form a dense ground cover in clearings and there is much bare, heavily eroded soil.

In west Malesia the forest over ultrabasic rocks is often much less distinctive. Ultrabasic rocks near Raub, east of the main range in Malaya, carry a high forest, with the structure and physiognomy of lowland evergreen rain forest (Whitmore), and the same is true of the ultrabasic hill north-east of Ranau in Sabah at the foot of Mt. Kinabalu, where the tallest tree, in a forest which included several dipterocarps, was 54 m and a deep soil had developed (Fox and Tan 1971). Meijer (1965) noted that the dipterocarp species found over lowland ultrabasics in

Sabah (*Shorea andulensis, S. kunstleri, S. laxa, S. venulosa, Dipterocarpus geniculatus,* and *D. lowii*) were quite different from those of different adjacent rocks, but that the same species occur in Brunei and Sarawak over other soil parent materials. A similar observation was made by Ashton (1964). Elsewhere in the lowlands of Sabah, especially on shallow soils, a low forest tending to heath forest in structure and physiognomy has been recorded, and pure stands of *Casuarina nobilis* occur on islands in Darvel Bay, on Malawali, and on Bangi Island (Fox 1972).

Although near Ranau forests on ultrabasic do not differ in structure or physiognomy from contiguous forests on different rock this is not the case nearby higher on the slopes of Mt. Kinabalu. For example, the trail to the summit enters an area of ultrabasic rocks at about 2400 m from an area of sandstone, and there is a sudden decrease in canopy height. Many species reach their lowest elevation on the mountain here, prominent among them *Leptospermum recurvum* and *Rhododendron ericoides*; but only *Dacrydium gibbsiae*, which is codominant with the *Leptospermum,* and the fern *Schizaea fistulosa* are restricted to this rock, the others extending on to the granodiorite above it (Meijer 1965, 1971). A similar sharp change occurs on the east ridge of Mt. Kinabalu at about the same elevation (Poore).

Soil–vegetation relations of ultrabasic areas, which have scarcely been studied, are briefly described in §9.8.

10.6. Beach vegetation

There are two kinds of beach vegetation (van Steenis 1957, 1961c). Along accreting coasts, where new sand is being continuously deposited, the initial stage of beach vegetation is the pes caprae association, a low herbaceous plant cover over a broad sand strand, of which most members are creeping plants with long, rooting stolons or stems. Typical species are: *Canavalia microcarpa, Cyperus pedunculatus, C. stoloniferus, Euphorbia atoto, Fimbristylis sericea, Ipomoea gracilis, I. pes caprae, Ischaemum muticum, Launaea sarmentosa, Lepturus repens, Spinifex littoreus, Thuarea involuta, Triumfetta repens,* and *Vigna marina.* Most of these species are confined almost or entirely to this habitat and are pantropical in distribution; some are rare in Malesia. Minor differences in composition reflect the origin of the sand, which may be from quartz, andesite (blackish in colour), or derived from coral and therefore calcareous.

Seedlings of beach trees, including coconuts from water-borne fruits, are found in the older part of the association, notably of the wind-dispersed *Casuarina equisetifolia,* itself a pioneer species which forms pure stands and is unable to regenerate on the litter carpet of its dead, fallen photosynthetic twigs.

On the beach wall, that is, the low (0.5–1 m) ridge at the inland margin of the sand beach, the second vegetation type, the *Barringtonia* association, is found.† On abrading coasts, where off-shore sea conditions ensure that no sand is being accumulated or that sand is being removed, this association is found without the pes caprae carpet in front, instead the narrow beach is inundated each flood-tide, and is shaded by the low-set, wide-branched crowns of trees of this association, commonly with their trunks lying out over the beach, and with the lowest branches often damaged by sea-water. As erosion continues trees are uprooted and crash down seaward. The width of this seaward forest fringe is seldom more than 25–50 m, and on rocky, steep shores it is confined to a very narrow strip. Inland it merges with lowland rain forest. Its composition is very uniform throughout Malesia, and many species extend from the coast of Africa through Malesia far into the Pacific (the so-called 'Indo–Pacific strand flora'); some indeed are pantropical. It is found in both perhumid and seasonally dry regions. Many species have seeds or fruits adapted to water-dispersal. Locally one or other species may become dominant, but a mixed association is more usual. The trees are sometimes loaded with epiphytes, among which are many ferns and orchids. Typical species are: *Ardisia elliptica, Barringtonia asiatica, Caesalpinia bonduc, Calophyllum inophyllum, Casuarina equisetifolia, Cocos nucifera, Colubrina asiatica, Crinum asiaticum, Cycas rumphii, Desmodium umbellatum, Dodonaea viscosa, Erythrina variegata, Guettarda speciosa, Heritiera littoralis, Hernandia nymphaeifolia (peltata), Hibiscus tiliaceus, Mammea odoratus, Maranthes corymbosa, Messerschmidia argentea, Morinda citrifolia, Pandanus bidur, P. tectorius, Pluchea indica, Pongamia pinnata, Premna corymbosa, Scaevola taccada, Sophora tomentosa, Tacca leontopetaloides, Terminalia catappa, Thespesia populnea,* and *Wedelia biflora.*

On small, low, coral islands the *Barringtonia* association may form the principal forest type. *Pisonia grandis* is especially common on small off-shore islets and is absent from the beach forest of the large islands; this has been ascribed to its needing guano, so that its occurrence is restricted to that of off-shore bird colonies (Airy Shaw 1953).

† This falls within the tropical littoral woodland Formation of Burtt Davy (1938)—cf. Symington (1943, p. xvii).

Tropical rain forests of the Far East

The *Barringtonia* association has been severely damaged over much of the Far East, but still survives extensively on the islands of the western Pacific. It is usually replaced by planted coconut groves under which are either grasses (*Ischaemum muticum, Thuarea involuta,* and *Zoysia matrella*) or ferns, often the common *Nephrolepis biserrata.*

There is no sharp demarcation between beach vegetation of sandy and rocky coasts, mangrove forest of muddy coasts, and brackish-water forests, because intermediate habitats occur and, furthermore, many coastlines are unstable and the nature of deposition subject to change. A few species are found in more than one vegetation type, notably *Hibiscus tiliaceus,* and, on the Sunda shelf, the big, clump-forming nibong palm *Oncosperma tigillarium.*

11 Forest Formations: (2) the wet-land rain forests

THERE ARE three main kinds of swamp forest. Mangrove forest is under the influence of sea-water; the other two Formations are fresh-water swamp forest and peat swamp forest. Fresh-water swamps receive water from streams and rivers which *ipso facto* has a certain amount of dissolved minerals. Peat swamps receive moisture solely from rainfall which only contains very much smaller amounts of dissolved minerals.

11.1. Mangrove forest

This essentially tropical type of vegetation has been very fully described in several excellent publications to which, for lack of space here, the reader is referred. Mangrove forest has long attracted the attention of scientists because of its habitat (silt-rich, saline, coastal waters), and the curious structures of many of its species (flying buttresses, stilt roots, pneumatophores, viviparous reproduction). It was the first forest Formation to be brought under intensive silvicultural management in Malaya, as a valuable source of firewood, charcoal, and cutch for tanning and of poles for piling and scaffolding; all uses except the last have markedly declined in recent years. The ecology of the Malayan mangrove forests, including a study of the complex zonation of different communities, is fully described in a classic monograph by Watson (1928), and their fauna (especially the invertebrate fauna), is elegantly covered by Berry (1972) and their birds by Nisbet (1968; see also Chapter 13). Van Steenis (1958c) has described mangrove ecology for the whole of Malesia, and McNae (1968) for the whole region of the Indian Ocean. Richards (1952) and Chapman (1973) give reviews for all the tropics. The specialized physiological mechanisms which enable mangrove species to tolerate salt-water conditions have recently been investigated by Scholander *et al.* (1962, 1964, 1966) and Atkinson *et al.* (1967) (see also the brief review in Chapman (1973)). Van Steenis (1958c) points out that mangroves are only facultative halophytes; several species have thrived and regenerated in fresh water at the Bogor Botanic Garden for over a century. Mangrove soils were briefly described in §9.9.

11.2. Brackish-water forest

The inland edge of the mangrove and the upper tidal limit of estuaries carries a forest with a number of distinctive species amongst which the palm *Nypa fruticans* (Fig. 11.1) is important, forming extensive pure stands mainly along water courses and as far east as New Britain, with scattered outliers extending to the Solomons and in the Marianas. In the mangrove forests of east Sabah *Nypa* forest is asso-

FIG. 11.1. The salt-water palm *Nypa fruticans* which ranges from Ceylon and the Bay of Bengal to the Solomons and Marianas. The fronds, about 3 m tall, are used for thatch; note the fruit clusters.

ciated with a very high density of the raised soil mounds of the mud lobster *Thalassina anomala* (Folland), but we do not yet know if the association is more than coincidental. The only *Phoenix* in our region, *P. paludosa*, 'the Mangrove Date Palm', is restricted to this Formation (Whitmore 1973*b*). A few species also occur in beach vegetation (§10.6). Brackish-water forest is well described by Wyatt-Smith (1963) and is mentioned in the references given above to the mangrove forest.

11.3. Peat swamp forest

Habitat and Far East distribution

The peat swamp forest Formation is of a very special type and with a rather restricted flora. The soil is peat, which may be defined as a soil with organic matter showing a loss on ignition greater than 65 per cent. Tropical peat is usually acid with a pH usually less than 4·0. The surface of a peat swamp is not subject to flooding and is normally markedly convex. The peat is usually at least $\frac{1}{2}$ m deep, and depths up to 20 m have been recorded. There is a solid, fibrous, sometimes-soft crust over a semi-liquid interior containing large pieces of wood, and the colour is commonly reddish-brown. The only incoming water is from rain, which is *ipso facto* extremely mineral deficient. The drainage water is black by reflected light and tea-coloured by transmitted light and is highly acid (pH $\leqslant$4).

Peat is also found in very wet mountain climates in the zone of prevalent cloud, where it is more compact, more highly humified, and usually blackish, and is associated mainly with upper montane rain forest (see §§9.12 and 9.16). Organic soils are histosols in terms of the new U.S.D.A. Classification (Soil Survey Staff 1968), many in tropical lowlands being troposaprists.

Lowland peat swamp forest is very extensive in east Sumatra, on both coasts of the Malay peninsula, and in Borneo. It is apparently absent from east New Guinea (Womersley; and references to §11.4) despite the very great extent of fresh-water swamp vegetation there which is described in the next section (11.4); but it occurs in the southern part of west New Guinea (Polak 1933*a*, in van Steenis 1957). There is some peat in the southern Philippines but not in the drier north-west. The total extent of peat swamp forest in Indonesia is estimated to be 17×10^6 ha (Coulter 1957), in Sarawak (where it occupies 12·5 per cent of the land area) $1·5 \times 10^6$ ha (Anderson 1963), and in Malaya about $0·5 \times 10^6$ ha (Wyatt-Smith 1963).

The classic work on peat swamps was by Polak,

who described the structure, hydrology, and chemical composition. This and other early work is reviewed by Richards (1952) and Anderson (1961*b*). More recently the ecology of the peat swamp forest Formation has been very fully investigated in Sarawak (Anderson 1958, 1961*a*, 1961*b*, 1963, 1964*a*, 1964*b*) and to a lesser extent in Malaya (Symington 1943; Wyatt-Smith 1959, 1963). In both countries, and especially the former, it is an extremely valuable forest resource which, because the land is in the main totally unsuitable for agriculture, is likely to remain as part of the forest estate. Peat swamp forest will therefore become relatively even more important in the future than it is today as progressively more and more of the dry lowlands are brought into agricultural use.

Because of its present and future economic importance and also because the results of the recent investigations illustrate clearly many of the aspects of rain-forest ecology discussed in general terms in earlier chapters, peat swamp forest will be described here in some detail.

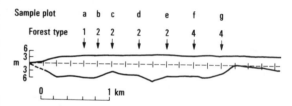

FIG. 11.2. Section through the peat swamp along a transect at Rantau Panjang, Rejang delta, Sarawak, showing the domed surface. Sample plots (a)–(g) and forests they carry indicated. (Based on Anderson 1964, Fig. 2.)

Peat swamps characteristically have a domed surface (Fig. 11.2), as do peat bogs of temperate climates, and have a stilted water table higher than that of the surroundings. The forests growing on most of the peat swamps in our region have evidence of concentric zones, the innermost one being a forest of stunted trees, commonly of markedly xeromorphic aspect. In the forest on the Paneh peninsula of Sumatra the central zone is a dwarf forest dominated by *Tristania* (Polak 1933*b*). In south Sumatra and east Borneo *Tristania obovata* and *Ploiarium alternifolium* are dominant (Endert 1920).

The peat swamp forests of Sarawak and Brunei

Zonation is very marked in the peat swamp forests of Sarawak and Brunei and has been very thoroughly studied by Dr. J. A. R. Anderson. Here it is only possible to give a brief summary of his more important findings. Peat swamp forests occupy nearly the entire coastline of these two countries. The biggest single swamp, on the Maludam peninsula, stretches 64 km inland from the mangrove forest fringe and covers 1070 km². These forests and those of north-west Kalimantan are unique in the presence of *Shorea albida*, whose range extends from the mouth of the Kapuas river south of Pontianak to the Tutong river in Brunei. This dipterocarp plays a major role in the swamp-forest communities, and no species is known to play the same part elsewhere.

The six forest types

In Sarawak and Brunei there exists a catena of forests from the edge to the centre of each peat swamp. Anderson divided this into six types (phasic communities) which are moderately sharply distinct in structure, physiognomy, and flora. Not all types are developed everywhere. The first type is found on the periphery, more or less confined to the outer steeper slopes of the dome surface. The last two types have formed only on the most highly developed swamps, which occur in the middle and upper reaches of the Baram estuary. Fig. 11.3 shows the concentric zonation of the forests of part of the Baram. Tea-coloured streams navigable by small boats penetrate the outermost community for several kilometres. Profile diagrams of the six forest types are shown in Figs 11.4 and 11.5 and photographs of the types in Figs 11.6–11.10. The sequential pattern of forest types represents, in brief, a change from an uneven-canopied high forest, similar in structure and physiognomy to lowland dipterocarp evergreen rain forest but with fewer species per unit area, a lower canopy (36–42 m), and fewer stems per unit area, to a similar forest (type 2) but dominated by enormous

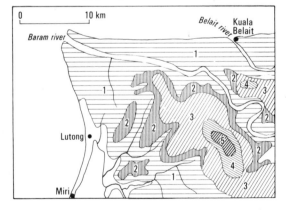

FIG. 11.3. Peat swamp forest around the Baram estuary, Sarawak. Successive forest types 1–5 (see text) shown. Type 6 only occurs further inland. (After Anderson 1961, map 4.)

trees of *Shorea albida*. This is followed by an even-canopied high forest (type 3) in which *Shorea albida* is the sole dominant, which in turn is replaced by a dense, even-canopied forest (type 4) with a xeromorphic and stunted aspect and in which few trees exceed 1·8 m girth. This type is itself succeeded, towards the centre of some of the Baram swamps, by a very dense pole-like forest (type 5) with a low canopy in which few trees exceed 0·9 m girth, and finally by an open savanna woodland (type 6) which shows a high degree of stunting and xeromorphism and in which only two species exceed 0·3 m girth. Accompanying these changes in forest structure and physiognomy there are also the following.

1. An almost complete change in flora, illustrated in Fig. 11.11 by the principal top-of-canopy trees. In fact only one species, *Dactylocladus stenostachys*, spans all six forest types; it grows as a tree of 2·7–3 m girth in type 1 and as a treelet 3 m tall or a shrub in type 6.

2. A reduction in the number of species per unit area (and also in the total number of species which has been recorded), but an increase in the number of stems (Fig. 11.12).

3. A decrease in the average girth of a species (Fig. 11.13), and in average crown diameter.

Flora

Most of the tree families of lowland evergreen dipterocarp rain forest are found in peat swamp forest; exceptions are Combretaceae, Lythraceae, Proteaceae, and Styracaceae. Palms are poorly represented and only occur in the peripheral communities. There are probably very few species restricted to peat swamp forest. The greatest similarity with lowland dipterocarp forest is in the peripheral mixed swamp forest (type 1), where drainage is best and the peat soil more fertile than further in. By contrast, species in the swamp centre are largely those found also on poor, frequently podzolized heath-forest soils, and to some extent on soils degraded by erosion and leaching after destruction of the primary forest cover. In total, 146 tree species have been recorded in both heath and peat swamp forest (Brunig 1973). The increasing percentage of heath-forest species along the catena is shown on the profile diagrams of Figs 11.4 and 11.5 (profile plots are all 232 m² in area). Eleven of the fifteen species of Dipterocarpaceae recorded in peat swamp forest have also been recorded in heath forest. Adaptations to the specialized habitat conditions of peat swamp forest include prominent pneumatophores (Fig. 11.14).

145

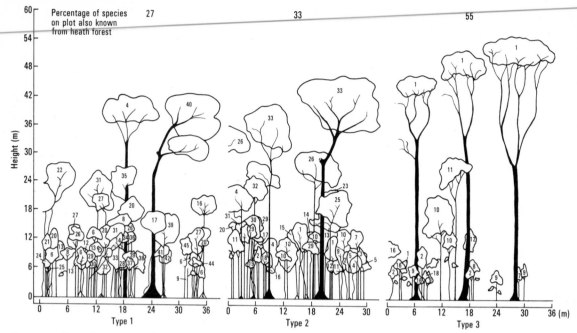

FIG. 11.4. Sarawak peat swamp forest catena, types 1–3. Type 1, mixed swamp forest: the *Gonystylus–Dactylocladus–Neoscortechinia* association. Type 2, alan forest: the *Shorea albida–Gonystylus–Stemonurus* association. Type 3, alan bunga forest: the *Shorea albida* consociation. See facing species list. (After Anderson 1961.)

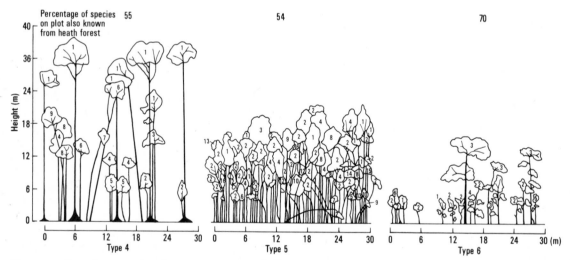

FIG. 11.5. Sarawak peat swamp forest catena, types 4–6. Type 4, padang alan forest: the *Shorea albida–Litsea–Parastemon* association. Type 5, the *Tristania–Parastemon–Palaquium* association. Type 6, padang keruntum: the *Combretocarpus–Dactylocladus* association. See facing species list. (After Anderson 1961.)

146

FIGS 11.4 and 11.5.   Identity of trees on the peat swamp forest profile diagrams. * indicates a species also known to occur in heath forest.

FOREST TYPE 1

4, *Gonystylus bancanus*
6, *Mangifera havilandii**
8, *Neoscortechinia kingii*
9, *Shorea inaequilateralis*
12, *Eugenia* aff. *havilandii**
13, *Diospyros maingayi**
14, *Dyera lowii*
16, *Mussaendopsis beccariana*
17, *Palaquium walsurifolium*
20, *Dryobalanops rappa**
21, *Samadera indica*
22, *Alseodaphne insignis*
24, *Blumeodendron tokbrai*
25, *Nephelium maingayi*
26, *Pometia pinnata*
27, *Ganua pierrei**
28, Unidentified
29, *Glochidion obscurum**
30, *Parishia sericea*
31, *Ctenolophon parvifolius*
32, *Alangium havilandii*
33, *Polyalthia glauca**
34, *Aromadendron nutans*
35, *Garcinia vidua*
36, *Blumeodendron subrotundifolium*
37, *Trigoniastrum hypoleucum*
38, *Croton laevifolius*
39, *Lithocarpus rassa*
40, *Shorea uliginosa*
41, *Xanthophyllum amoenum**
42, *Dillenia pulchella*
43, *Santiria rubiginosa*
44, *Garcinia* sp. (865)
45, Unidentified

FOREST TYPE 2

1, *Cyathocalyx biovalatus*
2, *Melanorrhoea beccarii**
3, *Palaquium pseudorostratum*
4, *Blumeodendron subrotundifolium*
5, *Xanthophyllum amoenum**
7, *Ganua pierrei**
9, *Ganua coriacea*
10, *Stemonurus umbellatus**
11, *Palaquium cochleariifolium**
12, *Sterculia rhoidifolia**
13, *Sandoricum emarginatum*
15, *Dryobalanops rappa*
16, *Campnosperma montanum*
17, *Neoscortechinia kingii*
18, *Garcinia* sp. (669)
19, *Arthrophyllum rubiginosum*
20, *Nephelium maingayi*
23, *Palaquium walsurifolium*
25, *Mezzettia leptopoda*
26, *Gonystylus bancanus*
29, *Lophopetalum rigidum*
30, *Shorea inaequilateralis*
31, *Garcinia vidua*
32, *Eugenia* sp. (479)
33, *Shorea albida**

FOREST TYPE 3

1, *Shorea albida**
2, *Xanthophyllum* sp. nov. (2614)
7, *Stemonurus umbellatus**
8, *Timonius peduncularis**
9, *Ilex hypoglauca*
10, *Xanthophyllum* aff. *citrifolium*
11, *Parastemon spicatum*
12, *Gonystylus bancanus*
16, *Eugenia* sp. (9274)
18, *Eugenia* sp. (479)

FOREST TYPE 4

1, *Shorea albida**
2, *Timonius peduncularis**
3, *Gonystylus bancanus*
4, *Lophopetalum rigidum*
5, *Palaquium cochleariifolium*
6, *Litsea crassifolia**
7, *Tristania obovata*
8, *Ternstroemia hosei*
9, *Calophyllum retusum*

FOREST TYPE 5

1, *Tristania maingayi**
2, *Parastemon spicatum**
3, *Litsea crassifolia**
4, *Palaquium cochleariifolium**
5, *Palaquium ridleyi**
6, *Xylopia coriifolia*
7, *Ilex sclerophylloides*
8, *Xanthophyllum* sp. nov. (2614)
9, *Diospyros evena*
10, *Dactylocladus stenostachys*
11, *Arthrophyllum rubiginosum*
12, *Canthium didymum**
13, *Ternstroemia hosei**
14, *Stemonurus umbellatus**
15, *Garcinia rostrata**
16, *Austrobuxus nitidus**

FOREST TYPE 6

1, *Parastemon spicatum**
2, *Dactylocladus stenostachys*
3, *Combretocarpus rotundatus**
4, *Tristania obovata**
5, *Litsea crassifolia**
6, *Garcinia rostrata**

147

FIG. 11.6.   Mixed peat swamp forest behind a riparian strip of low secondary forest on alluvium (Baram River, Sarawak).

The origin of the domed shape

Pollen analysis of peat cores (Anderson 1964*a*; Muller 1965, 1972) from swamps of the Baram delta has shown that the catenary sequence of forest types represents a succession in time. At the base of the cores stiff clay was reached at 13 m depth, overlain by mangrove, then a *Campnosperma coriaceum–Cyrtostachys lakka–Salacca conferta* association followed by the six communities in order, though types 2/3 and 5/6 could not be distinguished. The whole succession was shown by radio-carbon dating to have formed over 4500 years (Wilford 1960). It was possible also to show that the coastline of the Baram delta has been advancing over that period at a mean rate of 9 m/year. The average rate of accumulation of peat was 0·3 m/year, and it was distinctly faster in the early years (475 mm/year at 10–12 m depth, 223 mm/year at 0–5 m). This serves to explain the 'inverted-plate' shape of the bog surface (Fig. 11.2); the rapid initial formation of peat results in the steep sides (slopes of 0·2–0·6 m/km), the slow later rate accounts for the almost flat central bog plain.

The peat swamps have a biconvex shape, and the lower surface owes its concavity to the deposition of alluvium at the margins by the bordering rivers. It is noticeable that the peat swamps furthest from the coast, which are the oldest, are the thickest and most markedly lens-shaped.

Mode of origin of peat

It is thought that peat formation is probably initiated at the inland margin of mangrove swamp because the high sulphide and salt content of the underlying clay is toxic to the micro-organisms which would normally decompose falling plant debris (Anderson 1964*a*). It may also be significant that in Java, where the rivers drain base-rich, volcanic soils, there are no peat swamps (Mohr 1944; Mohr and van Baren 1954) whereas in Sarawak, Brunei, and elsewhere peat swamps have formed the rivers drain relatively mineral-poor hinterlands: but much of Java is seasonally dry and that may be more important.

Mineral nutrients

It has been shown (Muller 1972; Anderson) that there is a decrease towards the centre of the swamps in the amounts of mineral nutrients in the soil. The centre is very much poorer in particular in phosphorus and potassium. Peats of the Baram swamps (which are the most highly developed), with a loss on ignition of 98–100 per cent, have a much lower

---

FIG. 11.7 (see p. 148). Sarawak peat swamp forest interior (a), the outermost mixed swamp forest community. Large tree on the left is *Shorea inaequilateralis* and that on the right is *Gonystylus bancanus*. Note the strangling fig on the *Gonystylus*.

FIG. 11.8 (see p. 149). Sarawak peat swamp forest interior (b), alan bunga forest, the third community which is a consociation of *Shorea albida* trees about 60 m tall. Baram estuary.

FIG. 11.9 (see p. 150).   Sarawak peat swamp forest interior (c), padang alan forest, the fourth community. Here the canopy attains about 30 m tall and few trees exceed 1·8 m girth. Note man.

FIG. 11.10 (see p. 151).   Sarawak peat swamp forest (d), the ultimate community, type 6, padang keruntum, only developed in some of the Baram swamps. The forest is very stunted. The larger trees are all *Combretocarpus rotundatus*.

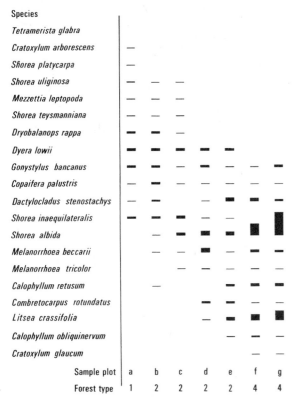

FIG. 11.11. Occurrence of commonest top-of-canopy species along the transect (Fig. 11.2) at Rantau Panjang peat swamp. (Anderson 1961, Fig. 8.)

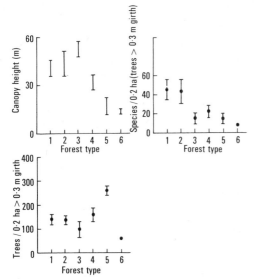

FIG. 11.12. Various features of the Sarawak peat swamp forest catena. (Anderson 1961, Table 26.)

mineral content than those of the Rejang. It was also found in the Baram swamps that the top 150 mm, where feeding roots form a dense mat above the water table, had more nutrients than deeper down. It is believed that the forests from perimeter to centre mirror conditions of increasing infertility. This is suggested by the decreasing canopy height and hence total biomass per unit area, the increasing sclerophylly, and the diminishing girth of individual species. The ultimate community (type 6), the open savanna woodland of some Baram swamps farthest from the coast (Fig. 11.10), has as additional signs of oligotrophy an abundance of plant species with supplementary means of mineral nutrition (myrmecophytes and pitcher plants), and the tree foliage appears distinctly chlorotic.

Similarities with heath forest.

There are conspicuous parallels in structure and physiognomy between the more central peat swamp forest types and heath forest, and there is an increase inwards in the percentage of species per unit area which also occur in heath forest (Figs 11.4 and 11.5).

As with heath forest, the relative importance of periodic water-stress and oligotrophy has not been certainly ascertained. In peat swamp forest the water table is perched, but below the surface. In the inner communities many of the tree roots form a platform which may periodically dry out above the water table. Further, it is possible that water uptake may be slow from waterlogged peat soil and that low transpiration rates may be essential to avoid uptake of toxic solutes from the highly acidic, phenol-rich ground water (Brunig 1971). Kerapah forest (§10.3), the variant of heath forest over waterlogged soil, possibly has particularly close similarities with peat swamp forest. Forest types 3, 4, and 5 have the canopy top more or less flat, especially type 3, the *Shorea albida* consociation, and in addition *Shorea albida* has a high albedo. It was shown in the discussion of ecophysiological studies on heath forest (§10.3) that both these features may be adaptive to conditions where water-stress is frequent.

The status of Shorea albida

In forest types 2, 3, and 4 *Shorea albida* is dominant or codominant (Figs 11.4 and 11.5). In forest type 3 it is the sole species which attains the canopy top, reaching 45–57 (–60) m tall and 0·9–3 m girth, with the clear bole generally over 30 m, the crown small, and the canopy surface rather even (Fig. 11.8). In type 4 the trees are slender and sinuous, and few exceed 1·8 m girth (Fig. 11.9);

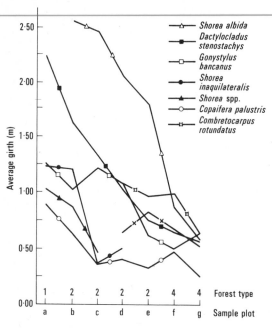

FIG. 11.13. Mean girths of principal canopy-top tree species along the transect (Fig. 11.2) in Rantau Panjang peat swamp forest. (Anderson 1961, Fig. 16.)

FIG. 11.14. *Calophyllum obliquinervium* in peat swamp forest of Brunei showing its prominent pneumatophores.

here all *S. albida* trees have light timber (of density 450–510 gm/m³), as do the smaller trees in type 3, but the bigger ones there have a peripheral shell of denser timber (640–710 gm/m³).

In forest type 2 most *S. albida* trees are huge specimens, 3·6–6 m girth and taller than 45 m, with stag-headed, wind-ravaged crowns and boles from which the inner light timber has been entirely eaten by termites or has rotted away, leaving just a hollow, dense shell. These trees give every appearance of being moribund. Apart from them type 2 is essentially the same as the peripheral mixed swamp forest, type 1.

The bottom of the peat dome is above sea-level in all swamps except those of the Rejang delta. The forests here mostly lack the *Shorea albida* consociation (type 3) and show the sequence 1–2–4, with type 2 very extensive. It is believed that in the Rejang area there has been extensive coastal subsidence during the last 200 years or so, which has lowered the whole of the peat swamp complex so that the water table is nearer the surface. This has altered soil conditions in such a way that the *S. albida* consociation (3) has been invaded by mixed swamp species (1) to produce type 2, in which *S. albida* persists solely as big old specimens. In the Baram delta and elsewhere subsidence has been less (the bottom of the peat dome is below river-level but above sea-level), and type 3 still persists in many areas (see the map, Fig. 11.3).

Forest dynamics, economics, and silviculture

The first type to be exploited, from about 1945, was the peripheral mixed swamp forest. *Gonystylus bancanus* is the most valuable species by far although it was at first unmarketable and was left behind in the forest to be poisoned. Other important timber species are *Copaifera palustris, Dryobalanops rappa, Shorea platycarpa, S. rugosa, S. scabrida,* and *S. uliginosa*. These species together comprise 70 per cent or more of all trees over 1·8 m girth. In virgin forest established seedlings and saplings can be found but there are virtually no poles of 0·2–0·3 m girth. It appears that this is because all these species are strong light-demanders; established regrowth grows vigorously after felling, though *Gonystylus* tends to be over-topped and suppressed by the Shoreas which are faster growing. In the most open places, along the rail extraction lines, *Cratoxylum arborescens, C. glaucum,* and *Dactylocladus steno-stachys* form pure stands; quite clearly they are the pioneer species of this Formation together with the small tree *Macaranga caladiifolia* (see §6.2). Fast-growing weed trees come to dominate the regrowth where big tree regeneration is absent; these are mainly *Antidesma coriaceum*, *Elaeocarpus obtusifolius*, *Litsea cylindricocarpa*, *L. gracilipes*, *L. nidularis*, *L. resinosa*, and *Phoebe* sp.

More recently, since about 1961, the *Shorea albida* consociation has come to be exploited. Seedlings and saplings are very rare, but are occasionally seen in gaps. Poles are absent. This is the forest type, more than any other, which is prone to extensive damage from wind and lightning, as was discussed in §6.1. No species other than *S. albida* has the ability to reach the canopy top of this type. Unless they occur over established seedlings or saplings, gaps apparently remain open until a *S. albida* fruiting year (cf. §4.2), when they are colonized, and the seedlings grow very fast up into trees, the characteristic very light timber being a sign of this rapid growth. (In most rain forests such gaps would, of course, be filled immediately by established seedlings or saplings of one of many species—cf. §6.1.) It has been possible by statistical analysis of a 7·2 ha block of this forest to detect groups of trees of similar girths, but growth is so rapid that no groups of poles have ever been found. After the 1955 seed year 81 600 seedlings per hectare of *S. albida* were counted in type 3 forest; by 1958 all had died except a few sited where light reached the forest floor through a gap. It is impossible to delay felling until after a seed year, which is only about once a decade, and regeneration of this forest type presents major problems.

S. albida regeneration is generally negligible in forest type 2, which has a denser middle and lower canopy than type 3, but 64 800 seedlings per hectare were recorded after a heavy seed year. The canopy is less liable to serious wind damage, and complete gaps rarely form. Natural regeneration of *S. albida* in this forest type appears distinctly rare. After felling, the species of type 1 regenerate.

In forest type 4 natural regeneration of *Shorea albida* and of two other common big trees of this community, *Combretocarpus rotundatus* and *Litsea crassifolia*, is mainly vegetative, by suckers or coppice shoots. *S. albida* trees of all girths are present and saplings and poles are more frequent than elsewhere. This forest type has no value for timber, but with its high volume per hectare and low extraction costs has potential as a source of pulp or chip wood.

Leo and Lee (1971) estimated that the total timber resource of *S. albida* in Sarawak, allowing for 50 per cent defect, was about 8×10^6 tonne.

The Malayan peat swamp forests

The Malayan peat swamp forests are less highly developed than those of Sarawak and Brunei; all of them carry mixed swamp forest, type 1. Soils have been investigated by Coulter (1950a, 1957). On the west coast the huge trans-Perak swamp is not domed, and river levées still protrude in parts. The Langat swamp in Selangor is domed. These swamps lie over stiff clay which is generally above sea-level, and in which diatoms of the mangrove environment were found at Telok in Selangor, now lying several kilometres inland (Webber 1954). The west coast of Malaya is sinking (Tjia 1973), and it is possible that this has prevented development of forests comparable to the inner zones elsewhere. The only sign of concentric zonation is at Hutan Melintang in south Perak where *Shorea uliginosa* increases from 4·8 per hectare near the margin to 30–51 per hectare 2–4 km inland, in one area as poles only, reminiscent of *S. albida* (Wyatt-Smith 1963).

On the east coast the peat has formed over sand behind coastal sand spits, and is most extensive between the Pahang and Rompin Rivers where the coastline is advancing rapidly.

There are floristic differences between the west and east coasts. Over all, the forests have the same economic species as the Sarawak mixed swamp forest, except that some are absent. The Malayan peat swamps are a very valuable timber resource. Their floristic poverty compared to dry-land forest means that the timber produced is of relatively uniform quality, and yields are very high—up to 61 tonne/ha. Natural regeneration of all sizes is excellent, and the first managed rotation should have even higher yields with minimal silvicultural treatment. Only *Gonystylus bancanus* and *Tetramerista glabra* are not found naturally regenerating in virgin forest. As in Sarawak, the fast-growing *Shorea* spp. and *Cratoxylum arborescens* predominate in regrowth forest.

Shallow peat has been converted to pineapple (in Johore) or rubber plantations. Peat over 3 m thick cannot be successfully brought into agricultural use, and there is no doubt that it should remain under forest.

World distribution

Peat swamp has been recorded in the Amazon basin, on some of the Caribbean islands, and on the north coast of South America (the pegass swamps of Guyana), but is apparently rare and restricted in tropical Africa (Richards 1952; Anderson 1961b). In neither continent has it been closely studied, and in both continents it is less extensive and with lesser economic importance than in the tropical Far East.

11.4. Fresh-water swamp forest

The soil surface of land covered by the fresh-water swamp forest Formation is regularly to occasionally inundated with mineral-rich, fresh water of fairly high pH (6 upwards), and the water level fluctuates, thus allowing periodic drying of the soil surface. A few centimetres of peat or muck† soil may occur, but these forests are not to be confused with peat swamp forest (described in the preceding section), which have deep peat and are more or less entirely dependent on rain as the water source. A very shallow peat layer usually has little effect on the species-composition of fresh-water swamp forest.

The extremely heterogeneous nature of the fresh-water swamp environment including its soils was described in §9.10. The floristic composition and the structure of the vegetation also varies enormously from floating grass mats (in the Bornean lakes and believed to be a fire-climax (van Steenis 1957)) and open sedge or grass plains (especially in New Guinea), to pandan or palm swamp (also especially extensive in New Guinea), and to scrub and forest. In Malaya, for example, fresh-water swamp forest varies from a low scrub with scattered 20–30 m tall trees to a forest similar in structure to that of mixed species peat swamp forest. Stilt roots, knee roots, and sinuous plank buttresses are present but infrequent. Where flooding is brief the forest approaches lowland evergreen rain forest in composition, via an intermediate Formation which may be designated seasonal swamp forest. The distinctive riparian forests of the middle reaches of rivers in Sarawak, which are known as *empran,* fall into this intermediate category. Empran forest is described in §15.3.

Far East distribution

The greatest extent of the fresh-water swamp habitat is where the biggest rivers are, that is, on the continent in Indo-China, Thailand, and Burma (especially the Mekong and Irrawaddy) and in New Guinea (especially the Fly and Sepik), but the habitat occurs throughout the region, associated with river valleys and, except where the coasts are very steep, also with alluvial coastal plains. Fresh-water swamp forest is not restricted to the wettest climates; it is found also in seasonally dry parts of New Guinea and

in east Java. Over much of its range, and especially on the Asian continent, fresh-water swamp vegetation has been destroyed and replaced by rice paddies or, to a lesser extent, by rubber plantations, and only tiny vestiges of the former forest remain.

World distribution

Fresh-water swamp forest also covers large areas in the African and South American humid tropics (Richards 1952); the Amazon River has a substantial

FIG. 11.15. *Campnosperma coriaceum* in secondary peat swamp forest (Brunei).

---

† Muck: organic soil with loss on ignition of 35–65 per cent.

annual fluctuation in water level and is lined throughout its length by swamp (*igapo*) and seasonal swamp (*varzea*) forest.

General floristics

The enormous range in habitat and vegetation is coupled to great diversity in floristic composition. Fresh-water swamp forest is not distinct, at family and genus level, from that of dry-land lowland forest of the same region. Some species are confined to swampy sites; many others grow also on dry land.

There is a distinct tendency to gregariousness in primary fresh-water swamp forest, and to species-poor associations or even to consociations. In Malaya and Borneo *Mallotus leucodermis* and *M. muticus* are very common gregarious trees. Throughout New Guinea *Camnosperma brevipetiolatum* occurs in pure or nearly pure stands and the Sago palm, *Metroxylon sagu*, also occurs in huge stands; in some places these two species grow together. *Campnosperma coriaceum* (Fig. 11.15) is a swamp species found through the region. *Alstonia* is another genus with several swamp species. Fresh-water swamp forest in narrow depressions in the heath forest of east coast Malaya, which receive very acid water, has floristic affinity with peat swamp forest.

Of particular interest is the occurrence along the north coast of Papua of pure stands of 48 m tall *Casuarina* aff. *cunninghamiana* as a pioneer species on swampy alluvial fans, resulting from destructive floods, and standing high over a mixed species forest 30 m tall (Paijmans 1967; Taylor 1964*b*).

Secondary swamp forest communities

Some pure stands of single tree species undoubtedly have a secondary origin. Throughout the region, especially in south Sumatra, Malaya, south and south-east Borneo, and New Guinea there occur forests of *Melaleuca cajuputi* (plus several other *Melaleuca* species in New Guinea). This grows as an understorey tree in primary swamp forest and becomes gregarious after repeated burning, owing to its production of root suckers and coppice shoots. Big *Melaleuca* trees have thick, loose, corky bark which affords protection against fire. Sloughed bark and other litter accumulates on the ground and becomes highly inflammable in dry weather. In Malaya mature *Melaleuca* forest has a 21 m high canopy and trees reaching 1·2 m girth. Associated species are *Alstonia spatulata*, *Cratoxylum cochinchinense*, *Excoecaria agallocha*, *Fagraea fragrans*, *Ilex cymosa*, *Macaranga*

pruinosa, *Ploiarium alternifolium*, and *Randia dasycarpa*, with *Scleria* spp. and *Stenochlaena palustris* common as ground flora. In Papua, where *Melaleuca* forest probably has its greatest extent, several communities have been described. Extensive pure stands of *Macaranga pruinosa* and *Campnosperma coriaceum* in Malaya, of same-size trees and an even canopy top, are believed to represent stages in a secondary succession back to mixed swamp forest after clearing. The pure stands in Malaya of *Ploiarium alternifolium*, to 15 m tall, on abandoned, poorly drained mining land (associated with *Alstonia spatulata* and *Glochidion obscurum*) are to be compared with the occurrence of this species in Sarawak both as a secondary species in heath forest (§10.3), and towards the centre of peat swamps (§11.3).

Economics

Fresh-water swamp forest has in general a lower timber-stocking than dry-land lowland rain forest as well as problems of access, and is consequently of low commercial value. Exceptions are some of the pure stands of species, either primary or secondary in nature. The *Campnosperma* forests of north-east Malaya are utilized as a source of timber for match splints, and the Malayan *Melaleuca* swamps are repeatedly cut for firewood and charcoal (Wyatt-Smith 1963) as are those of Indonesia, for example, round Bandiarmasin in south Kalimantan. A few of the New Guinea *Campnosperma* stands have been harvested. The vast Sago Palm swamps of New Guinea provide the prime food of the local inhabitants.

Important references

The published descriptions of fresh-water swamp forest are mainly floristic; little work has been done on the dynamics, or on the precise correlation of species with the great diversity of habitats. Wyatt-Smith (1963) described both primary and secondary swamp forest in Malaya and its silviculture. Van Steenis (1957) gave a brief summary for Indonesia with references to the early, mainly Dutch, literature. There is a lengthy series of reconnaissance reports prepared as part of land use appraisal projects which now cover a substantial area of east New Guinea (Taylor 1964*a,b*; Heyligers 1965, 1967, 1972*a*; Paijmans 1967, 1969, 1971; Robbins 1968*b*) and a separate publication (Taylor 1959) for part of north-east Papua. Richards (1952) gives an account of tropical hydroseres and swamp forests in general.

12 Monsoon forest Formations

12.1. Monsoon forests and savanna

MONSOON FOREST was introduced as a term by Schimper (Chapter 1). He also described savanna forest and thorn forest of even drier climates and two further lowland Formations not dominated by trees: tropical grassland and tropical desert. (For fuller discussion of these see Schimper (1903, p. 260, 1935) and Richards (1952, Chapter 15).) As with the term *rain forest*, which Schimper introduced at the same time, several distinct Formations can now be distinguished within each class (see especially Champion (1936), Burtt Davy (1938), Champion and Seth (1968)).

The different Formations occupy habitats of increasing severity of drought, but, as we have already noted, there is a complex interaction between local variations in rainfall, water held available in the soil (which is dependent on the depth, structure, and texture of the soil), and nutrient status of the soil. The same Formation may occur over different rocks in places with different degrees of drought. It follows that in seasonally dry climates there is an intricate mosaic of forest Formations (Fig. 12.1) which is made more complex by the great and greatly varying extent of alteration by man, resulting from the ready inflammability of these Formations in the dry season. In Java, for example, 'fire for hunting, for pleasure, for pestering neighbours or neighbouring villages, by carelessness, for clearing land, for making land passable, for converting forest into pasture land, in short for innumerable purposes, has played havoc within the monsoon forest', and it is doubtful if any of the original monsoon forest cover now remains (van

Fig. 12.1. The mosaic of forest types depending on physiography and aspect in a seasonally dry climate. Eastwards aerial view of a limestone area near Kanchanaburi 14° N in the Thailand–Burma border region. The light grey southern slopes carry *Thyrsostachys*-dominated forest; other, more sheltered and moister, areas carry *Thyrsostachys–Lagerstroemia* forest of darker colour. High, distant ridges carry a different evergreen forest type, which also occurs as gallery forest along the water courses in the foreground, where it is admixed with *Bambusa arundinacea*.

Steenis and Schippers-Lammertse 1965). It is most probable that all tropical grasslands, with the obvious exception of those found on some more-or-less permanently swampy sites (§11.4), are entirely derived from woodlands or forests as a result of long-continued burning by fires started by man or lightning and that there is no such thing as a tropical grassland climate (Richards 1952, Chapter 16).

Detailed consideration of these Formations of dry climates is beyond the scope of the present book, but they cannot be entirely ignored because they abut on the rain forests and because of the paramount commercial importance of teak (*Tectona*) and the tropical species of *Pinus*, both of which genera are indigenous to them.

Monsoon forest is used in this book as a convenient general term for those forests of the tropical Far East where water is periodically seriously limiting to plants (see Table 10.1, p. 121). In general, monsoon forests are of lesser stature than rain forests, with a lower biomass, and are deciduous to a considerable degree. The boundary against rain forest is often sharp owing to the action of fire, rain forests often penetrating the monsoon Formations as narrow strips of 'gallery forest' along water courses.

Monsoon forests (Fig. 12.2), and the savannas (grasslands with scattered trees) and grasslands derived from them by repeated burning, border the great Far East rain-forest zone in continental southeast Asia and are the principal vegetation types of Thailand, Burma, Indo-China, the Indian subcontinent, and Ceylon. (For descriptions see Stamp (1925), Champion (1936), Richards (1952), Walker and Pendleton (1957), and Champion and Seth (1968).)

On the eastern seaboard of Australia the rain forests occupy the wettest and most fertile sites and abut on to monsoon and sclerophyll forests (Webb 1959). In central Australia there is true desert. In central Burma is another very dry zone, centred on Mandalay and bearing thorn forest in its driest central part.

On the islands of the Pacific, monsoon forests and savanna occur in the Solomons in the rain shadow north of the high Kavo range on both Guadalcanal and Nggela, in parts of the New Hebrides (south-west Espiritu Santo and the western sides of Efate, Erromango, and Tanna) and parts of Fiji in the lee of the south-east winds, and also on some of the islands of Micronesia (several Marianas, Guam, and part of Palau (Hosokawa 1952, 1954*a,b*)).

The map of rainfall types (Fig. 3.1, p. 45) shows

FIG. 12.2. Monsoon forest in north Thailand, 3 km south of Boh Luang, Chiengmai, at 1000 m elevation. This is dry deciduous dipterocarp forest. *Pinus kesiya* is present in mixture with *Dipterocarpus obtusifolius* and *D. tuberculatus*, which are two of the commonest and most characteristic species of the Formation. Dry-season fires regularly sweep through these forests.

the parts of the tropical Far East which are seasonally dry, and provides a good base on which to describe the distribution of monsoon forests and savannas within the region.

The great Malesian rain-forest zone, occupying the ever-wet climates, is partially bisected by a north–south belt of seasonally dry climates and monsoon forests, in places forming an intricate mosaic with rain forests. This belt (Fig. 12.3) runs from west Luzon in the Philippines south through Celebes (where the Palu valley receives only 275 mm rain annually but well distributed). Monsoon forests also occur in central and east Java, diminishing westwards as a wedge along the north coast. In east Java and the Lesser Sunda Islands ever-wet climate and rain forest are in fact restricted to isolated patches on the south-facing sides of the mountains which receive rain from the on-shore winds. The Moluccas are ever-wet but with seasonally dry patches. New Guinea is wettest along the south side of the Central Cordillera, in a zone which reaches 160 km out onto the plain, and there is a central rain-forest block, with patches of monsoon forests and savanna along the north coast and in intermontane valleys as well as an extensive seasonally dry zone along the south coast. The western part of this southern zone stretches from the Oriomo plateau south of the Fly River into Irian Jaya west of Merauke, the eastern part centres on Port Moresby.

Within the western rain-forest block, which encompasses Sumatra, Malaya, and Borneo, there are only small markedly dry spots, caused by rain shadows cast by the mountains (around Bandjermasin in south Borneo, Sumatra west coast, Tapanuli, and Atchin), which bear monsoon vegetation. There are also extensive areas in the intermontane valleys of the Barisan range, west Sumatra, in Palembang (southeast Sumatra), and in south and east Borneo, which are mildly seasonally dry and probably have semi-evergreen rather than evergreen rain forest.

Where monsoon forests are burnt and tree species resistant to fire become predominant. Besides teak (considered in §12.2) the most important tree species in seasonally dry Indonesia is *Casuarina junghuhniana*, tjemera, which covers several hundred thousand hectares in vast open stands over grass at elevations above about 1400 m in east Java (cf. *Pinus merkusii* in Sumatra—Chapter 14). The importance of dry sites is seen in the occurrence of tjemera forest on ridge crests, and descending lower down from the summits on the northern rain-shadow side than on the south, so that from the air the appearance is of a star with unequal rays. It is estimated that about 4000 ha of tjemera forest are burned annually. Tjemera sprouts very freely even after severe fire damage. It can only regenerate under its own shade after fire; and where fire is excluded a succession to mixed oak–laurel forest begins in which *Dodonaea viscosa*, *Engelhardtia spicata*, *Homalanthus giganteus*, *Vernonia arborea*, and *Weinmannia blumei* are conspicuous early components (van Steenis 1972).

The flora of the monsoon forests is very different from that of the rain forests. Dipterocarpaceae are much less abundant; only 17 of 139 Malayan species

extend north of the Kra isthmus, and the total number of dipterocarps in the monsoon forests of Thailand is only 31 (Ashton 1967). Dipterocarpaceae are rare in Java, with only 4 genera and 10 species indigenous (Backer 1963). The major dominant trees of the Malesian monsoon forests are for the greater part derived from the monsoon belt of the continent to the north (van Steenis 1957). Typical species are: *Acacia leucophloea*, *A. tomentosa*, *Aegle marmelos*, *Albizia chinensis*, *A. lebbekioides*, *Azadirachta indica*, *Borassus flabellifer*, *Butea monosperma*, *Caesalpinia digyna*, *Cassia fistula*, *Corypha elata*, *Dalbergia latifolia*, *Dichrostachys cinerea*, *Feronia limonia*, *Garuga floribunda*, *Homalium tomentosum*, *Lannea grandis*, *Melia azedarach*, *Schleichera oleosa*, *Schoutenia ovata*, *Stereospermum suaveolens*, *Streblus asper*, *Tamarindus indica*, *Tectona grandis*, *Tetrameles nudiflora*, and *Zizyphus rotundifolia*. There is also an Australian element. This is most strongly developed in the south New Guinea monsoon belt, where various Myrtaceae, especially *Eucalyptus*, and Proteaceae (*Banksia*, *Grevillea*) occur (Heyligers 1972b). This element is represented by a few species in the Lesser Sunda Islands: *Eucalyptus alba* as far west as central Flores and *Casuarina junghuhniana* westwards to Mt. Lawau in east Java. *Santalum album* (Sandalwood) and *Melaleuca* are also typical Australian elements (van Steenis 1957). Thirdly, there is a small endemic Malesian element (for example, the genus *Semeiocardium*). However, many of the species of the monsoon climates have a much wider range, from India to Australia or even into Africa, for example, *Tamarindus*.

Certain groups of plants are distinct indicators of ever-wet conditions, for example, the filmy ferns (Hymenophyllaceae), *Dicranopteris*, *Gleichenia*, and *Nepenthes*; tea (*Camellia sinensis*) can only be cultivated in ever-wet climates. Mossy mountain forest and leaves encrusted with epiphyllous plants are also indicators of nearly permanent wetness. Other plants are definitely drought indicators, different species to a different degree. Sugar cane can only be successfully cultivated in seasonally dry places (van Steenis (1950b).

One interesting group of drought-indicators is those members of the Leguminosae, subfamily Papilionatae found in the monsoon forests of Malesia (van Meeuwen, Nooteboom, and van Steenis 1961), some of which are endemic to the region, or nearly so. The distribution of these, as of other monsoon-climate plants, is distinctly disjunct because between the monsoon climates of continental Asia and the Lesser Sunda Islands seasonally dry sites occur only

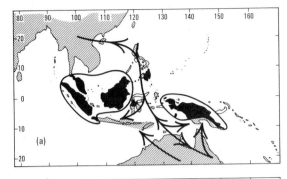

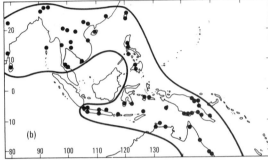

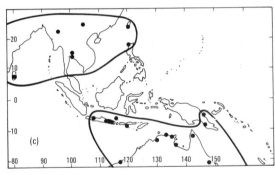

FIG. 12.3. Geographical ranges of two monsoon climate species. (a) The two big cores of ever-wet rain forest as barriers for distribution of seasonal plants; the hatched areas either dry or consisting of a mosaic of ever-wet and dry areas. (b) *Pycnospora lutescens*, requiring some degree of dry season. (c) *Rhynchosia minima*, requiring a much stronger dry season; the disjunction is much more marked. (From van Meeuwen, Nooteboom, and van Steenis 1961.)

as isolated, rather small 'stepping stones'. Species have distributions disjunct to different degrees, and two examples are shown in Fig. 12.3. As van Meeuwen and his colleagues point out, dispersal between these stepping stones is improbable, and therefore such distributions must imply greater extent of monsoon climates in the past, allowing an exchange of these drought plants between Asia and Australia. Drier climates probably coincided with lower sea-levels during the Pleistocene Ice Ages, when the perhumid blocks and their rain forests would have been of slightly reduced area with more extensive marginal pockets of monsoon climate and vegetation. Further examples of drought-indicators are afforded by certain Euphorbiaceae. For example, *Blachia andamanica*, *Melanolepis multiglandulosa*, and *Phyllanthus buxifolius* are restricted to seasonally dry parts of the archipelago and in Borneo only occur in the dry zone mainly on the south coast around Bandjarmasin (Airy Shaw, 1975). There are many more examples in other families which could be cited. Although seasonal drought is only one factor amongst many which control the distribution of species its importance has probably been underestimated.

Two sites on the Atherton Tableland in north Queensland which now carry rain forest have been shown from pollen analysis of deposits in small lakes to have borne sclerophyll forest between 10 000 years and 7000 years ago (Walker 1970). This too implies climatic change.

Finally, it is noteworthy that, in contrast with the Malesian tropical rain forest, both the Amazonian and African rain forests are now known to have been very much reduced in extent during dry epochs of the Pleistocene (see the discussion by Vanzolini (1973)). It is probably because of the strongly maritime climate of the tropical Far East region, with both the Indian and Pacific Oceans abutting on to it, that rain forest was not here also decimated. Moreover, the presence of numerous high mountains, which have probably always been humid and therefore forested, means that there have been refugia for perhumid species in the Far East which scarcely exist in America or Africa. It is of considerable interest in this connection that there is only one small genus of rain-forest-inhabiting grasses, *Leptaspis*, in the Far East and considerably more of both genera and species in South America. The important and interesting consequences of these differences in past climate on species distribution patterns and evolution are beyond the scope of this book. But in conclusion it may be remarked that if to the continuously hot, wet climate plus mountain refugia is added the presence of very ancient land surfaces in parts of the tropical Far East (for example, Malaya has been continuously above the sea since the Jurassic period) one begins to assemble some of the reasons which help to explain the fantastically rich and diverse fauna and flora of the region.

161

12.2. Tropical moist deciduous forest

General description

Tropical moist deciduous forest is closed high forest, commonly of good height (30–36 m or more), the dominant species being mostly deciduous, though often only briefly so compared with types of even drier places; although intimate mixture of species is the rule, a relatively small number of species together form the greater part of the canopy and relatively simple associations are fairly frequently met with. There are some evergreen big trees, but on the whole they are few (well under half), and the evergreen habit is more developed in the lower storey which gives the forest as a whole a more-or-less evergreen appearance most of the year. A bamboo undergrowth is characteristic though locally absent, in which case the evergreens are commonly better developed. Rattans are restricted to wet ground; other big woody climbers are abundant and large. The undergrowth has usually been greatly influenced by fires which result in the replacement of evergreen shrubs by grass and this is especially abundant where the canopy is open. Bamboos are also favoured by fire and other disturbances. The absence of small trees and saplings of the large-tree species is often very marked and is also ascribable to repeated burning and grazing.

Habitat and Far East distribution

This forest type is important in India, where it occupies a huge area of the north-east centred on Bihar (these are the highly valuable sal, *Shorea robusta*, forests) and lies in a narrow belt along the east side of the western Ghats. It also occurs in a broad zone round the central drought area of Burma, and in west Thailand runs down to the head of the peninsula (these are all teak forests). Within Malesia its delimitation against Formations of drier sites is not clear owing to the massive alteration it has suffered at the hands of man, but it must once have occurred in northern Java and in the central part of the Philippines adjacent to the rain forests of the eastern coasts. Nor has its precise extent been defined in the extensive areas of seasonal climate in New Guinea (see the map, Fig. 3.1, p. 45). It occurs in patches as part of the mosaic of monsoon forests and savanna.

World distribution

This Formation is extensive in both Africa and South America as one of the complex of Formations of seasonally dry climates.

General floristics

The most characteristic species in Burma, Thailand, and Java is teak, *Tectona grandis*, which on the continent is generally associated in the top of the canopy with *Lagerstroemia* spp., *Pterocarpus* spp., and *Terminalia* spp. (Champion 1936). In Java big trees may occur as isolated emergents and teak occurs with *Bombax*, *Duabanga*, and *Tetrameles* (van Steenis 1957). In Burma the main bamboos are *Bambusa polymorpha* and *Cephalostachyum pergracile* and Dipterocarpaceae are absent though they do occur in yet drier Formations not detailed here (Champion 1936).

Important references (tropical moist deciduous forest)

Champion (1936, pp. 65–88); Burtt Davy (1938, pp. 35–7); Beard (1944), as semi-evergreen forest; Webb (1959), as semi-evergreen mesophyll vine forest; Baur (1964*a*, pp. 82–4), as semi-evergreen rain forest; Champion and Seth (1968, pp. 103–55).

Teak forest

Teak is the most important economic species of tropical moist deciduous forest. It has marked habitat preferences (which have to be borne in mind by silviculturists (Sarlin 1963)) and occurs naturally only on certain sites. Teak is fire-resistant, its seedlings being able to survive repeated burning and also grazing. Gregarious stands arise from burning of the forest by man or natural agents. Silviculture of teak in Thailand and the more remote parts of Burma is by extraction on a selection system. In the more accessible parts of Burma clear-felling is practised followed by burning, and this is easiest when the bamboos which grow under the teak come gregariously into flower; good teak-regeneration results, and there are now extensive pure stands totalling some 300 000 ha. In Java earlier practice was to refine moist deciduous teak forests by burning, but more recently plantations have been established (mostly by the taungya system, p. 230). Space does not permit a full account of the various silvicultural practices in teak forests, of which a full review has been published by Haig, Huberman, and Aung Din (1958) and a full bibliography of over 1500 references by Mathur (1973). The teak forests of east and central Java, including plantations, cover about 700 000 ha, which in 1969 yielded 546 000 m³ of timber—over 90 per cent of the total timber harvest (Sweatman 1971). Teak plantations have been established widely through the tropics in seasonally dry climates, for example, in the extreme north-west of Malaya, in Perlis; and in Papua at Mount Lawes near to Port Moresby, about 1400 ha by 1973 (Anon. 1973).

12.3. Transition from rain to monsoon forest north of Malaya: the Kra ecotone

In the Malay peninsula in the region of the Kra isthmus north of the Thailand–West Malaysia border there is a change in forest type and also in flora, leading to the replacement of tropical lowland evergreen rain forest by tropical semi-evergreen rain forest. The change begins just north of the border between the two countries. It is due to decreasing rainfall and decreasing seasonality in climate northwards (see the map of rainfall types, Fig. 3.1, p. 45) and is complicated by the high degree of disturbance or destruction which the forests have suffered, as well as by areas of relatively wetter or drier climate and by azonal soil types, notably those formed over the limestone hills which run along the west coast for some distance north of the border.

Since the early botanical exploration by Boden Kloss (1920), the northern limit of the Malesian

flora has been taken to be at a line running from Alor Star (6° 8′ N) on the west coast north to Songkhla (7° 10′ N) on the east coast. Recent evidence collected mainly by P. F. Burgess (in 1973), with a few additional notes made by the author (in 1972) and in the unpublished record of a visit by F. W. Foxworthy in 1930, indicates that this boundary is not correct. The map (Fig. 12.4) shows the locations at which the rain forest has been observed by these three workers. Two types are distinguishable.

The Malayan-type forest is characterized by presence of the Red Meranti group of *Shorea* (of which *Shorea curtisii* is clearly visible from afar) and by the famous heavy hardwood *Balanocarpus heimii*, the palm *Eugeissona tristis* and the shade- and moisture-loving undergrowth arecoid palms *Areca, Iguanura, Nenga,* and *Pinanga*. The biggest trees are mostly evergreen and species are not gregarious except for *S. curtisii*.

The Thai-type forest differs from the Malayan by the absence of Red Meranti *Shorea*, by the abundance of the White Meranti group especially *S. hypochra* and (on limestone) *S. roxburghii*, and also by abundant, gregarious *Parashorea stellata*. The legumes *Intsia palembanica* and *Sindora* spp. and the dipterocarps *Anisoptera oblonga, Dipterocarpus kerrii*, and *Shorea guiso* are also very characteristic of these drier forests. The stature of the Thai forests is slightly less; huge emergent trees are rare, and the whole canopy tends to be slightly lower, denser, and hence less markedly layered.

The boundary between the two forest types, which is floristic as well as structural, is seen in Fig. 12.4 to run more or less west to east, from Kangar in Malaysia to Pattani in Thailand; Bukit Perangin, a granite hill in north Kedah, lies just to its south. The Kangar–Pattani line is believed to be a close approximation to the boundary between tropical lowland evergreen rain forest to the south (the Malayan type) and tropical semi-evergreen rain forest to the north (the Thai type) and to be a truer representation of the boundary than the line drawn by Boden Kloss.

The boundary, as already indicated, is complicated by several factors. First, several species do rarely transgress it, for example, *Shorea leprosula* and *S. parvifolia* (Red Meranti) are found at Khao Chong $(7\frac{1}{2}°\,N)$ north of the line, probably because this forest, which is on the central dividing range, is wetted by both monsoons (Smitinand); *S. parvifolia* has also once been found north of Bukit Perangin (Wyatt-Smith 1963). The White Meranti species, *Shorea roxburghii*, occurs south of the line in Kedah

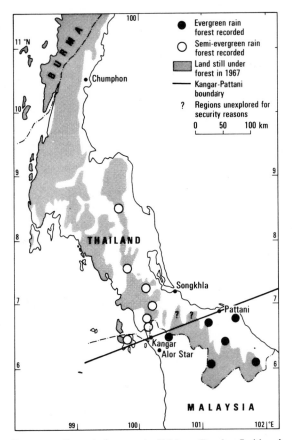

FIG. 12.4. Change in forest north of Malaya. (Based on Smitinand and Lamphun 1967 and unpublished observations of Burgess, Foxworthy, and Whitmore.)

163

and Perlis, extreme north-west Malaya, associated with limestone. Further, *Shorea hypochra* and *Parashorea stellata* occur, as scattered individuals, in central and north Malaya.

The second complication is that north of approximately the narrowest point of the isthmus ($10\frac{1}{2}°$N) the west coast of the peninsula, in lower Burma (Tenasserim), and the Mergui archipelago off-shore are markedly wetter than the east coast, resulting from the south monsoon blowing on-shore from the extensive stretch of the Bay of Bengal. Parts of this coast have, according to Champion (1936) and Champion and Seth (1968), true evergreen rain forest, though without the typically Malayan floristic groups; these authors note that there is a complex mosaic with semi-evergreen rain forest.

On the drier eastern side of the peninsula in Thailand, from Chumphon (11°N) northwards, the natural forest has been replaced on the coastal plain by a low scrub. It only persists as small relict patches in the valleys of the low mountain range which forms the spine of the peninsula and the border with

Burma (Smitinand). One can presume that seasonal drought is sufficiently severe in the rain shadow of this range to have permitted destruction by burning. At the top of the peninsula, from about $12\frac{1}{2}°$N northwards, the dry season is sufficiently marked for moist deciduous forest, which is dominated by teak, to replace semi-evergreen rain forest as the natural climax (Smitinand and Lamphun 1967).

Small isolated patches of semi-evergreen rain forest occur in central Thailand (notably at the Khao Yai National Park) and also in the south-east around Chantaburi (102°E, 12° 45′N), where, on the slopes and foothills of the Cardamon mountains as well as on the islands off-shore and extending eastwards into Cambodia, there is a small area with the typical Malayan undergrowth palm flora and a few bamboos (Rollet 1972). *Diospyros hermaphroditica*, a species of Borneo, Java, Sumatra, and Malaya, extends north to the head of the peninsula and reappears in the Chantaburi pocket. Elsewhere in Burma and the Indo-Chinese peninsula it is replaced by *D. ehretioides* (Ng 1971). These species perhaps indicate the occur-

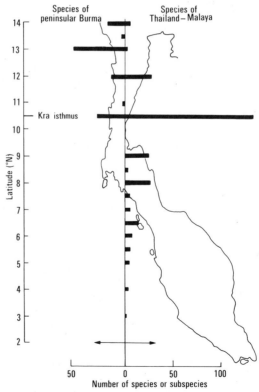

Fig. 12.5. Range limits of lowland rain forest birds in the Malay peninsula. The length of each horizontal bar is proportional to the number of species/subspecies reaching a limit at the latitude indicated. (From Wells 1974, Fig. 1.)

rence of an area of true evergreen rain forest in the Chantaburi pocket, probably as patches on particularly humid sites in a setting of more seasonal forest. Here too is found an impoverished, isolated, outlying pocket of the Malayan avifauna (Wells 1971). However, the rich Malayan *Macaranga* flora disappears north of the Kangar–Pattani boundary (Whitmore 1973*f*; Airy Shaw 1971) and does not reappear in the Chantaburi pocket, nor do the Red Meranti *Shoreas* and other truly Malayan dipterocarps.

South of the Kangar-Pattani boundary in the extreme north-west of Malaya most of the lowlands of Perlis and north-west Kedah bear a forest dominated by *Schima wallichii* and bamboo which also serves to obscure the line of the boundary. Symington (1943) in describing this forest (see also Wyatt-Smith (1963)) regarded it as derived from evergreen rain forest by intermittent cutting, grazing, cultivation, and burning and degraded to a drier type; floristically it is a mixture of the more adaptable rain-forest species together with colonists from secondary forest or from semi-evergreen rain forest or the monsoon forest Formations of Thailand and Burma. Structurally it is very heterogeneous. The bamboos are principally *Gigantochloa latifolia* and *G. ligulata*. *Schima* also occurs extensively in Bangka, south Sumatra, and Java in disturbed and secondary forest (van Steenis 1972).

The Langkawi Islands lie off the west coast just north of the Kangar–Pattani line (Fig. 12.4). The forest of the limestone outcrops on the Langkawis illustrates how dry sites accentuate the influence of seasonal climate. This forest is unique in west Malaysia in having pronounced 'autumn' coloration shortly before the leaves fall, with most species deciduous for a few weeks during January or February and also in being markedly spiny, like the Thorn forests of Burma (though one can only speculate on the functional significance of spines in strongly seasonal tropical climates). The granite of Langkawi (for example, Gunung Raya) bears semi-evergreen rain forest (Wyatt-Smith 1963).

The extreme north-west tip of Sumatra around Banda Aceh is seasonally even drier than the region just north of Malaya (Fig. 3.1, p. 45); it is an area of cultivation, and there appears to be no record of its natural vegetation cover.

The change in the lowland avifauna in the Kra isthmus is shown in Fig. 12.5. This parallels fairly closely the main changes in forest in two important respects. First, the greatest number of species or subspecies reach their northern limit at the northern limit of high forest, that is, at about the latitude of Chumphon (11° N). Secondly, the Burmese element reaches as far south as does the Burmese evergreen rain forest. The marked change which occurs in the amphibian fauna also has already been described (§1.2).

13 Animal life and forest Formations

OBSERVATIONS ON the extent to which animal life differs between the various Formations is still extremely fragmentary, and this chapter can do little other than chart the boundaries of our ignorance. The outlines of the zoogeography of the tropical Far East have already been described (§1.2), and some mention made of niche specialization within lowland evergreen rain forest (§2.7). Altitudinal zones of animals in the mountains will be discussed later (§16.7). In this chapter it is convenient to bring together observations on animal life in the primary lowland forests and in the secondary forest, scrublands, and savannas derived from them (Chapter 18). Most of the data are about the mammals and birds of Sarawak and Malaya.

The greatest number of animal species are adapted to life within the forest, presumably because this is the most complex vegetation type with the most niches and because, until man created extensive open and semi-open areas, it clothed nearly the whole landscape.

Dependence on the forest is well exemplified by the avifauna. Six hundred and sixty bird species are known, or presumed, to breed on the lands of the Sunda shelf (Wells 1971); 70 per cent are birds of inland forest and only 18 of these species inhabit open country as well as forest (Wells 1971). Within the present century 459 species of birds are known or assumed to have bred in Malaya; 297 (65 per cent) are species of inland forest (Wells 1974). In a 200 ha area of lowland dipterocarp rain forest at Kuala Lompat, Medway and Wells (1971) recorded 156 species of birds; 130 were forest or forest fringe species, 8 were riverine species, 9 were species associated with dwellings and large clearings, and 9 feed on insects above the forest canopy (6 of them having some dependence on forest). In this small area 141 species were breeding residents (Table 1.2, p. 11). In the same area 64 mammal species were recorded, of which all except two rats (*Rattus argentiventer*, *R. exulans*) are probably dependent on primary forest for survival.

In Borneo 183 species of amphibians are confined to primary forest. The other 8 recorded species are commensal with man and have wide ecological tolerance which is undoubtedly important to their success (Inger 1966).

We now turn to individual Formations.

Peat swamp forest

There is no evidence that any species of mammal or bird is confined to this forest Formation (Medway 1972c) despite its great extent (for example, it covers 12·5 per cent of the area of Sarawak—§11.3). Closer study is likely to show that here, as in other forest types, the proportional representation of species does differ from that in the evergreen rainforest Formation.

Heath forest

Coastal heath forest has been extensively degraded by man to open savanna woodland or a low scrub, to which the comments on secondary forest below apply. There is no evidence of a specialized mammal or bird fauna in heath forest. Extensive, isolated or depauperate stands can be expected to possess species in different proportions from evergreen rain forest, resulting from the distinctive flora and physiognomy of this Formation. But inland heath forest, mainly found in Borneo, occurs interdigitated with other forest Formations, and many of its stands are of small extent. These may have little faunistic difference from the surrounding forest, at least amongst more wide-ranging animals. An attempt to rehabilitate orang utan, confiscated from smugglers, to forest life failed at Bako National Park, Sarawak, but that is isolated on a coastal peninsula largely covered by an extreme kind of heath forest of low stature and with some areas of open savanna.

A comparative survey of three areas, one in heath forest and two in lowland dipterocarp rain forest, in Sarawak did show interesting differences amongst amphibians and reptiles; these are summarized in Table 13.1. The heath forest had no turtles and fewer species of frogs, lizards, and snakes. The difference was greatest for the snakes. Secondly, within these groups the heath forest had far fewer endemics than either of the dipterocarp forest areas. Thirdly, the two dipterocarp forest areas both had a high percentage of all three animal groups not shared with the heath forest; this was most marked amongst snakes and least amongst frogs. Snakes are tertiary consumers, feeding almost entirely on vertebrates. Their greater reduction in heath forest than lizards and frogs possibly indicates a relative shortage of food in heath forest which becomes more marked along the food chain and least affects the frogs, which

TABLE 13.1
Amphibians and reptiles in sample areas of heath and evergreen rain forest in Sarawak

	Heath forest Nyabau	Lowland evergreen rain forest	
		Pesu hill	Labang valley
Species numbers: frogs	24	53	33
lizards	13	31	33
snakes	13	35	38
turtles	0	1	2
Total	50	120	106
Percentage of spp. shared with the other two habitats	92	33	37
Percentage of spp. not shared with the heath forest: snakes		77	74
lizards		64	65
frogs		60	48

Unpublished data of R. F. Inger from the Fourth Division, based on prolonged trapping; communicated by D. H. Janzen.

are primary consumers feeding mainly on insects (Janzen).

Only further research will show whether the plants of heath forest possess a higher degree of toxicity to insects than those elsewhere, thereby reducing the food source available to animal consumers and hence their biomass.

Johnson (1967) found that in Malaya blackwater streams (that is, the kind which drain heath forest) had only about 100 species of fresh-water fish out of over 250 known from the Peninsula, a lesser diversity than in the clear or turbid streams draining dipterocarp rain forest. Several species were facultative air-breathers. The suspended polyphenols which give such streams their colour are possibly in some degree toxic to fish.

Mangrove forest

Mangrove forest in Malaya possesses a rather distinctive avifauna with only 27 species in common with inland forest (Nisbet 1968; Wells 1974) and largely composed of kingfishers, sunbirds, warblers, and woodpeckers. The abundant, mainly frugiverous, families of adjacent lowland dipterocarp evergreen rain forest are conspicuously rare, namely, babblers, barbets, bulbuls, leaf birds, hornbills, and pheasants. The inland boundary of the mangrove avifauna is very sharp, and many more species can be found a few metres inland from the ecotone than seawards. Several examples of replacement by obvious competitors are known. Throughout much of Malaya the kingfisher *Halcyon smyrmensis* replaces *H. chloris* in

dry-land forest, but in Borneo, where the former does not occur, *H. chloris* also ranges inland. In the New Hebrides *H. farquhari* similarly replaces *H. chloris* (Medway). The main interest of the Malayan mangrove avifauna is that it (plus species of forest fringes and the east coast padangs) and not the avifauna of the evergreen rain forest is the main source of the avifauna of the extensive open and semi-open country of villages, suburban gardens, riversides, and forest clearings. The 51 commonest mangrove-forest species are also found in these other habitats, and 85 per cent of the resident mangrove bird species also breed elsewhere in Malaya. Nisbet considers that the mangrove was also formerly the main habitat for migrant birds from the eastern Palaearctic wintering in Malaya; these also have now come to occupy the large tracts of man-made habitat. There is no evidence that the common practice of felling mangrove forest on a 30-year rotation affects the avifauna, except in reducing the number of nesting holes, many of which are made by woodpeckers and occur mainly in big trees of *Sonneratia*.

Secondary forest

Secondary forest is a much less complex ecosystem than primary forest. The canopy is lower and there are fewer, different species of plants (Chapter 18). Secondary forest existed originally as small, isolated patches on landslips and along rivers. Its extent has increased, and is increasing enormously, through man's influence, as will be described in Part V.

The primary lowland rain forest faunas appear on

the whole to be unable to take advantage of the vast new areas of secondary forest and its associated scrub and grassland, though Fogden (1972) pointed out that secondary forest provides a concentration of tree species with fruits edible to birds (especially *Macaranga, Mallotus, Melastoma, Rhodamnia,* and *Trema*) which, moreover, fruit most of the time (§6.2), and he suggested this might be significant for social and breeding behaviour. Wells (1971) noted how much more numerous birds are in secondary than primary forest, though of fewer species. McClure (1969) recorded 24 birds per hectare in suburban Kuala Lumpur and only 10 birds per hectare in primary forest a few kilometres away. These observations probably result because, in general, Malayan frugivorous birds occupy bigger territories than insectivores of comparable size so that more will be recorded in a given area, even though the biomass per unit area is not in fact greater (Medway). Stevens (1968) computed that in Malaya 53 per cent of the 115 ground-living mammal species are confined to primary forest, 25 per cent live in primary and tall secondary forest, 12 per cent live in primary or secondary forest and can also subsist in cultivated areas, and only 10 per cent live solely in cultivated or urban areas; amongst the 22 per cent that enter cultivated areas most are pests. Changes in the native mammal fauna were studied after clearance of a small area of lowland rain forest at Sungei Buloh in Malaya by Harrison (1965). A marked decline was found in the number of species, from 30 in primary forest to 10 in secondary forest to 4 in scrub and grassland, demonstrating that replacement of primary forest by secondary forest (or tree crops) causes a drastic reduction in the number, while complete elimination of the forest causes almost complete elimination of the native fauna and its replacement by a few species of commensal rats. Selective felling of primary forest, especially where a serious attempt is made to maintain the forest as a productive one, was found by Harrison not substantially to deplete the number of species, at least of the smaller mammals (cf. §17.4). Chivers has found that two gibbons (siamang and white-handed gibbon) are not affected either. However, monkeys appear better able than gibbons to make use of secondary forest and highly disturbed habitats.

Fire-climax *Imperata* grassland is very poor in mammal and bird life; though the rat *Rattus argentiventer* appears to be a grassland specialist. The fire-climax *Pinus merkusii* forests of Sumatra support little or no mammal life (Wilson and Wilson 1973).

The conclusion from these studies is, as Stevens (1968) pointed out, that the only way in which the majority of the native mammals and birds can be preserved is in the undisturbed lowland rain forest in which they evolved. If the habitat is entirely forfeited to agricultural or urban development the rich faunal heritage of the Sunda shelf countries will be lost. The only way it can be retained is by establishing large enough reserves, which must be permanent features of the landscape, 'because the treasures they protect have lived there for thirty million years and should have the right to expect a similar future.' We shall return to the subject of conservation in Chapter 19.

The sketchy nature of the preceding account will have strongly emphasized to the reader the point made in the introduction to this chapter. We really do still remain very largely in a state of complete ignorance both about the occurrence of animals and even more so about their interrelations with the rest of the rain-forest ecosystem.

14 Conifers in the forests

A NUMBER of tropical conifers hold considerable interest for foresters because of their major economic importance as a source of high-quality softwood timber (notably *Agathis* and *Araucaria*) or of fibres and cellulose for wood-based industries (notably *Pinus*). The economic importance of conifers is likely to increase even further in the future (cf. §19.1). Conifers are a more ancient and primitive group than the flowering plants and botanists have been concerned to investigate their place in the forests of the tropical Far East, which are predominantly composed of the much more diverse, successful, and numerous flowering plants.

All the conifer genera in the tropical Far East except one belong to families of essentially southern hemisphere distribution. Four of these, *Agathis*, *Dacrydium*, *Phyllocladus*, and *Podocarpus*, extend north of the equator. *Dacrydium* reaches Hainan and *Podocarpus* reaches as far as the Himalaya and Japan. *Phyllocladus* extends as far north-west as Sabah and Brunei. Pollen of *Podocarpus imbricatus* and *Phyllocladus* is first found in the Pliocene in Brunei which suggests they might be recent arrivals there (Muller 1972). The other southern-hemisphere

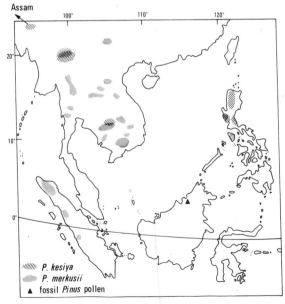

FIG. 14.1. Geographical range *Pinus kesiya* and *P. merkusii* (sens. lat.). (After Kowal 1966; Cooling 1968; Muller 1972; Turnbull 1972.)

conifers of the tropical Far East, *Araucaria* and *Papuacedrus*, are restricted to New Guinea, and consequently their ranges do not extend north of the equator.

Pinus extends southwards into the tropics from its centre in the north temperate zone in both Central America and the Far East. Two species, *Pinus kesiya (insularis)* and *P. merkusii*, reach the Malay archipelago (Fig. 14.1). *Pinus* pollen has been found in deposits in Brunei up till the Pliocene, associated with *Alnus*. Two other northern conifers, *Picea* and *Tsuga*, have been found as far as the Upper Miocene together with *Ephedra*. All these genera except *Pinus* are now not found nearer than 20°N on the Asian continent (Muller 1972); their geographical range has become more restricted.

In tropical lowland evergreen rain forest of the perhumid climate conifers are mostly found as scattered individuals, intermingled with the flowering plants. *Agathis* and *Podocarpus* are the commonest genera in this forest Formation; both extend in range into lower montane rain forest. *Agathis* is unusual in also frequently forming groves. In Malaya such groves occur between 300 m and 1500 m elevation and have always been found to be on thin, quartz-rich soils (for example, on sandstone plateaux on Kedah Peak and on Gunung Angsi) and associated with species restricted to or most abundant on these sites, for example, *Cratoxylum formosum*, *Eurycoma* spp., *Fagraea gigantea*, *Melanorrhoea* spp., *Pandanus recurvatus*, and *Tristania* spp., sometimes over ground cover of *Lycopodium cernuum*. The same species are often associated with *Shorea curtisii*, as will be discussed in §15.3.

Araucaria (Figs 14.6 and 14.7) is locally an important component of the evergreen and semi-evergreen rain forest of New Guinea, in the hills and mountains between about 500 m and 2500 m (that is, the lowland and lower montane Formations). The biggest and best-known stand, originally some 70 km long and containing an estimated 1.062×10^6 m³ of commercial timber, is centred on Bulolo. In a few localities *Araucaria* also occurs in upper montane rain forest.

Pinus is restricted to slightly seasonally dry parts of the archipelago (in B and C/D type climates, Fig. 3.1, p. 45), mainly in the zone of lower montane rain forest, occurring naturally on extreme sites

169

FIG. 14.2. *Pinus kesiya* regenerating after fire in dry deciduous dipterocarp forest in north Thailand. This stand includes *Dipterocarpus obtusifolius*, *Castanopsis* sp., *Dillenia* sp., *Shorea obtusa*, and *S. siamensis*.

and with its range expanded by man-made disturbance. It is rather more widespread in the monsoon forests of mainland south-east Asia (Figs 12.2 (p. 159) and 14.2).

Elsewhere in the lowlands, conifers are decidedly rare in all the Formations of swampy or seasonally swampy sites. Exceptions are *Podocarpus motleyi* in Malaya (Keng 1972) and Sarawak (Anderson 1963, as *P. blumei*) and *Dacrydium beccarii* var. *subelatum* (Fig. 14.3), which at Lawas in north Sarawak and in south-west Sabah south of Sipitang is gregarious

with *Casuarina nobilis* over shallow (3 m) peat but apparently dying out, perhaps owing to a rising water-level (Browne 1952; Anderson 1963; Fox 1972).

In heath forest, conifers are locally abundant, especially *Agathis* and *Dacrydium* and more locally *Podocarpus* (§10.3). They have also been recorded over limestone, possibly restricted to deep acid peat (§10.4). The only conifers recorded from ultrabasic rocks are *Dacrydium gibbsiae* restricted to this habitat on Mt. Kinabalu over 2400 m and a few stands of *Araucaria cunninghamii* in New Guinea and some of *Agathis* in east Kalimantan, Celebes (Malili), West Irian (Japen), and southern New Caledonia (*A. ovata*).

In New Guinea, which has a bigger conifer flora and much higher mountains than elsewhere in the tropical Far East, conifers are locally important. In the Wabag–Tari area of the highlands, for example, *Podocarpus* is a common component of the mixed lower montane forest (§16.1) and occasional in the 'beech' (*Nothofagus*) forest. Above about 2400 m there occur belts several scores of metres wide of forest mainly composed of the conifers *Dacrydium novoguineense*, *Papuacedrus* spp., *Phyllocladus hypophyllus*, and *Podocarpus* spp. These extend along valley sides, edging tongues of high mountain grassland which extend down the frost-prone valley floors, and pass abruptly into mixed broad-leaf forest on the upper slopes which do not get frosted. This conifer forest is 36 m tall, with about 12 trees of 1.5–2.4 m girth per hectare and a timber volume of 40 m³/ha. At elevations above 2100 m patches of either Myrtaceae or of the conifers *Dacrydium elatum* and *Podocarpus papuanus* 12–18 m tall are associated with boggy depressions, which are believed to be frost hollows, in the mixed lower montane rain forest. Trees of *Papuacedrus* occur as emergents from the 12–16 m tall canopy of upper montane forest and also from the mixed lower montane forest (Robbins and Pullen 1965; Grubb).

Wherever tropical forest is exploited big conifer trees are extracted for timber together with the broad-leaf species, but few species are sufficiently common to have attained commercial significance; the New Guinea stands just mentioned are still mainly inaccessible. The three genera which are exceptions to this generalization are *Agathis*,

FIG. 14.3 (opposite). The Lawas peat swamp forest, north Sarawak, dominated by *Casuarina nobilis* (umbrella-shaped crown) and *Dacrydium beccarii* var. *subelatum* (feathery crown).

Araucaria, and *Pinus*. These occur in habitats of increasing seasonal dryness in that order and will now be considered in turn. For all three, natural stands are now being augmented by plantations, for which purpose conifers hold great promise because of their high annual volume increment per unit area which exceeds that of all flowering plants except *Eucalyptus* (§8.1, Fig. 8.1, p. 89).

14.1. *Agathis*

Agathis has the most tropical distribution of all the genera of the Coniferae. It extends from Sumatra and Malaya, through the Malay archipelago to Queensland and Fiji, New Caledonia, and the northwest peninsula of North Island, New Zealand (*A. australis*, the Kauri Pine). It is apparently restricted to the regions without a marked dry season and is not native on Java, the Lesser Sunda Islands, or on the Kei, Tanimbar, and Aru groups of the Moluccas (Meijer Drees 1940; Manaputty 1955). The staple food of these last three groups is maize. *Agathis* grows in wetter climates on islands to their north, its area coincident with that where the semi-swamp Sago Palm is the staple crop (Manaputty 1955). Some 25 species have been described, but these are ill-defined. There is substantial variation in tree shape, growth rate, and ecological behaviour within *Agathis*, and this to some extent correlates with the taxonomy of the genus.

The most detailed ecological study is of *A. macrophylla* (Whitmore 1966c) (Fig. 14.4). This species is endemic to the Santa Cruz Islands in the south-west Pacific, where it occurs as groves and scattered trees over basalt on latosolic soil which shows no signs of podzolization. *A. macrophylla* seedlings require a small gap in the high forest canopy to grow up (see §6.5, Fig. 6.7, p. 77) and the species is apparently a normal, relatively shade-bearing component of primary rain forest not dependent for its survival on the occurrence of large gaps. Its behaviour is similar to many broad-leaf trees, and it appears to be successfully maintaining itself in competition. *A. microstachya* (Queensland), *A. obtusa* (New Hebrides), *A. vitiense* (Fiji), and *A. dammara* (Malaya) also occur as groves or individuals in predominantly flowering-plant rain forest. By contrast two species are known to form pure stands in heath forest over podzols, where, in terms of biomass per unit area, they are highly successful. Of these *A. borneensis* is said to occupy 30 000 ha in the lowlands in south Kalimantan (Manaputty 1955), mainly in huge stands of several thousand hectares each; though it does not form

stands bigger than 40 ha in Sarawak and Brunei (Fig. 14.5) (Browne 1952). Secondly, *A. labillardierei* is found from 200–1700 m in the Star Mountains of central New Guinea on sandy terraces, some with impeded drainage (Reynders 1964b), and also occurs over limestone on Waigeo Island (van Royen 1963), presumably on deep, acidic peat. Its habitat elsewhere in New Guinea remains mainly uninvestigated. In addition *A. flavescens* is a species of small or dwarf trees locally common in, and restricted to, upper montane rain forest on the summit plateaux of the sandstone and quartzite mountains Tahan and Rabong in central Malaya, probably over similar soils.

There are two species with ecology intermediate between that of these two groups. *A. australis* in New Zealand is reputed to develop podzols over acidic rocks (rhyolite and various sedimentaries) and brown loams over basic rocks (basalt) (Taylor, Dixon, and Seelye 1950). Secondly, *A.* 'sp. A' (Meijer Drees 1940) grows scattered in dense lower montane forest on the slopes of Mt. Kinabalu in Sabah. In some places the soils below it show signs of podzolization, for instance on the more gently sloping sites of the east ridge at 1260 m. In other places, for instance on valley sides which are subject to continual erosion and on recent river terraces, the soil shows no signs of podzolization (Askew 1964). In the mountainous interior of Brunei *A. borneensis* is restricted to plateau sites which are stable and therefore have non-renewing, leached soils which are podzolized (Ashton 1964).

Leaf leachate of *A. australis* has been shown experimentally to mobilize iron (Bloomfield 1953), and this is probably true of all species. It seems likely that the species of *Agathis* interact with the soil on which they grow and cause podzolization over acidic, base-poor parent materials but not on more base-rich substrata.

Agathis stands have been heavily exploited wherever they are accessible, mainly for the very high-grade timber, but also extensively in west New Guinea, Celebes, and Borneo for copal. *A. dammara* (*loranthifolia*) has been planted on a commercial scale in west and central Java, where there are 17 000 ha in the moister regions, mainly on the wetter south slopes of the mountains. The very high growth increment of 25 m³/ha/year at 35 years has been recorded on these young, base-rich volcanic soils (Ferguson 1949, cf. Fig. 8.1.). The trees have been raised for two or three generations from wayside trees which originally came from Ambon in the Moluccas. There are also about 400 ha of plantations

FIG. 14.4. A mature tree of *Agathis macrophylla* on Vanikolo, Santa Cruz Islands.

FIG. 14.5. *Agathis borneensis* forest in Brunei. The tree on the extreme right is a *Tristania*.

in Queensland (*A. robusta*). Trial plots have been widely established throughout the region and elsewhere in the tropics, but fuller use of *Agathis* awaits selection of superior strains of good tree-form and rapid growth rate, especially in youth, which in its turn awaits a fuller understanding of morphological and ecological plasticity in the genus.

It is of interest that some other very widely ranging woody plants in the Far East have proved as intractable as *Agathis* to taxonomic analysis. Two examples are *Pometia*, one of the prime timber trees

174

of New Guinea where it is very abundant and which ranges from Ceylon to Samoa (Jacobs 1962), and *Ficus deltoidea*, a complex species of shrubs, epiphytes, and small trees which ranges from Thailand to Celebes (Corner 1970).

14.2. *Araucaria*

Araucaria is a genus of about 14 species of which 2 are South American and the other 12 are restricted to the south-west Pacific region, 7 of the species being endemic to New Caledonia.

Two species occur in tropical rain forest in New Guinea, *A. hunsteinii* (*klinkii*), the Klinki Pine and *A. cunninghamii* (including *A. beccarii* of the Arfak mountains), the Hoop Pine (Figs 14.6 and 14.7). The latter species, which has poorer form, extends to tropical and subtropical rain forest in Australia. Both species occur gregariously. They do not usually grow together in the same stand.

A. hunsteinii is apparently restricted to eastern New Guinea, from the Jimi River southwards 5° to the Wamira River. It occurs between about 520 m and 2100 m on the slopes of the central cordillera mainly in inland valleys. *A. cunninghamii* is found through the whole extent of the island of New Guinea and also on Fergusson Island off the north coast of Papua. It ranges also down the eastern seaboard of Australia to the Hastings River at 33° S in northern New South Wales. With a latitudinal range of over 30° it is the widest-ranging species of *Araucaria*. Its altitudinal range from 90 m to 2800 m is greater than that of *A. hunsteinii*; the main stands lie between 500 m and 1900 m. The highest stands, at nearly 2800 m, are on Mts. Suckling and Dayman in south-eastern Papua (Paijmans 1967; Gray 1973).

Both species are most abundant in the Wau and Watut valleys of the Bulolo River and upper Watut River in east New Guinea where they have been heavily exploited. Their ecology has been described by Havel (1971). Most other stands are small and inaccessible, but a few almost of equal size have recently been discovered (Gray 1973). None of these have yet attained major commercial importance.

On the floor of the Wau and Watut valleys, *A. hunsteinii* occurs in semi-evergreen forest which includes deciduous species of *Cordia*, *Erythrina*, *Pterocymbium*, *Spondias*, *Terminalia*, and *Toona*. In the Wau valley this forest merges into a shorter, sparser rain forest on ridges and slopes which is over-topped by Araucarias, especially *A. hunsteinii*, at fairly high densities; this ridge forest is characterized by abundant Meliaceae (*Aglaia*, *Amoora*, *Chisocheton*, *Dysoxylum*, *Toona*) and Lauraceae (*Actinodaphne*,

FIG. 14.6. Giant *Araucaria cunninghamii* trees towering over the broad-leaf rain forest (Waris, Sepik, New Guinea, near the frontier). Note the monopodial construction. Arrows point to *Agathis labillardierei* in the foreground.

Beilschmiedia, Cinnamomum, Cryptocarya, Endiandra) with leathery notophylls the most conspicuous leaf size.

With increasing elevation this forest type merges into *Castanopsis–Quercus* lower montane rain forest in which *Cryptocarya, Elaeocarpus, Elmerillia, Eugenia, Garcinia, Gordonia*, and *Sloanea* are also common. *A. cunninghamii* replaces *A. hunsteinii* upwards within this forest and on ridges forms almost pure stands. Throughout New Guinea *A. cunninghamii* is commonest in this forest type and the two species apparently grow in a similar relationship to each other. On Mt. Dayman between 2050 m and 2450 m *A. cunninghamii* occurs in a mossy upper montane rain forest with *Decaspermum, Ficus, Ilex, Quintinia, Schizomeria*, and *Xanthomyrtus*. It has a very wide ecological range at lower elevations and has been recorded on ultrabasic rocks, in swampland (supposedly), and (at Daribi) on limestone. This last locality is the only place where pure stands have been found (Gray 1973).

These two New Guinea Araucarias are amongst the most noble trees in the world. At maturity they stand as giant columns 3 m in girth and 60 m tall (*A. cunninghamii*) or 65–75 m (*A. hunsteinii*)† with their crowns above the 30 m high flowering-plant forest (Fig. 14.8). Havel found that natural regeneration is best in places where the flowering-

† The tallest tree recorded in the tropics is one of *A. hunsteinii*, measured as 88·9 m in 1941 (Gray).

FIG. 14.7. The emergent crowns of *Araucaria hunsteinii* in the Jimi valley, New Guinea, rain forest seen from above. Note the regular radial branching.

175

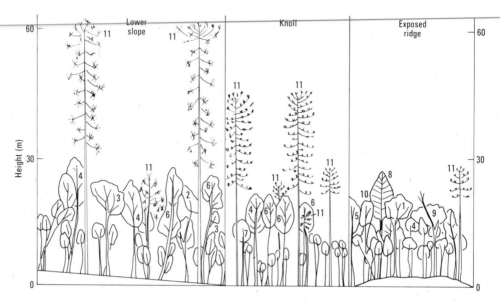

FIG. 14.8. Profile diagrams of New Guinea *Araucaria* forest. Topographical gradient from Watut Valley, 980–1300 m elevation. 1. *Cryptocarya*; 2. *Dysoxylum*; 3. *Sloanea*; 4. *Elaeocarpus*; 5. *Engelhardtia*; 6. *Castanopsis*; 7. *Eugenia*; 8. *Papuacedrus*; 9. *Xanthostemon*; 10. *Gordonia*; 11. *Araucaria cunninghamii*|*hunsteinii*. (Havel 1971, Fig. 4.)

plant canopy is rather open, such as steep slopes, rocky ridges, and disturbed sites. In high forest *Araucaria* occurs as stands of mixed size, seedlings and saplings together with trees (see Fig. 14.8), and apparently requires small gaps to grow up.

In Australia *A. cunninghamii* is abundant in some semi-evergreen rain forest and monsoon forests. It is not found in the wettest areas on deep soils of high fertility, except as big isolated trees with scanty regeneration (Webb and Tracey 1967) which have been estimated from girth growth measurements to be 400–500 years old (McGrath). It is not known whether these trees became established at a time when the climate was slightly drier (Webb 1964) or, alternatively, as pioneers following fire or cyclone damage to the forest, seeding-in from mother trees growing on skeletal soils on nearby ridges.

The Bulolo–Watut *Araucaria* forests are the single most important source of timber in New Guinea. The monthly coupe in 1967 was 4700 m³, of which 1400 m³ came from plantation thinnings (Morel 1967). Much is peeled for veneer which is made into plywood, a total of 18 000 m³ in 1967. Extensive plantations have been established to replace the virgin stands; 3235 ha and 3265 ha respectively of *A. cunninghamii* and *A. hunsteinii* by 1973 (Anon. 1973). The plantations are partly on land which was formerly forested and partly (along with *Eucalyptus deglupta*) on nearby valley-floors in long-grass (*Coelorachis, Imperata, Ophiuros, Saccharum*), fire-climax savanna (Morel 1967). Recently, young *A. cunninghamii* plantations have become seriously damaged by a Scolytid leaf miner (§2.8), to circumvent which this species is now being cultivated in mixed stands with flowering plants (Morel 1967). There were considerable problems initially in seed storage (§5.2) and in seedling establishment, until it was discovered that a very acid seed-bed is necessary. The annual planting programme now uses 1500 kg of Klinki and 2000 kg of Hoop Pine seeds, and 570 ha are planted up. Large-scale plantations of *A. cunninghamii* have been made in Australia, and experimental ones of both species have been established in various parts of the tropics (Ntima 1968). *Araucaria* seems assured of an important place in the man-made tropical forests of the future, despite the expense and difficulty of handling its large seeds: for further information on this aspect see Nikles (1973).

14.3. *Pinus*

Pinus extends from the north temperate zone into the seasonally dry tropics in central America as well as south-east Asia. Two species,† *P. kesiya* and *P. merkusii*, occur in continental south-east Asia and

† The continental populations of *P. merkusii* are consistently different in several characters from the island ones and were segregated as a new species *P. merkusiana* by Cooling and Gaussen (1970).

both extend into the Malay archipelago (Fig. 14.1). Of these *P. kesiya* has a more northerly distribution, and reaches south as far as the Cordillera Central and Zambales mountains of Luzon in the Philippines, where it occurs from 900 m elevation downwards. *P. merkusii*, with a more southerly distribution, occurs in the Philippines from 600 m downwards on Mindoro as well as on the Zambales and Caraballo mountains, and also at three localities (Aceh, Tapanuli, and Kerintji) in Sumatra at between 800 m and 2000 m elevation. Of these, the Kerintji population, occurring at 2°S, is the only extension of the genus into the southern hemisphere (Cooling 1968; Kowal 1966). In south China *P. massoniana* and *P. yunanensis* form extensive secondary forests replacing cut-over evergreen broad-leaf forest (Wang 1961). Two Indian species *P. wallichiana* (*excelsa*) and *P. roxburghii* (*longifolia*) occur in the drier parts of monsoon forests along the length of the Himalaya from Afghanistan to Bhutan and south-east Tibet. They are pioneer species, colonizing landslides and abandoned cultivations, and are favoured by fire (Champion 1936; Stainton 1972).

P. kesiya in the Luzon Cordillera Central (Kowal 1966) and *P. merkusii* in Sumatra (van Steenis 1957; Cooling 1968) have been shown to occupy a similar niche to these continental species. In the virgin forest they are very rare, and are restricted to steep, stony ridges with (usually podzolic) well-drained soils, landslides, and in Sumatra also to lahars (mud-streams) and lava streams, all of which they colonize as typical pioneers, not regenerating in the same place. Seedlings can only develop on mineral soil and cannot tolerate shade, they are fairly resistant to fire once over 3 m tall. Mature trees are generally immune to fire-damage owing to their extremely thick outer bark. However, short cycles of shifting cultivation and regular annual fire prevent satisfactory regeneration and can lead to the elimination of pines (Cooling 1968). The several pines of the Caribbean and central America have similar ecology. All these tropical pines remain dominant so long as fires occur at intervals of between about 5 years and 20 years (Kowal 1966).

In Sumatra *P. merkusii* (tusam) can attain 70 m height in a century, and giant trees are found emerging from broad-leaf forest. Man has increased its habitat by felling and burning the forest (cf. *Casuarina junghuhniana*, §12.1), and *P. merkusii* groves develop in grassy patches (blangs), from seedlings 'as densely packed as hairs on a dog'. The blangs are sharply bounded against the surrounding mountain rain forest and are maintained by fire. The

Sumatran pine forests are estimated to cover 220 000 ha, of which some 17 000 ha are plantations around Lake Toba.

In the Luzon Cordillera Central *P. kesiya* (Benguet Pine) forest has almost completely replaced lower montane rain forest and is itself replaced downwards by grasslands maintained by frequent burning. Its extent is estimated as about 180 000 ha of which over half is under logging licence. The *P. merkusii* forests of the Philippines still remain too inaccessible to fell (Lizardo 1957).

The Sumatran pine forests were first exploited for turpentine and resin, and a substantial industry had been established by the time of the Japanese invasion in 1943. At the present day *Pinus* is used more than any other genus for establishing tree plantations in the humid and monsoon tropics, but *Pinus* is used for its wood not its turpentine or resin. For example, the Indonesian annual target is to plant 20 000–30 000 ha of *P. merkusii*, which requires some 3000 kg of seed (Cooling 1968), and Peninsular Malaysia is on the verge of a massive planting programme. *Pinus* is favoured above all other trees mainly because of its very high annual timber volume increment per hectare. Further, besides providing a useful general-purpose timber, the wood has long fibres and so is easily made into paper, and it is also suitable as a cellulose source for particle-board manufacture; thus there is usually a ready market for thinnings. Moreover, the features *Pinus* has as a pioneer (§6.1) make it easy to handle in plantation forestry.

It is, however, a genus of strongly seasonal tropical climates which only extends into the humid tropics in seasonally dry places where it naturally occupies dry sites. The range has extended where man has burned these seasonally inflammable forest types. A comparison of the map of climate types (Fig. 3.1, p. 45), with the distribution of *Pinus* in the tropical Far East (Fig. 14.1), shows that it is not found in the wettest 'A' type climates. Difficulties have arisen in the attempt to grow pines in the perhumid 'A' climate of Malaya. First, very little seed is formed, because there is no annual climatic stimulus for cone formation and a little pollen is formed continuously, and this is apparently inadequate for complete fertilization. Secondly, tall leading shoots without side branches very commonly develop (evocatively named foxtails), probably owing to an auxin imbalance, and such trees may perform poorly (Ibrahim and Greathouse 1972). Thirdly, pines are unable to compete with the lush regrowth which follows the clearing of the Malayan rain forest and require very expensive weeding for a year or more before a canopy is established. There are substantial differences between the Sumatran and mainland populations of *P. merkusii* in ecology, morphology, timber, and resin chemistry (Cooling 1968 and footnote, p. 176). Care must be taken to select seed of the most suitable provenance for planting in any given locality.

15 Variation within tropical lowland evergreen rain forest

In CHAPTERS 10, 11, and 12 the lowland forest Formations of the tropical Far East were described in order to exemplify their very distinct habitats, physiognomy, structure, and flora. Their habitats are in the main sharply bounded, so it follows that there is usually little problem in recognizing the Formations from the air, from aerial photographs, or on the ground, even though the spatial scale of the forest dwarfs the human form.

In the present chapter variation within the principal lowland forest Formation will be investigated. This has proved very much more difficult to study because it is on the whole continuous. No one denies that lowland evergreen rain forest varies from place to place, but there are seldom sharp boundaries to aid perception of distinct types. The nature of variation and its causes is still not fully understood.

Most of the concentration of ecological effort has been in the temperate regions, where vegetation is of much simpler structure and comprises far fewer species than in the humid tropics. Concepts tend to be constrained by the limitations imposed by the restricted subject matter. Tropical rain forests, containing the most complex and most species-rich ecosystems of this planet, have received relatively little attention, although it would have been logical to have examined them first, framing concepts which could then be extended to the impoverished types of higher latitudes. Fortunately, studies (mainly of the last fifteen or so years), have begun to redress the balance. Many of these studies have been made in the Far East, and probably more is now known of the rain forests of our region than of any other.

There has been a great deal of interest in the extent to which discrete species associations or consociations are correlated with site factors in tropical rain forest. This was sharpened by the publication of Richards' book in 1952 (see Richards 1963). In addition, ecologists have been curious to discover the mechanism whereby such species-rich plant communities perpetuate themselves. It was suggested by Aubréville (1938), from his extensive knowledge of African rain forests, that the observed pattern of floristic variation from place to place in species-rich tropical rain forest is perpetuated by variation in species composition in time at any one spot. This suggestion has become known as the 'mosaic' or 'cyclical' theory of regeneration (Richards 1952) and has been much discussed. To know the extent to which a group of species growing together is perpetuating itself is clearly of the greatest importance in unravelling the nature of communities in the rain forest. The matter cannot be directly investigated by a single set of observations. It is much better to have repeated measurements in order to build up a picture of any changes which are taking place. Few studies have yet been made on these lines, one of them in the Solomon Islands will be discussed in §15.4. There is a very urgent need that the very few sets of long-term ecological observation plots in the virgin rain forests of the Far East, at Sungei Menyala and Bukit Lagong in Malaya (Wyatt-Smith 1966), Kabili–Sepilok in Sabah (Nicholson 1965a, Fox 1973a), and on Kolombangara in the Solomons, are saved from logging and maintained as commercial pressures inexorably increase, so that they can continue to throw light on this fundamental problem.

With a paucity of precise data, two diametrically opposed views on the nature of variation in tropical rain forest have developed. On the one hand is the view that the tropical lowland evergreen rain forest of a given region is to be considered as one single, vast plant community varying haphazardly from place to place. At the other extreme the view has been expressed that most, if not all, species have highly precise habitat requirements and occupy distinct 'niches', so that variation in the forest mirrors the occurrence of these niches and can be interpreted once they have been elucidated. It is the purpose of the present chapter to examine recent evidence and to show that the true nature of rain-forest communities lies somewhere between these extremes.

The elucidation of the nature of variation in lowland evergreen rain forest is of considerable practical as well as scientific interest. On the wider scale, foresters are concerned with preparing inventories of virgin forests which are to be brought under management. This is done by enumeration of the trees on a small sample of the total area.† It would

---

† It is beyond the scope of this book to discuss the details of forest inventory survey, on which there now exists an extensive literature; the reader should consult Dawkins (1952, 1958), Loetsch, Zohrer, and Haller (1964, 1973), F.A.O. (1968), and Husch, Miller, and Beers (1972).

be a valuable aid to surveyors to know the manner in which species composition is likely to vary from place to place, for example, on different topographic sites. On a smaller scale, silviculture and management would both be facilitated by a knowledge of the factors controlling species composition within a forest stand.

Modern numerical methods of plant-community analysis, which have developed with the advent of electronic computers, have been utilized in several of the investigations to be described, but it is beyond the scope of this book to discuss the theory or methodology of the confusingly numerous approaches. Suffice it to say, these powerful tools, if carefully used, can be a valuable adjunct to other means of ecological enquiry, but in no way supplant them. Discussions of the numerical approach in tropical and subtropical contexts can be found in Webb *et al.* (1967*a,b*, 1970), Greig-Smith, Austin, and Whitmore (1967), Austin and Greig-Smith (1968), Williams, Lance, Webb, Tracey and Dale (1969*a*), Williams, Lance, Webb, Tracey and Connell (1969*b*), and Greig-Smith (1971).

Variation occurs in a multitude of ways which we shall try to separate, working from the grossest scale of broad geographical patterns downwards. The complexity is so great that general modes are best illustrated by concrete examples. Therefore we shall go on to describe a number of studies in dipterocarp rain forest and a study in a Solomon Islands rain forest. In the final section an attempt will be made to draw up a hierarchy of the kinds of variation and then to discuss the nature of rain-forest communities and their perpetuation. Throughout the discussion we shall be able to refer to topics and themes described in earlier chapters.

The appendix contains a list of descriptions of lowland rain forest in the various countries of the tropical Far East, complementing those which are analysed in this chapter.

15.1. Variation through the region

At the broadest level there is the variation through the region, mentioned in Chapter 1 and §10.1, which is manifest principally as differences between the western and eastern rain-forest blocks, centred respectively on the Sunda and Sulu continental shelves, plus the increasing poverty of the flora eastwards into the Pacific.

Most plant species have discrete ranges and do not extend throughout the whole geographic range of their habitat, because of the ineffectiveness of dispersal whatever mechanism the propagules possess.

This was described in §5.1. The rich forests of the tropical Far East are notorious for the numerous very-localized endemic species, and even genera, some of which are very rare. Amongst the many examples cited in the new *Tree flora of Malaya* (Whitmore 1972*b*, 1973*c*,) the genera *Maingaya* and *Pachylarnax* on Penang Hill (to which must be added *Hexapora*) are especially noteworthy.

Only those species present within dispersal range *can* grow together in a given area of rain forest, so, underlying all other variation, is that arising from the availability of flora. This has ultimate historical causes which are now known, at least in outline.

Climate changes during the Pleistocene period, marked by the successive Ice Ages, have caused major differences in sea-level and consequently in the extent to which present-day islands have been joined together and plants have been more free to disperse (Chapter 1). Climatic changes, possibly plus different dispositions of land and sea, have affected the extent of monsoon climates and their associated plant species (§12.1) and also their animals (Medway 1972*b*). The tree line was lowered in the Ice Ages (in New Guinea by at least 550 m, §16.2) and the mountain forest zones were compressed downwards.

As well as the vertical movement of sea-level and mountain vegetation belts it is now known that on a longer time-scale there has been relative horizontal movement of the land masses, which is still continuing. For example, since the early Tertiary period the islands of the western margin of the Pacific, including the major archipelago of the Solomons, have moved away from close proximity to the fringing land masses, to their present watery isolation (Whitmore 1973*a*). The changes which have occurred within the Malay archipelago have still not been resolved, in fact it is the most complex zone of the earth's crust (Hamilton 1973). It already seems clear that the Sunda and Sulu shelves respectively form part of the crustal plates on which Eurasia and Australia lie (Raven and Axelrod 1972). Historical plant geography will have to be reassessed once the plate-tectonic history has been worked out; then will be the time to reconsider, for example, the occurrence of north temperate conifers in Borneo until the late Tertiary period (Chapter 14), the major concentration of Dipterocarpaceae on the Sunda shelf, and the significance of the numbers of animal and plant species on the different islands of the south-west Pacific, which have given rise to considerable speculation (Peake 1969; Whitmore 1969*c*).

For a study of regional variation in more detail we shall take the dipterocarp forests, about which most is known. The lack of detailed knowledge about variation within the non dipterocarp forests of the eastern block is in fact one of the major gaps in present-day understanding.

15.2. Regional variation within dipterocarp forest

Family dominance of Dipterocarpaceae (Fig. 15.1) is most marked in the western block of lowland evergreen rain forest, with outliers of dipterocarp rain forest to the north and west and also to the east.

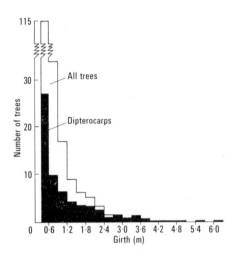

FIG. 15.1. Predominance of Dipterocarpaceae amongst the big trees in Sabah lowland rain forest. Data from five plots totalling 55·6 ha. (Burgess 1961.)

There is a dramatic decrease in the richness of the dipterocarp flora at the isthmus of Kra (§12.1). Beyond this, Dipterocarpaceae occur in small numbers throughout the rain forests of Burma, Ceylon,† and India, becoming progressively fewer in species and individuals away from Malaya. They are also found in some of the monsoon-forest Formations. Full details are given by Champion (1936) and Champion and Seth (1968). The northern limits of the family are the subtropical forests of southern China (Hainan has *Vatica astrotricha* and *Hopea hainanensis*, Kwangsi just *Hopea chinensis* growing in relict patches of hillside forest in moist valleys (Wang 1961). East of the Philippines there is also a diminution in the importance of Dipterocarpaceae. The eastern limits of the family are the Finisterre mountains of north-east New Guinea and the D'Entrecasteaux Islands north-east of the

† Which has the endemic genera *Vateria* (3 spp.; and shared with the Ghats) and *Stemanoporus* (15 spp.).

Papuan peninsula. In New Guinea dipterocarp rain forest is of limited extent and still not fully described. The most important timber species is *Anisoptera thurifera*, which is locally abundant. It is one of the principal hardwood timbers of New Guinea, with promise as a peeler for plywood veneer. *A. thurifera* is a fast-growing, light-demanding species which thrives best on well-drained soils. In the mountain foothills, for example, around Lae, it forms pure stands on ridge crests (Fig. 15.3) at the very high stocking of 470 m³/ha, the trees growing to 60 m tall,

FIG. 15.2. Interior of tropical lowland evergreen mixed dipterocarp rain forest: in west Sarawak, Sempadi forest. Note the open undergrowth. The big tree on the left is a *Shorea*.

with a clear bole of 48 m and girth sometimes reaching 3·6 m. 'The frequency here is quite Malayan' (Womersley) and the volume considerably exceeds that of any other dipterocarp forest known. Many of the stands have now been logged. *A. thurifera* is also found on alluvial plains, often in old secondary forest, and ranges up to 780 m altitude (Anon. 1951, Womersley and McAdam 1957, Paijmans 1967). Locally *Hopea* is also utilized for timber. In south New Guinea where the Fly River emerges from the mountains is a belt of mixed dipterocarp rain forest in which *Anisoptera*, *Hopea*, and *Vatica* occur, together with many non-dipterocarp species, principally of *Canarium*, *Eugenia*, and *Lithocarpus*. On steep slopes in the same locality *Vatica rassak* is the commonest tree species in all layers of the forest (Paijmans 1971).

From Sumatra to the Philippines Dipterocarpaceae are predominant amongst the big trees (Fig. 15.1) throughout the lowland evergreen rain forest Formation. The family attains its greatest richness in terms of abundance of species in the emergent stratum in Sarawak and Brunei, north-west Borneo (Fig. 15.2). In Sabah (north-east Borneo), and also in the Philippines, dipterocarps are numerous as individuals, but there are fewer species in any one small area. Further west in both Malaya and Sumatra the emergent stratum is shared with other families to a much greater degree, though little work has yet been done on the detailed ecology of this great island. Java has very few dipterocarps, and is largely outside the perhumid area (§12.1). In the dipterocarp forest zone the family is also an important component of other forest Formations (Table 10.1, p. 121), namely, of semi-evergreen rain forest (§10.2), heath forest (§10.3), some forests over ultrabasic rocks (§10.5), fresh-water, seasonal, and peat swamp forests (§§11.4, 11.3), and also the lower part of lower montane forest (§§16.1, 16.6). It is not well represented on limestone (§10.4).

In Malaya the emergent layer of the forest canopy of lowland rain forest contains besides Dipterocarpaceae appreciable numbers of Leguminosae (mainly *Dialium*, *Koompassia*, and *Sindora*) and a few species of other families, notably *Dyera costulata* (Apocynaceae), though Dipterocarpaceae undoubtedly do predominate amongst the larger trees even here (Table 15.1). The larger role of Dipterocarpaceae in Borneo is shown in Table 15.2, comparing counts of the bigger trees in extensive samples of mixed dipterocarp forest in Malaya and Sabah. In Sabah large tracts of forest are dominated by giant dipterocarps of a few species; for example, around

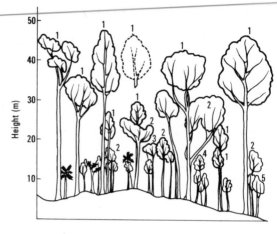

FIG. 15.3. Ridge forest in the *Anisoptera thurifera* consociation near Lae, New Guinea. 1. *A. thurifera*; 2. *Intsia bijuga*; 3. *Macaranga* sp.; 4. *Actinodaphne* sp.; 5. *Rhodamnia* sp. (After Havel 1972, Fig. 4A.)

Darvel Bay in the south-east *Parashorea malaanonan* forms about 80 per cent of the timber stand, with lesser amounts of *Shorea guiso* and *Hopea sangal* as emergents and locally *S. johorensis*, *S. leprosula*, and *S, parvifolia* (Fig. 15.4).

Enumerations of small as well as big trees (that is, all stems over 0·3 m girth) on two small plots, in Malaya and Sabah respectively, (Table 15.3), exemplify a greater over-all abundance of dipterocarps in Sabah forests in terms of species as well as tree numbers, but also a richer flora (fewer trees per species) in Malaya. The abundance of *Parashorea* spp. distinguishes the forests of Sabah from those of Malaya, Sarawak, and Brunei.

TABLE 15.1

Trees per 100 ha of 1·2 m or more girth of the ten commonest families in the lowland and lower montane mixed dipterocarp rain forest of Ulu Kelantan, north-east Malaya

1.	Dipterocarpaceae	1522
2.	Leguminosae	386
3.	Myrtaceae	293
4.	Lauraceae	182
5.	Anacardiaceae	175
6.	Burseraceae	173
7.	Euphorbiaceae	132
8.	Olacaceae	98
9.	Fagaceae	94
10.	Sterculiaceae	91

From a 676 ha strip sample (0·07 per cent) comprising 26 628 trees and spaced through a forest area of 10 100 km² ; mostly below 840 m, a few strips up to 1140 m. (After Whitmore 1973*i*, Table 2.)

TABLE 15.2

Tree numbers and percentages of dipterocarps in lowland mixed dipterocarp rain forest

		Tree numbers		
	Area (ha)	≥ 1·2 m girth	≥ 1·5 m girth	≥ 2·7 m girth
Malaya, Pangkor Island‡	63·13	4267 48†	—	—
Sabah, Segaliud-Lokan§	31·89	—	1000 76†	292 92†

† Percentages of dipterocarps.
‡ From Cousens (1958*a*).
§ From Fox (1967).

The Philippine dipterocarp forests, like those of Sabah, have abundant *Parashorea*. Here too, most of the emergents are Dipterocarpaceae, with only a few species predominant in any one locality. All the Philippine islands except Mindanao, the southernmost, lie in a cyclone belt (§6.1). Cyclones cause complete destruction over a narrow zone plus peripheral zones where they defoliate the trees and damage the crowns. The over-all effect is to favour light-demanding species, which are mainly Dipterocarpaceae. The abundance of dipterocarp saplings and poles in the Philippines lowland rain forests, which are so valuable for silviculture (§7.1), is cer-

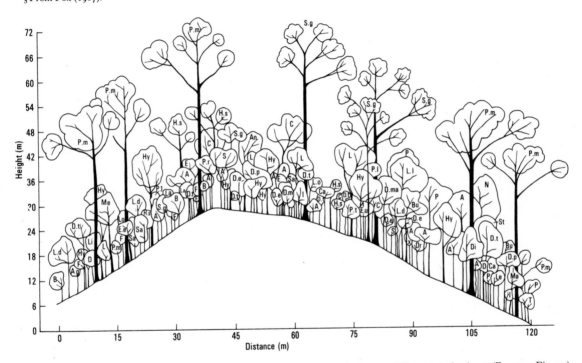

FIG. 15.4. Lowland mixed dipterocarp rain forest at Silam, Sabah; *Parashorea malaanonan* and *Shorea guiso* dominant. (Fox 1972, Fig. 11.)

A, *Aglaia affinis*
Ag., *Aglaia gamopetala*
An, *Annonaceae*
B, *Brownlowia stipulata*
Bu, *Buchanania fragrans*
C, *Cynometra elmeri*
Ca, *Casearia* sp.
D, *Dehaasia caesia*
D.e, *Dillenia excelsa*
Di, *Diospyros diepenhorstii*
D.m, *Diospyros macrophylla*
D.ma, *Diospyros malayana*
D.p, *Diospyros pyrrhocarpa*
Dr, *Drypetes* sp.
D.s, *Diospyros sumatrana*

D.t, *Diospyros toposioides*
E, *Enicosanthum erianthoides*
E.e, *Eugenia elopurae*
Eu, *Euphoria malaiensis*
F, *Fordia gibbsae*
H.s, *Hopea sangal*
Hy, *Hydnocarpus sumatrana*
I, *Ixora macrophylla*
L, *Lithocarpus gracilis*
La, *Lauraceae indet*
L.d., *Lansium domesticum*
Le, *Leea indica*
Li, *Litsea ochracea*
L.l., *Lithocarpus lucidus*
L.o, *Litsea oppositifolia*

Ma, *Mangifera* sp.
Me, *Meiogyne virgata*
N, *Neo-uvaia accuminatissima*
P, *Pentace* sp.
P.l, *Polyathia laterifolia*
P.m., *Parashorea malaanonan*
P.r, *Palaquium rostratum*
Pt, *Ptychopyxis arborea*
S, *Sindora irpicina*
Sa, *Saraca palembanica*
S.g, *Shorea guiso*
St, *Sterculia rubiginosa*
T, *Teijsmanniodendron holophyllum*
X, *Xanthophyllum excelsum*

FIG. 15.5. Storm forest at Kemahang, Kelantan, north-east Malaya, in 1968, 88 years after devastation. The two central trees are *Shorea parvifolia*. Many trees have a kink in the trunk believed to result from regeneration through a dense tangle of climbers.

TABLE 15.3

Tree, species, and genus numbers, 0·3 m girth and over, on small plots in lowland mixed dipterocarp rain forest

	Area (ha)	Spp.	Genera	Trees	Trees/spp.	Dipterocarps	
						spp.	trees
Malaya, Sungei Menyalat†	1·62	210	113	791	3·7	15	135 (= 17 per cent)
Sabah, Sepilok‡	1·90	198	99	1215	6·7	21	330 (= 27 per cent)

† From Wyatt-Smith (1966, Table 13).
‡ From Nicholson (1965*a*).

tainly in part, if not principally, a consequence of cyclone damage (Nicholson 1970).

Widescale variation in forest composition also occurs within the various countries. For example, the freak storm of November 1880 which struck parts of Kelantan in north-east Malaya devastated the forest over hundreds of square kilometres. The regrowth in the Kemahang forest (Fig. 15.5), (part of the devastated area and felled for timber in the late 1960s) has been studied in detail (Wyatt-Smith 1954*a*). It was very different from normal Malayan lowland dipterocarp forest in the reduced number both of dipterocarp species and of many normal main storey members of Burseraceae, Lauraceae, Myristicaceae, Myrtaceae, and Sapotaceae. The commonest species was the strongly light-demanding *Shorea parvifolia*.

There are many examples of restricted species ranges within the lowland rain forest of each country besides the highly localized endemics already mentioned. Within Malaya, *Koompassia excelsa*, tallest tree of the forest, is inexplicably absent south of a line across the centre of the peninsula from Kuala Lumpur to Kuantan, though it occurs south of this latitude in Sumatra (Whitmore 1972*d*). *Dryobalanops aromatica*, the Borneo camphorwood, is restricted to the eastern side of the country, except for a few small colonies on the west (mainly at Kanching) which were possibly planted by aborigines (Fig. 15.6); the genus has most species in Borneo (Symington 1943; Wyatt-Smith 1963). The giant, stemless undergrowth palm *Eugeissona tristis*, the diamond-fronded palm *Johannesteysmannia altifrons*, and some species of the tree genus *Parinari* have disjunct distributions through the lowlands which suggest partial extinction, possibly following secular climatic change (see §3.6).

In a 640 m × 420 m plot (Fig. 15.7) in the former Jengka forest (which was felled for settlement in the late 1960s) *Shorea leprosula*, a light-demander which

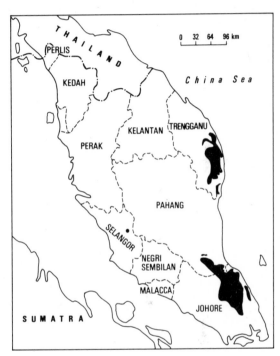

FIG. 15.6. Distribution of *Dryobalanops aromatica* in Malaya. (Wyatt-Smith 1963.)

grows fast and forms large trees, appeared to be invading from the west; it was clearly confined to the western half and had a preponderance of trees under 1·8 m girth and none over 2·4 m. Big trees were found outside the western limit of the plot, but not to its east. *Dipterocarpus crinitus* showed an opposite tendency, 17 of its 25 trees were over 2·7 m girth and only 5 trees were smaller than 1·2 m girth, suggesting that the species was dying out (Poore 1968). It is probably significant that *D. crinitus* is very common in parts of the Kelantan storm forest (Burgess).

One of the fascinations to the scientist working on primeval, lowland tropical forests, in vegetation

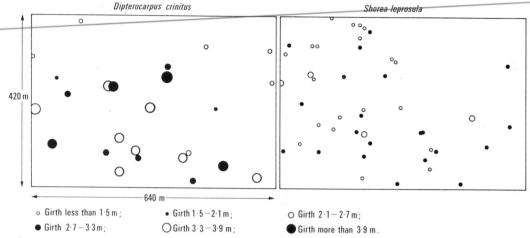

FIG. 15.7. The distribution of two dipterocarps at Jengka forest, Malaya. (a) *Diptocerpus crinitus*; (b) *Shorea leprosula*. (Poore 1968, Fig. 14.)

where man has been an insignificant factor and gross climatic change can be ruled out, has been the discovery of these 'invasion fronts' and other patterns and then the attempt to explain them. These patterns must have a historical explanation in terms of the evolution and spread of species, set against the backdrop of minor climatic change, sea-level change, and island movement which were described in §15.1. Doubtless, many more patterns remain undetected. Explanation and detection will probably now never come in most cases, because rain-forest scientists are few in number and the extensive tracts of forest which provide the scenario will have all been logged within the next few decades, as we shall describe in Part V.

15.3. Local variation within dipterocarp forest

It is at this smaller scale that variation occurs which bears most directly on the problem of whether discrete floristic communities exist or not within lowland rain forest.

Diverse kinds of variation can be clearly distinguished, contributing to the kaleidoscopic variety of the lowland evergreen rain forest Formation. Lowland dipterocarp rain forest is taken by way of the main example because it is the most throughly investigated; similar patterns can be expected everywhere.

Riparian forests

A number of forest communities are associated with water courses. At the edge of torrent streams, and on their rocky shoals, firmly rooted in clefts and crevices, is found the synusia of rheophytes. This

FIG. 15.8. Stenophyllous plants. (After Merrill 1945, Fig. 97.) A. *Neonauclea angustifolia* (Rubiaceae); B. *Fagraea stenophylla* (Loganiaceae); C. *Garcinia linearis* (Guttiferae); D. *Syzygium neriifolium* (Myrtaceae); E. *Saurauia angustifolia* (Actinidiaceae); F. *Erycibe stenophylla* (Convolvulaceae); G. *Homonoia riparia* (Euphorbiaceae); H. *Eugenia mimica* (Myrtaceae); I. *Psychotria acuminata* (Rubiaceae); J. *Tetranthera salicifolia* (Lauraceae).

is a life-form community of plants with narrow, willow-like leaves (Fig. 15.8), so called stenophylls, with water- or fish-dispersed fruits. Most are woody or semi-woody and of shrub form (Fig. 15.9). The colonies consist of several species of completely different taxonomic affinity, but remarkably similar appearance, growing together below the line of the high monsoon floods. For example, on the Sungei Tahan in Taman Negara, Malaya, can be seen *Aglaia salicifolia*, *Antidesma salicinum*, *Calophyllum rupicolum* var. *rupicolum*, *Dysoxylum angustifolium* (Fig. 2.30, p. 37), *Ficus pyriformis*, *Gomphandra quadrifida* var. *angustifolia*, and *Homonoia riparia*, plus the most extreme example, on rocks which are usually submerged, the recently discovered tiny herb of the Podostemaceae, *Indotristicha malayana* (Dransfield and Whitmore 1970). In Sarawak there

186

Fig. 15.9. *Garcinia cataractalis*, a rheophytic shrub with narrow, willow-like, stenophyllous leaves and crimson fruits. The species is restricted to the east coast of Malaya. It is locally common by rocky, swiftly flowing rivers. This plant, photographed in 1971, provided the specimen from which the species was described. (Whitmore 1973*j*.)

are even two stenophyllous palms, *Pinanga calami-frons* and *P. rivularis*. (Fuller details of rheophytes are given by Ridley (1893), Beccari (1904), van Steenis (1952), (1957), and Merrill (1945).)

Several tree species characteristically fringe watercourses. In Malaya rocky *Saraca* streams of the upper reaches give way down river to neram (*Dipterocarpus oblongifolius*) rivers and in the fresh-water tidal reaches there occur rassau (*Pandanus helicopus*) rivers (Corner 1940). Neram trees arch over the river (buttressed on the bank side, §2.5), supporting a wealth of epiphytes, with many ferns and orchids, including the gargantuan *Grammatophyllum speciosum*, the largest orchid in the world.

In Sarawak the raised, storm-deposited levées, where the hill torrents become slow-moving rivers, support a very distinctive forest called empran. The soil is fertile, deep, friable, and well-watered, and most empran has been cleared for cultivation. This is the habitat of the illipe nut trees (*Shorea*

macrophylla, S. seminis, and *S. splendida*) and of the Borneo ironwood, belian, *Eusideroxylon zwageri.* *Dipterocarpus apterus* and *Intsia palembanica* are frequent associates. Empran may carry commercial timber of up to 90 m³/ha, a very heavy stocking, further enhanced by the high proportion of important timbers. Empran is conspicous on aerial photographs from the very large, somewhat fluffy crowns of the emergents, not unlike little balls of cotton wool (Browne 1955). The significance of this very rough canopy surface was discussed in §10.3. Empran is frequently backed by swampy, alluvial, valley-floor forest and is itself inundated occasionally when the rivers are in spate. This habitat is thus somewhat intermediate to fresh-water swamp, and empran can be regarded as the least frequently inundated form of swamp forest (§11.4). Belian, one of the most valuable of heavy hardwoods, is not restricted to the alluvial clay soils of empran. It also occurs as scattered trees on clay hillsides up to about 360 m (where, however, the trees are of very poor form, and are locally named geriting (Anderson). It occurs throughout Borneo and is also abundant in Sumatra (van Steenis 1958*a*), though absent from Malaya.

Bare alluvium is first colonized by pioneer species, some of which develop potentially valuable timber stands of high stocking, namely, *Anthocephalus chinensis* and *Octomeles sumatrana* in Borneo†; plus *Eucalpytus deglupta* and *Casuarina* spp. in New Guinea (§7.2). In south New Guinea *Althoffia* sp. and *Timonius* sp. form pure stands along the Strickland and Fly Rivers as monsoon-climate riparian pioneers (Paijmans 1971).

Species associations on alluvial valley floors, distinct from those of hillsides and ridges, have been detected in numerical analysis of small plots at Jengka in Malaya (Poore 1968) and Andulau in Brunei (Austin, Aston, and Greig-Smith 1972), and by inspection at Sepilok in Sabah (Nicholson 1965*a*). In Malaya several common big trees are well known to prefer such sites, for example, *Pentaspadon* spp., *Pometia pinnata*, and *Pterygota alata*. *Shorea ovalis* is found near streams but not on alluvium.

Variation with rock type

The 26 628 trees enumerated in north-east Malaya on a 676 ha sample of lowland forest in Ulu Kelantan district (10 100 km², now almost entirely committed to felling) (Table 15.1) were analysed to see the extent to which species had different

---

† But at present not utilized owing to preference for dipterocarps.

preferences for four habitats; sedimentary or granite rocks and below or above 225 m elevation (Whitmore 1973*i*). This was an attempt to put on an objective basis the mainly subjective impressions held by foresters and botanists about species' habitats. The most important result was to show that nearly all species occur in all four habitats but that in most cases the frequency of occurrence varies. That is to say, qualitatively, on a presence or absence basis, the habitats have the same species composition, but, in more detail, there are quantitative differences. However, several easily recognized big-tree species which are common through Malaya were found to occur at about the same density in all four habitats. These were *Cynometra malaccensis, Dyera costulata, Intsia palembanica, Koompassia excelsa, Scorodocarpus borneensis,* and *Shorea pauciflora.* This survey thus clearly shows how the foresters' subjective impression, that Malayan timber tress can grow almost anywhere in the mesic climax forest, has arisen.

There are major differences in land-form and soil over sedimentary and granitic rocks. Granites tend to weather deeply to form well-structured soils, and

depths of 30 m are not unknown; there are huge core stones near the base. Sedimentary rocks tend to weather less deeply, especially where metamorphosed; shale-derived soils are much more finely textured than those derived from sandstones. The relief of granite country is characteristically less rugged, with broad, rounded ridges prone to landslides. Over sedimentary rocks precipitously sided, knife-edge crests are the rule. At this level of analysis, soil and topography are inseparable (cf. Lee 1969); both reflect the nature of the parent material and must exert an important influence on the differences which are found in species' distribution and abundance with elevation, operating partly at the stages of seedling establishment and survival in the way outlined in §§5.3 and 6.3; and also on big trees, which probably show differential sensitivity between species to the relatively unstable, continuously creeping soil of slopes. There are also important differences in soil depth and physical properties between parent materials which probably influence species mainly via water relations (see also below). All soils contain only very small amounts of available mineral

FIG. 15.10. Looking down on a stand of *Shorea curtisii* growing on shallow soil developed over conglomerate on the steep slopes of Bukit Cheraga, Ulu Telom, Pahang, Malaya. Mixed dipterocarp rain forest with much bamboo can be seen on the flat alluvial plain at the top of the picture.

nutrients, a consequence of continual leaching in a hot, wet climate, and probably chemical differences between soils are of lesser importance than physical ones. Much work remains to be done on the identification of soil factors which influence species abundance and distribution.

In both Malaya and Sabah a much higher proportion of timber trees are hollow on sedimentary rocks, and in Malaya there has been a significantly higher timber yield from forests over granite during the last 20 years (Pelinck 1970; Fox 1972).

The very deep, friable soils developed over basalt in east Sabah carry a forest which is unusually poor in species and of unusually enormous trees (Burgess 1961).

Shorea curtisii *in Malaya*

Shorea curtisii in Malaya is an example where the marked general restriction of a species to certain ridge crests, and its gregarious occurrence there has now been correlated with special features of the habitat. Symington (1943) distinguished hill from lowland dipterocarp forest by the presence of this species

(Fig. 16.1, p. 199) which occurs along ridge crests as groves, sometimes to the exclusion of other emergents, and is very readily spotted from its conspicuous grey crowns (Figs 15.10 and 15.11). Its lower limit of occurrence on the main ranges is about 225 m, but it is also found near sea-level on coastal hills. In fact there appears to be little consistent floristic difference between the lowland dipterocarp forests and the hill dipterocarp forests of Symington *except* on those ridges in the latter type which are dominated by *S. curtisii*, and it would perhaps be more correct to regard all forests in the Peninsula, up to an altitude corresponding to the lower limit of Symington's upper dipterocarp forest (about 750 m, Fig. 16.1, p. 199) as lowland dipterocarp forest, with the *S. curtisii* ridges an edaphic climax within it. P. F. Burgess (unpublished), in what is the most detailed autecological study of a tropical rain forest tree yet undertaken, has found considerable evidence that *S. curtisii* is restricted to dry sites. Water-shortage is most likely to be experienced in the annual early-year period of low rainfall (§4.1). Ridge crests are dry owing

Fig. 15.11. Mixed dipterocarp rain forest, on hill slopes in the upper valley of the river Batang Kali, Selangor, Malaya, at about 800 m elevation. The protruding giant trees, 50 m or more tall, on the spur ridges are *Shorea curtisii*.

FIG. 15.12. *Shorea curtisii* and the big, stemless, prickly bertam palm, *Eugeissona tristis*, commonly grow together (South Pahang, Malaya.)

to increased evaporation as windspeeds increase with increased exposure at higher elevations; to rapid run-off and drainage; and to shallowness or coarse texture of the soil found especially over sedimentary rocks and quartz-rich parts of granitic rocks respectively, and hence with a relatively low water-storage capacity (§3.3). Coastal hills are dry almost entirely because of high evaporation caused by constant unsaturated sea breezes (Nieuwolt 1965). The precise stage at which *S. curtisii* succeeds in competition with others has yet to be demonstrated. It develops its characteristic hard, waxy leaves only when it reaches the upper storey of the canopy. It is often, though not invariably, associated with the giant, prickly, stemless palm *Eugeissona tristis* which has fronds to 6 m long (Fig. 15.12). This palm shades the ground densely around its clumps and dries out the soil surface with its dense, shallow mass of fine roots. *S. curtisii* seedlings can survive these conditions for several years. The crown of *S. curtisii* has a high albedo (§10.3) which is perhaps significant for its water relations. It is sometimes associated with the same species if poor soils as *Agathis dammara* (§14.1) and indeed with *Agathis* itself which was the species amongst a number tested which best controlled the water loss from detached leafy twigs over 24 hours (Grubb). But experiments using Scholander's pressure-bomb technique have not shown any outstanding ability of *S. curtisii* to restrict water loss when compared with emergent dipterocarp species of lower hillsides and valley bottoms (Burgess). Nevertheless, cut twigs of *S. curtisii* in potometer experiments (where however water is limiting) have been shown to transpire at half to two-thirds the rate of other common hill-forest species (Burgess 1969a). Ridge crests besides being particularly prone to drought are also leached sites and therefore mineral-poor, as will be described in more detail in Chapter 16. It is not yet possible in the case of most species to distinguish the relative importance of periodic drought and oligotrophy (cf. the discussions of heath forest, §10.3, and of upper montane forest, Chapter 16). For *S. curtisii*, however, water relations do appear to be the main determinant of its habitat, despite the incompleteness of experiments on its transpiration. Analyses for major nutrients—nitrogen, phosphorus, and potassium—have shown no consistent difference between *S. curtisii* sites and others in the main ranges, and mineral deficiency does not explain its altitudinal depression on coastal hills. A study is still in progress to ascertain whether trace elements may be deficient.

Malayan foresters have long known that in the peninsula the heaviest timber-stocking is on ridges. This is largely because *S. curtisii* forms pure stands, is exceptionally wind-firm, and grows to huge size. That is to say, there is available in Malaya an exceptionally big tree well-adapted to this ecological niche. But other factors are also involved. One of these, seedling establishment, was discussed in §5.3. Additionally, middle and lower slopes are subject to continuous mass earth flow and slow surface creep. Slopes are also subject to landslides and periods of subsoil saturation during which big trees are especially prone to wind-throw (§6.1). For all these reasons giant (that is, old) trees are less likely to be common than on ridges (Burgess). It is noteworthy that heavy ridge stands are a marked feature of granite country, where lower hillside slips due to the weight of core boulders in a matrix of weathered material saturated by rain are particularly common (Fitch 1952).

The Dryobalanops aromatica *consociation in Malaya*

In the east of Malaya (Fig. 15.6), mainly on sedimentary rocks, in the lowlands from about 50–400 m, *Dryobalanops aromatica* (kapur), with 60–90 per cent of the total timber volume, dominated the forest which until recently covered several thousand square kilometres (see Fig. 15.13). Within stands of *D. aromatica* some areas consisted predominantly of trees of similar girth, indicative of simultaneous regeneration; others consisted of 'family groups', of graded size from one or two giant trees downwards, indicative of regeneration by single individuals. There were more pole-sized stems than is the case with most dipterocarps. *D. aromatica* is known to flower and fruit more frequently than most other dipterocarps (§4.1). Its seedlings and saplings show unusually prolonged persistence in deep shade and respond quickly to increased light. From this evidence it would appear that the species maintained dominance by sheer 'reproductive pressure'; there were more likely to be small individuals awaiting release of it than other species. It is not known why *D. aromatica* had a restricted range, that is, why it had not spread to cover the whole country, though its general restriction to sedimentary rocks must have been significant. Stands were normally sharply bounded and consisted either of mainly small trees, suggesting an invasion front, or mainly large ones, suggesting retreat (cf. Fig. 15.7). In hilly country, where it was frequently associated with *Swintonia penangiana*, the heaviest stands of *Dryobalanops* were on the upper slopes of ridges, not the crests. This

FIG. 15.13. The *Dryobalanops aromatica* consociation within the tropical lowland rain forest of Malaya. Seen in silhouette on a sandstone ridge near Kuala Loh, Ulu Dungun, in 1968. This extremely valuable forest type has now been largely felled (cf. Fig. 17.4).

presents a contrast to *Shorea curtisii* (Symington 1943; Wyatt-Smith 1963; Lee 1967). Forests dominated by *D. aromatica* have also been reported from Sumatra (van Zon 1915).

Groves of dipterocarps.

Trees over 0·3 m girth were enumerated on ten plots of 200 m × 20 m (0·4 ha) spread across 2.4 km of gently undulating lowland forest at Pasoh in Malaya and encompassing the three major soil types of the lowlands (Fig. 15.14). Five dipterocarps (Table 15.4) and 11 other species all showed signs of clustering. Numerical analysis of the data reflected these patterns of distribution by showing a gradual change in species' associations across the area. From such small linear plots it was not possible to distinguish whether the species with clustered trees were in family groups or same-size stands. There was no sign of species groups correlated with the soil types (Wong and Whitmore 1970). At Jengka in Malaya, also in gently undulating lowland forest, several dipterocarps showed distinct family groups on a block 640 m × 420 m (Fig. 15.15); and this is a sign of 'reproductive pressure', because within a grove the seedlings most likely to be present, when perchance a gap forms, are those of the species forming the grove (cf. *Dryobalanops aromatica* above). The degree of aggregation at Jengka was found to reflect the efficiency of the species' dispersal mechanism (Poore 1968).

192

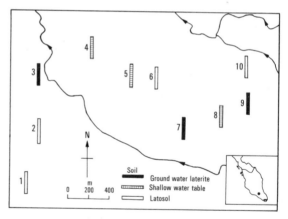

FIG. 15.14. Plot layout at Pasoh forest, Malaya. (From Wong and Whitmore 1970, Fig. 1.)

TABLE 15.4
Distribution of dipterocarps showing signs of clustering at Pasoh forest, Malaya

Plot number (see Fig. 15.14)	1	2	3	4	5	6	7	8	9	10
Shorea macroptera							1	9	1	
Shorea parvifolia						1	5	12	1	3
Shorea ovalis		1		3				3	5	2
Dipterocarpus sublamellatus	22	3		1						
Shorea multiflora	11									

The figures are numbers of stems per 0·4 ha plot.
After Wong and Whitmore (1970, Table 3).

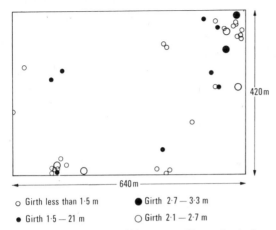

○ Girth less than 1·5 m   ● Girth 2·7 — 3·3 m

● Girth 1·5 — 21 m   ○ Girth 2·1 — 2·7 m

FIG. 15.15. Family groups of *Shorea maxwelliana* at Jengka forest,
Malaya. (From Poore 1968, Fig. 15f.)

Species associations and soil types.

The Andulau forest in Brunei lies on a dissected peneplain. The trees over 0·3 m girth were enumerated on plots of 100 m × 40 m (0·4 ha) sited on the alluvial valley bottoms (Fig. 15.16). In this case numerical analysis revealed that species associations were correlated with complex soil factors, which could not, however, be clearly defined (though all the usual physical and chemical factors were measured). Similar and equally cryptic results were obtained for ridge and hillside plots (considered together) in the same forest (Austin, Ashton, and Greig-Smith 1972).

These last two kinds of variation within lowland rain forest are the most subtle of all. The intensity of sampling, plot layout, and mode of analysis are probably crucial to their detection. The hilly terrain and the siting of the plots at Andulau (Fig. 15.16) probably determine that, here, soil

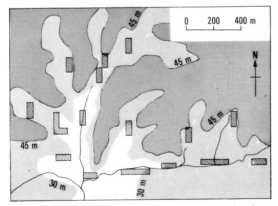

FIG. 15.16. Layout of valley-bottom plots at Andulau forest,
Brunei. (After Ashton 1964, Fig. 1.)

rather than pattern of trees resulting from mode of regeneration controls the associations which were detected between species. The low sampling intensity at Pasoh (Fig. 15.14) probably minimized the influence of soil on the results,† and no soil data were collected at Jengka.

In conclusion it can be noted that in northern Borneo marked relief is far commoner than flat to low undulating terrain and that there may in consequence be real differences in local variation in species composition between northern Borneo and Malaya.

15.4. Variation within a rain forest in the Solomon Islands

The studies of lowland dipterocarp rain forest have mainly consisted of detecting patterns of variation from sample-plot enumerations, followed by interpretation of their significance.

The species associated together in a patch of forest are those which have successfully established and grown up there, as was discussed at length in Chapter 6. Additional insight into species' associations therefore comes from a knowledge of the ecological requirements and preferences of trees at all stages of life, which is obtained by keeping populations under continual observation. This enables one to build up a picture of changes in time which can then be compared with fluctuations in the environment.

The most comprehensive attempt to interpret associations from a knowledge of the autecology of individual tree species has been the study in the lowland rain forest of Kolombangara in the Solomons, already discussed in §6.3 (Whitmore 1974). The twelve species, whose populations on 13.7 ha were monitored for 6·6 years, comprise the greater part of the top of the canopy. Kolombangara is a fairly symmetrical extinct Pleistocene volcano, 30 km across, with slopes rising gently near the shore and progressively more steeply inland to the crater rim of about 16 km diameter and at 1500–1650 m elevation. The 22 sample plots were located on the north and west slopes between sea-level and 420 m (Fig. 15.17).

Numerical analysis of an enumeration of trees of 0·3 m girth and greater on the sample plots resolved the lowland forests into six floristic types, I–VI

---

† P. S. Ashton (in press) has subsequently made a more detailed survey of part of the same area at Pasoh and has been able to show correlation between species composition and soil factors thus confirming these remarks.

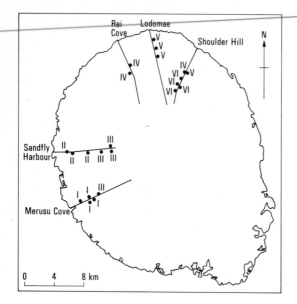

FIG. 15.17. Kolombangara Island in the Solomons showing location of forest types. (From Whitmore 1974, Fig. 8.1.)

(Greig-Smith, Austin, and Whitmore 1967). The greatest difference was between the forest types of the west (I–III) and north (IV–VI) coasts respectively (Fig. 15.17). Within each major group the plots at highest altitude and furthest inland, III and VI, were the next most distinct. Variation was found with topography both between types and between stands within types.

The observations on the autecology of the twelve common big-tree species have been described in §6.3 and summarized in Table 6.1 (p. 74). There were found to be substantial differences in the representation of these species in the different forest types. Principally, the north-coast forests had a predominance, amongst the trees of 1·5 m girth and over, of species requiring or favoured by canopy gaps for their regeneration (groups (c) and (d) in Table

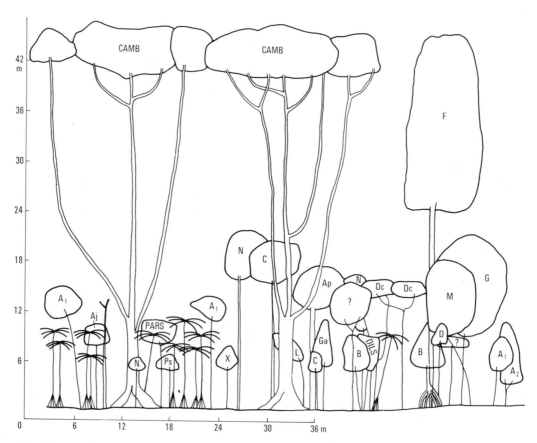

FIG. 15.18. Forest on Kolombangara, Solomon Islands, dominated by overmature trees of the light-demander *Campnosperma* *brevipetiolatum* (CAMB) which is not regenerating itself. See species list for Fig. 15.19. (From Whitmore 1974, Fig. 2.3.)

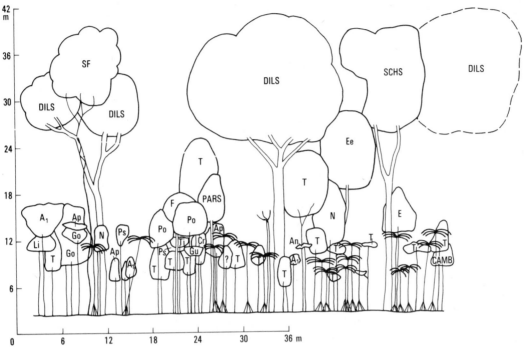

FIG. 15.19. Forest on Kolombangara, Solomon Islands, dominated by the shade-bearers *Dillenia salomonensis* (DILS) and *Schizomeria serata* (SCHS) which are regenerating themselves. (From Whitmore 1974, Fig. 2.4.) A1, A2, *Aglaia* spp.; Aj, *Alangium javanicum*; An, *Anacolosa papuana*; Ap, *Aporusa papuana*; B, *Belliolum haplopus* (abundance of this very primitive angiosperm is characteristic of Solomons' lowland rain forest); C, *Chisocheton* sp.; Cr, *Cryptocarya* sp.; D, *Dysoxylum* sp.; Dc, *Dysoxylum caulostachyum*; E, *Eriandra fragrans*; Ee, *Erythroxylum ecarinatum*; F, *Finschia chloroxantha*; G, *Gynotroches axillaris*; Ga, *Garcinia* sp.; Go, *Gomphandra* sp.; Gu, *Guoia* sp.; L, *Lepinia solomonensis*; Li, *Litsea* sp.; M, *Macaranga polyadenia*; N, *Neoscortechinia forbesii*; Po, *Polyosma* sp.; Ps, *Prunus schlechteri*; T, *Teijsmanniodendron ahernianum*; Ti, *Timonius pulposus*; X, *Xylopia peekelii*. The palm is *Physokentia insolita*.

6.1), including the pioneer species. By contrast, the west-coast forests had a predominance of species which do not require gaps to regenerate, but can perpetuate themselves *in situ* (groups (a) and (b) in Table 6.1). These shade-bearers were represented solely by small trees on the north coast. The two contrasting sorts of forest are represented by the profile diagrams of Figs 15.18 and 15.19. The clear conclusion appears to be that the north-coast forests owe their present composition to major disturbance, are progressively changing as shade-bearers come in, and will come to resemble the west-coast forests unless the disturbance is repeated. A cyclone which occurred after 3.3 years caused much more damage to the north-coast forests than the west ones. It is possible that intermittent cyclones maintain them at approximately their present composition. Differences in climbers and epiphytes between the northern and western forest, which also reflect disturbance differences, have been described in §2.6. More subtle differences were also detected. For example (Fig. 15.20), in types II

and III on the west coast, *Campnosperma brevipetiolatum*, which must have gaps for its seedlings to grow up (Table 6.1, p. 74), was represented solely by big trees, but in type I there was in addition a stand of small trees. The indication is that the canopy of all the three west-coast forest types was at one time damaged enough to allow *C. brevipetiolatum* to grow up, and that forest type I has experienced a repetition of the damage. It is probable that cyclones which pass directly over the northern forest and cause them major damage also cause minor damage to the west-coast forests peripheral to their path (cf. §§6.1 and 15.2).

It was also possible to demonstrate that some of the lesser differences in forest types Kolombangara were correlated with differences between the twelve species in efficiency of dispersal, seedling establishment, and onward growth of seedlings into trees.

The forest type (II) least affected by disturbance had the greatest floristic heterogeneity, and the deduction can be made that, in the absence of this important unifying ecological factor, chance has been

195

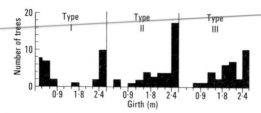

Fig. 15.20. Population structure in 1964 of *Campnosperma brevipetiolatum* in the three west-coast forest types on Kolombangara. (From Whitmore 1974, Fig. 7.3.)

important in determining which species regenerated at a particular spot.

The study clearly showed that perpetuation of the forest types as they now exist depends on the disturbance factor continuing to operate at the same level as in the past. The mosaic theory of forest regeneration, which postulates that variation in space is due to different groups of species succeeding each other in any one place, is seen, even for these species-poor Solomons' forests, to be an oversimplification. In the absence of the major unifying factor of disturbance species associations would be much less clear-cut.

In an area with more species, such as the New Guinea lowland evergreen rain forest or the mixed dipterocarp rain forest, the spectrum of response to gaps which is spanned on Kolombangara by only twelve common big-tree species is covered by a much greater number, many with very similar ecological amplitudes. This is shown best by long series of taxonomically very similar species, for example, of *Parinari* (discussed in detail by Prance and Whitmore (1973)) and the subgroups of *Shorea*, especially the Red Merantis (Symington 1943; Ashton 1964, 1965, 1968; Meijer and Wood 1964). In these species-rich rain forests clearly-defined species associations are therefore inherently less likely to occur, even where a major unifying factor such as disturbance is or has been in operation.† As there are likely to be several species within a given area which are ecologically suited to a given niche, an element of chance may determine which one actually comes to occupy a given spot (Poore 1963). This is one facet of the complexity in the association between species, to which we now return in the concluding section of this chapter.

† And in Malaya only the storm forest of Kelantan is comparable to north Kolombangara. The lowland dipterocarp forest of the rest of the country is more comparable to the various forest types of west Kolombangara.

15.5. On the nature of variation within lowland rain forest

Variation within a forest can only operate on the species present within the area. Thus, the availablity of flora (§§15.1 and 15.2) overrides all other reasons for variation.‡ In large measure it is due to historical causes which are now comprehended at least in outline and which operate on a wide regional scale as well as within a country.

Other factors which underly variation have been exemplified by particular cases in the discussions of dipterocarp forest and the Kolombangara forest in §§15.3 and 15.4. These can be arranged roughly into a hierarchy of diminishing importance.

Where there has been major disturbance this factor is the most important, as is clearly seen in the difference between the forests on north and west Kolombangara and in the storm forest of Kelantan in Malaya. The disturbed forests are dominated by long-lived pioneer or near-pioneer species (§6.2) whose life-span may exceed a century (§8.2). The effects of disturbance are thus very long-persistent. It is seen that rare climatic events (§3.5) can have very important consequences on forest composition. Secondary forest (Chapter 18) is, similarly, vegetation resulting from disturbance, often at the hands of man; commonly, short-lived pioneers are dominant at first, but again the effects of the disturbance may persist for more than a century. Gaps of various sizes resulting from various causes are colonized by species light-demanding to different degree, as we discussed at length in Chapter 6, especially §6.2.

Secondly, where not obscured by major disturbance, we can distinguish variation within lowland forest due to topography. This is a complex expression of intertwined factors manifesting themselves in several ways.

The differences in topography over granite and sedimentary rocks, from which differences in soil cannot be separated, were described in the discussion of the Ulu Kelantan survey (§15.2), and most species were shown to be commonest on one site type. Special water relations, resulting from topographic and soil factors, were shown to determine the sites occupied by *Shorea curtisii* in Malaya. Several examples of distinctive species associations on valley floors were mentioned. On Kolombangara Island variation correlated with topography was also detected, and as a minor kind.

‡ Possibly the most dramatic instance of this effect is the highly peculiar peat swamp forests of the north coast of Borneo within the geographical range of *Shorea albida*, which were discussed in detail in §11.3.

At a lower level, two further factors affect forest composition, operating within the framework of gross disturbance and topography-related variation. These are, first, variation due to 'reproductive pressure' and, secondly, that due to soil differences within a topographically uniform site. *Dryobalanops aromatica* dominated extensive tracts of forest in east Malaya, probably owing to a variety of factors which cumulatively ensured that it, rather than other species, was more likely to grow up when the chance occurs. Family groups of dipterocarps and other species at the Jengka and Pasoh forests in Malaya result from the same cause. By contrast at the Andulau forest in Brunei minor variations in soil have been shown to dominate the detected species associations. The relative importance of these two causes is likely to differ from place to place. The investigation necessitates discovering the ecological behaviour of each species, covering its frequency of fruiting, range of dispersal, seed dormancy, seedling establishment, and seedling ongrowth to tree, all of which aspects of tree biology have been fully discussed in Chapters 4, 5, and 6. The role of predators and parasites has to be considered too (§2.8).

From this discussion we can refine the question of the nature of the rain-forest community posed at the beginning of the chapter. The forest cannot be considered as one extensive fluctuating association. Environment-correlated variation occurs as a result of the success in competition of those species within dispersal range which are best adapted to a particular habitat, and there may be several species equally well suited. Here comes into play the important element of haphazard variation, which operates first and coarsely at the level of major canopy-destruction due to the chance occurrence of major disturbing agents such as cyclones. It also operates finely at the level of the chances concomitant with ripe-seed availability (flowering being commonly less often than annual), seed dispersal, seedling establishment, etc., and in the sheer chance of a suitable gap developing at the right place and the right time for seedling ongrowth (§6.1).

Discrete species associations do occur within the lowland evergreen rain forest Formation for various reasons, some of which also apply to differences between different Formations.

Phytosociological analysis, including that which depends on numerical techniques, works well at the level of major discontinuities between and within forest Formations and is an inappropriate tool for the investigation of the lesser more subtle variation

(cf. Webb *et al.* 1972). In fact it has been shown that, in species-rich tropical vegetation, the more subtle the variation the more likely the particular numerical technique used will colour the results (Austin and Greig-Smith 1968). Plot layout is also very important, as the Andulau–Brunei and Pasoh–Malaya studies show, but we have now sufficiently unravelled the modes of variation which can operate within lowland rain forest to realize how very carefully we need to pose the questions to be solved in any study under contemplation.† Only after one has a clear idea of exactly which facets are to be investigated can the sample design and techniques of enumeration and analysis be decided. The problems of species–area curves, minimal area, and indices of diversity are seen to be abstractions which take second place to analysis of the forest in terms of the ecological behaviour of the available species, coupled with the manifold roles of chance. It was this technique which proved so fruitful in the Kolombangara study. The importance of the study of rain-forest dynamics has been too little appreciated (Dawkins 1958).

We have described in this chapter several examples of lowland evergreen rain forest dominated by a single big-tree species instead of a broad mixture of species. It was at one time believed (Richards 1952) that these consociations were found on sites with non-optimal soil conditions, where the habitat has sifted, or selected out, the best-adapted from the numerous potential dominants. Knowledge has now advanced enough to show that consociations result from several causes, not solely from soil conditions. The *Shorea curtisii* ridge forest of the Malayan foorhills *is* associated with a special suboptimal site, as are the *Casuarina* forests of some limestone hilltops and some ultrabasic outcrops (§§ 10.4 and 10.5). *Campnosperma-brevipetiolatum*-dominated forest in the Solomons results from the aggressive response of this species to major canopy gaps, and is comparable to the pure stands of short-lived pioneers (*Macaranga*, etc.) in young secondary forest (Chapter 18). *Dryobalanops aromatica* dominates climax rain forest in Malaya, with no major disturbance to aid it, probably owing to its 'reproductive pressure'. In other Formations too, single-dominant forests have several causes. The *Shorea albida* consociation of the Sarawak peat swamp forest is sited halfway along the soil catena from

† And for further discussions see van Steenis (1961*b*), Poore (1963, 1964, 1968), Cousens (1965), Williams *et al.* (1969*b*), Webb *et al.* (1972 and Whitmore (1974).

relatively favourable to extremely unfavourable conditions (§11.3). *Melaleuca* forest is a fire–climax derivative of fresh-water swamp forest throughout the region (§11.4), and *Ploiarium alternifolium* is favoured in secondary forest over waterlogged soil by repeated cutting (§§10.3 and 11.4).

16 Mountain rain forests

16.1 Montane forest Formations

As ONE climbs a tropical mountain one successively encounters forests of different structure, physiognomy (Table 16.1), and flora (Figs 16.1 and 16.2). The most dramatic change, partly so because it usually occurs sharply over a short distance, is from mesophyll-dominated forest with an uneven, billowing, canopy surface to microphyll-dominated forest (Figs 16.3 and 16.4) with a lower, flattish canopy surface, the trees more slender, usually with gnarled limbs and very dense subcrowns. This latter Formation is called upper montane rain forest. It is encountered first on knolls and narrow ridge crests with mesophyll forest occupying the valleys, saddles, and broader crests. Upwards it comes to clothe the entire landscape. It is as clearly distinctive on aerial photographs or from an aeroplane as to the traveller on foot.

Upper montane rain forest is frequently only 10 m tall or less (range 1·5–18 m), and its shorter *facies* are sometimes called elfin woodland (Fig. 9.1, p. 105). On outlying spurs and on isolated peaks upper montane forest occurs at lower elevations than on big mountain massifs. In these sites it abuts directly on to tropical lowland evergreen rain forest, for example, on Mts. Belumut and Ophir and on Kedah Peak in Malaya; on Mt. Tinggi on Bawean, Mt. Ranai on Natuna (van Steenis 1972); smaller mountains of the Solomon archipelago; and ridges in the plain of the Fly River in south New Guinea (Brass 1938). By contrast, on all major mountains there is an intermediate Formation, lower montane rain forest (Fig. 16.5), below the upper montane rain forest and which itself merges downwards with lowland rain forest, usually through a broad ecotone.

TABLE 16.1

Characters used to define the principal montane forest Formations

Formation	Tropical lowland evergreen rain forest†	Tropical lower montane rain forest	Tropical upper montane rain forest
Canopy height	25–45 m	15–33 m	1·5–18 m
Emergent trees	Characteristic, to 60 (80) m tall	Often absent, to 37 m tall	Usually absent, to 26 m tall
Pinnate leaves	Frequent	Rare	Very rare
Principal leaf size class of woody plants‡	Mesophyll	Mesophyll	Microphyll
Buttresses	Usually frequent and large	Uncommon, small	Usually absent
Cauliflory	Frequent	Rare	Absent
Big woody climbers	Abundant	Usually none	None
Bole climbers	Often abundant	Frequent to abundant	Very few
Vascular epiphytes	Frequent	Abundant	Frequent
Non-vascular epiphytes	Occasional	Occasional to abundant	Often abundant

† Included for comparison.
‡ Following Raunkiaer (1934).

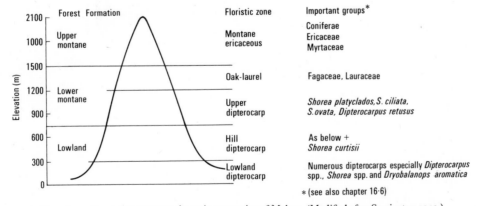

FIG. 16.1. Vegetation zones on the main mountains of Malaya. (Modified after Symington 1943.)

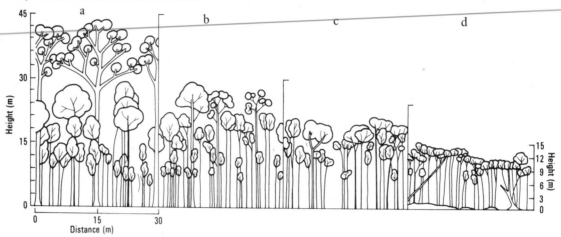

FIG. 16.2.   Altitudinal forest Formation series in Malaya: (a) lowland evergreen rain forest, 150 m elevation, 'lowland dipterocarp'; (b) lower montane rain forest, 780 m, 'upper dipterocarp'; (c) lower montane rain forest, 1500 m, 'oak laurel'; (d) upper montane rain forest, 1800 m, 'montane encaceous'. (Robbins and Wyatt-Smith 1964, Fig. 1.)

FIG. 16.3.   Upper montane rain forest, 2020 m elevation on the summit of Gunung Benom, Malaya. Note the flattish canopy surface, gnarled limbs, dense subcrowns, and small leaves. The conspicuous trees in the centre are *Leptospermum flavescens*.

Lower montane differs from lowland rain forest in having a lower canopy (15–33 m as against 25–45 m), with fewer, smaller emergent trees. Fewer trees are buttressed and the buttresses are much smaller, big woody climbers are usually absent, vascular epiphytes are abundant (as opposed to frequent), and cauliflory is much less common and so are species with compound leaves. We do not yet know the reasons for these differences. They are diagnostic when considered *in toto* although not individually striking, and forests of intermediate nature occur in the ecotone. It is interesting to note that Burtt Davy (1938) placed lower montane rain forest as a sub-Formation of lowland evergreen rain forest.

There is, in general, an increase in cloudiness with elevation on tropical mountains. Above the level where a cloud cap prevailingly develops on any particular mountain, conditions are for much of the time very moist. **Here** bryophytes (mostly hepatics and filmy ferns) develop luxuriantly, and may swathe tree boles and crowns in great festoons, as well as lying thickly underfoot (Figs 16.6 and 16.7). The bog moss *Sphagnum* sometimes occurs as one of the ground mosses and is frequently associated with *Corybas*, *Nertera*, and *Utricularia*. This eerie vegetation is called mossy forest, and it is most commonly found as a *facies* of upper montane rain forest, though mossy lower montane rain forest is known, for example, in the Solomons, and even mossy lowland rain forest occurs, patchily in damp canyons and more extensively in extremely wet climates such as on the Santa Cruz Islands (where rainfall is over 6000 mm/year).

'Mossiness' is often better developed in saddles, through which the moisture-laden air blows, than on adjacent ridges. Mossy forest is better developed in west than east Java, its luxuriance declines in parallel with the increasingly dry climate eastwards shown in Fig. 3.1 (p. 45). In the Lesser Sunda Islands, east of Java, where the climate is even drier, no mossy forest is found in the mountains, the only sign of the cloud zone in east Timor, for example, is the occurrence of epiphytic beards of the lichen *Usnea* (van Steenis 1972).

Upper montane rain forest is commonly very short and dense on knolls and sharp ridge crests, the saddles between carrying a much taller forest yet of identical floristic composition (Fig. 16.8). This variation is to be compared with that found at lower elevations where upper montane forest on knolls alternates with lower montane in the saddles. At still lower elevations lower montane forest itself

FIG. 16.4. *Leptospermum flavescens* with an undergrowth of low bushes, ferns, and sedges. Summit of Gunung Benom, Malaya, at 2020 m. This upper montane forest is poor in epiphytes and is believed to be climatically slightly dry. (Whitmore 1972*a*.)

exhibits similar variation with topography. In addition, as a further stunting effect, on many mountains in Malaya a narrow zone at the uppermost limit of lower montane forest is shorter than the main part, and similar stunted lower montane forest actually covers a few summits, for example, of Gunung Mandi Angin (1436 m (Cockburn 1969)).

The study of tropical montane forests is especially important in the Far East because so much more of the region is mountainous than are either the African or Amazonian tropical rain forest regions. The elucidation of correlations between observed changes with elevation in forest and in environment has proved to be much more intricate than was at one time suspected. Here it is only possible to discuss the main factors as they are at present understood, with reference to some of the more detailed studies. These investigations have a general importance in rain-

FIG. 16.5.   Lower montane rain forest, Gunung Ulu Kali, Malaya, at 1290 m elevation.

FIG. 16.6. Mossy forest *facies* of upper montane rain forest, at 1350 m elevation on Bukit Tibang, the topographical centre of Borneo.

forest ecology, especially for the insight they give into climate–soil–plant relationships.

Zonation in New Guinea

Richards (1952) has given excellent summaries of the classic descriptions of forest zones on the mountains of Malesia. On the biggest mountains, the huge cordillera which runs the length of New Guinea and which has several peaks over 4000 m high, the forest zones attain their greatest altitudinal extent. The ecotone between the lowland and lower montane forest Formations is at about 1500 m, and upper montane forest is found from about 3000 m upwards.

Zonation occurs in the lowland rain forest, especially between plains and foothill forest. For example, in the former *Pometia pinnata* is the most important timber species, locally with *Intsia palembanica*; in the latter *Anisoptera thurifera* and *Hopea* spp. form a widespread association on ridges (cf. §15.2). Zonation within lower montane rain forest also occurs and has now been elucidated in a

number of places. In the Wabag–Tari area of the Highlands (Robbins and Pullen 1965; Grubb) at the lower levels (900–2250 m), 'oak' forest is prevalent, containing much *Castanopsis acuminatissima*, with lesser abundance in the top of the canopy of species of the mixed forest (see below). The canopy is 18–24 m tall. Upwards, between 2100 m and 2700 m, 'beech' forest prevails, comprising *Nothofagus* spp. mainly as multi-species stands and occupying ridges either as discrete groves or as continuous tracts; the canopy is 30–36 m tall; mosses and ferns are more luxuriant than in the oak forest. Interspersed with the beech forest, and best developed in valleys, is a mixed forest of some 40–50 tree species in about as many families and with a predominance of Cunoniaceae, Elaeocarpaceae, Lauraceae, Myrtaceae, Podocarpaceae, Rubiaceae, and Rutaceae. The canopy is about 30 m tall; ferns, mosses, and herbaceous flowering plants are abundant. Mixed forest gives way abruptly to the upper montane Formation at elevations above 3000 m, and extends

203

FIG. 16.7. Mossy forest *facies* of upper montane rain forest, at 1800 m elevation on Gunung Murud, Sarawak.

FIG. 16.8. Upper montane rain forest with *Dacrydium* dominant and markedly taller in gullies than on ridge crests. Summit plateau, Gunung Ulu Kali, Malaya, 1700 m elevation.

downwards as low as 900 m. The upper montane flora is much poorer than the lower montane one. Elaeocarpaceae are much less abundant and Lauraceae are distinctly rare, while ground-dwelling Ericaceae are fairly common. The canopy only reaches 12–18 m tall. Ground ferns are much less common. At its lower elevations emergent *Papuacedrus* is locally present. Similar zonation to that at Wabag–Tari has been reported from a number of other peaks on the New Guinea cordillera (Hynes 1974). On this great mountain chain the upper montane rain forest can itself be divided into two rather distinct floristic zones; the 'cloud forest' at 3000–3300 (3350) m and the 'lower subalpine forest' at 3300 (3350)–3550 (3600) m, first recognized by Wade and McVean (1969) on Mt. Wilhelm. On the highest mountains a third zone has been distinguished: the 'upper subalpine forest' (Wade and McVean 1969) which lies between 3550 (3600) m and 3900 (3950) m on Mt. Wilhelm. This forest is 4·5 m tall and has even smaller leaves preponderant, namely, nanophylls (Grubb 1974). It is composed mainly of species of *Coprosma*, *Dimorphanthera*, *Drimys*, *Eurya*, *Olearia*, *Quintinia*, *Rapanea*, *Rhododendron*, *Styphelia*, *Trochocarpa*, and *Vaccinium*. The subalpine forest Formation is represented on the bigger mountains of Sumatra and Java at the uppermost limits of forest by a forest with low, dense canopy containing a strong microtherm element in the flora (van Steenis 1972) but does not apparently occur elsewhere in the Far East. Comparable forests occur on the highest peaks of the Andes.

Zonation elsewhere in the region

On the smaller main mountain ranges of Malaya (few peaks over 1800 m) zonation is much compressed in comparison with New Guinea. The Formations do not extend so high, and there is not so much variation with elevation within them. Zonation was well described by Symington (1936, 1943) who recognized floristic zones within the forest Formations (see Figs 16.1 and 16.9; see also Richards 1952; Whitmore and Burnham 1971; Whitmore 1972*a*).

Mt. Makiling in the Philippines has zones similar to those on a small Malayan mountain (Brown 1919; see also Richards 1952). On the big mountains of Sumatra and Java (with some peaks over 3000 m but none over 4000 m) zonation is intermediate between New Guinea and Malaya and the lower limit of upper montane rain forest is at about 2000 m (van Steenis 1972).

Forest zonation occurs in seasonally dry as well as perhumid climates and mountain monsoon forests have already been mentioned several times in earlier chapters. On many of the mountains in Java upper montane forest is periodically burned. After a mild fire there is much regeneration from stumps; more

FIG. 16.9. *Leptospermum flavescens* is a common species of upper montane rain forest in the tropical Far East. Note the tiny, hard leaves.

frequent fire increases the abundance of grasses, and ultimately savanna develops. The only tree which is favoured by burning is *Albizia lophantha*, whose regeneration was described in §5.2. Mossy forest is less often burned, which is hardly surprising. At lower elevations burning leads to the replacement of lower montane forest with *Casuarina junghuhniana* forest or savanna (§12.1). *Pinus* and *Araucaria* in our region both occupy seasonally dry sites in the lower montane zone (Chapter 14). Intermontane valleys, as in the Barisan range of Sumatra and the main ranges of New Guinea, are drier than the outer slopes. There are extensive seasonally dry montane forests in Thailand, Burma, and Indo-China.

Zonation summarized

In summary, three major and parallel changes in forest structure and physiognomy with increasing elevation can be observed. First, there is a decrease in stature and in biomass; the giant emergents of the lowlands are absent from lower montane rain forest, and there is a further decrease in stature to upper montane and subalpine forest. This progressive diminution has sometimes been referred to as a three-layered forest being replaced by a two-layered and ultimately by a one-layered one (Robbins 1968*a*, 1969), which is an evocative but rather crude description of the change (cf. §2.4). Secondly, leaf size decreases. Thirdly, there is an increase in the amount of epiphytes, especially of bryophytes and filmy ferns. There are also parallel changes in flora which will be discussed in §16.3, but first we must briefly consider the uppermost forest limits.

16.2. The tree line and beyond

The altitudinal limit of tree growth is only reached on a few of the biggest mountains of New Guinea where it lies at about 3720–3840 m (Walker 1970). Near its upper limit forest occurs as a low subalpine type as described above. Most if not all of these highest mountains have a short, very dry spell each year during which the mountain-top alpine vegetation is usually burned by native hunting parties, for it is the habitat of small mammals, including the possibly genuinely wild dog of New Guinea (Womersley and McAdam 1957). On Mt. Wilhelm the dry weather lasts for about 2 months (McVean 1974). Over large areas subalpine forest remains as patches in fire-climax alpine grassland, and fire-resistant woody plants such as *Cyathea* spp. and *Podocarpus brassii* stand as isolated survivors (Wade and McVean 1969; Gillison 1969; Kalkman and Vink 1970). The altitude at which the tree limit occurs is

further complicated by the occurrence of grassland in so-called 'frost-pockets' in hollows and along valley floors below the climatic tree line (see Chapter 14 for further details and also van Steenis (1968) for examples from the craters of extinct volcanoes in Java above 2000 m).

Alpine vegetation above the tree line is a complex, edaphically determined mosaic of dwarf shrub heath, short alpine grassland, moss tundra, and fern meadow. Many of the genera are mainly temperate in their distribution. Wade and McVean (1969) give a full description for Mt. Wilhelm (4510 m), highest mountain in east New Guinea, and Walker (1968) gives a short account. Precipitation may fall as snow above about 4000 m, and the line at which snow permanently lies is slightly above 4500 m, only a few peaks in west New Guinea reach above it. There are signs on Mt. Wilhelm and other high peaks of glaciation, and pollen analysis has revealed the former existence at lower elevation than today of alpine herb communities. From these two separate lines of evidence it has been deduced that the snowline was depressed during the Pleistocene period by at least 550 m (pollen analysis) and possibly by over 1000 m (geomorphology) (Flenley 1972).

The transition zone between grassland and subalpine forest has been investigated in the Doma Peaks region in central New Guinea. A number of species reach their greatest abundance in the transition zone. The forest is currently advancing into the grassland because fire is less frequent than formerly. Several of the woody species propagate themselves by layering (Gillison 1970).

Outside New Guinea no other mountains in the region extend above the climatic tree line. The uppermost slopes of the numerous high, active volcanoes in Indonesia are bare due to a continual supply of ash, lava, and other ejectamenta. Some montane forests have been converted to fire-climax savanna as was described in §16.1. Mt. Kinabalu (4101 m), the only major mountain in Borneo, has a bare rocky summit, with signs of having been ice-scoured and with herbs and dwarf shrubs growing in crevices (Meijer 1971).

16.3. The mountain floras

The changes in forest structure and physiognomy with elevation (§16.1) are paralleled by equally striking changes in floristic composition which are, as far as we at present know, also generally gradual within the lowland and lower montane forest Formations; abrupt to upper montane and then, in New Guinea, abrupt again to the subalpine forest.

At the broadest level of generalization, families of predominantly tropical distribution (megatherms) are restricted, or almost restricted, to elevations below about 1000 m. These include Anacardiaceae, Burseraceae, Capparidaceae, Combretaceae, Connaraceae, Dilleniaceae, Dipterocarpaceae, Flacourtiaceae, Marantaceae, Myristicaceae, and Rhizophoraceae.

Conversely, a number of families of predominantly temperate distribution (microtherms) and numerous genera are only found above about 1000 m (van Steenis 1972). Of north hemisphere distribution may be mentioned the genera *Anemone*, *Aster*, *Berberis*, *Cirsium*, *Galium*, *Lonicera*, *Myosotis*, *Primula*, *Ranunculus*, *Stellaria*, *Valerianella*, *Veronica*, and *Viola*, and of south hemisphere distribution *Caladenia*, *Gaultheria*, *Gunnera*, *Microlaena*, *Nertera*, *Thelymitra*, and *Wahlenbergia*. Van Steenis has dealt in great detail with the origin of the Malesian mountain flora, which is beyond our present scope, and reference should be made to his papers (van Steenis 1934, 1936, 1962, 1964). Tree families which are better represented at middle and high elevations than in the lowlands include Aceraceae, Araucariaceae, Clethraceae, Cunoniaceae, Ericaceae, Fagaceae, Lauraceae, Myrtaceae, Pentaphylacaceae, Podocarpaceae, Symplocaceae, and Theaceae. Montane forests have floristic affinity at family and genus level with the warm temperate and subtropical forests of south China and southern Japan (Wang 1961), though, as shown below (§16.5), there are in fact major differences in the climate more important than the superficial similarities.

Analysis of the altitudinal range by forest Formation of 1759 species, the Malayan representatives of 43 flowering plant families, (Table 16.2) showed that very nearly all are restricted in occurrence to a single Formation, with only 3 per cent occuring in both the lowlands and the lower montane rain forest, and fewer than 1 per cent extending from the lowlands to upper montane forest. This is, of course, as would be expected because the physiognomy and structure of each Formation is determined by the species which comprise it. Such zonation is probably typical of that found throughout the region. *Albizia lophantha* of Sumatra and the Sunda Islands has a total altitudinal range from 1100 m to 3100 m but occurs exclusively on mountains of which the highest peak exceeds 2500 m. *Casuarina junghuhniana* similarly ranges from 1400 m to 3100 m but is restricted to mountains which attain 2550 m.

TABLE 16.2
Altitudinal ranges of species in Malaya

Total number of species investigated	1759	
Lowlands † and lower montane rain forest	55	3 per cent
Lowlands † to upper montane rain forest	7	0.4 per cent
Disjunct range: lowlands† and upper montane rain forest only	4	0.2 per cent

Based on Whitmore (1973*k*); data from *Tree flora of Malaya* (Whitmore 1972*b*, 1973*c*).
† All lowland forest Formations grouped together.

Van Steenis (1961*a*, 1972, Chapter 6) points out that this is because these species, and others he cites, have an optimal altitudinal range within which they can grow and reproduce, plus a marginal zone below this which can be colonized, for instance, in shady gorges and by waterfalls and where conditions are adequate for growth but unsuitable for reproduction. Persistence in the marginal zone depends on continual replenishment from above. The zone of establishment extends below the zone of reproduction, and these species do not occur on mountains that do not reach sufficiently high. In addition, in Indonesia the upper limit of some species extends above its usual elevation in 'open-air hothouses', the warm humid atmosphere around the fumaroles of active volcanoes (van Steenis 1935). It is clear from this mass elevation effect, as van Steenis calls it, that studies on species zonation which are based simply on altitudes are not very informative.

Fuller details on altitudinal zonation of species in New Guinea and Malaya are given in §§16.1 and 16.6 respectively.

16.4. The upper montane and heath-forest Formations compared

Upper montane and heath forest have many features of structure and physiognomy in common. Some species also occur in both Formations. The forest canopy of both Formations is rather even, dense, and commonly with a high albedo (of pale colour on aerial photographs). Trees have dense crowns, microphyll (Raunkiaer 1934) is the predominant leaf size, and the leaves tend to be held obliquely vertical, often closely placed on the twigs. The plant community of both Formations is of low biomass in comparison with others. Paths made by animals or travellers remain open for a long time, and many species have hard, dense wood—two factors which suggest that growth rate is slow. Big woody climbers are absent or rare in both Formations.

Pachyphylly (see §16.5), which has been demonstrated to be frequent in Malayan and New Guinea upper montane and subalpine forest, has not yet been looked for in heath forest.

Amongst the sample of 1759 Malayan species already mentioned (§16.3, Table 16.2) four have a disjunct distribution between heath and upper montane rain forest. These are *Styphelia malayana*, *Austrobuxus nitidus*, *Myrica esculenta*, and *Lithocarpus lampadarius*.† Taking the whole Malayan flora, a few more tree and shrub species can be added to the list, namely, *Baeckia frutescens* and several species of *Rhododendron* and *Vaccinium*. Open sites in the mountains and inland heath-forest sites on quartz and quartzite ridges in the lowlands have a number of highly distinctive herbs in common especially *Dianella* spp. (Liliaceae), the ground orchids *Arundina graminifolia*, *Bromheadia* spp., and *Spathoglottis aurea*, and the ferns *Dipteris conjugata*, *Matonia pectinata*, and *Oleandra pistillaris* (s.l.).

In a comparison in Brunei of the forests of mountain tops with heath forest on rocky, sandstone ridges at various elevations, as well as near the coast on alluvium, Ashton (1964) found several species of wide altitudinal range. Examples are several *Eugenia*, *Rhododendron*, and *Vaccinium* spp., *Horsfieldia polyspherula*, *Myrsine umbellata*, *Stemonurus umbellatus*, *Ternstroemia aneura*, and *Tristania pentandra*. Some other species were found which are of restricted altitudinal range. For example, none of the heath-forest dipterocarps extends above 1500 m and, conversely, several species of mountain ridges are not found in lowland heath forest, for example, *Ascarina philippinensis*, *Dacrydium falciforme*, *Drimys piperita*, *Elaeocarpus fulvotomentosus*, *Phyllocladus hypophyllus*, *Podocarpus imbricatus*, *Weinmannia dulitensis*, and *Xanthomyrtus taxifolia*.

From these observations it appears that for some species either the montane or the lowland environment is necessary, that is, they are microtherms or megatherms (§16.3), whilst others are responding to features of the environment which are common to both the heath and upper montane Formations. We shall investigate what these features are in §16.6.

Some of the bryophytes of mossy forest also have restricted altitudinal ranges. *Herberta* and *Lepicolea* are found above 1000 m, *Pallavicinia zollingeri* is always found at 2000 m or higher, and *Breutelia chrysocoma* from 3000 m upwards. *Bazzania uncigera*

† In Sarawak, where there is a much greater extent of sandstone and of podzols at intermediate elevations, the first three of these species are found at all elevations without disjunction; cf. the observations in Brunei described in the next paragraph.

is abundant around 2000 m and replaced upwards by *B. praerupta*, 2800–3000 m. Other genera are found in both low- and high-elevation mossy forest, examples are *Frullania*, *Mastigophora*, *Riccardia*, *Schistochila*, and *Trichocolea* (Meijer 1961).

It must also be recalled that heath forest has numerous species in common with peat swamp forest (§11.3) and some in common with the forests on deep peat on the summits of limestone hills (§10.4). Furthermore, many of the *Rhododendron* and *Vaccinium* species of heath and upper montane forest also grow as epiphytes.

A few species span the complete altitudinal range from lowlands to upper montane rain forest. Of these, *Rhodoleia championii* in Malaya is restricted in the lowlands to rocky outcrops and *Dacrydium beccarii* var. *subelatum* in Borneo is restricted to heath forest and the Lawas peat swamp forest in the lowlands (Fig. 14.3, p. 171), and in Malaya extends down only as far as lower montane forest where it occurs along ridge crests.

16.5. The montane environment

Tropical montane climates

In Chapter 3 the term 'tropical' was taken to connote continuous warmth. It can also be taken to imply tropical latitudes. The importance of the second definition is that it denotes a certain insolation regime, the midday sun high in the sky all the year round, and only slight variation through the year in day-length (Blumenstock 1958). The diurnal range in temperature is usually greater than the annual range of the means. The climate of high tropical mountains has therefore been evocatively, but crudely, described as 'every day a summer, every night a winter'.

The biggest mountains in the tropical Far East have their summits above the snow line, which is at about 4500 m, and the upper parts of all the bigger mountains are certainly not tropical in the temperature sense; but because they have a tropical insolation regime, which is quite different from that of any temperate latitude, their climate is best considered as tropical montane rather than temperate.

Changes with elevation

In summary the aerial environment becomes progressively cooler and moister with increasing elevation, with a sharp change at the level of prevalent cloud.

Temperature. Temperature decreases with increasing elevation, the rate of fall, or lapse rate, is generally about 0·67 °C per 100 m but this varies from place to place, with season, time of day, water vapour content of the air, and other factors. Below the condensation level on mountains the dry adiabatic lapse rate is about 1·0 °C per 100 m, but above this level (which is generally about 1200 m) the saturated adiabatic lapse rate is only about 0·5 °C per 100 m, which however slowly increases again until it approaches the dry rate at about 12 000 m. The *Massenerhebung*, or mass elevation heating effect, of large mountains, is well known and was first recorded in the Alps. This is the phenomenon that large mountains and the central parts of large ranges are warmer at a given elevation than small mountains and outlying spurs. In temperate mountains the effect of the small temperature rises due to mass heating is accentuated since the consequent decrease in the incidence of frost results in a considerable extension of the annual growing season. Such conditions do not apply to most tropical mountains. But it has been demonstrated that the influence of elevated heating surfaces can be very considerable in the tropics. Hastenrath (1968) found, from analysing 10 years of observations with radiosonde balloons, that temperatures over the huge massif of the Mexican Meseta which has a substantial surface of high mean elevation heated by radiant solar energy were considerably higher than over adjacent lowlands. By contrast, the Cordillera de Talamanca of Costa Rica, 3900 m high and 320 km long but only 80 km wide, showed no such mass elevation effect, and this is because if offers only a small heating surface of high mean elevation. By analogy, and in the absence of direct measurement, it may be surmised that the huge mass of the New Guinea cordillera is the only mountain range in the tropical Far East likely to show a substantial *Massenerhebung* heating effect, and the Barisan range of Sumatra probably shows a slight one. The much smaller main mountain ranges of Malaya and isolated peaks are almost certainly too small.

Moisture. The degree of saturation of a given air-body increases as its temperature falls. With increasing elevation the dew-point (that is, the temperature at which condensation occurs and cloud forms) depends on the temperature lapse rate and the initial moisture content. As noted above, the cloud line is commonly reached at about 1200 m. Where the lowland air is highly humid, as it is around isolated peaks set in the sea or in an expanse of lowland rain forest (which has potential evapotranspiration approaching that of a free water surface—Chapter 3), the cloud cap tends to form at a lower elevation. Examples were given above in the discussion on the occurrence of mossy forest (§16.1). Burgess (unpublished) found over a year's observations a decrease in potential evaporation of 47 mm per 100 m between 150 m and 900 m in the main range of Malaya. He found there was no simple relationship between annual rainfall and elevation in the same range up to about 1500 m, owing to rain relief and rain-shadow effects. McVean (1974) found similar complications in a study of the rainfall received by Mt. Wilhelm in New Guinea from 1000 m to the summit region at 4400 m. Commonly, rainfall received by a mountain will exceed that of adjacent plains owing to the effect of relief (Chapter 3); Beckinsdale (1957) has given the average figure of a 100 mm increase per 30 m up to about 1500 m elevation, but generalization can be misleading owing to local variation.

Radiation. There has been no work yet done on the radiation regime of high tropical mountains. The thick blanket of moist air which shields the lowlands diminishes upwards, and more ultraviolet wavelengths, for example, reach the ground, which accounts for the rapidity with which a human becomes suntanned. Its effects on plants remain to be explored; there may be effects on growth via light-sensitive plant hormone systems.

Pressure. The direct effect of reduced barometric pressure has not been investigated either. It has been shown that transpiration can increase with reduced barometric pressure under isothermal conditions and that, for at least some Mediterranean plants, reduced barometric pressure has a depressing effect on the amount of carbon dioxide available for photosynthesis (Gale 1972*a,b*), but there are numerous variables and direct observation is required.

Fog. Cloud at ground level is fog, and has several direct effects. Light is greatly reduced, and may be so low as to limit assimilation (Brown 1919; Grubb and Whitmore 1966; Gates 1969). Cloud blown through foliage is strained of much of its moisture—so-called 'fog-stripping'; crowded foliage, dense crowns, and needle leaves may perhaps be viewed as adaptations to enhance the efficiency of the process. Direct experiment and observation remains scant, but it now seems probable that some forests receive a considerable amount of moisture from this source (Blumenstock 1958, Ekern 1964—Hawaii;

Kerfoot 1968; Brunig 1971—plateau edges of Sarawak heath forest; Ellis 1971—Australia). Fog-stripping may be more important in saddles through which winds are channelled than on adjacent ridge crests. Fog will tend to leach minerals from leaves unless the plants have protective impermeable cuticles. The over-all influence of fog must depend on its duration. Despite the extreme wetness of atmosphere and soil during fog periods, many sites above the cloud line may be seasonally dry and the vegetation suffer temporary water-stress. For example, McVean has reported 2 dry months annually on Mt. Wilhelm (§16.2). The summit plateau of Gunung Tahan, highest mountain of Malaya (2189 m), and nearby Gunung Rabong suffer annual water-stress (Wyatt-Smith 1963). Mossy forest does not develop above the cloud line in seasonally dry Timor (§16.1).

Soils. Soils also change with elevation, as was described in some detail in §9.12. In general they become more humic, with available minerals diminishing in amount. These changes are correlated with the cooler and moister aerial environment. Termites do not extend high into the mountains, nor in many places do earthworms. In the Malayan main range neither of these groups of soil mixers is found higher than about 1200 m (Whitmore and Burnham 1969). Surface accumulation of peat is a sign of the decreased rate of decay and mixing of leaf litter. Some minerals are held in the peat in a form unavailable to plants, especially phosphorus and nitrogen, possibly also copper and zinc (Grubb 1971). The tendency for peat to accumulate is accentuated by wetness, because anaerobic conditions inhibit decay, and its thickness commonly increases dramatically at the cloud line. Soils are typically waterlogged and anaerobic near the surface, becoming better drained at depth. Peaty podzols are common in which iron becomes reduced to the soluble ferrous state, moves down the profile, and is reprecipitated as a pan. *Sphagnum* and other peat-forming mosses occur above the cloud line and increase peat formation. Some montane species, including members of the Coniferae and Myrtaceae which are common families of peat soils, have leathery leaves, resistant to decay and which therefore tend to accumulate after falling, as undecomposed leaf litter on the ground.

In conclusion, it can be seen that there are a number of self-reinforcing factors, whose operation is accentuated by frequent fog, which lead to oligo-trophic conditions in mountain soils. It is unlikely however that all these factors always operate.

Ridges, knolls, and summits at all elevations are stable sites in which the soil is not being continually rejuvenated by slip or creep. The only water received is from the atmosphere, the soils are continually leached and do not receive soil water from higher sites. It follows that the soils of these places will tend to be more oligotrophic and drier than those of hillsides, saddles, and valleys. Peat formation may be triggered in such sites if the oligotrophic soil is *ipso facto* poor in litter-decaying organisms, and, as described above, once started the process tends to become self-reinforcing.

16.6. Correlations between elevational changes in forest and environment

Considering the mountain ranges, the forest zones are most extended on the largest mountains of all, the New Guinea cordillera, most compressed on low ranges, such as the mountains of Malaya, and of intermediate extent on mountains of intermediate height in Indonesia, especially the Barisan range of Sumatra (§16.1). It seems probable that this at least partly results from a *Massenerhebung* heating effect (§16.5) with the temperature lapse rate lowest on the biggest mountain systems and consequently the increase with elevation of coolness and moistness of the aerial and soil environment lowest there. The situation is complicated by regional differences in the incidence of moisture-laden airstreams (Chapter 3).

The occurrence of upper montane forest

Upper montane rain forest reaches below its general level along the ridges on big mountains, and its lowest occurrences are on knolls and sharp ridge crests where it is set amongst lower montane rain forest in the saddles. On the smallest mountains the upper montane Formation abuts directly on to lowland rain forest (§16.1). Further, within both upper and lower montane rain forest, knolls and sharp ridge crests commonly carry forest of lower stature.

It was described above (§16.5) how knolls and mountain summits are oligotrophic sites which also are more prone to periodic water deficit than hillside, saddle, and valley sites. It was also shown (§16.4) that upper montane forest has strong structural and physiognomic resemblances to heath forest and also has some species in common. It was demonstrated in an earlier chapter (§10.3) that many of the specialized features found in heath forest can be considered adaptive to periodic water-stress and that there are also indications of adaptation to oligotrophic conditions. Furthermore, the central forests on highly-developed, raised-peat bogs in Sarawak and the summit forest of limestone hills were noted also to have many similarities. It seems likely that the same features are similarly adaptive in upper montane forest, and that the species which occur in these situations (§16.4) are those which succeed in either a periodically dry environment or an oligotrophic one, or both.

The discovery (Grubb 1974) that some upper montane and subalpine species in New Guinea and Malaya have a unique type of thick, fleshy leaf strengthens the view that water may be periodically limiting. These leaves, called pachyphylls, have most of the lamina $300\,\mu m$ thick or more, usually have a hypodermis, and have well-developed palisade tissue and markedly thickened outer walls of the epidermal cells. These characters are considered to maximize the rate of carbon-dioxide uptake (and hence photosynthesis) relative to water loss while the stomata are open. Thus they may be an adaptation to maximize growth in conditions where water is at times limiting. No investigation has yet been made to see whether pachyphylls occur in heath forest.

Analysis has shown that markedly reduced amounts of certain major nutrients (nitrogen, phosphorus, and sometimes potassium) are found in leaves taken from upper montane forest on highly organic soil, compared with samples from lower montane and lowland forest (Grubb 1974). This is strong evidence that in such sites mineral supply may be less than elsewhere.

In conclusion, it can be seen that either or both of two groups of factors can give rise to the site conditions which support upper montane forest. In the case of oligotrophy some upper montane forest species themselves reinforce this state. Without detailed examination of particular forests the relative importance of a shortage of mineral nutrients and of periodic drought cannot be surmised. The following examples illustrate likely differences in the relative importance of the two groups of factors.

On Kolombangara, a small island in the Solomons reaching 1662 m elevation, the summit soils are excessively impoverished by leaching in the continuously wet climate (estimated annual rainfall 8250 mm (Whitmore 1969a)) and have reached a stage of degradation beyond that of similar soils described from other places (Lee 1969). The vegetation is a low, very mossy, upper montane rain forest. The bottom level of persistent cloud is at about 800 m on Kolombangara, and oligotrophy is undoubtedly

more important than periodic water-stress. Kolombangara is in some ways comparable with the Ecuadorian Andes (Grubb and Whitmore 1966).

The summit of Gunung Belumut, an isolated 1009 m granite peak in south Malaya, lies above the line of prevalent cloud. Upper montane forest abuts on lowland forest at 810 m, and the latter has a narrow stunted zone just below the ecotone. On Gunung Gua Rimau, a southern spur of the same mountain, the ecotone is at about 600 m. The lowlands surrounding the Belumut massif experience 2 months every year when potential evapotranspiration exceeds precipitation (Burgess). The high sandstone and quartzite summit plateaux of Gunung Tahan (2190 m) and Gunung Rabong (1536 m) in central Malaya are very wet indeed for much of the year, but in most years experience a period of up to 8 weeks from February onwards with no rain and little cloud. Kedah Peak (1200 m), an isolated coastal mountain in north-west Malaya, has a cap of white sandstone-quartzite which weathers to give soils only 0·1 m deep; the mountain top is often shrouded in cloud. Gunung Santubong (797 m), a coastal sandstone peak in west Sarawak near Kuching, is similar. In the cases of all these five Malaysian mountains both oligotrophy and drought might contribute to produce site conditions for upper montane rain forest. Only observation can decide their relative importance.

To complete the spectrum, one can perhaps cite the high Javan volcanoes which suffer water-stress in all or most years (Chapter 3) but have highly fertile periodically rejuvenated soils (Chapter 9). On these peaks it is likely that drought is a more important determinant of zonation than oligotrophy.

Richards (1952) suggested that the features of upper montane forest might be due to some chemical characteristic of the soil such as extreme mineral deficiency or poor nitrification. It was not realized at that time that drought periods are a feature of even the wettest tropical climates (Chapter 3), and that these extend up certainly some mountains and possibly most. Eco-physiological investigations on the water balance, the nutrient balance, and the heat balance of montane forests are now required to carry this subject further.

The ecotone between lower and upper montane forest

The change in forests with elevation is not gradual. Upper montane forest usually has an abrupt lower boundary, and the reasons for this are now well established.

Upper montane rain forest is frequently associated,

as we have seen, with special sites. These oligotrophic ridge crests, knolls, and summits, some of which are liable to periodic drought, are fairly sharply bounded. If site conditions lead to peat formation then, as has been described, certain upper montane tree species are favoured which themselves stimulate peat formation, and the effect is self-reinforcing, tending to sharpen even further the boundary with the adjacent forest.

One factor which is likely to initiate peat development, where it occurs, is waterlogged soil conditions, arising from frequent cloud. We have seen that the cloud cap tends to form at a particular level on any given mountain. It follows that marked liability to waterlogging will start rather abruptly at this elevation. Again, once peat has begun to form, the self-reinforcing process commences and a sharp boundary forms. *Sphagnum* frequently grows in these water-logged places and also accentuates peat accumulation.

Thus, there are several different reasons why the lower boundary of upper montane forest may be abrupt, and without examination it is not possible to say which factors are acting in any particular site. It is probably significant that the lower boundary is gradual on the volcanoes of Java (van Steenis 1972) which have a nutrient-rich soil (Chapter 9).

The ecotone between lowland and lower montane forest

The differences in structure and physiognomy between lowland and lower montane forest are slight, and Burtt Davy (1938) had the latter as a sub-Formation only. The ecotone is generally broad, so far as is known, but in Malaya it is abrupt, for reasons connected with the ecological preferences of the emergent dipterocarp species. In Malaya the ecotone occurs at the elevation of the replacement of all the emergent dipterocarp species of lowland forest with their enormous cauliflower-like crowns, plus the hill-ridge species *Shorea curtisii* (§15.3), by a smaller number of different big dipterocarps, which are slightly less massive and have smaller, less prominently emergent crowns (Fig. 16.1). The principal valley and slope species which disappear are *Anisoptera scaphula, Shorea acuminate, S. bracteolata, S. hopeifolia, S. leprosula, S. longisperma,* and *S. ovalis.* The main replacements are *S. ovata* and *S. platyclados* with lesser numbers of *S. ciliata, S. submontana, Dipterocarpus costatus,* and *D. retusus* (Symington 1943; Burgess 1969*b*). *S. platyclados,* which is by far the commonest lower montane dipterocarp, is a vigorous, aggressive, light-demanding species which comes in first in valleys and at

slightly higher elevations on ridges, where it replaces *S. faguetiana, S. laevis, S. macroptera, S. parvifolia, Dipterocarpus grandiflorus,* and the association of *S. curtisii* with the big stemless undergrowth palm *Eugeissona tristis* (Burgess 1969*b*). The ecotone is at about 750 m in the main ranges. It appears that *S. platyclados* becomes successful in competition with the lowland dipterocarps as conditions become moister and cooler, because it comes in first in valleys and is also found as isolated trees in moist sites as low as 300 m. It grows vigorously in plantations in the lowlands on fertile soils (Burgess). *S. platyclados* and its associated big dipterocarps themselves drop out upwards at about 1200 m, apparently because their seedlings cannot successfully establish on peat (§5.3). They are replaced by forest dominated by Fagaceae and Lauraceae (Fig. 16.1).

16.7. Zonation of animals on tropical mountains

The most detailed study of zonation has been made in Malaya, on Gunung Benom (2075 m), a large isolated mountain near the centre of the Peninsula. Findings there are believed typical of the main mountains of the country (Medway 1972*d*). On Gunung Benom both birds and mammals show a sharp disjunction between a lowland and a mountain fauna. Of 191 species of birds identified, 141 species (74 per cent) were found only below 750 m. Of 81 species of mammals, 69 (85 per cent) were recorded within this range. Thirty species of birds and 29 species of mammals were recorded only below 300 m, and there was a progressive attenuation upwards within the lowland zone. Very little of either of these lowland faunas extended above 750 m, only 3 per cent of the lowland birds, for example, reaching 1200 m. The montane avifauna was much smaller; only 48 species were found above 1200 m, of which 39 reached 1500 m and 31 reached 1800 m. Among the mammals also, the highland fauna above 1200 m was impoverished. Several mammals range widely, amongst them the gibbons, tapir, and pig, and elsewhere in Malaya the elephant (Symington 1936; Medway 1969).

The transition between the two altitudinal zones occurs fairly abruptly between 750 m and 1050 m and corresponds to the boundary on Gunung Benom between lowland and lower montane rain forest (Whitmore 1972*a*). A similar zonation occurs in the butterflies of Malaya, which exist as a rich homogeneous fauna in forested country from the lowlands to about 900 m and a small montane fauna of species never found below 900 m; the former group are only found as passengers or casual visitors above 900 m (Corbet and Pendlebury 1934).

On the main range of Malaya, though not on Gunung Benom, a minor discontinuity in the avifauna occurs at the ecotone between lower and upper montane rain forest. Many montane species, especially canopy feeders, do not occur in upper montane forest, which does however have several species not found elsewhere (Wells 1971).

The minor lowland disjunction at 300 m on Gunung Benom is comparable to a disjunction in the avifauna at 150 m in the main-range foothills (Wells 1971), where it coincides with the elevation at which the land becomes considerably hilly (the so-called 'steep-land boundary').

On Gunung Benom there are a few distinctive middle-altitude bird species, which tends to obscure the main zonation, and this is the case with mammals as well as birds in the country as a whole (Medway 1964).

Of the four giant rats (*Rattus*) in Malaya, two species (*R. muelleri*, *R. sabanus*) are abundant to 600 m and occasionally found as high as 900 m; a third is only occasionally found below 900 m (*R. edwardsii*), while the fourth (*R. bowersii*) has a wide altitudinal range. The overlapping species have different habitat and food preferences (Lim 1970). There are many other examples amongst the mammals (especially the rodents) of lowland and montane species pairs, and also amongst birds, reptiles, and amphibians (see Medway 1964).

In conclusion, zonation in the animal groups so far studied in Malaya correlates well with zonation in the forest Formations. The cooler, moister montane forests are utilized by smaller and less diverse faunas. The total animal biomass per hectare is certainly less. Amongst conspicuous absentees are cicadas and leeches. The upper limit of the lowland forest Formation where the major disjunction occurs is also more or less the upper altitudinal limit of many megatherm families of plants, that is, it is a major floristic boundary although it is only a minor structural–physiognomic boundary. It would be interesting to investigate the extent to which preference for particular plant foods, for examples, fruits and seeds, is the determining factor for animal ranges, and to extend the observations made in Malaya to other parts of the region.

Part V: Man and the tropical rain forest

17 Man and the tropical rain forest

MAN'S IMPACT on the rain forest is the subject for a book in itself. We conclude this one with a sketch to show his increasing effect through historical time, an examination of secondary forest, and a glimpse into the future. The reader will be referred to fuller accounts published elsewhere.

17.1. The three ages of man

The forest has been a feature of man's environment from time immemorial—taken for granted, sometimes preserved, more often cleared. It has provided many of his basic needs, shelter and water, food from wild animals, protection for his crops.... Until quite recent times the forest has been regarded as limitless, because renewable. It is only in the last twenty-five years that the rate of disappearance of the world's forests has been recognized as an imminent danger to the whole global environment. (F.A.O. 1972.)

Man's march forward to increasing domination of the forests of the Far East can be divided conveniently, albeit only crudely, into three stages: the primeval, traditional, and modern phases of civilization.

Primeval cultures

In the earliest stage man lived in the rain forest as a nomad, hunting animals and gathering food plants, making use of limestone caves (as at Niah in Sarawak and in east Java) for shelter and cemeteries. He made no attempt at cultivation. Today a few tribes of negroid pygmies still live this way (the Andaman Islanders,† the Acta of the Philippines, and some tribes in north-east Malaya) as also do some other peoples (the Kubu of Sumatra, the Toala of Celebes, and the Punan of northern Borneo (Pelzer 1945)). The Punans subsist largely on the starch from the stems of the giant wild palm *Eugeissona utilis*. Only about 2 per cent of the Malayan aborigines are nomadic (though with recognized territories). Primeval, nomadic man had no more effect on the forest ecosystems than other animals. Perhaps his arrival as a successful ground-living primate drove

† Who, incidentally, have not discovered how to make fire and have to keep naturally occuring fires alight.

the orang utan up from the forest floor into the trees, for fossils show that this ape, which is the largest truly arboreal animal in the world, was larger in the Pleistocene period and it has other traits indicative of a terrestrial past (MacKinnon 1972).

Traditional cultures

Slowly man mastered the problems of agriculture. In alluvial plains settled societies evolved, mostly based on irrigated rice fields, established on former swamp and seasonal swamp forest land. Elsewhere, the art of shifting agriculture was developed. Twenty-eight per cent of Malaya's aborigines, including most of the tribes of negroids, exhibit various stages in the progression to semi-permanent villages and shifting agriculture which is practised by some 70 per cent of the total aborigine population (Williams-Hunt 1952). The impact of man on the forests of the New Guinea mountains has been dated to about 5000 years ago by the rise of importance then in peat deposits of the pollen of ephemeral herbs and grassland plants (Walker 1970). Man's greatest power to disturb the balance of nature lay in his employment of fire (Bartlett 1955a,b, 1957, 1961). His influence was greatest where the resistance was least, and the natural ability for the forest to regenerate was weak. This was in the seasonally dry monsoon forests. Civilizations waxed which have since disappeared, sometimes leaving little direct trace. In east Java, species-poor monsoon forest with only a few dominant species (*Acacia leucophloea, A. tomentosa, Borassus flabellifer*) occurs in a region where a far richer mixed forest would be expected. It is believed to be derived from regrowth on ancient fields abandoned when, in a fanatical religious war, Muslims replaced Hindus several centuries ago (van Steenis 1961b). In Cambodia, monsoon forest has regrown to cover the vast temple of Angkor Wat and city of Angkor

217

Thom, heart of the medieval Khmer empire (Fig. 17.1). In the dry zone of Ceylon a civilization practised agriculture from 300 B.C. to A.D. 1200 and left behind it a complex network of reservoirs and canals; the area then reverted to climax forest and is now re-invaded by shifting agriculturists (de Rosayro 1962).

The lofty rain forests proved a much greater obstacle to progress and to the development of civilization. Here, however, shifting agriculture progressively destroyed great tracts. The forest itself was culled for materials to construct houses and household goods, thereby becoming depleted of useful plants near to centres of population. Jungle produce for trading was widely collected. Rattans, resins, edible birds nests from caves, latex, poisons and medicines, and parts of animals—rhinoceros horn, pelts, hornbill casques, ivory, bezoar stones (Burkill 1935, 1966)—all found their way out of the forest, and were traded down to the coasts.

The scattered remaining nomadic, hunting–gathering societies exist today alongside sedentary cultivators; the technology of cultivation is available to them yet they prefer to maintain a pre-agricultural life-style. Amongst their reasons no doubt cultural inertia is important, but hunting and gathering may provide a better diet for less labour. It is possible that in at least some cases an agricultural way of life is forced on forest peoples through population pressure which results in their previous livelihood ceasing to be viable, as will be discussed further in §18.1.

These early peoples brought many plants into cultivation (cf. Barrau 1962). The most important world food plants originating from the south-east Asian rain forest region are sugar cane, the banana, and, from its continental margin, rice. These are followed in primacy by the coconut and mango. Within the Sunda-shelf rain forests there is a host of kinds of fruit tree (cf. Meijer 1969). Some are not cultivated—their fruits are gathered from the forest (for example, *Dialium* spp., *Elateriospermum*

FIG. 17.1. A strangling fig, grown over a stupa at the abandoned giant temple of Angkor Wat, Cambodia.

TABLE 17.1
Fruit trees of Kampong Melor, Malaya

(a) Cultivated, also found wild in rain forest (12)
Artocarpus integer (chempedak)
Baccaurea griffithii (tampoi)
B. motleyana (rambai)
Bouea macrophylla (kundang)
Durio malaccensis (durian melaka), (Fig. 17.2)
Garcinia atroviridis (asam gelugor)
Nephelium lappaceum (rambutan)
N. mutabile (pulasan)
Pangium edule (kepayang kayu)
Parkia speciosa (petai)
Pithecellobium jiringa (jiring)
Sandoricum koetjape (sentul)

(b) cultivated, wild ancestors of same species in rain forest (6)
3 *Eugenia* spp. (jambu bertek, j. melaka, j. padang)
Lansium domesticum (duku, langsat)
Mangifera sp. (machang)
Sandoricum koetjape (sertapi)

(c) cultivated, indigenous to the tropical Far East, but wild ancestors unknown (5)
Areca catechu (pinang siri)
Artocarpus heterophyllus (nangka)
Cocos nucifera (kelapa)
Durio zibethinus (durian)
Garcinia mangostana (manggis)

(d) introduced (3), all from the New World
Annona muricata (durian belanda)
Averrhoa bilimbi (belimbing)
Carica papaya (betek)

Data compiled by the author on a short visit on 2 July 1971.

FIG. 17.2. *Durio malaccensis* grows wild and is cultivated and has not been improved by selection.

tapos). Others are planted in and around villages. For example, at Kampong Melor in the Trengganu mountains in east Malaya 29 different kinds of fruit tree are cultivated (Table 17.1). The biggest group, 12 species, have not been altered by selection and identical plants grow wild in the forest (see Fig. 17.2). Six species have been developed from wild types and have superior fruit quality. Five species (including the durian, *Durio zibethinus*, most famous fruit of the East) are indigenous to the region but are known only in cultivation, and 3 species are introductions from the New World.

Large tracts of the tropical lowland evergreen dipterocarp rain forest do not have signs of extensive interference by man. This is unusual, on a world scale, and is one of the reasons these forests have such a powerful fascination for scientists. By contrast, a great deal of the New Guinea lowland and lower montane rain forest and perhaps most of it, at the centre of the eastern evergreen rain forest block, does show signs of disturbance (White 1973). *Pometia pinnata*, one of the commonest big trees

there, is believed to be a late seral species (Womersley and McAdam 1957).

Modern cultures

The arrival of western man in the Far East heralded the change to the modern period. At first his impact was slight but it increased and modern societies of the region are heavily influenced by the increasing interdependence of West and East.

At first western man came for trade and took to Europe spices (especially cloves and nutmegs) and the other jungle products. He introduced many crop plants. Before Columbus discovered the New World in 1492 there was 'not a single cultivated basic food plant common to the two hemispheres, and only one domestic animal, the dog' (Merrill 1945).[†] Nowadays, maize, cassava, and sweet potatoes (*Zea mays*, *Manihot esculenta*, *Ipomoea batatas*) are important New World crops in the Far East, and the two last-named have become the staple food of many of the shifting cultivators, for example, replacing the aroids collectively known as taro (species of *Cyrtosperma* and *Colocasia*) in the Solomons; and *Pandanus* spp. in the New Guinea highlands (Keleney 1962).

The trade with Europe brought firearms to the Far East; forest animals were hunted in increasing numbers. Probably everywhere there have been bigger animal populations living in and feeding on the rain forest within the life-span of many of the currently living big trees than there are today. What effect this will have on future composition (Chapter 15) remains imponderable. It was estimated by Stevens in 1968 that of the 117 ground-living Malayan mammals two (the Javan rhinoceros, *Rhinoceros sundaicus*, and the banteng, *Bos javanicus*) had 'almost certainly become extirpated (by hunting) within the previous thirty years'; of the remainder, 38 per cent were rare, 34 per cent common and 28 per cent abundant; 21 species (54 per cent) of the carnivores and ungulates—groups which include many game animals or objects of the chase—were rare; the populations of the Sumatran rhinoceros (*Didermoceros sumatrensis*) and gaur (*Bos gaurus*) were approaching the critical state.

Western man introduced plantation agriculture, initially to grow spices, later to grow other cash crops, with coffee, tea, rubber, and oil palm pre-

[†] This is not strictly true. Sweet potatoes were in Polynesia before 1492 but reached the Malay archipelago at the hands of the Spaniards from South America, through Manila. The bottle gourd *Lagenaria siceraria* was in both Africa and America much earlier. See Herklots (1972).

219

dominating. This led to a great expansion in the area of open, disturbed habitats in which weeds flourish. And many of the weeds were brought by him, often unwittingly, from the New World. They are distinguished in the Far East by the paucity of native names. Many came along the Spanish galleon route from Acapulco in Mexico to Manila via the Marianas and Carolines. Others have been more recently introduced and have spread rapidly this century. The first published record in the region of the herb *Borreria laevis* is from Java in 1924; between 1925 and 1929 specimens were collected from Sumatra, Singapore, the Philippines, New Guinea, New Britain, and Samoa. *Eupatorium odoratum*, called Siam weed in Malaya, is still spreading south down the peninsula. Such plants are aptly described as having 'Napoleonic ambitions'. Merrill (1945, Chapter 8) gives a good account of weeds.

Clearance of the primary forest for railways, roads, and plantations, many of which were later abandoned, vastly extended the area under secondary forest. This is largely composed of indigenous pioneer species (§6.2), though in some deflected successions and on islands of the Pacific (for example, New Hebrides, Hawaii), with a species-poor indigenous pioneer flora, introduced shrubs and trees dominate, prominent amongst them are *Lantana camara* and *Psidium guajava*. The introduction of western medicine has led to the increase in human populations in the tropical Far East (which currently is accurately described as explosive), largely by depressing the death rate. (World population doubled or trebled between 1863 and 1963. Between 1958 and 1963 it increased 10·9 per cent; in the less industrialized countries by 12·7 per cent; in the more industrialized ones by 'only' 6·6 per cent (F.A.O. 1963, 1966).) His larger populations have increased man's impact on primary tropical lowland rain forest by increasing locally the demand for land on which to grow food or cash crops and by increasing the world demand for wood and wood products.

Until the Second World War timber extraction made little impact on the Far East rain forests, relative to their vast extent. Extraction under Forest Departmental control was selective; scattered heavy hardwoods were felled and hauled out by men or buffaloes (Chapter 7). Around settlements the forest did often become depleted by uncontrolled extraction of firewood and timber for construction; for example, in the hills of west Java the selective removal of *Altingia excelsa* has led to temporary dominance by *Castanopsis* and *Quercus* spp. (van Steenis 1950). The picture changed dramatically and progressively from the 1950s onwards. Light hardwoods gained favour, and for the first time extraction began over large areas at the rate of many trees per hectare (Chapter 7).

17.2. Man's current impact on the forest

South-east Asia now supplies a large proportion of the quality and large-sized hardwoods of the world; in total over 20 per cent of the world's hardwood logs come from this region. The export of tropical hardwood logs increased five-fold between 1953 and 1967, most of the increase coming from south-east Asia. During this period the United States became for the first time a net importer of hardwoods, as her own temperate deciduous mixed broad-leaf forests neared exhaustion (Pringle 1969).

The buoyant market with a novel demand for light hardwoods coincided with important technological advances, namely, the introduction of the one-man chain-saw, and the increasing power and reliability of road-making and log-hauling vehicles. Timber extraction became quicker, cheaper, more extensive, and more intensive. In 1971 it was estimated that the timber from nearly 2 km^2 of lowland dipterocarp forest was being exported on logging trucks across the causeway from Peninsular Malaysia to Singapore every day (Burgess 1971) and additional amounts were exported from her own ports. Much of the timber from south-east Asia went to Japan and from there, after processing, to North America. In 1969 the United States imported 60 per cent of its plywood requirements, and 90 per cent of this was made of dipterocarp timber. After 1967 Korea, Taiwan, and the Philippines overtook Japan in dipterocarp plywood exports to the United States (Stadelman 1969).

The third component leading to the rocketing forest exploitation rate was the acknowledged role, by the international development agencies of the United Nations, of forests and forest-based industries 'as of special importance in the attack on economic under development' (F.A.O. 1972). Wood itself is a versatile raw material from which a wide variety of products can be made. Forest-based industries provide jobs and generate valuable international trade. Table 17.2 shows the amount of timber produced and exported from the main countries of the region in 1966. Fig. 17.3, compiled from several sources, exemplifies the very rapidly increasing rate of extraction, its predicted further increase in all the principal countries, and the expected increase in demand by Japan. The graph of the anticipated increase in world demand for timber (Fig. 17.3(a)) rises much less steeply than any of the others; this clearly demon-

TABLE 17.2

Hardwood production and exports in 1966 in thousands of cubic metres from the main tropical rain forest lands of the Far East

	Production			Export		
	Roundwood	Processed wood	Total	Roundwood	Processed wood	Total
Indonesia	5563	1781	7344	228	5	233†
Philippines	7395	1172	8567	5882	112·5	5994·5
Malaysia West	3893	1385	5278	1402	479	1881
Sabah	5979	135	6114	4855	3	4858
Sarawak	3037	450	3487	1932	221	2153
Papua–New Guinea	474	88	562	120	2	122
Totals	26341	5011	31352	14419	822·5	15241·5

From F.A.O. 1968 Year Book of Forest Products, quoted by Stacey (1969).

† In 1969 exports had increased to $3685 \times 10^3\,\mathrm{m}^3$ due to the rapid opening-up of Riau and Djambi provinces, Sumatra, and east Kalimantan from 1967 onwards (Sweatman 1971).

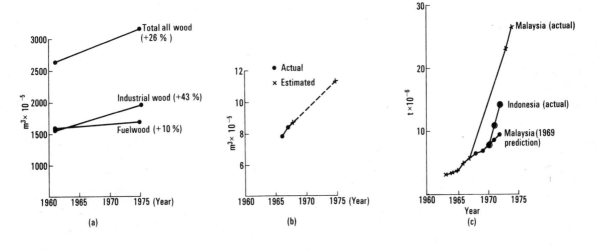

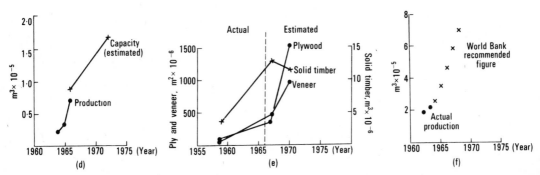

FIG. 17.3. Trends in timber consumption and production. (a) Estimated world consumption 1961–75 (F.A.O. 1966). (b) Japan: wood demand 1965–75 (Stacey 1969). (c) Malaysia and Indonesia: total timber exports (Malaysia 1963–7 and prediction: Stacey 1969; 1972–1973: Anon. 1974; Indonesia: Direktorat Pemasaran 1971, 1972). (d) Malaysia: ply and veneer industry 1965–75 (Stacey 1969). (e) Philippines: timber exports 1959–70 (Stadelman 1969). (f) Papua—New Guinea: advised log production 1964–9 (Morel 1967).

strates the increasing demand the world is making of the rain forests of the tropical Far East. Between 1953 and 1967 world timber removals (saw-wood, veneer, and sleepers) increased 43 per cent from $133 \times 10^6 \, \text{m}^3$ to $191 \times 10^6 \, \text{m}^3$; removals from tropical countries increased from $40 \times 10^6 \, \text{m}^3$ to $70 \times 10^6 \, \text{m}^3$ (+80 per cent), and from south-east Asia from $23 \times 10^6 \, \text{m}^3$ to $52 \times 10^6 \, \text{m}^3$ (+126 per cent) (Pringle 1969). Actual extraction has frequently outstripped predictions. Fig. 17.3(c) shows this strikingly for Malaysia. In 1969 it was estimated that by 1972 timber exports would be 9.4×10^6 tonne, whereas actually they were nearly $2\frac{1}{2}$ times (250 per cent) higher, at 22.5×10^6 tonne, and increased a further 3.5×10^6 tonne in 1973.

What the graphs in Fig. 17.3 do not show is the effects which are likely to follow if China enters the international timber trade. Analysis of the data available led Richardson (1966) to conclude that the present main source of timber in China, the products of clear felling primary forest, is likely to become exhausted by about 1977. Requirements will then have to be met either by imports or from recutting low-volume ($50 \, \text{m}^3/\text{ha}$) forest from which big trees have previously been 'creamed'. There will be a noticeable deficit in big logs, the commodity which

south-east Asia produces in abundance. Richardson estimated that China's plantations will not yield more than firewood, some pulpwood, and roundwood for domestic usage for two or three decades (widespread failures attended attempts at afforestation in the first decade after the Revolution). Firm statistics are not available, but the sheer magnitude of China in size and population makes her current awakening to the outside world a vitally important factor for the future of the Far East tropical rain forest. Richardson estimated that by 1975 China's timber requirements will be $150 \times 10^6 \, \text{m}^3$ (roundwood equivalent), of which only $107 \times 10^6 \, \text{m}^3$ will be available from her own resources. The deficit of $43 \times 10^6 \, \text{m}^3$ compares with his estimates of surpluses on then current trends of only $7.6 \times 10^6 \, \text{m}^3$ from continental south-east Asia and $12.4 \times 10^6 \, \text{m}^3$ from insular south-east Asia. China may clearly come to severely distort the international trade flows and dramatically increase the rate at which the Far Eastern primary tropical rain forest is cut down.

It is widely realized that forest extraction at the rate of the early 1970s (Fig. 17.4) cannot long go on. On present trends primary rain forest is doomed to disappear within our lifetime. In Malaya the lowland dipterocarp rain forest is unlikely to last until the

FIG. 17.4. Dipterocarp logs, many of them of *Dryobalanops aromatica*, at Sungei Chukai, Malaya, from the virgin lowland rain forest nearby; cf. Fig. 15.13.

FIG. 17.5. Lowland rain forest on Vanikolo, Santa Cruz Islands, 8 months after the timber was extracted. Note regrowth of *Macaranga aleuritoides* on the right. In the very wet climate of Vanikolo, climbers and epiphytes are much more abundant than in most lowland rain forests of the tropical Far East.

L

mid-1980s, and there is an excess of processing plant installed (Fig. 17.3(d)). In Indonesia, by the end of 1970, 70 concessions had been granted covering 0.65×10^6 ha and final approval given on 100 more, covering a further 13×10^6 ha, mainly in Riau and Djambi provinces of Sumatra and in east Kalimantan (Sweatman 1971). Since then the process has accelerated. In the Philippines it was estimated in 1969 that 172 000 ha/year of forest were disappearing, largely by unlicensed logging plus some shifting cultivation; this was 9 times the rate of reaforestation; a total of 1.4×10^6 ha were estimated to have been denuded and only 146 140 ha to have been reaforested (Anon. 1969). More than half the remaining dipterocarp forest was on Mindanao. Timber and its products were the country's most valuable export (Stadelman 1969).

The statistics in this section, the most recent available to the author, are already mostly several years out of date, and the trends they show are all continuing.

17.3. Effect of intensive logging on the rain forest

In mixed species-rich lowland rain forest only a small proportion of the trees is removed for timber even under modern 'intensive' methods. For example, in Malaya (Burgess 1971; Whitmore 1972c) there are some 2500 tree species of which some 700 reach a size large enough to be utilizable (basal girth 1.35 m) and less than 150 of these species are regularly exploited, the remainder being either very

FIG. 17.7. Dense bamboos which have replaced lowland mixed dipterocarp rain forest after repeated disturbance (Pahang, Malaya).

uncommon or with unsuitable timber characteristics. These figures mean that in average Malayan dipterocarp rain forest about 14 trees are felled per hectare (giving a stump every 25.5 m if the trees were evenly spaced). This figure rises in the *Dryobalanops aromatica* and *Shorea curtisii* consociations (Chapter 15) to 72, giving a stump every 12 m, and falls to 7 at the lower limit of exploitability (a stump every 36 m). But the felled trees are all large emergents with crowns often 15 m across, and when they fall they smash up a considerable amount of the lower layers of the forest. After felling the timber trees one is left with an irregular pattern of islands of almost undisturbed forest, pock-marked with patches where the tree crowns have fallen, and interwoven by the extraction tracks (Fig. 17.5). Fig. 17.6 shows the effects of logging as measured in one area of the Malayan rain forest. In the species-poor Solomons'

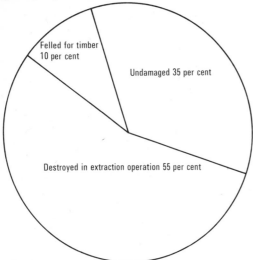

FIG. 17.6. The effect of logging on the basal area (trees over 0.1 m diameter) of lowland mixed dipterocarp rain forest on Gunung Tebu, Malaya. (Burgess 1971, Fig. 1.)

forests most top-of-canopy big trees are taken for timber and the residual stand contains fewer little-disturbed islands of forest.

Felling at this intensity favours light-demanding species, and they are further favoured by the Malayan Uniform and related silvicultural systems (§7.1). It follows that the forest regenerated after felling will in many places have different proportions of species from the virgin stand, especially amongst the emergents. The difference between north and west Kolombangara (§15.4) and between the Kelantan storm forest and the rest of the Malayan mixed dipterocarp forest (§15.3) is similar to that which current logging is likely to produce. Pockets of virgin forest, inaccessible or uneconomically poor in merchantable trees, will persist. Unless there is full-scale poisoning as part of the silvicultural treatment, most species, if not all, will still be present in any extensive area. In Malaya there has been a firm Forest Department policy of reserving a tiny but representative fraction of the lowland forest as Virgin Jungle Reserves (Wyatt-Smith 1950) to act as 'reservoirs' of species and as controls of silviculture.

Repeated logging is highly undesirable from a silvicultural viewpoint owing to the damage it does to the new growing crop (Chapter 7). Some of the more accessible forests in Malaya have been logged several times (for example, those on the Ulu Gombak and Gap roads). They have become progressively poorer in timber species and progressively richer in weed species, including short-lived pioneers (§ 6.2) and bamboos (*Dendrocalamus pendulus* and *Gigantochloa scortechinii* (Fig. 17.7) plus *Schizostachyum grande* (Fig. 17.8) at higher elevations). The foresters' aim should be to increase exploitation at one single felling operation, for which there is great scope. In the late 1960s in Malaya dipterocarps provided some 80 per cent of the timber (50 per cent from *Shorea* spp.), and some 60–65 per cent of the total of merchantable-size trees were left unfelled. In areas being cleared for agriculture up to 80 per cent of merchantable boles were on occasion burned (Fig. 17.9) (Sargent 1970).

17.4. The effects of logging on the rain-forest animals

The intensive logging currently practised seriously damages the structure of the forest, most so where the percentage of exploitable emergent trees is greatest. In dipterocarp rain forest the damage is greatest in the local consociations in Malaya, and more generally in Sabah and the Philippines where light and medium hardwood species of *Dipterocarpus*,

FIG. 17.8. *Schizostachyum grande*, a very elegant bamboo which invades seriously disturbed lowland rain forest in the main range of Malaya between about 600–800 m elevation.

Parashorea, and *Shorea* commonly make up nearly all the top of the canopy (§15.2).

There has been no full study of the consequences of logging on the rain-forest animals. It is of vital importance that such studies are initiated. In the interim, tentative suggestions on probabilities can be made.

Arboreal mammals will be the most seriously affected group, and this means that the consequences of logging are more serious in the western Sunda shelf rain forests than in the eastern Sahul shelf block (§1.2). Browsing mammals are less likely to be seriously affected, and the invasion of lush herbaceous growth (grasses, bananas, gingers, etc.) in the most open places may actually enhance the habitat for grazing animals, such as the banteng (*Bos javanicus*) or gaur (*Bos gaurus*) and elephant. Stevens

225

(1968) estimated that, of the 115 non-flying mammals in Malaya, 37 per cent are tree-dwellers.) This gives a measure of the problem. Extensive logging on the slopes of the Malayan main range in Selangor in the late 1960s was probably the cause of the abnormally high numbers of siamang in the Ulu Gombak valley where logging had been almost completed earlier (Chivers). After the northern half of the Ulu Segama forest orang utan sanctuary in Sabah was logged the resident orang utans called more, apparently owing to crowding, and showed a lower ratio of infants per female (0·3 instead of 0·8), indicating less breeding (MacKinnon 1972). On the Mentawi Islands west of Sumatra all four endemic primates (*Hylobates klossii*, *H. potenziana*, *Macaca pagensis*, *Simias concolor*) are endangered following widescale logging (Wilson and Wilson 1973). Removal of dipterocarps, which are apparently little used by animals for food (§2.8), by logging from the Ulu Telom valley in the Malayan main range stimulated (as always) flowering and fruiting of the remaining big trees, including the highly prized fig trees, without apparently completely shattering the forest frame, for the siamang and white-handed gibbon there appeared to be unaffected (Chivers).

Birds are possibly more seriously upset by logging (Wells 1971), and this is most likely for those specialized to live in the top of the canopy (§2.7). After part of the Pasoh forest in Malaya had been logged the affected populations became agitated and wandered, seemingly at random, through the surrounding forest. Selective felling 30 km away on the slopes of Gunung Angsi caused the disappearance of trogons. Some canopy-top birds, such as hornbills and eagles, roam widely and need large areas of forest for the maintenance of a breeding stock adequate to prevent extinction. It has been estimated that for hornbills the area is about 10^4 km^2 (Medway and Wells 1971), and these birds also need hollow trees to breed in. The avifaunas of small islands lying off the Malayan coast are far smaller than those of comparable areas on the mainland. These facts also point to the need for extensive forest tracts.

Complete replacement of primary forest by secondary has drastic, regressive effects on the fauna, as was described in Chapter 13.

Fig. 17.9 (opposite). Low undulating country cleared of virgin tropical lowland mixed dipterocarp rain forest for an oil palm plantation (Jerangau, Trengganu, Malaya, September 1966).

L*

18 Secondary forest and shifting cultivation

RAIN FOREST can be destroyed to varying degrees. Natural events cause gaps (§6.1), and the operations of contemporary timber extractors produce results which do not differ greatly from those of extensive high winds (apart from the local compaction of soil by extraction machinery, which can be ecologically important). The selective logging of an earlier era created small gaps and resulted in depletion in the rain forest of certain species. In *depleted forest*, as well as in much of today's more completely logged forest, seedling trees of the primary forest persist in variable numbers and commence upwards growth in the gaps, often with silvicultural assistance (Chapter 7). *Secondary forest* differs from logged and depleted forest in that it is forest regrown after complete clearance, and characteristically it consists of stands of one or a few species of same-age, more-or-less same-size trees. The most extreme logging operations do remove virtually the whole canopy, and this is certainly the case along extraction routes and at log 'landings', so there is a merging of the kinds of regrowth forest. Secondary forest is formed of pioneer species which grow from seed after the gap forms, not from pre-existing seedlings (§6.2). Epiphytes are rare. Often secondary vegetation is very heterogeneous, stands of trees are interspersed with patches of giant herbs (especially bananas and gingers), sedges (especially *Scleria*), and tangles of big, woody, light-demanding climbers (especially *Merremia* and *Uncaria*), whose growth is also stimulated by removal of the primary forest canopy. Floristically, secondary forest is of very different composition from primary, because most pioneer species belong to relatively few families, and many to genera which are scarce or absent in primary forest (§6.2). In the Far East very few palms grow in secondary forest; in Malaya, out of the 220 indigenous palm species, only *Caryota mitis* is characteristic of secondary forest (Whitmore 1973b).

The main cause of secondary forest is still the practice of shifting cultivation, where clearance of the primary forest has been followed by burning and the cultivation of one or more crops. Secondary forest also arises after the abandonment of plantations (for example, the hundreds of square kilometres of *Rhus taitensis* forest in the Solomon archipelago growing under coconuts which were abandoned at the onset of the Second World War), or after a cyclone has completely flattened a swathe of forest, or after fire has destroyed primary forest. This last has almost certainly occurred in Queensland (Ridley and Gardner 1961; Webb 1964), but primary rain forest within the principal ever-wet parts of the Far East appears to be mainly non-inflammable.

Trees left dead in clearings slowly lose their limbs and branches and the bark often loosens and falls off, before the trunk itself falls. The old bole sometimes becomes swathed in woody climbers to form a green leafy 'climber tower'. This has recently happened extensively in forests in Vietnam killed by herbicides sprayed from the air by the military forces of the United States (Richards).

Repeated interference with the forest by felling and burning, plus cultivation or grazing, causes a deterioration in the regrowth vegetation; the secondary succession is 'deflected' to a fire climax or biotic climax which in extreme cases may be shrubs or grassland (Fig. 18.1).

There has been remarkably little general advance in our knowledge of secondary successions in the two decades which have elapsed since Richards' book was published (Richards 1952). There have been several additional detailed studies, but still enormous gaps remain in our understanding. Foresters on the whole shun secondary forest. Their principal and considerable contribution to our contemporary understanding of rain-forest ecology has come from investigations of the autecology of trees of economic significance (Part III). Forest ecologists have in addition been interested to study the nature of the rain-forest communities (Chapter 15), as a direct result of the stimulus given by Richards' book, or else to extend the foresters' findings to the dynamics of whole communities (§§6.3, 6.4, and 15.4). University scientists, most of them newly on the scene, unfortunately have also rather avoided the secondary forest and have not risen to its challenge; the majority of them have been more concerned with laboratory studies. Yet the thorough understanding of depleted and secondary rain forest is of the highest importance. These kinds of vegetation are rapidly increasing in extent as a result of the increasingly rapid felling of primary rain forest. If present-day trends continue these will be the principal kinds of forest in the

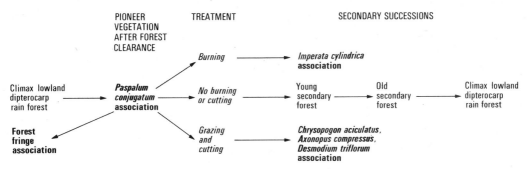

PIONEER VEGETATION AFTER FOREST CLEARANCE   TREATMENT   SECONDARY SUCCESSIONS

Fig. 18.1. Summary of the four main grassland associations (shown in bold) derived from lowland dipterocarp rain forest by different management regimes in Pahang, Malaya (Verboom 1968).

(For an account of the conditions leading to succession back from *Imperata* grassland to forest see Eussen and Wirjahardja 1973.)

tropical Far East within a few decades. A thorough understanding of their ecology is an essential pre-requisite to utilization by mankind, whether it be for their products or for the conservation of indigenous plant and animal species or as vegetative cover to prevent erosion in water catchments.

In this field alone amongst those covered in the present book the time is not ripe for a new synthesis. In the present chapter a résumé will be given, and some major gaps indicated. For an introductory description the reader is referred to Richards (1952, Chapter 17).

18.1. Shifting cultivation

Shifting cultivation has attracted a great deal of attention, largely of its socio-economic aspects. The fullest accounts for our region (and giving reference to this literature) are to be found in Pelzer (1945), Spencer (1966), and the published proceedings of a symposium held at Goroka, New Guinea (UNESCO 1962).

The basic principle of all shifting agriculture is the cultivation of a patch of ground for a short period, often only a year, followed by its fallowing for a period of several years. It has been aptly described therefore as 'rotation of fields rather than crops'. The cultivated patches give their name to the practice in the various parts of the region: chena (Ceylon), taungya† (Burma), tamrai (Thailand), ray (Indo-China), huma (Java), kaingin (Philippines), and ladang (Malay-speaking countries). Some big trees are usually left standing, for superstitious or practical reasons, for example, *Koompassia excelsa* (Sunda-shelf region: hard, useless timber, crown with bees'

† In the specialized foresters' sense, taungya involves planting timber-tree seedlings with the food crop and thus establishing a timber plantation; see King (1968) for a review. This has been very extensively practised for teak culture (§12.2).

nests), *Gmelina moluccana* (Solomons: for dugout canoes), and big banyan and strangling figs.

The natural secondary succession which commences after the field has been abandoned is relied upon to restore the soil fertility during the fallow period. In the New Guinea Highlands the first step to a managed crop rotation has been taken in that seedlings of *Casuarina papuana*, a local pioneer tree found on landslips, are planted, fenced to keep pigs out, and when grown ring-barked, felled, and utilized for firewood (*Casuarina* species have nitrogen-fixing root nodules).

Shifting agriculture is practised throughout the tropics and subtropics of the whole world. Its universality is one of its most remarkable features. It is certainly one of the oldest of all agricultural systems, which indicates that it must be, or have been until recently, more or less in equilibrium with the habitat. It has been estimated that about one-third of the total agricultural area in south-east Asia is under shifting cultivation (Dobby 1950) (cf. Fig. 18.2), though at any one time the greater part is lying under tree fallow. The density of population this system can support is low, about 7 persons per square kilometre. By contrast, at the other extreme, the Tonkin delta has about 9×10^6 people on $3630 \, \text{km}^2$, 354 times as many per square kilometre.

Continued cultivation leads to declining yields. Erosion becomes more likely (Fig. 18.3). In Malaya the yield of hill rice from virgin land declined from 1800–2240 kg/ha to 900–1340 kg/ha in 3 successive years (Grist 1953). This can be ascribed to various causes, principally deterioration of the nutrient status of the soil (due partly to changes in its microflora and fauna), erosion of the top-soil, deterioration of physical condition of the soil, multiplication of pests and diseases, and increase of weeds (Coulter 1950*b*; Nye and Greenland 1960; Soerinegara 1970). It now

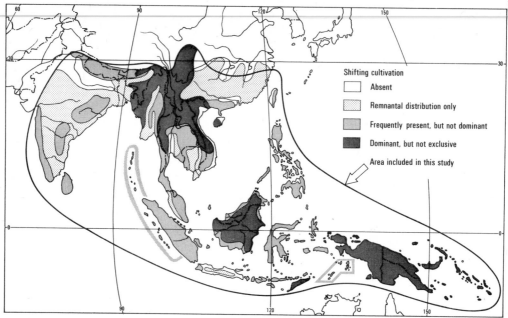

FIG. 18.2. Extent of shifting cultivation, India to the Solomons. (Spencer 1966, Fig. 1. Originally published by the University of California Press; reprinted by permission of the Regents of the University of California.)

seems that weed-invasion is the main reason why a farmer abandons his field. Primitive agriculturists work to get maximum return for minimum effort. A second burn with a second cultivation deflects the succession and increases the probability of invasion by the aggressive Asiatic variety (*major*) of the grass *Imperata cylindrica* (alang alang, cogon, kunai, lalang (Gray 1944; Fig. 18.1)) by largely eliminating seedlings of pioneer tree species and regrowth from suckers of the former forest. In places with an annual rainfall exceeding about 2500 mm and with no marked dry season, man cannot defeat the forest by burning and instead works with it. In the absence of any climatic cycle which he can use to help eliminate weeds he has created a cyclic agricultural system in which the forest fallow serves to clean the ground of weeds.

There is a demonstrable increase in the vegetation store of plant mineral nutrients in the fallow period, and especially during the first 5 years, when the mass of twigs and leaves where they are concentrated is being restored. The reasons for yield decline and the mechanisms which restore fertility during the fallow period have been reviewed as part of a world survey of the soil under shifting agriculture by Nye and Greenland (1960).

Shifting cultivators sometimes fell primary rain forest rather than old secondary forest, which brings them into conflict with Government. Their numbers

are increasing (for example, by 1–3 per cent/year in the New Guinea Highlands), and their demands also increase (cf. Carey 1962); large-scale plantation agriculture is increasingly infringing on their traditional homelands. They themselves are increasingly planting tree crops on part of their land to provide a cash income, for example, rubber is planted by the Iban of Sarawak. These several factors serve to increase pressure on the land, which is usually met by decreasing the length of the fallow period rather than lengthening the cropping period. Nye and Greenland had few data from south-east Asia for their review, and many important details are still unknown. For example, there is a nutrient decline during cropping, but it is not known how and how far the soil can sustain the losses. We have very little information on the partitioning of nutrients between different fractions of the forest and the soil or on the rate of cycling. These are vital subjects for study.

The conditions which lead societies to change from shifting to permanent cultivation have been the subject of much discussion in recent years, following the postulation by Boserup (1965) that increasing population pressure forces the change. She argued that a better technology is needed at each stage of the progression from cultivation with a long fallow to cultivation with no fallow in order to maintain soil fertility despite the increasingly short fallow period. The yields per unit of land improve as agriculture

Fɪɢ. 18.3.   Serious gully erosion in an area of shifting cultivation in the sparsely populated interior of Borneo (Ulu Ai, Sarawak).

231

becomes more intensive, but capital investment is required and the yields per unit of effort decline. As a result, there is always a resistance to change. Geertz (1963) contrasted the agricultural mainstays of Indonesia: wet rice padi and shifting cultivation. He showed that the cultivation of wet rice is able to absorb increasing inputs of labour and continue to show increasing marginal productivity. By contrast, shifting agriculture tends to break down under increasing population pressure; the essentials of the system are destroyed when the land is utilized too intensively. Provided the forest fallow is adequately long, shifting cultivation is a stable system. The crops protect the land from excessive leaching, and even to some extent mimic the forest in the diversity of species and life-forms which are grown together. The later stages of cultivation merge gradually into a secondary forest succession.

All these more recent investigations completely change the once-held conception that shifting cultivation is a wholly bad practice (*raubbau*, that is, robber economy, of the Dutch in Java (Pelzer 1945)).

18.2. General course of secondary successions

Prolonged cultivation, or repeated cultivation after only short fallow periods, affects the secondary succession, and here too there are great gaps in our knowledge. Nevertheless, it is possible to describe tentatively the course of secondary successions under different conditions.

Felling, followed by burning and the cultivation of a single crop, allows the re-establishment of forest. The bare ground is usually initially colonized by ephemeral grasses and other herbs. Soon these are shaded out by woody plants which are either sucker shoots or pioneer species growing from seed. For instance, in the Cordillera Central of Luzon the commonest small stems in regrowth were *Lithocarpus jordanae* and *Symplocos luzonensis* which sprout from cut stumps (Kowal 1966). In the lowlands to about 1000 m elevation (higher in New Guinea) *Macaranga* species are amongst the commonest pioneer invaders (cf. §6.2). Above about 1000 m secondary forest has a rather different species composition; *Macaranga* is much less common, *Homalanthus* spp., and tree ferns are conspicuous—*Cyathea contaminans* in Java and Malaya, plus also *C. elmeri* in Mindanao (Kellman 1970). (In the extremely wet Santa Cruz Islands, where annual rainfall is about 6000 mm, *C. lunulata* is a common component of secondary forest at sea-level (Whitmore 1966c).)

In secondary forest, pure stands of single species

form, and it seems that chance plays an important role, with those species whose seed happened to be present at the correct moment pre-empting the site. Where long-lived pioneer tree species invade, the site can be occupied for perhaps a century or more. Seedlings of shade-bearing species establish beneath the canopy of pioneers (Kochummen 1966; Kellman 1970; north Kolombangara, see §15.3) and as the latter die grow up to replace them. The availability of seeds of shade-bearing species is thus of great importance and determines the species composition of the later stages of the succession. The complete return to primary forest is likely to take centuries rather than decades.

Repeated cultivation and concomitant burning causes site-deterioration, including soil erosion, and leads to the development of stands of shrubs, including *Melastoma malabathricum*, *Lantana camara* (which establishes in full light on compacted soil (Webb *et al.* 1972)), *Rhodamnia cinerea*, *Rhodomyrtus tomentosa*, and locally *Dillenia suffruticosa*; or it can ultimately lead to open grassland of *Imperata cylindrica* (Fig. 18.1), which has underground diffuse rhizomes and can thereby survive fires. In parts of the New Guinea Highlands *Themeda australis*, Kangaroo Grass, has been found to indicate sites undergoing sheet erosion (Havel 1962). Because burning is easier in monsoon climates grasslands are most extensive there (Chapter 12). Gregarious bamboos are a sign of repeated interference with primary rain forest, for example, in the parts of the Malayan main ranges where there are most aborigines. In seasonally dry climates they also characterize fire-climax forests (Chapter 12) such as are especially common on the Asian continent. Once established, many bamboo species, from their smothering habit, preclude establishment of the seedlings of most tree species and so form self-perpetuating communities.

The skeletal nature of the preceding account clearly indicates just how fragmentary our knowledge of secondary forest successions remains. A major difficulty which has faced investigators is to ascertain the past history of an area so as to build up a picture of succession after different treatments. The study of secondary forest along logging roads, which can be readily dated and which show a clear succession along their edges, is an unexplored possibility. The study by continual sampling of permanent plots subjected to different cultivation regimes, which has been initiated in Sarawak (Anderson 1962), offers a second, longer term solution.

Important fields of investigation are as follows:

1. Whether propagules of pioneer species arrive

after a gap is created or are there and are released from dormancy (discussed in §5.2).

2. The whole question of nutrient partition, nutrient cycling, and the role of the forest fallow in building up the nutrient status of the top-soil and vegetation.

3. Autecological studies to ascertain the ecological amplitude of particular pioneer species and hence to interpret commonly associated groups of pioneer species. Studies in Singapore and Malaya give some indications: Kent Ridge, Singapore, is a shale and sandstone hill with very poor soils (Holttum 1954*b*). Pioneer herbs (*Dicranopteris linearis, Eriachne pallescens, Gahnia tristis, Lycopodium cernuum, Scleria levis*) are supplemented by shrubs of *Adinandra dumosa, Dillenia suffruticosa, Ficus grossularioides* (*alba*), *Melastoma malabathricum, Myrica esculenta, Ploiarium alternifolium,* and seedlings of *Fagraea fragrans.* It is not known whether, and if so how, site conditions determine that this community exists

rather than the more familiar Malayan closed secondary forest of mixed *Macaranga* spp., *Mallotus paniculatus, Trema* spp., etc. (for example, Burkill 1919; Symington 1933). But *Adinandra* and *Ploiarium* are common elsewhere on wet ground and may be responding to the poorly aerated clays. The one *Macaranga, M. heynei,* present on Kent Ridge is unique in Malaya in being associated with exposed rocky subsoils (Whitmore 1967*a*); and a species of *Nepenthes* is present, possibly indicative of poor nutrient status. It is possibly significant that *Macaranga heynei* and *Melastoma malabathricum* are the only two of the woody species on Kent Ridge which also invade peat after 10 years of pineapple cultivation in nearby Johore (Wee 1970). Investigations to follow leads such as these are clearly called for. A great advantage for secondary-forest studies is the immense extents of such vegetation easily accessible and the relatively simple species composition.

19 Looking ahead

THERE IS A slowly growing global awareness that man's exploitative days are numbered. His inheritance from the past of mineral resources and of plant resources, both living and in the form of coal, gas, and oil, is now realized by some to be by no means inexhaustable.

Nomadic man lived in equilibrium with the rain forest, much as the other animals. Traditional cultures achieved a new equilibrium through either settled agriculture or shifting cultivation. The modern period differs. Man's demands on natural resources have increased and continue to do so. It is essential for his wellbeing that a new state of equilibrium is achieved. Timber cannot be mined from the world's tropical rain forests for many more decades at the rates prevailing in the mid-1970s. In this final chapter we shall look briefly at trends in human development as they effect the forests of the tropical Far East, and hope to demonstrate why it is essential that adequate samples of these important ecosystems are conserved in perpetuity.

19.1. Trends in forestry and forest industry

Managed forests

'As the forests are brought under systematic management the day of the old giants draws to a close . . . future generations of both foresters and loggers may regard girths exceeding 1·8 m as exceptional' (Browne 1952), though the full height will be maintained (§2.5). A second important difference between the first managed tree crop and the virgin forest it replaces is the larger proportion of light-demanding species (§§7.1, 17.3). In many countries tree-felling is now proceeding so fast that silvicultural operations cannot keep up, and large areas are left untreated.

Plantations

However, managed semi-natural forests are likely to become less important in the future. There are strong financial attractions for Forest Departments to establish plantations of pioneer species (§7.2), especially conifers or eucalypts (§8.1, Fig. 8.1, p. 89), rather than expend resources on natural forest silviculture, and it seems inevitable that the trend towards plantation forestry will increase (Dawkins 1958; Baur 1964b). The money available is thereby

spent on the establishment of compact blocks of merchantable species, in monoculture, which are easier to establish and manage than are extensive natural forests and which yield more. The cost of road maintenance is minimized, as are harvesting costs. Thinnings of low intrinsic value can increasingly be utilized as timber-based industries develop. The results of tree-breeding can be readily utilized. Plantation establishment should ideally take place to compensate in timber volume for natural forests as the latter are felled, but this is not being achieved.

Unless the world is more or less to go without choice cabinet hardwoods these will have to be planted on a much greater scale than at present, as they are mostly not favoured by currently practised silvicultural systems. There is an especially strong case in the tropical Far East for making plantations of *Pterocarpus indicus,* a widespread indigenous leguminous species with superb grain and figure which grows fast from large woody cuttings (Whitmore 1972d).

There is no evidence that pests and diseases cause serious damage in mixed-species rain forests. Foresters have been traditionally cautious in 'refining' mixed-species tropical lowland rain forests under management in case such problems are introduced. In §2.8 several instances of serious pest damage in plantations and species-poor natural forest were reported, and these are omens of what lies in the future if narrow economic considerations come to prevail. The reduction of species diversity also reduces the range of food plants available for forest animals, as well as the range of species and strains of species potentially valuable to man, a topic to be discussed in the next section.

Chips

In 1955 Japan imported 85 per cent of her pulp-wood requirements in the form of softwoods (conifers). By 1967 85 per cent was hardwoods, of which more than half was as chips, including some rubberwood (*Hevea brasiliensis*) from Malaya (Abdul Latif and Harun 1970). Chipwood production for pulp and liner board began on a 49 200 ha concession in the mixed lowland Gogol rain forest, near Madang, New Guinea, in 1973, and chipwood exports were

234

expected to be worth 4×10^6 Australian dollars per year (Anon. 1972a). By 1974 in various other islands major concessions were either being worked or were under negotiation, including in the latter category a concession with a probable 800 tonne/day intake for paper pulp, to be based on the *Shorea albida* peat-swamp forest at Belait, Brunei. There is little doubt that, as paper-making technology advances, almost total utilization of the above-ground biomass of mixed tropical rain forest will also become feasible. Nicholson (1970) has advocated removal of small trees from Philippines dipterocarp forest for chipping, prior to the main felling for timber (§7.1). Most of the minerals of rain-forest ecosystems are in the vegetation, not the soil (Chapter 9), and there is a considerable danger of very serious, long-persisting degradation of the site, making regrowth of high forest impossible if a substantial proportion of the biomass is removed and the site then left alone for natural processes of succession to take place. Until research has shown the consequences of this kind of exploitation in a particular forest type the risks cannot be assessed and it cannot be condoned on scientific grounds. Log extraction, even where all the big trees are utilized, causes relatively far less drastic removal because there is a concentration of mineral nutrients in the smaller branches, twigs, and leaves, that is, just those plant parts left in the forest in conventional lumbering operations (Greenland and Kowal 1960).

19.2. Importance of the rain forest

It is difficult for a scientist to conceal his alarm at the rate at which the Far East tropical rain forests, especially the dipterocarp forests, are disappearing (Fig. 17.3, p. 221) and when even areas that had been set aside for posterity are being destroyed. There are important reasons why selected forests, including some of considerable extent, should be left intact for all time.

The protective role

On the regional and perhaps also the global level forests play a complex role in the heat balance of the earth's surface and in its water balance, which cannot be discussed here. More locally, forests are important in the hydrological cycle, breaking the impact of heavy rainstorms on the soil, increasing penetration of water into the soil, slowing down run-off, and minimizing erosion (to which the very deep soils found even in some hilly tracts bear witness). Felling operations frequently lead to serious erosion, especially on slopes, mainly along extraction tracks and

consequent silting up of streams and rivers (Burgess 1971; Poore 1961). Water-catchment areas, dams, and filter plants have already been damaged. Flooding, because of siltation and the increased rate of run-off, is likely to become an increasingly serious problem.

The steeper hills need to be kept clothed with protective forest to prevent serious damage by spectacular erosion once the forest cover is removed and soil creep (which gives the predominant convex land forms) is replaced by sheet and gully erosion.

The productive role

Although plantations will become ever more important, the continuing world appetite for timber from tropical countries ensures a role for forest regrown after the virgin stand has been felled; but this growth will often have had minimal silvicultural treatment, if any. Minor forest products, mainly rattans, will continue in demand for so long as they are available.

Tropical rain forest is a great storehouse of plant species, only a tiny fraction of which are at present utilized by man. The indigenous fruit trees of the Far East are forest plants, and many of them have been slightly or not at all improved by selection from their wild ancestors (Table 17.1, p. 218). We can expect greatly increased activity in plant breeding, for disease- and pest-resistance as well as quality, and this is dependent on utilizing variation which exists in the wild, forest populations, the 'gene pools' as they are termed (Frankel 1969). We can also expect breeding to be undertaken to develop superior strains of the tree species chosen for timber plantations. Further, there are wild fruit trees in the forest not yet utilized by man, for example, species of *Garcinia* in Malaya (Whitmore 1973g), and our descendants can be expected to wish to investigate these. The rain forests are an increasingly important source of drug plants, as western medicine progressively explores, modifies, and adopts traditional cures (for example, *Rauvolfia* as a treatment for high blood-pressure—see Whitmore (1973d)). Growing interest can also be expected in rain-forest species as sources of food dyes, essential oils, and pesticides (moulting hormones are present in tree bark, for example, many Podocarpaceae; roteone is obtained from *Derris*, *Millettia*, and *Tephrosia*). Lowry (1971) has recently summarized the field.

Forests are also a biochemical storehouse. In the longer prospect they can be expected to play an increasing part in maintaining the world's civilizations. As world population increases and as the non-renewable resources of coal and oil become depleted and more difficult to utilize, probably within the next century, man will of necessity make much greater use of organic production. Wood will remain valuable as a versatile raw material, and more species than at present will be merchantable. Forests can also be expected to become a major source of raw materials for the new biochemical technology which will develop to replace oil and coal as sources of complex molecules for food and manufactures. Already, edible protein can be extracted from leaves; and lignin is already utilized for the manufacture of plastics, ion-exchange resins, soil stabilizers, rubber reinforcers, fertilizers, vanillin, tanning agents, stabilizers for asphalt emulsions, and dispersants for oil-well drilling and for ceramics processing. Cellulose can be utilized for rayon and plastics and as a raw material for hydrolysis to sugar (Bray and Gorham 1964). Complex organic molecules such as steroids are conveniently obtained from plant sources (Lowry 1971). It is true that the technology exists to synthesize complex organic molecules from simple inorganic ones, but this involves the expenditure of enormous quantities of energy which still comes, and for a long while yet will come, from non-renewable sources. It is thus of crucial importance to utilize plants to perform the initial reduction of carbon dioxide using solar energy and to restrict man's intervention to manipulating plant products.

The prestigious role

The tropical rain forests of the Far East include the most complex and species-rich ecosystems which have ever existed on this planet. This is not questioned. Scientists have scarcely begun to unravel the intricacies of the multiple interactions between the many co-existing plants and animals. Enough has been discovered for it to be realized that for many animals the rain-forest habitat is essential and that they cannot live in secondary forest (Chapter 13). The same applies to many plant species, especially those of the dark cool forest interior.

The south-east Asian rain forest is in many respects unique, as this book has sought to show. It has a grandeur and diversity unexcelled elsewhere. In the coming decades tourists from both within and outside the region can be expected to wish to enter the rain forests in increasing numbers, just as the East African savanna woodlands and their huge animal populations have become internationally popular since the early 1960s. Penang received 1500 international tourists in 1969 and 100 000 in 1972 (Mabbett 1973); it will not be many years before numerous visitors want to see not an island city but the forests which are Malaysia's very special charm.

19.3. A plan for the future

'The dominant image of the age in which we live is that of the earth rising above the horizon of the moon—a beautiful, fragile sphere which provides the home and sustains the life of the entire human species.' (Strong 1972.)

'Conserve adequate habitat' is the underlying principle. If this simple plea, to set aside adequate and representative areas of the various rain-forest ecosystems, is followed, the future existence of rain-forest animals and plants is assured, and tropical rain forest will continue to help sustain and enrich the life of man. The habitat is conserved if sufficient and representative samples of virgin tropical rain forest be set aside as National Parks, inviolate in perpetuity. Such National Parks are the forest areas in which adequate populations will be retained to maintain the full genetic diversity of animal and plant species, especially those which occur at very low density, such as hornbill, tapir, and tiger, or have large territories, such as gaur and elephant. Very little research has been done on the size of area needed (Table 19.1). Wild fruit trees occur in the Malayan lowland rain forest at very low density (Table 19.2). In a sample survey of 676 ha in Ulu Kelantan few species exceeded 24 trees per 100 ha and 11 out of 18 species had fewer than 13 trees per 100 ha

TABLE 19.1

Density of hornbills and primates at Kuala Lompat, Malaya, and estimated areas to support viable breeding populations

	Numbers at Kuala Lompat	Area (km²) to support 5000 individuals
Hornbills: Helmeted	1	10 000
Rhinoceros	about 1	about 10 000
Southern Pied	2	5000
Black	4	2500
Bushy-crested	5	2000
Monkeys: Banded Leaf; troops	4	—
individuals at 10 per troop	40	250
Dusky Leaf: troops	4	—
individuals at 5 per troop	20	500
Long-tailed macaque	22	500
Pig-tailed macaque	3	3333
White-handed gibbon: groups	2	—
individuals at 3 per group	6	167
Siamang	5	2000

Medway and Wells (1971, Table 3); area surveyed 200 ha; 5000 individuals is provisionally suggested as an approximate minimum size for a viable population.

TABLE 19.2

Frequency of occurrence of species and genera of trees with horticultural or pharmacological potential in the rain forest of Ulu Kelantan, Malaya

(a) With horticultural potential		
Anacardiaceae	*Mangifera* (machang)	6·7
Bombacaceae	*Coelostegia* (punggai)	0·5
	Durio (durian)	3·7
Euphorbiaceae	*Baccaurea griffithii* (tampoi)	2·3
	Elateriospermum tapos (perah)	33·0
Guttiferae	*Garcinia* (kandis, manggis)	0·9
Leguminosae	*Parkia* (petai, p. meranti)	8·8
Meliaceae	*Lansium domesticum* (langsat)	0·2
	Sandoricum koetjape (sentul)	0·8
Moraceae	*Artocarpus integer* (bangkong; chempedak)	1·3
	A. lanceifolius (keledang)	18·0
	A. rigidus (temponek)	7·4
	A. scortechinii/elasticus (terap)	3·4
Sapindaceae	*Nephelium lappaceum* (rambutan)	5·9
(b) With pharmacological potential		
Apocynaceae	*Alstonia* (pulai)	0·8
	Dyera costulata (jelutong)	7·2
Moraceae	*Antiaris toxicaria* (ipoh)	0·5

Figures quoted are trees ≥ 1·2 m girth per 40 ha. Survey included 26 628 trees in a 676 ha sample of 10 100 km² of mainly lowland evergreen rain forest (Whitmore 1971*b*).

(Whitmore 1971*b*). It can be seen that if, as is likely, for each species 10 000 trees are needed to provide an adequate gene pool (Toda in Richardson 1970) huge tracts must be conserved. A large proportion of the mammals and birds occur only at low elevations, as do the majority of the plants with greatest potential for human use. It is essential, therefore, to conserve representative samples of lowland evergreen rain forest (the most valuable kind for logging) and other lowland Formations and totally inadequate solely to conserve montane Formations.

Some National Parks have been established in the tropical rain forests of the Far East (see van Steenis 1971) but several exist in name only,[†] and it is important that, as logging pressures continue to mount, enough are conserved intact. Amongst the most important parks including lowland evergreen rain forests are the Loeser reserve in Aceh, north Sumatra, Taman Negara in the centre of Malaya (see Ho, Soepadmo, and Whitmore 1971), Kinabalu in Sabah, and East Kutai in north-east Kalimantan. It has been estimated that Taman Negara (4340 km²) contains 60 per cent of the local, specialized endemic mammals of the Sunda-shelf region, 142 of the 198 species being dependent on forest for their existence

[†] Permanent agriculture is reported, for example, from within the Mt. Data National Park in Luzon (Kowal 1966).

and a major proportion of them living below 330 m elevation (Medway 1971); 172 of the 241 known lowland forest birds and 52 out of 76 known mountain species which breed in Malaya have also been recorded within this Park (Wells 1971). The most valuable lowland forest, covering perhaps 30 per cent of Taman Negara, contains timber valued in 1971 at about 1 000 000 Malaysian dollars per square mile (2·6 km²). The pressures in the future to extract this timber can be expected to be powerful indeed, but if Taman Negara is to serve its function they will have to be resisted (Ho *et al.* 1971).

It is unreasonable to expect the nations of the tropical Far East to conserve more than a small proportion of their forested land surface inviolate as National Parks (Taman Negara covers 4 per cent of the area of Peninsular Malaysia) despite the increasing benefits which can be expected to accrue from tourism and advancing technology. A graded series of sanctuaries is required, from National Parks at the head to smaller areas conserved for special purposes (such as the Virgin Jungle Reserves of Malaya (Wyatt-Smith 1950)); such sanctuaries already exist, at least on paper, for several countries.

At the same time the fundamental importance of the observation plots which have been established in rain forest must be realized. The principal plots in virgin lowland rain forest are at Bukit Lagong and Sungei Menyala in Malaya, Kabili–Sepilok (Sabah), and Kolombangara (British Solomons), all of which have been repeatedly referred to in this book. In 1970 additional plots were established in Malaya at the International Biological Programme forest at Pasoh. The older the plot gets the more valuable it becomes. The two older Malayan plots have now been under continual observation for quarter of a century, longer than most others in the world. Silvicultural treatment plots also become progressively more valuable. Numbers of these were established during the 1960s in Sarawak and Sabah. All these plots are of inestimable value to scientists and foresters for monitoring long-term changes and the effects of silviculture.

In the developed countries of the temperate regions of the world urbanized man is increasingly turning to the rural areas in which to spend his leisure time, and multiple use of forests is rapidly extending. There is no reason why some areas of the Far East rain forest should not be managed for multiple use, producing timber on a rotation of about 70 years and at the same time providing habitats for many animal species (Dawkins 1958; Stevens 1968). Too little is yet known about the effect of purified, simplified, managed forests on animal populations, though some species certainly survive and others may even be favoured by carefully controlled logging operations (§17.4); at least in the first managed rotation, a large number of tree species is likely to be present. Research should be initiated into the problems arising from managing a tropical rain forest for timber production, the life of the indigenous animals, and visits by tourists. F.A.O. increased its numbers of forest wild-life specialists from 2 in 1962–3 to 50 in 1968–9; these men are largely charged with 'developing the non-timber potential of forested land' (F.A.O. 1972).

The outlook then is not completely gloomy. More and more the importance of forests and the real possibility that man can cause irreversible destruction on a scale which endangers his own future is being realized, though as yet the realization is mainly amongst scientists and has not got through to the decision makers. But time is short, as the fast-rising trends of forest exploitation clearly show. Increased awareness and action to conserve is needed in the decade of the 1970s, or it will for many places, including the Sunda shelf region with its grand dipterocarp forests, be too late. 'One cannot bring to life extinct plants or animals. Once destroyed they are gone forever' (van Steenis 1971). And, as Richards (1970) has eloquently pleaded, 'Why save the jungle?—Come with an observant eye and the question will answer itself.'

Appendix: Select list of publications containing descriptions of tropical rain forests in the Far East

Full references to all the publications referred to elsewhere in the book will be found in the bibliography, here author and date are given.

Andaman Islands

BHARGAVA, O. P. (1958). Tropical evergreen virgin forests of Andaman Islands. *Indian Forester* **84**, 20–9.
CHATURVEDI, M. D. (1952). *Report on the forests of the Andamans*. Delhi.

Australia

WALKER, D. (ed.) (1972). *Bridge and barrier: the natural and cultural history of Torres Straits*. Research School of Pacific Studies, Australian National University, Pubn BG/3 (1972).
Webb (1959, 1968).

Borneo

Beccari (1904).

Brunei

Ashton (1964).
ANDERSON, J. A. R. (1957). The enumeration of 235 acres of dipterocarp forest in Brunei. *Malay. Forester* **20**, 144–50.

Sabah

Burgess (1961); Fox (1972, 1973a); Meijer (1965).
Meijer (1965, 1971).
Ho, C. C. and POORE, M. E. D. (1966). The value of Mt. Kinabalu Park Malaysia to plant ecology. *Malay. Nat. J.* **19**, 195–202.

Sarawak

Anderson (1961b, 1964a); Ashton (1971); Brunig (in press); Richards (1936).

Burma

Champion (1936); Champion and Seth (1968); Stamp (1925); Walker and Pendleton (1957).
KURZ, S. (1877). *Forest flora of British Burma* (2 vols), Calcutta.

Ceylon

HOLMES, C. H. (1958). The broad pattern of climate and vegetation distribution in Ceylon. In *Proceedings of the Symposium on humid tropics vegetation, Kandy*. UNESCO, Paris.

China

Hou, Chen, and Wang (1956); Walker and Pendleton (1957); Wang (1961).
FEDEROV, A. A. (1958). (The tropical rain forest of China.) *Botanitcheskii J.* **43**, 1385–408 (Russian with English summary).

Christmas Island

MITCHELL, B. A. (1974). The forest flora of Christmas Island. *Commonw. For. Rev.* **53**, 19–29.

Fiji

BERRY, M. J. and HOWARD, W. J. (1973). Fiji forest inventory (3 vols). *Land Resource Study* 12. Foreign and Commonwealth Office, Overseas Development Administration.
MEAD, J. P. (1928). The forests of the Fiji islands. *Emp. For. J.* **7**, 47–54.

Indo-China

Rollet (1972); Walker and Pendleton (1957).
ROLLET, B. (1953). Notes sur les forêts claires du sud de l'Indochine. *Bois Forêts Trop.* **31**, 3–13.
ROTHE, P. L. (1947). La forêt d'Indochine. *Bois Forêts Trop.* **1**, 25–30; **2**, 18–23; **3**, 17–23.
VIDAL, J. (1973). Bibliograph survey of taxonomic and phytogeographic studies related to Indo China (Cambodia, Laos, Vietnam) from 1955 to 1969. *Proc. Precongress Conference Bogor of the Pacific Science Association 1971*.
VIDAL, J. (1960). Les forêts du Laos. *Bois Forêts Trop.* **70**, 5–21.
VIDAL, J. (1934–60). La végétation du Laos. *Trav. Lab. for. Toulouse* t. 5 v.1 (3).

Java

van Steenis (1972); van Steenis and Schippers-Lammertse (1965).

Sumatra

BUNNING, E. (1947). *In den Waldern Nord-Sumatras*. Bonn. Bonn.

Malaya

Cousens (1958a); Robbins and Wyatt-Smith (1964); Symington (1936, 1943); Whitmore (1972a); Wyatt-Smith

(1959, 1963, 1966).

WYATT-SMITH, J. (1949). A note on tropical evergreen rain forest in Malaya. *Malay. Forester* **12**, 58–64.

WYATT-SMITH, J. (1952–3). Malayan forest types. *Malay. Nat. J.* **7**, 42–55; **8**, 52–8; **9**, 1–8.

WYATT-SMITH, J. (1964). A preliminary vegetation map of of Malaya with descriptions of the vegetation types. *J. trop. Geog.* **18**, 200–13.

Micronesia

Hosokawa (1952, 1954*a,b*).

New Guinea

Womersley and McAdam (1957); White (1973).

ANON. (1973). *New horizons—forestry in Papua New Guinea*. Brisbane.

BRASS, L. J. (1941). The 1938–39 expedition to the Snow Mountains Netherlands New Guinea. *J. Arnold Arbor* **22**, 271–95, 297–324.

BRASS, L. J. (1956). Results of the Archbold Expeditions. No. 75. Summary of the Fourth Archbold Expedition to New Guinea (1953). *Bull. Am. Mus. nat. Hist.* **111**, 80–152.

BRASS, L. J. (1959). Results of the Archbold Expeditions. No. 79. Summary of the Fifth Archbold Expedition to New Guinea (1956–7). *Bull. Am. Mus. nat. Hist.* **118**, 1–70.

BRASS, L. J. (1964). Results of the Archbold Expeditions. No. 86. Summary of the Sixth Archbold Expedition to New Guinea (1959). *Bull. Am. Mus. nat. Hist.* **127**, 145–215.

C.S.I.R.O. LAND RESOURCE SURVEYS: see bibliography under: Taylor (1964*a,b*); Heyligers (1965, 1967, 1972); Robbins and Pullen (1965); Paijmans (1967, 1969, 1971); Robbins (1968, 1970).

LANE-POOLE, C. E. (1925). The forests of Papua and New Guinea. *Emp. For. J.* **4**, 206–34.

McADAM, J. B. (1952). The forests of the territories of Papua and New Guinea. *Aust. Timber J.* **18**, 674–704.

PAIJMANS, K. (in preparation). *Vegetation*. In *The vegetation of New Guinea*. C.S.I.R.O., Canberra.

RIDSDALE, C. E. (1968). Botanical results of the New Guinea border demarcation expedition 1967. *Trans. Papua New Guinea sci. Soc.* **9**, 3–22.

New Hebrides

JOHNSON, M. S. (1971). New Hebrides Condominium, Erromango Forest Inventory (2 vols). *Land Resource Study 10*. Land Resources Division, Overseas Development Administration, Foreign and Commonwealth Offices, Tolworth.

Philippines

Brown (1919).

BEDARD, P. W. (1958). Reconnaissance, classification and mapping of Philippines forests. *Proceedings of the Symposium on humid tropics vegetation, Kandy*. UNESCO, Paris.

Solomons and Santa Cruz

Heyligers (1967); Whitmore (1966*a,c*, 1969*a*).

Thailand

SMITINAND, T. (1966). The vegetation of Doi Chiengdao, a limestone massive in Chiengmai, north Thailand. *Nat. Hist. Bull. Siam Soc.* **21**, 93–128.

SMITINAND, T. (1968). The vegetation of Khao Yai National Park. *Nat. Hist. Bull. Siam Soc.* **22**, 289–305.

SMITINAND, T. (1973). Conditions of the lowland tropical forests of Thailand. *Proc. Precongress Conference Bogor of the Pacific Science Association 1971*.

Timor

MONTEIRO GOMES, R.C.V. (1950). Reconhecimento preliminar das formaçoes florestais no Timor Português. *Estudios Ensaios e Documentos Ministerio Colonias Junta de Investigaçoẽs Colonias*. Ministerio Colonias, Lisbon.

Bibliography

TEXT SECTIONS where the reference is mentioned are indicated in square brackets and also all mentions in tables, figures, and the Appendix [App.]. A reference to, for example, 'Chapter 14' means the reference occurs in the un-numbered introductory section to that chapter.

ABDUL LATIF BIN NORDIN and HARUN BIN ISMAIL (1970). Utilisation of rubber wood and waste from primary wood based industries for chips. *Malay. Forester* 33, 334–41. [§ 19.1.]

AIRY SHAW, H. K. (1953). On the distribution of *Pisonia grandis* R. Br. (Nyctaginaceae), with special reference to Malaysia. *Kew Bull. 1953*, 87–97. [§ 10.6.]

—— (1971). The Euphorbiaceae of Siam. *Kew Bull.* 26, 191–363. [§ 12.3.]

—— (1975). The Euphorbiaceae of Borneo. *Kew Bull. Suppl. Series.* [§ 12.1.]

ALLEE, W. C. (1926). Measurement of environmental factors in the tropical rain-forest of Panama. *Ecology* 7, 445–68. [§ 3.6.]

ALVIM, P. de T. (1964). Tree growth periodicity in tropical climates. In *Formation of wood in forest trees* (ed. M. H. Zimmerman). Academic Press, New York. [§ 4.1.]

AMADON, D. (1973). Birds of the Congo and Amazon forests: a comparison. In *Tropical forest ecosystems in Africa and South America: a comparative review* (eds B. J. Meggers, E. S. Ayensu, and W. D. Duckworth). Association for Tropical Biology, Washington. [Table 1.2.]

ANDERSON, J. A. R. (1958). Observations on the ecology of the peat-swamp forests of Sarawak and Brunei. In *Proceedings of the Symposium on humid tropics vegetation.* UNESCO, Tjiawi. [§ 11.3.]

—— (1961a). The destruction of *Shorea albida* forest by an unidentified insect. *Emp. For. Rev.* 40, 19–29 [§§ 2.8, 6.1, 11.3.]

—— (1961b). *The ecology and forest types of the peat swamp forests of Sarawak and Brunei in relation to their silviculture.* Ph.D. thesis, Edinburgh University. [§§ 2.8, 4.1, 6.1, 11.3; Fig. 11.3, Fig. 11.4, Fig. 11.5, Fig. 11.11, Fig. 11.12, Fig. 11.13, App.]

—— (1962). Research on the effects of shifting cultivation in Sarawak. In *Proceedings of the Symposium on the impact of man on humid tropics vegetation.* UNESCO, Goroka. [§ 18.2.]

—— (1963). The flora of the peat swamp forests of Sarawak and Brunei including a catalogue of all recorded species of flowering plants, ferns and fern allies. *Gdns Bull., Singapore* 20, 131–228. [§§ 10.1, 11.3, 11.14.]

—— (1964a). The structure and development of the peat swamps of Sarawak and Brunei. *J. trop. Geogr.* 18, 7–16. [§ 11.3, Fig. 11.2, App.]

—— (1964b). Observations on climatic damage in peat

swamp forest in Sarawak. *Emp. For. Rev.* 43, 145–58. [§§ 6.1, 11.3.]

—— (1965). Limestone habitat in Sarawak. In *Proceedings of the Symposium on ecological research into humid tropics vegetation.* UNESCO, Kuching. [§ 10.4.]

—— (1966). A note on two tree fires caused by lightning in Sarawak. *Malay. Forester* 29, 18–20. [§ 6.1.]

ANDRIESSE, J. P. (1969). A study of the environment and characteristics of tropical podzols in Sarawak (East Malaysia). *Geoderma* 2, 210–27. [§ 9.6.]

ANON. (1951). *The resources of the territory of Papua and New Guinea.* Dept. of National Development, Division of Regional Development, Canberra. [§ 15.2.]

—— (1964). *Prospective pulpwood species for plantation in the Philippines.* Forest Products Research Institute (Laguna, Philippines). Technical Note 60. [§ 7.2.]

—— (1965a). *Ann. Rpt Singapore bot. Gdn* 55. Government Printer, Singapore. [§ 6.1.]

—— (1965b). *Handbook of selective logging.* Manila. [§ 7.1.]

—— (1969). *Philipp. Lumberm.* 15, 9–14. [§§ 7.1, 17.2.]

—— (1972a). Forthcoming events. New Guinea and Papua. *For. Abstr.* 215. [§ 19.1.]

—— (1972b). Ecology. In *Penyata Tahunan Perhutanan di-Malaysia Barat 1968.* Kuala Lumpur. [§ 5.1.]

—— (1973). *Ann. Rpt 1972–3 Dept Forests Papua New Guinea.* [§§ 12.2, 14.2.]

—— (1974). Malaysia, a special report on investment and development. 31.viii.74. *The Times, London.* [Fig. 17.1.]

ARNOTT, G. W. (1957). The Kelantan deficiency area. *Malay. agric. J.* 40, 60–91. [§ 9.10.]

ASHTON, P. S. (1964). Ecological studies in the mixed dipterocarp forests of Brunei State. *Oxf. For. Mem.* 25, [§§ 1.1, 10.3, 10.5, 14.1, 15.4, 16.4; Fig. 1.5, Fig. 1.6, Fig. 2.1, Fig. 10.11, Fig. 15.16, App.]

—— (1965). *Manual of the dipterocarp trees of Brunei State.* Oxford University Press, London. [§ 15.4.]

—— (1967). Climate versus soil in the classification of south-east Asian tropical lowland vegetation. *J. Ecol.* 55, 67P–8P. [§ 12.1.]

—— (1968). *A manual of the dipterocarp trees of Brunei State and Sarawak—supplement.* Government Printer, Kuching. [§ 15.4.]

—— (1969). Speciation among tropical forest trees: some deductions in the light of recent evidence. *Biol. J. Linnean Soc. London* 1, 155–96. [§ 2.8.]

—— (1971). The plants and vegetation of Bako National Park. *Malay. Nat. J.* 24, 151–62. [§ 10.3, App.]

241

ASKEW, G. P. (1964). The mountain soils of the east ridge of Mt. Kinabalu. *Proc. R. Soc. B* **161**, 65–74. [§ 9.12.]

ATKINSON, D. J. (1953). The natural control of forest insects in the tropics. *Int. Congr. Ent.* **9** (2), 220–3. [§ 2.8.]

ATKINSON, M. R., FINDLAY, G. P., HOPE, A. B., PITMAN, M.G., SADDLER, M. D. W., and WEST, K. R. (1967). Salt regulation in the mangroves *Rhizophora mucronata* Lam. and *Aegialitis annulata* R. Br. *Aust. J. Biol. Sci.* **20**, 588–99. [§ 11.1.]

AUBERT, G. and DUCHAUFOUR, P. (1956). Projet de classification des sols. *Int. Congr. Soil Sci.* **6** (5), 597–604. [Chapter 9.]

AUBRÉVILLE, A. (1938). La forêt coloniale: les forêts de l'Afrique occidentale française. *Annls Acad. Sci. colon.* **9**, 1–245. [Chapter 15.]

—— (1961). *Étudé ecologique des principales formations végétales du Brésil.* Centre Technique Forestier Tropical. Nogent sur Marne. [§ 10.3.]

AUSTIN, M. P., ASHTON, P. S., and GREIG-SMITH, P. (1972). The application of quantitative methods to vegetation survey III. A re-examination of rain forest data from Brunei. *J. Ecol.* **60**, 305–24. [§ 15.3.]

—— and GREIG-SMITH, P. (1968). The application of quantitative methods to vegetation survey II. Some methodological problems of data from rain forest. *J. Ecol.* **56**, 827–44. [Chapter 15; § 15.5; Fig. 1.5.]

BACKER, C. A. (1963). Dipterocarpaceae. In *Flora of Java* (eds C. A. Backer and R. C. van der Brink Bakhuizen). Vol. 1, pp. 328–33. Groningen. [§ 12.1.]

BAILLIE, I. C. (1970). *Report on a reconnaissance soil survey of the Pelagus protected forest 3rd Division.* Soil Survey Report F 2, Forest Dept., Kuching. [§ 10.3.]

—— (1972a). *Report on soil observations made in forest reconnaissance inventory units 1 and 3 in the Upper Rejang basin.* Soil Survey Report F 5, Forest Dept., Kuching. [§ 10.3.]

—— (1972b). *Further studies on the occurrence of drought in Sarawak.* Soil Survey Report F 7, Forest Dept., Kuching. [§§ 3.4, 4.1.]

BAKER, H. G. (1973). Evolutionary relationships between flowering plants and animals in American and African tropical forests. *Tropical forest ecosystems in Africa and South America: a comparative review* (eds B. J. Meggers, E. S. Ayensu, and W. D. Duckworth). Association for Tropical Biology, Washington. [§ 2.8.]

—— and HARRIS, B. J. (1957). The pollination of *Parkia* by bats and its attendant evolutionary problems. *Evolution* **11**, 449–60. [§ 2.8.]

BALGOOY, M. M. J. VAN (1971). Plant geography of the Pacific. *Blumea supplement* **6**, 1–222. [§ 1.1.]

BAREN, F. A. VAN (1961). The pedological aspects of the reclamation of tropical and particularly volcanic soils in tropical regions. In *Proceedings of the Symposium on tropical soils and vegetation.* UNESCO, Abidjan. [§ 9.1.]

BARRAU, J. (1962). The selection, domestication and cultivation of food plants in tropical Oceania in the pre-European era. In *Proceedings of the Symposium on the impact of man on humid tropics vegetation.* UNESCO, Goroka. [§ 17.1.]

BARTLETT, H. H. (1955a). Fire, primitive agriculture and grazing in the tropics. In *Man's role in changing the face of the earth.* Chicago. [Chapter 10; § 17.1.]

—— (1955b, 1957, 1961). *Fire in relation to primitive agriculture and grazing in the tropics.* Vols 1–3. Ann Arbor. [Chapter 10; § 17.1.]

BATE-SMITH, E. C. (1971). Attractants and repellants in higher animals. In *Phytochemical ecology* (ed. J. B. Harborne). Academic Press, London. [§ 2.8.]

—— and WHITMORE, T. C. (1959). Biochemistry and taxonomy in Dipterocarpaceae. *Nature* **184**, 795–6. [§ 2.8.]

BAUR, G. N. (1964a). *The ecological basis of rain forest management.* Sydney. [Chapters 1, 7; §§ 10.1, 10.2, 10.3, 12.2; Fig. 1.7.]

—— (1964b). Rain forest treatment. *Unasylva* **18**, 18–28. [Chapter 7; § 19.1.]

BEADLE, N. C. W. (1953). The edaphic factor in plant ecology with a special note on soil phosphates. *Ecology* **34**, 426–8. [§ 10.3.]

—— (1954). Soil phosphate and the delimitation of plant communities in eastern Australia. *Ecology* **35**, 370–5. [§ 10.3.]

—— (1962). Soil phosphate and the delimitation of plant communities in eastern Australia II. *Ecology* **43**, 281–8. [§ 10.3.]

—— (1966). Soil phosphate and its role in molding segments of the Australian flora and vegetation with special reference to xeromorphy and sclerophylly. *Ecology* **47**, 992–1007. [§ 10.3.]

BEARD, J. S. (1944). Climax vegetation in tropical America. *Ecology* **25**, 127–58. [§§ 10.1, 10.2, 12.2.]

BECCARI, O. (1904). *Wanderings in the great forests of Borneo* (Transl. E. H. Giglioli, revised and ed. F. H. H. Guillemard). Constable, London. [§ 15.3; App.]

BECKINSDALE, R. P. (1957). The nature of tropical rainfall. *Trop. Agric., Trin.* **34**, 76–98. [§ 16.5.]

BEERS, W. F. J. VAN (1962). Acid sulphate soils. *Bull. int. Inst. Ld Reclam.* [§ 9.9.]

BERNHARD, F. (1970). Étude de la litière et de sa contribution au cycle des éléments minéraux en forêt ombrophile de Cote d'Ivoire. *Oecol. Plant.* **5**, 247–66. [§ 8.3.]

BERRY, A. J. (1972). The natural history of west Malaysian mangrove faunas. *Malay. Nat. J.* **25**, 135–62. [§ 11.1.]

—— WELLS, D. R., and WYCHERLEY, P. R. (in press). Environmental stimuli for triggering developmental cycles of plants and animals in the humid tropics. *Proceedings of the Symposium on developmental biology today.* University of Malaya, Kuala Lumpur. [§ 4.2.]

BEVERIDGE, A. E. (1953). The Menchali forest reserve. *Malay. Forester* **16**, 87–93. [§ 10.3.]

BIRRELL, K. S. and WRIGHT, A. C. S. (1945). A serpentine soil in New Caledonia. *N. Z. Jl Sci. Technol. A* **27**, 72–6. [§ 9.8.]

BJÖRKMAN, O. and LUDLOW, M. M. (1972). Characterization of the light climate on the floor of a Queensland rain forest. *Carn. Inst. Yb. 1971–2* **71**, 85–94. [§§ 3.6, 8.4.]

—— and MORROW, P. A. (1972). Photosynthetic performance of two rain forest species in their native habitat and analysis of their gas exchange. *Carn. Inst. Yb. 1971–2* **71**, 94–102. [§ 3.6.]

BLACK, C. C. (1971). Ecological implications of dividing plants into groups with distinct photosynthetic production capacities. *Adv. Ecol. Res.* **7**, 87–114. [§ 8.4.]

BLATTER, E. (1929). The flowering of bamboos. *J. Bombay nat. Hist. Soc.* **33**, 889–921. [§ 4.1.]

—— (1930*a,b*). The flowering of bamboos. *J. Bombay nat. Hist. Soc.* **33**, 447–67, 889–921; **33**, 135–41. [§ 4.1.]

BLOOMFIELD, C. (1953). A study of podsolisation. II. The mobilisation of iron and aluminium by the leaves and bark of *Agathis australis* (Kauri). *J. Soil Sci.* **4**, 17–23. [§ 14.1.]

BLUMENSTOCK, D. I. (1958). Distribution and characteristics of tropical climates. *Proc. Pacif. Sci. Congr.* **9** (20), 3–24. [§§ 3.1, 16.5.]

BOARDMAN, N. K., ANDERSON, J. M., THORNE, S. W., and BJÖRKMAN, O. (1972). Photochemical reactions of chloroplasts and components of the photosynthetic electron transport chain in two rain forest species. *Carn. Inst. Yb. 1971–2* **71**, 107–114. [§ 8.4.]

BODEN KLOSS, C. (1920). In Ridley, H. N. Peninsula Siamese plants. *J. fed. Malay St. Mus.* **10**, 65–126. [§12.3.]

BOSERUP, E. (1965). *The conditions of agricultural growth.* London. [§ 18.1.]

BRASS, L. J. (1938). Botanical results of the Archbold Expeditions. IX. Notes on the vegetation of the Fly and Wassi Kussa Rivers. British New Guinea. *J. Arnold Arbor.* **19**, 174–190. [§ 16.1.]

BRAY, J. R. and GORHAM, E. (1964). Litter production in forests of the world. *Adv. Ecol. Res.* **2**, 101–57. [§§ 9.1, 19.2.]

BROOKFIELD, H. E. (1969). Some notes on the climate of the British Solomon Islands. *Phil. Trans. R. Soc. B* **255**, 207–10. [§ 4.1.]

BROWN, W. H. (1919). *Vegetation of Philippine mountains.* Forest Bureau, Manila. [§§ 16.1, 16.5; App.]

BROWNE, F. G. (1937). A note on the defoliation of sendok-sendok (*Endospermum malaccense*). *Malay. Forester* **6**, 267–9. [§ 2.8.]

—— (1949). Storm forest in Kelantan. *Malay. Forester* **12**, 28–33. [§§ 6.1, 6.5, 8.2.]

—— (1952). Kerangas lands of Sarawak. *Malay. Forester* **15**, 61–73. [Chapter 14; §§ 10.3, 14.1, 19.1.]

—— (1955). *Forest trees of Sarawak and Brunei and their products.* Government Printer, Sarawak, Kuching. [§§ 10.3, 15.3.]

BRUNIG, E. F. (1964). A study of damage attributed to lightning in two areas of *Shorea albida* forest in Sarawak. *Emp. For. Rev.* **43**, 134–44. [§ 6.1.]

—— (1965). A guide and introduction to the vegetation of the kerangas forests and the padangs of the Bako National Park. In *Proceedings of the Symposium on ecological research into humid tropics vegetations.* UNESCO, Kuching. [§ 10.3.]

—— (1968). Some observations on the status of heath forests in Sarawak and Brunei. *Proceedings of the Symposium on recent advances in tropical ecology.* Varanasi. Vol. 2, pp. 451–7. [Fig. 10.4.]

—— (1969*a*). Forestry on tropical podzols and related soils. *Trop. Ecol.* **10**, 45–58. [§ 10.3.]

—— (1969*b*). On the seasonality of drought in the lowlands of Sarawak (Borneo). *Erdkunde* **23**, 127–33. [§ 3.4.]

—— (1970). Stand structure, physiognomy and environmental factors in some lowland forests in Sarawak. *Trop. Ecol.* **11**, 26–43. [§ 10.3.]

—— (1971). On the ecological significance of drought in the equatorial wet evergreen (rain) forest of Sarawak (Borneo). In *The water relations of Malesian forests* (ed. J. R. Flenley). Department of Geography, University of Hull. [§§ 10.3, 11.3, 16.5.]

—— (1973). Species richness and stand diversity in relation to site and succession of forests in Sarawak and Brunei (Borneo). *Amazoniana* **4**, 293–320. [§§ 10.1, 10.3.]

—— (in press). *Ecological studies in the Kerangas forests of Sarawak and Brunei.* Government Printer, Kuching. [§ 10.3; App.]

—— (in preparation). *Silvics and silvicultural management in humid tropical forests.* [§§ 6.5, 7.1; Fig. 10.12.]

BURGESS, P. F. (1961). The structure and composition of lowland tropical rain forest in North Borneo. *Malay. Forester* **24**, 66–80. [§§ 8.1, 15.3; Fig. 7.1, Fig. 15.1; App.]

—— (1969*a*). Preliminary observations on the autecology of *Shorea curtisii* Dyer ex King in the Malay peninsula. *Malay. Forester* **32**, 438. [§§ 2.8, 15.3.]

—— (1969*b*). Ecological factors in hill and mountain forests of the States of Malaya. *Malay. Nat. J.* **22**, 119–28. [§ 16.6.]

—— (1969*c*). Colour changes in the forest 1968–69. *Malay. Nat. J.* **22**, 171–3. [§ 4.1.]

—— (1970). An approach towards a silvicultural system for the hill forests of the Malay peninsula. *Malay. Forester* **33**, 126–34. [§§ 5.1, 7.1.]

—— (1971). Effect of logging on hill dipterocarp forest. *Malay. Nat. J.* **24**, 231–7. [§§ 17.2, 17.3, 19.2; Fig. 17.6.]

—— (1972). Studies on the regeneration of the hill forests of the Malay Peninsula. The phenology of dipterocarps. *Malay. Forester* **35**, 103–23. [§ 4.1.]

BURINGH, P. (1968). *Introduction to the study of soils in tropical and subtropical regions.* Landbouwhogeschool, Wageningen. [Chapter 9.]

BURKILL, I. H. (1919). The composition of a piece of well-drained Singapore secondary jungle thirty years old. *Gdns Bull. Straits Settl.* **2**, 147–57. [§ 18.2.]

—— (1935). *A dictionary of the economic products of the Malay peninsula,* Vols 1 and 2. Crown Agents for the Colonies, Oxford. [§ 17.1.]

—— (1966). *A dictionary of the economic products of the Malay peninsula* (reprinted with different pagination).

Ministry of Agriculture and Co-operatives, Kuala Lumpur. [§ 17.1.]

BURNHAM, C. P. (1968). Landscape and soils in Malaya. *Malay. Agriculturist* **7**, 64–9. [§ 9.6.]

—— (1974). Altitudinal changes in soils on granite in Malaysia. *Int. Congr. Soil Sci.* **10** (6), 290–6. [§ 9.12.]

BURTT DAVY, J. (1938). *The classification of tropical woody vegetation types.* Imperial Forestry Institute, Paper 13. [Chapters 1, 10; §§ 10.1, 10.2, 10.6, 12.1, 12.2, 16.1, 16.6.]

CACHAN, P. (1963). Signification écologique des variations microclimatiques verticales dans la forêt sempervirente de basse Côte D'Ivoire. *Annls Fac. Sci. Dakar* **8**, 89–155. [§ 3.6.]

—— and DUVAL, J. (1963). Variations microclimatiques verticales et saisonnières dans la forêt sempervirente de basse, Côte d'Ivoire. *Annls Fac. Sci. Dakar* **8**, 5–87. [§ 3.6.]

CAREY, T. Y. (1962). Methods of cultivation among the Kelantan Temiar. In *Proceedings of the Symposium on the impact of man on humid tropics vegetation,* UNESCO, Goroka. [§ 18.1.]

CARTER, D. B. and MATHER, J. R. (1966). Climatic classification for environmental biology. *C. W. Thornthwaite Associates Laboratory of Climatology publications in climatology* **19**. [§ 3.1.]

CHAMPION, H. G. (1936). A preliminary survey of the forest types of India and Burma. *Indian Forest Rec.* (New Series) **1**, 1–286. [Chapter 10; §§ 10.1, 10.2, 12.1, 12.2, 12.3, 14.3, 15.2; App.]

—— and SETH, S. K. (1968). *A revised survey of the forest types of India.* Manager of Publications, Delhi. [Chapter 10; §§ 10.1, 10.2, 12.1, 12.2, 12.3, 15.2; App.]

CHAPMAN, V. J. (1973). Mangrove vegetation. *Proc. Precongress Conference Bogor, of the Pacific Science Association 1971.* [§ 11.1.]

CHINTE, F. O. (1971). Silvicultural studies of four pulpwood species. *Philipp. Lumberm.* **17**, 8–26. [§ 7.2.]

CHIVERS, D. J. (1971). Spatial relations within siamang group. In *Congr. Primatol.* **3**, 14–21. [§§ 2.8, 4.2.]

—— (1972). The siamang and the gibbon in the Malay peninsula. In *Gibbon and siamang* (ed. D. M. Rumbaugh). Karger, Basel. [§ 2.7.]

CHUA, S. E. (1970a). *The physiology of periodicity, foliar senescence and abscission in* Hevea brasiliensis *Muell. Arg.,* Ph.D. thesis, Singapore University. [§ 4.1.]

—— (1970b). *The physiology of foliar senescence and abscission in* Hevea brasiliensis *Muell. Arg.* Rubber Research Institute of Malaya, Research Archives Document 65. [§ 4.1.]

CLARKE, G. R. and BECKETT, P. H. (1971). *The study of soil in the field* (5th edn). Clarendon Press, Oxford. [Chapter 9.]

COCKBURN, P. F. (1969). Gunong Mandi Angin, Trengganu: a botanical visit. *Malay. Nat. J.* **22**, 164–70. [§ 16.1.]

—— and WONG, S. M. (1969). Germination in *Shorea curtisii* Dyer (seraya). *Malay. Forester* **32**, 266–8. [§ 5.2.]

COODE, M. J. E. (1973). Notes on *Terminalia* L.

(Combretaceae) in Papuasia. *Contrib. Herbarium Australiense* **2**. [§ 5.3.]

COOLING, E. N. G. (1968). Pinus merkusii. *Fast growing timber trees of the lowland tropics* 4. Department of Forestry, Oxford. [§§ 5.2, 14.3; Fig. 14.1.]

—— and GAUSSEN, H. (1970). In Indochina: *Pinus merkusiana* sp. nov. et non *P. merkusii* Jungh. et de Vriese. *Trav. Lab. for. Toulouse* Tome I, 8, art. 7. [§ 14.3.]

COOMBE, D. E. (1960). An analysis of the growth of *Trema guineensis. J. Ecol.* **48**, 219–31. [§ 8.4.]

—— and HADFIELD, W. (1962). An analysis of the growth of *Musanga cecropioides. J. Ecol.* **50**, 221–34. [§ 8.2.]

CORBET, S. A. and PENDLEBURY, H. M. (1934). *The butterflies of the Malay peninsula.* Kyle Palmer, Kuala Lumpur. [§§ 2.8, 4.2, 16.7.]

CORNER, E. J. H. (1935). The seasonal flowering of agarics in Malaya. *Gdns Bull. Straits Settl.* **9**, 70–88. [§ 4.2.]

—— (1940). *Wayside trees of Malaya.* Government Printer, Singapore. [§§ 2.5, 2.8, 4.1, 15.3; Fig. 2.24.]

—— (1949). The durian theory or the origin of the modern tree. *Ann. Bot.* **52**, 367–414. [§§ 2.5, 2.8.]

—— (1962). The classification of Moraceae. *Gdns Bull., Singapore* **19**, 187–252. [§ 2.8.]

—— (1966). *The natural history of palms.* Wiedenfield and Nicholson, London. [§ 2.8.]

—— (1970). The complex of *Ficus deltoidea*; a recent invasion of the Sunda Shelf. *Phil. Trans. R. Soc. B* **256**, 281–318. [§ 14.1.]

COSTER, C. (1923). Lauberneuerung und andere periodische Lebensprozesse in dem trockenen Monsun-gebiet Ost-Javas. *Annls Jard. bot. Buitenz.* **33**, 117–89. [§ 4.1.]

—— (1925). Eendagsorchideen. *Trop. Natuur* **14**, 121–6. [§ 4.1.]

—— (1926). Periodische Blüteerscheinungen in den Tropen. *Annls Jard. bot. Buitenz.* **35**, 125–62. [§ 4.1.]

COULTER, J. K. (1950a). Peat formations in Malaya. *Malay. agric. J.* **33**, 63–81. [§ 11.3.]

—— (1950b). Organic matter in Malayan soils: a preliminary study of the organic matter content in soils under virgin jungle, forest plantations and abandoned cultivated land. *Malay. Forester* **13**, 189–202. [§ 18.1.]

—— (1957). Development of the peat soils of Malaya. *Malay. agric. J.* **40**, 188–99 [§ 11.3.]

COUSENS, J. E. (1951). Some notes on the composition of lowland tropical rainforest in Rengam Forest Reserve, Johore. *Malay. Forester* **14**, 131–9. [Fig. 1.5.]

—— (1958a). A study of 155 acres of tropical rain forest by complete enumeration of all large trees. *Malay. Forester* **21**, 155–64. [Table 15.2; App.]

—— (1958b). *A pilot sampling scheme in the regenerated forests of Perak—1956. Project M8—research programme.* Malayan Forestry Dept. Research Pamphlet 23. [§ 7.1, Table 8.3.]

—— (1965). Some reflections on the nature of Malayan lowland rain forest. *Malay. Forester* **28**, 122–8. [§ 15.5.]

DALE, W. L. (1959). The rainfall of Malaya I. *J. trop. Geogr.* **13**, 23–37. [§§ 3.5, 4.1, 6.1.]

—— (1960). The rainfall of Malaya II. *J. trop. Geogr.* **14**, 11–28. [§ 4.1.]

DAMES, T. W. G. (1955). The soils of east central Java. *Contr. gen. agric. Res. Stn Bogor* **141**. [§ 9.10.]

DANSER, B. H. (1939). A revision of the genus *Phacellaria* (Santalaceae). *Blumea* **3**, 213–34. [§ 2.6.]

DARLINGTON, P. J. (1965). *Zoogeography.* Wiley, New York. [§ 1.2.]

DAVIS, D. E. (1945). The annual cycle of plants, mosquitoes, birds and mammals in two Brazilian forests. *Ecol. Monogr.* **15**, 245–95. [§ 4.2.]

DAVIS, T. A. W. and RICHARDS, P. W. (1933–4). The vegetation of Moraballi Creek, British Guiana; an ecological study of a limited area of tropical rain forest I, II. *J. Ecol.* **21**, 350–84; **22**, 106–55. [§ 2.3.]

DAWKINS, H. C. (1952). Experiments on low percentage enumerations of tropical high forest. *Emp. For. Rev.* **31**, 131–45. [Chapter 15.]

—— (1956). Rapid detection of aberrant girth increment of rain forest trees. *Emp. For. Rev.* **35**, 449–54. [§ 8.1.]

—— (1958). *The management of natural tropical high forest with special reference to Uganda.* Commonwealth Forestry Institute, Paper 34. [Part III heading; Chapter 7; §§ 7.1, 8.1; Chapter 15; §§ 15.5, 19.1, 19.3.]

—— (1959). The volume increment of natural tropical high forest and limitations on its improvement. *Emp. For. Rev.* **38**, 175–80. [§ 8.1.]

—— (1963*a*). *The productivity of tropical high forest trees and their reaction to controllable environment.* D. Phil. thesis, Oxford University. [§ 8.1.]

—— (1963*b*). Crown diameters, their relation to bole diameter in tropical forest trees. *Emp. For. Rev.* **42**, 318–33. [§§ 2.5, 8.1.]

—— (1964*a*). The productivity of lowland tropical high forest and some comparisons with competitors. *J. Oxf. Univ. Forest Soc.* **12**, 15–18. [§ 8.1; Fig. 8.1.]

—— (1964*b*). *Productivity of tropical forests and their ultimate value to man.* I.U.C.N. Publications, Morges. n.s. 4, 178–82. [§§ 8.1, 8.3.]

—— (1966). The time dimension of tropical forest trees. *J. Ecol.* **53**, 837P–38P. [§§ 2.4, 6.5.]

DICKERSON, R. E., MERRILL, E. D., McGREGOR, R. C., SCHULTZE, W., TAYLOR, E. H., and HERRE, A. W. C. T. (1928). Distribution of life in the Philippines. *Bur. Sci. Monogr. Manila* **21**. [§ 1.2.]

DIREKTORAT PEMASARAN (1971). *Statistik Pemasaran Hasil Hutan.* Jakarta. [Fig. 17.3.]

—— (1972). *Statistik Pemasaran Hasil Hutan.* Jakarta. [Fig. 17.3.]

DOBBY, E. H. G. (1950). *Southeast Asia.* London. [§ 18.1.]

DOCTERS VAN LEEUWEN, W. M. (1954). On the biology of some Javanese Loranthoideae and the role birds play in their life history. *Beaufortia* **4**, 102–207. [§ 2.8.]

DORE, J. (1959). Responses of rice to small differences in length of day. *Nature* **183**, 413–4. [§ 4.1.]

DOUGLAS, I. (1971). Aspects of the water balance of catchments in the Main Range near Kuala Lumpur. In *The water relations of Malesian forests* (ed. J. R. Flenley).

Department of Geography, University of Hull. [§§ 3.3, 3.4.]

DRANSFIELD, J. and WHITMORE, T. C. (1970). A Podostemacea new to Malaya: *Indotristicha malayana. Blumea* **18**, 152–5. (§15.3.)

DUDAL, R. and MOORMAN, F. R. (1964). Major soils of south east Asia. *J. trop. Geogr.* **18**, 54–80. [§§ 9.1, 9.2, 9.11; Table 9.2.]

—— —— and RIQUIER, J. (1974). Soils of humid tropical Asia. *Natural resources of humid tropical Asia.* UNESCO, Paris. [§ 9; Table 9.2.]

—— and SOEPRAPTOHARDJO, M. (1957). Soil classification in Indonesia. *Contrib. gen. Agric. Res. Stn Bogor* **148**. [Chapter 9; §§ 9.1, 9.2.]

—— —— (1960). Some considerations on the genetic relationship between latosols and andosols in Java, Indonesia. *Int. Congr. Soil Sci.* 7 (4), 229–37. [§ 9.5.]

DUVIGNEAUD, P. (ed.) (1971). *Productivity of forest eco-systems.* UNESCO, Paris. [§ 8.3.]

EDWARDS, J. P. (1930). Growth of Malayan forest trees as shown by sample plot records, 1915–1928. *Malay. Forest Rec.* **9**. [Table 8.3.]

EKERN, P. C. (1964). Direct interception of cloud water on Lanaihale, Hawaii. *Proc. Soil Sci. Soc. Am.* **28**, 419–21. [§ 16.5.]

ELLENBERG, H. and MUELLER DOMBOIS, D. (1967). Tentative physiognomic-ecological classification of plant formations of the earth. *Ber. geobot. Forsch Inst. Rübel* **37**, 21–55. [Chapter 10.]

ELLIS, R. C. (1971). Rainfall, fogdrip and evaporation in a mountainous area of southern Australia. *Aust. For.* **35**, 99–106. [§ 16.5.]

ENDERT, F. H. (1920). De woudboomflora van Palembang. *Tectona* **13**, 113–60. [§ 11.3.]

EUSSEN, J. H. H. and WIRJAHARDJA, S. (1973). Studies on an alang-alang (*Imperata cyclindrica* (L.) Beauv.) vegetation. *Biotrop. Bull.* **6**, 1–24. [Fig. 18.1.]

EVANS, G. C. (1956). An area survey method of investigating the distribution of light intensity in woodlands, with particular reference to sunflecks. *J. Ecol.* **44**, 391–428. [§ 3.6.]

—— (1966). Temperature gradient in tropical rain forest. *J. Ecol.* **54**, 20P–1P. [§ 3.6.]

—— (1972). *The quantitative analysis of plant growth.* Blackwell, Oxford. [§§ 2.5, 8.3, 8.4.]

—— WHITMORE, T. C., and WONG, Y. K. (1960). The distribution of light reaching the ground vegetation in a tropical rain forest. *J. Ecol.* **48**, 193–204. [§ 3.6.]

EYLES, R. J. (1967). Laterite at Kerdau, Pahang, Malaya. *J. trop. Geogr.* **25**, 18–23. [§ 9.4; Fig. 9.7.]

FAEGRI, K. and PIJL, L. VAN DER (1966). *Principles of pollination ecology.* Pergamon Press, London. [§ 2.8.]

—— —— (1971). *Principles of pollination ecology* (2nd edn). Pergamon Press, London. [§ 2.8.]

F.A.O. (1963). *World forest inventory 1960.* [§ 17.1.]

F.A.O. (1964). *Meeting on the classification and correlation of soils from volcanic ash, Tokyo.* World Soil Resources

Report no. 14, Rome. [§ 9.5.]

F.A.O. (1966). Wood: world trends and prospects. *Unasylva* **20**, 1–136. [§ 17.1; Fig. 17.3.]

F.A.O./UNESCO (1968). Definitions of soil units for the Soil Map of the World. World Soil Resources Report no. 33, Rome. (Also supplement dated 29th September 1970.) [§ 9; Table 9.2.]

F.A.O. (1968). *Handbook on forest inventory.* [Chapter 15.]

F.A.O. (1972). *Environmental aspects of natural resources management: forestry.* Paper for U.N. Conference on the human environment [§§ 17.1, 17.2, 19.3.]

FEDEROV, A. A. (1966). The structure of the tropical rain forest and speciation in the humid tropics. *J. Ecol.* **54**, 1–11. [§ 2.8.]

FERGUSON, J. H. A. (1949). Productiever-wachtingen en dunning van *Agathis loranthifolia* Salisb. in zuivere opstanden. *Tectona* **39**, 368–82. [§ 14.1.]

FITCH, F. H. (1952). The geology and mineral resources of the neighbourhood of Kuantan, Pahang. *Mem. Geol. Surv. Dep. Fed. Malay.* **6**. [§ 15.3.]

FITZPATRICK, E. A., HART, D., and BROOKFIELD, H. C. (1966). Rainfall seasonality in the tropical southwest Pacific. *Erdkunde* **20**, 181–94. [Fig. 3.1.]

FLENLEY, J. R. (1972). Evidence of Quaternary vegetational change in New Guinea. In *The quaternary era in Malesia* (eds P. Ashton and M. Ashton). Department of Geography, University of Hull. [§ 16.2.]

FOGDEN, M. P. L. (1972). The seasonality and population dynamics of equatorial forest birds in Sarawak. *Ibis* **114**, 307–43. [§ 4.2; Chapter 13.]

FOLLAND, C. J. and ACRES, B. D. (1972). *The soils of Sandakan and Kinabatangan districts.* Land Resources Division, Overseas Development Administration, Tolworth. [§§ 9.2, 9.3.]

FOX, J. E. D. (1967). An enumeration of lowland dipterocarp forest in Sabah. *Malay. Forester* **30**, 263–79. [Table 15.2.]

—— (1968). Some data on the growth of *Anthocephalus cadamba* (Roxb.) Miq. in Sabah. *Malay. Forester* **31**, 89–100. [§ 7.2.]

—— (1971). *Anthocephalus chinensis* the Laran tree of Sabah. *Econ. Bot.* **25**, 221–33. [§ 7.2.]

—— (1972). *The natural vegetation of Sabah and natural regeneration of the dipterocarp forests.* Ph.D. thesis, University of Wales. [§§ 2.8, 4.1, 5.1, 5.2, 5.3, 6.1, 6.2, 6.5; Table 6.4, Table 8.1, Table 8.2; §§ 10.5; Chapters 14, 15; § 15.3; Fig. 6.8, Fig. 15.4.]

—— (1973*a*). A handbook to Kabili-Sepilok Forest Reserve. *Sabah For. Rec.* **9**. [§ 10.3; Chapter 15; App.]

FOX, J. E. D. (1973*b*). Dipterocarp seedling behaviour in Sabah. *Malay. Forester* **36**, 205–14. [§ 6.5.]

—— and TAN, H. (1971). Soils and forest on an ultrabasic hill north east of Ranau, Sabah. *J. trop. Geogr.* **32**, 38–48. [§ 9.8, 10.5.]

FOXWORTHY, F. W. (1926). The size of trees in the Malay Peninsula. *J. Malay. Brch R. Asiat. Soc.* **4**, 382–4. [§ 2.4.]

FRANKEL, O. H. (1969). Pacific centres of genetic diversity. *Malay. Forester* **32**, 356–60. [§ 19.2.]

GALE, J. (1972*a*). Effect of altitude on the availability of CO_2 for photosynthesis. Theoretical considerations. *Ecology* **53**, 494–7. [§ 16.5.]

—— (1972*b*). Elevation and transpiration: some theoretical considerations with special reference to Mediterranean-type climate. *J. appl. Ecol.* **9**, 691–701. [§ 16.5.]

GANE, M. (1970). Hurricane risk assessment in Fiji. *Commonw. For. Rev.* **49**, 253–6. [§ 6.1.]

GARNER, W. W. and ALLARD, H. A. (1923). Further studies in photoperiodism, the response of the plant to relative length of day and night. *J. agric. Res.* **23**, 871–920. [§ 4.1.]

GATES, D. M. (1969). The ecology of an elfin forest in Puerto Rico. 4. Transpiration rates and temperatures of leaves in cool humid environment. *J. Arnold Arbor* **50**, 93–8. [§ 16.5.]

GAUSSEN, H., LEGRIS, P., and BLASCO, F. (1967). *Bioclimats du sud-est Asiatique.* Institut Français Pondicherry Travaux, Section Scientifique et Technique 3. [§ 3.2.]

GEERTS, H. C. (1963). *Agricultural involution.* Berkeley. [§ 18.1.]

GERASSIMOV, P. and IVANOVA, E. N. (1959). Three scientific trends in the study of the general problem of soil classification and the inter relation between these trends. *Soils Fertil.* **22**, 239–48. [Chapter 9.]

GILLETT, J. B. (1962). Pest pressure, an underestimated factor in evolution. *Syst. Ass. Pubns* **4**, 37–46. [§ 2.8.]

GILLISON, A. N. (1969). Plant succession in an irregularly fired grassland area, Doma Peaks region, Papua. *J. Ecol.* **57**, 415–28. [§ 16.2.]

—— (1970). Structure and floristics of a montane grassland/forest transition, Doma Peaks region, Papua. *Blumea* **18**, 71–79. [§ 16.2.]

GOODCHILD, D. J., BJÖRKMAN, O., and PYLIOTIS, N. A. (1972). Chloroplast ultrastructure, leaf anatomy, and content of chlorophyll and soluble protein in rain forest species. *Carn. Inst. Yb. 1971–2* **71**, 102–7. [§ 8.4.]

GOPINATHAN, B. (1968). Terrace and alluvial soils in West Malaysia. *Proceedings of the Malaysian Soils Conference,* Vol. 3, pp. 45–50. [§ 9.10.]

GRAY, A. P. (1944). Ecology. Imperata cylindrica, *taxonomy, distribution, economic significance and control,* Chap. 4. Imperial Agriculture Bureaux Joint Publication 7. Imperial Agricultural Bureau, Oxford and Aberystwyth. [§ 18.1.]

GRAY, B. (1972). Economic tropical forest entomology. *A. Rev. Ent.* **17**, 313–54. [§ 2.8.]

—— (1973). *Distribution of* Araucaria *in Papua, New Guinea.* Dept. of Forestry, Papua, New Guinea, Research Bulletin 1. [§ 14.2.]

GREENLAND, D. J. and KOWAL, J. M. L. (1960). Nutrient content of the moist tropical forest of Ghana. *Pl. Soil* **12**, 154–74. [§ 19.1.]

GREIG-SMITH, P. (1971). Application of numerical methods

to tropical forests. In *Statistical ecology* 3 (eds G. P. Patil, E. C. Pielou, and W. E. Waters). Pennsylvania State University Press. [Chapter 15.]

—— AUSTIN, M. P., and WHITMORE, T. C. (1967). The application of quantitative methods of vegetation survey. I. Association analysis and principal component ordination of rain forest. *J. Ecol.* **53**, 483–503. [§ 6.3; Chapter 15; § 15.3.]

GRIJPMA, D. (1967). *Anthocephalus cadamba*, a fast growing industrial tree species for the tropics. *Turrialba* **17**, 321–9. [§7.2.]

GRIJPMA, P. (1969). *Eucalyptus deglupta*, a promising forest species for the humid tropics of Latin America. *Turrialba* **19**, 267–83. [§ 7.2.]

GRIST, D. H. (1953). *Rice*. Longman-Green, London. [§ 18.1.]

GRUBB, P. J. (1971). Interpretation of the 'Massenerhebung' effect on tropical mountains. *Nature* **229**, 44–6. [§ 16.5.]

—— (1974). Factors controlling the distribution of forest types on tropical mountains—new facts and a new perspective. In *Altitudinal zonation of forests in Malesia* (ed. J. R. Flenley). Department of Geography, University of Hull. [§§ 9.12, 16.1, 16.6; Fig. 10.14.]

—— LLOYD, J. R., PENNINGTON, T. D., and WHITMORE, T. C. (1963). A comparison of montane and lowland rain forest in Ecuador. I. The forest structure, physiognomy and floristics. *J. Ecol.* **51**, 567–601. [§ 2.6.]

—— and WHITMORE, T. C. (1966). A comparison of montane and lowland forest in Ecuador. II. The climate and its effects on the distribution and physiognomy of the forests. *J. Ecol.* **54**, 303–33. [§§ 16.5, 16.6.]

—— —— (1967). A comparison of montane and lowland forest in Ecuador. III. The light reaching the ground vegetation. *J. Ecol.* **55**, 33–57. [§ 3.6.]

GUHA, M. M. (1969). A preliminary assessment of moisture and nutrients in soil as factors for production of vegetation in West Malaysia. *Malay. Forester* **32**, 423–33. [§§ 3.3, 3.4.]

HADFIELD, W. (1974*a*). Shade in North-East Indian tea plantations. I. The shade pattern. *J. appl. Ecol.* **11**, 151–78. [§§ 8.1, 10.3.]

—— (1974*b*). Shade in North-East Indian tea plantations. II. Foliar illumination and canopy characteristics. *J. appl. Ecol.* **11**, 179–99. [§§ 8.1, 10.3.]

—— (1975). Shade in North-East Indian tea plantations. III. Leaf temperatures in the field. *J. appl. Ecol.* (In press.) [§§ 8.1, 10.3.]

HADLEY, C. J. (1959). *A study of girth with age in sample plots of Kauri pine (Agathis macrophylla) in the Solomon Islands*. Special subject thesis, Dept. Forestry, Oxford University. [§ 8.2.]

HAIG, I. T., HUBERMAN, M. A., and AUNG DIN, U. (1958). Tropical silviculture. I. *Forestry and forest products studies*, No. 13. F.A.O., Rome. [§ 12.2.]

HAILE, N. S. (1971). Quaternary shorelines in West Malaysia and adjacent parts of the Sunda Shelf. *Quaternaria* **15**, 333–43. [§ 1.1.]

HALLÉ, F. (1971). Architecture and growth of tropical trees exemplified by the Euphorbiaceae. *Biotropica* **3**, 56–62. [§ 2.5.]

—— and OLDEMAN, R. A. A. (1970*a*). Essai sur l'architecture et la dynamique du croissance des arbres tropicaux. *Collect. Monogr. bot. biol. Veget.* **6**. Paris. [§ 2.5.]

—— —— (1975). Essai sur l'architecture et la dynamique du croissance des arbres tropicaux. *Collect. Monogr. bot. biol. Veget.* **6**. (Translation into English by B. C. Stone, currently under publication by University of Malaya Press, Kuala Lumpur.) [§ 2.5.]

HAMILTON, W. (1973). *Tectonics of the Indonesian region*. Bulletin of the Geological Society, Malaysia 6, pp. 3–10. [§ 15.1.]

HARRISON, J. L. (1962). The distribution of feeding habits among animals in a tropical rain forest. *J. anim. Ecol.* **31**, 53–63. [§ 2.7, Fig. 2.26.]

—— (1965). *The effect of forest clearance on small mammals*. Bangkok Conference I.U.C.N. (mimeo.). [Chapter 13.]

HASTENRATH, S. (1968). Certain aspects of the three-dimensional distribution of climate and vegetation belts in the mountains of central America and southern Mexico. *Colloquium geogr.* **9**, 122–30. [§ 16.5.]

HAVEL, J. J. (1962). In: general discussion on 'the nature of the secondary communities resulting from the activities of early man and the methods of their detection'. In *Proceedings of the Symposium on the impact of man on humid tropics vegetation*. UNESCO, Goroka. 1960. [§ 18.2.]

—— (1971). The *Araucaria* forests of New Guinea and their regenerative capacity. *J. Ecol.* **59**, 203–14. [§§ 5.1, 5.2, 14.2; Fig. 14.8.]

—— (1972). New Guinea forests—structure, composition and management. *Aust. For.* **36**, 24–37. [§ 2.8; Fig. 15.3.]

HEATHER, W. A. (1955). The kamarere (*Eucalyptus deglupta*) forests of New Britain. *Emp. For. Rev.* **34**, 255–78. [§ 7.2.]

HELLINGA, G. (1950). Aanplant soorten op bedrijesgrootte. *Tectona* **40**, 196–9. [§ 7.2.]

HENDERSON, M. R. (1939). The flora of the limestone hills of the Malay Peninsula. *J. Malay. Brch R. Asiat. Soc.* **17**, 13–87. [§ 10.4.]

HENWOOD, K. (1973). A structural model of forces in buttressed tropical rain forest trees. *Biotropica* **5**, 83–93. [§ 2.5.]

HERKLOTS, G. A. C. (1972). *Vegetables in south-east Asia*. London. [§ 17.1.]

HERZOG, T. (1950). Hepaticae Borneenses (Oxford University expedition to Sarawak, 1932). *Trans. Br. bryol. Soc.* **1**, 275–326. [§ 10.3.]

HEYLIGERS, P. C. (1965). Vegetation and ecology of the Port Moresby-Kairuka area, Territory of Papua and New Guinea. In *Land Research Series* 14. C.S.I.R.O., Melbourne. [§ 11.4.]

—— (1967). Vegetation and ecology of Bougainville and

Buka islands, Territory of Papua and New Guinea. In *Land Research Series* 20. C.S.I.R.O., Melbourne. [§§ 2.4, 11.4; App.]

—— (1972*a*). Vegetation and ecology of the Aitape-Ambunti area. In *Land Research Series* 30. C.S.I.R.O., Melbourne. [§ 11.4.]

—— (1972*b*). Analysis of the plant geography of the semi-deciduous scrub and forest and the eucalypt savannah near Port Moresby. *Pacif. Sci.* **26**, 229–41. [§ 12.1.]

Ho, R. (1962). Physical geography of the Indo-Australian tropics. In *Proceedings of the Symposium on the impact of man on humid tropics vegetation.* UNESCO, Goroka. [Chapter 3; § 3.1.]

Ho, T. H., SOEPADMO, E., and WHITMORE, T. C. (1971). (ed.) National Parks of Malaysia. *Malay. Nat. J.* **24**, 111–259. [§ 19.3.]

HOLTTUM, R. E. (1940). Periodic leaf change and flowering of trees in Singapore. *Gdns Bull. Straits Settl.* **11**, 119–75. [§ 4.1.]

—— (1949). Gregarious flowering of the terrestrial orchid *Bromheadia finlaysoniana. Gdns Bull., Singapore* **12**, 295–302. [§ 4.1.]

—— (1953). Evolutionary trends in an equatorial climate. *Symp. Soc. exp. Biol.* **7**, 154–73. [§§ 4.1, 5.2.]

—— (1954*a*). *Plant life in Malaya.* Longman–Green, London. [§ 4.1.]

—— (1954*b*). *Adinandra* belukar. *J. trop. Geogr.* **3**, 27–32. [§ 18.2.]

—— (1955). Growth habits of Monocotyledons—variation on a theme. *Phytomorphology* **5**, 399–413. [§ 2.5.]

HORN, H. S. (1971). *The adaptive geometry of trees.* Princeton. [§ 2.5.]

HOSOKAWA, T. (1952). A plant sociological study in the mossy forests of Micronesian islands. *Mem. Fac. Sci. Kyushu Univ.* Series E **1**, 65–82. [§ 12.1; App.]

—— (1954*a*). On the structure and composition of the *Campnosperma* forests in Palau, Micronesia. *Mem. Fac. Sci. Kyushu Univ.* Series E **1**, 199–218. [§ 12.1; App.]

—— (1954*b*). On the *Campnosperma* forests of Yap, Ponape, and Kusaie in Micronesia. *Mem. Fac. Sci. Kyushu Univ.* Series E **1**, 221–43. [§ 12.1; App.]

HOU, H. Y., CHEN, C. T., and WANG, H. P. (1956). The vegetation of China with special reference to the main soil types. *Int. Congr. Soil Sci.* **6**, A 55. [§ 10.1.]

HUSCH, B., MILLER, C. I., and BEERS, T. W. (1972). *Forest mensuration* (2nd edn) Ronald Press, New York. [Chapter 15.]

HYNES, R. A. (1974). Altitudinal zonation in New Guinea *Nothofagus* forest. In *Altitudinal zonation of forests in Malesia* (ed. J. R. Flenley). Department of Geography, University of Hull. [§ 16.1.]

IBRAHIM, S. and GREATHOUSE, T. E. (1972). Foxtailing in exotic pines—preliminary results of a study in West Malaysia. *Malay. Forester* **35**, 17–23. [§ 14.3.]

INGER, R. F. (1966). The systematics and zoogeography of the amphibia of Borneo. *Fieldiana, Zool.* **52**, 1–402. [§ 1.2; Chapter 13.]

—— and BACON, J. P. JR. (1968). Annual reproduction and clutch size in rain forest frogs from Sarawak. *Copeia* **68**, 602–6. [§ 4.2.]

—— and GREENBERG, B. (1963). The annual reproductive pattern of the frog *Rana erythraea* in Sarawak. *Physiol. Zoöl.* **36**, 21–33. [§ 4.2.]

—— —— (1967). Annual reproductive patterns of lizards from a Bornean rain forest. *Ecology* **47**, 100–21. [§ 4.2.]

JACOBS, M. (1962). *Pometia pinnata*: a study in variability. *Reinwardtia* **6**, 109–144. [§ 14.1.]

JANZEN, D. H. (1971*a*). The fate of *Scheelea rostrata* fruits beneath the parent tree: predispersal attack by brucids. *Principes* **15**, 89–101. [§ 2.8.]

—— (1971*b*). Seed predation by animals. *A. Rev. Ecol. System.* **2**, 465–92. [§ 2.8.]

JARRETT, F. M. (1959). Studies in *Artocarpus* and allied genera. III. A revision of *Artocarpus* subgenus *Artocarpus. J. Arnold. Arbor.* **40**, 113–55. [Fig. 1.8.]

JARVIS, P. G. and JARVIS, M. S. (1964). Growth rates of woody plants. *Physiologia Pl.* **17**, 654–66. [§ 8.4.]

JENNINGS, J. N. (1972). The character of tropical humid karst. *Z. Geomorph.* **16**, 336–41. [§ 9.7.]

JENSEN, L. A. (1971). Observations on the viability of Borneo camphorwood *Dryobalanops aromatica* Gaertn. f. In *Proc. Int. Seed Test. Ass.* **36**, 141–6. [§ 5.2.]

JOHNSON, D. S. (1967). Distributional patterns of Malayan freshwater fish. *Ecology* **48**, 722–30. [§ 10.3; Chap. 13.]

JONES, E. W. (1956). Ecological studies on the rain forest of southern Nigeria. IV. The plateau forest of the Okumu Forest Reserve (contd). *J. Ecol.* **44**, 83–117. [§ 5.1.]

KALKMAN, C. and VINK, W. (1970). Botanical exploration in the Doma Peaks region New Guinea. *Blumea* **18**, 87–135. [§ 16.2.]

KALSHOVEN, L. G. E. (1953). Important outbreaks of insect pests in the forests of Indonesia. *Int. Congr. Ent.* **9**, 229–34. [§ 2.8.]

KEAY, R. W. J. (1959). *Vegetation map of Africa. Explanatory notes.* Oxford University Press. [Fig. 1.1.]

—— (1960). Seeds in forest soils. *Niger. For. Inf. Bull.* (n.s.) **4**, 1–12. [§ 6.2.]

KELENY, G. P. (1962). Notes on the origin and introduction of the basic food crops of the New Guinea people. In *Proceedings of the Symposium on the impact of man on humid tropics vegetation.* UNESCO, Goroka. [§ 17.1.]

KELLMAN, M. C. (1970). *Secondary plant succession in tropical montane Mindanao.* Research School for Pacific Studies, Australian National University, Publication BG/2. [§§ 6.2, 18.2.]

KELLOGG, C. E. (1949). Preliminary suggestions for the classification and nomenclature of great soil groups in tropical equatorial regions. *Tech. Commun. Commonw. Bur. Soil Sci.* **45**, 16–35. [Chapter 9.]

KEMMERLING, G. L. L. (1921). De uitbarsting van den G. Keloet in den nacht van den 19den op den 20sten

Mei 1919. *Vulk. Meded. Dienst. Mijnw.* **2**, 1–120. [Fig. 9.10.]

KENG, H. (1972). Coniferae. In *Tree flora of Malaya* (ed. T. C. Whitmore), Vol. 1. Longman, Kuala Lumpur and London. [Chapter 14.]

KENWORTHY, J. B. (1971). Water and nutrient cycling in a tropical rain forest. In *The water relations of Malesian forests* (ed. J. R. Flenley). Department of Geography, University of Hull. [§§ 2.6, 3.3.]

KERFOOT, O. (1963). The root systems of tropical forest trees. *Emp. For. Rev.* **42**, 19–26. [§ 2.5.]

—— (1968). Mist precipitation on vegetation. *For. Abstr.* **29**, 8–20. [§ 16.5.]

KERLING, L. C. (1941). The gregarious flowering of *Zephyranthes rosea* Lindl. *Ann. Jard. Bot., Buitenz.* **51**, 1–42. [§ 4.1.]

KHOO, S. G. (1974). Scale insects and mealy bugs: their biology and control. *Malay. Nat. J.* **27**, 124–30. [§ 2.8.]

KING, K. F. S. (1968). Agri-silviculture (the taungya system). *Bull. Dept. For. Univ. Ibadan* **1**. [Chap. 18.]

KIRA, T. (1969). Primary productivity of tropical rain forest. *Malay. Forester* **32**, 375–84. [§ 8.3.]

—— and OGAWA, H. (1971). Assessment of primary production in tropical and equatorial forests. In *Productivity of forest ecosystems* (ed. P. Duvigneaud). UNESCO, Paris. [§ 8.3.]

—— —— YODA, K., and OGINO, K. (1967). Comparative ecological studies on three main types of forest vegetation in Thailand. IV. Dry matter production, with special reference to the Khao Chong rain forest. *Nature Life S. E. Asia* **5**, 149–74. [§ 8.3.]

—— and SHIDEI, T. (1967). Primary production and turn-over of organic matter in different forest ecosystems of the western Pacific. *Jap. J. Ecol.* **17**, 70–87. [§§ 8.3, 9.12.]

KLINGE, H. (1968). *Report on tropical podzols*. F.A.O., Rome. [§ 9.6.]

KOCHUMMEN, K. M. (1966). Natural plant succession after farming in Sungei Kroh. *Malay. Forester* **29**, 170–81. [§§ 5.1, 6.2, 18.2.]

—— (1972). Annonaceae. In *Tree flora of Malaya* (ed. T. C. Whitmore), Vol. 1. Longman, Kuala Lumpur and London. [§ 2.6.]

KOELMEYER, K. O. (1959, 1960). The periodicity of leaf change and flowering in the principal forest communities of Ceylon. *Ceylon Forester* **4**, 157–89, 308–64. [§ 4.1.]

KÖPPEN, W. (1918). Klassifikation der Klimate nach Temperatur, Niederschlag und Jahreslauf. *Petermanns Mitt.* **64**, 193. [Chapter 3.]

—— (1936). Das geographische System der Klimate. In *Handbuch der Klimatologie* (eds. W. Köppen, and W. Geiger). Vol. 1, Teil C. Berlin. [Chapter 3.]

KORIBA, K. (1958). On the periodicity of tree growth in the tropics with reference to the mode of branching, the leaf fall and the formation of the resting bud. *Gdns Bull., Singapore* **17**, 11–81. [§§ 2.5, 4.1.]

KOSTERMANS, A. J. G. H. (1972). A synopsis of the Old World species of *Trichospermum*, Tiliaceae. *Trans. Proc. bot. Soc. Edinb.* **41**, 401–30. [§ 6.2.]

KOWAL, N. E. (1966). Shifting cultivation, fire and pine forests in the Cordillera Central Luzon, Philippines. *Ecol. Monogr.* **36**, 389–419. [§§ 14.3, 18.2, 19.3; Fig. 3.2, Fig. 3.3, Fig. 14.1.]

KRAMER, F. (1926). Onderzoek naar de natuurlijke verjonging in den uitkap in Preanger gebergte-bosch. *Med. Proefst. Boschw. Bogor* **14**. [§ 6.2.]

—— (1933). De natuurlijke verjonging in het Goenoeng Gedeh complex. *Tectona* **26**, 156–85. [§ 6.2.]

LAMB, H. H. (1972). *Climate, present, past and future*, Vol. 1. Methuen, London. [§ 6.1.]

LANDON, F. H. (1955). Malayan tropical rain forest. *Malay. Forester* **18**, 30–8. [§ 6.5.]

LEAMY, M. L. (1966). *Proposals for a technical classification of Malayan soils*. Malayan Soil Survey Report 3. Ministry of Agriculture and Co-operatives, Kuala Lumpur. [§§ 9.2, 9.3.]

—— and PANTON, W. P. (1966). Soil survey manual for Malayan conditions. *Bull. Ministry of Agric. Co-op. Malaysia. Div. Agric.* **119**. [Chapter 9.]

LEE, K. E. (1969). Some soils of the British Solomon Islands Protectorate. *Phil. Trans. R. Soc. B.* **255**, 211–58. [§§ 9.3, 9.8, 9.12, 15.3, 15.6.]

LEE, P. C. (1967). *Ecological studies on* Dryobalanops aromatica *Gaertn. f.* Ph.D. thesis, University of Malaya. [§ 15.3.]

LEMÉE, G. (1961). Effets des caractères du sol sur la localisation de la végétation en zones équatoriale et tropicale humide. In *Proceedings of the Symposium on tropical soils and vegetation, Abidjan*. UNESCO, Paris. [§ 9.1.]

LEO, C. and LEE, H. S. (1971). The alan (*Shorea albida*) resources, their properties and utilisation. *Malay. Forester* **34**, 20–35. [§ 11.3.]

LEVIN, D. A. (1971). Plant phenolics: an ecological perspective. *Am. Nat.* **105**, 157–81. [§ 2.8.]

LIEW, T. C. (1971). Letter to the editor. *Malay. Forester* **34**, 154–5. [§ 7.1.]

—— and WONG, F. O. (1973). Density, recruitment, mortality and growth of dipterocarp seedlings in virgin and logged-over forests in Sabah. *Malay. Forester* **36**, 3–15. [§ 6.5.]

LIM, B. L. (1970). Distribution, relative abundance, food habits and parasite patterns of giant rats (*Rattus*) in West Malaysia. *J. Mammal.* **51**, 730–40. [§ 16.7.]

LIZARDO, L. (1957). The Philippine pine forests. In *Trop. Silvic.* **2**, 57. [§ 14.3.]

LLOYD, M., INGER, R. F., and KING, F. W. (1968). On the diversity of reptile and amphibian species in a Bornean rain forest. *Am. Nat.* **102**, 497–516. [§ 1.2.]

LOCKWOOD, J. G. (1971). Does Malaysia really have a hot wet climate? In *The water relations of Malesian forests* (ed. J. R. Flenley). Department of Geography, University of Hull. [§ 3.4.]

LOETSCH, F., ZOHRER, F., and HALLER, K. E. (1964). *Forest inventory*, Vol. 1 *Statistics of forest inventory and information from aerial photographs* (transl. E. Brunig and

B. Brunig). BLV Verlagsgesellschaft, Munich. [Chapter 15.]

——— ——— (1973). *Forest inventory*, Vol. 2 (transl. K. F. Panzer). Munich. [Chapter 15.]

LÖHR, E. (1969). Respirations intensität in Stämmen, Zweigen und Blättern von Laubbäumen im tropischen Regenwald und in temperierten Wäldern. *Physiologia Pl.* **22**, 86–93. [§ 8.3.]

—— and MÜLLER, D. (1968). Blatt-Atmung der höheren Bodenpflanzen im tropischen Regenurwald. *Physiologia Pl.* **21**, 673–765. [§ 8.4.]

LOW, K. S., and GOH, K. C. (1972). The water balance of five catchments in Selangor, West Malaysia. *J. trop. Geogr.* **35**, 60–6. [§ 3.3.]

LOWE-MCCONNELL, R. H. (1969). (ed.) Speciation in tropical environments. *Biol. J. Linnean. Soc., Lond.* **1**, 1–246. [§ 2.8.]

LOWRY, J. B. (1971). Conserving the forest—a phytochemical view. *Malay. Nat. J.* **24**, 225–30. [§ 19.2.]

MABBETT, H. (1973). Tourist invasion took travel industry unawares. In Supplement on Malaysia, 31 August 1973. *The Times, London*. [§ 19.2.]

MCCLURE, H. E. (1966). Flowering, fruiting and animals in the canopy of a tropical rain forest. *Malay. Forester* **29**, 182–203. [§§ 2.8, 4.1.]

—— (1969). An estimation of a bird population in the primary forest of Selangor, Malaysia. *Malay. Nat. J.* **22**, 179–83. [Chapter 13.]

MACKINNON, J. A. (1971). The orang utan in Sabah today. *Oryx* **11**, 141–91. [§ 2.7.]

—— (1972). *The behaviour and ecology of the orang utan* (Pongo pygmaeus). D.Phil. thesis, Oxford University. [§§ 2.7, 17.1, 17.4; Fig. 2.26.]

—— (1974). The behaviour and ecology of wild orang utan, *Pongo pygmaeus. Anim. Behav.* **22**, 3–74. [§ 2.7.]

MCNAE, W. (1968). A general account of the fauna and flora of mangrove swamps and forests in the Indo-West-Pacific. *Adv. Marine Biol.* **6**, 74–270. [§ 11.1.]

MCVEAN, D. N. (1974). Mountain climates of the southwest Pacific. In *Altitudinal zonation of forests in Malesia* (ed. J. R. Flenley). Department of Geography, University of Hull. [§§ 16.2, 16.5.]

MANAPUTTY, D. N. (1955). Keluarga *Agathis* di Indonesia. *Rimba Indonesia* **4**, 132–88. [§§ 10.3, 14.1.]

MARTEN, K. D. (1972). *A summary of the performance of various species in Departmental trial plots*. Forest Dept., British Solomon Islands, Technical note 1/72. [Table 8.3.]

MARTIN, W. E., VLAMIS, J., and STICE, W. W. (1953). Field correction of calcium deficiency on a serpentine soil. *J. Am. Soc. Agron.* **48**, 204–8. [§ 9.8.]

MASTAN, K. M. (1969). *Prospects of* Anthocephalus cadamba (*Roxb.*) *Miq. as a plantation species*. Special subject thesis, Commonwealth Forestry Institute, Oxford. [§ 7.2.]

MATTHEW, K. M. (1971). The flowering of the strobilanth, Acanthaceae. *J. Bombay nat. Hist. Soc.* **67**, 502–6. [§ 4.1.]

MATHUR, J. B. L. (1973). *Teak bibliography*. Forest Research Institute and Colleges, Dehra Dun. [§ 12.2.]

MAYR, E. (1944). Wallace's line in the light of recent zoogeographic studies. *Q. Rev. Biol.* **19**, 1–14. [§ 1.2; Fig. 1.9.]

MEDWAY, LORD (1960). The Malay tapir in Quaternary Borneo. *Sarawak Mus. J.* **9**, 364–7. [§ 1.2.]

—— (1964). The fauna. In *Malaysia—a survey*, Chapter 3 (ed. W. Gungwu). London. [§ 16.7.]

—— (1969). *The wild mammals of Malaya*. Oxford University Press, Kuala Lumpur. [§§ 1.2, 2.8, 5.1, 6.1, 8.3, 16.7.]

—— (1971). Importance of Taman Negara in the conservation of mammals. *Malay. Nat. J.* **24**, 212–4. [§ 19.3.]

—— (1972a). Phenology of a tropical rain forest in Malaya. *Biol. J. Linnean. Soc., Lond.* **4**, 117–46. [§§ 2.8, 4.1, 4.2; Table 4.1, Table 4.2, Table 4.3.]

—— (1972b). The quaternary mammals of Malesia: a review. *The quaternary era in Malesia* (eds P. Ashton and M. Ashton). Department of Geography, University of Hull. [§§ 1.2, 15.1.]

—— (1972c). *The quaternary era in Malesia* (eds P. Ashton and M. Ashton), p. 61. Department of Geography, University of Hull. [Chapter 13.]

—— (1972d). The Gunong Benom expedition 1967. 6. The distribution and altitudinal zonation of birds and mammals on Gunong Benom. *Bull. Br. Mus. nat. Hist. D.* **23**, 105–54. [§ 16.7.]

—— and WELLS, D. R. (1971). Diversity and density of birds and mammals at Kuala Lompat, Pahang. *Malay. Nat. J.* **24**, 238–47. [Chap. 13; § 17.4; Table 19.1.]

MEEUWEN, M. S. VAN, NOOTEBOOM, H. P. and STEENIS, C. G. G. J. VAN (1961). Preliminary revisions of some genera of Malaysian Papilionaceae. *Reinwardtia* **5**, 419–56. [§ 12.1; Fig. 12.3.]

MEIJER, W. (1959). Plant sociological analysis of montane rain forest near Tjibodas, west Java. *Acta. bot. neerl.* **8**, 277–91. [§ 8.2.]

—— (1961). On the flora of Mount Sago near Pajakumboh, central Sumatra. *Penggemar Alam* **40**, 3–13. [§ 16.4.]

—— (1965). Forest types in North Borneo and their economic aspects. In *Proceedings of the Symposium on ecological research into humid tropics vegetation.* UNESCO, Kuching. [§ 10.5; App.]

—— (1969). Fruit trees in Sabah (North Borneo). *Malay. Forester* **32**, 252–65. [§ 17.1.]

—— (1971). Plant life in Kinabalu National Park. *Malay. Nat. J.* **24**, 184–9. [§§ 10.5, 16.2; App.]

—— and WOOD, G. H. S. (1964). Dipterocarps of Sabah. *Sabah For. Rec.* **5**. [§ 15.4.]

MEIJER DREES, E. (1940). The genus *Agathis* in Malaysia. *Bull. Jard. bot., Buitenz.* **16**, 455–74. [§ 14.1.]

MERRILL, E. D. (1945). *Plant life of the Pacific world*. Macmillan, New York. [§§ 2.5, 2.8, 7.2, 15.3, 17.1; Fig. 15.8.]

MITCHELL, B. A. (1963). Forestry and tanah beris. *Malay. Forester* **26**, 160–70. [§ 10.3.]

MOHR, E. C. J. (1933). Debodem der tropen in het

algemeen en die van Ned.-Indie in het bijzonder. *Meded. Kon. Ver. Kol. Inst. Afd. Handelsmuseum* 31, Dl.1, 1e stuk. [§ 3.1.]

—— (1944). *The soils of equatorial regions with special reference to the Netherlands East Indies.* (trans. R. L. Pendleton). J. W. Edward S, Ann Arbor, Michigan. [§ 11.3.]

—— and BAREN, F. A. VAN (1954). *Tropical soils.* Interscience, London. [§ 3.1; Chapter 9; §§ 9.3, 9.4, 9.5, 9.12, 11.3; Fig. 9.9.]

—— —— and SCHUYLENBORGH, J. VAN (1972). *Tropical soils* third edn. Mouton, The Hague. [Chapter 9; §§ 9.5, 9.8.]

MONSALUD, M. R. and LOPEZ, F. R. (1967). Kaatoan bangkal, *Anthocephalus cadamba. Philipp. Lumberm.* 13, 60–4. [§ 7.2.]

MONTEITH, J. L. (1972). Solar radiation and productivity in tropical ecosystems. *J. appl. Ecol.* 9, 747–66. [§ 8.3.]

MOREL, J. (1967). Notes sur le territoire de Papouasie et Nouvelle Guinée. *Bois Forêts Trop.* 115, 15–31. [§§ 2.8, 5.2, 7.1, 14.2; Fig. 17.3.]

MULLER, J. (1965). Palynological study of Holocene peat in Sarawak. In *Proceedings of the Symposium on ecological research into humid tropics vegetation.* UNESCO, Kuching. [§ 11.3.]

—— (1972). Palynological evidence for change in geomorphology, climate and vegetation in the Mio-Pliocene of Malesia. In *The quaternary era in Malesia* (eds P. Ashton and M. Ashton). Department of Geography, University of Hull. [§ 11.3; Chapter 14; Fig. 14.1.]

MÜLLER, D. and NIELSON, J. (1965). Production brute, pertes par respiration et production nette dans la forêt ombrophile tropicale. *Forst. ForsVaes. Danm.* 29, 69–160. [§ 8.3; Fig. 8.6.]

MURPHY, D. H. (1973). Animals in the forest ecosystem. In *Animal life in Singapore* (ed. C. H. Chuang). Singapore. [§§ 2.7, 4.2.]

NG, F. S. P. (1966). Age at first flowering in dipterocarps. *Malay. Forester* 29, 290–5. [§ 4.1.]

—— (1971). *A taxonomic study of the Ebenaceae with reference to Malesia.* D.Phil. thesis, Oxford University. [§ 12.3.]

NICHOLSON, D. I. (1958). One year's growth of *Shorea smithiana* in North Borneo. *Malay. Forester* 21, 193–6. [§§ 4.1, 8.1.]

—— (1960). Light requirements of seedlings of five species of Dipterocarpaceae. *Malay. Forester* 23, 344–56. [§ 5.3.]

—— (1965a). A study of virgin forest near Sandakan, North Borneo. In *Proceedings of the Symposium on ecological research into humid tropics vegetation.* UNESCO, Kuching. [Chapter 7; 8.1; Table 8.4; Chapter 15; § 15.3; Table 15.3; Fig. 8.5.]

—— (1965b). A review of natural regeneration in the dipterocarp forests of Sabah. *Malay. Forester* 28, 4–25. [Table 6.7; § 7.1.]

—— (1970). *Forest management.* Technical Report 3. In *Demonstration and training in forest, forest ranges and watershed management, the Philippines.* F.A.O., Rome. [§§ 6.2, 7.1, 7.2, 15.2, 19.1.]

NIEUWOLT, S. (1965). Evaporation and water balances in Malaya. *J. trop. Geogr.* 20, 34–53. [§§ 3.4, 15.3; Fig. 3.4.]

—— (1966). A comparison of rainfall in the exceptionally dry year 1963 and average conditions in Malaya. *Erdkunde* 20, 169–81. [§ 3.5.]

NIKLES, D. G. (1973). Biology and genetic improvement of *Araucaria cunninghamii* Ait. in Queensland, Australia. In *Selection and breeding to improve some tropical conifers* (eds J. Burley and D. G. Nikles), vol. 2. Commonwealth Forestry Institute Oxford and Department of Forestry, Queensland. [§ 14.2.]

NISBET, I. C. T. (1968). The utilization of mangroves by Malayan birds. *Ibis* 110, 348–52. [Chapter 13; § 11.1.]

NTIMA, O. O. (1968). The araucarias. *Timber trees of the lowland tropics* 3. Department of Forestry, Oxford. [§§ 5.2, 14.2.]

NYE, P. H. and GREENLAND, D. J. (1960). The soils under shifting cultivation. *Tech. Commun. Commonw. Bur. Soil Sci.* 51. [§§ 2.5, 9.1, 18.1.]

ODUM, H. T. (1970). Rain forest structure and mineral cycling homeostasis. In *A tropical rain forest* (eds H. T. Odum and R. F. Pigeon). U.S. Atomic Energy Commission, Tennessee. [§§ 2.5, 2.6.]

—— LUGO, A., CINTRON, G., and JORDAN, C. F. (1970). Metabolism and evapotranspiration of some rain forest plants and soils. In *A tropical rain forest* (eds H. T. Odum and R. F. Pigeon). U.S. Atomic Energy Commission, Oak Ridge, Tennessee. [§ 8.4.]

OGAWA, H., YODA, K., KIRA, T., OGINO, K., SHIDEI, T., RATANAWONGSE, D., and APASUTAYA, C. (1965a). Comparative ecological study on three main forest types of forest vegetation in Thailand. I. Structure and floristic composition. *Nature Life S.E. Asia* 4, 13–48. [§ 8.3.]

—— —— —— —— —— (1965b). Comparative ecological studies on three main types of forest vegetation in Thailand. II. Plant Biomass. *Nature Life S.E. Asia* 4, 49–80. [§ 8.3.]

ORYNESS, C. T. (1967). Erodibility and erosion potential of forest watersheds. In *Proceedings of the International Symposium on forest hydrology, Oxford.* [§ 6.1.]

PAA, N. F. and GERARDO, J. A. (1968). Silvic characteristics of kaatoan bangkal *Anthocephalus cadamba* (Roxb.) Miq. *Philipp. Lumberm.* 14, 57–63. [§ 7.2.]

PAIJMANS, K. (1967). Vegetation of the Safia-Pongani area. In *Land Research Series* 17. C.S.I.R.O., Melbourne. [§§ 11.4, 14.2, 15.2.]

—— (1969). Vegetation and ecology of the Kerema–Vailala area, territory of Papua and New Guinea. *Land Research Series* 23. C.S.I.R.O., Melbourne. [§§ 10.4, 11.4.]

—— (1970). An analysis of four tropical rain forest sites in New Guinea. *J. Ecol.* 58, 77–101. [Fig. 1.3, Fig. 1.5.]

—— (1971). Vegetation, forest resources and ecology of the Morehead–Kiunga area, territory of Papua and New

Guinea. In *Land Research Series* 29. C.S.I.R.O., Melbourne. [§§ 11.4, 15.2, 15.3.]

PANTON, W. P. (1957). Types of Malayan laterite and factors affecting their distribution. *Int. Congr. Soil Sci.* 6 (5), 419–23. [§ 9.4.]

PARKHURST, D. F. and LOUCKS, O. L. (1972). Optimal leaf size in relation to environment. *J. Ecol.* **60**, 505–37. [Chapter 10.]

PATON, T. R. (1961). A reconnaissance soil survey of the Semporna peninsula, North Borneo. *Colonial Research studies* 36. Dept. Technical Co-operation, London. [§ 9.3.]

PEAKE, J. F. (1969). Patterns in the distribution of Melanesian land mollusca. *Phil. Trans. R. Soc. B* **255**, 285–306. [§ 15.1.]

PELINCK, E. (1970). An analysis of commercial out turn from forest reserves in West Malaysia. *Malay. Forester* **33**, 374–86. [§ 15.3.]

PELZER, K. J. (1945). *Pioneer settlement in the Asiatic tropics*. American Geographical Society special publication. 29. New York. [§§ 17.1, 18.1.]

PENDLETON, R. C. (1946). Analysis of some Siamese laterites. *Soil Sci.* **62**, 423–40. [§ 9.11.]

PENMAN, H. L. (1949). The dependence of transpiration on weather and soil conditions. *J. Soil Sci.* **1**, 74–89. [§ 3.1.]

PENMAN, H. L. (1949). The dependence of transpiration on weather and soil conditions. *J. Soil Sci.* **1**, 74–89. [§ 3.1.]

—— (1956). Estimating evaporation. *Trans. Am. geophys. Un.* **37**, 43–50. [§ 3.1.]

—— (1963). Vegetation and hydrology. *Tech. Commun. Commonw. Bur. Soil Sci.* **53**. [§ 3.1.]

PIJL, L. VAN DER (1956). Remarks on pollination by bats in the genera *Freycinetia*, *Duabanga* and *Haplophragma* and on chireptophily in general. *Acta bot. neerl.* **5**, 135–44. [§ 2.8.]

—— (1957). The dispersal of plants by bats (chiropterochory). *Acta bot. neerl.* **6**, 291–315. [§ 2.8.]

—— (1969). *The principles of dispersal in higher plants*. Berlin. [§ 2.8.]

POLAK, B. (1933*a*). Een tocht in het zandsteen gebied bij Mandor (West Borneo). *Trop. Natuur* **22**, 23–8. [§ 11.3.]

—— (1933*b*). Ueber torf und moor in Niederlandisch Indien. *Verh. K. Akad. Wet.* **30**, 1–85. [§ 11.3.]

POORE, M. E. D. (1961). River control and conservation in Malaysia. In *Nature conservation in western Malaysia* (eds J. Wyatt-Smith and P. R. Wycherley). Malayan Nature Society, Kuala Lumpur. [§ 19.2.]

—— (1963). Problems in the classification of tropical rain forest. *J. trop. Geogr.* **17**, 12–19. [§§ 15.4, 15.5.]

—— (1964). Integration in the plant community. *J. Ecol. (Suppl.)* **52**, 213–26. [§ 15.5.]

—— (1968). Studies in Malaysian rain forest. I. The forest on the Triassic sediments in Jengka Forest Reserve. *J. Ecol.* **56**, 143–96. [§§ 2.3, 4.1, 5.1, 15.2, 15.3, 15.5; Fig. 15.7, Fig. 15.15.]

PRANCE, G. T. and WHITMORE, T. C. (1973). Rosaceae.

In *Tree flora of Malaya* (ed. T. C. Whitmore), Vol. 2. Longman, Kuala Lumpur and London. [§§ 3.5, 15.4.]

PRESCOTT, J. A. and PENDLETON, R. L. (1952). Laterite and lateritic soils. *Tech. Commun. Commonw. Bur. Soil Sci.* **47**. [§ 9.4.]

PRINGLE, S. L. (1969). World supply and demand of hardwoods. In *Proceedings of the Conference on tropical hardwoods, Syracuse*. [Chapter 1; § 17.2.]

PROCTOR, M. C. and YEO, P. F. (1973). *The pollination of flowers*. Collins, London. [§ 2.8.]

RAO, A. N. (1973). Studies on growth of certain trees in Singapore. *Proc. of the Precongress Conference Bogor, of the Pacific Science Association 1971*. [§ 4.1.]

RAUNKIAER, C. (1934). *The life forms of plants and statistical plant geography*. Oxford University Press. [§§ 6.2, 16.4; Table 16.1.]

RAVEN, P. H. and AXELROD, D. I. (1972). Plate tectonics and Australasian paleobiogeography. *Science, N.Y.* **176**, 1379–86. [§ 15.1.]

REYNDERS, J. J. (1964*a*). *A pedo-ecological study of soil genesis in the tropics from sea level to eternal snow. Snow Mountains, central New Guinea*. Brill, Leiden. [§§ 9.7, 9.12.]

—— (1964*b*). A soil sequence in the tropics from sea level to eternal snow. *Int. Congr. Soil Sci.* **8** (5), 733–9. [§§ 9.12, 10.3, 10.4, 14.1.]

RICHARDS, P. W. (1936). Ecological observations on the rain forest of Mount Dulit, Sarawak. I, II. *J. Ecol.* **24**, 1–37, 340–60. [§ 10.3; App.]

—— (1952). *The tropical rain forest*. Cambridge University Press. [Preface, §§ 2.2, 2.5, 2.6, 3.1, 3.2, 3.6, 5.1, 10.3, 11.1, 11.3, 11.4, 12.1; Chapter 15; §§ 15.5, 16.1, 16.6; Chapter 18; Fig. 1.1, Fig. 1.5.]

—— (1961). The types of vegetation of the humid tropics in relation to the soil. In *Proceedings of the Symposium on tropical soils and vegetation, Abidjan*. UNESCO, Paris. [§ 10.3.]

—— (1962). Plant life and tropical climate. In *Biometeorology*. Pergamon Press, Oxford.

—— (1963). What the tropics can contribute to ecology. *J. Ecol.* **51**, 231–43. [Chap. 15.]

—— (1970). *The life of the jungle*. McGraw-Hill, New York and London. [§ 19.3.]

RICHARDSON, S. D. (1966). *Forestry in communist China*. Johns Hopkins Press, Baltimore. [§§ 10.1, 17.2.]

—— (1970). Gene pools in forestry. In *Genetic resources in plants* (eds O. H. Frankel and E. Bennett). London. [§ 19.3.]

RIDLEY, H. N. (1893). On the flora of the eastern coast of the Malay Peninsula. *Trans. Linn. Soc., Lond. (Bot.)* Ser. II, **3**, 367–408. [§ 15.3.]

—— (1930). *Dispersal of plants throughout the world*. Reeve, Ashford. [§§ 2.8, 5.1.]

RIDLEY, W. F. and GARDNER, A. (1961). Fires in rain forest. *Aust. J. Sci.* **23**, 227–8. [Chap. 18.]

ROBBINS, R. G. (1968*a*). The biogeography of tropical rain forest in south east Asia. *Proceedings of the Sym-*

posium on recent advances in tropical ecology. Varanasi. Vol. 2, 521–35. [§ 16.1.]

—— (1968*b*). Vegetation of the Wewak–Lower Sepik area, Territory of Papua and New Guinea. In *Land Research Series* 22. C.S.I.R.O., Melbourne. [§ 11.4.]

—— (1969). A prerequisite to understanding tropical rain forest. *Malay. Forester* 32, 361–7. [§ 16.1.]

—— and Pullen, R. (1965). Vegetation of the Wabag–Tari area, territory of Papua and New Guinea. In *Land Research Series* 15. C.S.I.R.O., Melbourne. [§ 10.4; Chapter 14; § 16.1.]

—— and WYATT-SMITH, J. (1964). Dry land forest Formations and forest types in the Malay peninsula. *Malay. Forester* 27, 188–217. [§ 10.3; Fig. 16.2; App.]

ROBINSON, M. E. (1934). The flowering of *Strobilanthes* in 1934. *J. Bombay nat. Hist. Soc.* 38, 117–22. [§ 4.1.]

ROLLET, B. (1972). La végétation du Cambodge. *Bois Forêts Trop.* 144, 3–15; 145, 23–38; 146, 3–20. [§ 12.3; App.]

ROSAYRO, R. E. de (1962). The nature and origin of secondary vegetational communities in Ceylon. In *Proceedings of the Symposium on the impact of man on humid tropics vegetation*, UNESCO, Goroka. [§ 17.1.]

ROTHSCHILD, M. (1971). Some observations on the relationship between plants, toxic insects and birds. In *Phytochemical ecology* (ed. J. B. Harborne). Academic Press, London. [§ 2.8.]

ROYEN, P. VAN (1963). *The vegetation of the island of New Guinea.* Department of Forests, Lae (mimeo.). [§§ 10.4, 10.5, 14.1.]

RUINEN, J. (1953). Epiphytosis, a second view on epiphytism. *Ann. Bogor.* 1, 101–58. [§ 2.6.]

SANTAPAU, J. (1962). Gregarious flowering of *Strobilanthes* and bamboos. *J. Bombay nat. Hist. Soc.* 59, 688–95. [§ 4.1.]

SARAWAK SOIL SURVEY STAFF (1966). *A classification of Sarawak soils.* Technical paper 2. Research Branch Dept. Agriculture, Kuching, Sarawak. [§ 9.2.]

SARGENT, K. (1970). *Forest industries development Malaysia. An analysis of problems affecting the development of forestry and forest industry in west Malaysia.* Technical Report 1, F.A.O., Rome. [§ 17.3.]

SARLIN, P. (1963). La pedologie forestiere applique aux reboisements. *Bois Forêts Trop.* 90, 17–31. [§ 12.2.]

SCHIMPER, A. F. W. (1898). *Pflanzengeographie auf physiologischer Grundlage.* Jena. [Preface; Chapter 1.]

—— (1903). *Plant-geography upon a physiological basis* (transl. W. R. Fisher, P. Groom, and I. B. Balfour). Oxford University Press. [Preface; Chapter 1; § 12.1.]

—— (1935). *Pflanzengeographie auf physiologischer Grundlage* (3rd edn) (revised F. C. van Faber). Jena. [§ 12.1.]

SCHMIDT, F. H. and FERGUSON, J. H. A. (1951). Rainfall types based on wet and dry period ratios for Indonesia with western New Guinea. *Verh. Djawatan Met. dan Geofisik. Djakarta* 42. [§ 3.1; Fig. 3.1.]

—— —— and GAREY, W. (1962). Salt balance in mangroves. *Pl. Physiol., Lancaster* 37, 722–9. [§ 11.1.]

SCHOLANDER, P. F., BRADSTREET, E. D., HAMMEL, H. T., and HEMMINGSEN, E. A. (1966). Sap concentrations in halophytes and some other plants. *Pl. Physiol. Lancaster* 41, 429–32. [§ 11.1.]

—— HAMMEL, H. T., HEMMINGSEN, E. A., and BRADSTREET, E. D. (1964). Hydrostatic pressure and osmotic potential in leaves of mangroves and some other plants. *Proc. natn. Acad. Sci. U.S.A.* 52, 119–25. [§ 11.1.]

SCHULZ, J. P. (1960). Ecological studies on the rain forest of northern Surinam, *The vegetation of Surinam*, Vol. 2. North-Holland, Amsterdam. [§§ 3.6, 4.1.]

SCHUYLENBORGH, J. VAN and RUMMELEN, F. F. F. E. VAN (1955). The genesis and classification of mountain soils developed on tuffs in Indonesia. *Neth. J. agric. Sci.* 3, 192–45. [§ 9.12.]

SELF, M. B. and TRENAMAN, K. W. (1972). *Wood remaining after logging (Kolombangara area and Viru/Kalena).* British Solomon Islands Forestry Department Technical Note 2/72. [Table 1.1.]

SETTEN, G. G. K. (1953). The incidence of buttressing among Malayan tree species when of commercial size. *Malay. Forester* 16, 219–21. [§ 2.5.]

—— (1954*a*). *The height of buttress structure on trees of kempas,* Koompassia malaccensis *Maing. ex Benth.* Malayan Forestry Department Research Pamphlet 11. [§ 2.5.]

—— (1954*b*). *The effect of situation on the height of buttress structure on trees of* Shorea parvifolia *Dyer,* Shorea leprosula *Miq.,* Shorea curtisii *Dyer ex King,* Dryobalanops aromatica *Gaertn. f. and* Koompassia malaccensis *Maing. ex Benth.* Malayan Forestry Department Research Pamphlet 12. [§ 2.5.]

SHIM, P. S. (1973). *Octomeles sumatrana* in plantation trials in Sabah. *Malay. Forester* 36, 16–21. [§ 7.2.]

SIBIRTSEV, N. M. (1899). *Pochvovedenie* (Soil Science). St. Petersburg. Reprinted 1951 in *Izbranye sochineniya*, Vol. 1. Sel' Khozgiz, Moscow. [Chapter 9.]

SINGH, K. G. (1966). Ectotrophic mycorrhiza in equatorial rain forests. *Malay. Forester* 29, 13–18. [§ 2.5.]

SIVARAJASINGHAM, S., ALEXANDER, L. T., CADY, J. G., and CLINE, M. G. (1962). Laterite. *Adv. Agron.* 14, 1–60. [§ 9.4.]

SMITH, A.M. (1909). On the internal temperature of leaves in tropical insolation, with special reference to the effect of their colour on the temperature; also observations on the periodicity of the appearance of young coloured leaves of trees growing in Peradeniya Gardens. *Ann. R. bot. Gdns Peradeniya* 4, 229–98. [§ 4.1.]

SMITINAND, T. and LAMPHUN, A. N. (1967). *Map of Thailand showing types of forest* (1:250 000). Environmental Science Division, Thai Military Research and Development Center. [§ 12.3; Fig. 12.4.]

SOCHARLAN, A. (1967). Preliminary stand table of *Anthocephalus cadamba* Miq. *Rimba Indonesia* 12, 37–46. [§ 7.2; Fig. 8.2.]

SOERIANEGARA, I. (1970). Soil investigation in Mt. Hondje F.R. W. Java. *Pengum. Lemb. Pusat Penjel. Kehut.* 93. Also in *Rimba Indonesia* 15, 1–16. [§ 18.1.]

SOIL SURVEY STAFF (1951). *Soil survey manual.* Handbook 18, U.S. Dept. Agriculture, Washington. [Chapter 9.]

—— (1960). *Soil classification, a comprehensive system, 7th approximation.* Soil Conservation Service, U.S. Dept. Agriculture, Washington. [Chapter 9; §§ 9.1, 9.10.]

—— (1967). *Supplement to soil classification system, 7th approximation.* Soil Conservation Service, U.S. Dept. Agriculture, Washington. [Chapter 9; 9.1, 9.3, 9.10, 9.11, 9.12; Table 9.1, Table 9.2.]

—— (1968). *Supplement to soil classification system, 7th approximation, histosols.* Soil Conservation Service, U.S. Dept. Agriculture, Washington. [§ 11.3.]

SPENCE, D. H. N. and MILLAR, E. A. (1963). An experimental study of the infertility of a Shetland serpentine soil. *J. Ecol.* **51**, 333–43. [§ 9.8.]

SPENCER, J. E. (1966). *Shifting cultivation in southeastern Asia.* University of California Press, San Francisco. [§ 18.1; Fig. 18.2.]

STACEY, D. L. (1969). South east Asia's forests—their significance to Australia. *Aust. Timb. J.* **35**, 129–45. [Table 17.2; Fig. 17.3.]

STADELMAN, R. C. (1969). Hardwood timber supply—south east Asia. In *Proceedings of the Conference on tropical hardwoods, Syracuse.* [§ 17.2; Fig. 17.3.]

STAINTON, J. D. A. (1972). *Forests of Nepal.* London. [Chapter 1, §§ 7.1, 14.3.]

STAMP, L. D. (1925). *The vegetation of Burma.* Calcutta. [§ 12.1; App.]

STAUFFER, P. H. (1973). Late Pleistocene age indicated for volcanic ash in West Malaysia. *Geolog. Soc. Malaysia Newsletter* **40**, 1–3. [§ 5.1.]

STEBBINS, G. L. (1950). *Variation and evolution in plants.* Columbia, New York. [§ 4.1.]

STEENIS, C. G. G. J. VAN (1934). On the origin of the Malaysian mountain flora 1. *Bull. Jard. bot. Buitenz. sér. 3,* **13**, 135–262. [§ 16.3.]

—— (1935). Open air hothouses in the tropics at 3100 m. *Gdns Bull. Straits Settl.* **9**, 64–9. [§ 16.3.]

—— (1936). On the origin of the Malaysian mountain flora. 3. Analysis of floristical relationships (first instalment). *Bull. Jard. bot. Buitenz. sér. 3,* **14**, 56–72. [§ 16.3.]

—— (1942). Gregarious flowering of *Strobilanthes* (Acanthaceae) in Malaysia. *Ann. R. bot. Gdn, Calcutta* (150th Anniversary volume), 91–7. [§ 4.1.]

—— (1950*a*). The delimitation of Malaysia and its main plant geographical divisions. *Flora Malesiana* Ser. I, 1, *lxx–lxxv.* [§ 1.1; Fig. 1.2.]

—— (1950*b*). On the hierarchy of environmental factors in plant ecology. In *Int. bot. Congr.* 7. [§§ 6.2, 12.1, 17.1; Table 10.1.]

—— (1952). Rheophytes. *Proc. R. Soc. Queensland* **62**, 61–8. [§ 15.3.]

—— (1953). Datiscaceae. *Flora Malesiana* ser. I 4, 382–7. [§§ 7.2, 10.2.]

—— (1957). Outline of vegetation types in Indonesia and some adjacent regions. *Proc. Pacif. Sci. Congr.* 8 (4), 61–97. [§§ 10.3, 10.6, 11.3, 11.4, 12.1, 12.2, 14.3, 15.3.]

—— (1958*a*). *Vegetation map of Malaysia* (in collaboration with UNESCO Humid Tropics Research Project). [§ 15.3.]

—— (1958*b*). Rejuvenation as a factor for judging the status of vegetation types. The biological nomad theory. In *Proceedings of the Symposium on humid tropics vegetation, Kandy.* UNESCO, Paris. [§ 6.2.]

—— (1958*c*). In Ding Hou, Rhizophoraceae. *Flora Malesiana* Ser. I, **5**, 431–6. [§ 11.1.]

—— (1961*a*). An attempt towards an explanation of the effect of mountain mass elevation. *Proc. K. ned. Akad. Wet.* **64**, 435–42. [§ 16.3.]

—— (1961*b*). Axiomas and criteria of vegetatiology with special reference to the tropics. *Trop. Ecol.* **2**, 33–47. [§ 15.5, 17.1.]

—— (1961*c*). Discrimination of tropical shore formations. In *Proceedings of the Symposium on humid tropics vegetation.* UNESCO, Tjiawi. [§ 10.6.]

—— (1962). The mountain flora of the Malaysian tropics. *Endeavour* **21**, 183–93. [§ 16.3.]

—— (1964). Plant geography of the mountain flora of Mt. Kinabalu. *Proc. R. Soc. B* **161**, 7–38. [§ 16.3.]

—— (1968). Frost in the tropics. In *Proceedings of the Symposium on recent advances in tropical ecology, Varanasi* 1, 154–67. [§ 16.2.]

—— (1971). Plant conservation in Malaysia. *Bull. Jard. bot. nat. Belg.* **41**, 189–202. [§§ 1.1, 19.3.]

—— (1972). *The mountain flora of Java.* Brill, Leiden. [§§ 2.5, 2.6, 2.8, 4.1, 5.2, 6.2, 12.1, 12.3, 16.1, 16.3, 16.6; App.]

—— and SCHIPPERS LAMMERTSE, A. F. (1965). Concise plant geography of Java. In *Flora of Java* (eds C. A. Backer and R. C. van der Brink Bakhuizen), Vol. 2. Leiden. [§ 12.1; App.]

STEPHENS, G. R. (1968). Assimilation by kadam (*Anthocephalus cadamba*) in laboratory and field. *Turrialba* **18**, 60–3. [§ 8.4.]

STEVENS, W. E. (1968). *The conservation of wild life in west Malaysia.* Office of the Chief Game Warden, Federal Game Department, Ministry of Lands and Mines, Seremban. [Chapter 13; §§ 17.1, 17.4, 19.3.]

STONE, B. C. and WHITMORE, T. C. (1970). Notes on the systematy of Solomon Islands' plants and some of their New Guinea relatives. XI. *Tapeinosperma* (Myrsinaceae). *Reinwardtia* 8, 3–11. [§ 2.5.]

STREETS, R. J. (1962). *Exotic forest trees in the British Commonwealth.* Oxford University Press. [§ 7.2.]

STRONG, M. F. (1972). Opening statement to the first plenary meeting. *United Nations Conference on the human environment, Stockholm.* [§ 19.3.]

SUDARMO, M. K. (1957). Preliminary yields table of *Anthocephalus cadamba* Miq. *Commun. Forest Res. Inst., Bogor* **59**. [§ 7.2.]

SWART, E. R. (1963). Age of the Baobab tree. *Nature* **198**, 708–9. [§ 8.2.]

SWEATMAN, H. C. (1971). *Report to the Government of Indonesia on forestry in Indonesia.* F.A.O., Rome. [§§ 12.2, 17.2; Table 17.2.]

SYMINGTON, C. F. (1933). The study of secondary

growth on rain forest sites in Malaya. *Malay. Forester* **2**, 107–17. [§§ 6.2, 18.2.]

—— (1936). The flora of Gunong Tapis, Pahang; with notes on the altitudinal zonation of the forests of the Malay Peninsula. *J. Malay. Brch. R. Asiat. Soc.* **14**, 333–64. [§§ 16.1, 16.7; App.]

—— (1943). Foresters' manual of dipterocarps. *Malay. Forest Rec.* **16**. [§§ 10.1, 10.2, 10.3, 10.4, 10.6, 11.3, 12.3, 15.2, 15.3, 15.4, 16.1, 16.6; Fig. 16.1; App.] (New edn (1974), Univ. Malaya Press.)

SYS, C. (1961). *La cartographie des sols au Congo et Ruanda Urundi, ses principles et ses methodes.* Publication I.N.E.A.C. sér. Technique **63**. [Chapter 9.]

—— (1967). The concept of ferrallitic and fersiallitic soils in Central Africa. *Pédologie, Gand* **17**, 284–325. [§ 9.2.]

TAGUDAR, E. T. (1966). A silvicultural treatment of a tropical virgin forest in the Philippines for sustained yield management, with special reference to the operations of the Bislig Bay Lumber Company. *Proceedings of the world forestry Conference* **6** (2), 2553–6. [§ 7.1.]

TAMESIS, E. V. and SALITA, D. C. (1971). Some aspects of lateritic soil formation in the Dahican–Alayao area, Camarines Norte Province, Philippines. Soils and tropical weathering. In *Proceedings of the Bandung Symposium.* UNESCO, Paris. [§ 9.3.]

TAN, K. H. and SCHUYLENBORGH, J. VAN (1961). On the classification and genesis of soils developed over acid volcanic material under humid tropical conditions. II. *Neth. J. agric. Sci.* **9**, 41–54. [§ 9.12.]

TANG, H. T. (1971). Preliminary tests on the storage and collection of some *Shorea* species seeds. *Malay. Forester* **34**, 84–98. [§ 5.2.]

—— and TAMARI, C. (1973). Seed description and storage tests of some dipterocarps. *Malay. Forester* **36**, 113–28. [§ 5.2.]

TANSLEY, A. G. (1935). The use and misuse of vegetational terms and concepts. *Ecology* **16**, 284–307. [§ 2.1.]

TAYLOR, B. W. (1957). Plant succession on recent volcanoes in Papua. *J. Ecol.* **45**, 233–43. [§ 8.2.]

—— (1959). The classification of lowland swamp communities in north eastern Papua. *Ecology* **40**, 703–11. [§ 11.4.]

—— (1964a). Vegetation of the Buna-Kokoda area, territory of Papua and New Guinea. In *Land Research Series* 10. C.S.I.R.O., Melbourne. [§ 11.4.]

—— (1964b). Vegetation of the Wanigela–Cape Vogel area, territory of Papua and New Guinea. In *Land Research Series* 12. C.S.I.R.O., Melbourne. [§ 11.4.]

TAYLOR, N. H., DIXON, J. K., and SEELYE, F. T. (1950). The soils of north Auckland peninsula, New Zealand. *Int. Congr. Soil Sci.* **4** (1), 293–6. [§ 14.1.]

TERCINIER, G. (1962). *Les sols de la Nouvelle Caledonie* 1, (*Pedologie*). Institut France d'Oceanie. ORSTOM, Paris. [§ 9.8.]

THAPA, R. S. (1969). *Notes on some insect pests of laran* Anthocephalus chinensis *in Sabah.* In Annual Report of the Research Branch (Forest Department), Sabah. [§ 7.2.]

THORNTHWAITE, C. W. (1931). The climates of north America. *Geogrl Rev.* **21**, 633–55. [§ 3.1.]

—— (1948). An approach toward a rational classification of climate. *Geogrl Rev.* **38**, 55–94. [§ 3.1.]

—— (1954). A re-examination of the concept and measurement of potential transpiration. In The measurement of potential evapo-transpiration (ed. J. R. Mather). *C. W. Thornthwaite Associates Laboratory of Climatology publications in climatology.* [§ 3.1.]

TJIA, H. D. (1973). Geomorphology. In *Geology of the Malay Peninsula* (eds D. J. Gobbett and C. S. Hutchinson). Wiley, New York. [§ 11.3.]

TRACEY, L. G. (1969). Edaphic differentiation of some forest types in eastern Australia. 1. Soil physical factors. *J. Ecol.* **57**, 805–16. [§ 10.3.]

TROUP, R. S. (1952). *Silvicultural systems* (2nd edn) (ed. E. W. Jones). Clarendon Press, Oxford. [Chapter 7.]

TURNBULL, J. W. (1972). *Pinus kesiya* Royle ex Gordon (syn. *P. khasya* Royle; *P. insularis* Endicher) in the Philippines. Distribution, characteristics and seed sources. In *Selection and breeding to improve some tropical conifers* (eds J. Burley and D. G. Nikles), Vol. 1. Commonwealth Forestry Institute, Oxford and Department of Forestry, Queensland. [Fig. 14.1.]

UNESCO (1962). *Symposium on the impact of man on humid tropics vegetation, Goroka 1960.* [§ 18.1.]

—— (1973). *International classification and mapping of vegetation.* UNESCO, Paris. [§ 10.]

VANZOLINI, P. E. (1973). Palaeoclimates, relief and species multiplication in equatorial forests. In *Tropical forest ecosystems in Africa and South America: a comparative review* (eds B. J. Meggers, E. S. Ayensu, and W. D. Duckworth). Association for Tropical Biology, Washington. [§ 12.1.]

VERBOOM, W. C. (1968). Grassland successions and associations in Pahang, central Malaya. *Trop. Agric.* (*Trinidad*) **45**, 47–59. [Fig. 18.1.]

VERSTAPPEN, H. T. (1960). Some observations on karst development in the Malay archipelago. *J. trop. Geogr.* **14**, 1–10. [§ 9.7.]

VINCENT, A. J. (1961a). *A note on the growth of three meranti* (*LHW* Shorea) *hill forest species in naturally and artificially regenerated forest, Malaya.* Malayan Forestry Dept. Research Pamphlet 37. [Table 8.3.]

—— (1961b). *A note on the growth of eleven individual species of the genus* Dipterocarpus (*keruing*) *in naturally and artificially regenerated forest, Malaya.* Malayan Forestry Dept. Research Pamphlet 38. [Table 8.3.]

VISHER, S. S. (1925). Tropical cyclones of the Pacific. *Bull. Bernice P. Bishop Mus.* **20**. [6.1.]

WADE, L. K. and McVEAN, D. N. (1969). *Mt. Wilhelm Studies. I. The alpine and sub-alpine vegetation.* Research

School of Pacific Studies, Australian National University Publication BG/1. [§§ 16.1, 16.2.]

WALKER, D. (1966). Vegetation of the lake Ipea region New Guinea highlands. *J. Ecol.* **54**, 503–33. [§ 8.2.]

—— (1968). A reconnaissance of the non-arboreal vegetation of the Pindaunde catchment, Mount Wilhelm, New Guinea. *J. Ecol.* **56**, 445–66. [§ 16.2.]

—— (1970). The changing vegetation of the montane tropics. *Search. Australia and New Zealand Association for the Advancement of Science* **1**, 217–21. [§§ 12.1, 16.2, 17.1.]

WALKER, E. H. and PENDLETON, R. L. (1957). A survey of the vegetation of south eastern Asia. The Indo-Chinese province of the Pacific Basin. *Proc. Pacif. Sci. Congr.* **8** (4), 99–114. [§ 12.1; App.]

WALL, J. R. D. (1964). Topography—soil relationships in lowland Sarawak. *J. trop. Geogr.* **18**, 192–9. [§ 9.6.]

WALLACE, A. R. (1860). On the zoological geography of the Malay archipelago. *J. Linnean Soc., Lond.* **4**, 172–84. [§ 1.2.]

WALTER, H. (1964). Die tropischen und subtropischen Zonen. *Die Vegetation der Erde in ökophysiologischer Betrachtung, Vol. I.* (2nd edn) Jena. [§ 2.6.]

—— (1973). *Vegetation of the earth*. English University Press, London. [§§ 2.5, 2.6.]

—— and LEITH, H. (1960). *Klimadiagramm Weltatlas*. Jena. [Fig. 3.1.]

WALTON, A. B. (1948). Some considerations for the future management and silvicultural treatment of Malayan forests. *Malay. Forester* **11**, 68–74. [§ 6.5.]

WANG, C. W. (1961). *The forests of China*. Maria Moor Cabots Foundation publication 5, Boston. [Chapter 1; §§ 10.1, 14.3, 15.2, 16.3; App.]

WARD, P. (1969). The annual cycle of the yellow-vented bulbul *Pycnonotus goiavier* in a humid equatorial environment. *Proc. Zool. Soc. Lond.* **157**, 25–45. [§ 4.2.]

—— and POH, G. E. (1968). Seasonal breeding in an equatorial population of the Tree Sparrow *Passer montanus*. *Ibis* **110**, 359–68. [§ 4.2.]

WATSON, J. G. (1928). The mangrove swamps of the Malay Peninsula. *Malay. Forest Rec.* **6**, [§ 11.1.]

WATT, A. S. (1924). On the ecology of British beechwoods with special reference to their regeneration. II. *J. Ecol.* **12**, 145–204. [§ 2.3.]

—— (1947). Pattern and process in the plant community. *J. Ecol.* **35**, 1–22. [§ 2.3.]

WATTS, I. E. M. (1954). Line squalls of Malaya. *J. trop. Geogr.* **3**, 1–14. [§ 6.1.]

WEBB, L. J. (1958). Cyclones as an ecological factor in tropical lowland rain forest, north Queensland. *Aust. J. Bot.* **6**, 220–8. [§§ 4.1, 6.1.]

—— (1959). A physiognomic classification of Australian rain forests. *J. Ecol.* **47**, 551–70. [Chapter 1; §§ 6.2, 10.2, 12.1, 12.2, App.]

—— (1964). An historical interpretation of the grass balds of the Bunya mountains south Queensland. *Ecology*, **45**, 159–62. [§ 14.2; Chapter 18.]

—— (1965). The influence of soil parent materials on rain forest distribution in south east Queensland. In *Proceedings of the Symposium on ecological research into humid tropics vegetation*. UNESCO, Kuching. [§ 10.3.]

—— (1968). Environmental relationships of the structural types of Australian rain forest vegetation. *Ecology* **49**, 296–311. [Chapter 1; § 10.3; App.]

—— and TRACEY, J. G. (1967). An ecological guide to new planting areas and site potential for hoop pine. *Aust. For.* **31**, 224–39. [§ 14.2.]

—— —— and WILLIAMS, W. T. (1972). Regeneration and pattern in the subtropical rain forest. *J. Ecol.* **60**, 675–95. [§§ 6.2, 15.5, 18.2.]

—— —— and LANCE, G. N. (1967a). Studies in the numerical analysis of complex rain forest communities. I. A comparison of methods applicable to site/species data. *J. Ecol.* **55**, 171–91. [Chapters 10, 15.]

—— —— —— (1967b). Studies in the numerical analysis of complex rain forest communities. II. The problem of species sampling. *J. Ecol.* **55**, 525–38. [Chapter 15.]

—— —— —— (1970). Studies in the numerical analysis of complex rain forest communities. V. A comparison of the properties of floristic and physiognomic structural data. *J. Ecol.* **58**, 203–32. [Chapter 15.]

WEBBER, M. L. (1934). Fruit dispersal. *Malay. Forester* **3**, 18–19. [§ 5.1.]

—— (1954). The mangrove ancestry of a fresh water swamp forest suggested by its diatom flora. *Malay. Forester* **17**, 25–6. [§ 11.3.]

WEE, W. C. (1970). Weed succession observations on arable peat land. *Malay. Forester* **33**, 63–9. [§ 18.2.]

WELLS, D. R. (1971). Survival of the Malaysian bird fauna. *Malay. Nat. J.* **24**, 248–56. [§ 1.2, Table 1.2; §§ 2.7, 12.3; Chapter 13; §§ 16.7, 17.4, 19.3.]

—— (1974). Resident birds. Chapter 1 in *Birds of the Malay Peninsula* (Lord Medway and D. R. Wells), Witherby, London. [Fig. 4.4, Fig. 12.5.]

WENT, F. W. (1940). Soziologie der Epiphyten eines tropischen Urwaldes. *Ann. Jard. bot. Buitenz.* **50**, 1–98. [§ 2.5.]

—— and STARK, N. (1968). Mycorrhiza. *BioScience* **18**, 1035–9. [§ 2.5.]

WERGER, M. J. A. (1972). Species-area relationship and plot size: with some examples from South African vegetation. *Bothalia* **10**, 583–94. [§ 1.1.]

WHITE, K. J. (1973). The lowland rain forest in Papua and New Guinea. *Proc. Precongress Conference Bogor, of the Pacific Science Association 1971*. [§ 17.1, App.]

WHITEHEAD, C. (1959). The rambutan, a description of the characteristics and potential of the more important varieties. *Malay. agric. J.* **42**, 53–75. [§ 4.1.]

WHITMORE, T. C. (1962a,b). Studies in systematic bark morphology. I. Bark morphology in Dipterocarpaceae. II. General features of bark construction in Dipterocarpaceae. *New Phytol.* **61**, 191–207, 208–20. [§ 2.5.]

—— (1962c). Why do trees have different sorts of bark? *New Scient.* **16**, 330–1. [§ 2.5.]

—— (1962d). Bark morphology as an aid to forest

recognition and taxonomy in Dipterocarpaceae. *Flora Malesiana Bull.* **18**, 1017–9. [§ 2.5.]

—— (1963). Studies in systematic bark morphology. III. Bark taxonomy in Dipterocarpaceae. *Gdns Bull., Singapore* **19**, 321–71. [§ 2.5.]

—— (1966a). *Guide to the forests of the British Solomon Islands.* Oxford University Press, London. [§§ 1.1, 2.5, 2.8, 4.1, 10.4; App.]

—— (1966b). A study of light conditions in forests in Ecuador with some suggestions for further studies in tropical forests. *Light as an ecological factor* (eds R. Bainbridge, G. C. Evans, and O. Rackham), British Ecological Society Symposium, Vol. 6. Blackwell, Oxford. [§ 3.6.]

—— (1966c). The social status of *Agathis* in a rain forest in Melanesia. *J. Ecol.* **54**, 285–301. [§§ 6.5, 14.1, 18.2; Fig. 6.7; App.]

—— (1967a). Studies in *Macaranga*, an easy genus of Malayan wayside trees. *Malay. Nat. J.* **20**, 89–99. [§§ 2.8, 6.2, 18.2.]

—— (1967b). *Piper aduncum* in Malaya. *Malay. Nat. J.* **20**, 83–4. [§ 2.8.]

—— (1969a). The vegetation of the Solomon Islands. *Phil. Trans. Roy. Soc. B.* **225**, 259–70. [§§ 1.1, 10.4, 10.5, 16.6; App.]

—— (1969b). Geography of the flowering plants. *Phil. Trans. R. Soc. B.* **255**, 549–66. [§ 2.5.]

—— (1969c). The island theory of biogeography. *Phil. Trans. R. Soc. B.* **255**, 613–14. [§ 15.1.]

—— (1969d). First thoughts on species evolution in Malayan *Macaranga* (Studies in *Macaranga* III). *Biol. J. Linnean Soc. Lond.* **1**, 223–31. [§ 6.2.]

—— (1970). *Liberbaileya gracilis. Principes* **14**, 97–107. [§ 10.4.]

—— (1971a). *Maxburretia rupicola. Principes* **15**, 3–9. [§ 10.4.]

—— (1971b). Wild fruit trees and some trees of pharmacological potential in the rain forest of Ulu Kelantan. *Malay. Nat. J.* **24**, 222–4. [Table 19.2; § 19.3.]

—— (1972a). The Gunong Benom Expedition. 2. An outline description of the forest zones on north east Gunong Benom. *Bull. Br. Mus. nat. Hist. D* **23**, 11–15. [§§ 16.1, 16.7; Fig. 16.4; App.]

—— (1972b). (ed.). *Tree flora of Malaya*, Vol. 1. Longman, Kuala Lumpur and London. [§§ 1.1, 15.1; Table 16.2.]

—— (1972c). Prologue. In *Tree flora of Malaya* (ed. T. C. Whitmore), Vol. 1. Longman, Kuala Lumpur and London. [§§ 2.5, 4.1, 17.3.]

—— (1972d). Leguminosae. In *Tree flora of Malaya* (ed. T. C. Whitmore), Vol. 1. Longman, Kuala Lumpur and London. [§§ 2.4, 15.2, 19.1.]

—— (1972e). Gnetaceae. In *Tree flora of Malaya* (ed. T. C. Whitmore), Vol. 1. Longman, Kuala Lumpur and London. [§ 2.6.]

—— (1973a). Plate tectonics and some aspects of Pacific plant geography. *New Phytol.* **72**, 1185–90. [§ 15.1.]

—— (1973b). *Palms of Malaya.* Oxford University Press, Kuala Lumpur. [§§ 1.1, 2.8, 3.5, 4.1, 10.4, 11.2; Chapter 18; Fig. 1.8.]

—— (1973c). (ed.). *Tree flora of Malaya*, Vol. 2. Longman, Kuala Lumpur and London. [§§ 1.1, 15.1; Table 16.2.]

—— (1973d). Apocynaceae. In *Tree flora of Malaya* (ed. T. C. Whitmore), Vol. 2. Longman, Kuala Lumpur and London. [§§ 6.2, 19.2.]

—— (1973e). Datiscaceae. In *Tree flora of Malaya* (ed. T. C. Whitmore), Vol. 2. Longman, Kuala Lumpur and London. [§ 10.2.]

—— (1973f). Euphorbiaceae. In *Tree flora of Malaya* (ed. T. C. Whitmore), Vol. 2. Longman, Kuala Lumpur and London. [§§ 2.8, 4.1, 6.2, 12.3.]

—— (1973g). Guttiferae. In *Tree flora of Malaya* (ed. T. C. Whitmore), Vol. 2. Longman, Kuala Lumpur and London. [§ 19.2.]

—— (1973h). Santalaceae. In *Tree flora of Malaya* (ed. T. C. Whitmore), Vol. 2. Longman, Kuala Lumpur and London. [§ 2.6.]

—— (1973i). Frequency and habitat of tree species in the rain forest of Ulu Kelantan. *Gdns Bull., Singapore* **26**, 195–210. [§ 15.3; Table 15.1.]

—— (1973j). Notes on the systematy of Malayan phanerogams. XVIII. Guttiferae—*Garcinia. Gdns Bull., Singapore* **26**, 271–8. [Fig. 15.9.]

—— (1973k). A new tree flora of Malaya. *Proc. Precongress Conference Bogor, of the Pacific Science Association 1971.* [§ 1.1; Table 16.2.]

—— (1974). *Change with time and the role of cyclones in tropical rain forest on Kolombangara, Solomon Islands.* Commonwealth Forestry Institute, Paper 46. [§§ 2.6, 5.1, 5.3, 6.1, 6.3; Table 6.1, Table 6.2; §§ 8.1, 15.4, 15.5; Fig. 1.5, Fig. 6.4, Fig. 8.5, Fig. 15.17, Fig. 15.18, Fig. 15.19, Fig. 15.20.]

—— (1975). *Macaranga.* In The Euphorbiaceae of Borneo (H. K. Airy Shaw). *Kew Bull. Suppl. series.* [§ 6.2.]

—— and AIRY SHAW, H. K. (1971). Studies in *Macaranga*. IV. New and notable records for Malaya. *Kew Bull.* **25**, 237–42. [§ 6.2.]

—— and BURNHAM, C. P. (1969). The altitudinal sequence of forests and soils on granite near Kuala Lumpur. *Malay. Nat. J.* **22**, 99–118. [§§ 5.3, 9.12, 16.1, 16.5; Fig. 9.15.]

—— SOH, K. G. and JONES, B. M. G. (1970). Studies in *Macaranga*. III. Chromosome counts. *Taxon.* **19**, 255–6. [§ 6.2.]

—— and WONG, Y. K. (1959). Patterns of sunlight and shade in tropical rain forest. *Malay. Forester* **21**, 50–62. [§ 3.6.]

WILFORD, G. E. (1960). *Radiocarbon age determinations of Quaternary sediments in Brunei and north east Sarawak.* British Borneo Geological Survey Annual Report, 1959. [§ 11.3.]

—— and WALL, J. R. D. (1965). Sarawak karst topography, *J. trop. Geogr.* **21**, 44–70. [§ 9.7.]

WILLIAMS, W. T., LANCE, G. N., WEBB, L. J., TRACEY, J. G., and DALE, M. B. (1969a). Studies in the numerical analysis of complex rain forest communities. III. The analysis of successional data. *J. Ecol.* **57**, 513–35. [Chapter 15.]

—— —— —— and CONNELL, J. H. (1969*b*). Studies in the numerical analysis of complex rain forest communities. IV. A method for the elucidation of small-scale forest pattern. *J. Ecol.* **57**, 635–54. [Chapter 15; § 15.5.]

WILLIAMS-HUNT, P. D. R. (1952). *An introduction to the Malayan aborigines*. Government Press, Kuala Lumpur. [§ 17.1.]

WILSON, W. L. and WILSON, C. C. (1973). *Final report: census of Sumatran primates*. University of Washington Seattle, (mimeo.). [§ 2.7; Chapter 13; § 17.4.]

WINKLER, H. (1914). Die Pflanzendecke Sudöst-Borneos. *Bot. Jb.* **50**, 188–208. [§ 10.3.]

WOMERSLEY, J. S. and MCADAM, J. B. (1957). *The forests and forest conditions in the territories of Papua and New Guinea*. Government Printer, Port Moresby. [§§15.2, 16.2, 17.1; App.]

WONG, Y. K. (1967). *Some indications of the total volume of wood per acre in lowland dipterocarp forest*. Malayan Forestry Dept. Research Pamphlet 53. [Table 1.1; Fig. 1.4.]

—— and WHITMORE, T. C. (1970). On the influence of soil properties on species distribution in a Malayan lowland dipterocarp rain forest. *Malay. Forester* **33**, 42–54. [§ 15.3; Table 15.4; Fig. 15.4.]

WOOD, G. H. S. (1956). The dipterocarp flowering season in North Borneo, 1955. *Malay. Forester* **19**, 193–201. [§§ 2.8, 4.1.]

WOOD, T. W. W. (1970). Wind damage in the forest of western Samoa. *Malay. Forester* **33**, 92–9. [§ 6.1.]

WYATT-SMITH, J. (1950). Virgin jungle reserves. *Malay. Forester* **13**, 40–5. [§§ 17.3, 19.3.]

—— (1953*a*). The vegetation of Jarak island, Straits of Malacca. *J. Ecol.* **41**, 207–25. [§ 5.1.]

—— (1954*a*). Storm forest in Kelantan. *Malay. Forester* **17**, 5–11. [§§ 6.1, 6.5, 8.2, 15.2.]

—— (1954*b*). Suggested definitions of field characters (for use in the identification of tropical forest trees in Malaya). *Malay. Forester* **17**, 170–83. [§ 2.5.]

—— (1959). Peat swamp forests in Malaya. *Malay. Forester* **23**, 5–32. [§ 11.3,; App.]

—— (1963). Manual of Malayan silviculture for inland forests (2 vols). *Malay. Forest Rec.* **23**. [§§ 2.8, 5.2, 6.1, 6.2, 6.5, 7, 7.1, 8.1, 10.2, 10.3, 10.4, 11.2, 11.3, 11.4, 12.3, 15.2, 15.3, 16.5; Fig. 15.6; App.]

—— (1966). *Ecological studies on Malayan forests. I.* Malayan Forestry Department Research Pamphlet 52. [§§ 2.3, 6.4; Table 6.3, Table 6.4, Table 6.5; § 8.1, Chapter 15; Table 15.3; Fig. 1.3, Fig. 1.5, App.]

WYCHERLEY, P. R. (1963). Variation in the performance of *Hevea* in Malaya. *J. trop. Geogr.* **17**, 143–71. [§ 4.1.]

—— (1967). Rainfall probability tables for Malaysia. *R.R.I.M. Planting Manual* [Chapter 12; §§ 3.2, 3.4.]

YANCEY, T. E. (1973). Holocene radiocarbon dates on the 3 meter wave cut notch in northwestern peninsular Malaysia. *Geol. Soc. Malaysia Newsletter* **45**, 8–11. [§ 1.1.]

YODA, K. (1967). Comparative ecological studies on three main types of forest vegetation in Thailand. III. Community respiration. *Nature Life S. E. Asia* **5**, 83–148. [§ 8.3.]

ZABALA, N. Q. and MANARPAAC, V. (1968). The effects of fertilization on growth of kaatoan bangkal seedlings. *Philipp. Lumberm.* **14**, 36–41. [§ 7.2.]

ZON, P. VAN (1915). Mededeelingen omtrent den kamferboom (*Dryobalanops aromatica*). *Tectona* **8**, 220–4. [§ 15.3.]

Index of plant names

THE PLANT names are listed according to the section in which they appear. A reference to, for example, 'Chapter 14' means the name occurs in the un-numbered introductory section to that chapter.

Acacia leucophloea (Roxb.) Willd., § 12.1, § 17.1, Leguminosae/ Mimosoideae
A. tomentosa (Roxb.) Willd., § 12.1, § 17.1
Acanthaceae, § 3.6
Aceraceae, § 16.3
Achras, § 2.8, Sapotaceae
Acronychia laurifolia B1., § 8.1, Table 8.4, Rutaceae
Actinidiaceae, Fig. 15.8
Actinodaphne, § 14.2, Fig. 15.2, Lauraceae
A. pruninosa Nees, Fig. 10.4
Adansonia digitata L., § 8.2, Bombacaceae
Adenanthera bicolor Moon, § 2.8, Leguminosae/Mimosoideae
A. pavonina L., § 4.1
Adinandra cordiifolia Ridley, Fig. 1.6, Theaceae
A. dumosa Jack, § 4.1, § 18.2
Aegle, § 2.8, Rutaceae
A. marmelos (L.) Corr., § 12.1
Aeschynanthus, § 2.8, Gesneriaceae
Agathis, Chapter 14, § 14.1, Fig. 8.1, Araucariaceae
A. australis Salisb., § 14.1
A. borneensis Warb., § 6.5, § 10.3, § 14.1, Fig. 14.5
A. dammara (Lamb.) L. G. Rich., § 14.1, § 15.3
A. flavescens Ridley, § 14.1
A. labillardierei Warb., § 10.3, § 10.4, § 14.1, Fig. 14.6
A. loranthifolia = dammara
A. macrophylla (Lindl.) Mast., § 6.5, § 8.2, § 14.1, Fig. 6.7, Fig. 14.4
A. microstachya J. F. Bailey, § 14.1
A. obtusa Mast., § 14.1
A. ovata Warb., Chapter 14
A. robusta F. Muell., § 14.1
A. vitiense (Seem.) Benth. & Hook., § 14.1
A. sp. 'A', § 14.1
Aglaia, § 14.2, Fig. 2.27, Figs 15.18 and 15.19, Meliaceae
A. affinis Merr., Fig. 15.4
A. gamopetala Merr., Fig. 15.4
A. salicifolia Ridley, § 2.8, § 15.3
Agrostistachys longifolia (Wight) Benth., § 10.3, § 10.4, Euphorbiaceae var. *leptostachya* (Pax & Hoffm.) Whitmore, Fig. 1.6
alang alang *see Imperata cylindrica*
Alangium havilandii Bloemb., Fig. 11.4, Alangiaceae
A. javanicum (K. & V.) Wang., Table 6.4
Albizia chinensis (Osb.) Merr., § 12.1, Leguminosae/Mimosoideae
A. falcata (L.) Back., § 2.5, § 6.2, § 8.2
A. lebbekoides (DC.) Benth., § 12.1
A. lophantha (Willd.) Benth., § 5.2, § 16.1, § 16.3
A. minahassae Koord., § 6.2
Algae, § 2.6
Alnus, Chapter 14, Betulaceae
Alocasia macrorhiza Schott, § 8.4, Araceae
Alphitonia sp., § 10.5, Rhamnaceae
Alseodaphne bancana Miq., § 8.1, Table 8.4
A. insignis Gamble, Fig. 11.4, Lauraceae
Alstonia, § 2.3, § 11.4, Table 19.2, Apocynaceae
A. scholaris (L.) R. Br., Fig. 2.8

A. spatulata Bl., § 8.3, § 10.3, § 11.4
Althoffia sp., § 15.3, Tiliaceae
Altingia excelsa Noroña, § 2.8, § 4.1, § 17.1, Fig. 8.1, Hamamelidaceae
Amoora, § 14.2, Meliaceae
Amaranthaceae, § 6.2
Amorphophallus, § 2.8, Araceae
Anacardiaceae, § 5.1, § 16.3, Fig. 1.6, Fig. 2.1, Table 15.1, Table 19.2
Anacardium occidentale L., § 10.3, Anacardiaceae
Anacolosa papuana Schellenb., Figs 15.18 and 15.19, Olacaceae
Anemone, § 16.3, Ranunculaceae
Anisophyllea sp., Fig. 10.8, Rhizophoraceae
Anisoptera, Chapter 7, § 10.1, § 15.3, Dipterocarpaceae
A. megistocarpa Sloot., § 6.1
A. oblonga Dyer, § 10.2, § 12.2, § 12.3
A. scaphula (Roxb.) Pierre, § 16.6
A. thurifera Bl., § 15.2, § 16.1, Fig. 15.3
Annona, § 2.8, Annonaceae
A. muricata L., Table 17.1
Annonaceae, § 2.4, § 2.5, § 2.6, § 2.8, § 8.1, Fig. 1.6, Fig. 2.1, Fig. 15.4
Anthocephalus cadamba = chinensis, Rubiaceae
A. chinensis (Lamk.) Rich. ex Walp., § 5.2, § 6.2, § 7.2, § 8.1, § 8.3, § 8.4, § 15.3, Fig. 7.2, Fig. 7.3, Fig. 8.2
A. macrophyllus Hav., § 7.2
Antiaris toxicaria (Pers.) Lesch., Table 19.2, Moraceae
Antidesma coriaceum Tul., § 11.3, Euphorbiaceae
A. salicinum Ridley, § 15.3
Apocynaceae, Table 19.2
Aporusa elmeri Merr., Fig. 1.6, Euphorbiaceae
A. nitida Merr., Fig. 2.1
A. papuana Pax & Hoffm., Figs 15.18 and 15.19
A. prainiana King ex Gage, Fig. 2.1
Araceae, § 2.6, § 2.8, Fig. 2.23
Araliaceae, § 2.5, Fig. 2.5
Araucaria, § 1.1, § 2.5, § 5.2, § 10.2, § 14, § 14.2, § 16.1, Fig. 8.1, Araucariaceae
A. beccarii Warb., § 14.2
A. cunninghamii Ait., § 2.8, § 5.2, Chapter 14, § 14.2, Fig. 14.6, Fig. 14.8
A. hunsteinii K. Schum., § 2.8, § 5.1, § 5.2, § 14.2, Fig. 14.7, Fig. 14.8
A. klinkii = hunsteinii
Araucariaceae, § 16.3
Ardisia elliptica Thunb., § 10.6, Myrsinaceae
A. hosei Merr., Fig. 10.4
A. sp., Fig. 2.1
Areca, § 8.3, § 10.1, § 12.3, Palmae
A. catechu L., Table 17.1
Arenga westerhoutii Griff., § 10.4, Palmae
Aristolochia, § 2.8, Aristolochiaceae
aroids *see* Araceae
Aromadendron nutans Dandy, Fig. 10.4, Fig. 11.4, Magnoliaceae
Arthrophyllum diversifolium Bl., Fig. 2.5, Araliaceae

259

A. rubiginosum Ridley, Fig. 11.4, Fig. 11.5
Artocarpus, § 2.8, Moraceae
A. anisophyllus Miq., Fig. 1.8
A. chaplasha Roxb., Fig. 1.8
A. elasticus Reinw. ex Bl., Table 19.2
A. heterophyllus Lam., § 1.1, Table 17.1
A. hispidus Jarrett, Fig. 1.8
A. integer (Thunb.) Merr., Table 17.1, Table 19.2
A. lanceifolius Roxb., Table 19.2
    ssp. *clementis* (Merrill) Jarrett, Fig. 1.8
    ssp. *lanceifolius*, Fig. 1.8
A. lowii King, § 4.1
A. melinoxylus Gagnep.
    ssp. *brevipedunculatus* Jarrett, Fig. 1.8
    ssp. *melinoxylus*, Fig. 1.8
A. odoratissimus Blco., Fig. 1.6, Fig. 1.8
A. rigidus Bl.
    ssp. *asperulus* Gagnep.) Jarrett, Fig. 1.8
    ssp. *rigidus*, Fig. 1.8, Table 19.2
A. scortechinii King, Table 8.3, Table 19.2
Arundina graminifolia (D. Don) Hochr., § 16.4 Orchidaceae
asam gelugor *see Garcinia atroviridis*
Ascarina philippinensis C. B. Rob., § 16.4, Chloranthaceae
Asplenium nidus L., Fig. 2.18, fern
Ashtonia excelsa Airy Shaw, Fig. 10.4, Euphorbiaceae
Aster, § 16.3, Compositae
Atriplex patula L., § 8.4, Chenopodiaceae
Austrobuxus nitidus Miq., § 16.4, Fig. 11.5, Euphorbiaceae
Averrhoa, § 2.8, Oxalidaceae
A. bilimbi L., Table 17.1
Avicennia, § 9.9, Avicenniaceae
Axonopus compressus Beauv., Fig. 18.1, Gramineae
Azadirachta indica A. Juss., § 12.1, Meliaceae

Baccaurea, § 2.8, § 4.1, Euphorbiaceae
B. griffithii Hk.f., Fig. 2.15, Table 17.1, Table 19.2
B. motleyana (M.A.) M.A., § 4.1, Table 17.1
B. parviflora (M.A.) M.A., § 2.5, Fig. 2.16, Fig. 2.17
Baeckia frutescens L., § 10.3, § 16.4, Myrtaceae
Balanocarpus heimii King, § 6.2, § 6.5, Chapter 7, § 12.3, Dipterocarpaceae
Balsa *see Ochroma lagopus*
Balsaminaceae, § 10.4
bamboos, § 2.8, § 4.1, § 12.2, § 12.3, § 18.2, Fig. 15.10, Fig. 17.7, Fig. 17.8
Bambusa arundinacea Willd., Fig. 12.1, Gramineae
B. polymorpha Munro, § 12.2
banana (s), § 4.1, § 8.4, § 17.1, § 17.4, Chapter 18
bangkong *see Artocarpus integer*
Banksia, § 12.1, Proteaceae
baobab *see Adansonia digitata*
Barringtonia, § 2.5, Fig. 1.6, Lecythidaceae
B. asiatica (L.) Kurz, § 10.6
Bauhinia, § 2.6, Leguminosea/Caesalpinoideae
Bazzania praerupta (Reinw., Bl. & Nees) Trevisan, § 16.4, Hepaticae
B. uncigera (Reinw., Bl. & Nees) Trevisan, § 16.4
Begoniaceae, § 10.4
Beilschmiedia, § 14.2, Lauraceae
belian *see Eusideroxylon zwageri*
belimbing *see Averrhoa bilimbi*
Belliolum haplopus (B. L. Burtt) A. C. Smith, Figs 15.18 and 15.19, Winteraceae
Berberis, § 16.3, Berberidaceae

betek *see Carica papaya*
Blachia andamanica (Kurz) Hk.f., § 12.1, Euphorbiaceae
Blumeodendron subrotundifolium (Elm.) Merr., Fig. 11.4, Euphorbiaceae
B. tokbrai (Bl.) J.J.Sm., Fig. 11.4
Boea, § 10.4, Fig. 10.15, Gesneriaceae
Bombacaceae, Table 19.2
Bombax, § 12.2, Bombacaceae
B. valetonii Hochr., § 2.8, § 4.1, Table 8.3
Borassus flabellifer L., § 12.1, § 17.1, Palmae
Borneo camphorwood *see Dryobalanops aromatica*
Borneo ironwood *see Eusideroxylon zwageri*
Borreria laevis (Lamk.) Griseb., § 17.1, Rubiaceae
Bottle Gourd *see Lagenaria siceraria*
Bouea, § 2.8, Anacardiaceae
B. macrophylla Griff., Table 17.1
Breadfruit, § 1.1
Breutelia chrysocoma (Hedw.) Lindb., § 16.4, Musci
Bromheadia, § 16.4, Orchidaceae
B. finlaysoniana Reichb. f., § 4.1
Brownlowia stipulata Kosterm., Fig. 15.4, Tiliaceae
Bryophyta, § 2.6, § 10.3, § 10.4, § 16.1, § 16.4
Buchanania fragrans Ridley, Fig. 15.4, Anacardiaceae
B. insignis Bl., Fig. 2.1
Burseraceae, § 2.4, § 15.2, § 16.3, Fig. 1.6, Fig. 2.1, Table 15.1
Butea monosperma (Lamk.) Taub., § 12.1, Leguminosae/Papilionatae
Caesalpinia bonduc (L.) emend Dandy & Exell, § 10.6, Leguminosae/Caesalpinoideae
C. digyna Roth, § 12.1
Caladenia, § 16.3, Orchidaceae
Calamus, Fig. 1.8, Palmae
Calophyllum, § 1.1, § 2.5, Fig. 2.1, Fig. 10.5, Guttiferae
C. depressinervosum Hend. & Wyatt-Smith, Fig. 2.1
C. inophyllum L., § 10.6
C. kajewskii A. C. Smith, § 5.3, § 6.3, § 10.4, Fig. 8.1, Table 6.1
C. obliquinervium Merr., Fig. 11.11, Fig. 11.14
C. retusum Wall., Fig. 11.5, Fig. 11.11
C. rubiginosum Hend. & Wyatt-Smith, Fig. 2.1
C. rupicolum Ridley var. *rupicolum*, 15.3
C. vitiense Turrill, § 5.3, § 6.3, Table 6.1
Calospatha, Fig. 1.8, Palmae
Camellia sinensis (L.) O.K., § 8.4, § 10.3, § 12.1, § 17.1, Theaceae
Campnosperma, § 2.5, § 6.2, Anacardiaceae
C. auriculatum Bl., Fig. 6.6, Table 8.3
C. brevipetiolatum Volk., § 1.1, § 6.5, Chapter 7, § 11.4, § 15.4, § 15.5, Fig. 6.7, Fig. 15.18, Fig. 15.19, Fig. 15.20, Table 6.1, Table 6.2, Table 8.3
C. coriaceum (Jack) Hallier f. ex Steenis, § 6.2, § 11.3, § 11.4, Fig. 11.15
C. montanum Ltb., Fig. 11.4
C. squamatum Ridley, Fig. 10.4
Canarium, § 15.2, Fig. 1.7, Fig. 2.4, Burseraceae
C. littorale Bl., Table 6.4
Canavalia microcarpa (DC.) Merr., § 10.6, Leguminosae/Papilionatae
Canthium, Fig. 1.6, Rubiaceae
C. didymum (Bedd.) Gaertn. f., Fig. 10.4, Fig. 11.5
Capparidaceae, § 16.3
Carallia brachiata (Lour.) Merr., § 8.3, Rhizophoraceae
Carica papaya L., § 4.1, Table 17.1, Caricaceae
Caryota mitis Lour., § 10.4, Chapter 18, Palmae
Casearia, Fig. 15.4, Flacourtiaceae
cassava *see Manihot esculenta*

Cassia fistula L., § 12.1, Leguminosae/Caesalpinoideae
Castanopsis, § 14.2, § 17.1, Fig. 14.2, Fig. 14.8, Fagaceae
C. acuminatissma Bl. (A.DC.), § 16.1
C. foxworthyi Schottky, Fig. 10.4
C. wallichii King ex Hk. f., Table 6.4
Casuarina, § 6.2, § 10.3, § 15.3, § 15.5, § 18.1, Casuarinaceae
C. aff. *cunninghamiana*, § 11.4
C. equisetifolia J. R. & G. Forst., § 10.6
C. junghuhniana Miq., § 12.1, § 14.3, § 16.1, § 16.3
C. nobilis Whitmore, § 10.3, § 10.4, § 10.5, Chapter 14, Fig. 10.4, Fig. 10.13, Fig. 14.3
C. papuana S. Moore, § 9.8, § 10.4, § 10.5, § 18.1
Casuarinaceae, § 2.5
Cecropia peltata L., § 8.4, Urticaceae
Celastraceae, Fig. 1.6, Fig. 2.1
Celtis, § 10.4, Ulmaceae
Centrospermae, § 8.4
Cephalostachyum pergracile Munro, § 12.2, Gramineae
Ceratolobus, Fig. 1.8, Palmae
chempedak *see Artocarpus integer*
Chief Tree *see Endospermum formicarum*
Chirita, § 10.4, Gesneriaceae
Chisocheton, § 14.2, Fig. 15.18 and 15.19, Meliaceae
C. princeps Hemsl., Fig. 2.7
Chrysopogon aciculatus Trin., Fig. 18.1, Gramineae
Cinnamomum, § 14.2, Lauraceae
Cirsium, § 16.3, Compositae
Cladium, § 10.3, Cyperaceae
Cleidion spiciflorum (Burm.f.) Merr., § 10.4, Euphorbiaceae
Cleistanthus winkleri Jabl., Fig. 1.6, Euphorbiaceae
Clerodendron fistulosum Becc., § 10.3, Verbenaceae
Clethraceae, § 16.3
coconut *see Cocos nucifera*
Cocos nucifera L., § 10.6, § 17.1, Chapter 18, Table 17.1, Palmae
Coelodepas sp., Fig. 1.6, Euphorbiaceae
Coelorachis, § 14.2, Gramineae
Coelostegia, Table 19.2, Bombaceae
Coffea, § 4.1, § 17.1, Rubiaceae
coffee *see Coffea*
cogon *see Imperata cylindrica*
Colocasia, § 17.1, Araceae
Colubrina anomala King, § 8.1, Rhamnaceae
C. asiatica (L.) Brongn., § 10.6
Combretaceae, § 11.3, § 16.3
Combretocarpus rotundatus (Miq.) Dans., § 11.3, Fig. 11.5, Fig. 11.10, Fig. 11.11, Fig. 11.13, Rhizophoraceae
Commersonia bartramia (L.) Merr., § 4.1, § 6.2, § 8.3, Sterculiaceae
Compositae, § 2.8, § 6.2
Coniferae, § 2.5, § 8.1, Chapter 14, § 16.5, § 19.1, Fig. 16.1
conifers *see Coniferae*
Connaraceae, § 2.8, § 16.3
Convolvulaceae, Fig. 15.8
Copaifera palustris (Sym.) de Wit, § 11.3, Fig. 11.11, Fig. 11.13, Leguminosae/Caesalpinoideae
Coprosma, § 16.1, Rubiaceae
Cordia, § 14.2, Verbenaceae
Cordyline rubra Hueg. ex Kunth, § 8.4, Liliaceae
Cornera, Fig. 1.8, Palmae
Corybas, § 16.1, Orchidaceae
Corypha elata Roxb., § 12.1, Palmae
C. umbraculifera L., § 4.1
Cotylelobium burckii (Heim) Heim, § 10.3, Dipterocarpaceae
C. malayanum Sloot., § 10.4
C. melanoxylon (Hk.f.) Pierre, § 10.3, Fig. 1.6

Cratoxylum arborescens (Vahl.) Bl., § 6.2, § 10.3, § 11.3, Fig. 11.11, Hypericaceae
C. cochinchinense (Lour.) Bl., § 10.3, § 11.4
C. formosum (Jack) Dyer, Chapter 14
C. glaucum Korth., § 6.2, § 11.3, Fig. 10.8, Fig. 11.11
C. sumatranum (Jack) Bl., Fig. 2.1
Crinum asiaticum L., § 10.6, Liliaceae
Croton laevifolius Bl., Fig. 11.4, Euphorbiaceae
Crudia, § 1.1, Leguminosae/Caesalpinoideae
Crypteronia griffithii C. B. Clarke, Fig. 2.1, Crypteroniaceae
Crypteroniaceae, Fig. 2.1
Cryptocarya, § 14.2, Fig. 14.8, Figs 15.18 and 15.19, Lauraceae
Ctenolophon parvifolius Oliv., Fig. 10.4, Fig. 11.4, Linaceae
Cunoniaceae, § 16.1, § 16.3
Cyathea, § 16.2, fern
C. contaminans (Wall. ex Hk.) Copel., 18.2
C. elmeri (Copel.) Copel., § 18.2
C. lunulata (Forst.) Copel., § 18.2
C. recommutata Copel., Fig. 10.4
Cyathocalyx, Table 8.3, Annonaceae
C. biovulatus Boerl., Fig. 11.4
C. pruniferus (Maing. ex Hk. f. & Thoms.) Sinclair, Table 6.4
Cycas rumphii Miq., § 10.3, § 10.6, Cycadaceae
Cynometra, § 2.8, § 4.1, Leguminosae/Caesalpinoideae
C. elmeri Merr., Fig. 15.4
C. malaccensis Meeuwen, § 15.3
Cyperus pedunculatus (R. Br.) Kern, § 10.6, Cyperaceae
C. stoloniferus Retz., § 10.6
Cyrtandra oblongifolia (Bl.) (B. & Hk.) ex Clarke, § 10.4, Gesneriaceae
Cyrtosperma, § 17.1, Araceae
Cyrtostachys lakka Becc., § 11.3, Palmae

Dacrydium, § 10.3, Chapter 14, Fig. 9.1, Fig. 10.7, Fig. 16.8, Podocarpaceae
D. beccarii Parl., § 10.4
  var. *subelatum* Corner, Chapter 14, § 16.4, Fig. 2.32, Fig. 14.3
D. elatum (Roxb.) Wall. ex Hk., Chapter 14, Fig. 10.4, Fig. 10.8
D. falciforme (Parl.) Pilg., § 16.4
D. gibbsiae Stapf, § 10.5, Chapter 14
D. novoguineense L. S. Gibbs, Chapter 14
Dacryodes expansa (Ridley) Lam, Fig. 1.6, Burseraceae
D. laxa (Benn.) Lam, Fig. 2.1
D. rostrata (Bl.) Lam, Fig. 2.1
Dactylocladus stenostachys Oliv., § 2.8, § 6.2, § 11.3, Fig. 11.5, Fig. 11.11, Fig. 11.13, Crypteroniaceae
Daemonorops, Fig. 1.8, Palmae
Dalbergia latifolia Roxb., § 12.1, Leguminosae/Papilionatae
Decaspermum, § 14.2, Myrtaceae
Dehaasia caesia Bl., Fig. 15.4, Lauraceae
Dendrobium crumenatum Swartz, § 4.1, Orchidaceae
Dendrocalamus pendulus Ridley, § 4.1, § 17.2, Gramineae
Dendromyza, § 2.6, Santalaceae
Dendrotrophe, § 2.6, Santalaceae
Derris, § 19.2, Leguminosae/Papilionatae
Desmodium triflorum DC., Fig. 18.1, Leguminosae/Papilionatae
D. umbellatum (L.) DC., § 10.6
Detarium, § 2.8, Leguminosae/Caesalpinoideae
Dialium, § 2.4, § 15.2, § 17.1, Leguminosae/Caesalpinoideae
D. laurinum Baker, Fig. 10.4
Dianella, § 10.3, § 16.4, Liliaceae
Dichrostachys cinerea (L.) W. & A., § 12.1, Leguminosae/Mimosoideae
Dicranopteris, § 12.1, fern

D. linearis (Burm. f.) Underwood, § 18.2
Dillenia, Fig. 14.2, Dilleniaceae
D. alata (DC.) Martelli, § 10.5
D. crenata (A. C. Smith) Hoogl., § 10.5
D. excelsa (Jack) Gilg, Fig. 15.4
D. pulchella (Jack) Gilg, Fig. 11.4
D. salomonensis (C. T. White) Hoogl., Fig. 15.18, Fig. 15.19, Table 6.1
D. suffruticosa (Griff.) Martelli, § 4.1, § 10.3, § 18.2
Dilleniaceae, § 16.3
Dimorphanthera, § 16.1, Ericaceae
Dinochloa, § 6.1, Gramineae
D. scandens (Bl. ex Nees) O.K., § 6.1
Diospyros, § 2.5, § 2.8, Fig. 1.6, Ebenaceae
D. bantamensis K. & V. ex Bakh., Fig. 1.6
D. buxifolia (Bl.) Hiern., Fig. 1.6
D. diepenhorstii Miq., Fig. 15.4
D. ehretioides Wall., § 12.3
D. evena Bakh., Fig. 10.5, Fig. 11.5
D. ferruginea Splitg. ex de Vriese, Fig. 1.6, Fig. 10.4
D. ferruginescens Bakh., Fig. 10.4
D. hermaphroditica (Zoll.) Bakh., § 12.3, Fig. 1.6
D. macrophylla Bl., Fig. 15.4
D. maingayi (Hiern.) Bakh., Fig. 11.4
D. malayana Bakh., Fig. 15.4
D. pyrrhocarpa Miq., Fig. 15.4
D. sumatrana Miq., Fig. 15.4
    var. *decipiens* (Clarke) Bakh., Fig. 2.1
D. toposoides King & Gamble, Fig. 1.6, Fig. 15.4
Dipteris conjugata Reinw., § 16.4, fern
Dipterocarpaceae, § 1.1, § 2.4, § 2.5, § 2.8, § 4.1, § 5.1, § 5.2, § 5.3, § 6.2, § 6.4, § 6.5, § 7.1, § 8.3, § 10.1, § 10.2, § 10.4, § 10.5, § 11.3, § 12.1, § 12.2, § 12.3, § 15.1, § 15.2, § 15.3, § 15.5, § 16.3, § 16.4, § 16.6, § 17.3, § 17.4, Fig. 1.6, Fig. 1.7, Fig. 2.1, Fig. 7.1, Fig. 15.1, Table 15.1, Table 15.2, Table 15.3, Table 15.4
dipterocarps *see* Dipterocarpaceae
Dipterocarpus § 2.4, § 5.1, § 5.2, § 6.4, § 6.5, Chapter 7, § 10.1, § 17.4, Fig. 16.1, Dipterocarpaceae
D. acutangulus Vesque, Table 8.4
D. apterus Foxw., § 15.3
D. caudatus Foxw., Fig. 2.1
D. caudiferus Merr., § 10.4
D. costatus Gaertn., § 16.6
D. costulatus Sloot., Fig. 1.7
D. crinitus Dyer, § 15.2, Fig. 2.2, Fig. 15.7
D. geniculatus Vesque, § 10.5
D. globosus Vesque, Fig. 1.6
D. grandiflorus Blco., § 16.6, Table 8.4
D. kerrii King, § 12.3
D. lowii Hk. f., § 10.5
D. oblongifolius Bl., § 15.3
D. obtusifolius Teysm. ex Miq., Fig. 12.2, Fig. 14.2
D. retusus Bl., § 16.6, Fig. 16.1
D. stellatus Vesque, § 5.3
D. sublamellatus Foxw., Table 15.4
D. tuberculatus Roxb., Fig. 12.2
Dischidia, § 2.8, Asclepiadaceae
Dodonaea viscosa Jacq., § 10.6, § 12.1, Sapindaceae
Dracaena, § 2.5, Liliaceae
Dracontomelum, § 2.8, § 7.2, Anacardiaceae
D. mangiferum = puberulum
D. puberulum Miq., § 7.1
Drimys, § 16.1, Winteraceae
D. piperita Hk. f., § 16.4

Drosera, § 2.8, § 10.3, Droseraceae
Dryobalanops, § 2.4, § 5.1, § 10.1, Dipterocarpaceae
D. aromatica Gaertn. f., § 2.4, § 2.5, § 2.8, § 4.1, § 5.1, **§ 5.2**, § 6.5, Chapter 7, § 15.2, § 15.3, § 15.5, § 17.3, Fig. 1.6, **Fig. 8.1**, Fig. 15.6, Fig. 15.13, Fig. 16.1, Fig. 17.4
D. lanceolata Burck, § 5.3
D. rappa Becc., § 10.3, § 11.3, Fig. 11.4, Fig. 11.11
Drypetes, Fig. 15.4, Euphorbiaceae
Duabanga, § 2.8, § 12.2, Sonneratiaceae
D. grandiflora (Roxb. ex DC.) Walp., § 4.1, Fig. 2.29
duku *see Lansium domesticum*
durian *see Durio zibethinus*
durian belanda *see Annona muricata*
durian melaka *see Durio malaccensis*
Durio, § 2.5, § 2.8, § 4.1, § 5.2, Table 19.2, Bombacaceae
D. griffithii (Mast.) Bakh., § 2.8
D. malaccensis Planch. ex Mast., Fig. 17.2, Table 17.1
D. zibethinus Murr., § 2.8, § 4.1, § 17.1, Table 17.1
Dyera costulata (Miq.) Hk. f., § 4.1, § 5.2, § 6.2, § 7.1, **§ 15.2**, § 15.3, Fig. 1.7, Table 8.3, Table 19.2, Apocynaceae
D. lowii Hk. f., Fig. 11.4
Dysoxylum, § 14.2, Fig. 14.8, Fig. 15.18, Fig. 15.19, Meliaceae
D. angustifolium King, Fig. 2.30
D. caulostachyum Miq., Fig. 2.14, Figs 15.18 and 15.19
D. motleyanum Ridley, Fig. 2.1
D. sp., § 14.2, Fig. 14.8, Figs 15.18 and 15.19

Ebenaceae, Fig. 1.6, Fig. 2.1
Elaeis guineensis Jacq., § 8.4, § 17.1, Fig. 17.9, Palmae
Elaeocarpaceae, § 16.1
Elaeocarpus, § 4.1, § 14.2, Fig. 10.4, Fig. 14.8, Elaeocarpaceae
E. angustipes Knuth, Fig. 10.4
E. fulvotomentosus Knuth, § 16.4
E. obtusifolius Merr., § 11.3
E. sphaericus (Gaertn.) K. Schum., Table 6.1, Table 6.2, **Table 8.3**
Elateriospermum tapos Bl., § 4.1, § 17.1, Table 19.2, Euphorbiaceae
Elmerrillia, § 14.2, Magnoliaceae
Endiandra, § 14.2, Lauraceae
Endospermum, § 2.5, § 2.8, § 6.2, Euphorbiaceae
E. formicarum Becc., § 2.8
E. malaccense M.A., § 2.8, § 6.2, § 7.1, Table 8.3
E. medullosum L. S. Smith, § 6.2, Fig. 6.4, Table 6.1, Table 8.3
Engelhardtia, § 1.1, Fig. 14.8, Juglandaceae
E. spicata Lechen. ex Bl., § 6.2, § 12.1
Enicosanthum erianthoides Airy Shaw, Fig. 15.4, Annonaceae
Ensete, § 2.8, Musaceae
Eperua falcata Aubl., § 10.3, Leguminosae/Caesalpinoideae
Ephedra, Chapter 14, Ephedraceae
Epiphyllum oxypetalum (DC.) Haw., § 4.1, Orchidaceae
Eriachne pallescens R. Br., § 18.2, Gramineae
Eriandra fragrans Royen & Steenis, Figs 15.18 and 15.19, **Poly-**galaceae
Ericaceae, § 1.1, § 16.1, § 16.3, Fig. 16.1
erima *see Octomeles sumatrana*
Erycibe stenophylla Hoogl., Fig. 15.8, Convolvulaceae
Erythrina, § 2.8, § 14.2, Leguminosae/Papilionatae
E. variegata L., § 10.6
Erythroxylum ecarinatum Burck, Fig. 15.18, Fig. 15.19, Erythroxylaceae
eucalypts *see Eucalyptus*
Eucalyptus, § 8.1, § 10.3, § 12.1, Chapter 14, § 19.1, Fig. 8.1, Myrtaceae
E. alba Reinw. ex Bl., § 12.1
E. deglupta Bl., § 6.2, § 7.2, § 14.2, § 15.3, Fig. 7.4, Table 8.3

E. grandis W. Hill ex Maiden, § 8.1
E. saligna J. E. Smith, § 8.1
E. tereticornis J. E. Smith, § 8.1
Eugenia, § 1.1, § 2.5, § 8.1, § 10.3, § 14.2, § 15.2, § 16.4, Fig. 1.6, Fig. 2.10, Fig. 14.8, Table 8.4, Table 17.1, Myrtaceae
E. corallina Merr., Fig. 10.4
E. cuneiforme Merr., Fig. 2.1
E. elopurae Ridley, Fig. 15.4
E. aff. *havilandii* Merr., Fig. 11.4
E. mimica Merr., Fig. 15.8
E. myrtillus Stapf, Fig. 10.4
E. cf. *myrtillus*, Fig. 10.4
E. oblata Roxb., Fig. 10.4
E. rosulenta Ridley, Fig. 2.1
E. spicata Buch.-Ham. ex Wall., Fig. 10.4
E. subdecussata Duthie, Fig. 10.4
E. cf. *syzygioides* (Miq.) M. R. Henderson, Fig. 10.4
E. sp. *479*, Fig. 11.4
E. sp. *9274*, Fig. 11.4
Eugeissona, § 1.1, Palmae
E. tristis Griff., § 3.5, § 12.3, § 15.2, § 15.3, § 16.6, Fig. 15.12
E. utilis Becc., § 17.1
Eupatorium odoratum L. f., § 2.8, § 17.1, Compositae
Euphorbia atoto Forst. f., § 10.6, Euphorbiaceae
E. heterophylla L., § 4.1
Euphorbiaceae, § 2.4, § 2.5, § 6.2, § 6.4, § 12.1, Fig. 1.6, Fig. 2.1, Fig. 15.8, Table 15.1, Table 19.2
Euphoria malaiensis Radlk., Fig. 15.4, Sapindaceae
Eurya, § 16.1 Theaceae
Eurycoma, Chapter 14, Simaroubaceae
E. longifolia Jack, Fig. 1.6
Eusideroxylon malagangai Sym., § 10.4, Lauraceae
E. zwageri T. & B., § 15.3
Excoecaria agallocha L., § 11.4, Euphorbiaceae

Fagaceae, § 1.1, § 16.3, § 16.6, Fig. 2.1, Fig. 16.1, Table 15.1
Fagraea, § 2.6, Loganiaceae
F. fragrans Roxb., § 10.3, § 11.4, § 18.2
F. gigantea Ridley, Chapter 14
F. stenophylla Becc., Fig. 15.8
ferns, § 10.4, § 10.6, § 16.1, Fig. 16.4
   filmy, § 2.6, § 3.6, § 16.1
   tree, § 18.2
Feronia, § 2.8, Rutaceae
F. limonia (L.) Swingle, § 12.1
Ficus, § 1.1, § 2.5, § 2.8, § 4.1, § 14.2, § 17.4, § 18.1, Fig. 17.1, Moraceae
F. alba = *grossularioides*
F. deltoidea Jack, § 14.1
Ficus glandulifera Summerh., Fig. 2.25
F. grossularioides Burm. f., § 18.2
F. pyriformis Hk. & Arn., § 2.8, § 15.3
F. variegata Bl., § 4.1
figs *see Ficus*
Fimbristylis sericea R. Br., § 10.6, Cyperaceae
Finschia chloroxantha Diels, Figs 15.18 and 15.19, Proteaceae
Firmiana, § 4.1, Sterculiaceae
F. malayana Kosterm., Fig. 2.28
Flacourtiaceae, § 16.3, Fig. 2.1
Fordia filipes Dunn, Fig. 2.1, Leguminosae/Papilionatae
F. gibbsiae Dunn & E. G. Baker, Fig. 15.4
Freycinetia solomonensis B. C. Stone, § 2.6, Pandanaceae
Frullania, § 16.4, Hepaticae

Gahnia, § 10.3, Cyperaceae
G. tristis Nees, § 18.2
Galium, § 16.3, Rubiaceae
Ganua coriacea Pierre ex Dubard, Fig. 11.4, Sapotaceae
G. kingiana (Brace) Assem, § 8.1, Table 8.4
G. palembanica (Miq.) Assem & Kosterm., Fig. 2.1
G. pierrei Assem, Fig. 11.4
Garcinia, § 1.1, § 4.1, § 14.2, § 19.2, Fig. 10.4, Figs 15.18 and 15.19, Table 19.2, Guttiferae
G. atroviridis Griff. ex T. Anders., Table 17.1
G. bancana (Miq.) Miq., Fig. 10.4
G. cataractalis Whitmore, Fig. 15.9
G. linearis Pierre, Fig. 15.8
G. mangostana L., § 4.1, Table 17.1
G. parvifolia (Miq.) Miq., Fig. 1.6
G. rheedii Pierre, Fig. 10.4
G. rostrata Hassk. ex Hk. f., Fig. 11.5
G. vidua Ridley, Fig. 11.4
G. sp. *669*, Fig. 11.4
G. sp. *865*, Fig. 11.4
Gardenia tubifera Wall., Fig. 1.6, Theaceae
Garuga floribunda Decne., § 12.1, Burseraceae
Gaultheria, § 16.3, Ericaceae
geriting *see Eusideroxylon zwageri*
Gesneriaceae, § 2.6, § 3.6, § 10.4
Gigantochloa latifolia Ridley, § 12.3, Gramineae
G. ligulata Gamble, § 12.3
G. scortechinii Gamble, § 4.1, § 17.2
gingers *see Zingiberaceae*
Gleichenia, § 10.5, § 12.1, fern
Glochidion, § 4.1, Euphorbiaceae
G. obscurum (Roxb. ex Willd.) Bl., § 11.4, Fig. 11.4
Gluta, § 8.1, § 8.2, Table 8.4, Anacardiaceae
G. laxiflora Ridley, Fig. 2.1
G. renghas L., § 4.1
Gmelina arborea Roxb., § 6.2, Table 8.3, Verbenaceae
G. moluccana Backer ex K. Heyne, § 6.2, § 18.1, Table 6.1
Gnetum, § 2.6, Fig. 2.21, Gnetaceae
Gomphandra, Figs 15.18 and 15.19, Icacinaceae
G. quadrifida (Bl.) Sleumer var. *angustifolia* (King) Sleumer, § 15.3
Gonocaryum, Fig. 1.6, Icacinaceae
Gonystylus bancanus (Miq.) Kurz, § 2.8, § 11.3, Fig. 11.4, Fig. 11.5, Fig. 11.7, Fig. 11.11, Fig. 11.13, Thymelaeaceae
G. nervosus Airy Shaw, § 10.4
G. velutinus Airy Shaw, Fig. 1.6
Gordonia, § 14.2, Fig. 14.8, Theaceae
Gramineae, § 6.2, § 8.4, § 10.3, § 11.4, § 17.4
Grammatophyllum speciosum Bl., § 15.3, Orchidaceae
Grass, Kangaroo *see Themeda australis*
grasses *see* Gramineae
Grevillea, § 12.1, Proteaceae
Grewia cinnamomifolia Stapf ex Burret, § 8.1, Tiliaceae
Guettarda speciosa L., § 10.6, Rubiaceae
Gulubia hombronii Becc., § 10.5, Palmae
Gunnera, § 16.3, Haloragidaceae
Guoia sp., Figs 15.18 and 15.19, Sapindaceae
Guttiferae, § 1.6, Fig. 2.1, Fig. 15.8, Table 19.2
Gymnacranthera eugeniifolia (A. DC.) Sinclair var. *griffithii* (Warb.) Sinclair, Fig. 10.4, Myristicaceae
Gynotroches axillaris Bl., Fig. 15.18, Fig. 15.19, Rhizophoraceae

Harmsiopanax aculeatus (Bl. ex DC.) Harms, § 6.2, Araliaceae
Helianthus annuus L., § 8.4, Compositae
Hepaticae, § 16.1

N

Herberta, § 16.4, Hepaticae
Heritiera littoralis Dryand. ex W. Ait., § 10.6, Sterculiaceae
H. macrophylla Wall. ex Kurz, § 4.1
H. simplicifolia (Mast.) Kosterm. Tab. 6.4
H. sumatrana (Miq.) Kosterm., Fig. 2.1
Hernandia nymphaeifolia (Presl) Kubitzi, § 10.6, Hernandiaceae
H. peltata = nymphaeifolia
Hevea brasiliensis (Willd. ex A. juss.) M.A., § 4.1, § 8.4, § 11.3, § 17.1,
   § 18.1, § 19.1, Euphorbiaceae
Hexapora, § 15.1, Lauraceae
Hibiscus rosa-sinensis L., § 2.8, Malvaceae
H. tiliaceus L., § 4.1, § 10.6
Homalanthus, § 6.2, § 18.2, Euphorbiaceae
H. giganteus Z. & M., § 12.1
Homalium tomentosum (Vent.) Bth., § 12.1, Flacourtiaceae
Homonoia riparia Lour., § 15.3, Fig. 15.8, Euphorbiaceae
Hopea, § 2.4, § 6.2, § 6.5, § 10.3, § 15.3, § 16.1, Fig. 1.7, Diptero-
   carpaceae
H. andersonii Ashton ssp. *andersonii*, § 10.4
H. argentea Meijer, § 10.4
H. beccariana Burck, § 8.2
H. bracteata Burck, § 2.3, Fig. 2.1
H. chinensis (Merr.) Hand.-Mazz., § 15.2
H. dasyrrachis Sloot., § 10.4
H. hainanensis Merr. & Chun, § 15.2
H. helferi (Dyer) Brandis, § 10.4
H. latifolia Sym., § 10.4
H. sangal Korth., § 15.2, Fig. 15.4
H. semicuneata Sym., § 10.3
Horsfieldia fulva (King) Warb., Table 6.4, Myristicaceae
H. polysperula (Hk. f. emend. King) Sinclair, § 16.4
H. superba (Hk. f. & Thoms.) Warb., Table 6.4
Hoya, § 2.8, Asclepiadaceae
H. parasitica Wall. ex Traill, § 5.1
Hydnocarpus pentagyna Sloot., Fig. 2.1, Flacourtiaceae
H. sumatrana Koord., Fig. 15.4
H. woodii Merr., Table 6.4
Hydnophytum, § 2.8, § 10.3, Fig. 10.8, Rubiaceae
Hymenophyllaceae, § 12.1
Hymenophyllum, § 2.6, fern
Hypericaceae, Fig. 2.1

Icacinaceae, Fig. 1.6, Fig. 2.1
Iguanura, § 1.1, § 8.3, § 10.1, § 12.3, Palmae
Ilex, § 14.2, Aquifoliaceae
I. cymosa Bl., § 10.3, § 11.4
I. hypoglauca (Miq.) Loes., Fig. 11.4
I. sclerophylloides Loes., Fig. 10.4, Fig. 11.5
illipe nuts, § 2.8, § 4.1, § 5.1, § 15.3
Impatiens, § 10.4, Balsaminaceae
Imperata cylindrica (L.) P. Beauv., § 10.2, Chapter 13, § 14.2,
   § 18.2, Fig. 18.1, Gramineae
     var. *major* (Nees) C. E. Hubbard, § 18.1
Indetermined SAR 18780, Fig. 10.4
Indotristicha malayana Dransfield & Whitmore, § 15.3, Podo-
   stemaceae
Intsia bijuga (Colebr.) O.K., Fig. 15.3, Leguminosae/Caesal-
   pinoideae
I. palembanica Miq., § 2.5, § 5.2, § 12.3, § 15.3, § 16.1, Fig. 4.1
ipoh *see Antiaria toxicaria*
Ipomoea alba L., § 2.8, Convolvulaceae
I. batatas (L.) L., § 17.1
I. bona-nox = alba
I. gracilis R. Br., § 10.6

I. pes caprae (L.) R. Br., § 10.6
Ischaemum muticum L., § 10.6, Gramineae
Ixonanthes beccarii H. Hall., Fig. 10.4, Linaceae
I. icosandra Jack, Table 6.4
I. reticulata Jack, Fig. 1.6
Ixora havilandii Ridley, Fig. 10.4, Rubiaceae
I. macrophylla Bartl. ex Koord., Fig. 15.4

Jack fruit *see Artocarpus integer*
jambu bertek
    melaka } *see Eugenia*
    padang
jelutong *see Dyera costulata*
Johannesteijsmannia, § 1.1, Palmae
J. altifrons (Reichb. f. & Zoll.) Moore, § 3.5, § 15.2

kaatoan bangkal *see Anthocephalus chinensis*
kadam *see Anthocephalus chinensis*
kamerere *see Eucalyptus deglupta*
kapur *see Dryobalanops aromatica*
Kauri Pine *see Agathis australis*
Kauri, Santa Cruz *see Agathis macrophylla*
kelapa *see Cocos nucifera*
keledang *see Artocarpus lanceifolius*
kelempayan *see Anthocephalus chinensis*
keypayang kayu *see Pangium edule*
Knema cinerea (Poir.) Warb.
    var. *patentinervia* (Sinclair) Sinclair, Fig. 1.6, Myristicaceae
K. kunstleri (Bl.) Warb., Fig. 1.6
K. latericia Elm., Fig. 2.1
Koompassia, § 2.4, § 15.2, Leguminosae/Caesalpinoideae
K. excelsa (Becc.) Taub., § 2.4, § 7.2, § 15.2, § 15.3, § 18.1, Fig. 4.2
K. malaccensis Maing. ex Benth., § 2.5, § 5.1, § 5.2, Fig. 1.7, Fig. 2.1,
   Chapter 7, Table 6.4
Korthalsia, § 2.8, Fig. 1.8, Palmae
Kostermansia malayana Soegeng, Fig. 2.9, Bombacaceae
kundang *see Bouea macrophylla*
kunai *see Imperata cylindrica*

Labiatae, § 2.8, § 6.2
Lagenaria siceraria (Moll.) Standl., § 17.1, Cucurbitaceae
Lagerstroemia, § 12.2, Fig. 12.1, Lythraceae
lalang *see Imperata cylindrica*
langsat *see Lansium domesticum*
Lannea grandis Engl., § 12.1, Anacardiaceae
Lansium, § 2.8, § 4.1, Meliaceae
L. domesticum Corr., § 2.5, § 4.1, Fig. 15.4, Table 17.1, Table 19.2
Lantana camara L., § 17.1, § 18.2, Verbenaceae
laran *see Anthocephalus chinensis*
Lauraceae, § 2.4, § 2.5, § 15.2, § 16.1, § 16.3, § 16.6, Fig. 2.1,
   Fig. 15.4, Fig. 15.8, Fig. 16.1, Table 15.1
Launaea sarmentosa (Willd.) Sch.–Bip. ex O.K., § 10.6, Compositae
Lawyer Vines *see* rattans
Lecanopteris carnosa (Reinw.) Bl., § 2.8, fern
L. sinuosa (Wall ex Hk.) Copel., § 2.8
Lecythidaceae, Fig. 1.6
Leea indica (Burm. f.) Merr., Fig. 15.4, Leeaceae
Leguminosae, § 2.4, § 2.5, § 2.8, § 5.2, § 15.2, Fig. 2.1, Table 15.1,
   Table 19.2
Leguminosae/Caesalpinoideae, § 2.5
Leguminosae/Papilionatae, § 2.8, § 12.1
Lepicolea, § 16.4, Hepaticae
Lepinia solomonensis Hemsl., Figs 15.18 and 15.19, Apocynaceae
Leptaspis, § 12.1, Gramineae

Leptospermum flavescens J. E. Smith, § 6.2, Fig. 16.3, Fig. 16.4, Fig. 16.9, Myrtaceae
L. recurvum Hk. f., § 10.5
Lepturus repens (Forst. f.) R. Br., § 10.6, Gramineae
Liberbaileya gracilis (Burrett) Burrett & Potzal, § 10.4, Palmae
Licania splendens (Korth.) Prance (ined.), § 10.3, Rosaceae
Licuala, § 2.8, Palmae
Linaceae, Fig. 1.6
Linociera evenia Stapf, Fig. 10.4, Oleaceae
Lithocarpus, § 1.1, § 15.2, Fagaceae
L. gracilis (Korth.) Soepadmo, Fig. 15.4
L. jordanae (Laguna) Rehd., § 18.2
L. lampadarius (Gamble) A. Camus, § 16.4
L. lucidus (Roxb.) Rehd., Fig. 15.4
L. rassa (Miq.) Rehd., Fig. 10.4, Fig. 11.4
L. sundaicus (Bl.) Rehd., § 6.2
Litsea, Fig. 2.1, Figs 15.18 and 15.19, Lauraceae
L. crassifolia (Bl.) Boerl., § 11.3, Fig. 10.4, Fig. 11.5, Fig. 11.11
L. cylindrocarpa Gamble, § 11.3
L. gracilipes Hk. f., § 11.3
L. nidularis Gamble, § 11.3
L. ochracea Boerl., Fig. 15.4
L. oppositifolia L. S. Gibbs, Fig. 15.4
L. resinosa Bl., § 11.3
Livistona saribus (Lour.) Chev., § 10.3, Palmae
Loganiaceae, Fig. 15.8
Lonicera, § 2.8, § 16.3, Caprifoliaceae
Lophopetalum beccarianum Pierre, Table 8.4, Celastraceae
L. javanicum (Zoll.) Turcz., Fig. 2.1
L. rigidum Ridley, Fig. 11.4, Fig. 11.5
L. subobovatum King, Fig. 1.6
Loranthaceae, § 2.6
Lycopodium cernuum L., § 10.5, Chapter 14, § 18.2, Lycopodiaceae
Lythraceae, § 11.3

Macaranga, § 2.8, § 6.2, § 7.2, § 10.3, § 12.3, Chapter 13, § 15.5, § 18.2, Fig. 15.3, Table 8.3, Euphorbiaceae
M. aleuritoides F. Muell., Fig. 17.5
M. caladiifolia Becc., § 6.2, § 11.3
M. conifera (Zoll.) M.A., Table 6.4
M. constricta Whitmore & Airy Shaw, § 6.2
M. gigantea (Reichb. f. & Zoll.) M.A., § 6.2, Fig. 6.1, Table 6.4
M. gigantifolia Merr., Fig. 6.3
M. heynei I. M. Johnston, § 18.2
M. polyadenia P. & H., § 6.5, Fig. 6.7, Fig. 15.18, Fig. 15.19
M. pruinosa (Miq.) M.A., § 11.4
M. triloba (Bl.) M.A., Fig. 2.31, Fig. 6.2
machang *see Mangifera*
Madhuca crassipes (Pierre) Lam, Fig. 1.6, Sapotaceae
Magnolia, § 4.1, Magnoliaceae
Magnoliaceae, § 2.8
mahogony *see Swietenia*
Maingaya, § 15.1, Hamamelidaceae
maize *see Zea mays*
Mallotus, § 6.2, § 7.1, § 10.3, Chapter 13, Fig. 2.1, Euphorbiaceae
M. glaberrimus (Reichb. f. & Zoll.) M.A., § 8.1, Table 8.4
M. griffithianus Hk. f., Fig. 1.6, Table 6.4
M. leucodermis Hk. f., § 11.4
M. muticus (M. A.) Airy Shaw, § 11.4
M. paniculatus (Lamk.) M.A., § 6.2, § 18.2
Malvaceae, § 6.2
Mammea, § 2.8, Guttiferae
M. calciphila Kosterm., § 10.4

M. odoratus (Rafin.) Kosterm., § 10.6
manggis *see Garcinia mangostana*
Mangifera, § 2.8, § 4.1, § 17.1, Fig. 1.6, Fig. 15.4, Table 17.1, Table 19.2, Anacardiaceae
M. havilandii Ridley, Fig. 1.6, Fig. 11.4
mango *see Mangifera*
mangosteen *see Garcinia mangostana*
mangroves, § 9.9, § 11.1
Manihot esculenta Crantz, § 17.1, Euphorbiaceae
Manilkara, § 2.8, Sapotaceae
Marantaceae, § 16.3
Maranthes corymbosa Bl., § 6.3, § 10.6, Table 6.1, Rosaceae
Mastigophora, § 16.4, Hepaticae
Matonia pectinata R. Br., § 16.4, fern
Maxburretia rupicola (Ridley) Ftdo., § 10.4, Palmae
Meiogyne virgata (Bl.) Miq., Fig. 15.4, Annonaceae
Melaleuca, § 11.4, § 12.1, § 15.5, Myrtaceae
M. cajuputi Powell, § 10.3, § 11.4
M. leucadendron = *cajuputi*
Melanolepis multiglandulosa (Bl.) Reichb. f. & Zoll., § 12.1, Euphorbiaceae
Melanorrhoea, Chapter 14, Anacardiaceae
M. beccarii Engl., § 10.3, Fig. 11.4, Fig. 11.11
M. inappendiculata King, § 10.3
M. torquata King, Fig. 1.6
M. wallichii Hk. f., § 8.1
Melastoma, Chapter 13, Melastomataceae
M. malabathricum L., § 2.8, § 4.1, § 10.3, § 18.2
Melastomataceae, Fig. 1.6
Melia azedarach L., § 12.1, Meliaceae
M. parasitica Osbeck, § 2.5
Meliaceae, Fig. 2.1, Table 19.2
Memecylon, Fig. 1.6, Melastomataceae
M. myrsinoides Bl., Fig. 10.4
meranti *see Shorea*
Merremia, § 2.6, 6.1, § 7.1, Chapter 18, Convolvulaceae
Messerschmidia argentea (L. f.) Johnston, § 10.6, Boraginaceae
Metroxylon sagu Rottb., § 11.4, Palmae
Mezoneuron, § 2.6, Leguminosae/Caesalpinoideae
M. sumatranum (Roxb.) W. & A. ex Miq., § 2.6, § 7.1
Mezzettia leptopoda (Hk. f. & Thoms.) Oliver, Fig. 11.4, Fig. 11.11, Annonaceae
Microlaena, § 16.3, Gramineae
Mikania cordata (Burm. f.) B. L. Rob., § 6.1, Compositae
Millettia, § 19.2, Leguminosae/Papilionatae
mistletoe, § 2.6
Monophyllaea, § 10.4, Gesneriaceae
Moraceae, § 6.2, Fig. 1.6, Fig. 2.1, Table 19.2
Morinda citrifolia L., § 10.3, § 10.6, Rubiaceae
moss, bog *see Sphagnum*
mosses, § 10.3, § 16.1
Moultonianthus leembrugianus (Boerl. & Koord.) Steenis, Table 8.4, Euphorbiaceae
Mucuna, § 2.8, Leguminosae/Papilionatae
Muntingia calabura L., § 2.8, Tiliaceae
Murraya paniculata (L.) Jack, § 4.1, Rutaceae
Musa, § 2.8, Musaceae
Musanga cecropioides R. Br., § 8.4, Urticaceae
Mussaenda, § 2.8, Rubiaceae
Mussaendopsis beccariana Baill., Fig. 11.4, Rubiaceae
Myrialepis, Fig. 1.8, Palmae
Myrica esculenta Buch.-Ham., § 10.3, § 10.4, § 16.4, § 18.2, Myricaceae
Myristica lowiana King, Fig. 1.6, Myristicaceae

Myristicaceae, § 2.4, § 2.5, § 2.8, § 8.1, § 15.2, § 16.3, Fig. 1.6,
  Fig. 2.1
Myrmecodia, § 2.8, § 10.3, Fig. 10.8, Rubiaceae
Myosotis, § 16.3, Boraginaceae
Myrsinaceae, Fig. 2.1
Myrsine umbellata (Wall.) Miez., § 16.4, Myrsinaceae
Myrtaceae, § 10.3, § 12.1, § 15.2, § 16.1, § 16.3, § 16.5, Fig. 1.6,
  Fig. 2.1, Fig. 15.8, Fig. 16.1, Table 15.1
Myrtella beccarii F. Muell., § 10.5, Myrtaceae

nangka see *Artocarpus heterophyllus*
Nenga, § 10.1, § 12.3, Palmae
Neonauclea angustifolia Merr., Fig. 15.8, Rubiaceae
Neoscortechinia forbesii (Seem. ex Harv.) Merr., Figs 15.18 and
  15.19, Euphorbiaceae
N. kingii (Hk. f.) P. & H., Fig. 11.4
Neo-uvaria acuminatissima (Miq.) Airy Shaw, Fig. 15.4, Annonaceae
Nepenthes, § 2.8, § 10.3, § 11.3, § 12.1, § 18.2, Nepenthaceae
N. albomarginata Lobb, § 10.4
N. ampullaria Jack, Fig. 2.32
Nephelium, § 4.1, Sapindaceae
N. lappaceum L., § 4.1, Table 17.1, Table 19.2
N. maingayi Hiern, Fig. 11.4
N. mutabile Bl., Table 17.1
Nephrolepis biserrata (Sw.) Schott, § 10.6, fern
neram see *Dipterocarpus oblongifolius*
Nertera, § 16.1, § 16.3, Rubiaceae
Nothofagus, § 10.4, Chapter 14, § 16.1, Fagaceae
N. pullei Steenis, § 8.2
Nypa fruticans Wurmb, § 11.2, Fig. 11.1, Palmae

Ochanostachys amentacea Mast., Fig. 2.1, Table 6.4, Olacaceae
Ochroma lagopus Sw., § 6.2, Fig. 8.1, Bombacaceae
Octomeles sumatrana Miq., § 2.5, § 6.2, § 7.2, § 8.2, § 15.3, Fig. 7.5,
  Datiscaceae
Olacaceae, Fig. 1.6, Fig. 2.1, Table 15.1
Oleandra pistillaris (Sw.) C. Chr., § 16.4, fern
Olearia, § 16.1, Compositae
Oncosperma tigillarium (Jack) Ridley, § 10.6, Palmae
Ophiuros, § 14.2, Gramineae
Orchidaceae, § 1.1, § 2.6, § 2.8, § 5.1, § 10.6
orchids see Orchidaceae
Oroxylum, § 2.8, Bignoniaceae

Pachylarnax, § 15.1, Magnoliaceae
Palaquium cochleariifolium Royen, Fig. 11.4, Fig. 11.5, Sapotaceae
P. leiocarpum Boerl., § 10.4, Fig. 10.4, Fig. 10.5
P. pseudorostratum Lam, Fig. 11.4
P. ridleyi King & Gamble, Fig. 11.5
P. rostratum (Miq.) Burck, Fig. 2.1, Fig. 10.4, Fig. 15.4, Table 6.4
P. walsurifolium Pierre ex Dubard, § 2.8, Fig. 11.4
Palmae, § 1.1, § 2.8, § 4.1, § 8.4, § 10.3, § 11.3, § 11.4, Chapter 18
  subfamily Arecoideae, § 1.1, § 12.3
  subfamily Caryotoideae, § 8.3
  subfamily Lepidocaryoideae see rattans
palm(s) see Palmae
  climbing see rattans
  Mangrove Date see *Phoenix paludosa*
  nibong see *Oncosperma tigillarium*
  oil see *Elaeis guineensis*
  undescribed genus, § 10.4
pandan see *Pandanus*
Pandanus, § 2.5, § 8.4, § 11.4, § 17.1, Fig. 10.4, Pandanaceae
P. bidur Jungh. ex Miq., § 10.6

P. epiphyticus Mart., Fig. 2.19
P. helicopus Kurz, § 15.3
P. lamprocephalus Merr. & Perry, § 10.5
P. recurvatus St. John, Chapter 14
P. scandens Sensu Brunig, Fig. 10.4
P. tectorius Soland. ex Park., § 10.6
Pangium edule Reinw., Table 17.1, Flacourtiaceae
papaya see *Carica papaya*
Papuacedrus, Chapter 14, § 16.1, Fig. 14.8, Cupressaceae
Paraboea, § 10.4, Gesneriaceae
Parartocarpus, § 2.8, Moraceae
Parashorea, § 5.1, § 6.5, § 7.1, § 10.1, § 15.2, § 17.4, Diptero-
  carpaceae
P. densiflora Sloot & Sym., § 5.3
P. malaanonan (Blco.) Merr, § 15.2, Fig. 15.4
P. stellata Kurz, § 12.3
P. tomentella (Sym.) Meijer, § 5.3, § 6.5, Fig. 6.8
Parastemon spicatum Ridley, Fig. 11.4, Fig. 11.5, Rosaceae
P. urophyllus (A. DC.) A. DC., Fig. 1.6, Fig. 10.4
Parinari, § 3.5, § 15.2, § 15.4, Rosaceae
P. salomonensis C. T. White, § 6.2, § 6.3, Fig. 6.4, Fig. 8.1, Table 6.1
Parishia insignis Hk. f., Fig. 1.6, Anacardiaceae
P. sericea Ridley, Fig. 11.4
Parkia, § 2.8, § 5.2, Table 19.2, Leguminosae/Mimosoideae
P. speciosa Hassk., § 5.2, Table 17.1
Paspalum conjugatum Berg., Fig. 18.1, Gramineae
Payena, Fig. 1.6, Sapotaceae
P. lucida (G. Don) DC., Fig. 1.6
Peltophorum pterocarpum (DC.) Backer ex Heyne, § 4.1, Legu-
  minosae/Caesalpinoideae
Pentace, § 8.1, Fig. 15.4, Table 8.4, Tiliaceae
P. macrophylla King, Fig. 2.1
Pentaphylacaceae, § 16.3
Pentaspadon, § 15.3, Anacardiaceae
P. officinalis Holmes, § 7.1
P. velutinum Hk. f., Fig. 4.3
perah see *Elateriospermum tapos*
Persea, § 2.8, Lauraceae
petai see *Parkia speciosa*
petai meranti see *Parkia*
Phacellaria, § 2.6, Santalaceae
Phoebe sp., § 11.3, Lauraceae
Phoenix paludosa Roxb., § 11.2, Palmae
Phyllanthus buxifolius (Bl.) M.A., § 12.1, Euphorbiaceae
Phyllocladus hypophyllus Hk. f., § 10.4, Chapter 14, § 16.4, Podo-
  carpaceae
Physokentia insolita Moore, Figs 15.18 and 15.19, Palmae
Picea, Chapter 14, Pinaceae
pigeon orchid see *Dendrobium crumenatum*
Pimelodendron amboinicum Hassk., § 10.4, Euphorbiaceae
P. griffithianum (M.A.) Benth., Fig. 1.6, Fig. 2.1
pinang siri see *Areca catechu*
Pinanga, § 2.8, § 8.3, § 10.1, § 12.3, Palmae
P. calamifrons Becc., § 15.3
P. disticha (Roxb.) Bl. ex Wendl., Fig. 10.4
P. rivularis Becc., § 15.3
pineapple, § 4.1, § 10.3, § 11.4, § 18.2
Pine, Benguet see *Pinus kesiya*
Pine, Hoop see *Araucaria cunnibghamii*
Pine, Klinki see *Araucaria husteinii*
Pinus, § 2.5, § 5.2, § 6.2, § 12.1, Chapter 14, § 14.3, § 16.1,
  Pinaceae
P. excelsa = *wallichiana*
P. insularis = *kesiya*

P. kesiya Royle ex Gordon, § 6.2, § 7.2, Chapter 14, § 14.1, § 14.3, Fig. 12.2, Fig. 14.2
P. longifolia = roxburghii
P. massoniana D. Don, § 14.3
P. merkusii Jungh. & de Vriese, § 2.8, § 5.2, § 6.2, § 7.2, § 12.1, Chapter 13, Chapter 14, § 14.3, Fig. 8.1, Fig. 14.1
P. roxburghii Sars., § 14.3
P. wallichiana A. B. Jackson, § 14.3
P. yunanensis Franch., § 14.3
Piper aduncum L., § 2.8, § 4.1, Piperaceae
Pisonia grandis R. Br., § 10.6, Nyctaginaceae
Pithecellobium jiringa (Jack) Prain, Table 17.1, Leguminosae/ Mimosoideae
Pittosporum ferrugineum W. Ait. § 10.3, Pittosporaceae
Platea fulignea Elm., Fig. 1.6, Icacinaceae
Plectocomia, Fig. 1.8, Palmae
P. griffithii Becc., § 4.1
Plectocomiopsis, Fig. 1.8, Palmae
Ploiarium alternifolium (Vahl) Melch., § 4.1, § 10.3, § 11.3, § 11.4, § 15.5, § 18.2, Fig. 10.4, Fig. 10.10, Theaceae
Pluchea indica (L.) Less., 10.6, Compositae
Podocarpaceae, § 16.1, § 16.3, § 19.2
Podocarpus, Chapter 14, Podocarpaceae
P. blumei, see P. motleyi
P. brassii Pilger, § 16.2
P. imbricatus Bl., Chapter 14, § 16.4
P. motleyi (Parl.) Dummer, Chapter 14
P. neriifolius D. Don, Fig. 10.4
P. papuanus Ridley, Chapter 14
P. polystachyus R. Br., § 10.3
Podostemaceae, § 15.3
Poinsettia, § 4.1, Euphorbiaceae
Polyalthia glauca (Hassl.) Boerl., Fig. 11.4, Annonaceae
P. laterifolia King, Fig. 15.4
P. sumatrana Miq., Fig. 1.6
Polyosma, Figs 15.18 and 15.19, Saxifragaceae
Pometia, § 14.1, Sapindaceae
P. pinnata J. R. & G. Forst., § 1.1, § 2.4, § 7.1, § 7.2, § 10.4, § 15.3, § 16.1, § 17.1, Fig. 11.4, Table 6.1, Table 8.3
Pongamia pinnata (L.) Pierre, § 10.6, Leguminosae/Papilionatae
Popowia pisocarpa (Bl.) Endl., Fig. 2.1, Annonaceae
Prainea frutescens Becc., Fig. 1.6, Fig. 2.1, Moraceae
Premna corymbosa (Burm. f.) Rottl. & Willd., § 10.6, Verbenaceae
Primula, § 16.3, Primulaceae
Proteaceae, § 11.3, § 12.1
Prunus arborea (Bl.) Kalkman, Fig. 10.4, Rosaceae
P. schlechteri (Koehne) Kalkman, Fig. 15.18, Fig. 15.19
Psidium, § 2.8, § 17.1, Myrtaceae
Psychotria acuminata Benth., Fig. 15.8, Rubiaceae
Pternandra capitellata Jack, Table 6.4, Melastomataceae
Pterocarpus, § 12.2, Leguminosae/Papilionatae
P. indicus Willd., § 4.1, § 7.1, § 7.2, § 19.1
Pterocymbium, § 14.2, Sterculiaceae
Pterospermum jackianum Wall. ex Mast., § 8.3, Sterculiaceae
Pterygota alata (Roxb.) R. Br., § 15.3, Sterculiaceae
Ptychopyxis arborea (Merr.) Airy Shaw, Fig. 15.4, Euphorbiaceae
P. costata Miq., § 6.4
pulai *see Alstonia*
pulasan *see Nephelium mutabile*
punggai *see Coelostegia*
Pycnospora lutescens Schindl., Fig. 12.3, Leguminosae/Papilionatae
Pyrrosia nummulariifolia (Sw.) Ching, § 2.6, fern

Quercus, § 14.2, § 17.1, Fagaceae

Q. argentata Korth., Fig. 2.1
Quintinia, § 14.2, § 16.1, Saxifragaceae

Rafflesia, § 2.8, Cytinaceae
rambai *see Baccaurea motleyana*
rambutan *see Nephelium lappaceum*
Randia anisophylla Hk. f., Table 6.4, Rubiaceae
R. dasycarpa (Kurz) Bakh. f., § 11.4
R. jambosoides Val., Fig. 1.6
R. scortechinii King & Gamble Tab. 8.3
Ranunculus, § 16.3, Ranunculaceae
Rapanea, § 16.1, Myrsinaceae
rasamala *see Altingia*
rassau *see Pandanus helicopus*
rattans, § 1.1, § 2.6, § 8.3, § 12.2, § 17.1, § 19.2, Fig. 1.8, Fig. 2.22
Rauvolfia, § 19.2, Apocynaceae
Rejoua aurantiaca Gaud., § 2.8, Apocynaceae
rengas, § 5.1
Rhapis, § 10.4, Palmae
Rhizophora, § 9.9, Rhizophoraceae
Rhizophoraceae, § 16.3
Rhodamnia, Chapter 13, Fig. 15.3, Myrtaceae
R. cinerea Jack, § 10.3, § 18.2, Fig. 10.4
R. trinervia = cinerea
Rhodoleia championii Champ. ex Hk. f., § 16.4, Hamamelidaceae
Rhododendron, § 1.1, § 10.4, § 16.1, § 16.4, Ericaceae
R. ericoides Low ex. Hk. f., § 10.5
Rhodomyrtus tomentosa (W. Ait.) Hassk., § 10.3, § 18.2, Myrtaceae
Rhopaloblaste, § 10.1, Palmae
R. singaporensis (Becc.) Moore, Fig. 10.3
Rhus taitensis Guill., Chapter 18, Anacardiaceae
Rhynchosia minima DC., Fig. 12.3, Leguminosae/Papilionatae
Riccardia, § 16.4, Hepaticae
rice, § 4.1, § 17.1
Rosaceae, Fig. 1.6
    subfamily Chrysobalanoideae, § 6.3
rotan kertong, Fig. 2.22
rubber *see Hevea brasiliensis*
Rubiaceae, § 2.4, § 4.1, § 16.1, Fig. 1.6, Fig. 2.1, Fig. 15.8
Rutaceae, § 16.1

Saccharum, § 14.2, Gramineae
Sago Palm *see Metroxylon sagu*
sal *see Shorea robusta*
Salacca conferta Griff., § 11.3, Palmae
Samadera indica Gaertn., Fig. 11.4, Simaroubaceae
Sandalwood *see Santalum album*
Sandoricum emarginatum Hiern., Fig. 11.4, Meliaceae
S. koetjape (Burm. f.) Merr., Table 17.1, Table 19.2
S. maingayi Hiern., Fig. 2.1
Santalaceae, § 2.6
Santalum album L., § 12.1, Santalaceae
Santiria laevigata Bl., Table 6.4, Burseraceae
S. rubiginosa Bl., Fig. 10.4, Fig. 11.4
Sapindaceae, Table 19.2
Sapium baccatum Roxb., Table 8.3, Euphorbiaceae
S. discolor (Champ. ex Benth.) M.A., § 6.4, Table 6.4
Sapotaceae, § 2.4, § 2.8, § 10.3, § 15.2, Fig. 1.6, Fig. 2.1
Saraca, § 4.1, § 15.3, Leguminosae/Caesalpinoideae
S. palembanica Baker, Fig. 15.4
Sararanga, § 2.5, Pandanaceae
Sarcotheca griffithii (Planch. ex Hk. f., Hall. f., Fig. 1.7, Oxalidaceae
Saurauia angustifolia Turcz., Fig. 15.8, Actinidiaceae
Scaevola taccada (Gaertn.) Roxb., § 4.1, § 10.6, Goodeniaceae

Scaphium macropodum (Miq.) Beumée, Fig. 2.1, Sterculiaceae
Scheelea rostrata Burrett, § 2.8, Palmae
Schefflera, § 2.5, § 2.6, Araliaceae
Schima wallichii (DC.) Korth., § 6.2, § 12.3, Theaceae
Schistochila, § 16.4, Hepaticae
Schizaea fistulosa Labill., § 10.5, fern
Schizomeria, § 14.2, Cunoniaceae
S. serrata (Hochr.) Hochr., Fig. 8.1, Fig. 15.19, Table 6.1
Schizospatha, Fig. 1.8, Palmae
Schizostachyum, § 4.1, Gramineae
S. grande Ridley, § 17.3, Fig. 17.8
Schleichera oleosa (Lour.) Oken., § 12.1, Sapindaceae
Schoutenia ovata Korth., § 12.1, Tiliaceae
Scitamineae, § 3.6, § 8.4
Scleria, § 11.4, Chapter 18, Cyperaceae
S. levis Retz., § 18.2
Scorodocarpus borneensis Becc., § 15.3, Olacaceae
Securinega flexuosa M.A., § 6.2, Euphorbiaceae
sedge, § 10.3, § 11.4, Chapter 18, Fig. 16.4
Semecarpus rufovelutinus Ridley, Fig. 1.6, Anacardiaceae
Semeiocardium, § 12.1, Balsaminaceae
sentul *see Sandoricum koetjape*
sertapi *see Sandoricum koetjape*
Shorea, § 1.1, § 2.4, § 2.5, § 2.8, § 5.1, § 5.2, Chapter 7, § 7.1, § 10.1, § 11.3, § 15.4, § 17.2, § 17.4, Fig. 2.4, Fig. 11.13, Fig. 15.2, Fig. 16.1, Dipterocarpaceae
    Balau group, § 6.2, § 6.5
    Light Red Meranti group, § 4.1, § 6.5, Chapter 7, § 7.1, Table 8.3
    Red Meranti group, § 5.1, § 6.4, § 6.5, § 12.3, § 15.4, Fig. 8.1
    White Meranti group, § 12.3, Table 8.3
    Yellow Meranti group, § 7.1
S. acuminata Dyer, § 5.2, § 16.6, Fig. 1.7
S. acuminatissima Sym., § 6.5
S. acuta Ashton, Fig. 1.6
S. agami Wood ex Ashton, Fig. 10.1
S. albida Sym., § 2.8, § 6.1, § 10.3, § 11.3, § 15.5, § 19.1, Fig. 10.6, Fig. 11.4, Fig. 11.5, Fig. 11.8, Fig. 11.11, Fig. 11.13
S. andulensis Ashton, § 10.5
S. argentifolia Sym., § 6.5, Table 8.4
S. beccariana Burck, Table 8.4
S. bracteolata Dyer, § 16.6
S. ciliata King, § 16.6, Fig. 16.1
S. coriacea Burck, § 10.3, § 10.4, Fig. 10.4
S. curtisii Dyer ex King, § 2.5, § 2.8, § 4.1, § 5.1, § 5.2, § 5.3, § 8.2, § 12.3, Chapter 14, § 15.3, § 15.5, § 16.6, § 17.3, Fig. 2.2, Fig. 2.6, Fig. 2.11, Fig. 15.10, Fig. 15.11, Fig. 15.12, Fig. 16.1
S. dolichocarpa Sloot., Fig. 1.6, Fig. 2.1
S. faguetiana Heim, § 16.6
S. fallax Meijer, § 5.1
S. geniculata Sym., Fig. 1.6
S. glauca King, § 10.3
S. glaucescens Meijer, § 2.3, Fig. 2.1
S. guiso (Blco.) Bl., § 10.4, § 12.3, § 15.2, Fig. 15.4
S. havilandii Brandis, § 10.3, § 10.4
S. hopeifolia (Heim) Sym., § 16.6
S. hypochra Hance, § 12.3
S. inaequilateralis Sym., Fig. 11.4, Fig. 11.7, Fig. 11.11, Fig. 11.13
S. isoptera Ashton, § 10.4
S. johorensis Foxw., § 5.3, § 6.5, § 15.2
S. kunstleri King, § 10.5
S. laevis Ridley, § 2.3, § 4.1, § 5.3, § 6.5, Chapter 7, § 16.6, Fig. 2.1
S. laxa Sloot., § 10.5

S. leprosula Miq., § 2.5, § 5.2, § 5.3, § 6.5, § 7.1, § 12.3, § 15.2, § 16.6, Fig. 1.7, Fig. 15.7, Table 6.4
S. lepidota (Korth.) Bl., Fig. 1.7
S. leptoclados = *johorensis*
S. longisperma Roxb., § 16.6
S. macrophylla (de Vriese) Ashton, § 4.1, § 8.1, § 15.3, Table 8.1
S. macroptera Dyer, § 5.2, § 6.5, § 16.6, Fig. 1.7, Table 6.4, Table 15.4
S. materialis Ridley, § 10.3
S. maxwelliana King, § 6.5, Chapter 7, Fig. 1.7, Fig. 15.15
S. mecistopteryx Ridley, Table 8.4
S. multiflora (Burck) Sym., § 6.5, § 10.4, Fig. 1.6, Table 8.4, Table 15.4
S. obtusa Wall., Fig. 14.2
S. ovalis (Korth.) Bl., § 5.2, § 15.3, § 16.6, Fig. 1.7, Table 15.4
S. ovata Dyer ex Brandis, Fig. 1.6, Fig. 16.1
S. pachyphylla Ridley ex Sym., § 10.3
S. parvifolia Dyer, § 2.3, § 2.5, § 6.5, § 7.1, § 12.3, § 15.2, § 16.6, Fig. 2.1, Fig. 15.5, Table 6.4, Table 15.4
S. platycarpa Heim, § 11.3, Fig. 11.11
S. platyclados Sloot. ex Foxw., § 4.1, § 5.2, § 5.3, § 16.6, Fig. 16.1
S. pauciflora King, § 6.5, § 10.4, § 15.3
S. robusta Gaertn. f., § 2.8, § 12.2
S. roxburghii G. Don, § 12.3
S. rugosa Heim, § 11.3
S. scabrida Sym., § 10.3, § 11.3, Fig. 10.4
S. seminis (de Vriese) Sloot., § 15.3
S. sericeiflora Fischer & Hutch., § 10.4
S. smithiana Sym., § 4.1, § 8.1, Table 8.4
S. siamensis Miq., Fig. 14.2
S. splendida (de Vriese) Ashton, § 15.3
S. submontana Sym., § 16.6
S. teysmanniana Dyer ex Brandis, Fig. 11.11
S. uliginosa Foxw., § 11.3, Fig. 11.4, Fig. 11.11
S. venulosa Wood ex Meijer, § 10.5
Siam weed *see Eupatorium odoratum*
Simaroubaceae, Fig. 1.6
Sindora, § 2.4, § 12.3, § 15.2, Leguminosae/Caesalpinoideae
S. irpicina de Wit, Fig. 15.4
Sloanea, § 14.2, Fig. 14.8, Elaeocarpaceae
Sonneratia, Chapter 13, Lythraceae
Sophora tomentosa L., § 10.6, Leguminosae/Papilionatae
Spathodea campanulata Beauv., § 2.8, Bignoniaceae
Spathoglottis aurea Lindl., § 16.4, Orchidaceae
Sphagnum, § 16.1, § 16.5, § 16.6, Bryophyta
Spinifex littoreus (Burm. f.) Merr., § 10.6, Gramineae
Spondias, § 2.6, § 2.8, § 14.2, Anacardiaceae
Stellaria, § 16.3, Caryophyllaceae
Stemonurus umbellatus Becc., § 16.4, Fig. 2.1, Fig. 11.4, Fig. 11.5, Icacinaceae
Stenochlaena, § 2.6, Fig. 2.23, fern
S. palustris (Burm. f.) Bedd., § 11.4
Sterculia, § 2.8, Sterculiaceae
S. rhoidifolia Stapf ex Ridley, Fig. 10.4, Fig. 11.4
S. rubiginosa Vent., Fig. 15.4
Sterculiaceae, § 2.5, § 6.2, Fig. 2.1, Table 15.1
Stereospermum suaveolens (Roxb.) DC., § 12.1 Bignoniaceae
Streblus asper Lour., § 12.1, Moraceae
Strobilanthes, § 4.1, Acanthaceae
S. cernua Bl., § 4.1
Strychnos, § 2.6, Strychnaceae
Styphelia, § 16.1, Epacridaceae
S. abnormis (Sond.) J. J. Smith, § 10.5
S. malayana (Jack) Spr., § 10.3, § 16.4

Styracaceae, § 11.3

sugar cane, § 8.4, § 12.1, § 17.1

sunflower *see Helianthus annuus*

sweet potato *see Ipomoea batatas*

Swietenia, Fig. 8.1, Meliaceae

Swintonia glauca Engl., Fig. 2.1, Anacardiaceae

S. penangiana King, § 15.3

S. schwenckii T. & B., Fig. 1.6

Symingtonia populnea (R. Br. ex Griff.) Steenis, § 6.2, Hamamelidaceae

Symplocaceae, § 16.3

Symplocos, § 8.1, Table 8.4, Symplocaceae

S. luzonensis Rolfe, § 18.2

S. sp. SAR 7327, Fig. 10.4

Syzygium nerifolium Becc., Fig. 15.8, Myrtaceae

Tabebuia serratifolia Nichols, § 4.1, Bignoniaceae

Tacca, § 2.8, Taccaceae

T. leontopetaloides (L.) O.K., § 10.6

Talauma, § 2.8, Magnoliaceae

Talipot palm *see Corypha umbraculifera*

Tamarindus indica L., § 4.1, § 12.1, Leguminosae/Caesalpinoideae

tampoi *see Baccaurea griffithii*

Tapeinosperma, § 2.5, Myrsinaceae

taro *see* Araceae

tea *see Camellia sinensis*

teak *see Tectona grandis*

Tectona grandis L. f., § 12.1, § 12.2, § 18.1, Fig. 8.1, Verbenaceae

Teijsmanniodendron, § 8.1, Table 8.4, Verbenaceae

T. ahernianum Bakh., Figs 15.18 and 15.19

T. coriaceum Kosterm., Fig. 2.1

T. holophyllum (Baker) Kosterm., Fig. 15.4

temponek *see Artocarpus rigidus*

Tephrosia, § 19.2, Leguminosae/Papilionatae

terap *see Artocarpus elasticus/scortechinii*

Terminalia, § 7.1, § 12.2, § 14.2, Combretaceae

T. brassii Exell, § 5.3, § 8.1, Fig. 8.4

T. calamansanai (Blco.) Rolfe, § 5.1, § 6.5, Chapter 7, Table 6.1, Table 8.3

T. catappa L., § 4.1, § 10.6

Ternstroemia aneura Miq., § 16.4, Theaceae

T. hosei Ridley, Fig. 11.4, Fig. 11.5

T. magnifica Stapf ex Ridley, Fig. 10.4

T. sp. nov., Fig. 10.4

Tetractomia montana Ridley, Fig. 10.4, Rutaceae

Tetrameles nudiflora R. Br. ex Benn., § 10.2, § 12.1, § 12.2, Datiscaceae

Tetramerista glabra Miq., § 11.3, Fig. 11.11, Theaceae

Tetranthera salicifolia Roxb. ex Wall., Fig. 15.8, Lauraceae

Thelymitra, § 16.3, Orchidaceae

Themeda australis (R. Br.) Stapf, § 18.2, Gramineae

Theobroma cacao L., § 8.4, Sterculiaceae

Thespesia populnea (L.) Soland. ex Correa, § 4.1, § 10.6, Malvaceae

Thrixspermum arachnites (Bl.) Reichb. f., § 4.1, Orchidaceae

Thuarea involuta (Forst. f.) R. & S., § 10.6, Gramineae

Thymelaeaceae, Fig. 1.6

Thyrsostachys, Fig. 12.1, Gramineae

Tiliaceae, § 6.2, Fig. 2.1

Timonius, § 2.6, § 15.3, Rubiaceae

T. borneensis Val., Fig. 2.1

T. peduncularis (Wall.) Ridley, Fig. 11.4, Fig. 11.5

T. pulposus C. T. White, Figs 15.18 and 15.19

tjemera *see Casuarina junghuhniana*

Toona, § 14.2, Meliaceae

Trema, § 6.2, Chapter 13, § 18.2, Ulmaceae

T. cannabina Lour., Fig. 6.5

T. guineensis (Schumach. & Thonn.) Ficalho, § 8.4

Trentepohlia, § 2.6, Chlorophyceae

Trichocolea, § 16.4, Hepaticae

Trichomanes, § 2.6, fern

Trichospermum, § 6.2, Tiliaceae

Trigoniastrum hypoleucum Miq., Fig. 11.4, Polygalaceae

Tristania, § 2.5, § 10.3, § 11.3, Chapter 14, Fig. 14.5, Myrtaceae

T. grandifolia Ridley, Fig. 10.4

T. maingayi Duthie, Fig. 11.5

T. obovata R. Br., § 10.4, § 11.3, Fig. 10.4, Fig. 11.4, Fig. 11.5

T. orientalis (L.) Bl., § 4.1, § 6.2

T. pentandra Merr., § 16.4

T. stellata Ridley, § 10.3

Triumfetta repens (Bl.) Merr & Rolfe, § 10.6, Tiliaceae

Trochocarpa, § 16.1, Epacridaceae

Tsuga, Chapter 14, Pinaceae

tusam *see Pinus merkusii*

Ulmaceae, § 6.2

Uncaria, § 2.6, Chapter 18, Rubiaceae

Urticaceae, § 6.2

Usnea, § 16.1, lichen

Utricularia, § 11.3, § 16.1, Lentibulariaceae

Vaccinium, § 1.1, 2.6, § 10.4, § 16.1, § 16.4, Ericaceae

V. bracteatum Thunb., § 10.3

Valerianella, § 16.3, Valerianaceae

Vatica, § 2.4, § 6.2, § 6.5, § 15.3, Fig. 2.12, Dipterocarpaceae

V. astrotricha Hance, § 15.2

V. brunigii Ashton, § 10.3, § 10.4

V. cinerea King, § 10.4

V. micrantha Sloot., Fig. 1.6

V. odorata (Griff.) Sym., Fig. 2.1

V. rassak (Korth.) Bl., § 15.2

V. umbonata (Hk. f.) Burck, Fig. 10.4

Verbenaceae, § 6.2, Fig. 2.1

Vernonia arborea Buch.–Ham., § 12.1, Compositae

Veronica, § 16.3, Scrophulariaceae

Vigna marina (Burm. f.) Merr., § 10.6, Leguminosae/Papilionatae

Viola, § 16.3, Violaceae

Viscum articulatum Burm. f., § 2.6, Loranthaceae

Vitex cofassus Reinw. ex Bl., § 2.4, Verbenaceae

V. pubescens Vahl, § 10.3

Wahlenbergia, § 16.3, Compositae

wallaba *see Eperua falcata*

Wallichia, § 8.3, Palmae

Wedelia biflora (L.) DC., § 10.6, Compositae

Weinmannia blumei Planch., § 6.2, § 12.1, Cunoniaceae

W. dulitensis Airy Shaw, § 16.4

Whiteodendron moultonianum Steenis, § 10.3, Fig. 1.6, Myrtaceae

Wightia, § 2.6, Scrophulariaceae

Xanthomyrtus, § 14.2, Myrtaceae

X. taxifolia (Ridley) Merr., § 16.4

Xanthophyllum amoenum Chod., Fig. 11.4, Polygalaceae

X. citrifolium Chod., Fig. 11.4

X. excelsum (Bl.) Miq., Fig. 15.4

X. sp. nov. 2614, Fig. 11.4, Fig. 11.5

Xanthostemon, § 10.5, Fig. 14.8, Myrtaceae

Xylopia coriifolia Ridley, § 10.3, Fig. 11.5, Annonaceae

X. ferruginea Hk. f. & Thoms., § 6.4
X. peekelii Diels, Figs 15.18 and 15.19

Zea mays L., § 8.4, § 17.1, Gramineae
Zephyranthes rosea (Spreng.) Lindl., § 4.1, Amaryllidaceae
Zingiberaceae, § 2.5, § 2.8, § 8.4, § 17.4, Chapter 18, Fig. 8.7
Zyziphus rotundifolia Lamk., § 12.1, Rhamnaceae
Zoysia matrella (L.) Merr., § 10.6, Gramineae

General Index

THE REFERENCES given are to section numbers, where not otherwise stated. Where a chapter number is given, the appropriate reference will be found towards the beginning of the chapter. Principal entries are shown in bold.

aborigines, § 8.3, § 10.1, § 15.2, § 17.1, § 18.2
Acapulco, § 17.1
aerial photographs, § 6.1, § 10.3, § 10.5, Chapter 15, § 15.3, § 16.1, § 16.4, Fig. 12.1
Afghanistan, § 14.3
Africa, Chapter 3, § 6.2, § 8.2, § 9.2, § 10.1, § 10.2, § 10.4, § 11.3, § 11.4, § 12.2, Chapter 15, § 16.1, § 17.1
    tropical lowland evergreen rain forest absent from, § 10.1
agriculture (see also plantation agriculture, shifting cultivation), § 3.1, § 9.3, § 9.9, § 10.3, § 11.3, § 17.1, § 17.3, § 18.1
    cash crops, § 17.1
    crop productivity, § 8.3
albedo, § 10.3, § 11.3, § 15.3, § 16.4
allophane, § 9.5
Alor Star, § 3.2, § 12.3
alpine vegetation, § 16.2
Alps, § 16.5
altitudinal range of species, § 16.3
altitudinal zonation
    of bryophytes, § 16.4
    of dipterocarps in Malaya, § 16.6
    of forest Formations, § 16.1, § 16.2, Fig. 16.1, Fig. 16.2, Table 16.2
    of soils, § 9.12
aluminium sensitivity, § 10.4
Amazon basin, Chapter 1, § 10.1, § 10.2, § 10.3
America, tropical lowland evergreen rain forest in, § 10.1; (see also Central America, South America)
Anamba Islands, § 10.3
Andaman Islands, Chapter 1, § 7.1, § 10.1, § 10.2, § 17.1
Andes, Chapter 1, § 10.1, § 16.1, § 16.6
andosols, § 7.2, § 9.5, § 9.12, Fig. 9.8, Fig. 9.9
Andulau forest, § 15.3, § 15.5, Fig. 1.6
angin besar see storm forest
animals, § 2.7, § 2.8, § 5.1
    amphibian, § 1.2, § 4.2, Chapter 13, Table 13.1
    grazing and production studies, § 8.3
    herbivorous, § 2.7, § 6.1, § 8.3
    invertebrate, § 2.1, § 2.7, § 8.3, § 11.1
    and man, Chapter 13, § 17.1, § 17.4, § 19.1, § 19.3
    minimal populations, § 17.4, Table 19.1
    and monsoon climates, § 15.1
    nearing extinction, § 17.1
    seasonal cycles in, § 4.2
    as seed dispersers, § 5.1
    zonation with elevation, § 16.7
Angkor Thom, Angkor Wat, § 17.1, Fig. 17.1
Anguédédou forest, § 8.3, Fig. 8.6
Antares Mountains, § 9.12
ants, § 2.8
apes, § 1.2, § 2.7, § 2.8, § 8.3, § 17.4; (see also gibbons, orang utan)
Arfak Mountains, § 14.2
Aru Islands, § 1.2
Assam, Chapter 1, § 7.2, § 10.1
Atchin, § 12.1

Atherton Tableland, § 12.1
Australia, Chapter 1, § 1.3, § 3.1, § 5.2, § 7.2, Chapter 10, § 10.2, § 10.3, § 14.2
    absence of tropical evergreen rain forest, § 10.1
    forest interdigitation on east coast, § 10.3, § 12.1
Australian floristic element, § 10.3, § 12.1
autecological studies, Chapter 18
    of Agathis macrophylla, § 14.1
    of common big trees of Solomon Islands, § 6.3, § 15.4, Table 6.1
    of secondary forest species, § 18.2
    of Shorea albida, § 11.3
    of Shorea curtisii, § 15.3
autotrophic plants, § 2.2, § 2.4
avifauna (see also birds)
    of Chantaburi pocket, § 12.3
    of different forests compared, § 1.2, Table 1.2
    of Kra isthmus, § 12.3
    of Malaya, Chapter 13
    of mangrove forest, Chapter 13
    of secondary vegetation, Chapter 13
    of Sundaland, § 1.2, Chapter 13

babblers, § 2.7, Chapter 13
bacteria, § 2.1, § 2.5
Baguio City, § 3.2, Fig. 3.2, Fig. 3.3
Bako National Park, § 10.3, Chapter 13
Bali, § 1.2, § 2.1, § 5.2
bamboo thickets, § 1.2, § 12.2
Banda Aceh, § 3.2, § 12.3
Bangi Island, § 10.5
Bandjermasin, § 12.1
Banka, § 10.3, § 12.3
banteng (Bos javanicus), § 17.1, § 17.4
Baram estuary, § 11.3, Fig. 11.3
barbets, § 1.2, § 2.7, Chapter 13
bare land, recolonization of, § 2.1, § 5.1
Barisan Range, § 12.1, § 16.1, § 16.5, § 16.6
bark, § 2.5, § 10.2, § 11.4, § 14.3, Fig. 2.11, Fig. 2.12
    associated epiphytes, § 2.5
barn owl, § 4.2
Barringtonia association, § 10.6
basal area, § 6.4, Chapter 7, § 8.1, § 8.3
bat flowers, § 2.8, Fig. 2.29
Batanta, § 1.2
bats, § 1.2
    fruit dispersal by, § 2.8, § 7.2
    seasonal breeding of, § 4.2
Bawean, § 16.1
beach vegetation, § 10.6, § 11.2, Table 10.1
beech forest, Chapter 14, § 16.1
    Danish, § 8.3, Fig. 8.6
bee flowers, § 2.8
bees nests, § 7.2, § 18.1
beetle flowers, § 2.8
Belait, § 6.1, § 19.1

Belalong forest, § 2.1, Fig. 2.1

berok *see* monkeys, macaque

Bhutan, § 14.3

Bihar, § 12.2

Billiton, § 10.3

biogeography of south-west Pacific, § 15.1

biological

    clock, § 4.1

    nomads *see* pioneer species

biomass and biovolume of rain forest, § 1.1, § 8.3, Table 1.1

biomass,

    decrease with elevation, § 16.1, § 16.4, § 16.7

    methods of estimation, § 8.3

    of heath forests, § **10.3**, 16.4

    of monsoon forests, § 12.1

    of peat swamp forests, § 11.3

    removed as wood chips, § 7.1, § 11.3, § 19.1

biosystematics, § 6.2

birds, § 1.2, § 8.3, § 11.1; *see also* avifauna

    canopy niches, § 2.7

    colonies offshore, § 10.6, § 17.4

    flowers, § 2.8, Fig. 2.28

    fruit dispersal by, § 2.8; § 5.1

    ranges in Kra isthmus, Fig. 12.5

    seasonal cycles of, § 4.2, Fig. 4.4

Bismarck Islands, § 1.1, § 5.3, § 9.7, Chapter 10

blackwater streams, § 10.3, § 11.3, Chapter 13

blangs, § 14.3

Bogor, § 7.2, § 11.1

boles, § 2.5, § 10.1

    ratio of diameter to crown diameter, § 2.5

    volume tables, § 2.5

Borneo, § 1.1, § 1.2, § 5.1, § 6.1, § 7.2, § 9.5, § 9.6, § 10.3, § 11.3, § 11.4, § 14.1, § 17.1, § 17.2

    dipterocarps in, § 10.1, § 15.2

Bougainville, § 2.4, § 9.5

brackish water forest, § 10.6, § 11.2, Table 10.1

Brazil, § 4.2

British Isles, § 1.1

Brunei, § 9.6, § 10.1, § 10.3, § 11.3, Chapter 14, § 14.1, § 16.4

bryophytes, § 10.1, § 10.3

Bubu forest, § 5.1

Bukit

    Lagong forest plot, Chapter 15, § 19.3

    Perangin, § 12.3

    Timah, § 2.7, § 4.2

bulbuls, § 2.7, Chapter 13

Bulolo, Chapter 14, § 14.2

Bulolo-Watut valleys, § 10.2

Burma, Chapter 1, Chapter 3, Chapter 7, § 9.2, § 9.10, § 9.11, § 10.1, § 10.2, § 11.4, § 12.1, § 12.2, § 16.1

    dipterocarps, § 15.2

    teak forests, § 9.11, § 12.2

butterflies, § 2.8, § 4.2

    zonation with elevation, § 16.7

butterfly flowers, § 2.8

buttresses, § **2.5**, § 7.2, § 10.1, § 10.2, § 10.3, § 11.1, § 11.4, § 15.3, § 16.1, Fig. 2.9, Fig. 2.10, Table 16.1

Butung, § 7.2

Cambodia, Chapter 1, § 9.10, § 10.3, § 12.3

Cameron Highlands, § 6.2, § 9.12

campinas, § 10.3

carbon dioxide, § 8.4, § 16.5

consumption by forest, § 8.3

diffusion rates in leaves, § 8.4, § 16.6

Cardamon mountains, § 12.3

Caribbean, Chapter 1, § 10.2, § 10.4, § 11.3

    Pinus in, § 14.3

carnivores, § 2.7

    fruit dispersal by, § 2.8

Caroline Islands, § 17.1

Carrascos, § 10.3

catena

    in Bornean lowland forest, § 10.3

    in peat swamp forest, § 11.3, § 15.5, Fig. 10.11, Fig. 10.12, Fig. 11.4, Fig. 11.5, Fig. 11.12

caterpillars, § 4.2

    defoliation by, § 2.8, § 6.1, § 7.2

catfish (*Clarias batrachus*), § 2.8

cauliflory, § 2.5, § 2.8, § 10.1, § 10.2, § 16.1, Fig. 2.14, Fig. 2.15, Fig. 2.16, Fig. 2.17, Table 16.1

Celebes, § 1.1, § 1.2, § 3.2, § 7.2, § 9.5, § 9.7, § 10.3, § 12.1, Chapter 14, § 14.1, § 17.1

cellulose, § 7.2, Chapter 14, § 14.3

Central America, *Pinus* in, Chapter 14

cerambycid borer (*Cyriopalus wallacei*), § 7.1

Ceylon, Chapter 1, § 3.2, § 4.1, § 9.11, § 9.12, § 10.1, § 10.2, § 10.3, § 12.1, § 14.1, § 15.2, § 17.1

chance, role of in determining forest composition, § 6.1, § 8.3, § 15.5, § 18.2

Chantaburi pocket, § 10.1, § **12.3**

chena, § 18.1

Chieng Mai, § 8.3, Fig. 12.2

Chimbu valley, § 7.2

China, Chapter 1, § 9.7, § 10.1, § 12.2, § 16.3, § 17.2, § 17.3

    dipterocarps of, § 15.2

    Pinus in south, § 14.3

Chumphon, § 12.3

Cibodas, § 2.5, § 2.6, § 8.2, Fig. 2.18

cicadas, § 16.7

civets, § 2.8

civilizations, disappeared, § 17.1

climates,

    delimited and defined, Chapter 3, § **3.1**, § 3.2, Chapter 10, § 12.1, Fig. 3.2

    indicator species of, § 12.1

    secular change in, § 3.5, § 6.1, § 12.1, § 15.1, § 15.2

    tropical grassland, § 12.1

    tropical maritime (oceanic), § 2.6, Chapter 3, § 12.1

    tropical montane, § 16.5

climatic rare events, § 3.5, § 15.4

climax (*see also* fire climax)

    biotic, Chapter 18

    defined, § 2.1

    secular changes in, § 2.1

climbers, § 2.1, § 2.2

    big woody, § **2.6**, § 6.1, § 10.1, § 10.2, § 10.3, § **12.2**, § 16.1, § 16.4, Chapter 18, Fig. 2.21, Table 16.1

    bole, § **2.6**, § 10.1, Fig. 2.23, Table 16.1

    colonizing gaps, § 6.1, Chapter 18

    reflecting disturbance, § 15.4

    in secondary forest, § 2.6

    and silviculture, § 6.5, § 7.1, § 8.1

    stratification of, § 2.6, § 8.3

    towers, Chapter 18

cloud

    forest in New Guinea, § 9.12, § 16.1

zone, § 3.2, § 9.12, § 11.3, § 16.1, § 16.5, § 16.6
coastal subsidence, § 11.3
coastline, rate of advance in Sarawak, § 11.3
cockatoos, § 1.2
coconut groves, § 10.6, Chapter 18
competition,
    between pioneer species, § 6.2
    between seedlings, § 5.3
    on limestone in Malaya, § 10.4
    slowing growth rate, § 8.1, Table 8.2
computer models, § 2.5, Chapter 10
Congo Basin, Chapter 1
conifers, § 8.1, **Chapter 14**, § 14.1, § 14.2, § 14.3, § 15.1, § 16.2, § 16.3, Fig. 6.7, Fig. 8.1
conservation, Chapter 13, Chapter 18, § 19.2, § 19.3
consumers defined, § 2.7
coppice shoots, § 10.3, § 11.3, § 11.4, § 12.1, § 16.1, § 18.1
coral islands, § 9.7, § 10.6
Cordillera Central, Luzon, § 18.2
Cordillera de Talamanca, § 16.5
cremnophytes, § 10.4
Cretaceous, § 2.8
crustal plates, § 15.1
cultural inertia, § 17.1
cyclical theory see regeneration
cyclones, § 6.1, § 6.3, § 14.2, § 15.2, § 15.4, § 15.5, Chapter 18
Cycloop mountains, § 10.5

Daribi, § 14.2
Darvel Bay, § 10.5, § 15.2
deciduous trees, § 4.1, § 10.1, § 10.2, § 10.3, § 12.1, § 12.2, Fig. 2.28, Fig. 4.1, Fig. 4.2
deer, § 1.2, § 8.3
deflected successions, § 17.1, Chapter 18
demarcation knot, § 1.1, Fig. 1.2
D'Entrecasteaux Islands, § 15.2
dependent synusiae, § 2.6
depleted forest, § 17.1, Chapter 18
deserts, § 12.1
dew, § 3.6
dew point, § 16.5
diatoms, § 11.3
Diptera, § 4.2
disjunct distributions, § 12.1, § 15.2, § 16.5, Fig. 12.3
dispersal, § 2.8, § 5.1, § 6.3, § 15.4, Fig. 2.30
    efficiency and species' aggregation, § 15.3, § 15.4
    of pioneer species, § 6.2
    range, § 5.3, § 15.1, § 15.5
disturbance, relationship to composition, § 15.4
disturbed forest, § 17.2, Fig. 17.7, Fig. 17.8
    extensive in New Guinea, § 17.1
dog, § 16.2, § 17.1
Doma Peaks, § 16.2
drip tips, § 2.6, Fig. 2.19
drought, Chapter 1, § 3.4, § 3.5, § 4.1, § 5.3, § 10.2, § 10.3, § 11.3, § 12.1; see also seasonally dry climate, water stress
    affecting amphibians, § 1.2
    decreasing inland, § 3.4
    in mountains, § 16.5, § 16.6
    and productivity, § 8.3
dryad species, **§ 6.2**, § 7.2
(dry) deciduous (dipterocarp) forest, § 10.2, Fig. 12.2
dynamic studies of forests, Part III, **§ 6.3**, **§ 6.4**, § 11.3, § 11.4, § 15.5, Chapter 18

eagles, § 17.4
earthworms, § 9.12, § 16.5
East Kutai Reserve, § 19.3
ecological strategy, Chapter 5, § 6.1, § 6.2, § 6.3, § 8.4
ecophysiological studies in heath forest, § 10.3
ecosystem, § 2.1, § 8.3
    in balance with aerial environment, § 8.3
ecotone, Chapter 10, § 10.2, Chapter 13, § 16.1, § 16.6, § 16.7
    at the Kra isthmus, § 12.3, Fig. 12.4
edaphic climax forest, § 15.3
elephant, § 1.2, § 16.7, § 17.4, § 19.3
    food consumption of, § 6.1, § 8.3
elfin woodland, § 16.1, Fig. 9.1
emergent trees, § 1.1, § 2.3, § 2.4, § 10.1, § 10.3, § 12.2, § 12.3, Chapter 14, § 14.3, § 15.2, § 15.3, § 16.1, § 16.6, § 17.4, Fig. 2.4, Table 8.4, Table 16.1
    decrease with elevation, § 16.1
    height at first flowering, § 4.1
empran, § 10.3, § 11.4, **§ 15.3**
energy flow, § 8.3
epharmony, Chapter 1, Chapter 10
epiphylls, § 2.6, § 12.1, Fig. 2.19
epiphytes, § 2.1, **§ 2.2**, § 2.5, **§ 2.6**, § 6.1, § 10.1, § 10.2, § 10.3, § 10.6, § 14.1, § 15.3, § 16.1, § 16.4, Fig. 2.18, Fig. 2.19, Fig. 17.5, Table 16.1
    hemi-parasitic, § 2.6
    increase with elevation, § 16.1
    rare in secondary forest, § 2.6, § 15.4, Chapter 18
equatorial rain forest see tropical lowland rain forest
erosion, § 9.1, § 9.6, § 9.10, § 9.12, § 10.10, § 11.3, § 14.1, Chapter 18, § 18.1, § 19.2, Fig. 18.3
evergreen seasonal (rain) forest see tropical semi-evergreen rain forest
evolution, § 2.8, § 4.1, Chapter 5, § 6.2, § 10.4, § 12.1, § 15.2
exploitation, § 7.1, § 8.3, § 10.1, § 10.2, § 15.2, **§ 17.3**, § 17.4, Chapter 18, Fig. 17.6
    of conifer forests, Chapter 14
    increasing pace of, § 1.1, § 10.1, § 17.1, § 17.2, Chapter 19, § 19.1, Fig. 17.3
extinction, § 3.5, § 15.2, § 17.1, § 17.4, § 19.3

family groups of trees, § 2.8, § 5.1, § 15.3, § 15.5, § 16.1, Fig. 15.15, Table 15.4; see also species consociations
fauna of Malesia, defined and described, § 1.2
faunistic richness discussed, § 1.2, § 12.1
felling see exploitation
Fergusson Island, § 14.2
fern meadow, § 16.2
figs
    banyan, § 2.6, § 18.1
    geocarpic, § 2.5
    strangling, § 2.6, § 18.1, Fig. 2.6, Fig. 2.24, Fig. 2.25, Fig. 17.1
Fiji, Chapter 1, § 3.2, § 6.1, § 12.1, § 14.1
Finisterre mountains, § 15.2
fire, § 6.1, § 7.2, § 8.2, Chapter 10, § 10.2, § 10.3, § 10.4, § 11.4, § 12.1, § 12.2, § 14.2, § 14.3, § 16.1, § 17.1, Chapter 18, § 18.1, § 18.2, Fig. 10.13, Fig. 10.15, Fig. 14.2, Fig. 17.9
    climax, § 11.4, § 15.5, § 16.2, Chapter 18
    and germination of *Albizia lophantha*, § 5.2
    resistant trees, § 10.2
firewood, Chapter 7, § 10.3, § 11.1, § 11.4, § 17.1, § 17.3
fishes, freshwater, § 1.2
fish, fruit dispersal by, § 2.8
floods, § 11.4, § 15.3, § 19.2

Flores, § 5.2, § 12.1

floristic

boundary (*see also* demarcation knot)

Alor Star–Songkhla line, § 12.3

Kangar–Pattani line, § 12.3

composition, § 1.1

change with elevation, § 16.3

effect of felling on, § 17.3

of secondary forest, Chapter 18

elements, § 15.1

Australian, § 10.3, § 12.1

Malesian and Melanesian, § 1.1

megatherm, § 16.1

microtherm, § 16.1

richness discussed, § 1.1, § 12.1

flowering, gregarious, § 4.1, § 6.5, § 11.3, § 12.2

of pioneer species, § 6.2

stimuli and conditions for, § 3.6, § 4.1, § 17.4, Table 4.2

Flowerpeckers (Dicaeidae), § 2.8

fly flowers, § 2.8

flying foxes (*Pteropus*), § 2.8

Fly River, § 11.4, § 15.2, § 16.1

fog, § 2.6, § 16.5

foliage,

biomass estimation, § 8.3

light interception by, § 8.1

food chain, Chapter 13

foothill forest in New Guinea, § 16.1

forest

canopy

after felling, § 17.3, § 17.4

defined, § 2.1

gaps *see* forest growth cycle

microclimates of, § 2.4

plan view, § 2.3, Fig. 1.7, Fig. 2.1

shrub layer of, § 2.5

stratification (storeys, layers) *see* stratification

Formations defined, Chapter 10, Table 10.1

growth cycle, § 2.3, § 6.1, § 8.1, Fig. 1.7, Fig. 2.1, Fig. 2.3, Fig. 8.3

gap phase, **§ 6.1**, § 15.3, § 15.4, § 15.5, Table 6.7

microclimates, § 3.6

and productivity, § 8.3

rate of rotation, § 8.2

inventory and survey, § 1.1, Chapter **15**

mosaic *see* forest growth cycle

foxtails, § 14.3

Fraser's Hill, § 6.2

freshwater swamp forest, § 5.3, § 9.9, § 9.10, § 11.3, § 11.4, § 15.2, § 15.3, § 17.1, Table 10.1

frost, Chapter 3, § 7.2, Chapter 14, § 16.2, § 16.5

fruiting

frequency, § 4.1, § 15.5, Table 4.3

gregarious, § 4.1, § 6.5, § 7.1, § 11.3, § 12.2

of illipe nut trees, § 4.1

monocarpic, § 4.1

stimulated by logging, § 17.4

fruit, dispersal and syndromes aiding it, § 2.8, § 5.1, § 10.6, § 15.3

fungal attacks,

creating canopy gaps, § 6.1

of pioneer species, § 7.2

fungi, § 2.1, § 4.2, § 8.3

seasonal reproduction of, **§ 4.2**

Fynbosch, § 1.1

Gabon, § 10.3

gallery forest, § 1.1, § 12.1, Fig. 12.1

game trails, § 6.1

Gap, § 17.3

gaps *see* forest growth cycle

colonization by climbers, § 2.6, § 6.1

formation, § 2.3, § 5.1, Fig. 2.3

microclimate, § 3.6, § 6.1

gaur *see* seladang

gene pools, § 19.2

gibbons, § 2.1, § 16.7, § 17.4, Fig. 4.1, Table 19.1

girth increment, § 7.2, § 8.2, Fig. 8.4, Fig. 8.5, Table 8.2, Table 8.3

in closed forest, Chapter 7

and crown size, § 8.1, Table 8.1

and production studies, § 8.3

sensitive measurement method, § 8.1

varying with age, § 8.1

varying with weather, § 4.1, § 8.1

glaciation, § 1.1, § 16.2

gley soils, § 9.6, § 9.7, § 9.9, § 9.10, § 9.12, Fig. 9.14, Table 9.1, Table 9.2

Gogol forest, § 19.1

grass mats, floating, § 11.4

grasses

ephemeral, § 18.2

within the rain forest, § 12.1

grasslands, § 9.11, § 10.2, § 11.4, § 12.1, § 12.2, Chapter 13, Chapter 14, § 14.3, § 16.2, Chapter 18, § 18.2, Fig. 18.1

animals of, § 1.2, Chapter 13

grazing, Chapter 10, § 10.3, § 12.2, Chapter 18

gregarious plants *see* species consociations

groves of trees *see* family groups

growth

flushes, § 4.1, § 8.2

in girth *see* girth increment

in height, § 2.4, § 6.3, § 6.4, § 6.5, § 7.2, § 8.1, Fig. 8.4, Table 6.2; *see also* growth rate

quantitative analysis of, § 6.5, **§ 8.4**

rate (*see also* girth increment, growth in height)

of mountain forest trees, § 16.4

of pioneer species, § 6.2

related to canopy conditions, § 8.1

of shade bearers, § 6.2

temperate and tropical plants compared, § 8.4

of understorey trees, § 8.1

rings, § 8.2

guano, § 10.6

Gulf of Guinea, Chapter 1

Gum Gum forest, § 8.1, Fig. 7.1

Gunung *see also* mountain,

Agong, § 2.1

Angsi, Chapter 14, § 17.4

Api, § 10.4, Fig. 10.16

Belumut, § 3.6, § 16.1, § 16.6

Benarat, § 10.4

Benom, § 6.2, **§ 16.7**

Besar, § 10.3

Gua Rimau, § 16.6

Mandi Angin, § 16.1

Mulu National Park, § 10.4

Panti, § 10.3

Rabong, § 14.1, § 16.5, § 16.6

Santubong, § 16.6

Sewu, § 9.7
Tahan, § 14.1, § 16.5, § 16.6
Guyana, § 10.1, § 10.3, § 11.3

Hainan, § 10.1
dipterocarps of, § 15.2
halloysite, Chapter 9, § 9.5
hardwoods,
cabinet, § 19.1
heavy, Chapter 7, § 7.2, § 10.3, § 15.3
heavy, response to silviculture, § 8.1
light, nowadays preferred, § 17.1, § 17.2
light, response to silviculture, § 8.1
production and export statistics, Table 17.2
Hastings River, § 14.2
Hawaii, § 17.1
heat balance, § 10.3, § 16.6, § 19.2
heath,
dwarf shrub, § 16.2
forest, § 2.8, § 9.6, § 10.1, § 10.3, § 10.5, Chapter 14, § 14.1, § 15.2, § 16.4, § 16.5, Fig. 10.4, Fig. 10.5, Fig. 10.6, Fig. 10.7, Fig. 10.10, Fig. 10.11, Fig. 10.12
animals of, Chapter 13
compared with other Formations, § 11.3, § 16.4, § 16.6, Table 10.1
Heidewald see heath forest
herbicide sprays in Vietnam, Chapter 18
herbs, § 2.2, § 2.4, § 8.4, § 10.1, § 10.4, § 10.6, § 16.4, Chapter 18
ephemeral, § 6.2, § 17.1, § 18.2
pioneer, § 18.2
rates, photosynthesis, of, § 8.4
heterotrophic plants, § 2.2
hill dipterocarp rain forest, § 5.3, § 7.1, § 10.1, § 15.3, Fig. 16.1
Himalayas, § 10.1, § 11.2, Chapter 14, § 14.3
Holocene, § 9.5
sea levels, § 1.1
homoiohydres, § 2.6
Honeyeaters (Meliphigidae), § 2.8
hormone systems, § 4.1
light sensitive, § 16.5
hornbills, § 2.7, Chapter 13, § 17.4, § 19.3, Table 19.1
huma, § 18.1
humus, Chapter 9, § 9.1, § 9.6, § 9.7
humirhizal, § 10.3
hurricanes, § 6.1
Hutan Melintang, § 11.3
hydrological cycle, § 19.2
hydroseres, § 11.4
hythergraphs, Fig. 3.2

Ibans, § 4.1, § 10.3
Ice Ages, § 12.1, § 15.1
igapo, § 11.4
ikan kli see catfish
illite, Chapter 9, § 9.9, § 9.11
India, § 3.1, § 3.2, Chapter 7, § 12.1, § 12.2
dipterocarps of, § 15.2
Indian Ocean, Chapter 3
indicator species, § 12.1
indices of diversity, § 15.5
Indo China, § 3.2, § 7.2, § 9.7, § 9.11, § 11.4, § 16.1
Indonesia, § 3.1, § 3.2, § 9.1, § 9.2, § 9.3, § 9.4, § 9.11, § 9.12, § 11.3, § 14.3, § 18.1, Table 17.2
Indo-Pacific strand flora, § 10.6
insectivorous plants, § 2.8, § 10.3

insects
damage by, § 2.8, § 6.5, § 7.2, § 14.2
pollinating, § 2.8, § 4.2
scale (Coccus), § 2.8
interactions between plants and animals, § 2.1, § 2.8, Chapter 13, § 19.3
intermontane valleys, § 3.2, § 10.2, § 12.1, § 16.1
introgressive hybridization, § 6.2
invasion fronts, § 15.2, § 15.3, Fig. 15.7
Irrawaddy River, § 9.10, § 11.4
Ivory Coast, § 3.6; see also Anguédédou forest

Jambu Bongkok, § 10.3
Japan, Chapter 1, Chapter 14, § 16.3, § 17.2
Japen Island, Chapter 14
Jarak Island, § 5.1
Java, § 1.2, § 3.1, § 4.1, § 5.2, § 6.2, § 7.2, § 9.7, § 9.9, § 9.10, § 9.11, § 10.4, § 11.3, § 11.4, § 12.1, § 12.2, § 12.3, § 14.1, § 16.1, § 16.6, § 17.1
dipterocarps in, § 15.2
Jengka forest, § 5.1, § 15.2, § 15.3, § 15.5
Jimi River, § 14.2, Fig. 14.6
Johore, § 4.2
Juliana mountains, § 9.12
Jurassic, § 2.8, § 12.1

Kabili–Sepilik see Sepilok
kaingin, § 18.1
Kalimantan see Borneo
Kampong Melor, § 17.1, Table 17.1
Kanching, § 15.2
kaolinite, Chapter 9, § 9.1, § 9.5, § 9.7, § 9.10, § 9.11, Fig. 9.16
Kapit, § 3.4
Kapuas river, § 11.3
Karimata Islands, § 10.3
karst see limestone
Kavo range, Guadalcanal, § 12.1
Kedah, § 9.4, § 10.4
Kedah Peak (Gunung Jerai), Chapter 14, § 16.1, § 16.6
Kei Islands, § 1.2
Kelantan, § 3.5, § 6.1, § 6.5, § 8.2, § 15.2, § 15.3, § 15.5, § 17.3, § 19.3, Fig. 2.21, Fig. 15.5, Table 15.1, Table 19.2
Kemahang forest see storm forest of Kelantan
Kemasul forest, Fig. 1.7, Table 1.1
Kent Ridge, § 18.2
Kepong, § 2.5, § 4.1
kera see monkeys, macaque
kerangas see heath forest
kerapah, § 10.3, § 11.3
Kerevat, § 7.1
Khao Chong forest, § 8.3, § 12.3
Khao Yai National Park, § 12.3
Khmer empire, § 17.1
kingfishers, Chapter 13
Kolombangara forests, § 2.6, § 5.1, § 6.3, § 8.1, § 9.12, Chapter 15, § 15.4, § 15.5, § 16.6, § 17.3, § 18.2, § 19.3, Fig. 6.4, Fig. 8.5, Fig. 15.15, Fig. 15.18, Fig. 15.19, Table 1.1, Table 6.1
Korea, § 17.2
Kra isthmus, Chapter 1, § 1.1, § 1.2, § 3.2, Chapter 10, § 10.2, § 12.1
Krakatau Island, § 5.1
Kuala Lompat, § 2.8, § 4.2, Chapter 13, Fig. 2.27, Table 1.2, Table 19.1
Kuala Lumpur, § 3.4, § 15.2

ladang, § 18.1

lahars, § 7.2, § 9.5, § 14.3

landslips, § 6.1, § 6.2, § 7.2, § 9.12, Chapter 13, § 14.3, § 15.3, § 16.5

Langat swamp, § 11.3

Langkawi Islands, § 3.2, § 10.4, § 12.3

laterite, Chapter 9, § **9.4**, § 9.5, § 9.10, § 9.11, Fig. 9.6, Fig. 9.7, Fig. 9.9, Table 9.1

latosols *see* oxisols

Lawas forest, § 10.3, Chapter 14, § 16.4, Fig. 14.3

leaching, § 2.6, § 9.1, § 9.2, § 9.10, § 9.12, § 11.3, § 14.1, § 15.3, § 16.5, § 16.6

leaf

    birds, Chapter 13

    miner (*Hylurdrectonus araucariae*), § 2.8, § 14.2

leaves

    change (flush) of, § 4.1, § 8.1, Table 4.1

    cooling of, § 10.3

    highly coloured, § 4.1, § 12.3, Fig. 4.3

    leachate mobilizing iron, § 14.1

    mineral contents, § 9.12, § 16.6

    pinnate, § 10.1, § 16.1, Table 16.1

    photosynthesis and respiration rates, different sorts and species, § 8.3, § 8.4

    of pioneer species, § 6.2

    scale, § 4.1

    shade, § 8.3, § 8.4

    size, Chapter 10, § 10.1, § 10.2, § 10.3, § 16.1, Table 16.1

    sun, § 8.3, § 8.4

leeches, § 16.7

leptocaul, § 2.5

Lesong forest, § 5.1

Lesser Sunda Islands, § 1.1, § 3.2, § 9.5, § 9.7, § 10.2, § 12.1, § 14.1, § 16.1

lichens, § 2.5, § 2.6, Fig. 2.13

light-demanding species, § 2.4, § 6.2, § 11.3, Fig. 6.4; *see also* pioneer species

    Albizzia lophantha, § 5.2

    basic physiological studies, § 8.4

    examples amongst Dipterocarpaceae, § 15.2, § 16.1

    favoured by modern felling methods, § 17.3

    growth rates in plantations, § 8.1

light

    compensation point, § 8.4

    composition and energy flux of in forest, § 3.6

    efficiency of utilization, § 5.3, § 8.1

    in heath forest, § 10.3

    and productivity, § 8.3

    reduced by fog, § 16.5

    ultraviolet, § 16.5

lightning, § 2.3, § 6.1, Chapter 10, § 10.4, § 11.3, § 12.1

limestone

    conifers of, Chapter 14, § 14.2

    consociations of, § 15.5

    dipterocarps of § 10.4, § 15.2

    hills and forest, Chapter 10, § 10.4, § 12.3, Fig. 10.15, Fig. 10.16, Table 10.1

    hill forest compared with other forest Formations, § 10.3, § 16.6

    and man, § 17.1

    soils, § 8.2, Chapter 9, § **9.7**, § 9.10, § 9.11, § 9.12

line planting, Chapter 7

litter, § 5.3, Chapter 9, § 9.1

    fall measured, § 8.3

lobang pusing *see* cerambycid borer

Loeser reserve, § 19.3

logging *see* exploitation

Lombok, § 1.2, § 5.2

lower montane rain forest, § 6.2, § 9.12, Chapter 14, § 14.1, § 14.3, § 15.2, § **16.1**, § 16.4, § 16.7, § 17.1, Fig. 2.18, Fig. 2.19, Fig. 16.1, Fig. 16.5, Table 10.1, Table 15.1, Table 16.2

    climate, Fig. 3.2, Fig. 3.3

    conifers, Chapter 14

    ecotone with upper montane and with lowland, Chapter 16, § 16.6

Lungmanis, § 5.1

Luzon, § 3.2, § 9.5, § 12.1, § 18.2

Madagascar, Chapter 1

Madai forest, § 8.1, Table 8.2

Malacca, § 3.5, § 9.4

    Straits, § 1.1, § 5.1

Malawali, § 10.5

Malaya, § 1.1, § 3.2, § 3.4, § 3.5, Chapter 5, § 5.1, § 6.1, Chapter 7, § 7.1, § 7.2, § 9.7, § 9.8, § 9.10, § 9.12, § 10.3, § 11.3, § 11.4, § 12.2, § 14.1, § 14.3, § 16.1, § 17.2, § 18.2, Table 16.2

    dipterocarps in, § 10.1, § 15.2, § 15.3

Malay Peninsula, § 1.1

Malaysia, § 1.1, § 9.2, § 17.2, Table 17.2

Maludam peninsula, § 11.3

Malesia, defined, § 1.1

mammals, § 1.2, § 2.7, § 2.8, § 6.1, § 8.3, § 16.2, § 17.4, Fig. 2.26

man

    as a direct forest influence, § 6.2, Chapter 10, Chapter 13

    population pressures of, Chapter 1, § 17.1, § 18.1

    primitive, § 1.2, § 10.4, § 17.1, Chapter 19

Mandalay, § 12.1

mangrove forest, § 9.9, § 10.6, § 11.1, § 11.2, Fig. 11.1

    avifauna of, Chapter 13

    lightning damage in, § 6.1

    relation to peat swamp forest, § 11.3

Manila, § 17.1

mass elevation

    effect of van Steenis, § 16.3

    heating effect *see* Massenerhebung

Massenerhebung heating effect, § 16.5, § 16.6

Mariana Islands, § 11.2, § 17.1

Mauritius, Chapter 1

medicinal plants, § 19.2

megatherms, § 16.3, § 16.4, § 16.7

Mekong River, § 9.2, § 9.10, § 11.4

Melanesia, Chapter 1, § 10.1

Menchali, § 10.3

Mentawi Islands, § 17.4

Merauke, § 12.1

Mergui archipelago, § 12.3

mesophyll vine forest *see* tropical semi-evergreen rain forest

Mexican Meseta, § 16.5

microclimates, § 2.1, § 2.4, § **3.6**, § 5.2, § 6.1

Micronesia, Chapter 1, § 3.2, § 10.1, § 12.1

micro-organisms, § 9.1, § 9.9, § 11.3, § 18.1

microrelief

    of flood plain, § 9.10

    of forest floor, causes, § 6.1

    of forest floor and seedling establishment, § 5.3

microtherms, § 16.1, § 16.3, § 16.4

mineral

    cycling, § 2.1, § 2.5, § 2.6, § 9.1, § 10.3, § 18.2

    deficiency *see* oligotrophy

nutrients, § 2.6, § 2.8, § 6.1, § 8.1, Chapter 9, § 9.1, § 9.8, § 9.11, § 10.4, § 11.3, § 15.3, § 16.5, § 16.6
  and shifting agriculture, § 18.1
  and wood chip extraction, § 19.1
  nutritional status and flower formation, § 4.1
Mindanao, § 6.1, § 6.2, § 7.1, § 7.2, § 9.5, § 17.2, § 18.1
minimal area, § 15.5
minor forest products, § 19.2
Miocene, Chapter 14
Miri, § 3.4
mixed dipterocarp forest *see* tropical rain forest
mixed (peat) swamp forest, § 11.3
Moluccas, § 3.2, § 7.2, § 9.7, § 12.1, § 14.1
mongooses, § 2.8
monkeys, § 1.2, § 2.7, § 2.8, § 8.3, Table 19.1
monocultures, § 19.1
monsoon
  climates, § 8.1, § 10.2, § 15.3, § 18.2, Fig. 3.2, Fig. 3.3
    defined, Chapter 3
    past extent of, § 12.1, § 15.1
  floods, § 15.3
  forests, Chapter 1, § 7.2, Chapter 10, § 12.1, § 17.1, Fig. 12.2, Table 10.1
    and conifers, Chapter 14, § 14.2, § 14.3
    dipterocarps, § 15.2
montane (mountain) forests, § 1.1, § 2.5, § 2.8, § 9.6, § 10.4, **Chapter 16**, Table 16.1
  ericaceous forest, Fig. 16.1
montmorillonite, Chapter 9, § 9.7, § 9.9, § 9.10, § 9.11
mor, Chapter 9
mosaic theory *see* under regeneration
mosses
  ground, § 16.1
  peat-forming, § 16.5
mossy (mountain) forest, § 9.12, § 12.1, § 14.2, § 16.1, § 16.5, § 16.6, Fig. 16.6, Fig. 16.7
mother trees, § 7.1
moth flowers, § 2.8
moths, day flying, § 2.8
Mount (*see also* Gunung),
  Austen plantations, Table 8.3
  Data National Park, § 19.3
  Dayman, § 14.2
  Dulit, § 10.3
  Kinabalu, § 9.8, § 9.12, § 10.5, Chapter 14, § 14.1, § 16.2, § 19.3
  Lawas, § 12.2
  Makiling, § 16.1
  Ophir (Gunung Ledang), § 16.1
  Ranai, § 16.1
  Suckling, § 14.2
  Tinggi, § 16.1
  Ulawa, § 7.2
  Victory, § 8.2
  Wilhelm, § 16.1, § 16.2, § 16.5
muck soil, § 11.4
mud lobster (*Thallassina anomala*), § 9.9, § 11.2
mull, Chapter 9, § 9.12
multiple usage of forests, § 19.3
Muna, § 7.2
mycorrhizas, § 2.5, § 5.3, § 9.1, § 10.3
myrmecophytes, § 2.1, § 2.8, § 10.3, § 11.3, Fig. 2.31, Fig. 10.8

naming kinds of forest,
  forest Formations, Chapter 10, Table 10.1

futile pursuit of, Part III
National Parks, Chapter 1, § 19.3
Natuna Islands, § 10.3, § 16.1
Nepal, § 7.2
net assimilation rate *see* unit leaf rate
New Britain, § 7.2, § 9.5, § 11.2
New Caledonia, § 9.8, Chapter 14, § 14.1, § 14.2
New Guinea, § 1.1, § 3.2, § 6.2, § 7.2, § 9.5, § 9.7, § 9.10, § 9.12, § 10.2, § 10.3, § 10.4, § 10.5, § 11.3, § 11.4, § 12.1, § 12.2, Chapter 14, § 14.1, § 15.4, § 17.1, Table 17.2
  central cordillera and Highlands, § 3.2, § 12.1, § 16.1, § 16.5, § 16.6, § 18.1
  dipterocarps in, § 10.1, § 15.1, § 15.2
New Hebrides, Chapter 1, § 3.2, § 6.1, § 9.5, § 12.1, Chapter 13, § 14.1, § 17.1
New Ireland, § 7.2
New South Wales, Chapter 1
New Zealand, Chapter 1, § 14.1
Nggela, § 12.1
Niah Caves, § 10.4, § 17.1
niche, § 8.4, § 14.3, Chapter 15, § 15.3, § 15.4
  of animals, § 2.7, Chapter 13
Nigeria, § 5.1, § 7.2
nitrogen fixation, § 9.8, § 18.1
nomad *see* pioneer species
numerical methods of plant community analysis, Chapter 15, § 15.4, § 15.5
nutrients *see* mineral nutrients

'oak' forest, § 16.1
oak-laurel forest, § 12.1, § 16.6, Fig. 16.1
oligotrophy, § 9.1, § 9.6, § 9.8, § 9.12, § 10.3, § 10.4, § 11.3, § 14.1, § 15.3, § 16.5, § 16.6
open-air hothouses, § 16.3
orang utan (*Pongo pygmaeus*), § 1.2, § 2.7, Chapter 13, § 17.4
  in competition with man, § 17.1
origin of Malesian mountain flora, § 16.3
Oriomo plateau, § 12.1
oxisols, § 9.1, § 9.2, § 9.3, § 9.4, § 9.5, § 9.10

pachycaul, § 2.5
  treelets, § 2.5
pachyphyll, § 16.4, § 16.5, § 16.6
Pacific Ocean, § 1.1, Chapter 3
padang, § 10.3
  avifauna of, Chapter 13
Pahang River, § 3.6, § 9.10, § 11.3
Palawan, § 1.1
Palembang, § 3.2, § 12.1
palms,
  dense stands, § 10.3
  stenophyllous, § 15.3
palm swamps, § 11.4
Palu valley, § 12.1
pandan swamps, § 11.4
Paneh peninsula, § 11.3
Pangkor Island, Table 15.2
Papua *see* New Guinea
parasites, § 2.1, § 2.2
Pasoh forest, § 15.3, § 15.5, § 17.4, § 19.3, Table 1.2, Table 15.4
peat, Chapter 9, § 9.9, § 16.5, Fig. 9.1, Fig. 9.16, Table 10.1
  dipterocarps not establishing in, § 5.3, § 16.6
  over limestone, § 9.7, § 10.4, § 16.4
  lowland, § 9.10, § 11.3, § 14.1

mountain, § 5.3, § 9.12, § 16.6

swamp forest, § 9.6, § 9.9, § 9.10, § 10.1, § 10.3, § 11.3, § 11.4, Chapter 14, § 15.3, § 15.5, § 18.2, § 19.1, Fig. 11.2, Fig. 11.3, Fig. 11.4, Fig. 11.5, Fig. 11.6, Fig. 11.7, Fig. 11.8, Fig. 11.9, Fig. 11.10, Fig. 11.11, Fig. 11.12, Fig. 11.13, Fig. 11.14, Table 10.1

  animals of, Chapter 13

  compared with heath and upper montane forest, § 10.3, § 16.4

  dipterocarps in, § 4.1, § 15.2

  lightning damage in, § 6.1

  myrmecophytes in, § 2.8

  net production of, § 8.3

pegass swamps, § 11.3

Penang Hill, § 15.1

penduliflory, § 2.8, Fig. 2.29

Peninsular Malaysia, § 1.1

Peradeniya, § 4.1

Perlis, § 10.4

permanent observation plots, Chapter 15, § 18.2, § 19.3

pes caprae association, § 10.6

pest pressure, § 2.8

pheasants, § 2.7, Chapter 13

Philippines, § 1.1, § 1.2, § 3.2, § 6.1, Chapter 7, § 7.1, § 9.3, § 9.5, § 9.12, § 10.2, § 11.3, § 12.2, § 14.3, § 15.2, § 17.1, § 17.2, § 17.3, § 19.1

  dipterocarps in, § 2.4, § 15.2

phosphate in soil, § 9.1, § 9.5, § 9.8, § 9.12, § 10.3, § 10.4, § 11.3, § 15.3, § 16.5, § 16.6

photosynthesis, § 3.6, § 5.3, § 6.5, § 8.1, § 8.4, § 10.3, § 16.5, § 16.6, Fig. 10.14

phyllosphere, § 2.6

phytophagy, § 2.8

phytosociological analysis, § 15.5

pigeons, § 2.7

pigs, § 1.2, § 2.8, § 5.1, § 16.7

pines

  Caribbean, § 14.3

  Chinese, § 14.3

  Indian, § 14.3

pioneer species, § 6.2, § 10.5, § 14.2, § 15.3, § 15.5, Chapter 18, Fig. 6.1, Fig. 6.2, Fig. 6.3, Fig. 6.5, Fig. 7.2, Fig. 7.3, Fig. 7.4, Fig. 7.5, Table 6.4; *see also* light-demanding species

  ages reached, § 8.2

  Casuarina papuana in New Guinea, § 18.1

  death of, § 6.4

  desirable properties of for plantations, § 7.2

  leaf features of, § 8.4

  photosynthetic rates of, § 8.4

  Pinus as, § 14.3

  in secondary forest, § 18.2

  seedling survival of, § 6.5

  short- and long-lived, § 6.2

  short-lived, favoured by repeated logging, § 17.3

  in various forest Formations, § 8.3, § 9.9, § 10.6, § 11.3, § 11.4, § 15.2, § 15.4, § 19.1

pitcher plants (*Nepenthes*), § 2.8, § 11.3, Fig. 2.32

pittas, § 2.7

plantation agriculture, Chapter 1, § 10.1, § 17.1, Chapter 18, § 18.1, § 19.1, Fig. 17.9

plantations (forest), Chapter 7, § 17.2, § 19.1

  attacked by insects, § 2.8, § 7.1

  in degraded heath forest, § 10.3

  growth rates, § 8.2, Table 8.3

  physiological interpretation of species performance, § 8.4

pioneer species for, § 7.2

teak, § 12.2

timber yields from, § 8.1, Fig. 8.1

of various conifers, Chapter 14, § 14.1, § 14.2, § 14.3, Fig. 8.1

varying productivity with elevation, § 8.3

plant

  geography, historical, § 15.1

plate tectonics, § 15.1

Pleistocene, § 2.1, § 9.5, § 10.3, § 12.1, § 15.1, § 15.4, § 16.2, § 17.1

  erosion surfaces in Africa, § 9.2

  extent of rain forest during, § 12.1

  fauna, § 1.2

  sea levels *see* sea-level changes

plinthite *see* laterite

Pliocene, Chapter 14

plywood, § 14.2, § 15.2, § 17.2

pneumatophores, § 9.9, § 11.1, § 11.3, Fig. 11.14

podzols, Chapter 9, § 9.6, § 9.10, § 9.12, Chapter 10, § 10.3, § 14.1, § 14.3, § 16.4, § 16.5, Fig. 9.11, Table 9.2, Table 10.1

poikilohydry, § 2.6, § 10.4

poison-girdling, § 7.1, § 8.1, § 11.3, § 17.3

poles, § 2.3, § 2.5, § 6.1, § 6.3, § 6.4, Chapter 7, § 7.1, § 8.3, § 10.3, § 15.2

  in *Dryobalanops* forest, § 15.3

  in heath forest, § 10.3

  in peat swamp forest, § 11.3

  population changes, § 6.3

  productivity of, § 8.3

pollen analysis, § 11.3, § 12.1, Chapter 14, § 16.2, § 17.1

pollination, § 2.1, § 2.8, Fig. 2.28, Fig. 2.29

Polynesia, Chapter 1, § 17.1

polyploidy, § 6.2

Pontianak, § 11.3

population structure of tree species, § 6.2, § 6.3, § 6.4

Port Moresby, § 3.2, § 12.1

primates, § 17.4; *see also* apes

prisere, § 2.1, § 7.2

producers, defined, § 2.7

productivity studies and definitions, § 2.3, § 2.5, § 8.3, § 10.3, Fig. 8.6

profile diagram, § 2.3, Fig. 1.6, Fig. 2.1, Fig. 2.2, Fig. 2.4, Fig. 6.7, Fig. 7.1, Fig. 10.4, Fig. 10.12, Fig. 11.4, Fig. 11.5, Fig. 14.8, Fig. 15.3, Fig. 15.18, Fig. 15.19, Fig. 16.2

protection forest, § 19.2

Puerto Rico, § 7.2

Queensland, Chapter 1, § 3.2, § 3.6, § 6.1, § 8.1, § 14.1, Chapter 18

radiocarbon (^{14}C), § 8.2, § 11.3

rain, Chapter 3, § 3.3, § 4.1, § 9.1, § 9.12, § 12.1

  convectional storms, § 3.5, § 5.1, § 6.1

  destroying illipe nut crop, § 4.1

  kinds of, § 3.2

  in mountains, § 9.12, § 16.5

  run-off from rain forest, § 3.3

  shadow, § 10.2, § 12.1

rainfall, Schmidt and Ferguson types, § 3.2, Fig. 3.1

ramiflory, § 2.5, § 2.8, § 10.1, § 10.2

Ranau, § 9.8, § 10.5

rats, § 4.2

Rattus, § 1.2

  ecology and zonation with elevation in Malaya, § 16.7

Raub, § 10.5

raubbau *see* shifting agriculture
ray, § 18.1
reaforestation, § 17.3
recreation, value of heath forests for, § 10.3
refinement of forest, Chapter 7, § 19.1; *see also* silviculture
relict trees after felling, § 7.1
refugia, § 12.1
regeneration improvement fellings (R.I.F.), Chapter 7
regeneration of *Albizia lophantha* after fire, § 16.1; *see also* silviculture
    mosaic or cyclical theory of, Chapter 15, § 15.4
    natural, § 5.2, Chapter 7, § 14.2
Rejang River, § 11.3, Fig. 11.2
relative growth rate, § 8.4
release of dipterocarps by canopy opening, Fig. 7.1
'reproductive pressure', § 15.3, § 15.5
reptiles, § 1.2, § 8.3, Chapter 13, Table 13.1
    putative pollination by, § 2.8
respiration, § 5.3, § 6.5, § 8.3, § 8.4, Fig. 10.14
Reunion, Chapter 1
rheophytes, § 15.3, Fig. 2.30
rhinoceros, § 17.1
rice, § 3.5, § 11.4, § 17.1, § 18.1
richness in species of rain forest, § 1.1, Chapter 7
Rio Negro, § 10.3
riparian (riverine) forests, § 1.1, § 10.4, § 11.4, § 15.3; *see also* gallery forests
rodents, § 1.2, § 2.8
Rodriguez, Chapter 1
Rompin River, § 11.3
root(s), § 2.5, § 3.3, § 9.1, § 9.4, § 9.5, § 10.3, § 11.3
    attacked by fungi, § 2.3, Fig. 2.3
    biomass, estimation of, § 8.3
    competition, § 5.3, § 6.1, § 6.2, § 6.3, § 6.5, § 8.1
    knee, § 11.4
    nodules, § 2.5, § 18.1
    plate, § 6.1
    stilt, § 11.1, § 11.4
    suckers, § 11.4
    tap, § 2.5
rubber plantations, § 11.3, § 11.4, § 18.1
Rumbia Island, § 5.1

Sabah, § 5.1, § 7.1, § 7.2, § 9.12, § 10.3, Chapter 14
Sahul Shelf, § 1.1, § 3.2, § 15.1, Fig. 1.9
salt licks, § 6.1
Santa Cruz Islands, § 2.6, § 6.5, § 14.1, § 16.1, § 18.2, Fig. 6.7, Fig. 17.5
Samoa, Chapter 1, § 6.1, § 14.1
saplings, § 2.3, § 2.5, § 4.1, § 6.1, § 6.3, § 6.4, § 7.1, § 10.3, § 11.3, § 12.2, § 15.3, Fig. 6.6, Fig. 7.3
saprolite, § 9.1, § 9.12
saprophytes, § 2.1, § 2.2
Sarawak, § 3.4, § 6.1, § 9.6, § 9.7, § 10.1, § 10.3, § 14.1, § 16.5, Table 13.1
Satun (Setul), § 10.3
saturation deficit *see* water balance
Savai'i, § 6.1
savanna, § 10.3, § 12.1, § 14.2, § 16.1, § 16.2
    mammals, § 1.2
    woodland, Chapter 1, § 7.2, § 8.2, § 11.3
Schima—bamboo forest, § 12.3
schopfbäumchen, § 2.5
sclerophyllous forests, § 10.3, § 12.1

sclerophylly,
    nutritional explanation of, § 10.3
    in peat swamp forests, § 11.3
scrub, § 9.11, § 11.4, § 12.3, Chapter 13
sea-level changes, § 1.1, § 1.2, § 9.7, § 10.3, § 12.1, § 15.1
seasonal
    cycles
        in animals, § 4.2
        in plants, § 3.5, § 4.1, § 5.3
    swamp forest, § 1.1, § 11.4, § 15.2, § 17.1, Table 10.1
    water stress *see* drought
seasonality complicating production studies, § 8.3
seasonally dry climate, § 7.2, § 8.3, Chapter 10, § 12.1, § 12.3, Chapter 14, § 14.3, § 16.1, § 16.5, Table 10.1
    complicating production studies, § 8.3
    on highest mountains, § 16.2
    indicator species of, § 12.1
    of Pleistocene, § 1.1
    soils of, § 9.4, § 9.5, § 9.11, § 9.12
secondary forest and successions (seral stands), § 6.4, § 7.2, § 8.2, § 8.3, § 9.11, § 10.3, § 11.4, § 12.1, § 15.5, § 17.1, Chapter 18, § 18.2, Fig. 17.5
    animals of, Chapter 13, § 17.4
    and *Agathis macrophylla*, § 6.5
    and *Anisoptera thurifera*, § 15.2
    on mining land, § 11.4
    and *Pinus*, § 14.3
    productivity of, § 8.3
sedge plains, § 11.4
seedlings, § 2.3, § 2.4, § 3.6, § 6.1, § 6.5, § 8.2, § 11.3, § 15.5, § 18.1, Table 6.1
    of *Agathis macrophylla*, § 6.5, § 14.1
    of *Pinus*, § 14.3
    population dynamics of, § 5.2, § 5.3, § 6.3, § 6.5, § 7.1, § 15.3, § 15.4, Fig. 6.8, Table 6.6, Table 6.7
    predation of, § 4.1
    survival, § 5.2, § 6.5, § 10.3
    of teak, § 12.2
    of *Terminalia calamansanai*, § 5.1
seeds,
    availability, § 7.2, § 15.5, § 18.2, Table 6.1
    conditions for storage, § 5.2, § 7.2, § 14.2
    dispersal of *see* dispersal
    dormancy and germination, § 4.1, § 5.2, § 6.1, § 6.2, § 15.5
    of *Anthocephalus chinensis*, § 7.2
    of *Eucalyptus deglupta*, § 7.2
    with food reserves, § 6.2
    of *Pinus*, § 7.2, § 14.3
    of pioneer species, § 18.2
    predation of, § 2.8, § 4.1
Segaliud–Lokan forest, Table 15.2
seladang (*Bos sundaicus*), § 1.2, § 17.1, § 17.4, § 19.3
selection pressure *see* evolution
selective felling, Chapter 7, § 17.1, Chapter 18
    effect on fauna, Chapter 13
    in heath forest, § 10.3
self-grafting, § 2.6
Semengo arboretum, § 3.6, § 4.2, Fig. 3.5
semi-evergreen mesophyll vine forest *see* tropical moist deciduous forest
semi-evergreen forest *sensu* Beard *see* tropical moist deciduous forest
semi-evergreen rain forest *sensu* Baur *see* tropical moist deciduous forest

Semporna peninsula, § 9.3
Sepik River, § 11.4
Sepilok forest, § 6.5, § 8.1, § 10.3, Chapter 15, § 15.3, § 19.3, Table 6.6, Table 8.4, Table 15.3
seral species *see* pioneer species
serpentine *see* ultrabasic rocks
Seychelles, Chapter 1
shade-bearing species, § 2.4, § 6.2, § 15.4, Fig. 6.4, Table 6.4
   Agathis macrophylla as a, § 14.1
   basic physiological studies, § 8.4
   colonization by, § 8.2
   in secondary successions, § 18.2
   seed characteristics of, § 5.3
   seedling survival, § 6.5
shade-intolerant species *see* light-demanding species
shade-tolerant species *see* shade-bearing species
shifting cultivation, § 10.1, § 14.3, § 17.1, § 17.2, Chapter 18, § 18.1, Chapter 19, Fig. 18.2, Fig. 18.3
shrubs, § 2.5, § 15.3, § 16.4, Chapter 18, § 18.2
siliceous vegetation *see* heath forest
silviculture
   aims of, § 8.1
   and contemporary exploitation, § 17.3, § 19.1
   and ecology, § 6.2, Chapter 7, § 8.1, Chapter 15
   first managed rotation, Chapter 7, § 19.1
   in lowland dipterocarp rain forest, § 7.1
   of mangrove forest, § 11.1
   of peat swamp forests, § 11.3
   problems caused by lack of seed dormancy, § 5.2
   of teak forests, § 12.2
silvicultural systems, Chapter 7, § 7.1
Singapore, § 1.1, § 2.7, § 3.4, § 3.5, § 3.6, § 4.1, § 4.2, § 17.2
   Garden's Jungle, § 6.1
Sipitang, Chapter 14
size class distribution *see* stand tables
snow line, § 16.2, § 16.5
soil, § 2.5, § 3.1, § 4.2, § 5.3, § 6.1, § 7.2, § 8.1, **Chapter 9**, § 9.12, § 10.3, § 10.4, § 10.5, § 12.1, § 15.3, § 16.6, § 18.1, § 18.2, Fig. 9.2, Fig. 9.3, Fig. 9.4, Fig. 9.5, Fig. 9.10, Fig. 9.12, Fig. 9.13
   classification, Chapter 9, § 9.1, Table 9.1, Table 9.2
   change with elevation, Chapter 9, § **9.12**, § **16.5**, § 16.6, Fig. 9.15
   compaction during timber extraction, Chapter 18
   intrazonal, Chapter 9
   red–yellow podzolic *see* ultisols
   and species composition, § 15.3, § 15.5
   water storage in, § 3.3, § 3.4, § 4.1, § 5.3, § 9.5, Chapter 10, § 10.3, § 12.1, § 15.3, Table 10.1
   zonal, Chapter 9, § **9.1**, Chapter 10, Table 10.1
solar radiation, utilization of, § 8.3, § 19.3
solfatara, § 5.2
Solomon Islands, Chapter 1, § 1.1, § 2.6, § 3.2, § 4.1, § 5.3, § 6.1, § 6.2, § 6.5, Chapter 7, § 7.2, § 8.2, § 9.3, § 9.5, § 9.7, § 9.8, § 11.2, § 15.1, § 16.1, § 17.1, Chapter 18
South Africa Cape region, § 1.1
South America, Chapter 3, § 10.4, § 11.4, § 12.2, § 17.1
spaceship earth, § 8.3
species–area curves, § 1.1, Fig. 1.3, § 15.5
species, aspects of richness in rain forest, § 2.8, § 10.1, § 11.3, Chapter 15, § 15.4, § 17.1, § 19.3, Fig. 1.4, Fig. 1.5
   associations, Chapter 15
     conditions of occurrence, § 15.4
     composition, fluctuation in time, § 6.4, § 15.4, § 15.5, Table 6.5
     consociations, § 10.1, § 10.2, § 10.3, § 10.4, § 11.4, § 12.2, § 14.2,

Chapter 15, § 17.4, § 18.2, Fig. 15.3, Fig. 15.10, Fig. 15.13; *see also* family groups
   of *Dryobalanops aromatica* in Malaya, § 15.3, § 15.5, § 17.3
   in secondary forest, § 18.2
   several reasons for, § 15.5
   of *Shorea albida*, § 11.3, § 15.5
   of *Shorea curtisii*, § 15.3, § 15.5, § 17.3
   diversity, dangers of reducing, § 19.1
squirrels, § 1.2, § 5.1, § 8.3
stand tables, § 6.2, § 6.4, Fig. 6.4
Star Mountains, § 9.12, § 14.1
steepland boundary of Malaya, § 16.7
stem borer, § 7.2
stenophylls, § 15.3, Fig. 15.8, Fig. 15.9
storm forest of Kelantan, § 2.5, § 3.5, § 6.1, § 6.5, § 8.2, § 15.2, § 15.4, § 15.5, § 17.3, Fig. 2.21, Fig. 15.5
strangling plants, § 2.1, § 2.2, § **2.6**
stratification, § **2.4**, § 2.6, § 2.7, § 6.2, § 8.1, § 8.3, § 10.1, § 10.3, § 12.2
   change with elevation, § 10.1
streams
   blackwater, § 10.3
   torrent, § 15.3
stunting of trees in mountains, § 16.1
subalpine forest, § 16.1, § 16.2, § 16.4, Table 10.1
subtropical rain forest, Chapter 1, § 3.6, § 14.2, § 16.3
sucker shoots, § 11.3, § 18.1, § 18.2
Sumatra, Chapter 1, § 1.1, § 1.2, § 3.2, § 5.2, § 7.2, § 9.7, § 9.10, § 11.3, § 11.4, § 12.3, § 14.1, § 14.3, § 16.1, § 16.3, § 17.1, § 17.2
   dipterocarps in, § 15.2, § 15.3
sunbirds (Nectariniidae), § 2.8, Chapter 13
Sunda Islands, § 9.5, § 16.3
Sunda Shelf (Sundaland), § 1.1, § 3.2, § 4.1, § 6.1, § 8.3, § 10.6, § 15.1, § 16.3, § 17.1, § 18.1, § 19.3, Fig. 1.8, Fig. 1.9
   dipterocarps, § 10.1
sunflecks, § 3.6, § 8.4
Sungei Kroh forest, § 5.1
Sungei Menyala forest, § 6.1, § **6.4**, § 8.1, Chapter 15, § 19.3, Fig. 2.3, Table 6.3, Table 6.4, Table 6.5, Table 15.3
Sungei Tahan, § 15.3
synusiae, defined, § 2.2

Tacloban City, § 3.2, Fig. 3.2, Fig. 3.3
Taiwan, Chapter 1, § 10.1, § 17.2
Talaud, § 7.2
Taman Negara, § 10.2, § 19.3
tamrai, § 18.1
tanah beris, § 9.6
Tanah Grogot, § 9.8
Tanjong Hantu, § 10.3
Tapanuli, § 12.1
tapir (*Tapirus indicus*), § 1.2, § 8.3, § 16.7, § 19.3
taungya, § 7.2, § 12.2, § 18.1
teak forests, § 9.11, § 12.2
Telok, § 11.3
Tembeling River, § 10.2
temperate deciduous forests, § 17.2, Fig. 8.6
temperate rain forest, Chapter 1
temperature,
   adiabatic lapse rates, § 16.5, § 16.6
   low, stimulating flowering, § 4.1
   and productivity, § 8.3
   within forest, § 3.6, § 6.1, Fig. 3.5

Tenasserim, § 12.3
Tenegang forest, § 8.1, Table 8.1
termites, § 2.1, § 2.8, § 3.3, § 9.1, § 11.3, § 16.5
Tertiary, § 15.1
Thailand, Chapter 1, § 3.2, §7.2, § 9.2, § 9.10, § 9.11, § 9.12, § 10.3, § 10.4, § 11.4, § 12.1, § 12.2, § 14.1, § 16.1
thinnings, § 8.3, § 14.3, § 19.1
thorn forest, § 12.1, § 12.3
thrushes, § 2.7
thunderstorms, § 2.3, § 3.2, § 3.5, § 6.1
Tibet, § 14.3
tiger, § 1.2, § 19.3
timber *see also* wood,
    constructional *see* hardwoods, heavy
    density and biomass estimates, § 8.3
    softwood, Chapter 14
    trade, § 17.1, § 19.1
    value of per square kilometre, § 19.3
    yields, stocking and increment, §7.2, §8.1, § 14.3, § 15.3, Fig. 8.1
Timor, § 16.1, § 16.5
Toba
    Lake, § 14.3
    volcano, § 5.1
Tonga, Chapter 1
topography—related variation in forest composition, § 15.3, § 15.5
tornadoes, § 6.1
Torres Straits, Chapter 10
tourism, § 10.3, § 19.3
trans Perak swamp forest, § 11.3
tree
    age, § 8.2, § 14.2, Table 8.4
    anchorage, § 2.5
    breeding, § 5.2, § 19.1, § 19.2
    crown, § 2.5, § 6.3, Chapter 7, § 7.2, § 8.1, § 16.1, § 16.4
        architecture and water relations, § 10.3
        crown/bole diameter ratio, § 8.1
        diameter in peat swamp forest, § 11.3
        structure and tree growth rate, § 8.1, § 8.4, Table 8.1
        monopodial, § 2.3, § 2.4, § 2.5, § 6.5, Fig. 2.1, Fig. 2.5, Fig. 2.7, Fig. 6.6, Fig. 14.6, Fig. 14.7
        pagoda, Fig. 2.8
        photosynthetic efficiency of, § 2.5
        wind damage to, § 6.1
    structure correlated with microclimate, § 3.6
    stratification, § 2.4
    sympodial, § 2.4, § 2.5, Fig. 2.6, Fig. 10.1
    fall, § 6.1, § 6.2, § 15.3
    form, § 2.5, § 8.3, § 8.4
    frequency, Table 19.2
    line, § 15.1, § 16.2
    mortality, § 6.1, § 6.4, Table 6.3
        and productivity studies, § 8.3
trees
    giant, § 2.4, § 14.2, § 15.2, Fig. 14.6, Fig. 14.7
    overmature, § 2.3
    percentage hollow and rock type, § 15.3
    'stagheaded', § 2.3, § 11.3
Tree Sparrow (*Passer montanus*), § 4.2
trogons, § 2.7
tropical littoral woodland *see* beach vegetation
(tropical) lowland (evergreen, mixed, dipterocarp) rain forest, Chapter 1, § 1.1, § 2.7, § 2.8, § 5.3, § 6.4, § 8.2, § 10.3, § 12.1, Chapter 13, § 15.2, § 15.3, § 17.1, Fig. 1.1, Fig. 1.6, Fig. 2.1, Fig. 2.2, Fig. 2.4, Fig. 10.12, Fig. 15.4, Fig. 15.11,
Fig. 16.1, Fig. 16.5, Table 10.1, Table 15.1, Table 15.2, Table 15.3, Table 16.2
    climate, Fig. 3.2, Fig. 3.3
    conifers in, Chapter 14, § 14.1, § 14.2, § 14.3
    current rate of destruction of, § 8.3, § 17.3
    dipterocarp, floristic comparison with heath forest, § 10.3
    ecotone with lower montane, Chapter 16, § 16.6
    at Kra isthmus, § 12.3
    productivity of, § 8.3, Fig. 8.6
    seral species of, in Java, § 6.2
    silviculture, § 7.1
tropical moist deciduous forest, Chapter 10, § 10.2, § 12.2, Table 10.1
tropical semi-evergreen rain forest, § 3.6, § 8.3, Chapter 10, § 10.2, § 12.1, § 12.3, Chapter 14, Table 10.1
    Araucaria in, Chapter 14, § 14.2
    dipterocarps in, § 12.3, § 15.2
    productivity studies in, § 8.3
tropical wet evergreen forest *see* tropical lowland rain forest
tropische Regenwald, Chapter 1
tundra moss, § 16.2
tussock moth (Hymantridae), § 2.8, § 6.1
typhoons, § 6.1
Tutong River, § 11.3

Uganda, Chapter 1
ultisols, § 9.1, § 9.2, § 9.4, § 9.10, § 10.4
ultrabasic rocks, soils and vegetation, § 9.8, Chapter 10, § 10.5, Chapter 14, § 14.2, § 15.5, Table 10.1
Ulu Gombak, § 2.8, § 3.3, § 3.4, § 4.1, § 4.2, § 17.3, § 17.4, Table 4.1, Table 4.2, Table 4.3
Ulu Kelantan forests, § 15.3, § 15.5, § 19.3, Table 15.1, Table 19.2
Ulu Segama, § 17.4
Ulu Sempan, § 4.2
Ulu Telom, § 17.4
ungulates, § 1.2
United Nations, § 17.2
unit leaf rate, § 8.4
upper dipterocarp rain forest, § 5.3, § 15.3, § 16.6, Fig. 16.1
upper montane rain forest, § 6.2, § 11.3, Chapter 14, § 16.1, § 16.4, § 16.6, § 16.7, Fig. 9.1, Fig. 9.15, Fig. 16.1, Fig. 16.3, Fig. 16.4, Fig. 16.8, Fig. 16.9, Table 10.1, Table 16.2; *see also* mossy (mountain) forest
    floristic comparison with heath forest, § 10.3
Usan Apau, § 9.6

varzea, § 11.4
vegetative reproduction, § 11.3
Vietnam, § 9.10, Chapter 18
Vigan, § 3.2, Fig. 3.2, Fig. 3.3
Virgin Jungle Reserves, § 17.3, § 19.3
Viru–Kalena forests, Table 1.1
Vogelkop peninsula, § 1.2, § 9.7

Wabag–Tari forests, § 16.1
Waigeo Island, § 1.2, § 3.2, § 10.4, § 10.5, § 14.1
Wallacea, § 1.2
Wallace's line, § 1.2, § 6.1, Fig. 1.9
warblers, Chapter 13
warm temperature forests, § 16.3
water
    availability and forest Formations, Chapter 3, Chapter 10
    balance, § 3.3, § 3.4, § 10.3, § 16.6, Fig. 3.4
    dispersal by, § 5.1, § 10.6

relations, § 3.1, § 3.3, § 3.6, § 6.1, § 10.3, § 15.3, § 15.5
stress, § 4.1, § 5.3, § 10.2, § 10.3, § 10.4, § 15.3, § 16.6; *see also*
    drought and seasonally dry climate
Wau–Watut valleys, § 14.2, Fig. 14.8
Weber's line, § 1.2, Fig. 1.9
weed trees, Chapter 7, § 8.1, § 11.3, § 17.3
weeds, § 17.1
    increase with continued cultivation, § 18.1
weevils, § 5.1, § 5.2
western Ghats, Chapter 1, § 10.1
White-eyes (Zosteropidae), § 2.8
wild fruit trees, § 2.7, § 4.1, § 17.1, § 19.2, § 19.3, Fig. 17.2,
    Table 17.1, Table 19.2
wildings, Chapter 7
wind, § 3.5; *see also* cyclone, hurricane, tornado, storm forest
    damage, § 4.1, § 6.1, § 11.3, § 15.3, Chapter 18, Fig. 2.3
    dispersal by, § 5.1, § 10.6
wintering *see* leaf change
wood, *see also* timber
    a versatile raw material, § 17.2, § 19.3

brittle-heart in, § 8.2
chips, § 7.1, § 11.3, § 19.1
compression, § 2.5
growth rings, § 4.1, § 8.2
of pioneer species, § 6.2
production, § 8.3
pulp, § 7.1, § 11.3, § 17.2, § 19.1
tension, § 2.5
volume increment, § 2.5
woodpeckers, § 2.7, Chapter 13

xeromorphic rain forest *see* heath forest
xeromorphism in peat swamp forests, § 11.3

yellow-vented Bulbul (*Pycnonotus goiavier*), § 4.2

zonation (*see also* altitudinal zonation)
    concentric of peat swamps, § 11.3
    in mangrove forest, § 11.1

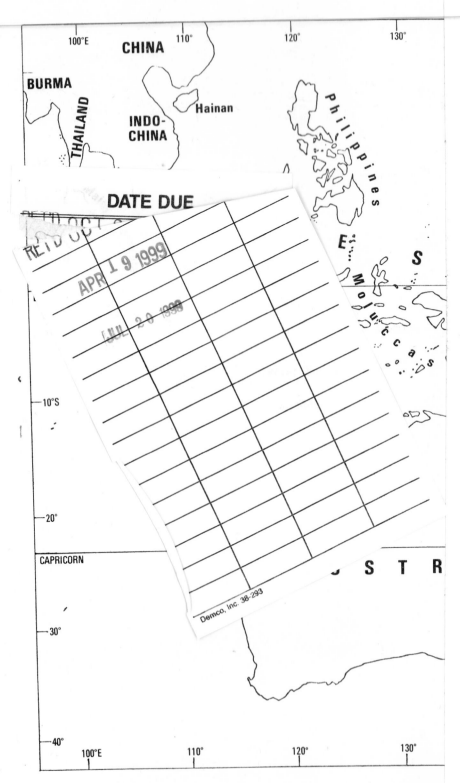

CHINA

BURMA

THAILAND

INDO-
CHINA

Hainan

Philippines

Moluccas

10°S

20°

CAPRICORN

30°

40°

100°E

110°

120°

130°

S T R